companion encyclopedia
of geography

This completely revised second edition of Routledge's very successful 1996 *Companion Encyclopedia of Geography* provides a comprehensive and integrated survey of the discipline. The revised edition takes the theme of place as the unifying principle for a full account of the discipline at the beginning of the twenty-first century.

The work comprises 64 substantial essays addressing human and physical geography, and exploring their inter-relations. The encyclopedia does full justice to the enormous growth of social and cultural geography in recent years. Leading international academics from ten countries and four continents have contributed, ensuring that differing traditions in geography around the world are represented. In addition to references, the essays also list recommendations for further reading. There is a comprehensive index guiding the reader to specific themes and concepts within the content.

As with the original work, the new *Companion Encyclopedia of Geography* provides a state-of-the-art survey of the discipline and is an indispensable addition to the reference shelves of libraries supporting research and teaching in geography.

Ian Douglas, **Richard Huggett** and **Chris Perkins** are based in the Department of Geography, School of Environment and Development, University of Manchester, UK.

See for ...

Sources [strong?] for every Source (anyone)
Get – photos / phone / notes
Not a traditional encyclopedia

Almost 5 million
international contributors

Though provides
essays – not merely
description or definition
as the source
topics differ ...

References – between
room & places
they are.

Cross reference in company – helps to unify
further reading   photos are overview
                                   – Slovenian codester

Brief

for – description of people & environment
"heart of geography"   truely – for beauty (.)

Multi-disciplinary – very many fields
                    not just for geography / journal

Witty – erudite

Geography in Middlesbrough   all depths
Heritage & relationship between homes & places ...
Definition remains ... time is otherwise inside

companion encyclopedia of geography

from local to global

second edition

edited by

ian douglas
richard huggett
chris perkins

volume 1

Routledge
Taylor & Francis Group

LONDON AND NEW YORK

First published 2007
by Routledge
2 Park Square, Milton Park, Abingdon, Oxon OX14 4RN
www.routledge.co.uk

Simultaneously published in the USA and Canada
by Routledge
270 Madison Avenue, New York, NY 10016
www.routledge-ny.com

Routledge is an Imprint of the Taylor and Francis Group, an informa business

© 2007 Routledge

Typeset in Bembo and Helvetica by Taylor & Francis Books
Printed and bound in Great Britain by MPG Books Ltd, Bodmin

British Library Cataloguing in Publication Data
A catalogue record for this book has been requested

Library of Congress Cataloging-in-Publication Data
A catalog record for this book has been requested

ISBN13: 978-0-415-43169-9 (set)
ISBN13: 978-0-415-33977-3 (volume 1)
ISBN13: 978-0-415-43171-2 (volume 2)

Contents

Volume 1

Part I: The nature of place

Part III: Actors in the process

Part IV: Nature, rate, and direction of change

Volume 2

Part V: The geographical imagination

Part VI: Responses to the geographical drivers of change

List of plates

List of figures

List of tables

Consultant editors

Professor Kay Anderson
Professor of Cultural Research, Centre for Cultural Research,
University of Western Sydney, Australia

Professor Thomas R. Leinbach
Department of Geography, University of Kentucky, USA

Professor Janice Monk
Women's Studies Department, The University of Arizona, USA

Professor Shii Okuno
University of Marketing and Distribution Sciences, Kobe, Japan

Professor Jamie Peck
Department of Geography, University of Wisconsin, USA

Professor Jonathan D. Phillips
Department of Geography, University of Kentucky, USA

Professor Eric Waddell
Département de Géographie, Université Laval, Québec, Canada

Professor Jim Walmsley
Division of Geography and Planning, School of Human and Environmental Studies,
University of New England, Armidale, Australia

Associate Professor Henry Yeung
Department of Geography, National University of Singapore, Hong Kong

Contributors

Stuart C. Aitken
San Diego State University, USA

Nigel W. Arnell
University of Southampton, UK

Sarah Atkinson
University of Durham, UK

Michael Batty
University College London, UK

Andy Bennett
Brock University, Canada

Gavin Bridge
University of Manchester, UK

William Cartwright
RMIT University, Australia

Vera Chouinard
McMaster University, Canada

Tim Cresswell
Royal Holloway, University of London, UK

Simon Dalby
Carleton University, Canada

Caitlin DeSilvey
The Open University, UK

Klaus Dodds
Royal Holloway, University of London, UK

Martin Dodge
University of Manchester, UK

Danny Dorling
University of Sheffield, UK

Ian Douglas
University of Manchester, UK

Chris Gibson
University of New South Wales, Australia

Howard Gillette
Rutgers University, USA

Peter Gordon
University of Southern California, USA

Jon Goss
University of Hawaii, USA

Colin Green
Middlesex University, UK

Bernd J. Haupt
Penn State University, USA

Lesley Head
University of Wollongong, Australia

Catherine Heppell
Queen Mary, University of London, UK

Jane Holgate
London Metropolitan University, UK

Phil Hubbard
Loughborough University, UK

Richard Huggett
University of Manchester, UK

Graeme Hugo
University of Adelaide, Australia

Helen Jarvis
University of Newcastle upon Tyne, UK

Martin Jones
University of Wales, Aberystwyth, UK

Maurie C. Kelly
Penn State University, UK

Philip Kelly
York University, Canada

Rob Kitchin
National University of Ireland, Maynooth, Eire

Lily Kong
National University of Singapore, Singapore

Richard J. Ladle
University of Oxford, UK

Ana C.M. Malhado
University of Oxford, UK

A.M. Mannion
University of Reading, UK

Janice Monk
University of Arizona, USA

Patrick Nunn
The University of the South Pacific, Fiji

Pau Obrador-Pons
University of Exeter, UK

Shii Okuno
University of Marketing and Distribution Sciences, Japan

Eric Pawson
University of Canterbury, New Zealand

Jan Penrose
University of Edinburgh, UK

Chris Perkins
University of Manchester, UK

Richard Phillips
University of Liverpool, UK

Marcus Power
University of Durham, UK

John Preston
University of Southampton, UK

Michael Pryke
The Open University, UK

Denise Reed
University of New Orleans, USA

Brian Robson
University of Manchester, UK

Paul Routledge
University of Glasgow, UK

D.A. Sear
University of Southampton, UK

Ian Simmons
University of Durham, UK

Victor F.S. Sit
University of Hong Kong, China

Ronald Skeldon
University of Sussex, UK

Richard G. Smith
University of Swansea, UK

Susan J. Smith
University of Durham, UK

Michael A. Summerfield
University of Edinburgh, UK

Jim Walmsley
University of New England, Australia

R.P.D. Walsh
University of Wales, Swansea, UK

Kevin Ward
University of Manchester, UK

Barney Warf
Florida State University, USA

Katie D. Willis
Royal Holloway, University of London, UK

Henry Wai-chung Yeung
National University of Singapore, Singapore

Kathryn Yusoff
The Open University, UK

Preface

The *Companion Encyclopedia of Geography* provides an integrated view of geography through a unifying theme of place and places at different scales. The highly praised first edition of the encyclopedia, subtitled *The Environment and Humankind*, centred on the theme of inter-relationships between physical and human factors. It adopted a chronological framework and sought an integrated and holistic view of the world as habitat. The second edition, with the subtitle *From Local to Global*, takes a fresh, forward-looking, but equally fundamental and unifying focus – the concept of place and the tensions of writing about local responses to different scales of change. It explores the nature of places, documents and exemplifies forces and actors producing different kinds and rates of change, and considers the role of the geographical imagination and responses to the challenges of the future. The emphasis is upon local regional and global pressures leading to change, and the ways in which nature and culture have responded to these. Carefully selected experts have written lucid and inviting chapters with international appeal that at once inform and provoke thought. These invited authors approached their individual contributions in the spirit of the entire volume – that the nature and understanding of places depends upon a variety of factors and upon individual and community responses that need analysing in an integrated manner.

Whilst not claiming comprehensiveness, we believe that this edition gives an integrated view of modern geography, drawing together many contemporary human and physical strands of the subject around the theme of place and change. It centres around six key areas. First, it explores ideas of place as human habitat, as landscape, as individual place, as social place, and as network. Second, it examines the natures of the different natural and human forces that produce change. Third, it investigates the ways in which organizations operating at different scales influence national policies, contrasting regional initiatives with governance of cities and discussing the significance of the firm, household and individual. Fourth, it probes the nature of change in particular circumstances, ranging from places of dramatic change to areas of stagnation, and the brand new places created in cyberspace. Fifth, it scrutinizes the ways in which people have imagined and communicated the character of places through different media – artistic, photographic, scientific or filmic – and through oral culture. Sixth, it explicates the remarkable diversity of responses to change.

We trust that by its unifying theme and by attention to such issues as integrative thinking, scale and multidisciplinary approaches, the book will appeal to teachers and students of geography and scholars and students in neighbouring disciplines that have an interest in contemporary geography and the relationships between society, the environment, and the Earth as human habitat.

Ian Douglas
Richard Huggett
Chris Perkins

How to use this book

The *Companion Encyclopedia of Geography* comprises 64 chapters of roughly equal length, arranged in six parts and two volumes. Volume 1 contains four parts – the nature of place, forces for change, actors in the process, and examples of the nature, rate and direction of change. Volume 2 contains two parts – the geographical imagination and responses to the geographical drivers of change. The editors introduce each part and provide an overview of the component chapters. To assist the reader, each chapter has cross-references to other chapters, where appropriate. In addition, each chapter has a further reading section, which contains useful introductory texts and articles. The index covers both volumes and enables the reader to find individual topics and to cross-reference ideas.

Acknowledgements

We should like to thank several people without whose efforts and support we should never have completed this large project. For asking us to edit a second edition and friendly assistance during its early stages, Dominic Shrayne and Gerard Greenway. For painstaking work in the preparation of diagrams and plates, Nick Scarle and Graham Bowden. For reviewing the mapping chapter, Martin Dodge. For gently keeping us on track, Jamie Ehrlich in Routledge's New York office. And for patience and politeness in the face of editorial pressure for them to 'produce the goods', the contributors.

Part I

The nature of place

Introduction

Chris Perkins

The introductory section of the encyclopedia sets out a number of different theoretical positions that have been adopted towards the concept of place. These five chapters frame different conceptions of place that are picked up later in the two volumes. Ecological notions of place are contrasted with contested views of place as landscape, more individual experiential approaches and the role of social power. The section concludes with a chapter reviewing non-dualistic and relational thinking of place as network.

The first chapter by Ian Simmons argues for an integration of people with environmental concerns. Charting the ecological history of the planet, he considers the changing role of landforms, soils, vegetation and wildlife as contributory elements of the Earth's ecosystems which reflect natural attributes and human ingenuity. It can be argued that this kind of environmental relationship is at the heart of geography. The chapter considers human control and symbolic relations as perhaps the most important lenses through which to understand changing environmental relations in different places.

Also, all places can be seen as segments of the landscape, with a physical form, and usually signs of human uses. However, landscape can also be seen as a metaphor, imagined as well as real. The ecologist, the landscape historian, the geographer, the artist, the planner, the sociologist: each has a very different response to the nature of places as landscapes. They read the landscape as place in a different way. Chapter 2 by Richard Huggett and Chris Perkins explores the contested nature of place as landscape. The natural is contrasted with the transformed, the imagined with the real. It traces the changing ways in which form, scales and functions of landscapes have been apprehended by different disciplines, and charts the interaction of people with physical landscapes to explore notions of cultural landscapes and histories of landscape change, and to unpack the stories embedded in differing places.

Place is also clearly experienced by the individual. Humanistic geographers in the 1970s focused upon these 'lived in' contexts in order to explore the meanings that places bring to people's lives. Tim Cresswell in Chapter 3 stresses the materiality and practice entangled with these meanings in order to reveal the nature of some of these links. Topophilia and exclusion are explored to reveal the nature of people's attachments and the key role of memory is highlighted. In an era supposedly characterized by the triumph of uniformity, and the rise of 'non-places', Cresswell argues that places continue to matter. He also stresses that the

1

humanistic focus upon the individual alone hugely underplays the profoundly social ways in which the materiality and meanings of place can become powerful social forces when they are enacted by individuals.

The next chapter picks up on these relations between societies and places. Phil Hubbard shows in Chapter 4 how the much-vaunted reassertion of space in social theory has been theorized. He focuses on exclusion, showing how social power makes places and in turn is reified in the ongoing relations between people and the societies in which they live. The chapter explores the ways in which locale is constructed, and how it impacts upon social and political practices. It shows how social norms exclude and create boundaries that define and prescribe appropriate behaviour, and discusses the ways in which representations reinforce and create particular places. Class, race, gender and sexuality are all employed as categories in this process. Hubbard stresses the dynamic qualities of this kind of approach to place and calls for a critical geographic engagement with the powerful forces of change.

Places may also be viewed as an outcome of relationships in a complex network: in this context all places are constituted by relations between natural and cultural actors. Chapter 5 by Richard G. Smith explores how network-based approaches to place have changed from scientific and Cartesian notions of density, connectivity, orientation, nodes, vectors and surfaces, to the more socially nuanced ideas embodied in actor-network theory and other poststructural approaches. Connections, relationships, flows and change have become more important than forms. Smith argues that focusing on places *in* networks is inadequate. Instead, every place can be seen as relational and, indeed, with relational effects – places *are*, he argues, networks. He concludes that it is time to challenge long-held assumptions about places and time to attend to the politics of connectivity!

1

Living on the Earth

Ian Simmons

Through a lens, mostly

Direct and unmediated experience of the world around us is rare. Our five senses receive stimuli like light, heat and texture, noise and flavour, but even these feed into a complex of mind which tells us what we might think about them and, much to the point, what words we might use when we communicate to others about them. It follows that any account of the past and present of our species and its relations to the non-human components of the world (like the atmosphere, soils, plants, animals, the oceans, freshwater) is mediated through human minds and their products, including technology. Some channels of knowing are very direct and probably give us an insight into the very essence of the object or process being examined, whereas others distance us in many ways other than the literal.

Our knowledge of the non-human world is dominated by what science tells us. There are other approaches: getting wet in the rain needs no science degree to inform us that we ought to have had an umbrella. Many non-western societies still have a body of shared information about plants, animals, weather and similar material phenomena which is reliable for their purposes and often more acceptable locally than imported 'science' imparted by ephemeral visits from development experts. Yet we mostly expect that science will give us the most reliable knowledge (albeit subject to ongoing modification) about what is 'out there', even though we know that our own minds are also limited in what they can understand. We need a label for the non-human world, to encompass all those facets of the universe which are outside our skins. 'Environment' is much used, though it tends to refer to this planet only or else to all kinds of other things like 'the business environment' or 'the learning environment' which derive from its basic meaning of something which surrounds. Perhaps better is 'nature' which, although also used in a multiplicity of ways ('human nature', 'things of this nature'), is available to encompass the phenomena of the physical world. However, its boundary with humankind is porous, like our skins, and care is needed in its use. Here it means 'the physical phenomena of the universe outside the physical manifestation of humans'. Those parts of nature which surround us and interact with us (actually or potentially) can be called environment, and this includes non-human living organisms.

The physical conditions of planet Earth have never been constant. Continents have moved, ice ages come and gone, oceans and mountains have changed places. Throughout those millions of years one key process has remained: the evolution of living forms. No matter what cataclysms or even gradual changes may have brought about extinctions, life has survived and new forms have emerged able to reproduce and survive in the new conditions. This continues to be the case even though human intervention in evolutionary processes is increasing: the rapid mutation of viruses and bacteria or the emergence of pesticide-resistant malarial mosquitoes reminds us of it. However, to consider the world as a set of human habitats, however, a datum line is needed, because not all geological time is relevant. The evolution of human beings from their ape-like ancestors some 4 million years ago provides one time horizon for consideration. Another time horizon might be the evolution of our own species (*Homo sapiens sapiens*) in the human lineage, at perhaps 50,000 years ago. Yet another might be the final disappearance of the major ice sheets from most of the northern hemisphere's landmasses around 10,000 years ago, which allowed the formation of most of the habitat types that were home to the human societies about which we know most from archaeology, anthropology, historical geography, palaeoecology and a myriad of historians' sources.

At around 10,000 years ago, the globe was emerging from a major ice age and the story of the next 3,000 years is of rapid adjustment to the warming world, sometimes with great speed (Alverson *et al.* 2003). Many tropical lowlands seem to have changed little during the million or so years of intermittent glaciations based on the present poles, but mountains in the tropics, many deserts, temperate zones, tundras and forests all shifted their basic vegetation type (e.g. the tundras of western Europe becoming clad with birch-pine woodland and then with deciduous forests dominated by oaks and beeches) or underwent species' shift within a vegetation type as cold-tolerant species were replaced by those better able to reproduce in warmer condition, as with the linden/lime (*Tilia* spp.) within the European forests. Somewhere about 5,000 BC the zones of vegetation and soils ('biomes') approximated those maps of 'natural vegetation' often found in atlases. One immediate relationship can be spotted: the influence of solar radiation on biome distribution, modified by the amount of precipitation received and by altitude. So, in a spatial sense as well as in time, climate is a major factor in deploying the products of organic evolution and their combination into locally and regionally interacting combinations of climate, soils, water, plants and animals which are labelled 'ecosystems'. Two further features must be noted: the planet is 70 per cent oceans and so the seas are always a relevant feature of any explanations at this level of generalization; and change is constant. Climates are rarely the same from millennium to millennium: many influences shift their patterns of incidence. The evolutionary processes in life-forms are rarely predictable as there is a random element in genetic recombination. Therefore, the world of Nature into which many human societies expanded and made their homes had two major characteristics: tremendous diversity at all spatial scales, and a lack of total equilibrium: the only unchanging context of life was change.

Not man apart

This was the plea of the US poet Robinson Jeffers talking of the love of Nature. He sometimes saw humans as contiguous parts of Nature, with the same characteristics as other animals. To be sure, the genus *Homo* shares many biological properties with other warm-blooded mammals: the need to maintain a constant core temperature, long periods of gestation and infant dependence are found in many, though not all, mammal species. Other traits which might be found in either group but whose crossover presences are vigorously debated in the scientific community include the propensity towards violence, altruism and sexual promiscuity. Historically, many writers have attempted to specify the uniqueness of humanity: animals that use tools to make tools, that cook their food, that laugh, that worry about the future, have all been candidates. Recent work on genetics has shown that approximately 98 per cent of human DNA is the same as that of chimpanzees. Anthropologists in particular are at pains to point out that this is to some extent a misleading indicator of human speciation as 25 per cent of human DNA is similar to that of dandelions and no great consanguinity is adduced from that. If we claim difference from or similarity to other animals then we must say which animals (Midgley 1995).

To say that human societies are simply a product of evolution in the same way that birds evolved from reptiles is counter to what we can observe; similarly, to say that human societies can float free of the non-human world is denied by every breath we take and every mouthful of food we eat. Better to argue in favour of a holistic approach in which human cultures in all their richness and diversity have a variety of linkages with the rest of the universe. Some are directly dependent, such as the supply of oxygen. Some are indirectly independent: food is a necessity and it depends eventually upon photosynthesis but the form in which it comes is culturally very variable. In Japan, raw sea slug is acceptable at dinner but blue cheese has very few takers. Others are indeed independent: the virtual worlds of the movies and TV drama can be created anywhere on Earth given the right bits of technology. Human cultures apprehend the rest of the universe (and especially the nearby parts of it) mostly through mediating 'lenses', of which language, memory and technology are integral and important parts. The role of the first two is amplified in later contributions to the present work: here it is sufficient to say that language, for example, is often critical in formulating human attitudes to Nature: different languages use what seem like equivalent words but which in fact carry variant meanings. Memory is critical in environmental histories with a human component, where it is often alleged, to put it crudely, 'that you cannot know where you are going unless you know where you have been'. The most obvious of this triad of cultural features is technology. There is again the possibility of direct connection: if you wish to dig a ditch then there is a difference between using a combined pick/shovel made from deer antler and making use of a JCB with a bucket attachment. There is once more indirect connection: experiencing the non-human world through TV wildlife or travel programmes is likely to change whole sets of attitudes about the objects portrayed and hence future actions. Floating free is another technological possibility: the journalist Nigel Calder suggested in the 1960s that the future of both Humanity and of Nature depended on their separation, with humans all living under plexiglass domes and letting the rest of the planet run itself (Calder 1967). Therefore, the shorthand term 'culture' used to encompass all those facets of human behaviour which are comprised of the total body of material artefacts and of their collective mental equivalents, which are transmitted and transmuted from generation to generation, is a useful working concept.

At every moment, be treated with respect

In the early millennia of the warm period known as the Holocene, which followed the last major ice age (in which the Holocene may well be an interglacial stage), the human cultures were dominated by those whose existence depended upon the gathering of wild plant material and the hunting of wild animals: that is, food collection. The term 'hunter–gatherer people' is often applied to such cultures. The succeeding economy, which revolved around the domestication of plants and animals ('agriculture') produced rather than collected food but did not replace the earlier type all at once: a few such groups persisted into the twentieth century, albeit on the margins (in every sense) of the modern world. That state of affairs contrasts with the period about 10,000–7,000 years ago when the food collectors had occupied most of the evolving biomes of the planet (Barnard 2004).

The success of the hunter–gatherers is reflected in their occupation of almost every habitat. On the bleak north slopes of North America and Eurasia, for example, the groups preceding today's Inuit and their equivalent Russian groups hunted seal, fish and caribou/reindeer together with a little summer plant material. In the semi-deserts of sub-Saharan Africa, it was possible to find enough plant material to stay well above starvation level, a situation which extended to the fringes of the Sahara where hunter–gatherers found conditions wetter than those of recent centuries. The lowland tropical forests of the Americas were once thought to have been desolate of hunter–gatherers but recent work has indicated their presence. In the Manaus region of the lowland Amazon basin, foraging societies who used caves have left evidence of paintings, pigments, carbonized fruits and wood in those sites, dating from 11,000–8,000 years ago. Virtually all of temperate Europe had stone- and wood-using groups who preceded the adoption of agriculture. Whenever humans lived by the sea, they developed ways of utilizing its diverse food resources.

About 50 years ago, it was common for hunter–gatherers to be regarded as 'children of Nature' who lived off the local ecosystems without any manipulation of Nature. This view has now changed so that environmental management by hunter–gatherers has been detected in many places. In the later Mesolithic cultures of upland Britain, 8,500–5,500 BP, evidence for forest recession is quite plentiful: the pollen of forest trees is partially replaced by species of open ground; there are many deposits with charcoal in them, and woodland is overtaken by bog vegetation. The upper edge of the woodland was the main scene of disturbance. Such a transition zone is of course always the most susceptible to climatic change, but this zone is also prone to the kinds of disturbance in which fire is implicated. The clearest indications of the processes at work come from central Pennine sites. At 6,000 BP, for example, there is a second temporary retraction of the limit of the upland forest which is associated with evidence of burning (Tallis and Switsur 1990).

Australia seems a more likely place than upland England and Wales for fire management by gatherer–hunters. In 1664, Abel Tasman sailed along the west coast and reported fire and smoke everywhere; one late nineteenth-century European traveller was so struck with the amount of Aboriginal burning that he wondered if the people 'lived on fire instead of water'. Reports from early European visitors to Australia suggest that the firestick was an important accompaniment of travel by Aborigines and that routes across country might be marked by burned swathes. One investigation reported some 5,000 separate bush fires per year in an area of 30 km². Some areas were not burned, so as to maintain a mosaic of vegetation patches, but a great number of plants became more accessible and better yielding to the gatherer economy. Firing also aided hunting, for thickets of spinifex could be set alight to flush out lizards, bandicoots and kangaroos; and the fire torch made night fishing possible (Pyne 1991). So, when an anthropologist described fire 'as the first great force employed by man', the food collectors were the pioneers.

The forces which hunter–gatherers were able to exert on their environments may have extended to the extirpation of several taxa of animals. In North America, soon after 11,000 BP, two-thirds of the large (adult weight over 50 kg) mammal fauna disappeared: it included three genera of elephants, six genera of armadillos, ant-eaters, and sloths, fifteen genera of ungulates and many carnivores dependent upon those groups. This mass extinction more or less coincides with one accepted set of dates for human colonization of Canada and the USA via the Bering land bridge and an ice-free corridor just east of the Cordillera. In contrast, the rapid fluctuations in climate of the terminal Pleistocene provide an alternative explanation. But were there enough people to kill off all those animals? Both views have been extensively canvassed, with the anthropogenic camp bringing in as validation the extinction of the moa bird in New Zealand (Aotearoa), the megafauna of Madagascar and dwarf elephants in Java and Sulawesi, because they all occurred soon after initial human colonization of those islands. Maybe climatic changes introduced considerable tension in the animal populations, which a new and socially adept predator then more easily wiped out. So, fire and humans together laid an impress upon the land even in the early millennia of the Holocene.

This imprint is an outcome of human cultures in their diversity as well as ecological possibilities. Richard Nelson (1983) wrote of the Koyukon Indians that they lived in a world of eyes, in which the surroundings were aware, sensate, personified. They could feel, and be, offended so that they must 'at every moment, be treated with respect'. If, therefore, the ecological relationships of this world are to be explored, then the social characteristics of any group must be examined with regard to their ecological consequences. But the difficulty is simply that for most gatherer–hunters this distinction does not exist. We find that the cultural and natural worlds are distinct but that they interpenetrate constantly; each depends upon the other and they must maintain a harmony. Supernatural means and the proper ritual can bridge any differentiation of the two worlds. The distribution of power is based on trust rather than on domination by rank and this confidence extends to the whole cosmos, including the food sources who, for example, may be conceived as humans in temporary disguise that have chosen to don animal skins in order to offer themselves to the human brethren. Similarly, the hunters' weapons were means of knowledge of Nature rather than a means of control.

Philosophy bakes no bread

However, once bread is assured then there is time for philosophy, and so one of the great achievements of agriculture was to free some people from getting their own food and having time to construct and, especially, to write down symbolic accounts of the multifarious natural and human worlds. The central fact is that a species which had been totally food-collecting became largely food-producing. In 10,000 BC the world population was perhaps 4 million, but in AD 1750 (an arbitrary but not unrealistic date for the onset of industrialization) it may have been 720 million, and solar-based agriculture was the economic foundation for that growth. The transfer from dependence upon food collection to food production, from the usufruct of the wild to the reproduction of the tamed, has misty beginnings with no sense of only one place or any one time. By about 10,000 BP there were some areas of the world that had shifted irrevocably to the new life: the hill lands of south-west Asia, moving downwards to the great river valleys of that region, together with south and east Asia where much land now below sea level had added to the space for human colonization (Harris 1990).

In environmental terms, the innovation never stayed put in the environments in which it first developed. In one group of expansions, the successful amplification was into water control. Its most spectacular results have been in the great river valleys such as the Euphrates, Nile, Yangtze and Indus, where elaborate systems of irrigation stored water from peak flows against a drier season when crops such as rice and wheat might then benefit from a hot sun under which to ripen. Another group of enlargements was into forests, where systems of shifting cultivation became established. Though associated mostly with tropical and semi-tropical lands, this system was present in European prehistory and in the coniferous forests of Finland until the nineteenth century. The last major augmentation of domesticate adoption was the use of herded animals to crop plants inedible to humans in lands that are very dry or very cold. This is collectively called pastoralism, and the animals herded range from the reindeer and yak through to the more familiar sheep and goats.

In practising agriculture, humans create new genotypes. Hunter–gatherers had experience in this practice with the dog, and this was extended to other animal species as well as a fairly wide range of plants. Domesticates need to be hardy since they have to survive the selective pressures of new conditions of soil, temperature, humidity, and infection by parasites and pests. They must be adaptable to living together as fields of wheat or herds of goats, be able to reproduce without too much human aid, and not require inputs of tending beyond that which the human community can supply. In the case of animals, they need preferably to be non-territorial, respond to a herd leader and be slow to flight when alarmed. Farming also creates new ecosystems. Like breeding, some creations are deliberate and some unintentional, though maybe more accidental consequences are found, or at any rate survive to be chronicled. The core of the first class is the permanent field in which a crop or crops are grown year on year (or more frequently) with or without a fallow period. This alters most of the characteristics of the soil and water regime of the field and adjacent area and in turn may require further selection among the genes of the selected crop plant. A variant of this system uses a shifting field which is abandoned when its fertility falls: the tropical versions in forest and savannah are best known. If fertility levels were maintained in these systems (which generally meant the levels of nitrogen and the crumb structure of the soil and hence the input of manure from one source or another) then it was often possible to produce a surplus. This freed people from growing their own food and so made possible many other kinds of land uses, as well as having social consequences. Thus societies had gardens for pleasure, hunting parks, managed woodland, and land devoted to high-status but unessential crops, for dyes, exotic fruits, drugs and above all, cities. Though most obvious in, for example, eighteenth-century Europe, the antecedents can be found in most of the ancient riverine civilizations such as Egypt, China and India.

The second class of relationships is the accidental. Many of these are apparent and have been so, it appears from sedimentary records, since the earliest days of cultivation. Higher rates of runoff entrain sediments, so floods are more frequent and erosion on slopes enhanced, with concomitant deposition in valleys and at the coast. On-site, a whole class of plants and animals are classified as unwanted and labelled as 'weeds' and 'pests'. On ranges used by pastoralists, grazing above a certain density and frequency means that some plants are unable to regenerate and their place is taken by species unpalatable to the herded beasts. An agricultural landscape is thus often one of a very large degree of makeover by human influences, the more so if it has been thus used for millennia.

Fire was still a key tool but wind- and water-mills, the plough, explosives and paper-making do not exhaust any list of inventions with environmental consequences. Similarly, it is not possible to list all the environments and all the makeovers for which our species was responsible even before industrialization. However, there is clearly a story of massive change over a long period, constantly bearing in mind that the predominant source of energy for human communities was the sun, mostly mediated via photosynthesis but also through wind and falling water. The environmental impact of humans was nevertheless increasingly channelled through technology and the possession of a hard metal such as iron being the key to many alterations and impacts: the term 'the iron age' deserves a wider circulation outside the discipline of archaeology.

Just as farming created new genotypes and new ecosystems, it also generated new patterns of thought and behaviour. We cannot know the psychological climates which engendered early agriculture, though we might accept the probability that there was an element of compulsion involved: think of the weeding, the storage problems and the organization of water control, the disposal of wastes and the gathering of firewood together with the likely accumulation of rats and fleas. Nevertheless, once agriculture had gained momentum and irreversibility, there was more food and more people, more concentrations of both, more specialization in food production and consumption and in people's occupations, more organizations allocating resources over greater distances, and crucially a differentiation of power among groups of people (Oelschlaeger 1991).

Accomplished in a few instants

Queen Victoria went to the Great Exhibition of 1851 and was so impressed by the machinery that she wrote in her diary:

> What used to be done by hand and take months doing is now accomplished in a few instants by the most beautiful machinery ... We saw hydraulic machines, pumps, filtering machines of all kinds, machines for purifying sugar – in fact every conceivable invention.

She was seeing the outcome of about 100 years of industrialization in an era which lasted until about 1950. The underlying essential of the industrial era is the human ability to supplement the flows of solar energy with that of fossil fuels which are essentially mineral in form. Like living tissue, which they once were, coal and oil (and the derivative natural gas) are carbon compounds; reflecting their geological heritage they are distributed world-wide, though not uniformly so. But their adoption meant that industrial energy was no longer dependent upon the use of surface area. Yet we often overlook the fact that the energy subsidy was also applied to agriculture since it is the transport and the manufacturing consequences that attract most attention. Producing more wheat per hectare may be ecologically as significant as producing millions of 'cheap tin trays', but the latter has a higher profile because the development of manufacturing is the new element. It implies the production of a high volume of goods and their fabrication in factories, i.e. on a concentrated site rather than piecemeal in workers' houses around a rural area. High-volume production also called forth the standardization of time and the fragmentation of manufacturing on the production line.

As neither the raw materials nor the social context were favourable everywhere, there were core areas of development of the new industrial ecology and an uneven spread in time and space via, mostly, trade and empire. So the cultural basis of the new economy cannot be overlooked, the more so as the changes wrought were truly Promethean in scale and in diversity of mode ('all the arts'), admitting to no sense of limits in any form or direction. Moreover, none of the previous energy supplies were lost and new technology gave added utility to such sources as falling water, once electricity became known and controllable (Grübler 1994).

The core areas of industrial growth are well known: they evolved where there was coal, iron ore and access to other raw materials such as the limestone used as a flux in blast furnaces. If

England was the core zone, then many other parts of Great Britain, Europe as far east as the Urals, eastern USA and eventually Japan followed by 1900. The 'benefits' of industrial production were spread outwards from these core territories through the media of trade and imperial direction, so that everywhere in the world knew about their existence even if only through new iron-edged tools or cheap guns. By 1950, even those countries without the basic industries of chemicals, iron and steel wanted factory-type production and so might develop electricity supplies from damming rivers or importing oil. Some larger nations, such as India, regarded heavy industry as essential to their post-independence economies. In cultural terms, it is interesting that very few nations turned their backs on industrialism even when they had a choice. There might be a short sharp debate about 'modernization' that resulted essentially in economic and political revolution, as with the restoration of the Emperor in Japan in 1867.

The ecology of the first 100 years of industrialism clusters around the processes of extraction (of mineral ores, coal and oil), of processing in factories, and in applying the goods in social and environmental fields. Each stage may need transport and each will have secondary effects: early coalfields not immediately near iron ore evoked canals to transport the coal, for example; the wastes from alkali plants poisoned fish in rivers many kilometres downstream; coal mines had a strong impact on forestry practices because of the demand for timber underground; every trend combined to foster the growth of towns and cities. Though the environmental consequences were inevitably strongest near to the centres of industrial activity, long-distance transport by water or railway meant that frontier industries sprang up well isolated from the burgeoning cities whose populations manned the new factories. The best example is probably logging of primary forests in lightly populated areas of North America during the nineteenth century. So it is impossible to overestimate the outreach of the industrial economy: where we do not detect it, then it may well be because the traces have been overlain by later changes. But look in the river sediments or in the layers of the peat bogs or in the health records of the populations and in the diaries that record the non-appearance of familiar species of wild animals.

The industrial era to 1950 can be seen as being one in which the human population came to demand three 'products' from its environments. The importance has varied in time and space and they are still present. The first is utility in the form of resources: energy as the binding resource that determines the availability of many others, including food, water and minerals. The second is sanitary, in the sense that environment is expected to receive and preferably process the wastes produced by industrial and urban conglomerations. Third, there is outdoor pleasure, once confined to a few social strata but increasingly becoming available to many in the industrial nations, if less so beyond them. To provide these social benefits, new genotypes and new ecosystems have been created. The new genotypes have mostly been deliberate creations, as with plant and animal breeding once these had been put on a scientific basis by an increasing knowledge of genetics. But incidental creations include species of plant adapted, for example, to grow on industrial wastes of high toxicity. One generalization which emerges is that some human-driven effects can be truly global: that material injected into the upper atmosphere can affect almost every part of the globe's environments.

The world as market

After about 1950, the term 'post-industrial' is normally used of societies in which the actual manufacture of goods carries less monetary value than that of services. (The acronym PIE will be used here.) The goods are still used but they are made in low- and middle-income places. Many parts of the world are nowhere near the same mix of making and consuming as 'western' nations like those of western and northern Europe, North America and Japan. However, because the western ways are so innovative and so much copied and as the west controls the media of advocacy of these ways of living, most countries aspire to them.

As with the nineteenth century, there are core areas and a constantly shifting periphery. In the case of the post-1950 world, the initial impetus lay without doubt with the USA. From there, the combination of corporate capitalism, high resource use, with rapid throughput of materials and a raised standard of material life for many (though never for all), has spread. Trade has been a major artery as always (plastics are ubiquitous) but the influence of film and TV is a difference from the preceding era. There was resistance to the American package in the shape of state socialism (in the USSR and its satellites, in a diluted form in the post-war Labour governments of the UK, in central America and in Cuba and above all in China) but most of these countries are now firmly in the grip of 'free trade' and neo-liberal thinking. This means that resources and their environmental linkages are deemed marketable and can have a price (Robertson 2003).

As in the entire Holocene, the numbers of humans are a basic element in environmental relations. In 1950, the annual growth rate was 1.5 per cent and between 1962 and 1972 rose to just above 2.0 per cent before dropping back to about 1.2 per cent by 2000. However, two-fifths of the world's population now lives in countries with a replacement level of population growth. Nevertheless, the 2,500 million (2.5 billion) people of 1950 grew to 6 billion in 1999, with just under 80 million being added to the total each year. As population growth is a key driver of environmental change, environmental writers and campaigners often adopt outspoken attitudes towards it. The high growth rates of the 1950s and 1960s, for example, led to a great deal of neo-Malthusian advocacy, with numerous campaigns and think-tanks aimed eventually at reducing growth rates in poorer countries but also in the rich nations whose consumption patterns were held to be destructive. Reduction of population growth rate is an interesting example of a social trend that loses its public high profile after a while. One attitude would be that this was a feedback process and that, indeed, the high visibility it gained resulted in the means being provided to most people to control their fertility. Pessimists have been heard to mutter that Malthus might be disapproved but was not disproved.

The technologies of the PIE era are in part continuations of the industrial decades and in part novel. Metals are still important but, for example, the centrality of steel is supplemented by the use of copper in wiring for a host of modern electrical applications. One ubiquitous set of materials since 1950 has been plastics, themselves offshoots of the refining of oil, and even in the worst situations (in refugee camps and after earthquakes) plastic sheeting is one of the first materials to appear. Trees are still the providers of paper, a demand propelled along by increasing literacy. In most of these mass material uses a different strand has arisen, namely that of re-use and recycling. This is not especially new in poor countries, where the picking-over of the city rubbish tip is normal, but an increasing practice in the rich in reaction to such things as the over-packaging of almost all consumer items.

The great technological novelty is miniaturization. In one literal sense this means that instrumentation in the environment (as elsewhere on Earth) can be placed in satellites or at the bottom of the oceans and thus accumulate measurements of a precision and a quantity hitherto impossible, and only manipulable because of the digital computer. At the same time, biotechnological techniques have allowed manipulation of living material at the molecular level so that engineering of the genetic characteristics of plants, animals, fungi, bacteria and viruses has become commonplace, albeit contested in some circumstances. The next step along this road (but not yet applicable, at any rate in unclassified contexts) is nanotechnology, using individual atoms as building-blocks. In spite of all this technology, the UNEP millennial overview listed a series of 'environmental surprises since 1950'. These were classified into unforeseen issues, unexpected events, new developments, and changes in trends (Table 1.1). There is another important aspect to this set of data, namely that perception is intimately connected with material events and processes. Many independent investigations and concerns (population, pollution and resource depletion, for example) were seen as related to each other and able to be viewed in ever wider contexts with labels such as sustainable development, climate change and loss of biodiversity. Moreover, the scale of focus shifted, as better knowledge and more concerned people showed that many substances had not only local but also national, international, world-wide and sometimes global pathways and storage pools (Millennium Ecosystem Assessment 2005).

More broadly still, there has been a continuing belief in the power of science and technology to solve problems. Rather than use less energy, for example, high-tech ways of sequestering carbon under the oceans are considered and money is invested in the possibilities of 'clean' energy from nuclear fusion, which is still 40 years off as it has been for the last

Table 1.1. Environmental surprises since 1950

Type of surprise	General examples	Cases
Unforeseen issues	CFC-induced ozone depletion	Hypothesized 1974, confirmed 1985
Unexpected events	Major oil spills	*Torrey Canyon* 1967; *Amoco Cadiz* 1978; *Exon-Valdez* 1989
	Accidental toxic events	Minamata disease 1959; PCB poisoning 1960s; Sveso dioxin leak 1976; Bhopal leak 1984; Basel chemical fire 1986
	Air pollution	London smog 1952; Indonesia forest fires 1997
	Nuclear accidents	Windscale 1957; Urals 1958; Three Mile Island 1979; Chernobyl 1986
	Biological invasions	Zebra mussel 1980s; mesquite in Sudan 1950s.
New developments	Pollution	Pesticide effects in birds 1962; Love Canal toxics; contaminants in Arctic ice 1970s
	Acid precipitation	Growing concern from 1972
	Climate change	1988 summer very hot; IPCC from 1990
	Tropical deforestation	Satellite images from 1980s
	Widespread consequences	Effects of Aswan High Dam 1970s; shrinkage of Aral Sea, 1980s
Changes in trends	Climate change: increase in occurrence of severe weather and El Niño events	1997–8 El Niño very severe
	Oil crisis from producer worries about depletion	1970s
	Fisheries collapse	Atlantic cod 1990s

Source: Adapted from UNEP (1999: 336).

40 years. Still, oil is cheap enough that baby sweetcorn can be flown from Thailand to Europe and Europeans can fly to Thailand for the weekend. Neither is without social and environmental consequences. Through all this, the pervasive power of the visual media has increased, pushing forward rising expectations of material anabasis.

All netted together

Two stories can be discerned. One is that Nature provides opportunities for humans but is at the same time indifferent to our presence. If humanity disappeared, then there would still be life on Earth and it would evolve in a Darwinian sense. The second is that humans recognize their dependence on Nature but mostly prefer not to acknowledge it. As the reserves of fossil fuel have enabled high-income economies (HIEs) to insulate themselves from the rest of the world, the day of open recognition of dependence has not yet come.

The upshot is, of course, that the two stories are woven together, 'all netted together' as Darwin wrote in one of his letters. Our impact upon Nature has been such that its integrity is now dependent upon our actions and that dependence seems to be extending to the global scale in the case of climate change and also the extinction of species on a world-wide scale. At the same time, we depend upon Nature to supply resources, to process wastes and to provide us with non-material benefits like for example, the chance sighting of a heron fishing if one happens to gaze from a window at the right time. Thus all geographical phenomena have an environmental component, as people eat and because they use some extra-somatic energy (though maybe not a lot in low-income economies) and they create wastes. So even in densely populated cities there are environmental linkages on hand and very probably at some distance as well: Manhattan is not self-sufficient for energy.

It is not enough to depict this netting together as if it were a simple weaving with even strands, regular knots and crisply defined spaces. The whole is uneven in every way and has changed through time. Understanding of these changes and their local and global implications helps us to make some sense of the diversity of our present world, and must be a precursor to all our attempts to find solutions. Yet just as a net will only work properly when under strain, when crises heighten the tension in the relations between humans and their surroundings, people attempt to learn lessons and manage those relations better, even if only for a short while. In this case, it looks as if particular movements in human societies have noticeable effects upon the natural world which result in greater fragmentations in that second world or, alternatively, produce coalescences. In the hunter–gatherers' era, the story is of an identification of human nature with 'natural' Nature: there is a felt flow from the stars to the next meal, and within that flow every component is important, particularly since without respect it may not be renewed. With the coming of agriculture, many relationships are changed. Time, for example, becomes linear rather than renewed annually. But the surpluses created by agriculture allow the stratification of society and the emergence of social elites, who in turn diversify the uses of the land and also intensify the demands upon it. Their technological development also creates coalescence as they can send out for products, and so plants and animals are transferred from continent to continent: the Americas obtained cattle and horses in return for maize and the potato. Botanic gardens can be seen as knots in the net. Each of these flows can cement the position of the recipients: new imports are status symbols before they are popular items.

The coming of industrialization makes these tensions even more apparent. The fragmentation of society is exacerbated by the difference between rich and poor at almost every scale, and the political divide is made plain in the surge of colonialism which the nineteenth century brought. Many management practices implanted fragmentation even further by, for example, the world-wide extinction of species such as the passenger pigeon and (almost) the North American buffalo, with regional equivalents such as the great bustard in southern England as downland was ploughed to feed industrial populations, or the osprey in Scotland as it ate the salmon favoured then as a sport fish by the rich. By contrast, the steamship and the railway allowed coalescence of people with their ideas (and their armies) and of goods, which in turn helped the movement of species, often in unexpected and undesired ways like the influenza epidemic which followed the First World War. Nature from time to time produced enforced coalescence: the first half of the nineteenth century was the worst phase of the 'Little Ice Age' in the northern hemisphere; there were at least eight severe El Niño episodes between 1828 and 1926, there was world-wide cooling after the eruption of Tambora (Indonesia) in 1815 (Davis 2001).

In today's world, these stresses are intensified. Any discussion of 'globalization' emphasizes the instant communication between distant places and the existence of 'virtual worlds' that is made possible by the miniaturization of electronic technology. This also means the further penetration of individualism, because there is less and less need for communal facilities when so many people can have an MP3 player to provide their own personal sound-bubble. The success of recorded music thus diminishes the need for the concert hall, for example. At the same time, the overall travel distance per head is increasing in all types of countries. Miniaturization is also affecting the biosphere. The collection of data from almost any organism is now possible, so that the nineteenth-century museum as a collection of information is superseded by computers. The genetic pool of the world's biota is seen as a resource for GM endeavours, including the creation of transgenic taxa. Thus eventually there will either be an enormous variety of 'tailored' spices (my special gut flora will be different from yours) or else the supermarket strategy of providing only a few very large stores might prevail: you can have the Durham gut flora, sir, but not the Manchester sort. The contribution of even smaller units in the shape of nanotechnology is yet to be explored. At the other extreme, there is a concern that the atmosphere's response to increased carbon loading does not reflect the source of the loading and that the unjust will probably be saved from the heavy rain. There seems at present little doubt that the higher the use of fossil fuels, the more species that become either extinct or at very low levels provide that ecosystems lose members with long-term consequences: the vacuuming of sand-eels from the North Sea basin affects the sea-bird populations as well as other fish all around the water body.

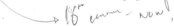

What sort of picture?

If we cannot but see the world through various lenses, then what kinds of pictures become visible? One constant factor links humanity and Nature through time and space: the desire of humans to control. If the control of Nature means the control of other humans first, then that is acceptable. Not even in the tenderest hunter–gatherer population is this wish absent, even though the means to achieve it are those of co-operation with Nature rather than conquest. So the habitats of human life on the planet are the spaces of control, with its exercise through all kinds of pathways and in hierarchies of dominance which usually now put Nature at the bottom, with occasional gestures at 'environmental impact'. Taken to extremes, there can be a desire to engineer the planet, in the sense of making all planned changes entirely predictable. So far, Nature seems to react with sets of unforeseen consequences, of the type that can get labelled 'fighting back' or the 'good whipping from Mother Nature' expressed after hurricane Katrina in the USA in 2005. The sharper the lens, the deeper in time human impacts can be traced: human-induced fire seems to have been significant in the global methane budget between AD 1 and AD 1700 (Ferretti *et al.* 2005).

Another constant is the wish of humans to formulate systems of symbols (words, music, money, clothing) to demonstrate their attitudes to each other and to the world around them. These can also counter the control of desires with those of celebration. The academic discipline of geography is one such collection of symbols and, as with all such collections, its fitness for its purposes needs careful examination at frequent intervals.

References

Alverson, K.D., Bradley, R.S. and Pederson, T.F. (eds) (2003) *Paleoclimate, Global Change and the Future.* Berlin: Springer.

Barnard, A. (ed.) (2004) *Hunter–Gatherers in History, Archaeology and Anthropology.* Oxford and New York: Berg.

Calder, N. (1967) *The Environment Game.* London: Secker and Warburg.

Davis, M. (2001) *Late Victorian Holocausts: El Niño Famines and the Making of the Third World.* London and New York: Verso.

Ferretti, D.F., Miller, J.B., White, J.W.C., Etheridge, D.M., Lassey, K.R., Lowe, D.C., MacFarling Meure, C.M., Dreier, M.F., Trudinger, C.M., van Ommen, T.D. and Langenfelds, R.L. (2005) Unexpected changes to the global methane budget over the past 2000 years. *Science* 309, 1714–17.

Grübler, A. (1994) Industrialization as a historical phenomenon. In R. Socolow (ed.) *Industrial Ecology and Global Change*, pp. 23–41. Cambridge: Cambridge University Press.

Harris, D.R. (1990) *Settling Down and Breaking Ground: Rethinking the Neolithic Revolution.* Amsterdam: Stichting Nederlands Museum voor Anthropologie en Praehistorie.

Midgley, M. (1995) *Beast and Man: The Roots of Human Nature*, revised edition. London and New York: Routledge.

Millennium Ecosystem Assessment (2005) http://www.millenniumassessment.org (accessed August 2005).

Nelson, R.K. (1983) *Make Prayers to the Raven: A Koyukon View of the Northern Forest.* Chicago: University of Chicago Press.

Oelschlaeger, M. (1991) *The Idea of Wilderness.* New Haven and London: Yale University Press.

Pyne, S. (1991) *Burning Bush: A Fire History of Australia.* New York: Holt.

Robertson, R. (2003) *The Three Waves of Globalization.* London and New York: Zed Books.

Tallis, J.H. and Switsur, V.R. (1990) Forest and moorland in the south Pennine uplands in the mid-Flandrian period. II. The hillslope forests. *Journal of Ecology* 78, 857–83.

UNEP (1999) *Global Environment Outlook 2000.* London: Earthscan.

2

Place as landscape

Richard Huggett and Chris Perkins

Consider the place shown in Plate 2.1 and Figure 2.1. Use these images to imagine the place, not as just as a photograph (see Chapter 37) or map (see Chapter 35). You may know the scene. In front of you is Wast Water, the deepest lake in England; straight ahead is Scafell Pike; close by is the wettest place in England. This is a landscape of physical superlatives, rocks and relief the legacy of the Ice Age and Borrowdale Volcanic geology, but it is also a cultured place. The small fields on the flatter ground in front of the lake are grazed by

Plate 2.1. Wasdale Head. Photograph by Rose Perkins.

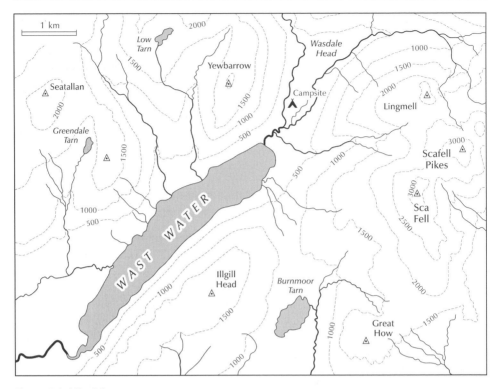

Figure 2.1. Wasdale.

Herdwick sheep and enclosed by dry-stone walls. These are pastures reclaimed from the wild, forming field patterns speaking of an age when farming made profits for tenant farmers. On the flat delta at the top of the lake you can pick out the wooded terrain around the National Trust campsite. The trees have only appeared in the last thirty years. This area was an open field used for camping within living memory. And the Lake District is now above all else a place where people take their leisure. Places change.

Some changes are allowed to happen; others are controlled more carefully. Unsightly footpath erosion is mitigated, repair teams preserve a particular idea of beauty and visitors come despite (and often because of) the difficult journey to this most remote and wildest corner of the Lakes. It is the romance of imagined wilderness that attracts visitors and tourists to the area. However, it also hides tensions as well as revealing pleasures. In the distance to the right are the cooling towers of Sellafield Nuclear Power Station, a legacy of an age before the North Sea Oil boom when technological progress was less questioned. The more immediate environment also hides turbulent undercurrents. In 2006 the National Park is suffering central government cutbacks and may be less able to resist development pressures and less able to support sustainable tourism or land management. The hill farmers and bed-and-breakfast owners are only just recovering from the catastrophic outbreak of foot-and-mouth disease.

This chapter is about the relations between place and landscape. It is about the many different ways places like Wasdale Head may be approached as landscapes. However, before considering landscape, what about the nature of place?

Place and space

Place is a multifaceted notion. At one level, it is simply a specific location identified by a referencing system or by a name on the map. At another level, individual places may bear some form of connection or relation to nearby places, forming spatial structures. Then again, place may connote much more than just a physical location or a spatial structure (e.g. Relph 1996); it may embody the character of a location – what is there – and how human cultures perceive the location and respond to it. And places like Wasdale are constantly *becoming*: rather than just existing they change and respond. So at a minimum, place has four facets:

1. locational
2. structural
3. cultural, and
4. perceptual and temporal.

As physical locations, places may be identified by reference to some grid system (e.g. eastings and northings) or by a name – Wasdale, the Mohave Desert, the Scilly Isles, Manchester. This locational view disregards scale or type of environment. Australia is a place as much as Uluru (Ayer's Rock) is a place. Place names are culture-laden. Many cultures name places after topographic features. In England, such place-name endings as –dale, –ford, –field and –ley betray a topographic origin. Wasdale is the valley with the lake. Family names may become associated with the topographically derived names. Macclesfield was founded by Anglo-Saxon settlers, whose headman may have been called Macca, a Saxon personal name, the place becoming known as 'Macca's field'. Cuffley is probably derived from a personal name, Cuffa, and *leah*, which is a clearing in a wood.

Structural facets of place concern links or relations between locations. They set places into wider landscape contexts and encompass the idea of geographical space. Space can be theorized in structural terms such as how flows, slopes, surfaces, networks, migration routes, trails, lines of communication, and so on, connect places. Physical geographers recognize many spatial structures – drainage basins, landforms, ecosystems, soil catenae, and so forth. Human geographers also recognize spatial structures – cities, nations, road networks, and so on. Throughout the history of geography, and particularly during the Quantitative Revolution of the late 1960s and early 1970s, spatial concepts have underpinned core areas of their discipline. For example, Coffey (1981) articulated a general spatial-systems theory arguing that concepts, rooted in spatial structure and spatial dynamics, underpin explanations of a wide range of phenomena in human and physical geography: spatial structure, comprising geometry, topology and dimensionality; and movements in space. Spatial structure and movements in space have been seen as expressions of spatial process, which involve growth and organization.

However, such schemes oversimplify the concerns of human geography. Cultural and social spaces do not lend themselves to a geometrical analysis (e.g. Hubert 1998, 1999). Cultural facets of place are captured in the following quotation:

> natural landscapes are the result of biophysical processes that shape the land and create the unmistakable differences between one place and another ... Similarly, human landscapes and settlements are the consequence of culture modifying and imposing its needs on natural or wild places.

(Hough 1990: 2)

In Australia, Aboriginal people have many sacred sites – rock clefts, valleys, water holes, rocks – that serve cultural and religious functions (Chatwin 1998). To the Aboriginals, the Australian landscape is laden with a cultural significance that is impalpable to people from other parts of the world.

Landscapes are also perceived and imagined, usually by being seen. They may have 'scenic' qualities, in which features of a place may be considered from an aesthetic angle (e.g. Downs and Stea 1974; Jackle 1987). Places like Wasdale are visited for these qualities. Romantic notions of scenic beauty emerged from eighteenth- and early nineteenth-century enlightenment encounters with places just like this (Whyte 2002: 70–121). The next chapter shows *how* people form bonds with places, focusing on the relations between individual and social constructions of places. Two constructs are important here: *topophilia*, the 'affective bond between people and place or setting', the 'human love of place ... diffuse as a concept, vivid and concrete as personal experience' (Tuan 1974: 92); and *topophobia*, its opposite, literally 'the fear of place'. Take the case of the people who use 'rail-trails', which are multi-use recreation trails established along disused railways. A study of such users suggested that place attachment has at least two dimensions: a place dependence, reflecting the importance of the place in facilitating a user's activity; and a more affective place identity, reflecting an individual's valuing of a setting for more symbolic or emotional reasons (Moore and Graefe 1994).

However, places are not only neutral static backdrops for human actions or imagining. Chapter 5 shows how they may also have agency, with relational qualities. And this agency is dynamic: places 'become' in a reflexive fashion, rather than being fixed and seen (Bender 2001). Places have 'rhythms', they shift and morph according to different patterns and influences (Mels 2004). Affectual responses bring landscapes into being, instead of simply working as a response to the place.

Landscape

It can be argued that the notion of landscape marries place with space, setting places within a geographical context. The term 'landscape' has several meanings that reflect views taken at different times and in different languages and societies. At root, however, core concepts of 'landscape' stem from European sources. Most Germanic languages used the word 'landscape' (*Landschaft* in German; *landschap* in Dutch) in the early Middle Ages as a counterpart for the Latin words *regio*, *patria* or *provincia*, meaning area, territory or region. By the end of the sixteenth century, a landscape also referred to a painted scene, in which the landscape was the subject of the painting and not merely a backdrop for the foreground figures. Landscape painting emerged as an art form during the fifteenth and sixteenth centuries and was an independent and popular genre in the seventeenth and eighteenth centuries (Casey 2002).

The first geographical notion of landscapes came from Alexander von Humboldt and others, who used the term 'landscape' to capture the total character of a region, including its natural, cultural and aesthetic qualities (e.g. Humboldt 1849: 252). This holistic meaning of 'landscape' emerged at a time when disciplinary boundaries were fluid and somewhat hazily defined. During the second half of the nineteenth century, increasing scientific specialization led to the waning of holistic concepts. However, holistic notions of landscapes enjoyed a renaissance in the first half of the twentieth century under the strong direction of such geographers as Paul Vidal de la Blache, Carl Ortwin Sauer and especially members of the German school led by Siegfried Passarge. For Sauer, a landscape is 'an area made up of a distinct association of forms, both physical and cultural (Sauer 1963: 321). Passarge considered the landscape to be geography's primary object of study and a synthesis of natural and cultural qualities of a region (see Antrop 2000). In the UK, the enormous influence of H.C. Darby led to a whole generation of geographers' becoming concerned with the empirical description and reconstruction of past cultural landscapes (e.g. Darby 1956, 1977). Meanwhile, W.G. Hoskins (1955) began the popularization of local historical studies in the UK and implicitly focused upon the description of the evolution of local cultural landscapes. Such work emphasized the case study, rather than seeking theoretical explanation.

The rebirth of holistic landscape concepts was short-lived. Academic disciplines continued to fragment during the twentieth century and holistic ideas faded. In their place evolved a range of different views, each serving the designs of a particular discipline. These views emerged in other natural and social sciences, in the humanities, and in the arts: aesthetics and art, ecology and soil science, history and archaeology, philosophy and psychology, geography and land survey, landscape architecture and planning. Each discipline concerned with landscapes has tended to develop its own applications and concepts. Approaches vary.

Landscape historian Richard Muir (1999), for example, identifies landscape history and heritage, the structure and scenery approach, landscapes of the mind, landscape politics and power, landscape evaluation, symbolic landscapes, landscape aesthetics, and landscape and place, but 'he largely ignores the more applied and empirical aspects of the practice of landscape ecology, landscape architecture and planning' (Huggett and Perkins 2004: 225). His account stresses the profound differences between those who view landscape as an objective reality, and those who use more subjective approaches.

In geography, some of the most influential 'scientific' approaches to landscape in the second half of the twentieth century came from Germany. In 1939, Carl Troll saw the landscape as a mixture of human enterprise and natural features and processes. This view harked back to the Humboldtian vision. We can trace two key concepts back to this root: *Landschaftsökologie*, linking geography and ecology, and *Landschaftshaushalt*. In French, *Landschaftshaushalt* has been translated as *économie des paysages* (landscape economy), and signifies the idea that a people look after a landscape (*Haushalt* means 'household'). This therefore implies a degree of management. Indeed, today the term 'landscape ecology' often includes landscape management. The International Association for Landscape Ecology's mission statement certainly conveys this impression: 'Landscape ecology is the study of spatial variation in landscapes at a variety of scales. It includes the biophysical and societal causes and consequences of landscapes heterogeneity' (IALE Executive Committee 1998).

It was in the Netherlands that an holistic view of landscapes was born in the 1970s. Antrop (2000) argues that new challenges in natural, ecological, cultural and social issues which emerged in this period were a justification for a new cross-disciplinary and holistic landscape agenda. More recently, there have been attempts from many different disciplines, including geography, to consolidate a cross-disciplinary approach to landscape that relies upon holistic understandings integrating natural sciences, human sciences and the arts under the umbrella of a systems approach (e.g. Décamps 2000; Naveh 2000; Naveh and Lieberman 1994; Tress *et al.* 2001). Technological advances towards the end of the century encouraged this holistic revival. Digital aerial photography, remote sensing and geographical information systems (GIS) facilitated a landscape-ecological approach that stresses the interactions between people and landscapes and focuses upon change. Indeed, it has been argued that this stress reaffirms a core concern for geographers and offers a unifying theme for future geographical enquiry, drawing together physical and human elements in the context of landscape form and process (Huggett and Perkins 2004). The reason for this is simple: 'Landscape is the prime sphere, where the combined effects of society and nature become visible' (Bürgi *et al.* 2004: 857).

However, artistic ideas of landscape as a human construct have also become more popular over the last thirty years. In the 1970s, geographers reacted against notions of spatial science by offering more humanistic approaches. They began to write about landscape as imagined as well as real, and humanistic approaches to landscapes became increasingly popular (e.g. Appleton 1975; Meinig 1979; Casey 2002).

Following the cultural turn in the 1980s, geographers began to adopt a more theoretical approach to landscape, one inspired by social theory. Attention shifted away from the *forms* of landscape and towards contested *meanings* of the processes underpinning their creation and reading (Huggett and Perkins 2004). Human geographers came to analyse power and interpret landscapes as texts imbued with symbolism (Duncan 1990; Cosgrove and Daniels 1988). In this kind of approach, the interpretation of a landscape depends upon one's worldview and varies across time, space, culture and belief (Bender 1993). For example, Aboriginal notions of the 'Dreaming' or 'Dream Time' could be seen as views of 'landscape', but also reflect a significantly different belief system, in which time is no longer separated from space and where creation myths are embodied in the landscape (Morphy 1993).

So despite pleas for unity from landscape ecologists, social scientists increasingly contest the 'landscape' as a concept and, moreover, the reading of landscape is consequently increasingly 'polysemic', open to multiple and contested interpretations (Huggett and Perkins 2004). These different readings are developed later in the chapter.

Landscapes admit of physical or cultural interpretations. Geomorphologists, landscape ecologists, pedologists and others are primarily concerned with the physical description and classification of landscape form and with landscape dynamics. Researchers concerned with the cultural landscape, with landscape history and with landscape architecture have also sought to recognize and to classify the landscape elements created by people and the processes occurring within them.

The forms and structures of landscape

Physical landscapes

Scientists from disciplines concerned with aspects of biological and physical landscape all tend to have their own conception of place and space. Geomorphologists, ecologists, pedologists and hydrologists conceive the landscape in different ways. Geomorphologists tend to see large structural units (mountains, plateaux, plains) or functional units such as drainage basins, hillslopes and dune systems. Pedologists focus on soil pedons (profiles) and large functional units (catenas, soil-landscapes). Hydrologists focus on drainage basins at various scales. Ecologists tend to focus more on landscape elements – patches, corridors and matrices – and large-scale units such as bioregions, which incorporate many elements of landscapes and have implication for sustainability (e.g. Bailey 2002). A practice shared by all these scientists is the identification of a set of basic landscape elements that in combination form various levels of regional landscape units. Geomorphologists combined landform elements (or a superabundance of equivalent terms) to form regional units such as sections, provinces, major divisions and continents (e.g. Linton 1949). Pedologists unite soil profiles or pedons to form polypedons and soilscapes (e.g. Buol *et al.* 1980). Hydrologists combine low-order drainage basins to form high-order drainage basins. Landscape ecologists combine patches, corridors and matrixes to form landscape mosaics and regions. In addition to these spatial landscape units, landscape ecologists identify landscape structures, which are sets of interrelated landscape elements (systems) that function as a whole. Examples are drainage networks, transport systems, urban settlements and agricultural systems.

Landscape ecology is hugely successful as a means of exploring spatial aspects of ecological systems. It forms a powerful model for viewing the structure and function of the physical landscape that, to some extent, integrates landforms, soils, hydrology and ecology, though it is primarily an ecological construct. At its core lies the patch–corridor–matrix model, which sees a heterogeneous mosaic of habitat islands connected by corridors and surrounded by a 'hostile' environment. This has had extraordinary success in explaining many features of species patterns and dynamics (e.g. Huggett and Cheesman 2002). Patches, corridors and matrixes – the landscape elements – are themselves made of individual plants (trees, shrubs, herbs), small buildings, roads, fences, small water bodies, and the like. Moreover, they include natural and human-made landscape components, so the patch–corridor–matrix model integrates the biological and physical aspects of landscapes. Patches are uniform (homogeneous) areas that differ from their surroundings – woods, fields, parks, ponds, rock outcrops, houses, gardens, and so forth. Corridors are strips of land that differ from the land to either side, such as roads and roadsides, powerlines, trails, hedgerows and rivers. They link inextricably with patches. Matrixes are the background ecosystems or land-use types in which patches and corridors are set, and are normally the dominant ecosystem or land-use – forest, grassland, heathland, arable, residential, greenhouses or whatever – in an area. Above the level of landscape elements are landscape mosaics, within which there is a range of landscape structures. These structures are distinct spatial clusters of ecosystems or land uses or both. Although patches, corridors and matrixes combine in sundry ways to create landscape mosaics, landscape ecologists recognize six fundamental types of landscape: large-patch landscapes, small-patch landscapes, dendritic landscapes, rectilinear landscapes, chequerboard landscapes and interdigitated landscapes.

Some landscape ecologists take the cultural landscape as their primary focus and do not use the patch–corridor–matrix approach. Instead, they classify form in relation to function. For instance, Willem Vos and Herman Meekes (1999) distinguish different landscape types, according to the intensity and nature of human control – 'industry', 'supermarket', 'historical museum', 'ruin' and 'wilderness'. They show how intensification has resulted in landscapes devoted to industrial production; in areas with increasing urban populations, landscapes increasingly support a wide range of functions serving urban consumption, including food production, industry, recreation, housing, mineral resource extraction and nature conservation. More traditional landscapes that have escaped intensification may survive where land is less suitable for production. In the most marginal areas like the Lake District, formerly cultural landscapes may be reverting to Nature. Natural landscapes survive as relicts, or have reverted from one of the other types. They also identify landscape elements that may be associated with each of these types. For example, the marginal 'ruined' landscapes are likely to be characterized by deserted settlements and disused field systems, whereas multifunctional landscapes in western urban hinterlands are most likely characterized by new elite housing estates, recreational land uses, second homes, specialist agricultural production and nature reserves.

Cultural landscapes

Elements of the cultural landscape may be described in a similar morphological and functional approach as that relating to the elements of biophysical landscapes. Muir (1999) shows how rural landscapes comprise surfaces linked by networks with nodes and argues these create local landscape distinctiveness. He identifies the use of land, boundaries, monuments and human constructions and settlements. In an English rural landscape fields might be enclosed or open, be irregular or geometric in shape, be organized locally or on a larger scale, be fenced, walled, hedged or ditched. Their form may reflect current practices or they may survive as a relict of the past. Other land uses might include woodland. Boundaries here may define ownership or responsibility for territory, and may be organized hierarchically (Muir 1999). They may alter how the land is used and reflect past cultural practice or environmental influences.

Cultural networks such as tracks, paths, roads, railways, canals, pipelines and other route-ways, carrying traffic, information or material goods allow the landscape to function. The form of the network is also likely to reflect past functions. At the nodes of this network may be cultural features such as settlements. Village forms and functions have for long been a productive focus of geographical research (e.g. Roberts 1987). Researchers have traced changing patterns of settlement and explored reasons for growth or decline. Settlement patterns have also been related to agricultural practices, and village functions and hierarchies charted. Monuments and features have been distinguished and characterized, such as houses, cemeteries or types of church. Indeed, this kind of emphasis has been central to the Berkeley School's approach to landscape (see Chapter 14 for a critique of this superorganic notion of culture).

Landscape processes

Landscape elements and regions are linked by flows of energy and materials, seeds, spores and individuals. As cultural landscapes, the political, legal, social, economic and cultural context is also always fluid. Interconnections occur at all levels and change is continuous.

Scientific approaches regard the landscape as a hierarchy of spatial structures and circulations – natural and human-made – that are constantly readjusting to one another and to changes in their environment. These circulations occur at local, regional and global scales. Wind and water transport involve mass flows driven by thermal and gravitational energy gradients. Wind and water carry heat, sound, gases, aerosols and particles within and between places and regions. Animal, human and machine transport involve the locomotion of 'individuals' using their own internal energy. The canalization of the flow of animals, people, machines and information leads to dispersal routes, migration routes, animal trails, human trails and transport and communication channels, described in Chapter 13. These routes help to tie landscapes and regions together. For instance, a city is a source of people, vehicles, goods and information that move out on radiating transport and communications systems, whilst rural people, water and agricultural products flow into the urban area. The spatial arrangement of landscape elements affects the landscape functions. Some flows are concentrated (such as water, silt or pollutants in rivers); other flows are dispersed (such as erosion, seeds and atmospheric pollutants). Some move fast; some move slowly. Landscape boundaries act as filters where movement rates change markedly. Different boundaries have different 'permeabilities' that regulate movements between different systems. Landscape patterns have a major effect upon regional flows; and, in turn, regional flows influence the landscape patterns.

The spatial structures and circulations in a landscape involve, and are created by, natural and cultural forces. Indeed, the different kinds of places described in Chapters 25–33 can all be seen as outcomes of a range of cultural and biophysical forces, acting at different time scales. For example the landscapes of places like Wasdale Head are preserved for the qualities of their physical landscape, but also as part of the Lake District National Park where romantic notions of the very idea of landscape itself were first articulated by poets such as Wordsworth. So landscape dynamics could be a highly eligible topic on which human and physical geographers could collaborate. Such a synergetic endeavour would build upon the venerable geographical tradition of landscape studies. Efforts in this direction are already proving rewarding. For instance, a recent major text explores how landscapes are produced by environmental change and population pressure; how humanized landscapes have evolved through such processes as woodland clearing, agriculture and the growth of urban–industrial complexes; and the ways in which landscapes at once represent and participate in social change (Atkins *et al.* 1998).

There have also been dynamic considerations of the cultural landscape. Vos and Meekes (1999: 8) argue for investigating the role of 'involution' and 'replacement' in this process of change. They see change taking place in an organic way in traditional systems with abundant labour power but limited technical resources, whereas elsewhere more advanced technology has allowed outside replacement of locally sustainable systems. More critical studies of the dynamics of change focus upon the work that the landscape itself achieves. Mitchell (1994: 1) for example, argues that we should investigate the political process by which social and political identities are formed and how these might be related to landscape.

Reading the landscape

The question of what these forms and processes might mean has long concerned geographers. How should we read the landscape? Approaches to landscape may best be explained through metaphor (Cosgrove and Daniels 1993), and the variety of approaches and meanings explored through stories currently being told about landscapes.

Landscape ecologists employing scientific methods have sought to explain the form and function of landscapes as a machine or system. Whilst their ideas have often been applied to the physical aspects of landscape, the cultural context can also be explained in this way (Vos and Meekes 1999). The systems approach described previously offers a unifying framework. Many of these scientifically grounded approaches to landscape rest upon assumptions about sustainable development, and normative notions of progress. Thus, landscape ecologists increasingly justify their call for transdisciplinary studies with references to aesthetic, ethical and environmental concerns for the future (e.g. Naveh 1995). Empirical studies of the values from practitioners, however, paint a more pragmatic picture. Ian Thompson (2000) concluded that landscape architects in practice often seek technocratic accommodation, instead of following normative principles. The other central feature of the systems-based work is that it is self-protecting. Little attempt is made to critique the metaphor, or to question the applied focus that is one of its major virtues.

Physical and cultural landscapes may also be explained by analysing the processes that have created them over time. Landscape historians and many archaeologists approach cultural landscapes as offering evidence of the past (e.g. Muir 1999; Whyte 2002). This kind of approach describes elements of the past that survive in present landscapes and sees the landscape as a palimpsest, 'whose real or authentic meanings can somehow be recovered with the correct techniques' (Cosgrove and Daniels 1988: 8). The cultural landscape itself becomes the focus of empirical attention, but is often divorced from any critical argument about social process or reading.

Aesthetic approaches to landscape and to representations of landscape continue to be used by landscape architects to justify approaches to management and construction of landscapes

25

(Herzog *et al.* 2000). But landscape taste and values can also be used in a more critical way to question shared cultural values and how they are embodied in differing landscapes (e.g. Setten 2001). Here the story focuses on the ways in which form, function and meaning of landscapes are constructed and contested (Egoz *et al.* 2001).

In a series of articles in the 1980s, Denis Cosgrove argued that landscapes could be theorized as a 'way of seeing', and that the concept reflects elite views grounded in the application of science and the rise of capitalism in early modern Europe (Cosgrove 1984, 1985; Cosgrove and Daniels 1988). This tradition of research drew upon artistic notions of landscape described in Chapter 36, and emphasized how a landscape comes to represent different sets of social and cultural values. This focus on landscape as a way of seeing drew attention to the role of vision in the construction of meaning, and the role of the observer. It has, however, been argued that earlier studies ignored the importance of gender in the construction of such elite views (Rose 1993; Nash 1996), and that focusing upon painterly traditions privileged Western and elite discourses (Cosgrove 1998).

In the 1980s and 1990s, social theory began to have an impact upon landscape research. Landscapes came to be seen as integral to social and political processes, and to represent social relations (Mitchell 1994). Researchers came to focus not only on the landscape as a backdrop for social action, but also on the active role it may play in the maintenance of power and the construction of identity (Wolch and Dear 1989). Research interrogated different aspects of power, varying widely across mode of production, social relations, cultures and landscapes. A plethora of research is now available, in which the complex relationships are mapped out between landscape and the state (e.g. Cartier 1999), class (e.g. Williamson and Bellamy 1987), ideology (e.g. Duncan 1990), gender (e.g. Rose 1993), ethnicity (e.g. Kaups 1995) and sexuality (e.g. Brown 2001). Most of these studies are grounded in material processes and many implicitly argue for a dialectical landscape (Mitchell, 2002). Very few are concerned with charting the morphology of the landscape, and there has also been a shift away from earlier rural obsessions towards a much more diverse range of contexts.

The shift towards social theory also led to increasing attention being paid to *how* a landscape might be interpreted. Literary metaphors became increasingly popular in studies of landscapes (Duncan 1990). The discursive construction of landscape, and the deconstruction of what this might mean, continues to be an important part of post-structuralist approaches to geography (see Barnes and Duncan 1992). Earlier studies in this tradition tended to draw upon semiotic approaches, but work that is more recent has focused upon the value of hermeneutic interpretations (e.g. Duncan and Duncan 2004), or upon the potential of allegorical readings (Auster 1997).

In the 1990s, an increasing focus in research across many disciplines came to investigate how identities were constituted in landscapes, and how landscapes themselves impacted upon the cultural identities of people. Religious belief was one important focus of attention (see Chapter 15; Cooper 1994; Jackson 1979). National identity formed another focus of study (e.g. Matless 1998; Kellerman 1996). Social and cultural historians continue to explore the links between changing national identities and human landscapes, focusing for example on landscape, myth and memory (e.g. Schama 1995), or landscape and the aesthetic and recreational experience in places like the Lake District (e.g. Darby 2000). Landscape can also be a commodity with an active role in the exercise of local elite identities (Duncan and Duncan 2004). While a Marxist emphasis upon the production can still be seen in this work, the cultural turn has led to an increasing emphasis upon the consumption of landscapes.

Bender (1998) argues that landscapes might best be understood as a result of *activities* rather than *representations*. Recent emphases in cultural geography have drawn upon the more complex and performative potential of landscape (Cresswell 1996; Nash 1996, 2000). Drawing upon anthropological work, landscapes, like places, can be seen as becoming and reflexive, rather than fixed and seen (Bender 2001). Attention in this metaphor shifts towards change, motion and action. No longer is human agency or social process separated from backdrop. Affectual responses bring landscapes into being, instead of simply responding to the place.

Conclusion

These examples relating to the reading of landscapes are mostly drawn from geographical research in the Anglo-American tradition and from contemporary scholarship. The anecdote with which this chapter started is itself part of this tradition, placed, just as much as the landscape it depicts and narrates, in an academic tradition in England in the year 2006. Metaphors are themselves social and cultural constructs and reflect changing times and places. The same researcher may use a number of different metaphors telling her or his story: identity, power, representation and aesthetic stories are, for example, often woven together in critical landscape research. Approaches to landscape and place are, however, often under-pinned by core 'meta-narratives' that allow these different metaphorical notions to speak authoritatively about places and in so doing reveal the continuing complexity and power of the landscape concept.

Scientific approaches to landscape emphasize a search for order and pattern, in which unique places might be understood, explained and managed. They imply a normative control over place, privilege the role of the expert and offer practical, distanced and knowable ways forward for researchers, in which human knowledge progressively advances, a landscape of research that denies subjectivity and argues for disciplinary unity under the umbrella of applied scientific progress. To save and manage the world and its landscapes we must collaborate and share scientific knowledge.

The relations between nature and culture form another core area in landscape studies. Differences between 'interpretation' and 'fact' also play an important role in helping us understand these stories. The physical geographer is more likely to employ the scientists' tool kit to explain nature and the world, whilst the human geographer emphasizes culture through interpretation, meaning and reading. Nature and culture may be seen as separate entities, with physical and cultural landscapes studied in isolation. It has been argued that neither approach is sufficient: both are necessary (Huggett and Perkins 2004); and indeed that increasingly landscape is best understood as a hybrid category (see Chapter 51).

Questions of scale are also critical to almost all of the metaphors described previously. The notion of landscape allows a bridge to be made between local places and bigger units, that are less unique, such as the region and the nation, or even to abstract notions of space and location.

The process by which landscapes are made and used is also central to these stories. A continuing interest in the cultural politics of landscape reflects this core concern. On the one hand, it can be argued that structural forces creating landscapes need to be apprehended; on the other hand, individual human agency may be important in determining the cultural reception of a particular place.

There is likely to be a continuing debate around these issues and around the best way forward for those wishing to study landscape like Wasdale. Perhaps a recognition of diversity will allow us to begin to tackle the grander scheme of harmonizing the artistic and scientific views of landscape, so building on the Humboldtian geographical tradition established around two centuries ago.

Further reading

Atkins, P., Simmons, I. and Roberts, B. (1998) *People, Land and Time: An Historical Introduction to the Relations between Landscape, Culture and Environment*. London: Arnold.

McIntyre, S. and Barrett, G.W. (1992) Habitat variegation, an alternative to fragmentation. *Conservation Biology* 6, 146–7.

Mitchell, W.J.T. (ed.) (1994) *Landscape and Power*. Chicago: Chicago University Press.

Muir, R. (1999) *Approaches to Landscape*. Basingstoke: Palgrave Macmillan.

Naveh, Z. and Lieberman, A.S. (1994) *Landscape Ecology: Theory and Applications*, second edition. New York: Springer.

Whyte, I. (2002) *Landscape and History*. London: Reaktion.

Winchester, H.P.M., Kong, L. and Dunn, K. (2003) *Landscapes: Ways of Imagining the World*. Harlow: Pearson.

References

Antrop, M. (2000) Geography and landscape science. *Belgian Journal of Geography* (special issue on the International Geographical Congress) 29 (1), 10–35.

Appleton, J. (1975) *The Experience of Landscape*. London: John Wiley and Sons.

Atkins, P., Simmons, I. and Roberts, B. (1998) *People, Land and Time: An Historical Introduction to the Relations between Landscape, Culture and Environment*. London: Arnold.

Auster, M. (1997) Monument in a landscape: the question of meaning. *Australian Geographer* 28, 219–27.

Bailey, R.G. (2002) Ecoregion-based Design for Sustainability. New York: Springer Verlag.

Barnes, T. and Duncan, J.S. (1992) *Writing Worlds: Discourse Text and Metaphor in the Representation of Landscape*. London: Routledge.

Bender, B. (ed.) (1993) *Landscape Politics and Perspectives*. Providence, Rhode Island: Berg.

——(1998) *Stonehenge: Making Space*. Oxford: Berg.

——(2001) Landscape on-the-move. *Journal of Social Anthropology* 1, 75–89.

Brown, M. (2001) *Closet Space: Geographies of Metaphor from the Body to the Globe*. New York: Routledge.

Buol, S.W., Hole, F.D. and McCracken, R.J. (1980) *Soil Genesis and Classification*, second edition. Ames, Iowa: The Iowa State University Press.

Bürgi, M., Hersperger, A.M. and Schneeberger, N. (2004) Driving forces of landscape change – current and new directions. *Landscape Ecology* 19, 857–68.

Cartier, C. (1999) The state, property development and symbolic landscape in high-rise Hong Kong. *Landscape Research* 24, 185–208.

Casey, E. (2002) *Representing Place: Landscape Painting and Maps*. Minneapolis: University of Minnesota Press.

Chatwin, B. (1998) *The Songlines*. London: Vintage.

Coffey, W.J. (1981) *Geography Towards a General Spatial Systems Approach*. London: Routledge, Chapman and Hall.

Cooper, A. (1994) Negotiated dilemmas of landscape, place and Christian commitment in a Suffolk parish. *Transactions of the Institute of British Geographers* 19, 202–12.

Cosgrove, D. (1984) *Social Formation and Symbolic Landscape*. London: Croom Helm.

——(1985) Prospect, perspective and the evolution of the landscape idea. *Transactions of the Institute of British Geographers* 10, 45–62.

——(1998) *Social Formation and Symbolic Landscape*, revised edition. Madison, Wisconsin: University of Wisconsin Press.

Cosgrove, D. and Daniels, S. (eds) (1988) *The Iconography of Landscape*. Cambridge: Cambridge University Press.

——(1993) Spectacle and text: landscape metaphors in cultural geography. In J. Duncan and D. Ley (eds) *Place/Culture/Representation*, pp. 57–77. London: Routledge.

Cresswell, T. (1996) *In Place/Out of Place: Geography, Ideology, and Transgression*. Minneapolis, Minnesota: University of Minnesota Press.

Darby, H.C. (1956) *The Draining the Fens*, second edition. Cambridge: Cambridge University Press.

——(1977) *Domesday England*. Cambridge: Cambridge University Press.

Darby, W.J. (2000) *Landscape and Identity: Geographies of Nation and Class in Britain*. Oxford: Berg.

Décamps, H. (2000) Demanding more of landscape research (and researchers). *Landscape and Urban Planning* 47, 10–19.

Downs, R.M. and Stea, D. (eds) (1974) *Image and Environment; Cognitive Mapping and Spatial Behaviour*. London: Edward Arnold.

Duncan, J.S. (1990) *The City as Text: the Politics of Landscape Interpretation in the Kandyan Kingdom*. Cambridge: Cambridge University Press.

Duncan, J.S. and Duncan, N.G. (2004) *Landscapes of Privilege: The Politics of the Aesthetic in an American Suburb*. New York: Routledge

Egoz, S., Browning, J. and Perkins, H.C. (2001) Tastes in tension: form, function and meaning in New Zealand's farmed landscapes. *Landscape and Urban Planning* 57, 177–96.

Herzog, T.R, Herbert, E.J., Kaplan, R. and Crooks, C.L. (2000) Cultural and developmental comparisons of landscape perceptions and preferences. *Environment and Behaviour* 32, 323–35.

Hoskins, W.G. (1955) *The Making of the English Landscape*. London: Hodder and Stoughton.

Hough, M. (1990) *Out of Place: Restoring Identity to the Regional Landscape*. New Haven, Connecticut, and London: Yale University Press.

Hubert, J.-P. (1998) À la recherche d'une géométrie de l'espace habité chez Camille Vallaux, Jean Gottman et Gilles Ritchot. *L'Espace Géographique* 3, 217–27.

——(1999) L'aménagement et le concept de structure. In A. Fischer and J. Malezieux (eds) *Industrie et Aménagement*, pp. 129–44. Paris: Éditions L'Harmattan.

Huggett, R.J. and Cheesman, J.E. (2002) *Topography and the Environment*. Harlow: Prentice Hall.

Huggett, R.J. and Perkins, C. (2004) Landscape as form, process and meaning. In J.A. Matthews and D.T. Herbert (eds) *Unifying Geography: Common Heritage, Shared Future*, pp. 224–39. London: Routledge.

Humboldt, A. von (1849) *Cosmos: A Sketch of a Physical Description of the Universe, volume 1*, translated from the German by E.C. Otté. London: G. Bohn.

IALE Executive Committee (1998) IALE mission statement. *Bulletin of the International Association for Landscape Ecology* 16, 1.

Jackle, J.A. (1987) *The Visual Elements of Landscape*. Amherst, Massachusetts: University of Massachusetts Press.

Jackson, J.B. (1979) The order of landscape: reason and religion in Newtonian America. In D.W. Meinig (ed.) *The Interpretation of Ordinary Landscapes*, pp. 153–63. Oxford: Oxford University Press.

Kaups, M.E. (1995) Cultural landscape: log structures as symbols of ethnic identity. *Material Culture* 27, 1–19.

Kellerman, A. (1996) Settlement myth and settlement activity: interrelationships in the Zionist land of Israel. *Transactions of the Institute of British Geographers* 21, 363–78.

Linton, D.L. (1949) The delimitation of morphological regions. *Transactions of the Institute of British Geographers, Publication* 14, 86–7.

Matless, D. (1998) *Landscape and Englishness*. London: Reaktion Books.

Meinig, D.W. (1979) *The Interpretation of Ordinary Landscapes*. Oxford: Oxford University Press.

Mels, T. (ed.) (2004) *Reanimating Places: A Geography of Rhythms*. London: Ashgate.

Mitchell, D. (2002) Cultural landscapes: the dialectical landscape: recent landscape research in human geography. *Progress in Human Geography* 26, 381–9.

Mitchell, W.J.T. (ed.) (1994) *Landscape and Power*. Chicago: Chicago University Press.

Moore, R.L. and Graefe, A.R. (1994) Attachments to recreation settings: the case of rail-trail users. *Leisure Sciences* 16, 17–31.

Morphy, H. (1993) Colonialism, history and the construction of place: the politics of landscape in Northern Australia. In B. Bender, *Landscape Politics and Perspectives*, 205–43. Providence, Rhode Island: Berg.

Muir, R. (1999) *Approaches to Landscape*. Basingstoke: Palgrave Macmillan.

Nash, C. (1996) Reclaiming vision: looking at landscape and the body. *Gender, Place and Culture* 3, 149–69.

——(2000) Performivity in practice: some recent work in cultural geography. *Progress in Human Geography* 24, 653–64.

Naveh, Z. (1995) Interactions of landscape and cultures. *Landscape and Urban Planning* 32, 43–54.

——(2000) What is holistic landscape ecology? A conceptual introduction. *Landscape and Urban Planning* 50, 7–26.

Naveh, Z. and Lieberman, A.S. (1994) *Landscape Ecology: Theory and Applications*, second edition. New York: Springer.

Relph, E. (1996) Place. In I. Douglas, R. Huggett and M. Robinson (eds) *Companion Encyclopedia of Geography*, pp. 906–22. London and New York: Routledge.

Roberts, B.K. (1987) *The Making of the English Village*. Harlow: Longman.

Rose, G. (1993) *Feminism and Geography*. Cambridge: Polity Press.

Sauer, C.O. (1963) *Land and Life: A Selection of the Writings of Carl Ortwin Sauer*, edited by J. Leighly. Berkeley: University of California Press.

Schama, S. (1995) *Landscape and Memory*. London: HarperCollins.

Setten. G. (2001) Farmers, planners and the moral message of landscape and nature. *Ethics, Place and Environment* 4, 220–5.

Thompson, I. (2000) Aesthetic, social and ecological values in landscape architecture: a discourse analysis. *Ethics, Place and Environment* 3, 269–87.

Tress, B., Tress, G., Décamps, H. and Hauteserre, A.-M. (2001) Bridging human and natural sciences in landscape research. *Landscape and Urban Planning* 57, 137–41.

Tuan, Y.F. (1974) *Topophilia: A Study of Environmental Perception, Attitudes, and Values*. Englewood Cliffs, NJ: Prentice-Hall.

Vos, W. and Meekes, H. (1999) Trends in European cultural landscape development: perspectives for a sustainable future. *Landscape and Urban Planning* 46, 3–14.

Whyte, I. (2002) *Landscape and History*. London: Reaktion.

Williamson, T. and Bellamy, E. (1987) *Property and Landscape*. London: George Philip.

Wolch, J. and Dear, M. (1989) *The Power of Geography: How Territory Shapes Social Life*. London: Unwin Hyman.

3

Individual place

Tim Cresswell

Geography is self-evidently about places – West Africa, Swansea, the West. For much of geography's history the term 'place' has been taken for granted as simply referring to the fact that the world is differentiated into unique and particular segments that can straightforwardly be called places. It was only in the 1970s that humanistic geographers began to ask what a place is (Tuan 1977; Relph 1976). They were interested in this question because humanists, inspired by the continental philosophies of phenomenology and existentialism, wanted to consider humans as subjects with intentions, feeling, emotions and attachments to the world. Through most of the 1960s and 1970s the majority of geographers had considered humans in the same way as a physical scientist might consider atoms or rocks – as objects subject to universal scientific laws. Humanistic geographers insisted on the centrality of human con-sciousness and subjectivity and the need to understand it. It was not the world in itself that they wanted to focus on but 'being-in-the-world'. Rather than seeing the world as a blank space, geographers turned to place as an idea that described human attachment to the world. Since then human geographers of all theoretical persuasions have grappled with how humans make places through the creation of meanings attached to locations. Much of human life is dedicated to making connections to the world we inhabit. We do not float through mean-ingless space but we live in and become attached to (or repelled by) place. This can be seen in the way we inhabit our homes, attempt to make our workplace comfortable and express-ive of who we are, and where we choose to go on holiday.

Since the 1970s place has generally been used to refer to segments of the Earth's surface which have become, in some way or other, meaningful to us. Places have material form (buildings, fields, roads, etc.) and more immaterial 'senses of place' – a term that refers to the meanings and sentiments that we attach to these material structures. When I write 'Baghdad' or 'New York' I am referring to fixed locations on the Earth's surface, to particular unique landscapes and to a whole host of ideas, meanings and emotions that circulate around them. Places are also practised. Every day we conduct life in place, and this conduct gives place some of its meanings. Place is experiential in the sense that we experience it through our senses and the multiple ways in which we use it. When writing about place, individual or otherwise, we evoke these three entangled dimensions – material structure, meaning and practice.

Materiality – meaning – practice

Let us take each of these three facets of place – materiality, meaning and practice – in turn. When I write 'Baghdad' or 'New York' I am referring to things in the world. These are clearly cities that have particular landscapes and can be located on a map of the world. Baghdad may bring to mind minarets, mosques, bombed-out ruins, market places, palaces, prisons. We know that New York has skyscrapers, a grid pattern of roads, the Statue of Liberty, shops, Central Park. This is perhaps the most obvious manifestation of place. Geography is about place insofar as it is about Africa, Exeter, the Lake District or New Orleans – places we can identify through their appearance – their solidity. But places need not be the obvious places on a map. My office is also a place. It has a particular location in space and is clearly bounded by four walls. Two walls are lined with books. Filing cabinets stand in the corner. My desk faces into the room and there are windows behind me. The walls are decorated with posters, postcards, maps (I am a geographer, after all) and important reminders of the academic calendar. I have four seats arranged around a table where I hold tutorials. Many of the postcards say things I think relate to me in some way like 'Normal is a Myth' or 'Where does History Happen?' On the door is an image of some official-looking graffiti that reads 'No loitering'. These are interspersed with pictures of my family and copies of my book covers. On my desk is an Apple computer rather than a PC. My desk is a mess. Five days a week I open the door and enter this place and feel more or less at home. My tutees come here every other week, my colleagues more often than that. Just as New York has its skyline so my office has its own micro geography – its own topography. While New York is obviously an object of geographical curiosity – obviously a place – my office is also, if less obviously, a place.

Meaning is perhaps the most important ingredient of place. As we have seen (previously) notions of place in human geography arose out of a critique of spatial science by humanistic geographers in the 1970s (Tuan 1974a; Relph 1976; Buttimer and Seamon 1980). Spatial science attempted to make law-like generalizations about the human world by treating the human world as abstract – as a set of locations, areas, lines and volumes (Abler *et al.* 1971). Humanistic geographers suggested that something was missing from this world. The main thing that was missing, they argued, was meaning. To Yi-Fu Tuan in his books *Topophilia* (Tuan 1974b) and *Space and Place* (Tuan 1977) places were not simply locations but 'centres of meaning' and 'fields of care'. Places were evidence of the way in which people make themselves at home in the world. They were material, to be sure, but they were also sites of emotion, security, attachment and sentiment. In this sense places could exist at any scale. A favourite armchair is an important place of comfort and belonging – every bit as much as my office is, or Aberystwyth. Similarly my home country makes sense to me in ways that other countries do not. Even the whole Earth has place-like qualities when viewed from the moon or a space-shuttle. There is an undeniable sense of attachment and care.

Recognizing that places – from a chair to the Earth – are meaningful raises the question of how they become meaningful. Meaning is a tricky business. Many meanings we attach to place are incredibly personal. The way my office speaks to me is surely unique and different from the meanings it may have for my colleagues or my tutees. Indeed, my tutees may enter it with trepidation. It may be a place they associate with difficult questions and the necessity to speak up when they would rather remain silent. The objects in my room are meaningful to me and I hope they project something about me to my tutees and others. But they may not realize that the 'No loitering' postcard on the door is ironic. However hard I try to make this place welcoming, they may interpret it as exclusionary – a professor's office. So meaning, at one level, is highly individualistic, and this is why places have variable significance to different people. But meanings are also shared. As well as constructing meanings in our heads we live in a world where symbols and signs surround us. This is why when I write 'New York' or 'Baghdad' we probably share something. We have watched movies about New York, we have seen news broadcasts about Baghdad. Relatively few of us have been to either place but they are still meaningful places and many of these meanings will be shared. In addition to the media, local governments and chambers of commerce deliberately try and create meanings for place in much the same way I do for my office. They want people to live in them (and thus pay taxes and improve the local economy) and they need businesses to locate there. Even an unremarkable place like my office – a place that has not featured in films or in news stories – has shared meanings. It is, after all, the office of an academic. Offices of academics appear fairly regularly on the news as a book-lined backdrop for an expert. Offices of academics as a general category are likely to exhibit a host of meanings that are, to some degree, shared.

The third ingredient of place is practice. Practice refers to the things people do. We have seen how places are material – they have shape and substance. Places are also meaningful – meanings which may be individual and may be shared. The same could be said of an artwork of a piece of fruit. A picture is constructed from the material of paper or canvas, ink or paint. It has been made to mean things by both the artist and the viewers who look at it. A piece of fruit is made up of cells and often bears meaning. Think of apples and think of Adam and Eve. Think of bananas and slapstick comedy. What completes the picture of place is that we do things *in* it, and this constant doing is both informed by the shape and meaning of place and has the potential to transform place.

One interesting way of thinking about this was developed by the humanistic geographer David Seamon. Seamon used the evocative term 'place-ballet' to describe the way in which places are performed (Seamon 1980). Individuals, he argued, conduct what he called 'time–space routines' in their everyday life. Often these mundane mobilities are habitual. People drive to work, walk to school or go shopping on an almost daily basis. These are not often the product of great thought. Take the way people can drive for miles without being aware of how they have travelled from A to B. People who have moved house sometimes return to their old address before realizing they have gone the wrong way. This is what Seamon means by 'habitual'. When these individual 'time–space routines' add up, they coalesce into a 'place-ballet'. In the centre of any busy town or city there are hundreds of people conducting their individual 'time–space routines' but they do so in the company of others in such a way that recognizable and regular patterns of practice emerge. Examples would be rush hour at a busy metro station, the 'school run' in the middle of the afternoon or the buzz of a city street on a summer evening. Seamon's argument is that places exhibit a kind of unchoreographed yet ordered practice that makes the place just as much as the place's object qualities or meaning qualities do. Indeed, the meaning of a place may arise out of the constant reiteration of practices that are simultaneously individual and social.

When we travel, and encounter places we do not know, all of these qualities appear different and unintelligible. The material structure of a place will be unfamiliar. Many Mediterranean countries, for instance, have wide pavements alongside and in the middle of roads. During the early afternoon old men will walk up and down them in intense conversation. These spaces appear different, they obviously have meanings we do not understand (by 'we' I mean people who do not participate in these practices) and are practised in ways that would not be evident in Cardiff or Baltimore. Buildings look strange, people act differently, we need guidebooks to figure out what places might mean.

Let us consider the object qualities, meaning qualities and practice qualities of a particular place. Think of a library. A library has a very definite physical structure. It is designed to hold books in a recognizable order and allow people to access them as easily as possible. It is also designed to allow people to read and study. The university library here, in Aberystwyth, has three floors. The ground floor is mostly taken up with the space dedicated to the librarians to monitor the flow of books and people and facilitate the library's functions. A significant portion I have never seen, because it is staff space and I am not a member of staff there. You cannot enter or exit the library without passing through this space. The other two floors contain hundreds of thousands of books and periodicals arranged so that science books are on the first floor and humanities/social science books are on the second floor. All the periodicals are on the first floor. The cataloguing of books means that they are ordered in a way that reflects deeply held assumptions about the order of knowledge in the modern West. I am unlikely to find a book on Hinduism next to a book on the General Theory of Relativity. Throughout the library there are plaques and inscriptions reminding us that this is a place of learning and knowledge and that these are serious qualities.

The library is a place that is practised. If you were to sit there all day observing the 'place-ballet' that goes on there, you would notice the times when it is busiest, the arrival and departure of staff, the characteristic ways in which the place becomes embodied. People are generally quiet. They whisper. We know that libraries are serious places and we act accordingly. I cannot recall if there are signs telling people to be quiet, but people generally remain silent anyway. We expect this of libraries and act accordingly without necessarily being conscious of it. The reiterative practice of silence leads to more silence, and so on. A sudden loud noise – laughter, for instance – might result in the perpetrator looking nervously around, aware that they have transgressed an unspoken boundary. The material structure, meaning and practice of this place are all intermingled – each reinforcing the other.

Libraries are, you might suggest, exceptional places with clearly defined boundaries and expectations. But all places share the three qualities I have outlined in the library. Streets, homes, workplaces, sports fields, pubs and public squares all carry with them unspoken expectations of behaviour – some more precise than others, some more or less formal. They have familiar material structures and meanings that are in some senses shared and understood. We negotiate them as individuals but in ways that make sense to others.

Topophilia and exclusion

To some geographers the ways that materiality, meaning and practice coalesce in place result in deep and abiding forms of care and attachment. To others they produce deeply problematic sites of social exclusion. Humanistic geographers have invested a considerable amount of moral worth in the notion of place. As centres of meaning and fields of care, places are given as evidence for human attachment to the physical world. Clearly this attachment to and love of place is a powerful force in human life. Tuan refers to this love of place as 'topophilia' (Tuan 1974b). The evidence for topophilia is everywhere. It is in the sense of place evoked by novelists, poets and film makers, in the ways people look after their gardens, and in the aesthetic details on even the smallest and most functional of human products. It is as evident in the placement of posters on my office wall as it is in the pomp and ceremony of national events. The degree to which topophilia is 'individual' is open to question. While it seems likely that each of us has idiosyncratic relationships to place based on our personal biographies, it is equally clear that the mediation of places means that attachments to place are also shared and social. This is particularly true of places we have never been to but have only experienced vicariously on television or in the pages of a favourite novel. It is equally true that many places evoke feelings of disgust or threat. Think of the places in which the Holocaust was enacted, or threatening neighbourhoods of unfamiliar cities. 'Topophobia' is also part of human life.

Whether it is love of or fear of place that is being considered, in the humanist lexicon place is a moral concept. Reading Tuan or Relph it is clear that they believe in the power of place to make human life meaningful, rich and full. The kinds of meanings in place they discuss are generally positive and life-affirming.

More recently, cultural geographers have criticized humanistic geographers for being too enamoured of place as a source of attachment. The problem with humanism, it is argued, is that is has so little to say about power relations that pervade society. Issues of class, gender, race, ethnicity and sexuality are overlooked or deliberately avoided. The next chapter develops and illustrates the significance of these social categories. The humans in humanistic geography are either strictly individual or unrealistically universal. People are not simply people but they are men and women, black people and white people, adults and children. Taking power relations into account, critical geographers suggest, would lead to a greater emphasis on the dark side of place – particularly its role in defining 'us' insiders against 'them' – the outsiders (Cresswell 1996; Sibley 1995). As individuals live in place and invest meaning in it, it is also the case that these meanings, and the practices that they support or discourage, often lead to forms of exclusion. Attachment suggests a deep affection, but it can also be possessive. My office is a case in point. Although I try to make it a place that welcomes me and those I choose to share it with, it is not so welcoming to those students who find tutorials a painful experience or who find me threatening. I do not necessarily choose these meanings for my place, but they are bolstered by the administrative structures that make up higher education in contemporary Britain. I am, after all, a professor. I mark their papers. I sit in judgement. They are not allowed to enter whenever they want. They have to be invited. This is not their place. A similar set of processes occurs with nation-states. Rituals and ceremonies of national belonging enact a form of topophilia. They encourage members of the nation-state to feel good about it – to celebrate it. But the very power of this attachment cannot help but exclude those who are not members of the nation-state or who do not sympathize with its aims and actions (see Chapter 19). Nation-states are places that are necessarily exclusionary. The borders are policed and elaborate systems of law and governance make sure that only the 'right kind of people' are allowed to enter. Every year thousands are forcibly removed.

The tensions between topophilia and place-based exclusion can be illustrated through the concept of 'home'. 'Home' is one of the key terms used in humanistic geography and dwelling has been a continuing focus for geographers (see Chapter 59). The characteristics of place as a centre of meaning and field of care are very close to a definition of home. Indeed, Tuan has referred to geography as the study of the Earth as a home for humanity. The key word, he suggests, is 'home' (Tuan 1991). The kinds of relations to place exhibited in topophilia are very much the way home has been constructed as an ideal – a place where we feel secure, warm, sheltered and comfortable. Home frequently appears in this guise as a source of universal attachment – as an ideal kind of place. Consider the way Tuan evokes home place in his book *Passing Strange and Wonderful*. He quotes Helen Santmyer reflecting on her childhood home town:

One's home or hometown need not be beautiful by artbook standards. Other values may be more important, such as comfort and security, a haven of human warmth. Yet even in the most humdrum town there are moments of beauty. 'You passed the doctor's office, and were at the corner of your own street, where you turned west, and saw the tree arched against a glowing sky.'

(Tuan 1993: 144)

Here home is a familiar and beautiful place – a 'haven of human warmth'. Note how the reaction to home seems intensely personal, yet it stands as an example of attitudes to home as place that are given as widespread, even universal. Tuan's reflections on Santmyer's musings on home are not given as a single, unrepeated instance of homeliness but as an example of what it is to be human.

This appreciation of home as place contrasts starkly with notions of home as place developed by critical cultural geographers concerned with the ways power operates in society. David Sibley, for instance, considers the kind of home as ideal place argument in his book *Geographies of Exclusion* (Sibley 1995). While he agrees that many people do derive satisfaction from their homes as sites of belonging, he worries that this rosy view of home obscures many of the less positive feelings home can evoke. He notes how homes also provide a context for 'violence, child abuse, depression and other forms of mental illness' (Sibley 1995: 94). At a more mundane level home, he points out, is also associated with strict, often cold, forms of ordering that can make home an uncomfortable place to be in, especially for children who have little power over the production of home as a place. Contrast Tuan's use of Santmyer's reflections on home with that provided by Sibley. He quotes the memories of 'David':

Dad had his special chair near the TV and radio in the living room and the rest of the family had their own recognized seating places. The other living room was a 'best room', reserved for visitors but not attractive in any case because it was always freezing. Mother organized the house. She likes everything neat and tidy. Feet were not allowed on chairs and neither food nor friends could be taken upstairs.

(David, quoted in Sibley 1995: 96)

Sibley uses David's experience to illustrate how home can be a site of strict boundary maintenance where the authority of 'father' is clearly signified and reinforced. Just as Tuan generalized from his positive image of the home to discuss forms of attachment and belonging to places at many different scales, so Sibley generalizes from his image of a strict and disciplinarian home to a wider sense in which society is built around strict hierarchical boundaries:

Inside the home and in the immediate locality, social and spatial order may be obvious and enduring characteristics of the environment. For those who do not fit, either children whose conceptions of space and time are at variance with those of controlling adults or the homeless, nomadic, or black in a homogeneously white, middle class space, such environments may be inherently exclusionary.

(Sibley 1995: 99)

This kind of thinking reminds us of the many ways in which the production of place as a site of belonging can reinforce, or even produce, social relations of systematically unequal power.

Much work has been done on the role of place in the production of norms that serve the lives and experiences of *included* people, as against others who are *excluded*. Examples include the marginalization of children, the disabled, racial others, gay and lesbian people, refugees and asylum seekers and animals (Philo 1995; Valentine 1997; Delaney 1998; Forest 1995; White 2002; Kitchin 1998). The idea of place as a rooted, bounded and stable locus of identity is linked to ways of thinking that clearly locate particular kinds of people in particular kinds of places. Arguments such as 'women belong at home' or 'black people belong in the city' are examples of this way of thinking. This 'sedentarist metaphysics' leads to people without place being necessarily labelled as threatening outsiders. The anthropologist Liisa Malkki, for instance, has discussed how the rooting of identities in national places has led to refugees being perceived as amoral beings who threaten the good order of place. If place is a moral concept then people who have no place appear to exist outside of morality (Malkki 1992). An example of this is the Chinese Exclusion Act of 1882 in the United States. The Act was passed to prevent Chinese people from entering the United States and gaining citizenship. It reflected considerable anti-Chinese sentiment at the time. Chinese people were associated with drugs, pollution and prostitution in the media and in the pronouncements of government officials (Craddock 2000). The Act stated that:

> Whereas, in the opinion of the Government of the United States the coming of Chinese laborers to this country endangers the good order of certain localities within the territory thereof: Therefore, Be it enacted by the Senate and House of Representatives of the United States of America in Congress assembled, That from and after the expiration of ninety days next after the passage of this act, and until the expiration of ten years next after the passage of this act, the coming of Chinese laborers to the United States be, and the same is hereby, suspended; and during such suspension it shall not be lawful for any Chinese laborer to come, or, having so come after the expiration of said ninety days, to remain within the United States.
> (Chinese Exclusion Act Forty-Seventh Congress. Session I. 1882, Chapter 126)

Here the rationale for the exclusion of a racial group from the United States is given as a threat to 'the good order of certain localities'. The mobility of the Chinese, in other words, was portrayed as a threat to place. This is a sedentarist metaphysics in action. An important place in the enactment of the Chinese Exclusion Act was the immigration detention centre at Angel Island in San Francisco Bay. It was here that arrivals from China and other Asian points of origin were 'processed' to see if they could be allowed in or would be sent home. Now the immigration station is a heritage museum providing an account of Asian immigration to the United States. On its walls can be seen graffiti in the form of elaborately carved poems in classical Chinese style. One poem reads in part:

> The low building with three beams merely
> shelters the body.
> It is unbearable to relate the stories
> accumulated on the Island slopes.
> Wait till the day I become successful and
> fulfill my wish!
> I will not speak of love when I level the
> immigration station.
> (Lai *et al.* 1980: 94)

This poem, written by an inmate, expresses powerful feelings about place. The politics and geography of exclusion results, in this instance, in topophobia of an extreme kind.

Place and memory

The author of this anonymous poem never achieved his wish. Ironically, the discovery of poems like this saved the building from being levelled and it is now a place of memory. Place has an intimate connection to memory (Foote 1997; Till 1999, 2005; Johnson 1996; and Chapter 26). Memory is a facility of the human brain that we might think of as individual. It is unlikely, after all, that my memories are exactly the same as anyone else's. They are intensely personal. My individual biography has its own trajectory through space made up of different places I have called home. These places evoke nostalgia when they are places I have enjoyed or where significant events have occurred. For other people the same places may mean nothing or may be associated with uncomfortable memories. But memory is also social. There are many ways in which social memories are produced. Museums, commemorative events and historical narratives all produce versions of the past in place. The materiality of place is perhaps the principal way in which shared memories are produced – memories of events which people, as individuals, may have no memory of whatsoever. Museums choose objects to display that link us to the past. Memorials remind us of events that were chosen as significant by other people. Most towns in Britain, for instance, have war memorials for the First World War listing the names of local people who died. Factories, almshouses, stately homes and statues have all been preserved to remind us of a past we were not a part of. The material fact of places associated with crime and evil also remind us of the events that took place there. Thus a place such as Auschwitz – where millions of Jews, Gypsies and gay people were killed during the Holocaust – has become a place of memory in order that we cannot forget the dark side of humanity (Charlesworth 1994). Kenneth Foote has reflected on this brute power of place to remind us. 'A bare stretch of ground in Berlin, once the Reichs-sicherheitshauptamt, the headquarters of the Nazi state security, or Gestapo, compels the visitor to reflect on genocide in the twentieth century' (Foote 1997: 5–6). It is the capacity of place to 'compel' that makes it a powerful tool in both the preservation and the invention of memories that are, in some sense, shared.

However, it is not just place's materiality that contributes to individual and shared memories. Places also compel practice. Consider the difference between a book and a place. A history book will remind us of past events and, if it is a good one, it will evoke something of what it was like to be in the past. But the only way a book is practised is by reading it. We may feel the book in our hands and, if we are in an archive, we may even smell something of its history. In a place, however, we are actually in it. All our senses are engaged. This is why many museums now feature complete structures that we can experience in a multi-sensory way rather than simply looking at exhibits. If the museum is actually the place where commemorated events happened, then these evocations may be all the more powerful. The urban historian Delores Hayden makes this point in her book *The Power of Place* (Hayden 1995). To her the power of place to evoke memories lies in its holistic qualities of practice rather than simply its material reminders of the past. She writes of a visit to the Lower East Side Tenement Museum in New York City. The museum memorializes the squalid living conditions in the New York tenements of the Lower East Side where recent immigrants would often be forced to live. It enacts this memorialization within one of the buildings where immigrants lived:

The building will be a more evocative source than any written records. One can read about unhealthy living conditions, but standing inside a tenement apartment – perhaps 400 square feet of living space for an entire family, minimal plumbing, only one or two exterior windows – leaves a visitor gasping for air and looking for light.

(Hayden 1995: 33–34)

Being there, in other words, has a particularly powerful hold on memory as the material qualities of place are entangled with the meanings and practices associated with it.

Individual responses to place in an era of non-place

Places of memory are now a familiar experience across the world. Heritage sites, museums, monuments, plaques marking the lives of famous people and historical theme parks have sprung up in even the most unlikely places. Indeed, this process of 'museumification' is one of the principal symptoms of what some observers describe as the proliferation of 'placelessness'. An argument is frequently made that as we enter the twenty-first century places are becoming less distinctive. This argument was first made in geography by Edward Relph in his 1976 book *Place and Placelessness* (Relph 1976). In this book Relph argued that places were becoming placeless. He gives many reasons for this – mass production, an increasingly mobile world, an emphasis on 'disneyfied' and 'museumified' places that were fake copies of more worthy originals. He described these places as 'inauthentic'. They are inauthentic, he argues, because it is impossible to be an existential insider in DisneyWorld or McDonald's or on a mass-produced housing estate. It is also impossible, he argues, to make significant attachments to place if we move about too much, never stopping to linger and create roots. Variations of this argument are now quite commonplace and have been variously described as 'McDonaldization' or 'Americanization'. More recently, the French anthropologist Marc Augé has used the term 'non-place' to refer to sites such as motorway service stations, airports and places of transit which never actually go anywhere but endlessly refer to other places indirectly (Augé 1995). Augé does not believe such 'non-places' are inauthentic but simply a condition of the way we lead our lives now.

While it is clearly the case that we live (in the West at least) in a way that is increasingly mobile and uprooted, it is surely not the case that place is no longer important. Given that place refers to a combination of materiality, meaning and practice that produces forms of affection and attachment (as well as fear and dislocation), we can still see place everywhere. Most of us still have places that are important to us – where we feel at home. Even the places most often thought of as placeless or non-place are capable of being loved and cared for. Motorways, for instance, display all the qualities of place I have referred to in this essay. Peter Merriman has recently shown how the British M1 motorway is every bit as much a place as anywhere else (Merriman 2004). An airport is another kind of space that has been described as a non-place, though some people clearly become attached to the shape, feel and performance of airports as places. Some academics reportedly do their best work in airports. I recently spent time in Schiphol Airport, near Amsterdam, conducting research (Cresswell 2006). There I met homeless people who found the airport to be warm, dry and interesting. One man, who had originally migrated to the Netherlands from Curacao, spent almost every day of the year there. To him, the airport was a place he called home.

Conclusion

It should be apparent from this short exploration of the notion of place that it is hard to clearly separate 'individual place' from more social notions of place. While it is clear that early accounts of place in humanistic geography sought to make geography more human by considering human characteristics of subjectivity, intelligence, emotion and attachment as central to our understanding of what it is to be-in-the-world, it is also clear that these human characteristics are often shaped and moulded in relation to other people. Places form part of our biographies, and we all attach particular significance to places where important things happen in our lives – where we were born, went to school, fell in love, split up, succeeded, failed, went on holiday or endured a tragedy. Even a vague smell or a familiar sound may take us back to these places. But unless we lead the life of a hermit many of the attachments we form through place are formed in relation to other people around us, the arts and media, politics and other forms of shared meaning production. It is impossible to separate the purely individual from the social. Just as Seamon's 'place-ballet' evokes the notion of a place being made out of a multitude of individual paths through time and space which are unorchestrated but, nevertheless, coherent, so the materiality and meanings of place can only become powerful social forces when they are enacted by individuals.

Further reading

Buttimer, A. and Seamon, D. (eds) (1980) *The Human Experience of Space and Place*. New York: St Martin's Press.

Cresswell, T. (1996) *In Place/Out of Place: Geography, Ideology and Transgression*. Minneapolis: University of Minnesota Press.

——(2004) *Place: A Short Introduction*. Oxford: Blackwell.

Sibley, D. (1995) *Geographies of Exclusion: Society and Difference in the West*. London: Routledge.

Tuan, Y.-F. (1977) *Space and Place: The Perspective of Experience*. Minneapolis: University of Minnesota Press.

References

Abler, R., Adams, J. and Gould, P (1971) *Spatial Organization: The Geographer's View of the World*. Englewood Cliffs, New Jersey: Prentice Hall.

Augé, M. (1995) *Non-Places: Introduction to an Anthropology of Supermodernity*. London, New York: Verso.

Buttimer, A. and Seamon, D. (eds) (1980) *The Human Experience of Space and Place*. New York: St Martin's Press.

Charlesworth, A. (1994) Contesting places of memory: the case of Auschwitz. *Environment and Planning D: Society and Space* 12, 579–93.

Craddock, S. (2000) *City of Plagues: Disease, Poverty, and Deviance in San Francisco*. Minneapolis: University of Minnesota Press.

Cresswell, T. (1996) *In Place/Out of Place: Geography, Ideology and Transgression*. Minneapolis: University of Minnesota Press.

——(2006) *On the Move: Mobility in the Modern Western World*. New York: Routledge.

Delaney, D. (1998) *Race, Place and the Law*. Austin: University of Texas Press.

Foote, K.E. (1997) *Shadowed Ground: America's Landscapes of Violence and Tragedy*. Austin: University of Texas Press.

Forest, B. (1995) West Hollywood as symbol: the significance of place in the construction of a gay identity. *Environment and Planning D: Society and Space* 13, 133–57.

Hayden, D. (1995) *The Power of Place: Urban Landscapes as Public History*. Cambridge, Mass.: MIT Press.

Johnson, N.C. (1996) Where geography and history meet: heritage tourism and the big house in Ireland. *Annals of the Association of American Geographers* 86, 551–66.

Kitchin, R. (1998) 'Out of place', 'knowing one's place': space, power and the exclusion of disabled people. *Disability and Society* 13, 343–56.

Lai, H.M., Lim, G., Yung, J. and Chinese Culture Foundation (1980) *Island: Poetry and History of Chinese Immigrants on Angel Island, 1910–40*. [San Francisco]: HOC DOI; distributed by San Francisco Study Center.

Malkki, L. (1992) National Geographic: the rooting of peoples and the territorialization of national identity among scholars and refugees. *Cultural Anthropology* 7, 24–44.

Merriman, P. (2004) Driving places: Marc Augé, non-places and the geographies of England's M1 motorway. *Theory, Culture and Society* 21, 145–67.

Philo, C. (1995) Animals, geography, and the city: notes on inclusions and exclusions. *Environment and Planning D: Society and Space* 13, 655–81.

Relph, E. (1976) *Place and Placelessness*. London: Pion.

Seamon, D. (1980) Body–subject, time–space routines, and place-ballets. In A. Buttimer and D. Seamon (eds) *The Human Experience of Space and Place*, pp. 148–65. London: Croom Helm.

Sibley, D. (1995) *Geographies of Exclusion: Society and Difference in the West*. London: Routledge.

Till, K. (1999) Staging the past: landscape designs, cultural identity, and Erinnerungspolitik at Berlin's Neue Wache. *Ecumene* 6, 251–83.

——(2005) *The New Berlin: Memory, Politics, Place*. Minneapolis: University of Minnesota Press.

Tuan, Y.-F. (1974a) Space and place: humanistic perspective. *Progress in Human Geography* 6, 211–52.

——(1974b) *Topophilia: A Study of Environmental Perception, Attitudes, and Values*. Englewood Cliffs, New Jersey: Prentice-Hall.

——(1977) *Space and Place: The Perspective of Experience*. Minneapolis: University of Minnesota Press.

——(1991) A view of geography. *Geographical Review* 81, 99–107.

——(1993) *Passing Strange and Wonderful: Aesthetics, Nature, and Culture*. Washington DC: Shearwater Books.

Valentine, G. (1997) Angels and devils: moral landscapes of childhood. *Environment and Planning D: Society and Space* 14, 581–99.

White, A. (2002) Geographies of asylum, legal knowledge and legal practices. *Political Geography* 21, 1055–73.

4

Social place

Phil Hubbard

Place has a rich but complex genealogy (Cresswell 2004; Hubbard 2005a; Agnew 2005). In some quarters, it is treated synonymously with terms like space, environment or even landscape, used to connote a specific portion of the Earth's surface. Yet against that, there is a widespread view that place is a term which foregrounds questions of being human and the inhabitation of space. Positing an opposition between generalized (nomothetic) *space* and particularized (idiographic) *place*, the argument in this chapter is that places are made through human agency, whether individual or collective. Viewed from such perspectives, place represents a distinctive (and more or less *bounded*,) type of space which is defined by (and constructed in terms of,) the lived experiences of people. As such, places can be seen as fundamental in expressing a sense of belonging for those who live in them, and providing a locus for identity; in short, there is a definite but complex relationship between the character of specific places and the identities of those who inhabit them.

As we have seen in previous chapters, varied traditions in regional, cultural and humanistic geography have explored the emotional and even spiritual ties binding people to places, feeding off philosophies such as existentialism and phenomenology (Holloway and Hubbard 2001). Reacting against these types of analysis, the historical and geographical materialism which initially emerged in the 1970s ushered in a rather different interpretation of the lived-in dimensions of place, with place deemed to be inherently caught up in social relations, both socially produced and consumed (Soja 1980; Harvey 1985). Explicitly critical of readings that focus on the individual at the expense of society, Marxist and feminist geographers trained their analytical spotlight on these hidden yet pervasive social structures that allowed people to make places, but not always under circumstances of their own choosing. Though Marxist and feminist geographers have often preferred to talk about spaces, localities and regions, there can be little question that both have generated important insights into the ways that places are constructed in the midst of social struggles of all kinds. Specifically, the work of geographers in these 'critical' traditions has demonstrated it is impossible to ignore the ways that places are shaped by the logics of capitalism, patriarchy, heterosexism, disablism, racism, post-colonialism and other 'structures' of difference. Each of these constitutes an ideology supportive of particular interests, be they men (patriarchy), specific white groups (racism), the 'able-bodied' (disablism), the bourgeois (capitalism) or the ex-colonizers (post-colonialism). Each has important implications for those whose lifestyle, bodies or identities do not concur with those of privileged social groups. One major outcome is the forcible exclusion of specific groups from particular places.

The idea that questions of *power* cannot be ignored in understanding the use and occupation of place is thus a cornerstone of contemporary social geography. So too is an interest in the *representation* of place (see Chapters 34–40). Here, the term representation may be taken to encompass the wide range of media – such as films, TV, books, Internet sites, music, radio broadcasts, magazines and newspapers – through which we come to understand the world and our place within it (Woodward 1997). In this sense, while social geographers are primarily interested in the way social relations create places, they recognize these relations have important symbolic dimensions. The social struggle for place is not just about the ways a place is used and occupied, it is also about the power to name place, to mythologize it and to represent it as belonging to a particular group (Shields 1991). Hence, representations cannot be dismissed as immaterial. Far from it – they have a material weight that affects the 'reality' of place in a number of ways. For some commentators, the very distinctions of material/immaterial or real/imagined are thus hard to sustain when exploring the social dimensions of place. Indeed, the growing rapprochement of social and cultural geography is testament to the difficulty of separating 'real' social inequalities from cultural questions that might once have been dismissed as irrelevant.

The coalescence of social and cultural geography around two key issues – first, the power and resistance played out in the everyday and, second, the politics of representation – has thus fuelled a staggeringly diverse and absorbing series of analyses of the multiple and contested identities of place. Moreover, while geographers have always been open to the idea that places may exist on both a micro- and macro-scale (from the smallest of rooms to entire regions), what is particularly remarkable is geographers' enthusiasm to explore the connections between processes of place-making at different scales (see Chapters 18–24). The notions of mobility central to globalization arguably demands this sensitivity, with Doreen Massey's (1996) much-cited notion of a 'progressive' sense of place dispelling any idea that we can separate what is going on in a given place from what is happening in the wider world. The idea that people move through place, and occupy it in different ways for different periods of intensity, is an important rejoinder to accounts that emphasize the fixity and boundedness of place. Being open to the world, and accepting that place is always in process, is thus vital as we try to pick apart the forms of power being played out in specific places.

Places of power and exclusionary places

Though we live in a world of unprecedented mobility, not all are free to move where they wish. Indeed, one of the key ways in which social relations can be expressed, maintained and reified is through the creation of exclusionary places. These are places which are (consciously or otherwise) designed and occupied so as to restrict access to particular groups who are regarded as dangerous or deviant. In contemporary Western societies, a widely noted trend is towards the creation of 'defensive' landscapes designed to repel those who are perceived as an unwanted or threatening presence (Gold and Revill 1999). Particular figures of contemporary concern include a variety of 'street people' – sex workers, the homeless, street traders and groups of teenagers – who, while they have committed no crime, provoke anxiety among those middle-class affluent consumers whose values directly inform the planning and design of the Western city (Clarke 2003).

Through combinations of CCTV surveillance, barricading and securitization, many city centres are now physically segregated into zones of protection and surveillance such as high security financial districts and segregated gated communities. Shopping centres too are routinely privatized, and subject to forms of policing designed to exclude those who might interrupt the atmosphere of leisurely consumption. Flusty (2001) thus concludes that the commercial privatization of space has been taken to an extreme as a strong fear of the public realm leads to highly exclusive urban spaces, constant surveillance and high-profile policing. Many urban geographers concur, suggesting urban space is becoming increasingly 'prickly' and unwelcoming, with post 9/11 anxieties about terrorist threat hardening the boundaries of urban space and creating an increasingly exclusionary landscape (Flusty 2001; Coaffee and Wood 2006).

Of course, acts of boundary-drawing and target-hardening are also implicated in the making of places on other scales. For instance, anxieties about social difference expressed at local scales may be mirrored in attempts to reaffirm the boundaries of the nation, as was the case in the immediate aftermath of the 9/11 attacks. At this time, instances of Islamaphobia and racism were noted throughout the urban West as (mainly white) citizens sought to generate a sense of security and order by rejecting those whom they regarded as different (Dunn 2001; Hubbard 2005b). In many senses, these instances of racism were encouraged by 'official' responses which talked of the need for tighter immigration controls and the battle to prevent the nation-state being over-run by incomers. In the UK, for example, anxieties about the 'flood' of asylum seekers seemingly threatening to 'swamp' the state have triggered a series of draconian measures designed to protect the boundaries of the nation: procedures for 'screening' those seeking political asylum have been tightened considerably and the National Asylum Support Service (NASS) offers only the barest level of subsistence to those who are waiting for their claim to be processed (working on the assumption that all asylum seekers are bogus).

Related to this is the physical 'tightening' of national boundaries, with closer scrutiny of bodies at airport and border zones linked to new biometric data surveillance systems determining whether someone has the right to enter (or leave) a territory (Dodge and Kitchin 2004 and Chapter 33). Indeed, airports are perhaps one of the most obvious exclusionary places, replete as they are with forms of surveillance intended to render them sterile, ordered and safe:

> The airport exposes people to what the average Westerner regards as either a nuisance or a reassurance – drug-sniffing dogs, X-ray machines, metal detectors, mandatory searches, restrictions on movement, security inspections and intense screening. Staring customs officers, sharp questioning, bio-identifiers, computerized facial recognition and other technological marvels are meant to produce an environment in which people's intentions are 'revealed' and suspicious behaviour is recognized.
>
> (Aaltola 2005: 263)

As Aaltola argues, the international airport is a place where all manner of social types are created and classified, and where 'terrorists, suspect Arabs, Third-Worlders, different ethnicities and illegal immigrants' may be subject to intensive scrutiny. The airport is thus a place of constant and intrusive surveillance, with constant signs and announcements reminding us we are being watched.

Yet not all exclusionary places belie their status so clearly. In many cases, socially excluded groups may simply be made to feel 'out of place' by the looks, language and practices of the groups who routinely inhabit them. For instance, the forms of 'natural' surveillance present in some exclusive suburban districts, where curtains twitch and middle-class aesthetics reign, mean that outsiders may be made to feel distinctly unwelcome in some neighbourhoods (Valentine 2002; Duncan and Duncan 2001). Strangers may stand out in such socially homogeneous places, with some suburban dwellers prepared to use the police to exclude those whose appearance marks them out as different. Here, suburban dwellers may draw on media images and stories about deviance. The UK media has recently played a crucial role in mapping anxieties about crime and disorder on to young people, who often find their presence on suburban streets at night challenged by those who suggest teenagers and children have little reason to be hanging around. The range of strategies now used to restrict young people from (specific) public places is quite remarkable, taking in curfews, the designation of dispersal areas and tagging.

Accordingly, specific groups may be demonized at particular times as a threat to the moral order of place. The role of the press is particularly important here as they collectively order the world into what is good and bad, desirable and undesirable, normal and 'Other', often whipping up a moral panic by representing a group in an exaggerated way. Critical media studies have therefore demonstrated that seemingly 'commonsense' representations construct hierarchies of difference, with the media using specific metaphors and descriptions to suggest certain social groups are somehow less than normal (Cresswell 1996). It is thus possible to identify a number of similarities in the way marginalized groups are depicted, with terms relating to pollution, dirt and disease frequently used to symbolize a distinction between order and disorder. Key metaphors relating to bodily imperfection, disease and 'naturalness' are invoked to suggest that asylum seekers or teenage yobs, for example, are beyond the realms of the acceptable (see Hubbard 2005b).

The importance of the body as a locus of meaning is thus something which has been explored by an increasingly large number of human geographers, perhaps mindful of the discipline's long-standing ignorance of corporeal matters. One of the topics where an embodied approach has helped illuminate the making of social place is the study of disability. Herein, a variety of studies have concluded that people living with a bodily impairment are disabled not by their impairment, but by a society that produces places which do not take account of the full range of bodily capacities. Western cities in particular have been identified as environments designed for 'normal' bodies, creating a multitude of mobility problems for those with partial sight or hearing, locomotion problems or learning difficulties (Imrie 1999). The fact many of the design features which cause major problems for those with disabilities – such as steep steps, dropped kerbs, uneven surfaces – are also problematic for the very young, the pregnant and the elderly underlines that those who produce the built environment often do so in a manner that normalizes middle-aged, able-bodied and male views of the world (see Longhurst 2000, 2005). In this respect, it should be noted that the media rarely – if ever – idealize impaired, obese or pregnant bodies, and routinely depict them as bodies of disgust rather than desire. For instance, the widespread media interest in the unveiling of Mark Quinn's sculpture of limbless artist Alison Lapper in London's Trafalgar Square (in September 2005) suggests the disabled body is still widely regarded as anomalous when encountered in many social places.

As Cresswell (1996) argues, such representation of people or acts as out of place has a great deal to do with power. Power can be defined as the ability to make rules for others. In this sense, a group's ability to influence the media depiction of another group as a social, administrative, welfare or security problem enables them to create imaginary geographies that reinforce social values. Sibley (1995) likewise suggests these representational geographies fuel exclusionary practices, arguing fears of the Self being defiled are projected on to those groups depicted by the media as polluting or dirty. This engagement with psychoanalytical theory offers geographers an important insight into social processes, suggesting that the creation of exclusionary places can only be understood with reference to the deep-seated urge people have to purify their surroundings. As we have seen, these urges are currently creating places that exclude groups who are demonized by the press (e.g. asylum seekers and teenage 'yobs'), as well as those whose exclusion is long-standing (e.g. those living with a disability). Yet geographers have also documented longer-standing geographies of exclusion which have created and sustained class, gender and racial divides.

Places of class conflict

Inspired by Marx, Engels and others in the 'Marxist' canon (notably Althuser), the radical social geography that emerged in the 1970s focused on the importance of social place as a vital ingredient in a wider story of class conflict and ideological control. In the writing of those geographers and urban theorists who most directly engaged with Marxism (e.g. Ed Soja, Manuel Castells and David Harvey), this type of reasoning was transformed into analyses of the role of place in this process of legitimation and crisis avoidance. These writers emphasized the importance of capitalism's *spatial fix* – the way that spatial differentiation and de-differentiation were implicated in capitalist relations. This perspective has been perhaps most fully elaborated by David Harvey, whose various works provide a sustained and critical engagement with Marx's oeuvre. Identifying place as an *active moment* – a unit of capital accumulation as well as a site of class struggle – Harvey's *Limits to Capital* (1982) focused on the idea that surplus profit can be used to make more goods for short-term gain (the 'primary' circuit) or invested in property (the 'secondary' circuit) for longer-term gain. Suggesting that in times of economic slump, profits could be most usefully ploughed into property, the implication was that place provides a major source of profit and loss:

> Under capitalism there is a perpetual struggle in which capital builds a physical landscape appropriate to its own condition at a particular moment in time, only to have to destroy it, usually in the course of a crisis, at a subsequent point in time. The temporal and geographical ebb and flow of investment in the built environment can be understood only in the terms of such a process. The effects of the internal contradictions of capitalism, when projected into the specific context of fixed and immobile investment in the built environment, are thus writ large in the historical geography of the landscape that results.
>
> (Harvey 1973: 124)

Harvey characterized urban places as subject to contradictory impulses of investment and disinvestment. In addition, he noted the capitalist imperative that segregates class communities so as to suppress working-class agitation. This segregation thus creates an urban mosaic of class communities ranging from the wealthiest enclaves and gated communities of the rich to the 'dump' estates and unpopular housing areas occupied by those who exist on the margins of poverty (and, it might be argued, those people whose disability renders them marginal to processes of capitalist production and consumption – see Gleeson 2001).

Subsequently, social geographers have done much to demonstrate the deliberately exclusionary nature of many wealthy neighbourhoods, noting their thoroughly aestheticized forms serve to mystify class relations by eliding social conflict in favour of issues of lifestyle, consumption, taste and visual pleasure (Duncan and Duncan 2001).There has also been considerable attention devoted to the sense of stigma and despair that accrues in the poorest neighbourhoods, with commentators suggesting the media rarely exposes the real reason that such places exist, and instead blames place-specific social problems on the feck-lessness and criminality of the population (Goodwin 1995; Taylor 1998). Significantly, the association of specific places with this criminalized 'underclass' drives down land prices in those locales, meaning subsequent development can realize the difference between actual ground rent and the potential rent offered by that place (the so-called 'rent gap'). This means that lower-class areas are often ripe for gentrification, with middle-class bridge-headers having often instigated a process which re-values these places, and ultimately displaces the original occupants.

In recent times, geographical interpretations of gentrification have focused on the pivotal role of corporate capital in this process (Smith 2002). In an era when fears about crime and risk are endemic, it has been noted that the state and the law often bend over backwards to encourage such corporate gentrification, typically by reassuring investors, tourists and business-people that central cities are safe and secure. This often requires high-profile 'reassurance' policing, with Zero Tolerance for perceived incivility or for those who might disturb the leisured ambience of the gentrified city. By way of example, Neil Smith (1996) gra-phically documents the way in which the 'improvement' and gentrification of New York's Lower East Side resulted in the systematic eviction of the homeless from a number of shelters, parks and streets. Most notably, he describes the forcible removal of homeless people from Tompkins Square Park, an area that had begun to be regularly used as a place to sleep by around fifty homeless people, recounting how the police waited until the coldest day of the year to evict the entire homeless population from the park, their belongings being hauled away by a queue of Sanitation Department garbage trucks (reiterating that notions of social purification rest on ideas that certain people are 'polluting'). The stigmatization of the homeless in this case thus resonates with the same kinds of metaphors that are used to describe unwanted and troublesome 'Others' throughout history, with ideas of the homeless as dirty, deviant and dangerous provoking fears about the potential of homeless people to 'lower the tone' (and the land values) in a particular place. He sees this heavy-handed treatment as symptomatic of the fears evident among the new middle-classes who had relo-cated to the Lower East Side, groups who regarded the unemployed, homeless or immigrants as a potential threat to their dream of urban living.

Smith (1996) describes attempts to exclude the street homeless from particular sites as symptomatic of the class-based *revanchism* (literally, 'revenge') evident in contemporary cities, where sometimes brutal attacks on 'Others' have become cloaked in the language of public morality, neighbourhood security and 'family values'. Revanchism is manifest throughout the urban West in the introduction of curfews, public order acts, by-laws and draconian policing designed to exclude certain 'Others' from spaces claimed by the affluent. In many US cities this has involved the passing of 'anti-homeless' laws designed to prevent people congregating in parking lots, making it illegal to panhandle or beg within range of a cash machine or even making sleeping in public an offence (see Mitchell 1997). Else-where, suitable sites for the congregation of the street homeless have been 'designed out' through the barricading of public parks at night and the removal of benches used for sleeping on. Collectively, these acts indicate the lengths which the authorities are pre-pared to go to in removing members of the 'underclass' from the planned spaces of the gentrified city.

Racialized place

Class-based perspectives suggest the upper classes possess the power to create places, reproducing their wealth and affluence in the process. The removal of lower-class populations from areas earmarked for redevelopment is one outcome; so too is the NIMBYism often displayed by wealthy suburban communities (Cox 1989). Simply defined, NIMBY ('Not in my backyard') protests are locally organized campaigns opposing a locally unwanted land use, whether an industrial installation, human service facility or new housing. Accordingly, NIMBYism is increasingly regarded as a social and spatial process in which wealthy groups seek to 'distance' themselves from stigmatized Others. Such processes of community opposition are seen to encourage the clustering of human service facilities in devalued places (Lake 1993). NIMBYism is often pronounced in the context of human service facilities (e.g. hostels for the homeless, hospitals and mental health facilities), where the social and spatial construction of stigma is seen to enhance the probability of local opposition:

> The embodiment and emplacement of stigma are central to the organized rejection that human service facilities encounter ... Places, along with persons and groups, experience processes of devaluation (and likewise valuation) whereby some places come to be seen as less worthy than others ... local responses to a large degree emanate from and further reinforce the time- and space-specific characterization of stigma.
>
> (Takahashi 1997: 903)

Western cultures characteristically equate whiteness with purity, order and cleanliness – and conversely, non-whiteness with disorder and incivility (Anderson 2000; Sibley 1995), so it is perhaps unsurprising that NIMBYism perpetuates racial divides as well as class ones. Indeed, within the literature on exclusionary reactions to proposed developments, increased attention has been devoted to the role of race, exposing the ways NIMBY actions often exclude people of colour (Wilton 2002). Though protagonists contesting the development of human service facilities rarely see themselves as having malicious or racist intentions, Pulido (2000) alleges NIMBYism maintains white ethnic privilege by constructing whiteness as the unnamed norm against which Otherness is gauged. Even when it is not characterized by hostile racism, NIMBYism may be a key means by which white populations protect the benefits of their whiteness (such as the enhanced value of their homes and properties in relation to those in 'non-white' areas). This is evident in a history of US segregation that has consistently pushed stigmatized facilities and populations towards coloured neighbourhoods, bequeathing a landscape of white suburban prosperity and black disinvestment (Dwyer and Jones 2000).

Accordingly, NIMBYism can be seen as one of the 'spatial effects' that Nast (2000) suggests arise from the desire of white populations to repress blackness. White anxieties about dark bodies and spaces have characterized the colonial histories of the US, and continue to fuel strategies designed to isolate, exploit and control blackness. Statistics suggest that US cities remain highly segregated on racial lines, with Afro-American people remaining more spatially concentrated than any other US ethnic minority. While the situation is improving in many areas, in some there is actually increasing division between white and Afro-American populations. Further, non-white populations are more likely to live in less affluent census tracts. In considering explanations for this in American cities, Massey (1985) suggests this is not simply a question of the over-representation of African-Americans in the poorer classes; instead, it results from a complex interaction of class and ethnicity manipulated by gatekeepers such as housing agencies, landlords, planners and police. In many US cities, white residents who can afford to, leave when non-white groups begin to gain a significant foothold in the area.

However, Wright *et al.* (2003: 460) argue that the racialization of US residential space is more complex than this black/white dualism implies, with the prevalence of multi-racial households and spaces demanding a serious re-evaluation of 'linguistic, physical and theoretical conceptions of singularly "black", "white", or "Asian" bodies'. Writing in a British context, Jackson (1998: 104) likewise warns against forms of racialized thinking where whiteness is automatically opposed to blackness, arguing instead for exploration of the 'complex cultural politics' of whiteness. While most white English populations do not see themselves as ethnically marked, many exhibit an ambiguous relationship with dominant notions of Englishness, and may be subject to forms of racialized exclusion based on their ancestry. Jackson (1998) thus argues for explorations that acknowledge the fluidity and plurality of white identities, recognizing that whiteness takes diverse forms. On similar lines, Bonnett (2000), has repeatedly called for attention to be devoted to the heterogeneity of white identities, suggesting that not all white people have historically achieved whiteness while others have struggled to claim and maintain its privileges.

Though both Bonnett (2000) and Jackson (1998) arguably overlook earlier attempts to study minority white ethnicities, their arguments have struck a chord with (white) geographers seeking to expose the contingency of white identities. Consequently, several recent studies have explored how different white places may be differently racialized in relation to a black/white binary, demonstrating that the privileges of an unmarked whiteness are denied to certain white groups as well as non-white. For example, Holloway (2003) has explored the racialization of a white ethnic minority – Gypsy travellers – in the late nineteenth and early twentieth century. Demonstrating historically specific processes of racialization served to label this white group 'out of place' in the English countryside, Holloway (2003: 712) suggests discourses more normally reserved for colonial descriptions of the non-white 'savages' of distant lands positioned this group as both noble and criminal. While Vanderbeck (2005) suggests the explicitly racist language of the past no longer features in government and media discourse, he notes that notions of cultural disadvantage and backwardness tend to be implicit in many descriptions of Gypsy and Traveller communities today, and inform policies relating to housing, education, health and welfare.

Other forms of whiteness may be subject to exclusionary urges. For instance, Haylett (2001) has scrutinized the contemporary political discourses that burden the poor white working class with an *abject* white ethnicity (that of a white 'underclass'). Depicted as embodying an excessive and offensive whiteness, the exclusion of the white working class has been crucial in the definition of a modern, multicultural Britain forged around white middle-class claims to moral and cultural superiority (see Nayek 2003). For instance, there was violent local opposition expressed towards newly arrived asylum seekers in several white working-class areas, sometimes reflected in voting for right-wing nationalist parties (Kudnani 2001).

The idea that it is only the white working class that harbours racist attitudes distracts from the latent forms of racism evident in places like the middle-class countryside. Significantly, opposition to the construction of asylum centres in the English countryside by middle-class white residents has been represented in the press as an instance of NIMBYism rather than racism, eliding the racial dimensions of anti-asylum discourse (Hubbard 2005b). Here, the imagined boundary between urban and rural places is significant, with the English countryside widely interpreted as the 'real' England in a construction that prevents a range of non-white groups from accessing the countryside (Cloke and Little 1997; Sibley 2003). The perceived absence of 'ethnic minorities' in rural spaces – as visitors, residents or in its symbolism – thus continues to belie the description of the UK as a multicultural society (Agyeman and Spooner 1997).

Gendered and sexualized place

The suggestion that class and race may intersect in a variety of complex ways to create places that are exclusive of particular social identities has provided a basis for many explorations of the placing of social relations. Yet these can seldom be divorced from issues of sexuality and gender, with (for example) dominant notions of respectable whiteness suggesting that men and women should adhere to different codes of sexual conduct, dress and behaviour. Indeed, Skeggs (1997) argues that the making of class, gender and race categories relies upon people identifying with certain modes of comportment and not others. Among the working-class women she interviewed, becoming respectable was most important, with many claiming that a respectable body is one that is 'looked after'. To be seen badly dressed, overweight, drunk or 'disorderly' in public view was thus frowned upon by interviewees, who felt it incompatible with respectability. Of course, such notions change over space and time. For example, Tinkler (2003) argues smoking was once a marker of refinement for women, with working-class smokers aping the habits of the middle and upper classes. However, in an era where people's appearance and health is increasingly valorized, this imagery of smoking has been reversed to the extent that images of working-class women smoking are used to mark it out as a signifier of disrespectability. The choreographies and geographies of smoking are thus gendered in a number of ways, with smoking bans supported by reference not just to the health risks but also the *undesirability* of smoking (Fisher and Poland 1998).

Longhurst's (2005) explorations of the corporeal dimensions of gender geography shed further light on the gendering of place by suggesting that the pressure to conform to an ideal body-image particularly has implications for women, discouraging them from displaying their body in particular places at particular times and especially when their body is considered overweight. Pregnant women interviewed by Longhurst recounted a series of anecdotes of feeling out of place, subjected to looks and gazes that suggested they should not be in places of work, leisure and consumption, but instead should be 'resting at home'. The example of the outcry provoked by a beauty contest in Australia when a group of pregnant women paraded in bikinis also suggests gendered expectations of display and comportment weigh heavily on women (though here it is, of course, important to note that masculinity also favours the display of slender and toned *ectomorphic* bodies) (Longhurst 2000).

This take on the embodied geographies of place has also been explored in Bell and Valentine's (1997) work on eating, which reveals a highly textured landscape of consumption where women and men may wish to be seen eating particular things in particular ways. Eating in public places, for instance, may be regarded as uncivilized and animalistic as street foods (whether burgers, sandwiches, kebabs or chips) rarely require the use of eating utensils, and dispense with the need for elaborate rituals of table manners. As a result of gendered expectations, many women deny themselves the pleasures of street food, particularly where they feel this may lead them to be seen as ill-disciplined and giving in to hunger.

Drinking too may be highly gendered, with concerns about binge drinking identifying young women as particularly at risk within a night-time economy that promotes drinking to excess. Moral conventions about drinking and eating thus create taken-for-granted expectations about who should consume what, where and how, particularly when in public view (see also Jayne *et al.* 2006).

Valentine (2002) makes the point that public space is also segregated in another way. She notes the group which is actually dominant in a public space varies depending on the time of day. Public space is particularly segregated according to gender and age, because of different lifestyles and hence time–space routines. One result is that women's fear of crime is heightened at night – not only because night reduces visibility and therefore increases the opportunity for attackers to strike unobserved, but because the nature of public space changes, being dominated in the evening by the group women have most to fear, namely men:

> During the daytime, public places are numerically dominated by women, housewives, young children and the elderly. As evening draws in, it is younger people, and particularly men, who are visible. Consequently, while women fear isolated places during the day, they express a fear of all public space alone at night.
>
> (Valentine 1989: 387)

Fear is accordingly a key theme in explorations of the gendered nature of public space. Moreover, debunking the dominant ideology that associates men with the public realm and women with the private has been a priority for feminist geographers (Bondi and Rose 2003; Duncan 1996; Day 1999). Feminists have suggested that this ideology can be traced back to the nineteenth century, when the new social mores and identities associated with industrial capitalism restricted women to the private sphere of the home and family, insisting that only men could cope with the hustle and bustle of modern city life. From that point, it was considered disreputable for bourgeois women to be unaccompanied in public spaces, especially at night (Domosh 1998). In effect, women in public space were described as women out of place – either dangerous or in danger – and subject to sanctions and negative connotations. The figure of the street prostitute, in particular, became a cipher for gendered anxieties about city life, with vice laws intended to limit the visibility of sex-working women lest their presence on the streets undermine male mastery of space (Hubbard 1999).

To highlight the differential sexual freedoms afforded to men and women on the streets is not to insist that the public realm is a solely male realm, nor the private realm exclusively female. Rather, as a multitude of feminist geographers have demonstrated, it is to assert that men and women occupy places in a profoundly different basis (Parsons 1997). Indeed, gender and sexual identities are always in flux, and the increased visibility of women in many places that were once exclusively male (e.g. sporting venues, pubs, clubs, company boardrooms, universities) suggests gender divisions are breaking down. Nonetheless, as the examples of public smoking, eating and drinking imply, men and women are still expected to behave in slightly different ways in different places. Further, in Western societies expectations about what is fitting in particular places – and what is out of place – overwhelmingly serve to reproduce male values.

Yet even if most places promote male values, feminist geography has suggested there are places that provide a basis for resisting male dominance. Women-run housing associations and refuges, community and neighbourhood associations and local trading networks may all create places of resistance (see Chapter 57). Such places may be important repositories of social 'capital' that allow women's groups to work co-operatively in resisting social, political and economic change. Accordingly, some of these places are sites from which the relatively powerless can organize themselves into self-supporting cultures of resistance and co-operation. For example, so-called 'lesbian villages' in the US (e.g. Grand Rapids or Provincetown) constitute relatively affluent centres of lesbian cultural life through political organization, creativity and activism, creating feminine identities in the process (Valentine 1997). In some ethnicized places women's co-operatives bring feminine values and ideas to the attention of wider audiences, making them less marginal in the process.

Male expectations about the use and occupation of place have also been challenged. For instance, many women's groups have been involved in attempts to 'reclaim the night' simply by walking on the streets of cities at night. As Cresswell (1996) demonstrates, transgressing place and disturbing assumptions about how particular groups should act in particular places remains a powerful tool for challenging established social categories, and this is as true for gender identities as it is for disabled, ethnic and classed categories of belonging.

Conclusion

The much-vaunted 'reassertion of space in social theory' (Soja 1989) has had the reciprocal effect of encouraging social geographers to work more closely with social theory and to consider the forms of identity politics played out in different places. This engagement has witnessed rich and varied attempts to theorize the ways place is caught up in power relations, and to consider the importance of place in the reproduction of social hierarchies. Further, empirical studies focusing on the cultural dimensions of place-making have suggested new ways of understanding the varied and multi-layered nature of place, stressing struggles for place are both real and imagined.

Hence, in this chapter I have highlighted some of the processes which shape the social characteristics of place, noting the impacts of media stigmatization, discrimination in the housing market, institutional prejudice, NIMBY politics and so on. It has been suggested that these processes segregate the powerful and the less powerful, with the former tending to include wealthy, white men. While such processes of exclusion and discrimination tend to carve up space in favour of powerful white men, in some instances excluded groups are able to resist these processes. For example, some excluded groups may resist forms of social closure by transgressing into the places of the powerful, challenging taken-for-granted expectations about where they should locate (Cresswell 1996). These actions may subtly change the social order (for instance, gay pride marches in Western cities have often drawn attention to homophobia in society, encouraging the repeal of discriminatory legislation, while Muslims have pursued a variety of public actions designed to topple the Islamaphobia that is rampant in the West).

Yet we have also seen that such transgressions may trigger a moral panic (such as that which surrounded asylum seekers in the early 2000s) and encourage the introduction of new forms of social and spatial control. In the final analysis, while it is important to note the asymmetry of power associated with a particular place, we should never assume that the social character of place is fixed. Indeed, one of the key contributions of human geography to the social sciences has been to show that identities are always becoming, being made and remade in different spatial contexts. Places too are always in process. Capturing this sense of dynamism and transformation while still making meaningful generalizations about the forms of oppression thus remains the key challenge for critical social geography in the twenty-first century.

Further reading

Bonnett, A. (2000) *White Identities*. Harlow: Prentice-Hall.

Cresswell, T. (1996) *In Place Out of Place: Geography, Ideology and Transgression*. Minneapolis: University of Minnesota Press.

——(2004) *Place – A Short Introduction*. London: Arnold.

Holloway, L. and Hubbard, P. (2001) *People and Place: The Extraordinary Geographies of Everyday Life*. Harlow: Longmans.

Panelli, R. (2004) *Social Geographies*. London: Sage.

Nayek, A. (2003) Last of the real Geordies? White masculinities and the subcultural response to deindustrialisation. *Environment and Planning D – Society and Space* 21, 7–25.

Sibley, D. (1995) *Geographies of Exclusion, Society and Difference in the West*. London: Routledge.

——(1999) Creating geographies of difference. In D. Massey, J. Allen and P. Sarre (eds) *Human Geography Today*, pp. 115–28. Cambridge: Polity.

Valentine, G. (2002) *Social Geographies*. Harlow: Pearson.

White, A. (2002) Geographies of asylum, legal knowledge and legal practices. *Political Geography* 21, 1055–73.

Winchester, H.P.M., Kong, L. and Dunn, K. (2003) *Landscapes: Ways of Imagining the World*. Harlow: Pearson.

References

Aaltola, M. (2005) The international airport: the hub-and-spoke pedagogy of the American empire. *Global Networks* 5, 261–78.

Agnew, J. (2005) Space/place. In P. Cloke and R.J. Johnston (eds) *Spaces of Geographical Thought*, pp. 81–96. London: Sage.

Agyeman, J. and Spooner, R. (1997) Ethnicity and the rural environment. In P. Cloke and J. Little (eds) *Contested Countryside Cultures*. London: Routledge.

Anderson, K. (2000) The beast within: race, humanity and animality. *Environment and Planning D – Society and Space* 18, 301–20.

Bell, D. and Valentine, G. (1997) *Consuming Geographies: We Are What We Eat*. London: Routledge.

Bondi, L. and Rose, D. (2003) Constructing gender, constructing the urban: a review of Anglo-American feminist urban geography. *Gender, Place and Culture* 10 (3), 229–45.

Clarke, D.B. (2003) *The Consumer Society and the Postmodern City*. London: Routledge.

Cloke, P. and Little, J. (eds) (1997) *Contested Countryside Cultures*. London: Routledge.

Coaffee, J. and Wood, D. (2006) Security and surveillance. In P. Hubbard, T. Hall and J.R. Short (eds) *The Urban Compendium*, pp. xx–xx. London: Sage.

Cox, K. (1989) The politics of turf and the question of class. In J. Wolch and M. Dear (eds) *The Power of Geography*, pp. 61–89. London: Unwin Hyman.

Cresswell, T. (1996) *In Place Out of Place: Geography, Ideology and Transgression*. Minneapolis: University of Minnesota Press.

Day, K. (1999) Embassies and sanctuaries: women's experiences of race and fear in public space. *Environment and Planning D – Society and Space* 17, 3: 307–28.

Dodge, M. and Kitchin, R. (2004) Flying through code/space: the real virtuality of air travel. *Environment and Planning A* 36: 195–211.

Domosh, M. (1998) Those glorious incongruities: polite politics and public space on the streets of nineteenth-century New York City. *Annals, Association of American Geographers* 88 (2), 209–26.

Duncan, J.S. and Duncan, N.G. (2001) The aestheticization of the politics of landscape preservation. *Annals of the Association of American Geographers* 91, 387–409.

Duncan, N. (1996) Renegotiating gender and sexuality in public and private places. In N. Duncan (ed.) *Bodyspace: Destabilizing Geographies of Gender and Sexuality*. London: Routledge.

Dunn, K.M. (2001) Representations of Islam in the politics of mosque development in Sydney. *Tijdschrift voor Economische en Sociale Geografie* 92, 291–308.

Dwyer, O.J. and Jones, J.P. III (2000) White socio-spatial epistemology. *Social and Cultural Geographies*, 1 (2), 209–22.

Fisher, B. and Poland, B. (1998) Exclusion, risk and social control. *Geoforum* 29 (2), 187–97.

Flusty, S. (2001) The banality of interdiction: surveillance, control and the displacement of diversity. *International Journal of Urban and Regional Research* 25, 658–64.

Gleeson, B. (2001) Disability and the open city. *Urban Studies* 38 (2), 251–65.

Gold, J. and Revill, G. (eds) (1999) *Landscapes of Defence*. Harlow: Pearson.

Goodwin, M. (1995) Poverty in the city, you can raise your voice, but who is listening? In C. Philo (ed.) *Off the Map, the Social Geography of Poverty in the UK*. London: Child Poverty Action Group.

Harvey, D. (1973) *Social Justice and the City*. London: Arnold.

——(1982) *The Limits to Capital*. Oxford: Blackwell.

——(1985) The geopolitics of capitalism. In D. Gregory and J. Urry (eds) *Social Relations and Spatial Structures*, pp. 128–63. Basingstoke: Macmillan.

Haylett, C. (2001) Illegitimate subjects? Abject whites, neoliberalism, and middle-class multi-culturalism. *Environment and Planning D – Society and Space* 19, 351–70

Holloway, S. (2003) Outsiders in rural society? Constructions of rurality and nature-society relations in the racialization of English gypsy-travellers. *Environment and Planning D – Society and Space* 21, 695–715.

Hubbard, P. (1999) *Sex and the City: Geographies of Prostitution in the Urban West*. Chichester: Ashgate.

——(2005a) Space/place. In D. Sibley, P. Jackson, D. Atkinson and D. Washbourne (eds) *Critical Terms in Cultural Geography*, pp. 41–48. London: I.B. Tauris.

——(2005b) Inappropriate and incongruous: opposition to asylum centres in the English countryside. *Journal of Rural Studies,* 21, 3–17.

Imrie, R. (1999) The body, disability and Le Corbusier's conception of the radiant environment. In R. Butler and H. Parr (eds) *Mind and Body Spaces: Geographies of Illness, Impairment and Disability*, pp. 25–46. London: Routledge.

Jackson, P. (1998) Constructions of whiteness in the geographical imagination. *Area* 30, 99–106.

Jayne, M., Bell, D., Holloway, S. and Valentine, G. (2006) Pleasure and leisure. In P. Hubbard, T. Hall and J.R. Short (eds) *The Urban Compendium*. London: Sage.

Kudnani, A. (2001) In a foreign land: the new popular racism. *Race and Class* 43, 41–60.

Lake, B. (1993) Rethinking NIMBY. *Journal of the American Planning Association* 59, 87–93.

Longhurst, R. (2000) Corporeo-geographies of pregnancy. *Environment and Planning D – Society and Space* 18, 453–72.

——(2005) Fat bodies: developing geographical research agendas. *Progress in Human Geography* 29, 247–59.

Massey, D.S. (1985) American apartheid: segregation and the making of the underclass. *American Journal of Sociology* 96, 329–57.

——(1996) Space/power, identity/difference, tensions in the city. In A. Merrifield and E. Swynge-douw (ed.) *The Urbanisation of Injustice*, pp. 190–205. London: Blackwell.

Mitchell, D. (1997) The annihilation of space by law: the roots and implications of anti-homeless laws in the United States. *Antipode* 29 (3), 303–35.

Nast, H. (2000) Mapping the unconscious: racism and the Oedipal family. *Annals, Association of American Geographers* 90, 215–55.

Parsons, C.O. (1997) Reputation and public appearance: the de-eroticisation of the urban street. In S.J. Drucker and G. Gumpurt (eds) *Voices in the Street: Explorations in Gender, Media and Public Space*. Cresskill: Hampton Press.

Pulido, J. (2000) Rethinking environmental racism: white privilege and urban development in South-ern California. *Annals, Association of American Geographers* 90, 12–40.

Shields, R. (1991) *Places on the Margin*. London: Routledge.

Sibley, D. (1995) *Geographies of Exclusion: Society and Difference in the West*. London: Routledge.

——(2003) Psychogeographies of rural space and practices of exclusion. In P. Cloke (ed.) *Country Visions*. Harlowe: Pearson.

Skeggs, B. (1997) *Formations of Class and Gender*. London: Sage.

Smith, N. (1996) *The New Urban Frontier, Gentrification and the Revanchist City*. London: Routledge.

——(2002) New globalism, new urbanism, gentrification as global urban strategy. *Antipode* 34, 434–57.

Soja, E. (1980) The socio-spatial dialectic. *Annals, Association of American Geographers* 70 (2), 207–25.

——(1989) *Postmodern geographies.* Oxford: Blackwell.

Takahashi L (1997) The socio-spatial stigmatisation of homelessness and HIV/AIDS: towards an explanation of the NIMBY syndrome. *Social Science and Medicine* 45, 903–14.

Taylor, M. (1998) Combating the social exclusion of housing estates. *Housing Studies* 13, 819–32.

Tinkler, P. (2003) Refinement and respectable consumption: the acceptable face of women's smoking in Britain 1918–70. *Gender and History* 15, 342–58,

Valentine, G. (1989) The geography of women's fear. *Area* 21, 385–90.

——(1997) Making space: lesbian separatist communities in the United States. In P. Cloke and J. Little (eds) *Contested Countryside Cultures.* London: Routledge.

——(2002) *Social Geographies: Space and Society.* London: Prentice Hall.

Vanderbeck, T. (2005) Anti-nomadism, institutions and the geographies of childhood. *Environment and Planning D: Society and Space* 23, 71–94.

Wilton, R. (2002) Colouring special needs: locating whiteness in NIMBY conflicts. *Social and Cultural Geography* 3, 303–21.

Winchester, H., Kong, L. and Dunn, K. (2003) *Landscapes: Ways of Imagining the World.* London: Prentice Hall.

Woodward, K. (1997) Concepts of identity and difference. In K. Woodward (ed.) *Identity and Difference,* pp. 8–59. London: Sage.

Wright, R., Houston, S., Ellis, M., Holloway, S. and Hudson, M. (2003) Crossing racial lines: geographies of mixed-race partnering and multiraciality in the United States. *Progress in Human Geography* 27, 457–74.

5

Place as network

Richard G. Smith

The town is the correlate of the road. The town exists only as a function of circulation and of circuits; it is a singular point on the circuits which create it and which it creates. It is defined by entries and exits; something must enter it and exit from it. It imposes a frequency. It effects a polarization of matter, inert, living or human; it causes the phylum, the flow, to pass through specific places, along horizontal lines. It is a phenomenon of transconsistency, a network, because it is fundamentally in contact with other towns.

> Deleuze and Guattari (1986: 195–96)

In 1931 Henry C. (Harry) Beck created a map of London's Underground tube network. Beck's now iconic subterranean map – still the template for today's journey-planner and copied around the world – is interesting to a geographer because it creates a London that is geographically different to the London one conventionally encounters above ground. The comical travel writer Bill Bryson (1995: 54) writes:

> Here is an amusing trick you can play on people ... Take them to Bank Station and tell them to make their way to Mansion House. Using Beck's map ... they will gamely take a Central Line train to Liverpool Street, change to a Circle Line train heading east and travel five more stops. When eventually they get to Mansion House they will emerge to find they have arrived at a point 200 feet further down the same street ... Now take them to Great Portland Street and tell them to meet you at Regent's Park (that's right, same thing again!), and then to Temple Station with instructions to rendezvous at Aldwych. What fun you can have!

At the heart of Beck's design is an abandonment of cartographic conventions – of street-level topography – in favour of a sequential and non-scalar topology. In other words, Beck realized that a passenger could be moved around the network by making him or her follow a given sequence of stations, a sequence that has relative autonomy from the physical geography of the city above ground. Further, on his map Beck played with scale, with the proximate and the remote, drawing his map as it would appear through a convex mirror:

outlying stations appearing near to each other and those in central London appearing further from each other (see Figure 5.1). Beck's map is important because it is analogous with the global world we live in. Globalization is made through the formation of networks, and those networks often do not correspond directly with 'real' geography, the kind of geography you were perhaps taught at school or possess as 'common sense' or take for granted: *our global world is no longer a configuration of fixed positions, neatly scalar, a Euclidean and Cartesian space;*

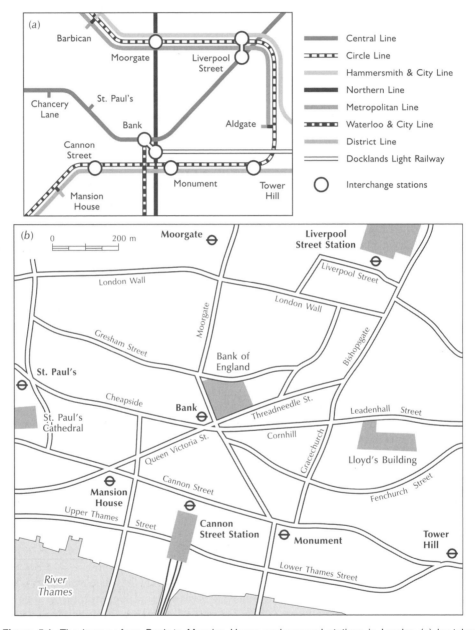

Figure 5.1. The journey from Bank to Mansion House underground stations in London (a) by tube; (b) on foot.

indeed, it is now only on obsolete maps that places retain an objective shape. We need to avoid falling into the trap of somehow reading Beck's map as 'imaginary' and in contradiction to the 'real' above-ground geography of London if we are to begin to understand places as networks.

Beck's map is just a starting point in our rethinking of places as networks because a non-Euclidean and non-Cartesian topological take on place as network has numerous consequences for how we understand the world's geography as a crumpled spatial configuration (see Smith 2003a). Two decades ago Peter Cook (1986: 436) wrote:

> My walkman is on my head for the whole of my weekly London–Frankfurt commute. I can't remember where I bought the tape. I wave on the escalator to friends at both ends. I select to eat Italian in Frankfurt and Indian in London, have heavy discussions in one and witty discussions in the other. In the late 20th-century city I can fuzz out my view from the bus window or choose to look. I choose certain indulgences in the late 20th-century city. Others choose completely other sets of indulgences. They switch in or out on a different set of criteria. Isn't it funny that we occasionally overlap.

Perhaps unwittingly, Cook here is making an important point about our global world: namely, that *your world is just one of many parallel worlds.* Latour (1997: 3) explains how in our global world there is no summation as such, no coherence, no longer is there one map for all:

> I can be one metre away from someone in the next telephone booth, and be nevertheless more closely connected to my mother 6000 miles away; an Alaskan reindeer might be ten metres away from another one and they might be nevertheless cut off by a pipeline of 800 miles that makes their mating for ever impossible; my son may sit at a school with a young Arab of his age but in spite of this close proximity in first grade they might drift apart in worlds that become at later grades incommensurable; a gas pipe may lie in the ground close to a cable television glass fiber and nearby a sewage pipe, and each of them will nevertheless continuously ignore the parallel worlds lying around them.

This is our global world – increasingly Hobbesian with no 'Leviathan' or other unifying figure – a world where proximity, propinquity and contiguity count for less and less in terms of what and whom we connect to. People in particular networks (e.g. bankers working and living in a global city, the super rich, a Pakistani living in Leicester) are often more connected to one another, even when half a world away, than to people who are far more spatially proximate to them (i.e. the near can be distant, and vice versa). In short, with globalization places have a topology of numerous parallel – sometimes intersecting – networks that do not necessarily correspond to a metric geography of stable and well-defined distances.

Having said all that, however, very little has been written about places as networks, let alone the distinctive topologies of networked places. Those writers that have mentioned networks in their thinking about places have by and large tended to conceptualize places and networks separately: places are treated as in networks, as fixed, rather than as constituted by networks themselves that are constantly in movement. To move towards a topological conceptualization of places as networks, this chapter will develop its argument in the following sequence. First, the ideas of two key theorists of globalization – Doreen Massey and Saskia Sassen – will be discussed. Both authors are interesting because whilst they argue for a topological take on globalization, on global networks, they nevertheless – like Manuel

Castells – conceptualize places as *in* networks, and so ultimately see places or nodes (usually privileged ones: key points such as global cities, world cities, international financial centres, etc.) as apart from networks. Second, ideas from poststructuralism, actor-network theory (ANT), and non-representational theory (NRT) will be mobilized to outline an alternative way of thinking about relations, connections and globalization that enables a conceptualization of places *as* networks: a way of thinking about Place that rejects the very idea of making any distinction at all between places and networks and so any need for the preposition 'in'. Finally, my rejection of the ontological category 'place', to rethink place as network is mobilized to illustrate how networked places are enacted and relational effects.

Place *in* network

Doreen Massey is a widely cited writer on Place and globalization, having written on the topic throughout the 1990s (1993, 1994, 1995, 1999). Indeed, Massey has written a great deal about Place, and so let us just examine one of her specific arguments about the different places of different people in globalization. In her writings she is keen to note the inequalities between individuals and groups in globalization and time–space compression (see 1993: 61; Massey's (1993) ideas developed as a critique of Harvey's (1989) idea of 'time–space compression'). She argues that the numerous asymmetries (what she calls power-geometries) of time–space compression are a product of control by some (those with wealth and power) over movement and communication. Massey is consistent in her argument. For example, in 1999 she writes that:

> the space–time of the banker zapping in and around with an internationalized set of contacts to Silicon Valley and Tokyo, is different from the space–time of the beggar who has connections to the village and the countryside beyond and who goes home to a very different housing area.
>
> (Massey 1999: 77)

In broader terms, what are counterpoised and presented by Massey as incommiscible are: first, the relational geographies of the transnational professional class who produce and circulate through a seemingly rapidly expanding network of global and world cities; and second, the relational geographies of the excluded and marginalized who are cut off from the glamorous side of neo-liberal global networks to participate in quite different networks altogether. In short, Massey is concerned with the inequalities *between* the different flows and interconnections of globalization. Different people find themselves in different space–times and so are locked into 'international or wider connections in different ways' (Massey 1999: 77).

Earlier, in 1993, Massey made a similar argument:

> For different social groups and different individuals are placed in very distinct ways in relation to these flows and interconnections. The point concerns not merely the issue of who moves and who doesn't, although that is an important element of it; it is also about power in relation *to* the flows and the movement. Different social groups have distinct relationships to this anyway-differentiated mobility: some are more in charge of it than others; some initiate flows and movement, others don't; some are more on the receiving end of it than others; some are effectively imprisoned by it.
>
> (Massey 1993: 61)

Her argument about this 'highly complex social differentiation' is illustrated through exam-ples. She identifies four groups that are more or less mobile and more or less in control: first, highly mobile transnational elites, 'wired' through hi-tech communications, and able to take advantage of time–space compression; second, economic migrants who also move frequently but are restricted by some national borders; third, poor UK pensioners living in high-crime inner cities who are scared to leave their homes but are consumers of goods and images from around the world; fourth, poor favela residents in Brazil who contribute to globalization through football, music and dance but nevertheless remain imprisoned and impoverished through time–space compression. Massey is keen to point to the differences between groups, and how some groups have power over others: 'the mobility and control of some groups can actively weaken other people' (Massey 1993: 62). However, whilst Massey is surely right to point to the idea that these groups – whilst existing in parallel worlds – might nevertheless be connected, she never quite reaches the idea *that people in different social groups, and perhaps in different places, are within the same asymmetrical networks.*

Saskia Sassen is famous for her research on global cities (Sassen 2000a, 2001) and has started to try to think about the complexity of these places:

In order to begin to understand what our large cities are about today and in the near future – in order to see what constitutes their complexity – it matters that we recog-nize the interconnections between urban forms that present themselves as uncon-nected.

(Sassen 2003: 117)

Her argument is quite simply that in our consideration of global cities more people need to be included and valued:

The top end of the corporate economy – the highly paid professionals and the cor-porate towers that project engineering expertise and precision – is far easier to recog-nize as necessary for an advanced economic system than are truckers and other industrial service workers, or maids and nannies, even though all of them are a necessary ingredient.

(Sassen 2003: 117)

Sassen is critical of the way in which the global city is often portrayed as containing many cities within cities, with some sectors (urban forms) being more highly valued as emblematic of an advanced post-industrial economy. For example, the corporate city with its 'signature architecture' and highly paid professional workforce is highly valued and separated from both the declining (de)industrial city with its 'flexible' workforce, and the expanding low-wage immigrant city with its various neighbourhood industries and cultural networks. Her point is that to understand the complexity of global cities one must recognize the interconnections and see through the negative discourse that labels some people and activities as backward and marginal. She points out how, while many people living and working in the global city are portrayed as living in different worlds, they actually belong to the same network. And that network only works because of the mix of people and activities within it, all of which are necessary 'to produce the capability for servicing and coordinating the global operations of firms and markets' (Sassen 2003: 114). In short, within the same network there are lawyers, truckers, nannies, accountants, janitors, consultants, cleaners, receptionists, bankers and maids, all of whom are paid and otherwise rewarded at highly differential rates. The case that these people are all parts of the same network is strongly made by Sassen, who points out how global staffing firms are adding household and childcare service staff to their portfolios so that 'the transnational professional class can access these [domestic] services in the expanding network of global cities among which they are likely to circulate' (Sassen 2003: 116).

In short, Sassen recognizes that all these people are in the same network, so highlighting the asymmetries *within* networks rather than just *between* networks (as with Massey). Clearly both Massey and Sassen have – in their own ways – moved the globalization debate forward. However, both authors' treatment of place in their accounts of globalization is still problematic: *both suggest that places are intersections or nodes.*

Sassen in particular has tended to privilege nodes (the global cities, world cities and international financial centres) rather than links or networks in her accounts of globalization and its consequences. More recently she has been convinced by the arguments of some urban geographers (Beaverstock *et al.* 1999, 2000, 2003) that with globalization more attention needs to be paid to the links, the relations, the connections and networks between cities: and in her work attention is now duly paid to the world's urban networks as a whole, not just to the attributes of certain cities, places or nodes (see Sassen 2000b, 2002). However, whilst this move to considering networks as well as nodes is the most important recent advance in urban studies, it is still not enough (see Smith 2005). Dematteis (2001: 113) summarizes this now standard approach in global urban studies which actually limits current thought:

> In a world dominated and controlled by networks of interaction and global flows, many of the assumptions upon which the territorial conception of cities was founded are increasingly fading away ... the key break with the past lies with the fact that while previously the city was thought of as a primary, taken-for-granted entity – stable in time – it can now only be envisioned as *one* possible, deliberate construction: a local geographical order born out of the turbulence of global flows and with which it must interact in order to continue to exist.

In other words, the argument is that globalization throws previous settled conceptualizations of place into doubt. Previous accounts that thought of place as bounded and consequently to some extent or another outside of the myriad of connections and networks that constitute globalization are redundant. However, that is not to say that the world is now somehow place-less but rather that with globalization place can no longer be thought of as bounded, self-contained, coherent, settled, a territorial package. Places – so the argument goes – should now be conceptualized as intersections or nodes interacting with networks: perhaps the most famous proponent of this style of thought is Manuel Castells (1996) with his idea of the network society (for a critique, see Smith 2003b). However, it is my contention that we now need to go even further than what Dematteis suggests is *de rigueur*: to move on to consider places as networks, not as fixed permanencies (somehow outside of networks) that are increasingly linked together through networks. Indeed, we need to abolish the distinction between interior and exterior, place and network, altogether if we are to fully appreciate the networked and topological organization of place.

Place *as* network

> A concept ... should express an event rather than an essence.
>
> (Deleuze 1995: 25)

A dictionary would begin as of the moment when it no longer provided the meanings of words but their tasks.

(Bataille 1995: 51)

Place is traditionally viewed, with space and environment, as central to the project of human geography. It should be no surprise, then, that a great deal has been written on Place, with some writers being particularly noted for their contributions to blazing new paths (e.g. for a recent overview, see Cresswell 2004). There are many key thinkers on Place (Heidegger, Relph, Tuan, etc.), but none of these thinkers provides an account of place as network, or even provides us with a starting point for thinking about places as networks. Only Nigel Thrift (1999) has started to forge a dynamic non-signifying sense of place through his development of Non-Representational Theory (NRT). In developing his NRT take on Place, Thrift's concern has been to emphasize processes, events, performances and practices in the making of places as networks, rather than to focus on the interpretation and representation of place which has been the predominant concern of cultural geography. For Thrift places are alive, they are made of relations that are constantly being performed, places are networks.

Consequently, my starting point for thinking about places as networks will be NRT and the philosophies of poststructuralism and actor-network theory (ANT) from which NRT was in part born – precisely because these intellectual movements are concerned with relations, connections, practices, performances and networks. However, these approaches also offer much more to a rethinking of place as network. Most writing on Place has, in one way or another, been concerned with the essence of Place, but poststructuralism, ANT and NRT are different because they offer a way of thinking about Place as *event* rather than *essence*. In other words, these philosophies are ones that guide you towards eschewing pure, bloodless, lifeless Platonic accounts of places (definitions, formulas, essences) to pay attention to the spacing and timing of places as events, practices, performances, relations, connections and networks. In other words, understanding places as networks is to be Deleuzian rather than Platonic. Indeed, places as networks can be conceptualized as Bodies-without-Organs where, if one were to invoke Shakespeare's Prospero from *The Tempest* (1968), or literally quote Marx and Engels from *Manifesto of the Communist Party* (1965: 37; where in the German the word 'solid' reads as the 'privileged and established'), 'all that is solid melts into air'. This idea is taken up in Smith (2007) where the privileged and established power of world and global cities is presented as distributed, decentred and relational. Indeed, nothing is solid – with poststructuralism there is no distinction between process and thing – there are only transitory hardenings, changeable (not inevitable) political attempts to regulate flows.

How we conceptualize key ideas in human geography really does matter and that is why some geographers (e.g. see Allen 2003, 2004; Amin 2004; Amin and Thrift 2002; Doel 1999; Doel and Hubbard 2002; Smith 2003a, 2003b; Thrift 2003; Whatmore 2002) have been developing what might be called a *new spatial grammar* through an engagement with ideas from poststructuralism, ANT and NRT to rethink space, time, scale, identity, environment and power. This chapter is a contribution to that endeavour, to propose a radical new direction for conceptualizing Place. In other words, this chapter is aligned with current efforts in critical social theory to undo established habits of thought (conceptual maps) that no longer – if they ever did – match current global realities. My argument is for a *relational* rather than a *representational* understanding of place (see Table 5.1).

Table 5.1. A new spatial grammar for place

Representational	Relational
distal	proximal
preformed	performed
present	absent, the figural presence of absence
essentialist	rhizomatic
framed	open
permanent	transitory
settled	nomadic
rooted	routed
centred	distributed
being	becoming
node	network

One of the key achievements of poststructuralist theory – which has shaped both ANT and NRT – has been an undoing of many of the dualisms that have shaped critical social theory. Poststructuralism is a purely materialist approach – naked without even a fig-leaf of ideology or any of the other mumbo-jumbo that has cluttered modern social science (e.g. class consciousness or other such essentialisms). Elsewhere (Smith 2003a, 2003b) an argument for a shift from a topographical to a topological perspective was advanced, as the binary of global and local was undone to argue for actant-networks and against an ontology based on geographical scale. That argument is extended here by undoing the separation of place and/in network. A poststructuralist-driven relational perspective is always aware that places are not somehow made *a priori*; rather, any place is always travelling without moving (toing and froing, stuttering and stammering, or voyaging in place, as Deleuze would say) as it is co-constructed with numerous other humans and non-humans. Place, like space and time (see Smith 2003b), is not passive and neutral but is constantly becoming made, unmade and remade. In other words, dualisms are irrelevant for thinking effectively about geographies of globalization. It is not the case that place is somehow outside of actant-networks and then becomes incorporated into forever combining and recombining networks, but is rather actively co-constructed through connections and relations. From this perspective, global and local, abstract network (space) and concrete place are redundant categories because places are actively co-constructed through actant-networks which are always distanciated and 'concrete, grounded, and real' because they are a product of connections, relations, practices and performances.

Previously (Smith 2003a, 2003b) a topological spatial formation emerged from an outlining of the co-relation of space and time as multiple (coherently or incoherently related) and constructed through networks with elsewhere, as always undergoing a series of transformations, translations and transductions in the process of becoming made, unmade and remade, as always incomplete and in movement. Thus, through an anti-essentialist and relational poststructuralist perspective place can now be conceptualized as a formless amorphous coacervate made up of all kinds of relations and movements: a hybrid and porous unbounded space of flows, always becoming and replete with loose ends and possibilities. Place can now be imagined as folding, refolding and unfolding through a hinge logic, as a rhizome: place as network is a plane of immanence. The rhizome means that places are not points or nodes in a network, where our task would be to 'join up the dots' so to speak, but to realize that it makes no sense even to distinguish between nodes and links, as all is lines of flight across the manifold. Places as networks are never given, ready-made, or preformed; they are always becoming and performed.

Let me be frank: the argument is not that place–local has been displaced or replaced by network–space–global, but rather that everything is folded together: *globalization is topological in organization and place is an effect of relations*.

Place as relational effect

Reporting on a visit to Istanbul, Baudrillard (2001) contends that there is something about that city which is special, a quality that is certainly not being erased by globalization. Baudrillard (2001: 40) writes that:

> The star system is one of the effects of globalization. And it applies not just to film stars and politicians, but to cities too. Looking beyond the concentration of economic and demographic forces that characterizes all cities that can be said to be 'global', we must ask wherein lies the singularity of some modern metropolises, what it is that makes them world cities and that, even boundless as they are, makes them resistant to globalization. It's to do with fame, not simply political and economic power.

According to Baudrillard, something about Istanbul's culture (not the museums or official heritage sites that are a part of globalization) resists its disappearance into the planetary conurbation, the mental diaspora of networks, the virtual world city, as Virilio (1997) puts it.

For Baudrillard, cities are not becoming homogenized and absorbed into the networks (or flows, if you like) of globalization. Baudrillard is not one of those who fetishizes the (surely dystopian) ideal of a truly global or world city, one who tries to sell the exaggerated narrative that the city to end all cities is the city network, a planetary horizontal conurbation of multiple networks, which produces – to invoke Relph – a common city of 'non-places and soulless urban spaces' (Baudrillard 2001: 40). Rather, Baudrillard points towards a different analysis altogether, a different definition of a global city, when he draws our attention to the 'elective affinities' between cities. He writes that:

> A truly fascinating city shares its fabric, its sky, its characteristic features, its memories with many others. It has with them elective affinities – and it's that which makes it a global city, not the fact of having been the centre of the world.
>
> (Baudrillard 2001: 40)

And it is that idea that there is something about Istanbul and other cities that makes them resistant to erasure on the spinning surface of globalization that is, I think, significant.

Baudrillard's 'elective affinities' between cities makes me think of Wittgenstein, of his *Philosophical Investigations* (2000) and his discussion of games. In remarks 66, 67 and others he discusses the category of 'games' (including board-games, card-games, ball-games, Olympic games, chess, tennis, ring-a-ring-a-roses, etc.) through the idea of 'family resemblances', arguing that all 'games' are related and belong to 'a complicated network of similarities overlapping and criss-crossing: sometimes overall similarities, sometimes similarities of detail' (Wittgenstein 2000: 32e). Further, Wittgenstein develops his thinking about categories to ask:

> Why do we call something a 'number'? Well, perhaps because it has a-direct-relationship with several things that have hitherto been called number; and this can be said to give it an indirect relationship to other things we call the same name. And we extend our

concept of number as in spinning a thread we twist fibre on fibre. And the strength of the thread does not reside in the fact that some one fibre runs through its whole length, but in the overlapping of many fibres.

But if someone wished to say: 'There is something common to all these constructions – namely the disjunction of all their common properties' – I should reply: Now you are only playing with words. One might as well say: 'Something runs through the whole thread – namely the continuous overlapping of those fibres,' (Wittgenstein 2000: 32).

With Wittgenstein, 'family resemblances' can be thought of as fibrous and overlapping connections. And so we can perhaps link together Baudrillard's 'elective affinities' with Wittgenstein's 'family resemblances' to realize that there is some kind of effect that is generated through connections; it is a particular arrangement of connections that makes a place special, familiar, famous. It is relations, the performance of relations, that produces the effect of this or that place: it has nothing whatsoever to do with embedment, historical or otherwise.

Wherein lies the singularity of some modern metropolises? In a discussion of Serres' interest in cities Hénaff (1997: 61–62) writes:

> What is at stake for our epoch is that the planet is being urbanized globally. Will we think about the entire world as a swelling city that invades space by homeothesis – in other words, will we see the world as the outgrowth of the *oecumene* only? Or will we think of the city as part of the world, that is, think of the built environment inhabited by humans in its relation to the totality of the landscape, including the spaces of the other species, the mineral elements, the continents and climates, not to mention its relation to older traditions, various ways of life – whether urban or not – and the arts and sensitivities that make for the extraordinary cultural diversity of the world?

For Serres – and, ironically, reminiscent of an argument Castells made many years ago – 'the question of the city goes far beyond the urban question' (Hénaff 1997: 63), the city should be considered as a part of both the human and non-human world. For Serres the city is a 'world object', an artefact with the capacity to intervene globally (other examples include banking, nuclear weapons and satellites; see Hénaff 1997). Serres highlights a broader sense of the significance of the city, of place, in the modern world through a myriad of connections: networks not only constitute cities but also touch the world, shape the world. Following this approach Istanbul can be considered as both connected and actant. Istanbul both resists and enables globalization; as a networked place it has a power to affect and modify the relations between people and materials, humans and non-humans.

Conclusion

> It is not drawn in any map, true places never are
>
> (Melville 2003: 61)

Any Place is made through connections, made up of, made by, nothing more than actant-networks of varying lengths and durability. Every place is both present and absent, an absent presence (see Hetherington (2002) on the importance of considering the effects of absence, not just the absence of presence, but the figural presence of absence). In other words, every place is never fully 'there' – it is there to some extent, but it is also not there insofar as its being is determined by its relation to the whole network of which it is a part, a network that does not appear to us (cf. a metaphysics of presence). It is for this reason that we should be concerned with the network as a whole, with places as networks, and not with individual places as such, with places in networks. Finally, the characteristics of any place are the effect of the relations that run through them: a city is famous because the relations that constitute that place have produced that particular spatial formation and effect.

It is time to challenge your long-held assumptions about Place. Places are networks, not simply open or perforated intersections. And if you accept that argument then the study of Place can never be the same again.

Coda

The new paradigm for Place that has been outlined is not just a different way of seeing Place, but a way of situating yourself, too. And so there is a politics involved in accepting places as networks. Approaching places as networks means that:

1 places are not 'framed' as local and weak;
2 any place is not 'explained away' as being shaped by, or a 'victim' of, some exterior force such as capitalism or the neo-liberal or neo-conservative, unbounded, 'free trade' discourse of globalization pushed by such institutions as the International Monetary Fund, World Bank, Western governments and the World Trade Organization (see Smith (in press) for my poststructuralist critique of such extrinsic approaches to urban studies); and
3 any place is no longer disempowered through being located within a 'big picture' or 'wider context'. A topological take on places as networks means that it makes no sense to think of – and portray – place as 'detailed' and context as somehow 'general' and so more important. And, of course, vice versa: it makes no sense either to think of the general or the large as more complex than the particular or small.

The current hegemonic rhetoric that presents and promotes one form of globalization as inexorably encroaching and inevitably driving towards open, barrier-less, friction-less, unfettered mobility and interaction (but paradoxically not the free movement of all people) needs to be challenged. In that discourse the global is commonly portrayed as an inevitable, unstoppable, virtual or abstract process that is intangible and untouchable. In contrast, places are seen as fixed, inherently local and ultimately weak, unable to stand up to the storm outside. Indeed, so ingrained is the hyper-globalizers' scalar argument that now many people seem to think that the global and the local have different and separate kinds of politics (that you can distinguish between a space of global politics and a space of local politics). However, if places are networks then it is harder to pretend that globalization simply overwhelms places. Rather, those considering places as networks need to be attentive to the politics of connectivity (see Amin 2004) that such a perspective brings.

Further reading

Amin, A. and Thrift, N. (2002) *Cities: Reimagining the Urban*. Cambridge: Polity Press.
Hetherington, K. (2002) Whither the World? In G. Verstraete and T. Cresswell (eds) *Mobilizing Place, Placing Mobility: The Politics of Representation in a Globalized World*, pp. 173–88. Rodopi: Amsterdam.

Ong, A. and Collier, S.J. (eds) (2005) *Global Assemblages*. Oxford: Blackwell.

Serres, M. with Latour, B. (1995) *Conversations on Science, Culture and Time*. Ann Arbor: Michigan University Press.

Smith, R.G. (2003) World city actor-networks. *Progress in Human Geography* 27 (1), 25–44.

——(2003) World city topologies. *Progress in Human Geography* 27 (5), 561–82.

——(2007) Poststructuralism, power and the global city. In P. Taylor, B. Derudder, P. Saey and F. Witlox (eds) *Cities in Globalization: Practices, Policies and Theories*, pp. 260–72. London: Routledge. (Available at http://www.lboro.ac.uk/gawc/rb/rb170.html).

Thrift, N. (1999) Steps to an ecology of place. In D. Massey, J. Allen and P. Sarre (eds) *Human Geography Today*, pp. 295–322. Cambridge: Polity.

Urry, J. (2000) *Sociology Beyond Societies*. London: Routledge.

References

Allen, J. (2003) *Lost Geographies of Power*. Oxford: Blackwell.

——(2004) The whereabouts of power: politics, government and space. *Geografiska Annaler B* 86 (1), 19–32.

Amin, A. (2004) Regions unbound: towards a new politics of place. *Geografiska Annaler B* 86 (1), 33–44.

Amin, A. and Thrift, N. (2002) *Cities: Reimagining the Urban*. Cambridge: Polity Press.

Bataille, G. (1995) Formless. In G. Bataille, M. Leiris, M. Griaule, C. Einstein and R. Desnos, *Encyclopaedia Acephalica*, pp. 51–52. London: Atlas Press.

Baudrillard, J. (2001) Sanctuary city. *Tate: The Art Magazine* 24 (Spring), 38–41.

Beaverstock, J.V., Smith, R.G. and Taylor, P.J. (1999) A roster of world cities. *Cities: The International Journal of Urban Policy and Planning* 16 (6), 445–58.

——(2000) World city network: a new metageography? Millennial issue of the *Annals of the Association of American Geographers* 90 (March), 123–34.

——(2003) The global capacity of a world city: a relational study of London. In E. Kofman and G. Youngs (eds) *Globalization: Theory and Practice*, second edition, pp. 223–36. London: Continuum.

Bryson, B. (1995) *Notes from a Small Island*. London: Black Swan.

Castells, M. (1996) *The Rise of the Network Society*. Oxford: Blackwell.

Cook, P. (1986) Questionnaire 4. In J. Crary, M. Feher, H. Foster and S. Kwinter (eds) *ZONE 1/2 The Contemporary City*, pp. 436–37. New York: Zone Books.

Cresswell, T. (2004) *Place: A Short Introduction*. Oxford: Blackwell.

Deleuze, G. (1995) *Negotiations*. New York: Columbia University Press.

Deleuze, G. and Guattari, F. (1986) City/state. In J. Crary, M. Feher, H. Foster and S. Kwinter (eds) *ZONE 1/2 The Contemporary City*, pp. 195–99. New York: Zone Books.

Dematteis, G. (2001) Shifting cities. In C. Minca (ed.) *Postmodern Geography: Theory and Praxis*, pp. 113–28. Oxford: Blackwell.

Doel, M.A. (1999) *Poststructuralist Geographies: The Diabolical Art of Spatial Science*. Edinburgh: Edinburgh University Press.

Doel, M.A. and Hubbard, P.J. (2002) Taking world cities literally: marketing the city in a global space of flows. *City* 6 (3), 351–68.

Harvey, D. (1989) *The Condition of Postmodernity*. Oxford: Blackwell.

Hénaff, M. (1997) Of stones, angels and humans: Michel Serres and the global city. *SubStance* 83, 59–80.

Hetherington, K. (2002) Whither the world? In G. Verstraete and T. Cresswell (eds) *Mobilizing Place, Placing Mobility: The Politics of Representation in a Globalized World*, pp. 173–88. Rodopi: Amsterdam.

Latour, B. (1997) *The Trouble with Actor-Network Theory*. (Available at http://www.ensmp.fr/~latour/artpop/p67.html). [Published as B. Latour (1997) Om aktor-netvaerksteroi. Nogle fa afklaringer og mere end nogle fa forvikinger. *Philsophia* (Danish philosophy journal) 25 (3 et 4), 47–64].

Marx, K. and Engels, F. (1965) *Manifesto of the Communist Party*. Beijing: Foreign Languages Press.

Massey, D. (1993) Power–geometry and a progressive sense of place. In J. Bird, B. Curtis, T. Putnam, G. Robertson and L. Tickner (eds) *Mapping the Futures: Local Cultures, Global Change*, pp. 59–69. London: Routledge.

——(1994) *Space, Place and Gender*. Cambridge: Polity Press.

——(1995) The conceptualization of place. In D. Massey and P. Jess (eds) *A Place in the World?* pp. 45–85. Milton Keynes: Open University Press.

——(1999) *Power-geometries and the Politics of Space–Time*. Heidelberg: Department of Geography, University of Heidelberg.

Melville, H. (2003) *Moby-Dick; or the Whale*. Harmondsworth: Penguin Books.

Sassen, S. (2000a) *Cities in a World Economy*, second edition. London: Pine Forge Press.

——(2000b) New frontiers facing urban sociology at the millennium. *British Journal of Sociology* 51 (1), 143–59.

——(2001) *The Global City: New York, London, Tokyo*, second edition. Princeton, NJ: Princeton University Press.

——(ed.) (2002) *Global Networks – Linked Cities*. London: Routledge.

——(2003) More than CitiBank: who belongs in the global city? *Topic Magazine* 3, 111–17.

Shakespeare, W. (1968) *The Tempest*. Harmondsworth: Penguin Books.

Smith, R.G. (2003a) World city topologies. *Progress in Human Geography* 27 (5), 561–82.

——(2003b) World city actor-networks. *Progress in Human Geography* 27 (1), 25–44.

——(2005) Networking the city. *Geography: An International Journal* 90 (2), 172–76.

——(2007) Poststructuralism, power and the global city. In P. Taylor, B. Derudder, P. Saey and F. Witlox (eds) *Cities in Globalization: Practices, Policies and Theories*, pp. 260–72. London: Routledge. (Available at http://www.lboro.ac.uk/gawc/rb/rb170.html).

Thrift, N. (1999) Steps to an ecology of place. In D. Massey, J. Allen and P. Sarre (eds) *Human Geography Today*, pp. 295–322. Cambridge: Polity.

——(2003) Space: the fundamental stuff of human geography. In S.L. Holloway, S.P. Rice and G. Valentine (eds) *Key Concepts in Geography*, pp. 95–107. London: Sage.

Virilio, P. (1997) *Open Sky*. London: Verso.

Whatmore, S. (2002) *Hybrid Geographies*. London: Sage.

Wittgenstein, L. (2000) *Philosophical Investigations*. Oxford: Blackwell.

Part II
Forces for change

Richard Huggett and Chris Perkins

The character of places constantly changes, often imperceptibly but sometimes violently and dramatically. Forces driving this change come from natural and human sources.

Natural forces of change are cosmic, geological and biological. Cosmic forces include energy from the sun and gravitational changes resulting from the jostling of planets and their satellites. Geological forces in the broadest sense include uplift, earthquakes and the power of flowing water and wind. Biological forces include the direct action of organisms in damaging soils and vegetation, and the action of microorganisms on biogeochemical cycles. The human species, by its sheer numbers and ability to alter the environment, has come to be a potent force of change in its own right. Humans exploit natural energy stocks, change ecosystems, modify habitats, alter biodiversity, manage soil fertility; they have also developed technologies, economic and social practices, and belief systems that themselves change the world. This block of chapters explores the nature of the different forces that together drive change.

Chapters 6–8 explore essentially natural drivers of global change. In Chapter 6, Richard Huggett gives an overview of global biogeochemical cycles and their role in transferring energy, water and matter across the surface of the Earth, between the oceans, atmosphere and the land. Human activities have affected these natural cycles and stocks. In Chapter 7, Mike Summerfield moves on to deep-seated geological processes and their effects on global change. Specifically, he considers plate tectonics, the creation of continental topography, the interactions between tectonics and surface processes, and topography, denudation and climate change. Richard Huggett, in Chapter 8, looks at climate and climatic change as a force for change. For many, the most readily apparent feature of a place is its climate, localities being seen as belonging to one of a set of climatic regions based on combinations of temperature and rainfall. Real understanding of climate only derives from understanding the general circulation, its perturbations and its relationship to ocean currents. Climatic variability across timescales from days to millennia is also an important aspect of places, given the legacies of the last Ice Age that are relevant to everyday life, from fossil sand dunes in the wet tropics to fossil glaciofluvial sand and gravel resources in the temperate zone.

Human forces for change include population growth, disease, economic and social development, economic globalization, changes in transport systems, cultural and ideological change, and light-speed advances in information technology and biotechnology. Graeme

Hugo (Chapter 9) discusses the human population, the growth and increasing wealth of which are probably the most powerful drivers of current global change. Human distribution across the globe is uneven, ranging from the crowded lands of south, south-east and east Asia through the sparsely peopled areas of Australia, parts of Africa and south-west Asia, to the almost uninhabited Antarctic continent. Within the broad distribution is enormous variation in population growth, age-distribution and migration. A major shift of population from rural areas to towns and cities is continuing in many parts of the world. International migration is a major factor in the growth of some recipient countries, while remittances from migrants help to sustain the character of places in many others. Sarah Atkinson (Chapter 10) examines human health and disease. The huge inequality of life expectancy between places reflects an unequal geography of health, and disease relates to access to health care and the ecological conditions affecting the spread of disease. Atkinson focuses upon four case studies to illustrate these links. The social and spatial consequences of the epidemic of HIV/AIDS; the effects of long-term ill-health on residence patterns; the impact of stigma on individual life-courses and places; and the production or reproduction of social relations and values through meanings that have come to be associated with health and healing are all considered.

Chapters 11–13 consider the chief economic drivers of global change. Environments, societies, cultures and economies of different places have all changed because of inexorable modernization. Former colonial powers with mature economies still control much of the development process and enjoy the fruits of having developed first. Here people enjoy higher standards of living, administered through liberal democratic political systems, with economies that have shifted from primary through secondary to an emphasis upon tertiary and qua-ternary services and information. Meanwhile, newly industrializing countries aspire to western patterns of consumption and the poorer nations struggle under often-autocratic regimes, social and economic inequalities, and penal debt burdens. Katie Willis in Chapter 11 focuses on different ways of understanding this process of economic and social development. She contrasts views of development as economic modernization with structuralist approaches. The domination of neo-liberalist orthodoxy is explained and contrasted with sustainable development, grassroots development and post-development discourse. Willis shows how these many different ways forward reflect and in turn create powerful voices.

Phil Kelly (Chapter 12) argues that perhaps the most significant influence on how places have changed in the last century has come from the pervasive forces of economic globalization. Throughout modernity, trade has created places. However, globalization touches all places. Kelly explores contested meanings of the term and situates these changes in the historical process. He focuses upon the geographical pervasiveness, the interconnectivities that are central to the process, the speed of flows and the impacts of globalization. The institutions enacting these powerful changes are described and the geographical imagination around the concept explored.

John Preston (Chapter 13) explores the transport of goods and people as a powerful influence on changing geographies. Industrialization depended on the development of transport infrastructures that linked the increasingly global economy and facilitated the movement of people and goods. However, the impact of transport systems is uneven and dependent upon technological progress, regulation and the particular local context. Preston highlights changing mobilities, costs, urban transport, inter-urban transport and the new places that emerge from the nexus of transport changes. He concludes with a consideration of the implications for sustainability.

Cultural and ideological change are, and always have been, strong shapers of places. Eric Parson (Chapter 14) argues that skilled human activity, the arts, ideas, fashion, ways of life and language all change and constitute local difference. Differences in landscapes, in settlements, in thought, in societies, all reflect culture. Colonialism and emerging post-colonial contexts continue to represent locally distinct places.

Belief and religion, discussed by Chris Perkins in Chapter 15, has also always exerted an influence on the location and design of human settlements and other sites. For some, the end of the Cold War signalled the end of history, but the last decade of the twentieth century saw many places increasingly built according to local custom and belief. Ideology matters. Nations and individuals take positions on conflicts that relate to religious belief or ethnic identity. Fundamentalist thought has risen as a major social force. From the West Bank to Kashmir, geographies are changing because of people's beliefs. Many places remain dominated by symbols of religious hopes and fears. Religious buildings still dominate settlements. Cities have developed around temples and cathedrals, and many are now centres of tourism, hotel building and place transformation.

To conclude the catalogues of forces for change, Chapters 16 and 17 turn to information technology and biotechnology respectively. As Mike Batty (Chapter 16) shows, information technologies change the way people see places and experience separation and distance. The application of different processing, storage, communications and display technologies in the second half of the twentieth century encouraged a shift to a global economy operating around the processing of information. In recent years, remote sensing and surveillance, personal and distributed computing, the Internet, mobile technologies, global positioning systems and electronic mail have altered every aspect of life and have profoundly altered geographies. Mike examines the geographical significance of these technological shifts. In like manner, and as Antoinette Mannion explains in Chapter 17, biotechnology – from plant and animal breeding to xenotransplantation and genetically modified organisms – is transforming lives, nutrition, medicine and landscapes, and altering our social relationship with Nature. As biotechnology expands, it affects people–environment relationships, changing farming from a culture and way of life to a precise, highly regulated form of commodity production. Agricultural yields in many places have doubled or tripled since 1950, but this has required massive changes to local ecosystems, biogeochemical flows, farming methods and ways of life. Although farmers are unevenly affected by these technical changes, virtually none escapes in some way or another from the new technologies, even if it is only to walk to a neighbour's to borrow a mobile phone to contact a sick relative in hospital.

6

Drivers of global change

Richard Huggett

Energy from the sun, energy from the inside the Earth and gravitational energy power the transformation and flow of materials through the ecosphere in solid, liquid and gaseous forms. The chief flows are of water, rock and rock waste, and elements essential to life (bioelements). These materials flow from one store to another, sometimes transforming in the process. The water cycle involves stores and fluxes of water as ice, liquid and vapour. The rock cycle comprises stores and fluxes of rocks and their weathered products. Bioelements, such as carbon and nitrogen, move repeatedly back and forth from non-living to living parts of the ecosphere in biogeochemical cycles. These three main types of cycle are interconnected. For instance, water stores and fluxes help carry fragments of weathered rock material through the land-surface leg of the rock cycle, and these fragments often transfer bioelements from one part of the ecosphere to another. Moreover, plants take up some products of rock decay, which then enter part of a biogeochemical cycle.

Water, rock and biogeochemical cycles have run at least since life first evolved. Humans make an increasingly material impact on the stores and fluxes in these cycles at local, regional and global scales. In doing so, they have themselves become a potent driver of global change, largely through activities related to food production, urbanization, industrialization and water management. Humans use more than one-half of all accessible surface freshwater. They have caused accelerated soil erosion in many parts of the world; and they have nearly exhausted some non-renewable resources and placed some renewable resources in jeopardy. Since the beginning of the Industrial Revolution, the concentration of carbon dioxide in the atmosphere has increased by nearly 30 per cent. Humanity fixes more atmospheric nitrogen than is fixed by all natural nitrogen-fixing processes. Humans affect global biogeochemical cycles, including the carbon, nitrogen and sulphur cycles; they mobilize such metals as arsenic and mercury. Global change wrought by the human species is so thoroughgoing that some writers consider it appropriate to designate the last two hundred years as the dawn of a new geological epoch – the Anthropocene. To be sure, human actions have transformed about one-half of the land surface (Table 6.1). Regional variations are marked: Europe is by far the most transformed continent, with about 16 per cent remaining undisturbed; Antarctica is the least transformed continent, with almost 100 per cent undisturbed.

Table 6.1. Human disturbance of habitats by continent

Continent	Area (millions km^2)	Habitat		
		Undisturbed (%)	Partially disturbed (%)	Dominated by human (%)
Europe	5.8	15.6	19.6	64.9
Asia	53.3	43.5	27.0	29.5
Africa	34.0	48.9	35.8	15.4
North America	26.1	56.3	18.8	24.9
South America	20.1	62.5	22.5	15.1
Australasia	9.5	62.3	25.8	12.0
Antarctica	13.2	100.0	0.0	0.0
World total	**162.0**	**51.9**	**24.2**	**23.9**
World total less area of bare rock and barren land	**134.9**	**27.0**	**36.7**	**36.3**

Source: Adapted from Hannah *et al.* (1994).

The water cycle

Water is indispensable to all life on Earth. It is stored as vapour in the atmosphere, as a salty liquid in oceans and seas, as a freshwater liquid in life, clouds, rain, rivers, soils and rocks, and as a solid in snow, icecaps, ice sheets, glaciers and other forms where freezing conditions prevail. Water moves between the stores by evaporation, condensation and precipitation, and by gravity. This cycle of water helps to drive biogeochemical cycles and the rock cycle.

Water stores

The hydrosphere is the totality of Earth's waters. It includes liquid water, water vapour, ice and snow. Water in the oceans, in rivers, in lakes and ponds, in ice sheets, glaciers and snowfields, in the saturated and unsaturated zones below ground, and in the air above ground is all part of the hydrosphere. At present, and averaging out variations over a long period of years, the hydrosphere holds about 1,400,000,000 km^3 of water in various states (Table 6.2). By far the greatest portion of this volume is stored in the oceans. A mere 2.5 per cent (35,029,000 km^3) of the hydrosphere is freshwater. Of this, 68.70 per cent is water frozen in the ice and snow cover of the Antarctic, the Arctic and mountainous regions. Fresh groundwater accounts for 30.06 per cent, leaving a tiny fraction stored in the soil, lakes, rivers, the biosphere and the atmosphere. Nonetheless, the relatively small volumes of soil, lake, reservoir and river water are the most accessible for humans and essential resources for many ecosystems. The usable water amounts to about 200,000 km^3, or less than 1 per cent of the freshwater total.

Water flows

Water, even in its solid state, seldom stays still for long. Meteoric water circulates through the hydrosphere, atmosphere, biosphere, pedosphere and upper parts of the lithosphere. This

Table 6.2. Water stocks in the hydrosphere

Water	Water volume (km³)	Percentage of all water	Percentage of freshwater
Salt water stocks			
Oceans	1,338,000,000	96.54	–
Saline and brackish groundwater	12,870,000	0.93	–
Saltwater lakes	85,000	0.006	–
Freshwater stocks			
Glaciers and permanent snow	24,064,000	1.74	68.70
Fresh groundwater	10,530,000	0.76	30.06
Ground ice and permafrost	300,000	0.022	0.86
Freshwater lakes	91,000	0.007	0.26
Soil moisture	16,500	0.001	0.05
Atmospheric water vapour	12,900	0.001	0.04
Marshes and wetlands	11,500	0.001	0.03
Rivers	2,120	0.0002	0.006
Within living things	1,120	0.0001	0.003
Total freshwater	**35,029,000**		**100**
Total water in hydrosphere	**1,386,000,000**	**100**	

Source: Adapted from Laycock (1987) and Shiklomonov (1993).

water circulation – the water cycle – involves evaporation, condensation, precipitation and runoff. The Earth's surface water balance is:

$$\text{Precipitation } (P) = \text{Evaporation } (E) + \text{Runoff } (D) + \text{Storage } (S)$$

In the long term, storage is fairly constant and ignored in drawing up a global inventory of annual water fluxes. It is reasonable to assume that world water reserves have not changed substantially in recent times. This being the case, it follows that the quantity of water evaporated from the entire planetary surface must be replaced by an equal amount of precipitation; and it must be true that the annual global precipitation equals the annual global evaporation, so there is no net runoff.

Water and humans

From the perspective of human use, water stores are either static reserves or renewable reserves. The distinction depends on the turnover time of the store (Table 6.3). River water is hugely important in the global water cycle and in supplying water to humans because it has a fast turnover rate compared to most other water stores and is usually accessible. It takes about 2,000–4,000 years to replenish the water stored in oceans and seas, and about 10,000 years to replenish that stored in ice caps. Lake and reservoir water replenishes in 10–20 years and river water in a couple of weeks.

Static water resources usually include freshwater that takes many years or decades to replenish completely, such as large lakes, groundwater or glaciers. If used intensively, stores of static water dwindle with adverse consequences. An example is the falling of water tables in heavily used aquifers. Once depleted, static water reserves may take decades or centuries to return to their original state. Static reserves tend to be used where surface water is meagre. Desalination comprises several processes that remove salt from water, usually from static

Table 6.3. Water stores and their turnover times

Store	Volume (km³)	Turnover time
Biosphere	1,120	Several hours to a week
Atmosphere	12,900	10 days
Rivers	2,120	16 days
Marshes and wetlands	11,500	1–10 years
Lakes and reservoirs	176,400	10–20 years
Soil	16,500	2 weeks to 1 year
Ice caps, ice sheets and permanent snow	24,064,000	10,000 years
Mountain glaciers	40,600	1,500 years
Oceans and seas	1,338,000,000	2,000–4,000 years
Groundwater	23,400,000	2 weeks to 10,000 years

Source: Adapted from Laycock (1987).

water reserves. In 1999, the countries with the greatest desalination capacity were: Saudi Arabia (5,106,742 m³day⁻¹), USA (3,234,042), United Arab Emirates (2,184,968) and Kuwait (1,285,527) (Gleick 2000: 288). Of the world's total desalination capacity (22,696,068 m³day⁻¹), about 59 per cent comes from seawater and 26 per cent from brackish water (Gleick 2000: 290). Groundwater mining refers to the withdrawal of underground water at rates that significantly exceed its natural recharge rate. In Saudi Arabia, 90 per cent of water comes from groundwater sources built up thousands of years ago but currently replenishing at negligible rates. Similarly, vast underground water resources in Libya, which finished accumulating about 3,000 years ago, provide the Great Man-Made River that carries water from desert wells through two main pipelines to coastal towns. In the USA, the High Plains aquifer or Ogallala covers 450,000 km² from South Dakota to Texas. Water mined from this aquifer system helped transform the mid-western prairies into a productive grain-producing region, but a slow natural recharge and a high demand for water is leading to falling water tables, escalating pumping costs and the loss of irrigated land.

Renewable water resources include waters replenished each year. They are mainly river runoff formed within a specific region or coming from external sources, such as groundwater inflow. They also include the annual renewable upper aquifer groundwater not drained by the river systems, although these resources are tiny compared with river runoff volumes and significant only in specific regions.

Humans impede and impound river flow to create reservoirs of water for power generation, for agriculture and for human consumption. They also manage waterways for transport, to control floods and to dilute chemical wastes. All these activities alter freshwater ecosystems, in some cases to a considerable degree. For instance, in 1997, some 267,727,000 ha were irrigated worldwide, with variations between continents (Table 6.4). In places, irrigation has led to salinization of soils. Worldwide, 20 per cent of irrigated land is affected by salinization.

The impoundment of water is a worldwide phenomenon with growing environmental impacts. In 2005, there were more than 45,000 dams higher than 15 m capable of holding back more than 6,500 km³ of water, which represented some 15 per cent of the total river runoff. Of these dams, over 300 were giant dams standing over 150 m high, or having a volume in excess of 15 million cubic metres, or reservoir storage of over 25 km³. The Three Gorges Dam on the Chang Jiang (Yangtze) in China is the world's largest dam. It is 181 m high and stores more than 30 km³ of water. By building dams, humans appreciably affect the

Table 6.4. Irrigated area by continent in 1997

Country and region	Area irrigated (ha)
Africa	12,314,000
North and Central America	30,552,000
South America	9,902,000
Asia	187,194,000
Europe	24,777,000
Oceania	2,988,000
Total	**267,727,000**

Source: Adapted from Gleick (2000: 265).

flow of half of the world's major rivers. A study of 292 large river systems on all continents, which drain 54 per cent of the land area and carry 60 per cent of the runoff, revealed the impact of dams on river flow (Nilsson *et al.* 2005). Of the world's ten largest river systems, dams strongly affect river flow in four and moderately affect river flow in the other six.

Dams have impacts on ecosystems upstream and downstream as a result of flooding, flow manipulation, and the fragmenting of river habitats (e.g. World Commission on Dams 2000; see also Graf 2005; Petts and Gurnell 2005). Flooding destroys terrestrial ecosystems and eliminates turbulent river reaches, so affecting river biota. It may cause anoxia, release of greenhouse gases, sedimentation and a bout of nutrient release in new reservoirs. Flow manipulations may hamper channel development, drain floodplain wetlands, reduce flood-plain productivity and modify aquatic communities. Fragmentation disrupts the upstream and downstream migration of animals, which in some cases leads to extinction of freshwater fish species, and the flooding of areas behind dams and the drying out and fertility loss in wetland areas below dams. Matters are likely to get worse because further large dams are either planned or under construction in 46 large river systems, 40 of them in developing countries. Nearly half these new dams affect just four rivers: China's Chang Jiang (49 new dams), the Rio de la Plata in South America (29 new dams), the Shatt Al Arab in the Middle East (26 new dams), and the Ganges–Brahmaputra in South Asia (25 new dams).

Humans alter the chemical load of rivers. Environmental problems may arise where such rivers discharge into shallow seas. In the Yellow Sea and Bohai Sea of China, algae harmful to fish commonly form a bloom or 'red tide'. Similar blooms of harmful algae occur in the North Sea, where agricultural pesticides washed in by rivers cause problems for marine life.

The rock cycle

Humans have become increasing adept at ploughing land and at excavating and moving materials in construction and mining activities. Indeed, humans are so efficient at unintentionally and deliberately moving soils and sediments that they have become the leading geomorphic agent of erosion (e.g. Hooke 2000). Placing human-induced erosion in a geological perspective demonstrates the point (Wilkinson 2005). The weathered debris stored in continental and oceanic sedimentary rocks suggests that, on average, continental surfaces have lowered through natural denudation at a rate of a few tens of metres per million years. By contrast, construction, mining and agricultural activities presently transport sediment and rock and lower all ice-free continental surfaces by a few hundred metres per million years.

Therefore, the human species is now more important at moving sediment than all other geomorphic processes put together by an order of magnitude.

The key areas of human influence on the rock cycle are in mining and construction, agriculture and dam building.

Mining and construction

Locally and regionally, humans transfer solid materials between the natural environment and the urban and industrial built environment. Robert Lionel Sherlock, in his book *Man as a Geological Agent: An Account of His Action on Inanimate Nature* (1922), recognized the role of human activity in geomorphic processes, and supplied many illustrations of the quantities of material involved in mining, construction and urban development. Recent work confirms the potency of mining and construction activities in Earth surface change. In Britain, such processes as direct excavation, urban development and waste dumping are driving landscape change: humans deliberately shift some 688–972 million tonnes of Earth-surface materials each year; the precise figure depends on whether or not the replacement over overburden in opencast mining is taken into account. British rivers export only 10 million tonnes of solid sediment and 40 million tonnes of solutes to the surrounding seas. The astonishing fact is that the deliberate human transfers move nearly fourteen times more material than natural processes. The British land surface is changing faster than at any time since the last ice age, and perhaps faster than at any time in the last 60 million years (Douglas and Lawson 2001).

Every year humans move about 57 billion tonnes of material through mineral extraction processes. Rivers transport around 22 billion tonnes of sediment to the oceans annually, so the human cargo of sediment exceeds the river load by a factor of nearly three. Table 6.5 gives a breakdown of the figures. The data suggest that, in excavating and filling portions of the Earth's surface, humans are at present the most efficient geomorphic agent on the planet. Even where rivers, such as the Mekong, Ganges and Yangtze, bear the sediment from accelerated erosion within their catchments, they still discharge a smaller mass of materials than the global production of an individual mineral commodity in a single year. Moreover, fluvial (river-borne) sediment discharges to the oceans from the continents are either similar in magnitude, or smaller than, the total movement of materials for minerals production on those continents.

Table 6.5. Natural and mining-induced erosion rates of the continents

Continent	Natural erosion (Mt per year)[a]	Hard coal, 1885 (Mt)	Brown coal and lignite, 1995 (Mt)	Iron ores, 1995 (Mt)	Copper ores, 1995 (Mt)
North and Central America	2,996	4,413	1,139	348	1,314
South America	2,201	180	1	712	1,337
Europe	967	3,467	6,771	587	529
Asia	17,966	8,990	1,287	1,097	679
Africa	1,789	993	None	156	286
Australia	267	944	505	457	296
Total	**26,156**	**18,987**	**9,703**	**3,357**	**4,442**

Note: [a] Mt = Megatonne = 1 million tonnes.

Source: Various, including Douglas and Lawson (2001).

Soil erosion

In transporting sediment to the oceans, rivers maintain a vital leg of the rock cycle and a key component of the global denudation system. The amount of sediment carried down rivers is a measure of land degradation and the related reduction in the global soil resource. Many factors influence fluxes of river sediments, including reservoir construction, land clearance and land-use change, other forms of land disturbance (such as mining activity), soil and water conservation measures and sediment control programmes, and climate change. Land clearance, most land-use change and land disturbance cause an increase of sediment loads; soil and water conservation, sediment control programmes and reservoir construction cause a decrease in sediment loads. A study by Walling and Fang (2003) provided a first assessment of current trends in the sediment loads of the world's rivers. Analysis of longer-term records of annual sediment load and runoff assembled for 145 major rivers revealed that some 50 per cent of the sediment-load records contain evidence of statistically significant upward or downward trends, though the majority display diminishing loads. The evidence pointed to reservoir construction as probably the most important influence on land–ocean sediment fluxes, although the influence of other controls resulting in increasing sediment loads were detectable.

In North America, agricultural land-use typically accelerates erosion tenfold to a hundredfold through fluvial and aeolian processes. Much of this high sediment yield is stored somewhere in the river system, mainly in channels, behind dams and as alluvium and colluvium. Many other reports in the literature support this conclusion. With the maturation of farmlands worldwide, and with the development of better soil conservation practices, it is probable that the human-induced erosion is less than it was several decades ago (e.g. Trimble 1999). Overall, however, there has been a significant anthropogenic increase in the mobilization of sediments through fluvial processes. Global estimates of the quantities vary considerably. Using a range of scenarios, Stallard (1998) suggests a range from 24 to 64 billion tonnes per year of bulk sediments; Smith *et al.* (2001) estimate that as much as 200 billion tonnes of sediment move every year.

Dam building

The construction of dams, and other human activities, alters the amount of sediment carried by rivers to coastal environments, so affecting marine ecology, fisheries and coastal geomorphology. Dams reduce the amount of sediment carried to coasts by about 1.4 billon tonnes per year, although soil erosion and mining and construction activities have increased it by about 2.3 billion tonnes per year (Syvitski *et al.* 2005). Excessive sediment may suffocate coral reefs and sea grasses, leading to declines in fish populations. Less sediment, however, can make coastal areas more vulnerable to erosion. The positive and negative influences of human activities on river flow could balance each other out, but the net global result at present is that rivers carry less sediment to the coastal zone, with considerable differences on the regional level. In Indonesia, where fewer dams have meant fewer sediment-trapping reservoirs, more sediment is building up along the coastline because of human activities, chiefly deforestation. In general, Africa and Asia have seen the largest reduction in sediment to the coast.

A study of the impacts of 633 of the world's largest reservoirs (with a maximum storage capacity of 0.5 km^3 or more), and the potential impacts of the remaining >44,000 smaller reservoirs highlights the issues (Vörösmarty *et al.* 2003). It used the residence time change (the time that otherwise free-flowing river water stays in a reservoir), in conjunction with a sediment retention function, as a guide to the amount of incoming sediment that is trapped. Across the globe, the discharge-weighted mean residence time change for individual impoundments is 0.21 years for large reservoirs and 0.011 years for small reservoirs. The large reservoirs intercepted more than 40 per cent of global river discharge, and approximately 70 per cent of this discharge maintains a theoretical sediment-trapping efficiency in excess of 50 per cent. Half of all discharge entering large reservoirs shows a local sediment trapping efficiency of 80 per cent or more. Between 1950 and 1968, global sediment trapping in large reservoirs tripled from 5 per cent to 15 per cent; it doubled to 30 per cent between 1968 and 1985, but then stabilized. Several large basins such as the Colorado and Nile show almost complete trapping caused by large reservoir construction and flow diversion. From the standpoint of sediment retention rates, the most heavily regulated drainage basins lie in Europe. Large reservoirs also strongly affect sediment retention rates in North America, Africa and Australia–Oceania. Worldwide, more than 50 per cent of basin-scale sediment flux in regulated basins is potentially trapped in artificial impoundments, with discharge-weighted sediment trapping caused by large reservoirs of 30 per cent, and an additional contribution of 23 per cent from small reservoirs. Taking regulated and unregulated basins together, the interception of global sediment flux by all 45,000 registered reservoirs is at least 4–5 billion tonnes per year, or 25–30 per cent of the total. There is an additional but unknown impact caused by the still smaller 800,000 or so unregistered impoundments. The study showed that river impoundment is a significant component in the global fluxes of water, sediment, carbon and nutrients.

Biogeochemical cycles

Biogeochemical cycles engage the storage and flux of all terrestrial elements and compounds except the inert ones. Material exchanges between life and life-support systems define biogeochemical cycles. At their grandest scale, biogeochemical cycles involve the entire Earth. An exogenic cycle involves the transport and transformation of materials near the Earth's surface; a slower and less well-understood endogenic cycle involves the transport and transformation of materials in the lower crust and mantle. As their component chemical species exist as gases for a leg of the cycle, cycles of carbon, hydrogen, oxygen and nitrogen are called gaseous cycles. Other chemical species follow a sedimentary cycle because they do not readily volatilize and move between the biosphere and its environment in solution. Humans have become a major biogeochemical force, materially altering the flows of biochemicals, which are having repercussions in the environment.

Carbon

Carbon is the basis of all life on Earth. The global carbon cycle is the return movement of carbon through living things, air, rocks, soil and water (Figure 6.1). In brief, the cycle runs as follows. Photosynthesizing plants convert atmospheric carbon, in the form of carbon dioxide, to carbohydrates. Producer respiration returns some plant carbon to the atmosphere in the form of carbon dioxide. Animals assimilate and metabolize some plant carbon. A portion of animal carbon returns to the atmosphere as carbon dioxide released through consumer respiration. The balance enters the decomposer food chain and either returns to the atmosphere through decomposer respiration or accumulates as organic sediment (e.g. peat and coal). Combustion during fires and volcanic eruptions releases carbon dioxide into the atmosphere.

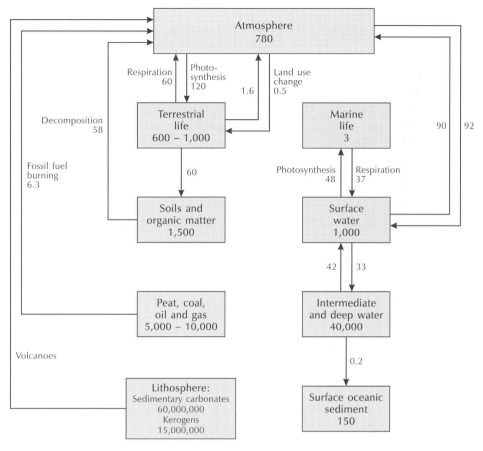

Figure 6.1. The carbon cycle. Stores are billion tonnes of carbon (GtC); flows are GtC per year.

Agricultural, industrial and domestic practices alter the stores and fluxes in the carbon cycle. Every year, the burning of fuelwood and fossil fuels pumps some 6.3 billion tonnes of carbon dioxide into the atmosphere. The growing atmospheric carbon dioxide store augments the greenhouse effect and contributes to global warming. Current knowledge of the carbon cycle within the oceans, on land and in the atmosphere is sufficient to conclude that, although natural processes can potentially slow the rate of increase in atmospheric carbon dioxide, they are unlikely to assimilate all the human-produced carbon dioxide during the twenty-first century. Forests hold out promise as carbon sinks (better than oceans and soils). Northern Hemisphere forests are absorbing 3.6 billion tonnes of carbon (GtC) per year. Further understanding requires greater knowledge of the relationship between the carbon cycle, other biogeochemical cycles and the climatic system.

Given the real threat of climatic changes associated with global warming, it is not surprising that much research goes into studying the effects of elevated carbon dioxide levels on ecosystems (e.g. Falkowski *et al.* 2000). Measurements of carbon stores and fluxes, and the understanding of carbon-cycling processes, are becoming ever more refined.

Modelling studies in the early 1970s suggested that, to balance the global carbon budget, carbon must be stored in terrestrial ecosystems. Further research in the 1990s confirmed that

83

terrestrial ecosystems play a vital role in regulating the carbon balance in the Earth system. The global carbon cycling research, so critical to the global warming issue, has stimulated a wealth of studies on several aspects of plant biology, including leaf photosynthesis, plant respiration, root nutrient uptake and carbon partitioning (the allocation of carbon to roots, trunks, leaves, etc.). The studies range from response to increased carbon dioxide concentrations at the molecular level, through impacts on species diversity in communities, to carbon fluxes in the ecosphere. At the global scale, global biosphere models take in experimental results to predict potential changes in terrestrial ecosystems as the globe warms up.

An interesting finding of current work illustrates the complexity of the carbon cycle and the difficulties of making unequivocal predictions about the impact of rising temperatures. Two opposing processes are associated with climatic warming (Figure 6.2). First, a negative feedback mechanism is the increase in plant growth and carbon sequestration resulting from stimulated nutrient mineralization and longer growing seasons. Second, the warming may trigger a positive feedback mechanism, stimulating biological metabolism in terrestrial vegetation, which in turn increases a greater release of heat-trapping gases to the atmosphere and augments human-induced warming. Recognition of the second mechanism partly explains the increased temperature rises predicted by the IPCC. An experiment to test this mechanism in the field, conducted in a tall-grass prairie in the Great Plains of the USA, revealed another complicating factor – acclimatization. The process here seems to be that, rather than soil respiration simply increasing with increasing temperature, the soil tends to 'acclimatize' to the higher temperatures, and does so more fully at high temperatures, so weakening the positive feedback effect. In addition, increased carbon dioxide levels increase microbial activity, which in turn promotes the formation of soil aggregates. As soil aggregates tend to protect particles of organic matter in the soil against microbial attack, an increase in soil

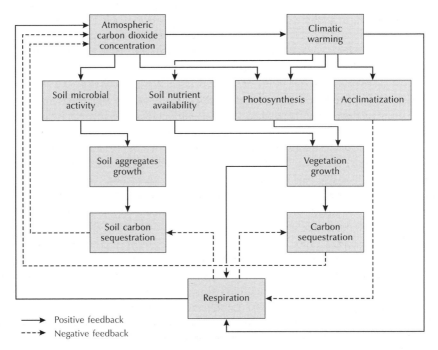

Figure 6.2. Main feedbacks between climate and the carbon cycle.

aggregation resulting from higher carbon dioxide levels may lead to a sequestration of soil carbon. This is another negative feedback mechanism.

Elevated carbon dioxide levels significantly enhance the growth and development of nearly all plants. Studies from field-grown trees suggest a continued and consistent stimulation of photosynthesis of around 60 per cent for a 300 ppm increase in atmospheric carbon dioxide concentration. Such enhanced growth may alter the concentrations of food-plant constituents related to animal and human health. The situation is complicated because a host of environmental factors and not just carbon dioxide levels affect the nature of plant constituents. However, some generalizations are possible. When soil nitrogen levels are below their optimum, an increase in atmospheric carbon dioxide concentration normally reduces the nitrogen and protein levels of animal-sustaining forage and human-sustaining cereal grains. In addition, higher atmospheric carbon dioxide levels tend to reduce oxidative stress in plants, which accordingly manufacture fewer antioxidants for protection, and increase the concentration of vitamin C in some fruits and vegetables. The quality of bread and wine made from plants grown in a carbon dioxide enriched atmosphere is affected. Likewise, the carbon dioxide enrichment increases the biomass of plants grown for medicinal purposes and at the same time increases the concentrations of disease-fighting substances produced with them, such as heart-helping digoxin (a cardiac glycoside) in the woolly foxglove (*Digitalis lanata*) and a suite of cancer-fighting substances found in the tropical spider lily (*Hymenocallis littoralis*). In summary, work to date suggests that rising carbon dioxide levels will increase food production while sustaining the nutritional quality of food and heightening the yield of certain disease-inhibiting plant compounds.

Nitrogen

The nitrogen cycle is the return movement of nitrogen through living things, air, rocks, soil and water. Nitrogen is unique among the chief elements required by living things in that a huge atmospheric reservoir of the element (in the form of N_2) can only be tapped if it is fixed (that is, combined with carbon, oxygen or hydrogen). The fixed nitrogen strongly influences the productivity, carbon storage and species composition of many ecosystems. Atmospheric diatomic nitrogen is fixed by combining with rainwater to form inorganic compounds, and by nitrogen-fixing bacteria (nitrifiers) that produce a reactive form that organisms can use. (Broadly defined, reactive nitrogen is all biologically active, photochemically active and radioactively active nitrogen compounds in the ecosphere; it includes reduced forms (e.g. NH_3, NH_4^+), inorganic oxidized forms (e.g. NO_x, HNO_3, N_2O, NO_3^-) and organic compounds (e.g. urea, amines, proteins)). Atmospheric chemists have a narrower definition of reactive nitrogen, restricting it to NO_y, which is any combination of nitrogen and oxygen except N_2O, so including NO_x, N_2O_5, HNO_2, HNO_3, nitrates, organic nitrates, etc. Animals and plants assimilate and metabolize reactive nitrogen. It then returns to the soil in nitrogenous animal wastes and in dead organisms. Nitrogen in the soil is subject to nitrification (conversion to nitrates and nitrites by nitrifying microorganisms), to mineralization or ammonification (the release of ammonia and ammonium from dead organic matter by decomposers) and to denitrification (the reduction of nitrate to gaseous nitrogen forms that return to the atmosphere).

Food production and energy production have both boosted the creation of reactive nitrogen (Figure 6.3). Legume and rice cultivation encourage high rates of biological nitrogen fixation. Energy production creates reactive nitrogen in the form of NO, which is a by-product of fossil fuel combustion (through either oxidation of atmospheric nitrogen or organic nitrogen in the fossil fuel). By the beginning of the twentieth century, demand for reactive nitrogen to sustain increasing food population was met by the development in

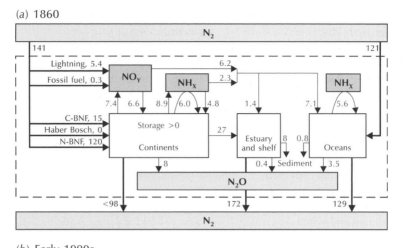

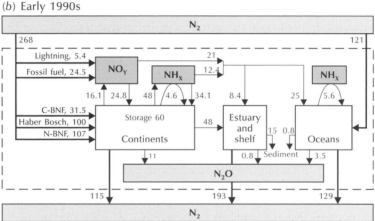

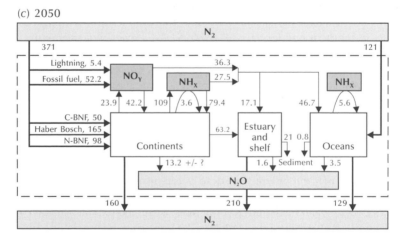

Figure 6.3. The nitrogen cycle. Shaded boxes are reservoirs of nitrogen species. Fluxes are in units of million tonnes of nitrogen per year (=Tg N per year) (a) in 1860; (b) in early 1990s; (c) estimates for 2050.

Source: After Galloway *et al.* (2004).

Germany of the Haber–Bosch process, which produces ammonia from diatomic nitrogen and H_2. Between 1860 and the early 1990s, reactive nitrogen production by natural terrestrial processes decreased by about 15 per cent (120 million tonnes of N per year to about 107 million tonnes per year). In the same period, human-based processes increased tenfold (from about 15 million tonnes per year to some 156 million tonnes) and humans came to dominate reactive nitrogen production on continents. By 2050, human-created reactive nitrogen is predicted to be 270 million tonnes of N per year. Much of the 'extra' reactive nitrogen generated by humans disperses to the environment – atmosphere, rivers, inland and coastal areas, and open oceans.

The increasing human domination of the nitrogen cycle has a host of consequences. In the atmosphere, nitrous oxide (a greenhouse gas), nitric oxide and ammonium gas concentrations have increased globally, and reactive forms of nitrogen have contributed to acid rain and to photochemical smog. Reactive nitrogen emitted into the atmosphere may be deposited downwind where it affects recipient ecosystems, to begin with boosting the productivity and carbon storage in those systems where fixed nitrogen was deficient, but eventually increasing nitrogen and cation losses from soils through a set of processes called nitrogen saturation that lead to forest decline and soil acidification (e.g. Aber *et al.* 1998). Human-created reactive nitrogen may move from agricultural land, sewage systems and nitrogen-saturated ecosystems into rivers, groundwater and the oceans.

Other elements

Humans alter all other biogeochemical cycles. For instance, by burning fossil fuels, humans are the largest supplier of sulphur gases to the atmosphere. This quickly oxidizes and falls as acid rain. Steps to remedy the acid-rain problem may reduce atmospheric sulphur concentrations. In consequence, it may become necessary to supplement soil sulphur through fertilizer applications. Under oxidizing conditions in soils, sulphates may form, including sulphuric acid. Acidification in sulphide-rich soils, as found on spoil-heaps of mines, is a serious problem. Mining mobilizes phosphorus and many metals, some of which, including arsenic, cadmium, lead and mercury, are highly toxic. For example, humans extract some 30,453 tonnes of arsenic globally each year for industrial purposes, mainly for pesticides and wood preservatives. Another 28,400 to 94,000 tonnes of arsenic finds its way back into soils and groundwaters in wastes of various sorts. Once the arsenic-bearing wastes are in the soil, arsenic sulphides cause soil acidification, which in turn increases the mobility of arsenic. Tailings from metal-sulphide mining operations are substantial sources for both heavy metal and arsenic contamination of groundwaters and surface waters.

Synthetic organic chemicals

Several synthetic compounds, designed to have beneficial effects, are toxic to humans and other species, some of them at concentrations as low as 1 part per billion. The compounds may spread from agricultural and industrial areas and persist in the environment for decades. Organochlorines (chlorinated hydrocarbons) include the best known of all the synthetic poisons – endrin, dieldrin, lindane, DDT and others. They are widely used as biocides. Plastics manufacturers use polychlorinated biphenyls (PCBs) as flame-retardants and insulating materials. A very worrying development is the high levels of organochlorines recorded in Arctic ecosystems, where they are biomagnified (become increasingly more concentrated as they pass up a food web) and have adverse effects on consumers. The organochlorines drift northwards from agricultural and industrial regions; they are carried by air and ocean currents, or such birds as northern fulmars (*Fulmarus glacialis*) carry them from more southerly latitudes in their digestive systems and deposit them in their droppings (Blais *et al.* 2005). They then enter Arctic ecosystems through plants and start an upward journey through the trophic levels, accumulating in a extensive variety of Arctic species. They accumulate in birds, including thick-billed murres (*Uria lomvia*), northern fulmars (*Fulmarus glacialis*) and black-legged kittiwakes (*Rissa tridactyla*) (e.g. Braune *et al.* 2001; Buckman *et al.* 2004), and in mammals, including Arctic fox (*Alopex lagopus*) (Hoekstra *et al.* 2003) and polar bears (*Ursus maritimus*) (Henriksen *et al.* 2001).

A worrying side-effect of some synthetic chemicals is their capacity to disrupt endocrine systems in animals. Endocrine disruptors cause such undesirable effects as reduced ability to reproduce, functional or morphological birth defects, cancer and changed immune functions. Many suspected endocrine disruptors are high-volume, economically important chemicals.

Interacting biogeochemical cycles

The grand cycles of bioelements variously interact. Many human activities alter these interactions in ways that add to major environmental problems, including climate change, acid precipitation, photochemical smog and anoxic areas in the coastal zone (Melillo *et al.* 2003). Often, the consequences of element interactions result from the interplay of several natural and human drivers acting at the same time. Understanding such consequences is essential to controlling the effects of human actions on the environment. The chief human-induced drivers that affect element interactions are agricultural intensification and extent, urbanization and industrialization, atmospheric chemistry, and species introductions, species harvesting and species losses (Austin *et al.* 2003). The consequences of these driving factors for element interactions include impacts of nitrogen deposition on the carbon balance of ecosystems, sedimentation and erosion, climatic change, and change in species composition.

Changes in species composition and species diversity may alter element interactions to the same degree as direct human actions on biogeochemical cycles. This is perhaps not surprising given the thoroughgoing mixing of species in the biosphere carried out by humans. Humans have introduced species to new areas, caused species extinctions, and affected species distributions by changing land use, climate, atmospheric composition and trophic interactions (see Chapter 50). Such species changes impact upon element interactions. At sites in North and South America, the introduction of the zebra mussel (*Driesenna polymorpha*) into aquatic ecosystems greatly boosted the filtration rate of water, causing a 80–90 per cent removal of algal biomass, a significant reduction in summertime dissolved oxygen concentrations, and doubled phosphate concentrations (e.g. Caraco *et al.* 2000). The introduction of the nitrogen-fixing fayatree (*Myrica faya*) to Hawaii in the 1800s has increased nitrogen input to mid and upper elevation ecosystems, so reducing the degree of nitrogen limitation and shifting the ecosystems towards limitation by phosphorus, and lowering the carbon–nitrogen ratio in live tissue (Vitousek *et al.* 1987).

Changing drivers, changing places

A message of this chapter is that humans are a hugely potent driver of change in the ecosphere. They significantly alter natural cycles of material flow in the water cycle, in the rock cycle, and in biogeochemical cycles. In mining and construction activities, humans move over twice the amount of sediment in a year that rivers transport to the oceans. By diverting water for irrigation, they have caused problems of salinization in large areas of the world. By damming streams, they have caused a series of ecological repercussions and encouraged sedimentation in reservoirs. Accelerated soil erosion has increased sediment loads reaching seas and oceans, precipitating problems in coastal ecosystems. Humans now play a leading role in many biogeochemical cycles. By pumping increasing amounts of carbon dioxide (and other greenhouse gases) into the atmosphere, they appear to have triggered a bout of sustained global warming with its attendant problems. They have become the primary source of nitrogen-fixation in the ecosphere and are responsible for environmental problems associated with nitrogen enrichment. In addition, they have managed to disperse toxic synthetic chemicals to remote parts of the planet where they accumulate in wildlife.

From a geographical perspective, it is important to note that natural and human-induced alterations to driving agencies cause changes in the nature of places. The data in Table 6.1 suggest the extent of such changes, which are many and various. For instance, modification of the water cycle can lead to areas drying up, as in the case of the Aral Sea. In the rock cycle, accelerated erosion of material from land may cause alteration to the character of coastal ecosystems. Disruptions to biogeochemical cycles may act positively, as when nutrients added to ecosystems increase productivity, or negatively, as when toxic metals released from mine waste kill vegetation or when acid rain causes forest decline. Plants and animals transported around the world by humans have changed many communities and landscapes: witness the invasion of goats in New Zealand and Indian balsam in many British rivers. Of course, places have changed throughout Earth history, but current human impacts appear to represent a new order of change that is refashioning landscapes and seascapes in unprecedented ways.

Further reading

Gleick, P.H. (2000) *The World's Water 2000–2001: The Biennial Report of Freshwater Resources.* Washington, Covelo, California: Island Press.

——(2003) Global freshwater resources: soft-path solutions for the 21st century. *Science* 302, 1524–28.

Melillo, J.M., Field, C.B. and Moldan, B. (eds) (2003) *Interactions of the Major Biogeochemical Cycles: Global Changes and Human Impacts* (SCOPE Report 61). Washington, Covelo, London: Island Press.

Morgan, R.P.C. (2005) *Soil Erosion and Conservation*, third edition. Oxford: Blackwell.

Sala, O.S., Chapin, F.S. III, Armesto, J.J., Berlow, E., Bloomfield, J., Dirzo, R., Huber-Sannwald, E., Huenneke, L.F., Jackson, R.B., Kinzig, A., Leemans, R., Lodge, D.M., Mooney, H.A., Oesterheld, M., Poff, N.L., Sykes, M.T., Walker, B.H., Walker, M. and Wall, D.H. (2000) Global biodiversity scenarios for the year 2100. *Science* 287, 1770–74.

References

Aber, J., McDowell, W., Nadelhoffer, K., Magill, A., Berntson, G., Kamakea, M., McNulty, S., Currie, W., Rustad, L. and Fernandez, I. (1998). Nitrogen saturation in temperate forest ecosystems. *Bioscience* 48, 921–34.

Austin, A.T., Howarth, R.W., Baron, J.F., Chapin III, S., Christensen, T.R., Holland, E.A., Ivanov, M.V., Lein, A.Y., Martinelli, L.A., Melillo, J.M. and Shang, C. (2003) Human disruption of element interactions: drivers, consequences, and trends for the twenty-first century. In J.M. Melillo, C.B. Field and B. Moldan (eds) *Interactions of the Major Biogeochemical Cycles: Global Changes and Human Impacts* (SCOPE Report 61), pp. 15–45. Washington, Covelo, London: Island Press.

Blais, J.M., Kimpe, L.E., McMahon, D., Keatley, B.E., Mallory, M.L., Douglas, M.S.V. and Smol, J.P. (2005) Arctic seabirds transport marine-derived contaminants. *Science* 309, 445.

Braune, B.M., Donaldson, G.M. and Hobson, K.A. (2001) Contaminant residues in seabird eggs from the Canadian Arctic. Part I. Temporal trends 1975–98. *Environmental Pollution* 114, 39–54.

Buckman, A.H., Norstrom, R.J., Hobson, K.A., Karnovsky, N.J., Duffe, J. and Fisk, A.T. (2004) Organochlorine contaminants in seven species of Arctic seabirds from northern Baffin Bay. *Environmental Pollution* 128, 327–38.

Caraco, N.F., Findlay, S.E.G., Fischer, D.T., Lampman, G.G., Pace, M.L. and Strayer, D.L. (2000) Dissolved oxygen declines in the Hudson river associated with the invasion of the zebra mussel (*Dreissena polymorpha*). *Environmental Science and Technology* 34, 1204–10.

Douglas, I. and Lawson, N. (2001) The human dimensions of geomorphological work in Britain. *Journal of Industrial Ecology* 4, 9–33.

Falkowski, P., Scholes, R.J., Boyle, E., Canadell, J., Canfield, D., Elser, J., Gruber, N., Hibbard, K., Högberg, P., Linder, S., Mackenzie, F.T., Moore III, B., Pedersen, T., Rosenthal, Y., Seitzinger, S., Smetacek, V. and Steffen, W. (2000) The global carbon cycle: a test of our knowledge of Earth as a system. *Science* 290, 291–96.

Galloway, J.N., Dentener, F.J., Capone, D.G., Boyer, E.W., Howarth, R.W., Seitzinger, S.P., Asner, G.P., Cleveland, C., Green, P., Holland, E., Karl, D.M., Michaels, A.F., Porter, J.H., Townsend, A. and Vörösmarty, C.J. (2004) Nitrogen cycles: past, present and future. *Biogeochemistry* 70, 153–226.

Gleick, P.H. (2000) *The World's Water 2000–2001: The Biennial Report of Freshwater Resources*. Washington, Covelo: Island Press.

Graf, W.L. (2005) Geomorphology and American dams: the scientific, social, and economic context. *Geomorphology* 71, 3–26.

Hannah, L., Lohse, D., Hutchinson, C., Carr, J.L., and Lankerani, A. (1994) A preliminary inventory of human disturbance of world ecosystems. *Ambio* 23, 246–50.

Henriksen, E.O., Wig, Ø., Skaare, J.U., Gabrielsen, G.W. and Derocher, A.E. (2001) Monitoring PCBs in polar bears: lessons learned from Svalbard. *Journal of Environmental Monitoring* 3, 493–98.

Hoekstra, P.F., Braune, B.M., O'Hara, T.M., Elkin, B., Solomon, K.R., Muir, D.C.G. (2003) Organochlorine contaminant ands stable isotope profiles in Arctic fox (*Alopex lagopus*) from Alaskan and Canadian Arctic. *Environmental Pollution* 122, 423–33.

Hooke, R.LeB. (2000) On the history of humans as geomorphic agents. *Geology* 28, 843–46.

Laycock, A.H. (1987) The amount of Canadian water and its distribution. In M.C. Healey and R.R. Wallace (eds) *Canadian Aquatic Resources* (Canadian Bulletin of Fisheries and Aquatic Sciences 215), pp. 13–42. Ottawa: Department of Fisheries and Oceans.

Mellilo, J.M., Field, C.B. and Moldan, B. (2003) Element interactions and the cycles of life: an overview. In J.M. Melillo, C.B. Field, and B. Moldan (eds) *Interactions of the Major Biogeochemical Cycles: Global Changes and Human Impacts* (SCOPE Report 61), pp. 1–12. Washington, Covelo, London: Island Press.

Nilsson, C., Reidy, C.A., Dynesius, M. and Revenga, C. (2005) Fragmentation and flow regulation of the world's large river systems. *Science* 308, 405–8.

Petts, G.E. and Gurnell, A.M. (2005) Dams and geomorphology: research progress and future directions. *Geomorphology* 71, 27–47.

Sherlock, R.L. (1922) *Man as a Geological Agent: An Account of His Action on Inanimate Nature*, with a foreword by A.S. Woodward. London: H.F. and G. Witherby.

Shiklomanov, I.A. (1993) World fresh water resources. In P.H. Gleick (ed.) *Water in Crisis: A Guide to the World's Fresh Water Resources*, pp. 13–24. New York: Oxford University Press.

Smith, S.V., Renwick, W.H., Buddemeier, R.W. and Crossland C.J. (2001) Budgets of soil erosion and deposition for sediments and sedimentary organic carbon across the conterminous United States. *Global Biogeochemical Cycles* 15, 697–707.

Stallard, R.F. (1998) Terrestrial sedimentation and the carbon cycle: coupling weathering and erosion to carbon burial. *Global Biogeochemical Cycles* 12, 231–57.

Syvitski, J.P.M., Vörösmarty, C.J., Kettner, A.J. and Green, P. (2005) Impact of humans on the flux of terrestrial sediment to the global coastal ocean. *Science* 308, 376–80.

Trimble, S.W. (1999). Rates of soil erosion. *Science* 286, 1477–78.

Vitousek, P.M., Walker, L.R., Whiteaker, L.D., Mueller-Dombois, D. and Matson, P.A. (1987) Biological invasion of *Myrica faya* alters ecosystem development in Hawaii. *Science* 238, 802–4.

Vörösmarty, C.J., Meybeck, M., Fekete, B., Sharma, K., Green, P. and Syvitski, J.P.M. (2003) Anthropogenic sediment retention: major global impact from registered river impoundments. *Global and Planetary Change* 39, 169–90.

Walling, D.E. and Fang, D. (2003) Recent trends in the suspended sediment load of the world's rivers. *Global and Planetary Change* 39, 111–26.

Wilkinson, B.H. (2005) Humans as geological agents: a deep-time perspective. *Geology* 33, 161–64.

World Commission on Dams (2000) *Dams and Development: A New Framework for Decision-making* (The Report of the World Commission on Dams). London: Earthscan.

7

Internal–external interactions in the Earth system

Michael A. Summerfield

Plate tectonics

(INTRODUCTORY

Since its development in the 1960s and 1970s from the earlier idea of continental drift, plate tectonics has been very successful in explaining the major topographic features of the Earth as well as a diverse suite of geological phenomena. These include the main structural components of the crust, the location of volcanic and seismic activity and the distribution of mountain belts (orogens). In essence, the plate tectonics model is simple: the Earth's outer layer consists of around a dozen large lithospheric plates, together with many smaller ones, which are in motion with respect both to each other and to the Earth's pole of rotation. Continents are carried on these plates and over geological time can join together to form supercontinents and then break up again – a sequence extending over hundreds of millions of years called the supercontinent cycle.

The lithosphere comprises a layer of crust underlain by the upper, rigid part of the mantle – the mantle being the zone, composed of dense silicate minerals, that extends from the base of the crust down to the Earth's core. The lithosphere moves over a relatively more deformable zone in the upper mantle termed the asthenosphere. In continental regions the crust, which is very largely composed of lower density minerals than the mantle, averages around 30–35 km thick, with the lithosphere overall extending to a depth of 200 km or more. Under the oceans the lithosphere is rather different; the crust is thinner and somewhat more dense than in continental areas, and the lithosphere overall is also less thick, rarely exceeding 100 km. The greater density of oceanic compared with continental crust (~3300 kg m^{-3} compared with ~2700 kg m^{-3}) is the primary control over the first-order topography of the Earth, as is evident in Earth's hypsometry. Figure 7.1 illustrates this dramatically by comparing the hypsometry (the proportionate areal distribution of elevation) of Earth to that of Mars and Venus. Earth with two crustal types has a bimodal distribution compared with the unimodal distribution for Mars and Venus, both of which have a more uniform crustal composition.

Oceanic lithosphere is generated along the system of mid-oceanic ridges that traverse the ocean basins as two plates move apart from each other, a process known as sea-floor spreading. Ridges form along these divergent plate boundaries because here the new oceanic

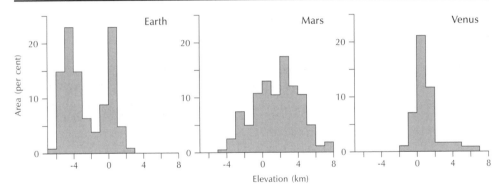

Figure 7.1. Hypsometry of the Earth, Mars and Venus.

crust formed by the eruption of basaltic magma rising from the mantle is thin, hot and buoyant. As it moves away from the mid-oceanic ridge the crust cools, thickens and becomes denser. This reduces the overall buoyancy of the lithosphere, so whereas mid-oceanic ridges flanked by young lithosphere are typically only about 2 km below sea level, the oldest litho-sphere underlying ocean basins is associated with ocean depths of 5 km or more. Where plates are in motion towards each other a convergent boundary is formed. If both plates are oceanic (that is, composed of oceanic lithosphere) the older, denser plate edge will be subducted below the younger, more buoyant plate along a subduction zone (marked by a deep trench on the ocean floor). The frictional heat generated along the upper surface of subducted plate causes melting and this leads to volcanic activity which produces arcuate chains of volcanoes (island arcs), such as those that festoon the south-west Pacific Ocean. Where oceanic lithosphere converges on lithosphere capped by continental crust (continental lithosphere), the former is subducted below the latter as it is denser and thus less buoyant. Here, too, frictional heating associated with subduction gives rise to melting and volcanism, but this is added to mountain building along the flank of the continental plate as the crust is compressed, folded and thickened.

What causes plates to move – at typical rates of 20–100 mm per year – is still not under-stood fully, but two mechanisms seem to be important. One involves the forces exerted at the edges of plates by the push of material injected at divergent margins along mid-oceanic ridges, and the pull of dense, cold lithosphere being subducted at convergent margins. The other major mechanism, which is probably less important, is the drag exerted on the base of the lithosphere by convective flow in the sub-lithospheric mantle. There is strong evidence that convection occurs in the mantle over geological time scales, with columns of warmer mantle rising between cooler, denser zones, but the detailed nature and depth of the con-vecting systems is unclear. A spectacular manifestation of mantle convection is the volcanism that occurs in locations remote from plate boundaries. Many researchers think these hot-spots, of which the Hawaiian Islands zone of volcanism in the Pacific Ocean is an example, result from masses of hot magma rising from deep within the mantle, possibly from the core–mantle boundary (e.g. Courtillot *et al.* 2003; see Foulger *et al.* 2005 for a different view). These mantle plumes, which are slow moving relative to the lithosphere, are thought to account for the lines of volcanic islands and submarine volcanoes (guyots) in the oceans that form as the lithosphere moves across the plume head. Highly active mantle plumes may also be responsible for the vast masses of basalt that have erupted occasionally over geological time both on to the ocean floor and on to the continents, forming major topographic features called large igneous provinces; the Deccan Plateau in western India and Parana Plateau in southern Brazil are examples.

A fundamental tenet of plate tectonics is that plates are sufficiently rigid for stresses to be transmitted across them with little internal deformation. This applies well to oceanic lithosphere since its composition renders it very strong, but the notion of rigid plates seems to work less well when we look at the behaviour of continental lithosphere. This is demonstrated dramatically by the deformation that has occurred as a result of the collision of India (moving northwards as part of the Indo-Australian plate) with the southern flank of Asia, which began around 50 million years ago. India has continued to move northwards into Asia since initial contact was made and, as is discussed later, this has had a number of consequences for the development of topography. But the resulting deformation is clearly visible in drainage patterns, such as those on the eastern margin of this collision zone where the form and alignment of three major rivers – the Mekong, Salween and Yangtze – appear to record the internal displacement of the crust since collision (Hallet and Molnar 2001).

Creating continental topography

What, then, are the processes involved in creating the topographic features of the continents? Tectonics alone plays an important role, but as we will see in the following section research since the 1990s has been revealing a much more fundamental role for surface processes than previously thought. Here we will examine the major tectonic processes that can create continental topography – crustal thickening, heating of the crust, and the dynamic effects of flow in the sub-lithospheric mantle.

Since the nineteenth century it has been known that regions of high topography are underlain by deep crustal 'roots'. While the average thickness of continental crust is around 30–35 km, in regions of very high terrain, such as the Himalayan–Tibetan Plateau orogen and the central Andes, crustal thickness reaches around 70 km. The formation of such thickened crust is a direct consequence of plate convergence; where convergence occurs the horizontal distance available for a given 'length' of crust is reduced (an effect termed crustal shortening) so to conserve mass the crust must become thicker (although, as we will see later, some of the shortening may be accommodated by lateral rather than vertical displacement). The elevation above sea level of crust of a particular thickness is controlled primarily by isostasy – the state of hydrostatic equilibrium between the crust and the mantle at the depth of compensation. One way to envisage this is as blocks of wood of different thicknesses floating in a tank of water. If the density of the wood is 90 per cent of that of water then 10 per cent will be exposed above the water surface and 90 per cent will be below, but the actual height of each block of wood above the water surface will depend on how thick it is even though the proportions above and below the water surface will remain constant.

For the Earth it is the difference between the density of the continental crust (ρ_c ~2700 kg m^{-3}) and the mantle at the depth of compensation (ρ_m ~3300 kg m^{-3}) that determines the elevation of crust of a given thickness. If an area of continental crust 35 km thick is at sea level, then a doubling of thickness to 70 km will increase elevation to a little over 6 km above sea level ($(1 - (\rho_c / \rho_m)) \times 35$ km) and there will be a supporting crustal root a little under 29 km deep ($(\rho_c / \rho_m) \times 35$ km). However, a number of factors complicate this simple picture, the most important of which is that the lithosphere has rigidity. This means that changes in load brought about by changes in crustal thickness are not just compensated locally (that is, just in the area over which the change in load occurs) but are accommodated by flexure of the lithosphere which distributes the load over a greater area. Imagine placing a pile of books on a plank of wood pinned at both ends; the plank will flex – how much will depend on the load exerted by the books and the thickness of the plank, with a thinner plank flexing more over a shorter wavelength. For the lithosphere, the concept of 'effective elastic thickness' is used to quantify this property of flexural rigidity. Such flexural isostatic effects are important where continents rift apart and new continental margins are formed; upward flexure of these margins can arise under certain conditions of extension of the lithosphere and this provides a possible explanation of why high topography can be found along many rifted continental margins.

Although crustal convergence is an important mechanism of crustal thickening, it can occur in other ways. Some researchers believe that when continents break apart along rift zones and eventually move away from each other as sea-floor spreading begins, additional crust can be accreted at the base of the crust along the new continental margin through the heating and conversion of minerals in the mantle to lower density forms. Another mechanism of crustal thickening is the extrusion of lavas, such as those of giant basalt plateaus, and the associated intrusion of igneous rocks, typically dolerite. As the density of basalt (~3000 kg m^{-3}) is higher than that of average continental crust, and therefore closer to the density of the mantle on which it 'floats', the amount of elevation change for a given increase in crustal thickness by this process is less (about 100 m for each kilometre of thickening). However, large igneous provinces represent prodigious quantities of erupted basalt and intruded dolerite which can extend over areas in excess of 1 million square kilometres. Although the thickness of erupted material rarely exceeds 2 km, accompanying intrusions may increase this significantly, so the resulting surface uplift can be substantial.

These major magmatic events, together with less spectacular forms of volcanic activity, are associated with heating of the crust which causes it to expand. This thermal uplift has been suggested as a mechanism generating high topography along the newly created margins of continents produced by continent rifting and breakup, such as the present-day margins of the Red Sea. There is certainly abundant heat present in the vicinity of divergent plate margins where the lithosphere is very thin and there is a high heat flow to the surface. Where this heat is conducted into adjacent continental crust it could produce uplift, but as the continental margin moves away from the spreading zone the heat source is removed and the continental margin will cool and subside. It takes a long time for such cooling to occur in the lithosphere (around 60 Ma); nonetheless, thermal uplift is a temporary uplift mechanism that cannot account for the high topography of older continental margins, such as those flanking the South Atlantic.

Dynamic flow in the mantle which could impinge on the base of overlying lithosphere is another possible cause of surface uplift. It has been suggested that the extensive area of elevated topography extending across southern and East Africa is related to a major buoyant zone originating deep in the mantle. Such deep Earth structures have been identified using seismic tomography, a technique analogous to that used to take a brain scan but where the behaviour of seismic waves generated by earthquakes is used to give a picture of the three-dimensional structure of the mantle. Interpreting such data is extremely difficult, but this mechanism may explain the extensive areas of moderately elevated terrain that do not have an obvious alternative explanation.

As with thermal effects, dynamic mantle flow is a 'temporary' mechanism in terms of geological time scales in that the elevated topography will only be sustained for as long as the process is active and its effects persist. Surface uplift associated with crustal thickening is often termed 'permanent' because once this has occurred it is difficult to remove. One way this can occur is by extension when the crust is subject to tensional stresses and is stretched and therefore thinned. This has occurred in the Basin and Range Province of the south-west USA, but in continental crust significant crustal extension is not a widespread phenomenon. By far the dominant process for reducing thickened continental crust is denudation by surface processes, but great depths of denudation are required to lower topography because of the effects of isostasy. Where typical continental crust is being eroded, denudation of 1 km will only lower the elevation by a little under 200 m, assuming local isostatic compensation. As the building of a high mountain range with a mean elevation of around 6,000 m requires crust to be thickened from about 35 to 70 km, it will be necessary to erode 35 km of crust to reduce the area to its pre-uplift elevation. Even with high rates of denudation this will take a long time, and this may be why remnants of mountain belts formed several hundred million years ago, such as the Ural Mountains of Russia, and the Appalachian Mountains of the eastern USA, still persist as topographic features. However, research since the 1990s has demonstrated that the role of surface processes in mountain belts is not simply limited to reducing topography originally formed entirely by tectonic processes.

Tectonic–surface process interactions

When the plate tectonics model was developed and then applied to orogens the emphasis was on the geological features that could be explained, such as the distribution of different rock types and the relationships of structures such as folds and faults. Geophysical models of plate convergence sought to account for these features, but very largely neglected the topography that was produced. The situation was effectively summarized by one geophysicist: 'In retrospect, it is difficult to understand how models of collision zones could be constructed without reference to the inevitable topography but somehow we managed' (Koons 1995: 389). The topography of mountain belts is perhaps the most obvious product of the tectonic processes of plate convergence, and if geophysical models of crustal deformation are to be regarded as successful they clearly have to account for the resulting topography. A number of questions need to be addressed. For instance, what controls the elevation of orogens, and why do the world's two highest orogens – the Himalayas–Tibetan Plateau and the Andes – incorporate large plateaus with extensive areas of internal drainage? And what is the role of denudation in shaping mountain belts at the large scale? Are its effects more fundamental than the minor modification of landforms that are essentially a product of tectonic processes?

Since the 1990s these questions have begun to be addressed using an approach that treats orogens, and landscapes more generally, as the product of a coupled tectonic-climatic system with the potential for feedbacks between climatically influenced surface processes and crustal deformation (Beaumont *et al.* 2000; Pinter and Brandon 1997; Willett 1999). It is clear that where there are high rates of crustal convergence, the resulting surface uplift will rapidly achieve an elevation that cannot be supported by the crustal strength of rocks. This limit seems to be around 6–7 km on the Earth, although individual mountain peaks can exceed this as they are supported by the strength of the surrounding crust. (On Mars this elevation limit is much higher because of a stronger crust and lower surface gravity which means a given mass of rock weighs less and therefore exerts less of a load on the crust.) In most mountain belts, this upper limit is not reached because of the effects of denudation. As tectonic uplift occurs and elevation increases, river gradients will steepen and this will tend to increase denudation rates. The growth of topography is also likely to increase precipitation (through the orographic effect) and therefore runoff, which will also tend to enhance denudation (Summerfield and Hulton 1994). In parts of highly active mountain ranges, such as the Southern Alps of New Zealand where the crust of the Pacific plate is being peeled off the underlying lithospheric mantle as it is thrust over the edge of the Indo-Australian plate along the Alpine fault, rivers actively incise and maintain, through frequent landsliding, the adjacent valley-slide slopes at their threshold angle of stability. This means that any increase in tectonic uplift rate will produce a rapid response in denudation rate as river channels cut down and set off landslides on adjacent slopes (Montgomery and Brandon 2002). Orogens seem to maintain a roughly steady-state topography where changes in tectonic uplift rate are (geologically speaking) rapidly matched by adjustments in denudation rates. The actual steady-state elevation will depend on climatic and lithological factors with higher overall elevations being attained where rocks are resistant and the climate is dry and produces limited runoff. Such orogens will never maintain a perfect steady-state as there will always be some delay in the response of topography to changing controlling variables such as climate, and especially to changes in tectonic uplift rate since the resulting fall in base level must be propagated along drainage systems to the axis of the range.

Modelling studies which attempt to show how spatial variations in rates of denudation across an orogen could affect patterns of crustal deformation and topographic form have produced some intriguing results (Beaumont *et al.* 2000; Willett 1999). For instance, for relatively simple orogens the prevailing direction of rain-bearing winds appears to be significant (Figure 7.2). On the windward side of the orogen the greater runoff resulting from more precipitation leads to higher rates of denudation than on the drier, leeward side. This has the effect of drawing up crustal rocks more rapidly on the windward than the leeward flank and this produces a marked asymmetry in depths of denudation across the orogen, and also produces a particular pattern of crustal deformation. Such modelling studies indicate that a reversal of prevailing rain-bearing winds will produce a change in topography, spatial patterns of denudation and the form of crustal deformation, and they demonstrate that the topographic and deformational evolution of orogens reflects complex feedbacks between tectonic and climatically driven surface processes.

The Andes

The Andes extend for 9,000 km along the entire length of the South American continent and in stretching from 10° north of the equator to 55° south different sections of the orogen are subject to markedly contrasting climates (Figure 7.3). In addition, the prevailing direction of rain-bearing winds switches from one side of the orogen to the other with changing latitude and this produces marked asymmetries in precipitation, with very high amounts on the windward flank and aridity in the rain-shadow of the leeward side. In the south the western side of the Andes is wet as a consequence of eastward-moving mid-latitude depressions coming in from the Pacific Ocean, with the eastern leeside being much drier. North of latitude 35° south the whole orogen becomes progressively more arid under the combined influence of the stable sub-tropical anticyclones that dominate in these latitudes and the cold, Humboldt current offshore. Under the dominant influence of this cold water mass offshore which reduces evaporation and enhances air mass stability, this west coast arid zone (the Atacama Desert) extends almost to the equator. However, on the eastern flank of the orogen humid air masses moving westward from the Amazon Basin produce heavy precipitation north of 15° south.

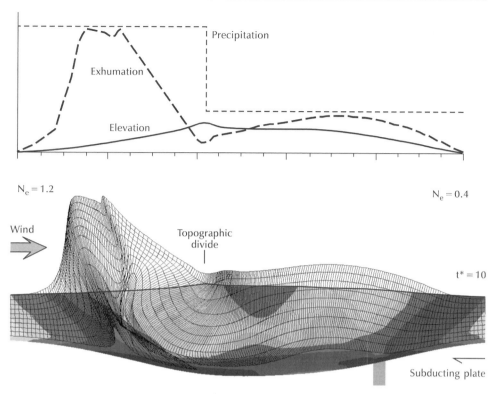

Figure 7.2. Modelling of the interactions between tectonics, climate, denudation and topography for an orogen at a convergent plate boundary.

Note: In the bottom diagram N_e represents relative erosion rate proportionate to the difference in precipitation across an orogen such as the Southern Alps, New Zealand (shown in top diagram). The grid mesh shows the crustal deformation and the grey tones represent the strain rate in the crust (darker = higher). The difference between the topographic profile and the deformed crust above it is the depth of denudation (labelled exhumation in the top diagram).

Source: After Willett (1999).

There is no doubt that tectonic, and related volcanic, processes play a fundamental role in creating the north–south variations in the topography of the Andes as a result of variations in crustal convergence rates and in the orientation and dip of oceanic lithosphere being subducted below the orogen. But the apparent correlation between precipitation rates and variations in the elevation and width of the Andes are intriguing and suggest that climate, along with tectonics, may be a first-order control (Montgomery *et al.* 2001). Analysis of variations in erosional regimes controlled by climate suggests that the Andes can be divided broadly into three zones. In the north, high runoff resulting from the prevailing wet climate has enabled fluvial denudation to match the tectonic uplift rate and maintain a relatively narrow orogen. In the south, abundant precipitation on the western flank of the orogen also maintains an efficient denudational system which is enhanced locally by glacial erosion that tends to reduce the maximum elevation of the range at its southern extremity. In many respects the most intriguing sector of the Andes is the predominantly arid central part of the orogen. Here denudation appears to be generally ineffective as a result of low rates of runoff, and

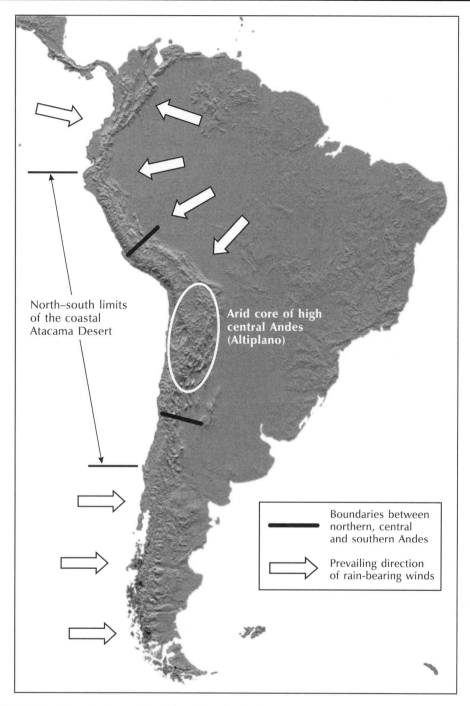

North–south limits
of the coastal
Atacama Desert

Arid core of high
central Andes
(Altiplano)

Boundaries between
northern, central
and southern Andes

Prevailing direction
of rain-bearing winds

Figure 7.3. Major climatic controls of denudation for the Andes.

Note: Topography is from digital elevation model (DEM) derived from Shuttle Radar Topography Mission data (JPL/NASA). Note that the orogen is widest in its central zone where the climate is most arid, and declines in width both to the north and south where precipitation is higher.

crustal thickening has advanced to the point where the elevation of the orogen has been limited not by denudation but by the mechanical strength of the crust. Much of the central Andes is around 5,000 m above sea level, and it appears that as crustal convergence has proceeded, the orogen has begun to spread laterally rather than building up further vertically. This lateral extension has produced basin structures which, when combined with the low erosive power of rivers under conditions of aridity and low runoff, has created large areas of internal drainage within this intra-orogen plateau known as the Altiplano. This idea of the climatic control of orogen morphology raises the question of what would be the consequences of changes in climate. It has, in fact, been suggested that a change to a more arid climate in the central Andes in the Cenozoic could have prompted the rise of this part of the orogen to its present lofty elevation (Lamb and Davis 2003). The proposed mechanism is based on an assessment of the balance of tectonic forces that support topography in the Andes and predicts that a significant reduction in the supply of sediment to the oceanic trench and subduction zone bordering the west of the range as a result of a change to a more arid climate would have focused the plate boundary stresses that support the topography of the high central Andes.

The Himalayan–Tibetan Plateau orogen

An even more spectacular example of an intra-orogen plateau is provided by the Tibetan Plateau immediately to the north of the Himalayas. It extends roughly 1,500 km north to south and 3,500 km east to west, and contains over 80 per cent of the Earth's land surface area over 4,000 m. Well over half of the Tibetan Plateau is drained internally and the mean elevation of this area is a little over 5,000 m. Of course, the highest peaks of the Himalayas to the south reach over 8,000 m, but when the deep intervening valleys between these peaks are taken into account the average elevation of the axis of the Himalayas is about the same as the Tibetan Plateau to the north. Rather than being a distinct topographic feature, it is perhaps more appropriate to regard the Himalayas as the deeply dissected southern flank of the Tibetan Plateau.

The reasons for the development of the Tibetan Plateau seem to be similar to that of the Altiplano Plateau in the central Andes. The Himalayas intercept the humid monsoon air flow from the Indian Ocean, dramatically reducing precipitation on the lee side of the range and forming a highly effective rain-shadow. The growth of the Himalayan–Tibetan Plateau orogen began after the initial collision of India and Eurasia about 50 million years ago. At some stage the rain-shadow effect of the Himalayas reduced precipitation and runoff to the point where denudation could not keep pace with tectonic uplift generated by crustal shortening as India continued to plough northwards into Eurasia. Once the critical elevation of around 5,000 m was attained, the crust began to accommodate shortening by lateral spreading rather than by crustal thickening. Seismic data reveal that Tibet is underlain by crust of double the normal thickness, and its current mean elevation is broadly what we would expect from 70 km-thick continental crust in isostatic equilibrium. But major strike-slip fault systems within the Tibetan Plateau which indicate lateral movement of continental blocks suggest that some of the crustal shortening brought about by the continued northward movement of India into Eurasia has been accommodated by the displacement of crustal blocks eastwards towards south-east Asia and the China Sea.

One of the most remarkable aspects of the Tibetan Plateau is the extensive development of internal drainage, especially in the centre and the west. The conditions favouring the establishment of this large internally drained area appear to be the presence of fault-bounded basins and the lack of runoff caused by the aridity of the climate. The erosive power of river channels became insufficient to maintain river courses across these developing structures, and the rivers now feed sediment into local basins, some of which have been depositional centres for millions of years (Sobel *et al.* 2003). Within this internally drained area there is no net export of mass through denudation (excepting a trivial amount by wind erosion) and so at the regional scale this part of the Tibetan Plateau represents a landscape determined solely by the mechanical properties and behaviour of the crust.

Landscape regimes in orogens

Modelling studies of orogens, coupled with more detailed analyses of their morphology and data on their denudational history, suggest that there are two basic modes of development (Figure 7.4). In regions with humid climates, runoff in river channels is likely to be sufficient to prevent crustal thickening reaching the point where it is the mechanical strength of the crust that limits further increases in elevation rather than the rate of denudation. Where climates are arid – a situation that will be enhanced where ranges are aligned across the direction of prevailing moisture-laden winds – river channel incision may be incapable of keeping pace with the rate of tectonic uplift. In such cases the elevation will continue to increase up to the limit of the mechanical strength of the crust, after which point the orogen will start to widen in the direction of crustal convergence, and may extrude laterally.

Landscape development after continental breakup

It is not only in active orogens where the effects of feedbacks between surface processes and tectonics can be observed in landscape development. The fragmentation of the super-continent of Pangaea which began around 250 million years ago created new continental blocks and so new coastlines to which rivers could drain. The southern part of Pangaea, known as Gondwana, eventually rifted apart to produce the southern continental blocks of

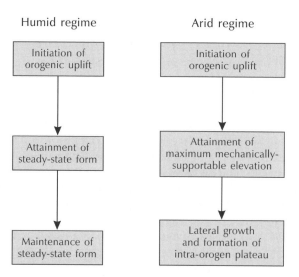

Figure 7.4. Schematic representation of the evolution of orogens under humid and arid climatic regimes.

South America, Africa, Antarctica, Australia and India. The coastline of southern Africa began to take shape around 130 million years ago as the landmass that was to become South America moved away to the west and the South Atlantic Ocean began to open. The topography of southern Africa today is characterized by dissected topography around the coast; this rises inland to a major escarpment zone which surrounds an interior plateau marked by predominantly subdued relief and with an elevation generally in excess of 1,000 m. There is uncertainty about the mechanisms responsible for the relatively high elevation of much of southern Africa, although as we discussed previously, dynamic flow in the mantle may play a role. However, there is no doubt when we look at the topography around the continental margin that much greater depths of denudation have occurred along the coastal zone than inland of the escarpment. Various lines of evidence support this interpretation, including that from thermochronology which can be used to infer the long-term history of denudation from the cooling history of rocks (Gleadow and Brown 2000). As much more rock has been removed from the coastal zone than inland, we would expect this to be reflected in the isostatic response of the lithosphere. When this is modelled using the concept of flexural isostasy, it is evident that the spreading of the change in load brought about by the removal of wedge of crust represented by denudation seaward of the escarpment results in surface uplift along the escarpment rim (Figure 7.5) (van der Beek *et al.* 2002). More generally, it has been shown that where major drainage divides coincide with continental margin escarpments, this uplift has the effect of back-tilting drainage inland (Tucker and Slingerland 1994). This is an important interaction between surface process-driven denudation and tectonics since it will tend to delay the incorporation of interior drainage into coastward-draining river systems, and this will help to preserve the landscape inland from aggressive denudation.

Topography, denudation and climatic change

Another type of interaction between internal and external processes arises from the way in which changes in topography and in rates of surface processes can influence climate (Ruddiman 1997). It has long been appreciated that changes in topography, such as the uplift of mountain belts, can influence regional climates, both by locally enhancing precipitation – especially on the windward side of the barrier – and through the cooling effect of raising the ground surface to higher elevations. Changes in topography could potentially have wide-ranging impacts if they interact with key components of the Earths's climatic system. It has been suggested, for instance, that the uplift of the Tibetan Plateau intensified the Asian monsoon through changes in atmospheric pressure at the land surface due to the elevation increase, and by imposing a barrier to air flow at high altitudes. The supposed regional climatic changes that resulted – which might have extended to a cooling effect which eventually led to the present ice age – were thought to have occurred around 8 million years ago, which correlated with some interpretations of the uplift history of the Tibetan Plateau. But subsequent estimates of elevation based on isotopic data have indicated that at least the central part of the Tibetan Plateau was close to its present elevation as far back as 35 million years ago (Rowley and Currie 2006).

A potentially much more pervasive influence of tectonics and landscape development on climate extending to the global scale is through the interaction of chemical weathering rates and the concentration of the 'greenhouse gas' carbon dioxide (Kump *et al.* 2000). The concentration of CO_2 in the atmosphere plays an important role in controlling global mean temperature, as

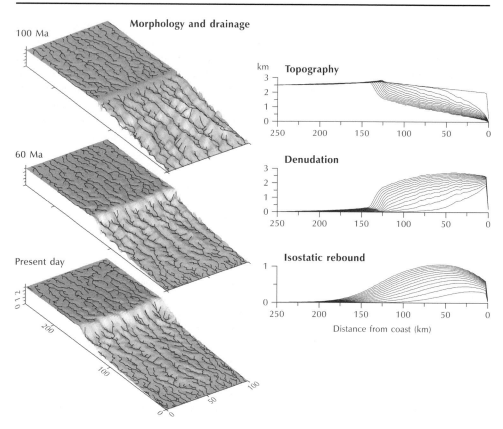

Figure 7.5. Predicted evolution of the south-east margin of southern Africa from 100 million years ago to the present day based on a flexural isostatic response to denudational unloading.

Note: Oblique views on the left show the predicted mode of landscape development, and the cross-sections on the right show changes in topography, denudation and isostatic rebound at 10 million year intervals.

Source: After van der Beek *et al.* (2002).

is evident from current concerns about rising levels of CO_2 and global warming. Over time scales up to hundreds of thousands of years, the concentration of atmospheric CO_2 is determined by complex interactions between the biosphere, the atmosphere and the oceans. However, over longer geological time scales these controls are unimportant because of the amount of carbon stored in rocks, especially limestones, which dwarfs storage in the biosphere. Over very long time scales the concentration of CO_2 in the atmosphere is controlled by the rate of output through volcanism (especially the rate of sea-floor spreading) and the rate of drawdown by the weathering of silicate minerals which consumes CO_2 through the process of carbonation. Changes in the amount of carbon stored in limestones appear to be less significant. Overall, it is thought that rates of outgassing of CO_2 through volcanism probably do not vary significantly over geological time scales, so attention has been focused on variations in the global rate of chemical weathering as a means of producing the significant variations that appear to have occurred in the atmospheric concentration of CO_2 throughout Earth history.

It was once thought that the highest rates of weathering occurred in tropical and equatorial environments, such as the Amazon Basin. This belief was based on the demonstrated effect of higher temperatures on chemical weathering rates revealed in laboratory studies, and the evidence of thick weathering mantles in such environments. But the depth of weathered material is a function of both its rate of production (by weathering) and rate of removal (by erosion). When rivers draining such regions were analysed it was shown that they carried very low concentrations of the solutes that would be produced by weathering reactions. In fact the highest rates of solute transport in river systems occur in regions of steep slopes and high runoff where there is little or no mantle of weathered rock. The reason for this appears to be that the key control on rates of rock weathering is the amount of water that passes through the weathering zone. Where a thick weathering mantle has already developed, the amount of water penetration of water from the surface to the weathering front where fresh bedrock is present is minimal, and therefore the rate of chemical weathering is low. On steep slopes, by contrast, weathered material is more likely to be removed by erosional processes, thus exposing the underlying unweathered rock to water penetrating from above. So it appears that chemical weathering rates will be at a maximum where there is little or no accumulation of weathered material and where precipitation and runoff are high.

The link with tectonics comes from the association with areas of active uplift with terrains characterized by steep slopes. The uplift of mountain belts will also tend to increase precipitation and runoff. It is therefore possible that variations in rates of mountain building through geological time could affect overall rates of global chemical weathering and thereby global mean temperatures by altering the concentration of atmospheric CO_2 (Figure 7.6). If chemical weathering rates increase due to increased tectonic uplift then CO_2 will be drawn out of the atmosphere, but there must be some overall negative feedback in the system

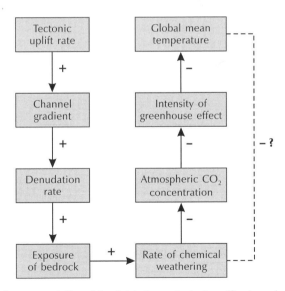

Figure 7.6. Schematic representation of the link between tectonic uplift rate and global mean temperature through the control of atmospheric CO_2 concentration by the rate of silicate weathering.

Note: The dashed line and question mark indicate the problematic feedback between temperature and weathering rate which is required to maintain terrestrial temperatures within the observed range over geological time.

otherwise atmospheric CO_2 would become exhausted, or would keep on increasing and cause a runaway greenhouse effect. Neither has occurred during Earth history and the required negative feedback probably occurs through an indirect effect of temperature on chemical weathering rates. It is likely that if global temperatures increase this will speed up the hydrological cycle and increase runoff. This will, in turn, tend to increase chemical weathering rates which will draw down atmospheric CO_2 and thereby reduce global mean temperature. It is also possible that variations in atmospheric CO_2 concentration may directly affect chemical weathering rates and this could provide another negative feedback mechanism.

Conclusions

Since the 1990s there has been an increasing realization that a number of major features on the Earth's surface previously considered to be the result of internal processes are, in fact, the product of complex interactions between internal and external mechanisms. Both the morphology and patterns of crustal deformation exhibited by mountain belts are now seen to be the consequence of complex feedbacks between tectonics and climatically driven surface processes. But climate itself may be influenced in the long term by tectonically driven variations in global rates of chemical weathering which control the concentration of CO_2 in the atmosphere. We are just beginning to unravel some of these complex interrelationships, and there are certain to be further surprises in store as researchers explore the workings of the Earth system in the future.

Further reading

Burbank, D.W. and Anderson, R.S. (2001) *Tectonic Geomorphology*. Malden: Blackwell.
Kearey, P. and Vine, F.J. (1996) *Global Tectonics*, second edition. Oxford: Blackwell.
Ruddiman, W.F. (ed.) (1997) *Tectonic Uplift and Climatic Change*. New York: Plenum.
Summerfield, M.A. (1991) *Global Geomorphology*. Harlow: Longman.
——(ed.) (2000) *Geomorphology and Global Tectonics*. Chichester: John Wiley and Sons.

References

Beaumont, C., Kooi, H. and Willett, S. (2000) Coupled tectonic–surface process models with applications to rifted margins and collisional orogens. In M.A. Summerfield (ed.) *Geomorphology and Global Tectonics*, pp. 29–55. Chichester: John Wiley and Sons.
Burbank, D.W. and Anderson, R.S. (2001) *Tectonic Geomorphology*. Malden: Blackwell.
Courtillot, V., Davaille, A., Besse, J. and Stock, J. (2003) Three distinct types of hotspots in the Earth's mantle. *Earth and Planetary Science Letters* 205, 295–308.
Foulger, G.R., Natland, J.H., Presnall, D.C. and Anderson, D.L. (eds) (2005) *Plates, Plumes, and Paradigms* (Geological Society of America Special Paper 388). Boulder, Colorado: The Geological Society of America.
Gleadow, A.J.W. and Brown, R.W. (2000) Fission-track thermochronology and the long-term denudational response to tectonics. In M.A. Summerfield (ed.) *Geomorphology and Global Tectonics*, pp. 57–75. Chichester: John Wiley and Sons.
Hallet, B. and Molnar, P. (2001) Distorted drainage basins as markers of crustal strain east of the Himalaya. *Journal of Geophysical Research* 106, 13697–709.

Kearey, P. and Vine, F.J. (1996) *Global Tectonics*, second edition. Oxford: Blackwell.

Koons, P.O. (1995) Modeling the topographic evolution of collisional belts. *Annual Review of Earth and Planetary Sciences* 23, 375–408.

Kump, L.R., Brantley, S.L. and Arthur, M.A. (2000) Chemical weathering, atmospheric CO_2, and climate. *Annual Review of Earth and Planetary Sciences* 28, 611–67.

Lamb, S. and Davis, P. (2003) Cenozoic climate change as a possible cause for the rise of the Andes. *Nature* 425, 792–97.

Montgomery, D.R. and Brandon, M.T. (2002) Topographic controls on erosion rates in tectonically active mountain ranges. *Earth and Planetary Science Letters* 201, 481–89.

Montgomery, D.R., Balco, G. and Willett, S.D. (2001) Climate, tectonics, and the morphology of the Andes. *Geology* 29, 579–82.

Pinter, N. and Brandon, M.T. (1997) How erosion builds mountains. *Scientific American* 276 (April), 60–65.

Rowley, D.B. and Currie, B.S. (2006) Palaeo-altimetry of the late Eocene to Miocene Lunpola basin, central Tibet. *Nature* 439, 677–81.

Ruddiman, W.F. (ed.) (1997) *Tectonic Uplift and Climatic Change*. New York: Plenum.

Sobel, E.R., Hilley, G.H. and Strecker, M.R. (2003) Formation of internally drained contractional basins by aridity-limited bedrock incision. *Journal of Geophysical Research*, DOI: 10.1029/2002JB001883.

Summerfield, M.A. (1991) *Global Geomorphology*. Harlow: Longman.

——(ed.) (2000) *Geomorphology and Global Tectonics*. Chichester: John Wiley and Sons.

Summerfield, M.A. and Hulton, N.J. (1994) Natural controls of fluvial denudation rates in major world drainage basins. *Journal of Geophysical Research* 99, 13871–83.

Tucker, G.E. and Slingerland, R.L. (1994) Erosional dynamics, flexural isostasy, and long-lived escarpments: a numerical modelling study. *Journal of Geophysical Research* 99, 12229–43.

van der Beek, P., Summerfield, M.A., Braun, J., Brown, R.W. and Fleming, A. (2002) Modelling post-break-up landscape development and denudational history across the southeast African (Drakensberg Escarpment) margin. *Journal of Geophysical Research*, DOI: 10.1029/2001JB000744.

Willett, S.D. (1999) Orography and orogeny: the effects of erosion on the structure of mountain belts. *Journal of Geophysical Research* 104, 28957–81.

8

Climate

Richard Huggett

As the sky is divided into two zones on the right hand, and two on the left, with a fifth in between, hotter than any of the rest, so the world which the sky encloses was marked off in the same way, thanks to the providence of the god: he imposed the same number of zones on earth as there are in the heavens. The central zone is so hot as to be uninhabitable, while two others are covered in deep snow: but between these extremes he set two zones to which he gave a temperate climate, compounded of heat and cold.

(Ovid 1955: 30)

What is climate? What is climatic change? These two big questions are crucial to any discussion of global change and underpin current debates about the influence of humans upon climate. Climate helps to shape the character of places and climatic change may alter the character of places.

Climate

Climatic zones and regions

Latitudinal zones

Climate is the average atmospheric conditions at a particular place. Mean temperatures, pressures, winds and so forth over a thirty-year period often define it. Planetary fields of temperature and wind create three basic climatic zones: the torrid zone of low latitudes, the temperate zones of middle latitudes, and the frigid zones of high latitudes. The ancient Greeks appreciated this fundamental zonary pattern, as the quotation from Ovid suggests.

The navigators and naturalist–explorers who sailed the oceans first established global patterns of basic atmospheric variables. The location of the chief wind belts (the sub-tropical easterly trade winds and the mid-latitude westerlies), the zonal pattern of temperature and the greater seasonal contrast of temperature over continents than over oceans were all charted by the early years of the nineteenth century. As scientists started to fill in the details of the spatial pattern of atmospheric variables, they realized that the distribution of land and sea and the presence of large-scale topographic features, chiefly mountain ranges and plateaux, hugely distort the fundamental zonary arrangement of climates.

During the early twentieth century, the coverage of the spatial distribution of atmospheric variables was sufficient to allow the first (and lasting) attempts at the classification of climate, such as that proposed by Wladimir Peter Köppen (1931). At present, the distortions to the three basic climatic zones produce some seven climatic regions, though the exact number varies from one authority to the next. The regions are:

1. humid tropical climate (equatorial rain zone);
2. savannah climate (tropical margin zone with summer rains);
3. desert climate (subtropical dry zone);
4. Mediterranean climate (subtropical zone of winter rain and summer drought);
5. temperate climate (temperate zone with precipitation all year round); this extensive zone is divisible into maritime climate (warm temperate subzone), nemoral climate (typical temperate subzone – a short period of frost), continental climate (arid temperate subzone – cold winter) and boreal climate (cold temperate subzone);
6. tundra climate (subpolar zone);
7. polar climate (polar zone).

Each climate zone produces physical constraints that help to dictate the distribution of soils, landforms and living things, including humans and their habitations.

Altitudinal climatic zones

As the general decline in temperature with increasing latitude produces latitudinal climatic zones, so decreasing temperature with increasing elevation produces altitudinal climatic zones. Starting at a mountain base, the zones are usually submontane, montane, subalpine, alpine and nival. In the tropics, altitudinal effects are strong enough to allow polar conditions on mountaintops, with permanent snow in, for example, the equatorial Andes and New Guinea and African mountains, and tropical glaciers on, for instance, Mount Kilimanjaro (e.g. Kaser 1999; Kaser *et al.* 2004). Moreover, the altitudinal depression of temperature defines the character of many significant tropical places that are around or over 2,000 m above sea level, such as Mexico City, Johannesburg, Nairobi, Quito and La Paz.

Local climates

All topographic features may sufficiently modify radiation fluxes, heat balances, moisture levels and aerodynamics in the local environment to create local climates (topoclimates). Radiation modification depends largely on the aspect and inclination of ground surfaces and the walls and roofs of buildings, on the albedo (the reflectivity of topographic features – different vegetation types, bare soil, human-made surfaces, water bodies), on shading effects and, in some cases, on local energy sources (domestic fires, industrial plants, and so on). Some parts of landscapes receive more sunlight than others receive and emit and absorb different amounts of long-wave radiation. In turn, the altered radiation balances produce hotter and cooler areas within landscapes by modifying local heat balances. Moisture levels vary because of spatial variability in precipitation receipt (caused by differing interception rates and shelter effects), in evaporation rates and in soil drainage. Aerodynamic modifications concern the physical effects of small-scale topographic features on airflow.

Urban areas commonly have a distinct local climate. The air in the urban canopy is often warmer than air in the surrounding rural areas, so creating an urban heat island. The precise form and size of urban heat islands are variable and depend upon meteorological, locational and urban factors. Heat islands occur in tropical and extra-tropical cities. Urban heat-island intensity (the difference between the peak temperature and the background rural temperature) depends on many factors, of which city size is one of the most important. The maximum heat island intensity of Dublin is about 8 °C, as is that for Barcelona; it is about 10 °C for metropolitan Washington DC and 17 °C for New York.

Climatic dynamics

Air moves relentlessly and atmospheric motion is fundamental to understanding Earth's climates. On a planetary scale, the temperature gradient between the equator and the poles is the foremost driver of air movements. This thermal gradient drives a vast overturning of air, first suggested by Edmund Halley in 1686 and elaborated by George Hadley in 1735, called the Hadley circulation. On Venus, there is one grand Hadley cell in each hemisphere: a huge convective current of air rises at the Venusian equator, moves polewards, sinks over the poles, and then returns at ground level to its equatorial origin. On the Earth, the Hadley circulation breaks down into three component cells in each hemisphere (Figure 8.1). Heat released as water evaporated from the tropical oceans condenses, mainly in the inter-tropical convergence zone (ITCZ) or equatorial low-pressure trough, and largely powers the equatorial Hadley cell. At ground level, the air returning towards the ITCZ produces the trade winds. The middle or Ferrel cell flows in the reverse direction: that is, equatorwards aloft and polewards at the surface. The third cell, known as the polar cell, is rather weak.

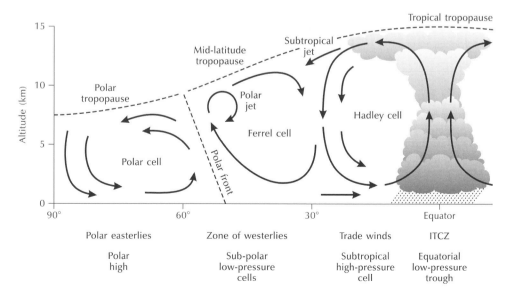

Figure 8.1. The general circulation of the atmosphere.

111

As a result of the Earth rotating, winds in the tropics tend to blow north-east to south-west (Northern Hemisphere) or south-east to north-west (Southern Hemisphere). In middle and high latitudes, where Corioli's force is strongest, they have a strong east-to-west component. In addition, easterly winds predominate in the upper troposphere in the tropics, and westerly winds elsewhere. The upper air westerlies are the main flow of the atmosphere. They form a circumpolar vortex, the fastest flowing ribbons of which are jet streams. This vortex progresses from shallow zonal waves rushing west to east to great meandering meridional loops. The full sequence of the 'index cycle', so named because the zonal index (the average hemispherical pressure gradient between 35° and 55° N) runs from low to high and back again over a four to six week period (Namias 1950). The tropical easterlies may also form jet streams, especially in summer.

The tripartite Hadley circulation has a smaller 'eddy' circulation superimposed upon it. Baroclinic instabilities and the development of standing waves create this eddy circulation. Baroclinic instabilities arise when steep temperature and pressure gradients cross one another. The result is that baroclinic waves develop, forming the disturbances known as the travelling cyclones and anticyclones characteristic of mid-latitudes. These disturbances play a major role in transferring heat to the upper troposphere and towards the poles. In tropical latitudes, large and intense wave cyclones are absent because of the weak Corioli's force. Instead, disturbances take the form of easterly waves, which are slow-moving troughs of low pressure within the trade wind belt (Dunn 1940; Riehl 1954); weak equatorial lows, which form at the heart of equatorial troughs and serve as foci for individual convective storms along the ITCZ; and powerful tropical cyclones.

The latitudinal temperature gradient and the general circulation serve to define broad hot, cold, wet and dry zones. However, seasonal climatic features, particularly those associated with tropical cyclones and the poleward swing of the ITCZ in the summer hemisphere and associated monsoon circulations, are enormously important in defining the climates of many places, including some of the densely populated ones. Tropical cyclones – called hurricanes in the Atlantic Ocean, typhoons in the Indian and Pacific Oceans, and willy-willies in Australia – are large-scale, though seasonal, features of the general circulation. They begin as weak low-pressure cells over very warm ocean water (27 °C and more) between 8° and 15° N and S that grow into deep circular lows. Tropical cyclones tend to define the character of such places as Taiwan, Luzon, several Pacific Islands, the Bay of Bengal, Florida, the Caribbean, and north-western and north-eastern Australia. Paradoxically, while tropical cyclones may cause severe coastal damage – witness the flooding of New Orleans resulting from hurricane Katrina in September 2005 – they can be the major rain-producing systems of the year some areas, including much of inland Australia.

The seasonal shift of the ITCZ in the summer hemisphere explains such seasonal rainfall patterns as summer rains in savannah zones, winter rains in west coast Mediterranean climates, summer rains in the east coast (China) climates and in the tropical margin zones like India and northern Australia. Monsoon circulations develop in parts of the tropics and are connected with the northward and southward swing of the ITCZ. In southern Asia, monsoons involve a changeover from north-east winds in winter to south-west monsoon winds in summer. The generation of stationary eddies (standing waves) by massive mountain ranges and plateaux, and by temperature differences between oceans and continents, influences atmospheric circulation patterns. The Rockies, for example, tend to anchor the westerly jet stream over North America. Similarly, the Tibet plateau affects the position of the jet stream, which in turn influences the invasion of the south-west monsoon, which occurs as the jet stream shifts from the south or southern edge of the Tibet plateau.

Seasonal temperature changes result partly from differences in thermal properties of land and sea. A landmass will have hotter summers and colder winters than an ocean occupying the same latitude. This is the effect of continentality. It arises because land has two to three times the heat capacity of sea, and because heat is conducted downwards more slowly from the land surface than it is by turbulent mixing from the ocean surface. For these reasons, the annual and diurnal ranges of surface and air temperatures are much larger in continental climates than in oceanic climates. The influence of oceans extends over continental areas lying next to oceans, especially non-mountainous areas on western seaboards where maritime air masses move inland. Various indices describe the degree of continentality. The Northern Hemisphere displays more marked effects of continentality than does the Southern Hemisphere, simply because the Northern Hemisphere contains about twice as much land as the Southern Hemisphere.

Smaller circulations of air include individual eddies revealed by the swirling of autumn leaves, thunderstorms, and land and sea breezes. These ride within the larger-scale hurricanes, fronts, cyclones and anticyclones, and hemispheric and global circulations.

Climatic models

The 1950s saw the building of the first numerical weather forecast models, the construction of which had been adumbrated thirty years earlier by Lewis Fry Richardson in his remarkable book *Weather Prediction by Numerical Process* (1922). These models, which involved the numerical solution of three-dimensional, time-dependent equations of atmospheric hydrodynamics, predicted the change in observed atmospheric temperature and pressure fields for several days ahead. They were chiefly concerned with adiabatic temperature changes resulting from air movement and pressure differences characteristic of cyclonic disturbances. Over longer periods, 'diabatic' heating terms – including the release of latent heat during condensation, atmospheric radiation processes and convective heating from the Earth's surface atmospheric temperature – greatly influence atmospheric temperature. The first general circulation models, built during the 1960s, combined these longer-term processes with the equations of the weather prediction models. Briefly, a general circulation model comprises a prognostic system of equations describing the physical and dynamical processes that determine climate. It usually includes also a heat and water balance model of the land surface, and a mixed-layer model of the ocean.

Four chief types of climate model exist: energy balance models (EBMs), radiative–convective models (RCMs), statistical dynamical models (SDs) and general circulation models (GCMs). Of these, GCMs are the most sophisticated climate models currently available. They simulate three-dimensional parcels of air as they move horizontally and vertically through the atmosphere. There are several types of GCMs (Table 8.1, Figure 8.2). Modellers often run these with carbon cycle models, biosphere models and atmosphere chemistry models. General circulation models are an exceedingly useful way of exploring past, present and future climates.

Climatic change

What is climatic change?

Climatic change is a change in average atmospheric conditions at a particular place or in a particular region. It is often difficult to distinguish from climatic variability, especially in strongly seasonal climates. Climatic variability (see Chapter 42) is the differences between mean atmospheric states of the same kind: for instance, between mean July temperatures or mean winter precipitation in different years. In the Mediterranean region, seasonal conditions fluctuate wildly from year to year. Mean summer temperatures vary some 5–7°C, and mean winter temperatures some 8–13°C, from one year to the next, while seasonal rainfall departs 80 per cent from the long-term mean.

Paradoxically, change in modern climates is difficult to perceive – it commonly hides in the welter of direct measurements taken over short time periods, whereas change of past

Table 8.1. Types of general circulation models

Type	Abbreviation	Details
Atmospheric general circulation models	AGCMs	Represent the atmosphere in three dimensions. Include the land surface and ice. Similar to models used for numerical weather prediction (weather forecasting). Useful for studying atmospheric processes, the variability of climate, and its response to changes in sea-surface temperature.
Atmospheric general circulation models coupled to a 'slab' ocean	–	Predict changes in sea-surface temperatures and sea ice by treating the ocean as a layer of water of constant depth (typically 50 metres). Heat transports within the ocean are specified and stay constant while climate changes. Useful for simulating the climate for a fixed level of carbon dioxide, but it cannot predict the rate of change of climate because that depends upon processes in the ocean interior.
Ocean general circulation models	OGCMs	Oceanic counterparts of an AGCM: a three-dimensional representation of the ocean and sea ice. Useful by themselves for studying ocean circulation, interior processes, and variability. They require data on surface air temperature and other atmospheric properties.
Coupled atmosphere–ocean general circulation models	AOGCMs	Most complex models in use, consisting of an AGCM coupled to an OGCM. Some recent models include the biosphere, carbon cycle and atmospheric chemistry as well. Used for predicting the nature and rate of change of future climate. Also used to study the variability and physical processes of the coupled climate system.
Regional climate models	RCMs	Local features such as mountains, poorly represented in global models because of their coarse resolution, greatly influence local climate change. Regional climate models with a higher resolution (typically 50 km) are constructed for limited areas and run for shorter periods (20 years or so). The current resolution for atmospheric section of a typical model is about 250 km horizontally and about 1 km vertically above the boundary layer; and for the oceanic section it is about 200–400 m vertically and 125–250 km horizontally. Figure 8.2 shows the chief physical processes and interactions, and the spatial structure, of a coupled atmosphere–ocean general circulation model.

Source: Adapted from http://www.metoffice.com/research/hadleycentre/models/modeltypes.html (last accessed 21 July 2005).

climates is unmistakable, owing to limited observations of proxy climatic indicators taken from rocks, sediments and soils. Past climates (palaeoclimates) are no easier to define than modern climates. Within the historical period, various written accounts and instrumental records may provide clues to climatic conditions in the recent past. The stratigraphic record contains evidence of historical and older climates, but it does not always register conditions on a yearly basis and seldom supplies an annual calendar of palaeoclimatic events and states. Another difficulty is that not all past climates appear to have modern analogues. The

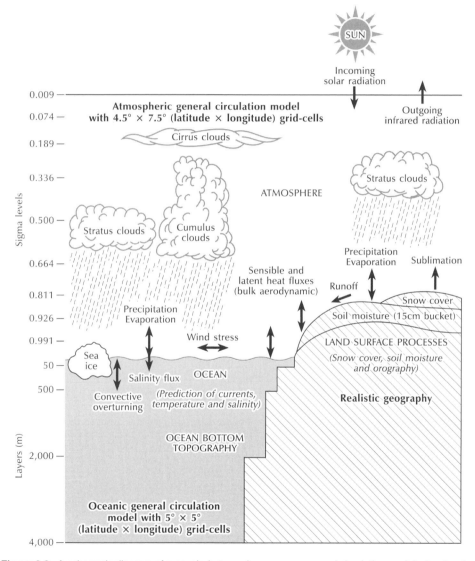

Figure 8.2. A schematic diagram of a coupled atmosphere–ocean general circulation model, showing the vertical structure of atmospheric and oceanic layers and the chief physical processes and interactions modelled.

Source: Adapted from Washington and Meehl (1991).

115

disposition of land and sea, the position of high land, and other physical conditions were different in the past and, in some cases, produced climates that do not exist today. A prime example is the 'boreal grassland' climate that occupied a broad belt immediately south of the Northern Hemisphere ice sheets.

Seventeenth-century scholars recognized geological changes of climate: tropical fossils unearthed in temperate climes suggested that the present climate was unlike the ancient climate. In the nineteenth century, the recognition of glacial and interglacial regimes indicated that the climate had changed drastically in the relatively recent past. A multitude of theories attempted to explain these long-term changes of climate. These theories, many of them highly inventive, were difficult to appraise because hard palaeoclimatic evidence was meagre, the interpretation of climatic indicators was problematic, and a sound chronology of events did not exist. Moreover, most of the theories were rather simplistic because many of the complex interactions and forcings of the climate system were only guessed at or remained unimagined, and because knowledge of the solar system and Milky Way galaxy was limited. Today, geochronometric dating techniques provide an absolute timescale of events that has helped to remedy some of the problems faced by earlier generations of theorists in trying to evaluate the worth of their palaeoclimatic conjectures. Ice cores, deep-sea sediments, cave sediments, bog and lake cores, tree rings and palaeosols yield up evidence of the climatic past. A better understanding of the relation between climate and Earth surface phenomena means that climatic indicators are reliable tools in the reconstruction of ancient climates. Computer models of the general circulation allow climates of the past to be simulated, and allow the effect of the Earth's changing orbital motions on solar input to be calculated quickly and accurately. Used in combination, all these new palaeoclimatological methods have unveiled a far more colourful spectrum of climatic changes than that considered by the earlier generations of climatologists. For a variety of reasons, weather and climate change over timescales ranging from less than an hour, as in short-lived but severe meteorological phenomena, to over tens of millions of years, as in protracted phases of global warming and cooling (Table 8.2). In addition, they follow secular trends lasting aeons.

Causes of climatic change

Scientists now understand the basic mechanisms of atmospheric change in broad terms, though the relative importance of various factors over different time-spans is still uncertain. Figure 8.3 summarizes the chief processes involved in atmospheric change. In the short term, over years, decades and centuries, the atmosphere may change owing to external forcings (cosmic, geological and anthropogenic) or to internal atmospheric dynamics. Cosmic forcing arises from changes in gravitational forces, by variations in electromagnetic and particulate radiation receipt from the sun and from space, and by the impact of asteroids and comets. Gravitational stresses may emanate from three sources – the solar system, our galaxy and other galaxies – but only interactions within the solar system will force the atmosphere in the short term when the overall motions and alignments of the planets in the solar system and by Earth–Moon motions modulates the delivery of energy. Geological forcing is, in the short term, caused by the injection of volcanic dust and gases into the stratosphere. Internal dynamics of the atmospheric system involve short-term cyclical components. Thus, climatic change can occur without the aid of external forcing. Sorting out signals from these potential sources of climatic change is very hard. Humans cause climate change largely by interfering with biogeochemical cycles, especially the carbon cycle, and by changing land cover.

Table 8.2. Major climatic variations, excluding secular trends

Variation	Period (years unless otherwise stated)	Nature of period	Nature of variation
Short-term variation			
Diurnal	1 day	Spike	Daily cycle of climate
Weekly[a]	3–7 days	Peak	Synoptic disturbances, chiefly in middle latitudes
Annual[b]	1	Spike	Annual cycle of climate
Quasi-biennial	~26 months	Peak	Wind shift (east phase to west phase) in tropical stratosphere (quasi-biennial oscillation – QBO)
Quinquennial	2–7 years	Peak	Rapid switch of pressure distribution across the southern Pacific Ocean. Linked with changes in temperature in the same region, and together termed El Niño–Southern Oscillation (ENSO). Average period is 4–5 years; 2–7 years is the range
Undecennial	~11	Peak	Quasi-periodic variation corresponding to the sunspot cycle
Nonadecennial	~18.6	Peak	Quasi-periodic variation corresponding to the lunar nodal cycle
Octogintennial	~80	Peak	Quasi-periodic variation corresponding to the Gleissberg cycle
Bicentennial	~200	Peak	Quasi-periodic variation corresponding to the solar orbital cycle
Bimillennial	~2,000	Peak	Quasi-periodic variation of uncertain correspondence
Medium-term variation			
Precessional	~19,000	Spike	A periodic component of the Earth's precession cycle
Precessional	~23,000	Spike	A periodic component of the Earth's precession cycle
Tilt	~41,000	Spike	Chief periodic component of the Earth's tilt (obliquity) cycle
Short eccentricity	~100,000	Spike	A periodic component of the Earth's orbital eccentricity cycle
Orbital plane inclination	~100,000	Spike	A periodic component of Earth's orbit
Long eccentricity	~400,000	Spike	A periodic component of the Earth's orbital eccentricity cycle
Long-term variation			
Thirty megayear	~30,000,000	Peak	Quasi-periodic fluctuations perhaps corresponding to a tectonic cycle
Warm mode–cool mode	~150,000,000	Peak	Quasi-periodic fluctuations from warm to cool climatic modes, possibly connected to half a galactic year
Hothouse–icehouse	~300,000,000	Peak	Quasi-periodic fluctuations from hothouse to icehouse conditions

Notes: [a] Strictly periodic variation dictated by astronomical cycles; [b] Quasi-periodic variation with preferred timescales of occurrence.

Source: After Huggett (1997: 109).

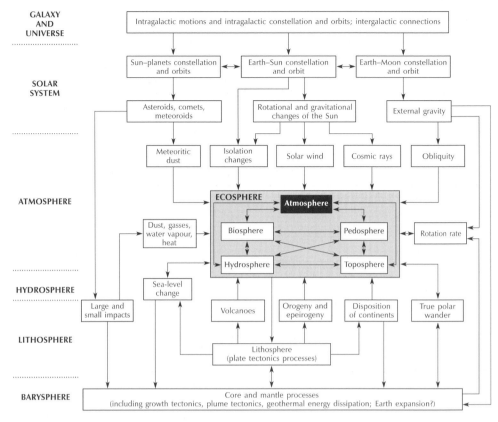

Figure 8.3. Geological, cosmic and ecological drivers of atmospheric change.

Source: After Huggett (1997: 7).

Medium- and long-term climatic change

In the medium and long term, over thousands to millions of years, cosmic and geological forcings and internal atmospheric dynamics cause climates to change.

Cosmic forcing

Cosmic forcing over medium and long timescales involves orbital variations, secular changes in solar output and, indirectly, large-body impacts that can influence geological processes. The Earth's orbital cycles wield a considerable influence over climate (Table 8.3) (Hays *et al.* 1976). They do so by changing seasonal and latitudinal patterns of solar radiation receipt, and possibly by altering geological processes. Orbital variations in the Croll–Milankovitch frequency band appear to have driven climatic change during the Pleistocene and Holocene epochs. Orbital forcing has led to climatic change in middle and high latitudes, where ice sheets have waxed and waned, and to climatic change in low latitudes, where water budgets and heat budgets have marched in step with high-latitude climatic cycles. Quaternary loess

Table 8.3. Orbital forcing cycles

Cycle	Approximate period (years)	Examples in climatic data
Tilt	41,000	Oxygen-isotope records from deep-sea cores
Precession	19,000 and 23,000	Oxygen-isotope records from deep-sea cores; magnetic susceptibility variations in deep-sea cores; loess deposits
Short eccentricity and orbital plane inclination[a]	100,000	Diatom temperature records in deep-sea cores
Long eccentricity	400,000	Diatom temperature records in deep-sea cores

Note: [a] See Muller and MacDonald (1995).

deposits, sea-level changes and oxygen-isotope ratios of marine cores record the 100,000-year cycle of eccentricity. The precessional cycle (with 23,000- and 19,000-year components) and the 41,000-year tilt cycle ride on the 100,000-year cycle. They, too, generate climatic changes that register in marine and terrestrial sediments. Oxygen isotope ratios in ocean cores normally contain signatures of all the Earth's orbital cycles, though the tilt cycle, as it affects seasonality, has a stronger signature in sediments deposited at high latitudes.

Variations in orbital parameters do not explain all aspects of Quaternary climatic change. Elkibbi and Rial (2001) identified five challenges to the astronomical theory of ice ages. Three relate to the '100,000-year problem'. First, 100,000-year variations of insolation forced by eccentricity changes are too small (less than 1 per cent) to drive the great ice ages. Second, 100,000-year oscillations have dominated the last 900,000 years but 41,000-year oscillations dominated the late Tertiary and early Quaternary (this is called the mid-Pleistocene transition). Third, over the last 500,000 years, glacial cycles some 80,000–120,000 years long do not correlate linearly with insolation. The fourth challenge is the '400,000-year problem', which is the absence of a 413,000-year signal in oxygen isotope from marine cores over the past 1.2 million years, despite that being the largest component of eccentricity forcing. The fifth challenge is the presence of signals for climatic cycles that appear unrelated to insolation forcing, which indicate nonlinear responses of the climate system.

Orbital forcing does not act in isolation. Greenhouse gases and atmospheric dust may have contributed to glacial–interglacial temperature changes. The biggest contributor is probably carbon dioxide. Reliable measurements of past carbon dioxide levels in the atmosphere come from air bubbles entrapped in Arctic and Antarctic ice cores. Carbon dioxide levels in the Vostok ice core, Antarctica, vary from between 190 and 200 ppmv during a glacial stage, and between 260 and 80 ppmv during an interglacial stage (Barnola *et al.* 1987). Carbon dioxide changes, which orbital variations might partly drive, could magnify orbitally induced insolation changes and bring a switch of climate.

Geological forcing

Geological forcing over medium and long time-scales involves plate tectonic processes powered by geological processes occurring in the Earth's core and mantle. In the long term, plate tectonics leads to changes in palaeogeography – the redistribution of continents and oceans, the formation of mountain ranges, changes in the volume of the oceans, changes of sea level, and so on – all of which may induce atmospheric change. Redistribution of mass within the Earth can lead to secular trends in true polar wander that will have repercussions in the atmosphere, too. Processes in the core and mantle, which drive many lithospheric processes, are themselves influenced by cosmic forcing: large-body impacts may force changes at the core–mantle boundary that, eventually, are felt in the atmosphere. The entire planet is subject to gravitational forcing that may effect long-term changes of axial tilt (astronomical pole shift), again with concomitant effects on the atmosphere. Gravitational forces also gradually change the position of the solar system relative to the centre of the Milky Way galaxy. This may lead to very long-term changes of climate. In addition, the atmosphere may change over thousands to millions of years because of processes going on inside it, such as changes in the salinity of the oceans, changes of sea-surface temperatures, the growth and decay of ice sheets and sea ice, the eustatic change of sea level, biological evolution, and changes in terrestrial biomass.

Short-term climatic change

Over years, decades and centuries, the atmosphere may change owing to external forcings from cosmic, geological and anthropogenic source, or to internal atmospheric dynamics.

Solar and lunar forcing

Solar activity varies over days and years. These short-term solar cycles leave their mark in many parts of the environment (Table 8.4). For this reason, a connection between the sunspot cycle and climate processes seems undeniable, though the causal links remain elusive. Periods of prolonged solar minima have occurred during the last several centuries (Figure 8.4). Some climatologists argue that they tend to be associated with periods of low temperatures (e.g. Eddy 1977). The Maunder Minimum, for example, coincides with the Little Ice Age, though the correlation between these two events is questionable. The solar orbital cycle may have triggered the collapse of the Mayan civilization in the ninth century by producing devastating droughts in the Yucatán Peninsula (Hodell *et al.* 2001).

The strong, 18.6-year beat given by the lunar nodal precession cycle appears to exert an influence on the atmosphere and its signal is present in many atmospheric variables (Table 8.2).

Table 8.4. Solar and lunar climatic cycles

Forcing cycle	Period (years)	Examples in climatic data
Sunspot	~11	Air temperature, permafrost temperature, annual minimum temperature, tree-ring width
Hale	~22	Varve thickness
Gleissberg	~80	Northern Hemisphere land and air temperatures
Solar orbital	~180	Air temperatures since Little Ice Age
Bimillennial	~2,000	Radiocarbon in tree rings over last 9,000 years
Lunar	~18.6	Air temperature, air pressure, tree-ring width

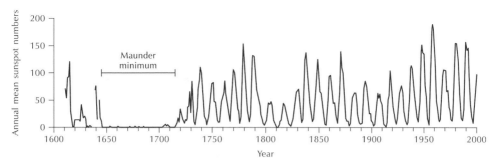

Figure 8.4. Annual mean sunspot numbers, 1610–2000.

Note: The period between about AD 1645 and 1715, when the sun seems to have been quiet and sun-spots to have been scarce, is the Maunder Minimum. However, this dearth of sunspots might reflect poor historical records. The 11-year sunspot cycle and the 80-year Gleissberg cycle may be picked out in the post-1800 data.

Volcanic forcing

Volcanoes, by injecting dust and gases into the air, may force atmospheric changes. The expectation is that violent volcanic explosions will cause a temporary depression of global temperatures. This was the case, for example, after the eruption of Mount Agung, Bali, in March 1963. By late 1964 and early 1965, the temperature of the tropical middle and upper troposphere dropped by 1°C. Contrarily, several great eruptions, such as that of Coseguina, Nicaragua, in 1835 and that of Mount St Helens, United States, in 1980, had no detectable effect on atmospheric temperatures (Robock and Mass 1982). A host of factors determine the impact of volcanic dust injections on climate, but the amount of sulphur volatiles released seems crucial (Rampino *et al.* 1988).

Without doubt, none of the historical eruptions was anything like as awesome as some of the eruptions in the geological past. Toba, in Sumatra, exploded some 73,500 years ago. This gigantic explosion may have injected some 1,000–10,000 Mt of sulphuric acid aerosols, and equal amounts of fine ash, some 27–37 km into the atmosphere (Rampino *et al.* 1988; Rampino and Self 1992). The Tambora eruption of 1815 was tame in comparison – it released a mere 100 Mt of sulphuric acid aerosols. While the Tambora event would have caused a dimming of the sun, the higher estimate for the Toba event would have led to the cessation of photosynthesis and a 3–5 °C temperature drop in the Northern Hemisphere.

Internal mechanisms

Short-term instabilities in the atmosphere–ocean system drive El Niño–Southern Oscillation events. Every few years, exceptionally warm waters appear off Ecuador and Peru and extend far westwards in equatorial regions. This is an El Niño event. It is associated with an air-pressure fall over much of the south-eastern Pacific Ocean, and an air-pressure rise over Indonesia and northern Australia. When cold water returns to the western South American seaboard – a La Niña event – the pressure gradient reverses over the Pacific and Indian Oceans. This flip-flopping of pressure is called the Southern Oscillation. The combined oceanic and atmospheric changes are the El Niño–Southern Oscillation, sometimes called ENSO events. The intervals between strong El Niño events range from two to seven years and average four to five years. This unusual variability may result from the interaction of two

121

pulses in the Pacific equatorial winds, one with a two-year beat and the other with a four to five-year beat (Rasmussen *et al.* 1990). A strong El Niño event may occur when these two cycles are in phase, and a weak El Niño event when they are out of phase.

ENSO events affect climates worldwide (Bjerknes 1969; Ropelewski and Halpert 1987). They do so by causing wavelike disturbances of airflow in the upper troposphere that extends into mid-latitudes. Mid-latitude mountains tend to amplify these wave disturbances (DeWeaver and Nigam 1995). The impacts of El Niño upon temperate climates are greatest during winter. For instance, most El Niño winters are mild over western Canada and parts of the northern USA, and wet over the southern USA from Texas to Florida. However, even during winter, El Niño is one of several factors influencing temperate climates, and consequently El Niño years do not always display 'typical' El Niño conditions in the way they tend to in tropical latitudes.

Instabilities in the atmosphere–ocean system may also cause abrupt climatic changes within Pleistocene glacial and interglacial stages, including the Dansgaard–Oeschger cycles and Heinrich events.

Human forcing

Humans unquestionably alter local climates, a prime example being the urban heat islands that sometimes develop in cities. There is growing evidence that the human population may be having a global climatic impact, triggering a warming of the atmosphere and oceans largely through increasing the concentration of atmospheric greenhouse gases. However, natural cycles of climatic change may also lead to fluctuations in atmospheric carbon dioxide levels and in the levels of some other greenhouse gases, which may bring about a warming and cooling of the atmosphere. Natural climatic cycles, such as the ones mentioned in previous sections, must provide a backdrop against which to assess the extent of human-induced global warming. Indeed, current global warming may have natural components related to orbital forcing that would keep temperatures rising even without an increase in greenhouse gases (Kukla and Gavin 2004).

Evidence that the Earth is warming is mounting. Strong observational indicators include the following. First, the global average surface temperature (the average of near-surface air temperature over land, and sea-surface temperature) has increased since 1861 (Figure 8.5). During the twentieth century, the increase was about 0.6°C, although the warming was not even, most of it taking place in the periods 1910–1940, and 1976–2000. Second, globally, it is likely the 1990s were the warmest decade and 1998 the warmest year in the instrumental record since 1861. Third, twentieth-century warming in the Northern Hemisphere is likely to have been the fastest for any time over the last 1,000 years, and the 1990s were the hottest decade and 1998 the warmest year (Figure 8.5).

Almost without exception, climate models that simulate the effect of much higher burdens of carbon dioxide and trace gases in the atmosphere predict that the Earth will be a warmer and more humid planet over the next century. Predictions suggest a globally averaged surface temperature in the range 1.4 to 5.8 °C over the period 1990 to 2100, depending upon the scenario used (Figures 8.6 and 8.7). The basic reasons for the increased temperature and humidity are not difficult to grasp. The higher the concentration of greenhouse gases in the atmosphere, the greater the amount of infrared radiation emitted from the Earth's surface absorbed by the atmosphere, and so the hotter the atmosphere. With a warmer atmosphere, evaporation of water from the world's oceans increases, so leading to a more vigorous pumping of water round the hydrological cycle. This results in an increased occurrence of droughts and of very wet conditions, the last created by deeper thunderstorms with greater

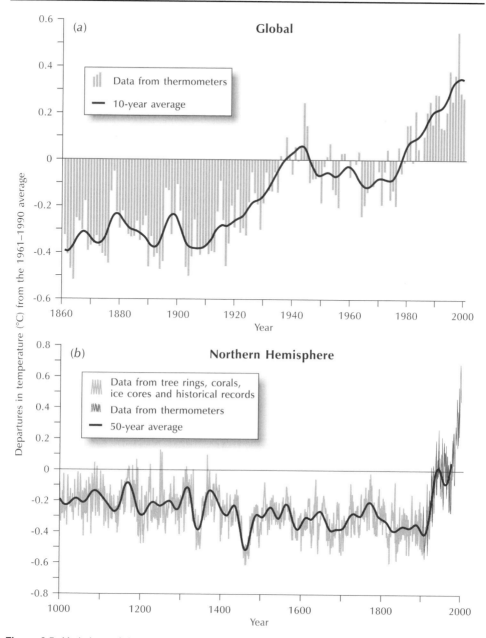

Figure 8.5. Variations of the Earth's surface temperature over (a) the last 140 years and (b) the last millennium.

Source: Adapted from Houghton *et al.* (2001).

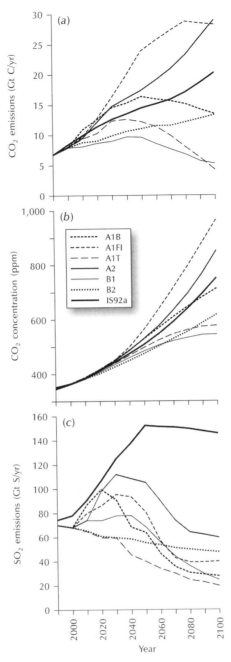

Figure 8.6. Selected climatic forcing emissions during the twenty-first century: (a) carbon dioxide emissions; (b) carbon dioxide concentrations; (c) sulphur dioxide emissions.

Note: Scenario A1F1 (fossil-fuel intensive) is the worst-case scenario; scenario B1 (the 'green scenario') is the best-case scenario.

Source: Adapted from Houghton *et al.* (2001).

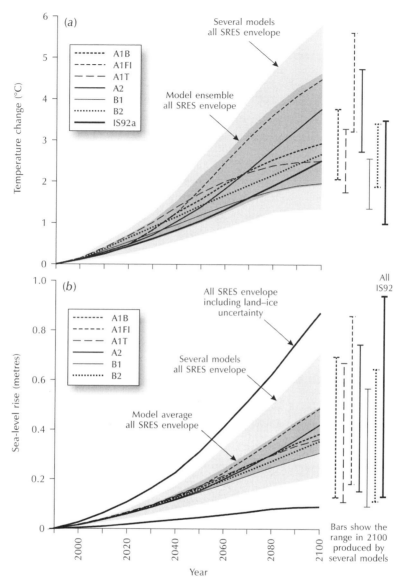

Figure 8.7. Predictions of climatic change during the twenty-first century: (a) temperature changes; (b) sea-level rise

Note: Scenario A1F1 (fossil-fuel intensive) is the worst-case scenario; scenario B1 (the 'green scenario') is the best-case scenario.

Source: Adapted from Houghton *et al.* (2001).

rainfall. Tropical cyclones also become more destructive. The increased humidity of the air may itself boost greenhouse warming since water vapour absorbs infrared radiation.

Importantly, climate models predict an uneven warming of the atmosphere, the land areas warming faster than the seas, and particularly the land areas at northern high latitudes during the cold season. Predictions indicate that the northern regions of North America and northern and central Asia will warm 40 per cent more than the global average. Conversely, south and south-east Asia in summer and southern South America in winter will warm less than the global mean. It also seems likely that surface temperatures will become more El Niño-like in the tropical Pacific Ocean, with the eastern tropical Pacific warming more than the western tropical Pacific. This differential warming should substantially alter the global pattern of evaporation and precipitation and cause radical changes of climate in most regions outside the tropical zone. The models suggest that the global average water-vapour concentration and precipitation will rise over the twenty-first century. After 2050, northern mid to high latitudes and Antarctica will have wetter winters. At low latitudes, some regions will become wetter and some drier. Large year-to-year variations in precipitation are likely in most regions where higher precipitation is predicted (see Table 8.5).

Table 8.5. Estimated confidence in observed and predicted extreme weather and climate events

Phenomenon	Confidence in observed changes (second half of twentieth century)(%)	Confidence in predicted changes (twenty-first century)(%)
Higher maximum temperatures and more hot days in nearly all land areas	66–90	90–99
Higher minimum temperatures, fewer cold days and frost days over nearly all land areas	90–99	90–99
Reduced daily temperature range over most land areas	90–99	90–99
Increase of heat index[a] over land areas	66–90, over many areas	90–99, over most areas
More intense precipitation events	66–99, over many Northern Hemisphere mid- and high-latitude land areas	90–99, over most areas
Increased summer continental drying and associated risk of drought	66–99, in a few areas	66–90, over most mid-latitude continental interiors (other areas lack consistent predictions)
Increase in tropical cyclone peak-wind intensities	Not observed in the few analyses available	66–90, over some areas
Increase in tropical cyclone mean and peak precipitation intensities	Insufficient data for assessment	66–90, over some areas

Note: [a] The heat index index is a measure of the combination of temperature and humidity effects on human comfort.

Source: Adapted from Houghton et al. (2001).

Conclusion

Climate influences the nature of places. Different climatic zones tend to foster particular types of soils, animals, plants, communities, agricultural systems and types of human habitation. The temperate gradient between the equator and poles drives global circulation of air. Climatic zones result from the general atmospheric circulation modified by the distribution of land and sea and the presence of lofty mountain ranges and plateaux. Mathematical general circulation models of varying degrees of sophistication successfully mimic features of real climates, past, present and future. Climates change over a wide range of timescales. Long-term climate changes taking millions of years produce climates of the geological past, which involve hothouse and icehouse episodes. Medium-term climate changes focus on orbital forcing producing climatic cycles lasting tens to hundreds of thousands of years. Within the cycles are bouts of abrupt change seen as Dansgaard–Oescher cycles and Heinrich events. Short-term climatic swings relate to solar forcing, lunar forcing, internal atmospheric dynamics and human-induced changes. The current phase of global warming, predicted to alter the nature of places considerably over the next century, is surely human-induced in part, but natural orbital cycles may play a substantial role.

Further reading

Barry, R.G and Chorley, R.J. (2003) *Atmosphere, Weather and Climate*, eighth edition. London: Routledge.

Burroughs, W. (ed.) (2003) *Climate: Into the 21st Century*. Cambridge: Cambridge University Press.

Fagan, B. (2002) *The Little Ice Age: How Climate Made History 1300–1850*. London: Basic Books

——(2004) *The Long Summer: How Climate Changed Civilization*. London: Granta Books.

Houghton, J.T. (2004) *Global Warming: The Complete Briefing*, third edition. Cambridge: Cambridge University Press.

Maslin, M. (2004) *Global Warming: A Very Short Introduction*. Oxford: Oxford University Press.

Rasmussen, E.M., Wang, X. and Ropelewski, C.F. (1990) The biennial component of ENSO variability. *Journal of Marine Systems* 1, 71–96.

References

Barnola, J.M., Raynaud, D., Korotkevich, Y.S. and Lorius, C. (1987) Vostok ice core provides 160,000-year record of atmospheric CO_2. *Nature* 329, 408–14.

Bjerknes, J. (1969) Atmospheric teleconnections from the equatorial Pacific. *Monthly Weather Review* 97, 163–72.

DeWeaver, E. and Nigam, S. (1995) Influence of mountain ranges on the mid-latitude atmospheric response to El Niño events. *Nature* 378, 706–8.

Dunn, G.E. (1940) Cyclogenesis in the tropical Atlantic. *Bulletin of the American Meteorological Society* 21, 215–29.

Eddy, J.A. (1977) The case of the missing sunspots. *Scientific American* 236, 80–92.

Elkibbi, M. and Rial, J.A. (2001) An outsider's review of the astronomical theory of the climate: is the eccentricity-driven insolation the main driver of the ice ages? *Earth-Science Reviews* 56, 161–77.

Hays, J.D., Imbrie, J. and Shackelton, N. J. (1976) Variations in the Earth's orbit: pacemaker of the ice ages. *Science* 194, 1121–32.

Hodell, D.A., Brenner, M., Curtis, J.H., and Guilderson, T. (2001) Solar forcing of drought frequency in the Maya lowlands. *Science* 292, 1367–70.

Houghton, J.T., Ding, Y., Griggs, D.J., Noquet, M., van der Linden, J.P., Dai, X., Maskell, K. and Johnson, C.A. (eds) (2001) *Climate Change 2001: The Scientific Basis: Contribution of Working Group I to the Third Assessment Report of the Intergovernmental Panel on Climate Change: The Scientific Basis.* Cambridge: Cambridge University Press and the Intergovernmental Panel on Climate Change.

Huggett, R.J. (1997) *Environmental Change: The Evolving Ecosphere.* London: Routledge.

Kaser, G. (1999) A review of the modern fluctuations of tropical glaciers. *Global and Planetary Change* 22, 93–103.

Kaser, G., Hardy, D.R., Mölg, T., Bradley, R.S. and. Hyera, T.M. (2004) Modern glacier retreat on Kilimanjaro as evidence of climate change: observations and facts. *International Journal of Climatology* 24, 329–39.

Köppen, W.P. (1931) *Grundriss der Klimakunde. Zweite, Verbesserte Auflage der Klimate der Edre.* Berlin: Walter de Gruyter.

Kukla, G. and Gavin, J. (2004) Milankovitch climate reinforcements. *Global and Planetary Change* 40, 27–48.

Muller, R.A. and MacDonald, G.J. (1995) Glacial cycles and orbital inclination. *Nature* 377, 107–8.

Namias, J. (1950) The index cycle and its role in the general circulation. *Journal of Meteorology* 17, 130–39.

Ovid (1955) *Metamorphoses*, translated by Mary M. Innes. Harmondsworth, Middlesex: Penguin Books.

Rampino, M.R. and Self, S. (1992) Volcanic winter and accelerated glaciation following the Toba super-eruption. *Nature* 359, 50–52.

Rampino, M.R., Self, S. and Stothers, R.B. (1988) Volcanic winters. *Annual Review of Earth and Planetary Sciences* 16, 73–99.

Richardson, L.F. (1922) *Weather Prediction by Numerical Process.* Cambridge: Cambridge University Press.

Riehl, H. (1954) *Tropical Meteorology.* New York and London: McGraw-Hill.

Robock, A. and Mass, C. (1982) The Mount St Helens volcanic eruption of 18 May 1980: large short-term surface temperature effects. *Science* 216, 628–30.

Ropelewski, C.F. and Halpert, M.S. (1987) Global and regional scale precipitation patterns associated with the El Niño/Southern Oscillation. *Monthly Weather Review* 115, 1606–26.

Washington, W.M. and Meehl, G.A. (1991) Characteristic of coupled atmosphere–ocean sensitivity experiments with different ocean formulations. In M.E. Schlesinger (ed.) *Greenhouse-gas-induced Climatic Change: A Critical Appraisal of Simulations and Observations*, pp. 79–110. Amsterdam: Elsevier.

9

Population

Graeme Hugo

Introduction

The twentieth century could justifiably be designated 'The Demographic Century'. It took more than a million years for the number of people to reach 1.8 billion by 1900, but over the next 100 years this number had increased over three times to reach 6.07 billion. The world will never see such a rapid growth of population again. The rate of increase rose from 0.5 per cent per annum between 1850 and 1900 to 2.06 in 1965–70 and had fallen to 1.4 per cent by 2000, and it is anticipated that global population will peak at 9.2 billion persons in 2075 (United Nations 2004a). These demographic shifts have been among the most remarkable and unanticipated events of the last century. This chapter examines shifts in the world's population and its changing pattern of distribution. It moves on to a consideration of the massive changes in the demographic processes – fertility, mortality and migration – which have underlain these shifts. The next section considers the major underlying drivers of these changes including economic changes, social shifts, environmental factors, health and disease, globalization and the increasing role of public policy. Some of the outcomes of recent and impending demographic change are then explored. Finally, some consideration is given to a range of future scenarios with respect to global population, and their implications discussed.

Population change

In 2004 the world's population stood at 6.5 billion and was increasing by 76 million persons per year (United Nations 2005a). Figure 9.1 shows that the bulk of the growth has occurred in recent times. Yet one of the most striking features of the contemporary demographic picture is the slowing down in the rate at which the global population is increasing. The length of time it took to add an extra billion to the world population telescoped until 1999, but the rate of which this occurred began to decline after 1974 (Table 9.1). Each successive billion added in the twenty-first century will take an increasing number of years as population growth slows down. This slowing rate of growth and the time taken to

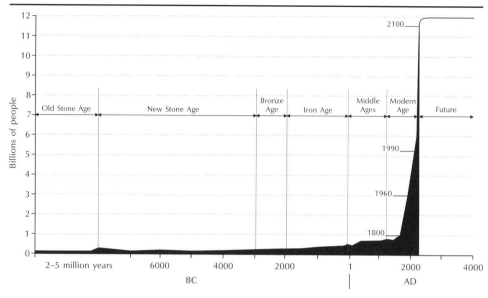

Figure 9.1. World population growth through history.
Source: Population Reference Bureau (2004a).

Table 9.1. World population growth

World population reached	*It is expected to reach*
1 billion in 1804	7 billion in 2012 (13 years later)
2 billion in 1927 (123 years later)	8 billion in 2027 (15 years later)
3 billion in 1960 (33 years later)	9 billion in 2050 (23 years later)
4 billion in 1974 (14 years later)	
5 billion in 1987 (13 years later)	
6 billion in 1999 (12 years later)	

Source: *Populi* (December 1998), p. 3; United Nations (2005a, 2005b).

achieve stability will be of critical importance to the world in the twenty-first century. The changing pace of population over the last century depicted in Table 9.2 shows that the third quarter of the twentieth century saw a sharp increase in the rate of population growth as mortality rates declined and fertility remained high in line with traditional demographic transition theory, the descriptive version of which originated with Notestein in 1945. This postulated that in the long term populations move from high stability (high mortality and fertility) through to low stability (low mortality and fertility). This transition involves a period with high population growth (reducing mortality, continuing high fertility) and then a period of reducing population growth (reducing mortality and fertility). This model is depicted in Figure 9.2.

The peak growth period for the global population saw the publication of a number of books such as Ehrlich's (1968) *The Population Bomb*, which depicted the apocalyptic results

Table 9.2. World population: per annum growth rates, 1900–50 to 2000–5

1900–50	0.85
1950–65	1.79
1965–70	2.06
1975–80	1.73
1985–90	1.74
1995–2000	1.35
2000–5	1.21

Source: United Nations (2005b).

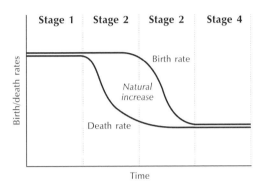

Figure 9.2. Stages of the demographic transition.

of a continuation of such rapid rates of population growth. However, no contemporary writers foresaw the 40 per cent reduction in the annual population growth rate between 1965–70 and 2000–2005.

While 1963–64 was the fulcrum period of change, the annual increment of population of the globe continued to increase. This was because of *demographic momentum* whereby population continues to increase even after fertility declines because numbers of women of child-bearing age continue to grow. Hence, while the number of babies per woman falls, this is affected by the number of woman bearing children. The annual increment to the global population peaked at 87.4 million in 1989–90 but thereafter started to fall (Figure 9.3).

Before analysing the processes which have brought about these far-reaching changes. it is necessary to point out the wide variations between different parts of the world. Over the period 1900–1950 a third of the global population lived in More Developed Countries (MDCs), but in the subsequent half-century this proportion fell to 19 per cent (Table 9.3). Population growth rates in the less developed and more developed worlds were similar up to 1950; subsequently the gap between them has grown. Indeed, 90 per cent of the population growth in the world between 1950 and 2004 occurred in Less Developed Countries (LDCs). Moreover, there have been significant changes in regional components of this growth. Europe's share of global population has fallen significantly whilst North America and Oceania increased their share of global population up to 1950, with a subsequent decline. In LDCs,

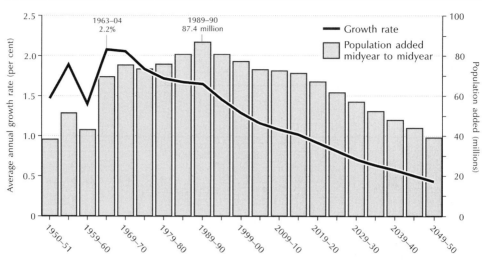

Figure 9.3. Annual additions and the annual growth rate of global populations, 1950–2050.
Source: US Census Bureau (2004: 15).

Table 9.3. Population changes in major world regions, 1900, 1950 and 2004

	1900		1950		2004	
	Million	%	Million	%	Million	%
World	1,650	100	2,519	100	6,396	100
More developed	539	33	813	32	1,206	19
Europe	408	25	547	22	728	11
North America	82	5	172	7	326	5
Japan, Australia and New Zealand	49	3	97	4	151	2
Less developed	1,111	67	1,706	68	5,190	81
Africa	133	8	221	9	885	14
Asia and Oceania	904	55	1,315	52	3,756	59
Latin America and Caribbean	74	4	167	7	549	9

Source: United Nations 2003a; Population Reference Bureau 2004a.

Asia is dominant increasing its share of global population. The fastest growth occurred in Africa between 1950 and 2004 when its population quadrupled.

These differentials are to become more marked over the next few decades. It is anticipated that over the 2004–50 period, the more developed world's share of the population will fall from 18.6 to 13.6 per cent, and in Europe it will fall from 11.4 to 7.2 per cent. On the other hand, in 2004, one in 12 global citizens (13.8 per cent) lived in Africa and by 2050 it will be more than one in five (20.9 per cent). Most global population growth over the 2004–50 period (98.9 per cent) will be in LDCs (Figure 9.4). By 2050 the 38.8 million increment in world population will almost all stem from LDCs with around two-thirds from Africa. It is also notable that 37.4 per cent of the world's population now live in China and India. The

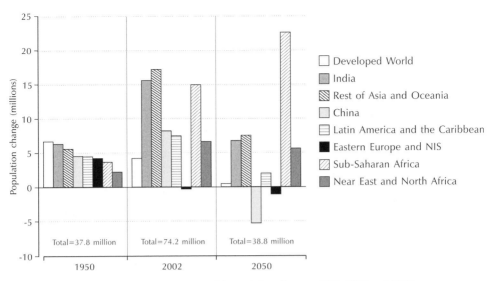

Figure 9.4. Regional contributions to net world population change: 1950, 2002 and 2050.
Source: US Census Bureau (2004: 16).

United Nations (2005c: 2) projects that 51 developed countries are expected to have a lower population in 2050 than in 2005 but the population of the 50 least developed nations will more than double from 0.8 to 1.7 billion. Half of the projected increase will be accounted for by nine countries – India, Pakistan, Nigeria, the Democratic Republic of Congo, Bangladesh, Uganda, USA, Ethiopia and China.

Natural increase – mortality

At the global level, population change is a function of fertility and mortality. It is perhaps one of the great achievements of the last half-century that global life expectancy[1] increased from 47 in 1950–55 to 65 in 2000–2005, with further projected increases to 75 years by 2050. However, as one would expect, there is considerable variation both between and within countries in the level of mortality. Some 22.4 years have been added to life expectancy in less developed nations. While the improvement was less in MDCs (9.7 years), life expectancy increased from 66.1 to 75.8. By 2050 life expectancy is expected to be 82 in MDCs; that in the least developed countries will increase to 67, while that in the remainder of less developed countries is projected to rise to 76 years.

The considerable variation between countries is apparent in Figure 9.5. Most striking are the persistent low levels of life expectancy in sub-Saharan Africa, where the impacts of low income are exacerbated by high prevalence of HIV/AIDS. In contrast, there are high levels of life expectancy in Japan (81.9 years), Singapore (78.6 years) and Taiwan (76.0 years). Mortality has actually increased in Eastern Europe, especially the Russian Federation and the Ukraine. The inter-country variation in life expectancy in world regions is shown in Figure 9.6 and contrasted with WHO goals for improvement in life expectancy. Again the distinctive situation in Africa is strongly in evidence. Mortality in Africa is increasing in countries most affected by HIV/AIDS, with life expectancy plummeting in Southern Africa. As a

133

result, in Botswana, Lesotho and Swaziland the population is projected to decrease over the next twenty years (United Nations 2005c: 4).

Within countries, too, there are substantial variations. In most countries life expectancy is greater in urban than in rural areas, especially in LDCs where urban/rural differences in access to health services are greater. In a majority of countries women outlive men, but there are important exceptions in LDCs where there is gender differentiation in access to food, health services and education. There are important socio-economic differentials, especially in LDCs with weak national provision of health services. Other differences exist between ethnic groups and regions within countries.

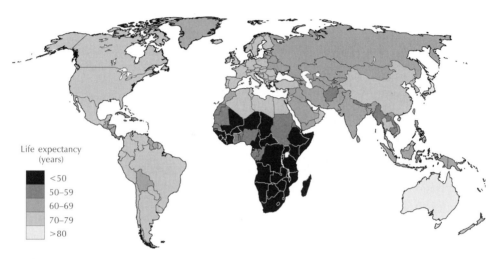

Figure 9.5. Life expectancy at birth across the globe, 2002.
Source: US Census Bureau (2004: 24).

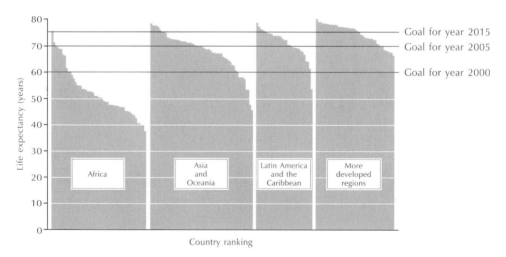

Figure 9.6. Life expectancy at birth.
Source: United Nations Population Division.

In MDCs mortality has declined as a result of health-related interventions such as advances in medical and pharmaceutical technology, immunization and improved access to health services, and lifestyle shifts such as reduction in smoking and increased levels of exercise. Most commentators predict that life expectancy will continue to steadily increase in MDCs, although there has been a suggestion that increasing obesity, especially among children, may reverse this trend (Olshansky *et al.* 2005). In LDCs large-scale health interventions, such as improvement in water supply, immunization and the control of infectious disease, and personal factors, such as better education and improved nutrition, have reduced fertility. However, access to health services remains one of the main causes of the MDC/LDC mortality inequality.

HIV/AIDS has significant regional impacts on mortality. Between 1981, when the first AIDS diagnosis was made, and 2004, some 20 million people had died from AIDS-related illnesses and another 40 million people were living with HIV (United Nations 2005c: 5). Sub-Saharan Africa has the highest rates of infection with 3 million new infections in 2004, although some parts of Asia and Eastern Europe have faster growing rates of infection from lower base levels (Population Reference Bureau 2004b). It is estimated that 15 million children worldwide have lost one or both parents to HIV/AIDS (United Nations 2005c: 6) and AIDS is now the fourth leading cause of death worldwide. It is difficult to predict the future scale and impact of HIV/AIDS, owing to complex interrelations between the disease with deprivation, disempowerment and low levels of health service provision. The prevalence of HIV is nine times higher in LDCs than MDCs. The United Nations (2005c) projects that Africa's population in 2050 will be 1 billion – 350 million less than it would have been without HIV/AIDS.

Natural increase – fertility

In 2004 the global Total Fertility Rate[2] (TFR) was 2.65 children per woman, about half the level which prevailed in 1950–55 – a decline which no commentator of the 1950s, 1960s and early 1970s had anticipated. This represents a massive shift in behaviour reflecting profound social and economic change. While there has been a fertility decline in virtually all of the world's nations, the patterns have varied (see Figure 9.7). In most developed countries the TFR fell below replacement level in the 1970s, stabilizing in some nations but falling even further in others. This has contributed to substantial ageing and concern with future labour force numbers and the ratio to the dependent aged population they support. It has been projected that in order to maintain the current workforce size in the European Union there would need to be an annual net migration of 949,000 (United Nations 2000). Accordingly, several MDCs have initiated programmes to lift fertility and the United Nations (2005c: 3) has assumed that the TFR in MDCs will rise from 1.56 in 2004 to 1.84 in 2045–50. The reasons for the decline of fertility reflect shifts in the role and status of women, changes in family structure and functioning, massive economic and social change, a changing policy environment and a revolution in consumerism.

However, it is the change which has occurred in LDCs which has been the most dramatic. Figure 9.7 shows how fertility has more than halved across Asia and Latin America over the last half-century, with substantial declines in the last 30 years. In Africa the fall in fertility came later, so the reduction has been less.

Notestein (1945) provided the first explanations for the changes in mortality and fertility. He argued that the reason why fertility was high in pre-transitional societies was to counteract high mortality. Fertility remained high when mortality declined because of the cultural

135

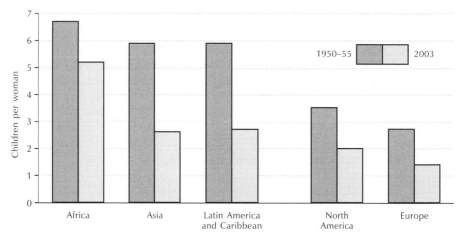

Figure 9.7. Fertility levels in major world regions, 1950 and 2003.
Source: Population Reference Bureau (2004b: 10).

props which had developed to support high fertility. The latter would only be eroded with economic development and hence fell long after mortality had begun to decline. For the next three decades it was believed that fertility would only decline if there were substantial increases in economic development reflected in large GDP per capita increases. A corollary was that it was a considerable waste of time to initiate family planning programmes unless countries had experienced 'economic take-off' and had increasing GNP per capita (Mamdani 1972). This orthodoxy was challenged in the 1970s when historical demographic study showed there was not necessarily a correlation between economic development and fertility decline (Coale 1973). Moreover, in some LDCs fertility began to decline without significant improvements in economic development (Caldwell 1976). Hence, demographers introduced new explanations for fertility decline in which economic development was a sufficient, but not necessary, condition for fertility decline. Social changes which involved substantial shifts in the structure and functioning of families and in the roles and status of women were particularly crucial in initiating fertility decline. The role of the spread of universal education and mass media were fundamental in bringing this about.

This shift in thinking about the causes of fertility decline had the important effect that family planning programmes could be anticipated to influence fertility even before economic development. Hence, national governments and development assistance in LDCs were encouraged to develop programmes, and these undoubtedly contributed to subsequent fertility decline. There was a massive increase in the proportion of women who use modern forms of contraception (see Figure 9.8).

The experience of fertility decline has varied according to economic development differentials and cultural and religious variations. Africa stands out as a region of high fertility (see Figure 9.9). The Middle East also has high fertility despite high economic status, as a result of cultural factors. High levels of fertility are expected by the United Nations (2005c: 2) to produce a tripling of national population in Afghanistan, Burkina Faso, Burundi, Chad, Congo, the Democratic Republic of Congo, Timor Leste, Guinea-Bissau, Liberia, Mali, Nigeria and Uganda. Countries with high fertility, all in LDCs, account for 10 per cent of the world's population. In contrast, Figure 9.9 shows that many LDCs have below replacement level – indeed 23 such countries account for 25 per cent of the global population. The world's largest nation, China, had a TFR in 2000–2005 of 1.7. All MDCs except Albania had below replacement level fertility. Within nations too there are significant fertility differentials between urban and rural communities, ethnic groups, religious groups and social class categories.

The course that fertility takes over the next few decades is of profound significance. Results of United Nations population projections based on four different fertility scenarios are presented in Table 9.4. A very wide range of outcomes are possible. The huge variations indicate the sensitivity of projections to shifts in fertility and the critical importance of government action in shaping the world's future population. The medium fertility scenario sees

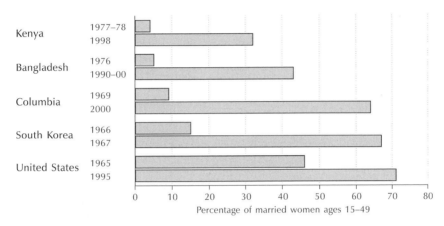

Figure 9.8. The reproductive revolution increase in modern contraceptive use in selected countries, 1960–2000.
Source: Population Reference Bureau (2004b: 8).

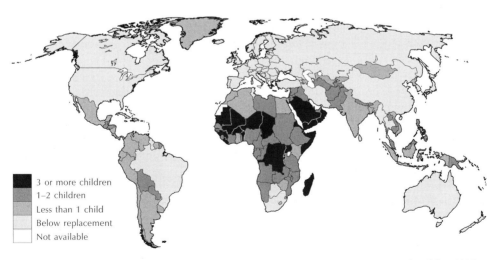

Figure 9.9. Total fertility rate relative to the replacement level for each country across the globe: 2002.
Source: US Census Bureau (2004: 24).

137

Table 9.4. World population projections based on four scenarios, 2000–2050 (in billions)

Year	Fertility scenarios			
	Medium	High	Low	Constant
2000	6.1	6.1	6.1	6.1
2050	9.1	10.6	7.7	11.7

Source: United Nations 2003b, 2005b.

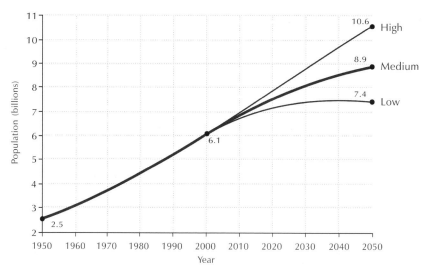

Figure 9.10. Estimated world population, 1950–2000, and projections: 2000–2050.
Source: United Nations (2004a: 5).

the world's population growing, stabilizing in 2100 and declining to 8.5 billion in 2150, then stabilizing again at around 9 billion persons around 2300. The annual population increment declined from its peak of 86 million in 1985–90 to 74 million in 2002. The rate of annual population growth will decline from a present level of 1.19 per cent to 0.42 per cent in 2045 to 2050.

Although the high and low fertility scenarios differ by just one child per couple, the size of the world population in 2150 would range from 3.9 billion persons to 16.7 billion! The crucial importance of maintaining fertility decline is evident in Figure 9.10, which shows the different trajectories of future population growth with different fertility levels.

International migration

One of the most dramatic changes in global population in the last two decades has been with respect to international migration. Before the late 1980s only a handful of nations had populations growing as a result of international migration – the traditional migration countries (Canada, United States and Australia) and those in the global south experiencing an influx of refugees. However, there has been a dramatic change in global migration trends. The first issue is that migration has increased greatly in scale and diversity. The United Nations (2002) estimated that between 1995 and 2000 MDCs received a 12 million net migration gain from less developed nations. Of the 2.3 million net gains per year, 1.4 million were in North America and 800,000 in Europe. One of the key results of these changes has been the rapid growth of communities of expatriates from less developed nations residing in more developed nations (see Figure 9.11). The censuses counted 46 million expatriates in OECD nations born outside of Europe and North America (Dumont and Lemaitre 2005). That these official figures represent only part of the expatriate population from south countries is reflected in Table 9.5, which shows estimates of the size of the diaspora of some of the larger countries.

In addition to the more or less permanent communities of expatriates in developed countries, there is also large-scale circulation of workers from less developed to more developed nations. High skilled, highly paid transnationals operating in an international labour market can be distinguished from low paid, lower skilled groups needed in labour markets in countries where fertility has fallen below replacement level and where local labour forces are inadequate (Castles and Miller 1998). Asia is the case *par excellence* here: at any one time over 20 million Asians are working on a temporary basis in more developed nations, especially in the Middle East and other Asian nations such as Japan, Singapore, Malaysia, Thailand, Hong Kong, Taiwan, Brunei and Korea.

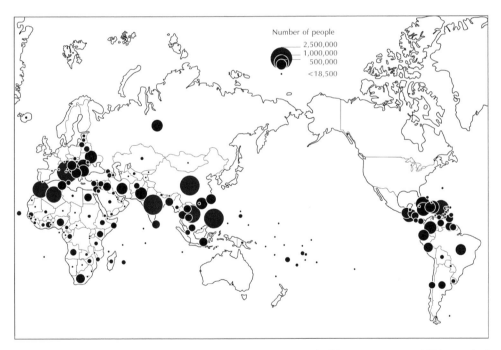

Figure 9.11. Persons born in 'South' nations enumerated in OECD nations at the 2000 round of censuses.

Source: OECD database on immigrants and expatriates, http://www.oecd.org/documents/51/0,2340,en _2649_33931_34063_91-1_1_1_1.–.html

Note that this represents a significant underestimate because data were not available for all OECD nations including some significant immigrant nations (e.g. Italy), and in most cases there was a significant under-enumeration of the overseas-born.

Table 9.5. National diasporas in relation to resident national populations

Country	Expatriates (millions)	Per cent of national population
Philippines	7.5	9.0
India	20	1.9
Pakistan	4	2.8
China	30–40	2.9
Mexico	19[a]	19
Vietnam	3	3.6

Note: [a] Mexican diaspora in the USA.

Source: Ministry of External Affairs, India, http://indiandiaspora.nic.in; Naseem 1998; Sahoo 2002; Gutièrrez 1999; Dimzon 2005; Nguyen Anh 2005.

While total numbers of international migrants have increased, 2004 saw the number of refugees recognized by the UNHCR (2005) decline to 9 million – the lowest figure for more than a quarter of a century. This does not mean, however, that forced migration reduced in significance since the number of 'people of concern' to UNHCR increased from 17 million in 2003 to 19 million in 2004. Much of the difference was made up of internally displaced persons (IDPs). Moreover, the ILO has reported that there are 12.3 million forced labourers in 'slave-like' situations, most in LDCs (*Asian Migration News*, 15–31 May 2005) and often associated with trafficking. Forced migration remains a substantial and volatile element in global migration.

It has been estimated that 49 per cent of international migrants are women (United Nations 2004b) of whom 10 per cent are refugees; 75 per cent of these travel with children (*Asian Migration News*, 1–15 March 2005). The significance of female migration has increased in recent decades and the proportion of women moving independently has also increased. While the diversity of female migration is increasing, female migrants tend to be more concentrated in particular occupations than their male counterparts. There has been a substantial increase in the numbers of women moving as 'mail order brides', especially out of Asian countries like the Philippines, Thailand and Vietnam. Women migrants are disproportionately vulnerable to exploitation in occupations such as housemaids, carers or sex workers.

These developments have resulted in a proliferation of social networks linking more and less developed countries. Such networks encourage and facilitate further migration and are significant conduits for two-way flows of money, information, goods, ideas and information. Modern information and communication technology has made it possible to maintain regular contact between diaspora and home countries. Moreover, cheaper and quicker international travel has made it possible for people to be transnational and move easily between countries, whilst maintaining a strong presence in more than a single country and keeping a significant stake in diaspora and origin.

The population of MDCs would have begun to decline in 2003 were it not for migration from the south. The labour markets of those nations have benefited from an influx of both skilled and unskilled workers, but there is an increasing focus of immigration policy on recruitment of skilled migrants and on excluding unskilled migrants. Some 2 million of 100 million tertiary students around the world study outside their native country, and the bulk of these are south–north migrants. While such migration has the potential to enhance human capital in LDCs there is a growing nexus between student migration and permanent settlement in north countries.

While aggregate numbers are significant it is also important to look at *who* moves. Is the migration especially selective of the 'brightest and the best', who are of critical importance in providing leadership as well as specific skills in the origin country's efforts to develop? Moreover, losses can be concentrated in particular skill areas that can impinge negatively on the well-being of origin populations as well as development potential. Particularly significant here is the net loss of doctors, nurses and other health personnel from south countries. With ageing OECD populations there have been shortages of medical workers and consequent recruitment of people with these skills from developing countries. In Australia, for example, in 2001, 21.7 per cent of the medical workforce were born in Asia, Africa and the Middle East compared with only 7.8 per cent of all workers (Hugo 2005a).

The global south faces a real dilemma with respect to the emigration of skilled persons and students. On the one hand, such movement can contribute to development while, on the other hand, large numbers never return. Human rights considerations and global realities make it impossible to prevent emigration. Nevertheless, the number of less and least developed nations that reported to the United Nations that they had policies to reduce emigration increased from 17 in 1976 to 43 in 2003 (United Nations 2004c: 47).

The question of remittances sent home by migrants has become an important issue in development discourse (Terry and Wilson 2005). Remittances have been associated with migration from time immemorial but have suddenly gained the attention of development economists. There has been a new appreciation of the scale of transfers, which were in the past often dismissed as peripheral and of limited effect. Only a fraction of total global remittances are ever counted in official statistics. The level of official global remittances has expanded exponentially with the increase in migration and increasing extent to which remittances flow through official channels. The latest estimates by the International Monetary Fund and the World Bank put global remittances at US $130 billion, $79 billion of which go to developing nations, while the International Organization of Migration estimates that if transfers through informal channels are included, remittances could be as high as $300 billion (*Asian Migration News*, 16–31 January 2005). Remittances have long been larger than Foreign Development Assistance (FDA) and probably now are larger than Foreign Direct Investment (FDI) in less developed countries (Figure 9.12).

In the past, the impact of remittances on development has been dismissed because field evidence indicated that the most were not invested in 'productive' enterprises but are spent on consumption, meeting basic needs and the building and refurbishment of houses. However, it has been shown (Taylor *et al.* 1996) that a dollar spent in such activity has multiplier effects which ripple through local and regional economies, having significant impacts on poverty and encouraging development.

There has also been a realization that remittances are effective in poverty reduction at a grassroots level: because they are passed directly from the migrant and received by families in less developed countries, they can be readily used to improve the situation of those people. In contrast, FDI and FDA are mediated by an array of institutions which can dilute local grassroots impacts. Hence, of all south–north financial flows, remittances have the greatest impact on everyday lives of ordinary people. In addition, the World Bank (2006) has demonstrated that remittances are often the means whereby people in less developed nations are introduced to formal financial institutions.

Migrants from the south are not drawn randomly from the entire population, so the impact of remittances tends also to be concentrated in particular parts of a country where its effect is amplified. These are often peripheral areas where remittances are the only source of foreign exchange and of capital inflow for development. With an increasing focus on

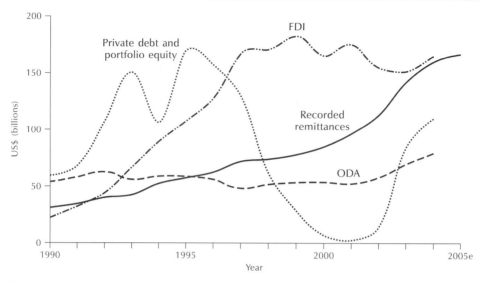

Figure 9.12. Resource flows to developing countries (in billions of US$).
Source: After Bridi (2005).

regional and decentralized development, there has been an enhanced realization of the significance of remittances.

There is a growing realization that the developmental effects of migration are complex. Networks set up by migrants between their destination and origin countries can be conduits for more than remittances and the developmental implications of other flows need to be considered. As Lucas (2001: n.p.) points out, 'a highly skilled diaspora may play several important roles in promoting development at home'.

A fundamental underlying issue concerns the growing mismatch between citizen populations and populations residing within their national boundaries. For some countries, their diaspora is a substantial and significant part of their citizenry and their involvement in national development is only part of a wider project of incorporation in the mainstream of national life.

One of the most prominent ways that diasporic communities influence development at home lies in promoting FDI from their new home to the origin country. Lucas (2001: i) maintains that the diaspora 'can act as middlemen enhancing information flows, lowering reputation barriers and enforcing capital arrangements resulting in an expansion of capital inflows from foreigners as well as from the diaspora and of trade links too'.

Another role of the diaspora is that they can be bridgeheads for better economic links with the home nation. Korean Americans were the entry points for the successful penetration of the United States market by Korean car, electronics and white goods manufacturers. Canadian-based studies have shown that a doubling of skilled migration from Asia saw a 74 per cent increase in Asian imports to Canada (Head and Reis 1998; Lucas 2001).

Diaspora networks have also become important in transmitting information in both formal and informal ways. Lucas (2001: 22) has shown how professionals in origin and destination countries maintain strong links so that ideas flow freely in both directions. In Taiwan, meetings of local and diasporic scientists are held. In the scientific world, flows of information are of utmost significance, and it may be that diaspora can play a role in technology transfers.

Transnational networks may also be vehicles for so-called 'social remittances'. There is some evidence that diaspora may be playing an important role in reshaping individual and social preferences, social norms and expectations in countries of origin (Kapur 2001: 270). The potential is there for the diffusion of attitudes towards education, change and innovation which could be positive for development. Kapur (2001: 273) credits the Indian diaspora with helping 'unleash an entrepreneurial culture in a country whose cultural (and later bureaucratic) ethos was long regarded as inimical to capitalism'.

One of the enduring myths of south–north migration is that there is an overwhelming desire for people from the south to relocate permanently to the north. In fact many migrants want to retain valued aspects of their heritage and to return to their homelands. One of the features of all diaspora is return migration to the homeland, although its incidence varies greatly. The extent of circularity in international migration is underestimated. Indeed, it has been argued that return migration is often constrained by destination country policies which make frequent return difficult (Hugo 2005b). There can be significant dividends to the home country if expatriates return, especially when they are skilled in areas in demand in the origin country labour market. They have extended their knowledge and experience and return with a network of overseas contacts which can benefit work at home. There would seem to be scope to introduce programmes that facilitate and encourage the return migration of skilled migrants. The role of government here is to facilitate. Certainly there may be scope for a government programme to provide some assistance to institutions and businesses that can make a strong case for 'bringing home' outstanding expatriate scientists, innovators and business people.

Changing age composition

The age composition of a population is of crucial significance since demands and needs for virtually all goods and services vary with age. Moreover, the proportion of the population in the economically active ages can influence the productivity and prosperity of nations. Figure 9.13 contrasts the age structure of a high fertility, high mortality region (West Africa) to that of a low fertility, low mortality region (Western Europe). In West Africa the concentration in young ages presents considerable challenges for the provision of education and places great pressure on labour markets. In contrast, in Western Europe the numbers entering school and workforce are reducing as the effects of below replacement fertility are felt, but the numbers poised to enter the older age groups are very large, creating challenges for health and aged support systems.

In West Africa numbers of women aged 15–49 will more than treble over the 2000–2050 period, while in Western Europe there will be a decline (Figure 9.14). Even if women in West Africa significantly reduce the number of children they bear, the increase in the number of women having children will ensure a continued increase in population. Contrarily, in Western Europe a reduction in the number of women of childbearing age, together with low fertility, ensures a 'natural decrease' in population. In West Africa the workforce will continue to grow rapidly, with each cohort adding more young people to the workforce. The opposite will apply in Western Europe. Some authors (Xenos 2001) have indicated that LDCs will benefit from population growth by having a younger and more productive workforce during this period. To take advantage of this demographic dividend requires nations to have education and labour market policies which allow young people to achieve their potential. The significance of the 'youth bulge' in assisting economic development has been especially demonstrated with respect to Asia (Hugo 2005c).

The dramatic shift which is occurring in global age structure is depicted in Table 9.6. There are clearly substantial differences between LDCs and MDCs. In contrast, the trends in

143

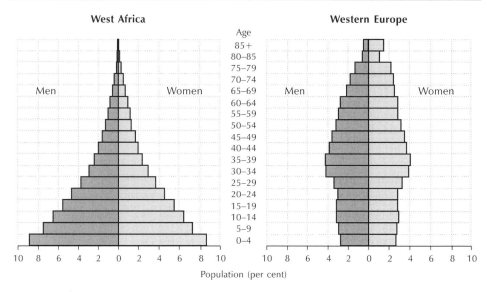

Figure 9.13. Age and sex profile for West Africa and Western Europe, 2000.
Source: Population Reference Bureau (2004b: 13).

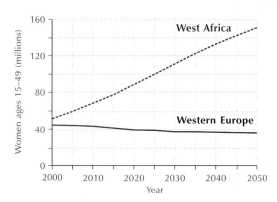

Figure 9.14. Women of childbearing age in Western Europe and West Africa, projected 2000–2050.
Source: Population Reference Bureau (2004b: 14).

Table 9.6. World population: percentages aged 0–14 and 65 years and over, 1970, 2004 and projected 2050

| | 0–14 | | | 65+ | | |
	1970	*2004*	*2050*	*1970*	*2004*	*2050*
World	37	30	20	6	7	16
Less developed countries	42	33	21	5	5	14
More developed countries	26	17	16	16	15	26

Source: United Nations 2003a; Population Reference Bureau 2004a.

the population in the 65+ age group show substantial increases in both LDCs and MDCs over the next 50 years after quite limited change between 1970 and 2004. The proportion aged 65+ will almost treble over the next 50 years in LDCs, and more than a quarter of MDC residents will be aged 65 or over by 2050. This presents a significant challenge for policy makers, despite measures to stabilize or increase fertility to ameliorate ageing.

Others are looking to migration, increasing the age of retirement, increasing labour force participation in groups currently with low levels of engagement. Many nations face greatly increased demand for health and aged care services. The median age of the world population will rise from 25.4 years in 1995 to 36.5 years in 2050 to 42.9 years by 2150. The proportion of the global population aged under 15 years will decline from 31 per cent in 1995 to 17 per cent by 2150, while the proportion aged 60 and over will increase from 9 to 30 per cent. Those aged over 80 will grow from 61 million in 1995 to 320 million in 2050. The proportion of the world's population aged 65 years and over is increasing at an unprecedented rate.

The variations between nations with respect to age structure are substantial. This is apparent in Figure 9.15 which shows that Africa and, to a lesser extent, part of Asia and Latin America, have greater concentration of youth in their population. Similar spatial patterns apply to the 0–14 age group, whereas the inverse pattern applies for the 65+ age group.

Population distribution within nations

One of the major global demographic shifts of recent decades has been an exponential increase in personal mobility. In MDCs there has been little change in the extent to which people move house. However, the level and complexity of non-permanent migration has increased massively. Commuting distances have increased. Circular migration between place of residence and place of work has also increased. Non-work-related circular migration has also grown, evidenced by an increase, for example, in the numbers of 'snowbirding' retirees

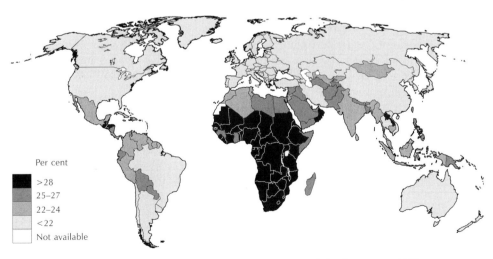

Figure 9.15. Youth (ages 15–29) as a percentage of the total population by country, 2025.
Source: US Census Bureau (2004: 42).

moving between north and south in the United States to winter in warmer southern cities, and retiree 'grey nomads' in Australia on extended camping/caravanning trips around the continent. In LDCs the changes have been even more dramatic, with significant increases in the extent to which people move on a permanent basis. Movers here often spend considerable periods working at destinations far removed from their 'permanent' residences. The origins are usually rural, closely settled areas and the destinations are often cities or mining, plantation and extensive agriculture areas in relatively remote, less densely settled areas. It is difficult to quantify this phenomenon because it is not detected in census and other standard population data collections.

What impact has this massive increase in mobility had on population distribution patterns? Globally the most striking trend has been in increasing urbanization. Table 9.7 shows that over the 1950–2000 period the proportion of the world's citizens living in urban areas increased from 29.7 to 47 per cent, and by 2010 the majority of people will reside in urban areas. While increasing urbanization has been substantial in MDCs, it has been even more rapid in LDCs and the pattern will continue over the next three decades so that by 2030, 60 per cent of all world citizens will live in urban areas. There are some difficulties, however, in using a rural–urban dichotomy to describe national settlement systems – it is a very blunt instrument to capture the complexity of evolving and changing patterns of human settlement. Countries vary greatly in the way they define urban areas and people move more frequently, blurring rural and urban differences (Champion and Hugo 2004).

In MDCs the 1970s saw a widespread phenomenon of counter-urbanization described in Chapter 32, whereby non-metropolitan populations grew faster than metropolitan populations (Champion 1989). This process has become more muted over subsequent decades and more geographically concentrated in particular non-metropolitan areas that are ecologically favourable (coasts, river areas, etc.) or are just beyond the fringes of major cities. In many OECD countries the major metropolitan areas are predominantly growing through net overseas migration gains and are experiencing net internal migration losses of all but the young adult ages (Frey 1994, 1995a, 1995b). Developments in transport, communication and information technology have made it possible for people living well beyond large cities to maintain substantial linkages with these cities. Complex patterns of linkages between cities are another important element of the contemporary settlement system in MDCs (Bourne and Simmons 2004; Champion 1997).

In LDCs one of the major developments has been the emergence of megacities with more than 10 million inhabitants that have grown to envelop surrounding rural areas and nearby smaller cities so that they take on a multi-nucleated nature. Asia currently has 11 of the world's cities with more than 10 million people (United Nations 2004d). The role of these cities in the development of their nations and linking them to the outside world is very

Table 9.7. World population: percentage of the population living in urban areas, 1950 to 2000 and projected, 2030

	1950	*2000*	*2030*
World	29.7	47.0	60.3
More developed regions	54.9	76.0	83.5
Less developed regions	17.8	39.9	56.2

Note: Almost all of global population increase between 2000 and 2030 will be absorbed by LDC urban areas whose population will increase from 1.9 to 3.9 billion.

Source: United Nations 2004d.

significant (Jones 2004). However, the majority of LDC urban populations live in smaller and medium-sized towns and cities. Nevertheless, it is significant that 90 per cent of global population growth over the next forty years will be in the urban areas of less developed countries.

Population policy

Policy intervention is playing an increasing role in shaping population trends. Efforts by government to influence the size and distribution of national populations have increased. Policy can and does influence the trajectory of population change. The United Nations (2004a) regularly polls nations regarding their views on, and policies regarding, population. Between 1976 and 2003 the proportion of nations having no policy interventions to influence the rate of population growth fell from 55 to 38 per cent, indicating an increasing recognition by government of the importance of population policy. In LDCs the proportion with policies to *reduce* rates of population growth increased from 34 to 51 per cent over this period, while in least development nations the change was even more pronounced, increasing from 14 to 67 per cent of countries. Contrastingly, in MDCs the proportion of nations with policies to *raise* their rate of population growth or maintain their current rate of population growth has doubled from 24 to 48 per cent (United Nations 2004a: 20).

Some of the most substantial policy interventions have come in the area of fertility where policies and programmes are becoming increasingly widespread. Figure 9.16 shows the number of countries which have policies designed to influence fertility. The percentage of nations not having any policy intervention on fertility almost halved between 1976 and 2003. Particularly striking is the increase from 27 to 43 per cent for countries with policies directed at reducing fertility. The introduction of family planning programmes has seen the median prevalence of use of contraception among women currently married or in union in developing countries increase from 27 per cent in the 1970s to 40 per cent in the 1950s (United Nations, 2004b). By 2001, 92 per cent of all governments supported family planning

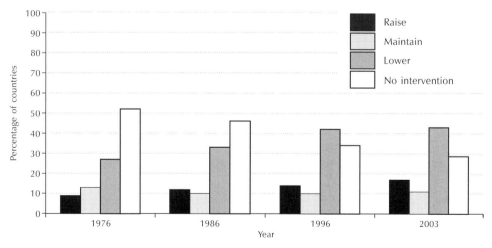

Figure 9.16. Government policies on the level of fertility, 1976–2003.
Source: United Nations (2004a).

programmes and the distribution of contraceptives, either directly through government facilities or indirectly by supporting the activities of non-governmental organizations such as family planning associations. The increasing influence of government policies to reduce fertility has not been without difficulty (e.g. see Hull 2005). Some programmes have been criticized for infringing the human rights of women. Others have been criticized for not taking sufficiently into consideration the individual situations of women, and as a result there has been a shift away from distribution of contraceptives to programmes more oriented to wider reproductive health of women. Funding from overseas development sources has been unreliable due to periodic intervention by conservative forces stopping money being directed to family programmes. In some nations cultural and religious barriers have militated against the introduction of family planning programmes.

Bongaarts (1994) has summarized the main interventions which are required in LDCs if the maximum demographic impact is to be achieved. These include reducing the number of unwanted pregnancies through continued support of family planning programmes; reducing the underlying demand for large families through investment in human development; and slowing down the momentum of population growth through raising the average age of child bearing and reducing family size.

There have been massive achievements in reducing fertility levels and population growth in LDCs but there is a danger that this success will breed complacency. Continued political and resource commitment is required if the transition to global population stability is to be achieved as quickly as possible. Bongaarts (1998) maintains that despite the achievements of lower fertility, population growth in developing countries remains a major problem and will continue to hamper ongoing efforts to reduce poverty and achieve sustainable development. As Gelbard et al. (1999: 40) have pointed out:

> One of the greatest success stories of the 20th century has been the dramatic decline in child bearing brought about by investments in family planning and other health programmes, in education and in greater social and economic opportunities, especially for women. In the 1990s, the world community made financial and program commitments to continue investments in these areas. Both the future size of the world's population and the quality of people's lives will be closely linked to the extent to which these commitments are met.

Turning to MDCs, Figure 9.16 shows that the proportion of nations with policies designed to increase fertility has doubled between 1976 and 2003. Fertility trends have major implications for future growth (or decline) of population and labour forces. Fears of impending population decrease and imbalance in age structure have been especially strong in Europe. The United Nations (2000: 6) has projected that 33 nations will experience population decline over the 1995–2005 period.

Overall these countries would have 127.3 million fewer inhabitants in 2050 than in 1995. The largest declines are anticipated to occur in the Russian Federation (25.7 million), Japan (21.8), Italy (16.1), Ukraine (11.1), Spain (9.4), Germany (8.9) and Romania (5.9). Among the EU nations, only Ireland and France are *not* anticipated to decline in population between 1995 and 2050.

An important dimension of the anticipated population decline is that it will be greatest among the economically active. Overall in MDCs over the 2000–2050 period there will only be a slight overall decline in population (-0.02 per cent per annum), but the population aged 15–59 will decline by 0.42 per cent per annum. In Europe the working age population will decline at twice the rate (-0.84 per cent per annum) that the total population will decrease (-0.37 per cent per annum) (United Nations 2001: 16).

Concerns with impending labour force decline have seen several nations initiate policies which seek to encourage women to have more children. Efforts to increase fertility can be divided into two broad patterns. Direct policies involve attempts to influence fertility by offering incentives to those who have children and disincentives to those who choose not to have children. Incentives include cash payments for each child, privileged access to housing, medical or education services, taxation incentives or disincentives, etc. Indirect policies seek to change the environment in which couples make decisions about the number of children they intend to have. Several governments have attempted to increase fertility by direct government intervention (McIntosh 1998). Most notorious were the fascist governments of Mussolini and Hitler, which compelled rather than induced people to have more children. Some of the most comprehensive direct pronatalist policies were introduced in Eastern European countries in the 1960s and 1970s. These varied greatly across countries (David 1982), but included restricting access to abortion; provision of paid or unpaid maternity leave; paying monthly allowances to families with children, in some cases with the amounts per child increasing with birth of each child; income tax reductions for families with children; subsidies and supports for childcare; children's transportation, school equipment, clothing and housing; and provision of loans to newly wed couples to buy and furnish homes. Some Western European countries have pronatalist policies at national and sub-national levels encompassing substantial family and single-parent allowances; privileged access to government housing for families with children; extended paid maternity leave; accouchement leave without loss of seniority or job security; provision of low-interest marriage loans with repayments being remitted with the birth of each child; subsidized nurseries and crèches and substantial tax reduction with successive births (Van de Kaa 1997; United Nations 1999). A similar range of policies has been enacted in Singapore for the last two decades, though with limited success (Saw Swee-Hock 2005).

Governments are tending to move towards more comprehensive approaches to fertility policy which combine fiscal measures with policies facilitating parents to combine work and family life (Kent and Haub 2005: 21). These include family allowances to compensate parents for the costs of children; income tax concessions for families; access to housing or housing loans; improving availability of child care; and flexible workplace arrangements. Family-friendly policies require commitment from employers, who in some countries have been slow to co-operate with governmental initiatives.

With respect to mortality, the key issue is the response of individuals, families, communities, nations and multilateral agencies to the HIV/AIDS epidemic. While the treatment and care of those living with the disease is important, the most critical pillar for action according to the United Nations (2005c: 6) is prevention, and a combination of strategies are needed to reduce the risk of infection. In particular, there is a need to raise public awareness; change risky behaviours; promote condom use and ensure adequate supplies; ensure blood safety; increase access to anti-retroviral treatment; and reduce the stigma and discrimination associated with infection.

With respect to international migration there have been some substantial changes in policy over the last three decades. As a result of the increased and increasing scale of international migration, nation-states have become more involved in attempting to influence its flow. There has been a substantial increase in the numbers of laws and regulations relating to migration enacted in the last decade. The United Nations (2002: 21) reports that in the 1990s over 100 countries enacted legislation or signed agreements relating to migration.

149

With respect to immigration, Figure 9.17 shows that a higher proportion of countries in 2003 were satisfied with the level of immigration compared to 1996. This reflects the fact that in the intervening period several mostly more-developed nations increased their intake of immigrants.

An important distinction in immigration policies is between those which involve permanent settlement of immigrants at the destination and those by which immigrants (predominantly workers) are granted temporary residence and required to return home after completing work. MDCs actively attract migrants who meet specific labour needs in science and technology, where skills are in short supply or where there is capital to invest (United Nations 2004b). However, there are increasing limits on the migration of low skilled groups even where there is a manifest demand for such workers. Ageing MDC populations, reductions in the number of native workers and rising expectations among those workers create labour shortages in fields such as agriculture, construction, service provision, domestic services and caring for elderly people. Some countries have responded to this demand by allowing temporary immigration of unskilled workers, while in others unskilled workers enter through family reunion, refugee-humanitarian and working holiday schemes. Others tolerate undocumented immigration to meet labour needs.

Many aspects of international migration are subject to national policies and laws. Nation-states control who is admitted to a country. However, there are some issues which are universal. Even if a nation admits migrants on a purely contractual basis, it is obliged to recognize the rights owed to the migrant workers under international law. There are increasing numbers of nations which are unable to meet their internal labour requirements through fertility decline, rapid economic growth and labour market segmentation. The majority of such nations have opted for policies which allow the entry of temporary migrant workers, but which do not allow permanent settlement, rarely grant citizenship to migrants and seek to protect national identity.

Measures designed to ensure the unskilled migrant worker returns home include disallowing family to accompany or visit the worker; limiting the worker's rights to travel within the country; tying them to a single employer; prohibiting marriage to citizens; and enforcing other restrictions on rights and movement.

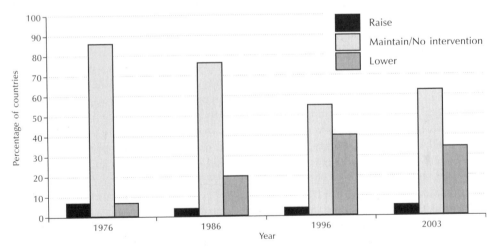

Figure 9.17. Government policies on immigration, 1976–2003.
Source: United Nations (2004c: 15).

The fear that temporary unskilled workers will stay grew out of the experience of post-war Europe, when several countries opted to cope with labour shortages by importing temporary guest workers: these groups subsequently developed substantial permanent communities. However, it is relevant to ask whether in the contemporary situation temporary migration is necessarily a prelude to permanent settlement. There is some evidence that this is less the case than in the past because modern forms of transport and communication have greatly reduced the friction of distance between origin and destination countries. Migrants are able to maintain closer links with their home area than ever before. Cheaper phone calls, the introduction of email and fax, and cheaper and faster international travel have made it possible for migrants to interact in real time with their home country on a regular basis and to visit home more frequently in emergencies and for breaks. This has reduced the imperative for temporary workers to want their family to join them in the destination. Indeed, many low skilled migrant workers see a number of advantages of maintaining a regular pattern of circular international migration in preference to permanent settlement at the destination. They are able to 'earn' in the high income, high cost destination and 'spend' in the low income, low cost origin and hence maximize the purchasing power of their earnings; they can retain traditional cultural language and other associations of their homeland and they can maintain strong family linkages, and this can be more easily done at home rather than at the destination.

In the right contexts, circulation can become a permanent strategy. However, this presupposes migrant workers are able to interact freely with home countries. Frequently, such interaction is made difficult, especially where the migrant workers are undocumented. For example, increasing policing of the Mexico–United States border has resulted in a reduction in circulation and an increase of Mexicans permanently settling in the United States (Cornelius 2003).

Turning to policies on emigration, over the last three decades there has been a doubling of the proportion of countries which perceive the level to be too high, with now a quarter of countries having some concern (United Nations 2004c). It is selective of the most educated and skilled, and so deprives originating countries of some of their most talented citizens and exacerbates the constraints which low levels of human capital have imposed on development in those countries. In contrast, global remittances in 2005 were estimated to be US $167 billion (World Bank 2006: 85) and have positive developmental effects in LDCs. Moreover, diasporic communities from LDCs can assist development in their homeland through encouraging FDI, technology transfer and trade. However, little has been done to facilitate the positive effects of emigration. Policies and programmes which seek to maintain contact with their diaspora, encourage their cultural and language maintenance and develop and enhance linkages with, and financial flows to, their homeland are not new. Greece and Italy, for example, have been involved in such activities for over a century. Nations have varied in whether they have engaged their diaspora and in the extent of engagement, and as Newland (2004: 3) points out, involvement has ranged from active courting of expatriates through indifference to hostility towards them. However, with the rapid growth of expatriate communities and new forms of information and communication technology it is possible to engage diaspora in an immediate and effective way.

There has been a significant shift in the attitudes of some 'south' nation-states towards their diaspora. In the Philippines, for example, the high level of emigration of contract labour and permanent settlers was depicted in national discourse in the 1970s and 1980s as a 'national shame' (Aguilar 1996). Migration was seen as a temporary phenomenon which had to be endured while the Philippines made the transition to a more developed economy. The fact that millions of Filipinos were forced to seek their destiny in other nations was perceived as a 'national failure'. However, in the last decade, Filipinos overseas have been reborn as 'national heroes' (Rosales 1999) who are making a crucial and important contribution to national prosperity. The Philippines now has a suite of policies and programmes to support the diaspora and encourage them to maintain strong linkages with, and return to, the Philippines. A similar transition was experienced in Mexico in relation to the large-scale migration to the United States. Governments of the Philippines and Mexico now recognize that emigration is a longstanding and structural feature of their economies and societies, and as a result are putting in place policies and programmes to enhance its positive effects and ameliorate its negative consequences.

Accordingly, some less developed nations have begun to develop policies which attempt to engage their diaspora. The focus in the migration and development literature has largely been on what origin countries can do to enhance the contribution of their expatriates to economic and social development at home. Such policies include facilitating transfer of remittances to home areas through reduction of transaction costs; encouraging return migration; making pensions more portable; supporting cultural and language links with the home country; and encouraging diasporic organizations. The crucial question is whether it is possible to develop policies whereby the migrant sending country and receiving country both gain from the process.

Notes

1 Life expectancy is defined as 'the average number of years a person of a given age can expect to live if the present mortality rate at all ages for a given period is maintained over their lifetime' (Hugo 1986: 19).
2 The Total Fertility Rate can be defined as the sum of age-specific fertility rates (live births at each age of mother per female population of that age). It represents the number of children a woman would bear during her lifetime if she experienced current age-specific fertility rates at each age of her reproductive life (Hugo 1986).

Further reading

Bongaarts, J. (1994) Population policy options in the developing world. *Science* 11 (263)(5148), 771–76.

Castles, S. and Miller, M.J. (1998) *The Age of Migration: International Population Movements in the Modern World*, second edition. London: Macmillan.

Champion, A.G. (ed.) (1989) *Counterurbanisation: The Changing Pace and Nature of Population Deconcentration*. London: Edward Arnold.

Haub, C. and Kent, M.M. (2005) *Frequently Asked Questions about the PRB World Population Data Sheet*. Washington: Population Reference Bureau.

Organization for Economic Co-operation and Development (OECD) (2005) *Trends in International Migration 2004*. Paris: OECD.

Population Reference Bureau (2004a) *2004 World Population Data Sheet*. Washington: Population Reference Bureau.

——(2004b) Transitions in world population, *Population Bulletin* 59 (1), 1–40.

Saw Swee-Hock (1990) *Changes in the Fertility Policy of Singapore* (Occasional Paper No. 2, Times Academic Press). Singapore: Institute of Policy Studies.

United Nations Economic and Social Commission for Asia and the Pacific (UNESCAP) (2000) *2000 ESCAP Population Data Sheet*. Bangkok: ESCAP.

United Nations High Commission for Refugees (UNHCR) (2005) *2004 Global Refugee Trends.* Geneva: UNHCR.

United Nations (2005a) *Population Challenges and Development Goals.* New York: United Nations.

——(2005b) *World Population Prospects: The 2004 Revision.* New York: United Nations.

References

Aguilar, F. Jr (1996) The dialectics of transnational shame and national identity. *Philippine Sociological Review* 44, 101–36.

Asian Migrant Centre (1999) *Asian Migrant Yearbook 1999.* Hong Kong: Asian Migrant Centre.

Bongaarts, J. (1994) Population policy options in the developing world. *Science* 11 (263) (5148), 771–76.

——(1998) Demographic consequences of declining fertility. *Science* 282, 419–20.

Bourne, L.S. and Simmons, J. (2004) The conceptualisation and analysis of urban systems: a North American perspective. In A. Champion and G. Hugo (eds) *New Forms of Urbanization: Beyond the Rural–Urban Dichotomy,* pp. 249–68. Aldershot: Ashgate.

Bridi, H. (2005) Consequences of labour migration for the developing countries: management of remittances. Presentation at Conference on Labour Migration, 26 February.

Caldwell, J.C. (1976) Toward a restatement of demographic transition theory. *Population and Development Review* 2 (3–4), 321–66.

Castles, S. and Miller, M.J. (1998) *The Age of Migration: International Population Movements in the Modern World,* second edition. London: Macmillan.

——(1997) The complexity of urban systems: contrasts and similarities from different regions. Paper presented to IUSSP's XXIIIrd General Population Conference, Beijing, China, 11–17 October.

Champion, A.G. and Hugo, G.J. (2004) *New Forms of Urbanisation: Beyond the Urban-Rural Dichotomy.* Aldershot: Ashgate.

Coale, A.J. (1973) The demographic transition reconsidered. *International Population Conference Liege* 1, 62–63.

Cornelius, W. (2003) Mexico, new security concerns, and implications for development. Presentation at the MPI Meeting on Remittances and Circular Migration as Drivers of Development, University of California at San Diego, 3 April.

David, H.P. (1982) Eastern Europe: pronatalist policies and private behaviour. *Population Bulletin* 36 (6), 1–49.

Dimzon, C.S. (2005) Philippine migration, remittances and development in the Philippines. Paper presented at *Workshop on International Migration and Labour Market in Asia* organized by the Japan Institute for Labour Policy and Training, Japan Institute of Labour, Tokyo, 20–21 January.

Dumont, J. and Lemaitre, G. (2005) Counting immigrants and expatriates in OECD countries: a new perspective. Paper presented at Conference on Competing for Global Talent, Singapore Management University, Singapore, 13–14 January.

Ehrlich, P.R. (1968) *The Population Bomb.* New York: Ballantine Books.

Frey, W.H. (1994) The new white flight. *American Demographics* April, 40–48.

——(1995a) The new geography of US population shifts: trends towards Balkanization. In F. Reynolds (ed) *The State of the Union: Social Trends,* pp. 271–336. New York: Russell Sage.

——(1995b) Immigration and internal migration 'flight': a California case study. *Population and Environment* 16, 353–75.

Gelbard, A., Haub, C. and Kent, M.M. (1999) World population beyond six billion. *Population Bulletin* 54 (4), 1–44.

Gutièrrez, C.G. (1999) Fostering identities: Mexico's relations with its diaspora. *Journal of American History* 86 (2), 545–67.

Head, K. and Reis, J. (1998) Immigration and trade creation: econometric evidence from Canada. *Canadian Journal of Economics* 31 (February), 47–62.

Hugo, G.J. (1986) *Australia's Changing Population: Trends and Implications*. Melbourne: Oxford University Press.

——(2005a) Asian experiences with remittances. In D.F. Terry and S.R. Wilson (eds) *Beyond Small Change: Making Migrant Remittances Count*, pp. 341–72. Washington: Inter-American Development Bank.

——(2005b) *Migrants in Society: Diversity and Cohesion, Thematic Project 4: Global Commission on International Migration*. Report to Global Commission on International Migration, February.

——(2005c) A demographic view of changing youth in Asia. In F. Gayle and S. Fahey (eds) *Youth in Transition: The Challenges of Generational Change in Asia*. Bangkok: UNESCO.

Hull, T.H. (ed.) (2005) *People, Population and Policy in Indonesia*. Singapore: Equinox.

Jones, G.W. (2004) Urbanization trends in Asia: the conceptual and definitional challenges. In A. Champion and G. Hugo (eds) *New Forms of Urbanization*. Aldershot: Ashgate.

Kapur, D. (2001) Diasporas and technology transfer. *Journal of Human Development* 2 (2), 265–86.

Kent, M. and Haub, C. (2005) Global demographic divide. *Population Bulletin* 60 (4), 1–24.

Lucas, R.E.B. (2001) *Diaspora and Development: Highly Skilled Migrants from East Asia*. Report prepared for the World Bank, Boston University, November.

McIntosh, A. (1998) European population policy in the twentieth century: is it relevant for Australia? *People and Place* 6 (3), 1–15.

Mamdani, M. (1972) *The Myth of Population Control: Family, Caste and Class in an Indian Village*. New York: Month Review Press.

Naseem, S.M. (1998) The diaspora view of the economy. *Dawn*, 30 December.

Newland, K. (2004) *Beyond Remittances: The Role of Diaspora in Poverty Reduction in their Countries of Origin. A Scoping Study*. Washington: Migration Policy Institute for the Department of International Development.

Nguyen Anh, D. (2005) *Enhancing the Development Impact of Migrant Remittances and Diaspora: The Case of Vietnam, Regional Seminar on the Social Implications of International Migration*. Bangkok, 24–26 August. Available at http://www.unescap.org/esid/psis/meetings/SIIM/VietNam.pdf

Notestein, F. (1945) Population – the long view. In T. Schultz (ed.) *Food for the World*, pp. 36–57. Chicago: Chicago University Press.

Olshansky, S.J., Passaro, D.J., Hershow, R.C., Layden, J., Carnes, B.A., Brody, J., Hayflick, L., Butler, R.N., Allison, D.B. and Ludwig, D.S. (2005) A potential decline in life expectancy in the United States in the 21st century. *New England Journal of Medicine* 352 (11), 1138–45.

Population Reference Bureau (2004a) *2004 World Population Data Sheet*. Washington: Population Reference Bureau.

——(2004b) Transitions in World Population. *Population Bulletin*, 59 (1), 1–40.

Rosales, L.A.P. (1999) *Legislative Agenda on Filipino Migrant Workers. Papers from the Public Forum on the Philippines. The Estrada Government Amidst the Crisis: Can it Deliver its Promises to the Poor?* Utrecht, Netherlands, 23 April. Available at http://www.philsol.nl/fora/NL99a-Rosales.htm

Sahoo, S. (2002) Can India catch up with China? From a diasporic perspective. *India-China Mirror* (Quarterly), VII (July–September).

——(2005)*Population Policies and Programmes in Singapore*. Singapore: Institute of Southeast Asian Studies.

Taylor, J.E., Hugo, G.J., Arango, J., Kouaouci, A., Massey, D. and Pellegrino, A. (1996) International migration and national development. *Population Index* 62 (2), 181–212.

Terry, D.F. and Wilson, S.R. (eds) (2005) *Beyond Small Change: Making Migrant Remittances Count*. Washington: Inter-American Development Bank.

United Nations (1999) *Population in Europe and North America on the Eve of the Millennium: Dynamics and Policy Responses*. New York and Geneva: United Nations.

——(2000) *Replacement Migration*. New York: Department of Economic and Social Affairs, Population Division.

——(2001) *World Population Prospects: The 2000 Revision Highlights*. Available at http://www.un.org/esa/population/unpop.htm

——(2002) *International Migration 2002*. New York: United Nations.

——(2003a) *World Population Prospects: The 2002 Revision*. New York: United Nations

——(2003b) *World Population in 2300, Highlights*. New York: United Nations.

——(2004a) *World Population Policies to 2300*. New York: United Nations.

——(2004b) *World Economic and Social Survey 2004: International Migration*. New York: United Nations.

——(2004c) *World Population Policies 2003*. New York: United Nations.

——(2004d) *World Urbanization Prospects: The 2003 Revision*. New York: United Nations.

——(2005a) *Population Challenges and Development Goals*. New York: United Nations.

——(2005b) *World Population Prospects: The 2004 Revision*. New York: United Nations.

——(2005c) *World Population Prospects: The 2004 Revision* (Population Newsletter 79, June). New York: United Nations.

US Census Bureau (2004) *Global Population Profile: 2002*. Washington: US Government Printing Office.

Van de Kaa, D.J. (1997) Options and sequences: Europe's demographic patterns. *Journal of the Australian Population Association* 14 (1), 1–30.

World Bank (2006) *Global Economic Prospects: Economic Implications of Remittances and Migration*, Washington: World Bank.

Xenos, P. (2001) *The National Youth Populations of Asia: Long Term Change in Six Countries* (East–West Centre Working Papers Population Series, 108–2). Honolulu: East–West Centre.

10

Health and disease

Sarah Atkinson

Introduction

Health and disease display uneven spatial patterns at all scales, between geo-political areas of the world, between countries, between sub-national units and within sub-national units. Health viewed as an outcome serves as a key indicator in assessments of well-being, development and policy impacts. The internationally agreed Millennium Development Goals, established to focus on eradicating poverty, give three of the eight goals to health outcomes (Sachs 2004). Geographers have sought to explore the particular influence of place in determining such patterning of health and disease at different scales (Curtis 2004; Davey Smith *et al.* 2001; Mitchell *et al.* 2000; Gordon *et al.* 1999; Thomas *et al.* 2002). The opposite relationship of health and disease on place has been researched in relation to population responses, such as adaptations in the built environment or labour protection laws, to natural hazards and risks to health arising from different kinds of places. However, the small-scale processes by which health and particularly disease themselves act as forces in shaping and changing communities and places are far less well explored. This potentially vast topic is the main concern of this chapter. Material presented here is by no means comprehensive. Rather, the chapter will showcase research on four topics which serve to illustrate some of the processes by which health and disease may act as a force for change in the geographies of communities and places. These topics are the social and spatial consequences of the epidemic of the human immunodeficiency virus and acquired immunodeficiency syndrome (HIV/AIDS); the effects of long-term ill-health on residence patterns; the impact of stigma on both individual life-courses and the emergence of stigmatized places; and the production or reproduction of social relations and values through meanings reflected, represented and enacted in specific places that have come to be associated with health and healing.

The HIV/AIDS epidemic

By the end of 2005, 40.3 million people were estimated to be living with HIV/AIDS worldwide, of which 4.9 million were new infections. In addition to this, there were an estimated 3.1 million AIDS deaths. As is well known, the distribution of those living with HIV/AIDS and deaths from AIDS is highly spatially patterned worldwide. Sub-Saharan Africa with just over 10 per cent of the world's population has experienced more than 60 per cent of all people living with HIV/AIDS. An estimated 2.4 million deaths from AIDS occurred in sub-Saharan Africa during 2005, over 77 per cent of all AIDS deaths in that year, while better general health and the availability of anti-retroviral treatments in high income countries results in slower disease progression and lower mortality rates (UNAIDS/WHO 2005). Much of the research on HIV/AIDS has focused on aetiology, transmission, prevention, treatment and possible cures. Efforts to understand the nature of the epidemic and its course have included work predicting likely impacts on population demography. This work is reviewed in the previous chapter and, as indicated there, HIV/AIDS makes its demographic impact through a combination of impacts on the reproductive age group and children, resulting in lower fertility rates, higher infant mortality rates and slower overall growth rates. Nonetheless, the absolute numbers affected and the fact that HIV/AIDS particularly affects adults in their main productive and reproductive years means the epidemic inevitably has and will continue to have far-reaching consequences for the economy and the social fabric of daily life at all scales of analysis. It is therefore surprising to find remarkably little empirical research by social scientists on the social and economic impact of HIV/AIDS (Barnett et al. 2001). The research that has been made predominantly concerns modelling exercises.

The first generation of models predicting the impact of HIV/AIDS on macro-economic growth suggested that the net effects of AIDS on output per capita or aggregate growth would be small relative to other factors. However, subsequent research criticized these early models for underestimating prevalence and ignoring a number of features peculiar to the HIV/AIDS epidemic. Such features include its impact predominantly on the active labour force, on the unskilled and semi-skilled labour categories, and its slower incubation time, compared with other infectious diseases, from infection to expression as AIDS (Gaffeo 2003). Models compare scenarios of predicted growth rates with AIDS with a fictitious scenario without AIDS and have estimated per capita income in scenarios with AIDS to be as much as two-thirds lower than those without (Bonnel 2000 cited in Gaffeo 2003; Arndt and Lewis 2000, 2001).

At the micro-economic scale, loss of health of the productive members of a household is well recognized as a major factor that may push households into poverty, trap them further in deepening poverty or result in their disintegration altogether. In rural Tanzania, one of the commonest responses to the death of the household head (in 44 per cent of cases) was the complete disintegration of the household, and whilst death of the household head from HIV/AIDS was not associated with a higher level of household disintegration, the scale of the HIV/AIDS epidemic means many more household heads are dying with substantial likely impacts on the continuity of social structures (Urassa et al. 2001). Interactions between reduced productivity, increased health costs, lower food intakes, chronic energy deficiencies and exacerbation of other health problems set up vicious circles that trap households in chronic poverty. However, the long-term nature of HIV/AIDS illness results in household assets being cumulatively eroded over time with more extensive impacts on household resources (Barnett et al. 2001; Gaffeo 2003). The International Labour Organization (ILO) (2000 cited in Gaffeo 2003) estimates that outputs in the traditional farming sector in many countries have been more than halved through the effects of HIV/AIDS. As the numbers of women affected by HIV/AIDS continue to increase (UNAIDS/WHO 2005) and women carry out the majority of agricultural work, this impact on the traditional agricultural sector looks set to deteriorate further.

The HIV/AIDS epidemic has implications and impact also on the inter-generational transmission of poverty (ITG). Such effects can be explored at different scales, as the private transmission of poverty within a family or the public transfer or lack of transfer of resources across generations (Harper *et al.* 2003), and can be viewed in a wider framework of transfers or non-transfers of different types of capital (Moore 2001). Children born into impoverished households are more likely to be undernourished, more susceptible to disease and less likely to progress through education, and will themselves develop with long-term and irreversible impaired capabilities. In the case of HIV/AIDS, increasing numbers of infants themselves die from infection, a total depletion of capabilities. Infection is passed from mother to child during pregnancy, birth or breast-feeding; for example, a study in rural Tanzania reported that 25 per cent of all newborns of HIV positive mothers had died by their second birthday (Urassa *et al.* 2001). Moreover, the HIV/AIDS epidemic leaves increasing numbers of children with at least one parent dead from the disease. In south-west rural Uganda, amongst children under 15 years of age who had had a parent die during a three-year follow-up study, 43 per cent had died from HIV/AIDS (Kamali *et al.* 1996). Orphans may be highly disempowered and lose property and other resources to which they may have entitlement. Other impacts include higher vulnerability to sexual abuse or exploitation with the concomitant risk of HIV infection (Barnett *et al.* 2001). The poor outlook for HIV/AIDS orphans relates to the dynamics of child care arrangements through the extended family. Some shifts in social structures are recorded as numbers of orphans increase and this puts stress on extended families. In Zimbabwe, orphans are now cared for by extended maternal and paternal families as opposed to depending in the past only on the paternal side. A second new feature is that of households headed by siblings rather than accommodated under an existing adult-headed structure: this also indicates stress on extended families' capacity to cope (Foster *et al.* 1995). Observed differentials in school enrolment between orphans and non-orphans have been attributed to breakdowns in orphan care arrangements within extended families. More detailed exploration of this relationship in South Africa (KwaZulu-Natal) and in rural Zimbabwe show that the most significant impact on children's school enrolment rates comes from the death of the mother rather than the father, or even of both parents (Nyamukapa and Gregson 2005; Case and Ardington 2004). In the case of a paternal or double parental death, orphans tend to end up living with female-headed households which typically invest more in education and having greater access to external welfare resources as a result of having poorer socio-economic status (Nyamukapa and Gregson 2005).

At the same time, various services that aim to assist the poor, such as microfinance institutions, or to invest in human capital, such as education and health care, are themselves undermined and eroded by the epidemic. Microfinance institutions have proved an effective support for the poor, particularly women, to invest in improved livelihoods through small loans with an excellent record of repayments. However, in high prevalence communities, client groups are highly likely to include at least one person living with HIV/AIDS. In this context people are less likely to be able to repay loans, which in turn decreases the quality of services of the institutions and indeed threatens their survival. Institutions in turn must spend increasing percentages of their resources on health care for their own staff (Gaffeo 2003). Other services that invest in human capital, such as health care and education, are understaffed or closed down as the pool of health professionals and teachers is reduced by the epidemic (Gaffeo 2003). The size of the epidemic also consumes resources and budgets for welfare and health care. On tea estates in Malawi, 40 per cent of employee benefits such as medical care provision is accounted for by HIV/AIDS, illustrating how other needs are

159

pushed out and systems overwhelmed by the epidemic (Bollinger and Stover 1999, cited in Gaffeo 2003). The burden of AIDS patients was shown in a longitudinal study in Kenya to damage other health care provision through displacing others in need of care from hospitals (Gilkes *et al.* 1998 cited in Barnet *et al.* 2001).

This section has illustrated just some of the ways in which HIV/AIDS impacts on economic and social aspects of everyday life of households, trapping them into deeper and more vicious cycles of poverty during a life-course and across generations. Without dramatic policy intervention, the scale of the HIV/AIDS epidemic in some districts and countries of the world, and the relatively slow progression of the disease, implies that profound changes to social structures, household dynamics and economic performance are likely, with a long-term polarization of wealth distributions.

Health and housing

In the very different context of high income countries, the spatial distributions of a range of socio-economic indicators over time reflect a scenario in the UK in which neighbourhoods are becoming more homogeneous, at the same time as differences between these communities are growing (Dorling and Rees 2003). Spatial distributions of inequalities in health and their association with place are most commonly understood as reflecting deprivation charted by a range of social and economic variables. The examination of ill-health as not only an outcome of deprivation but also a contributing factor through health-selective mobility and migration has been unpopular and under-researched (Norman *et al.* 2004; Smith and Easterlow 2005).

Understanding the processes contributing to this trend centres on factors affecting residential options and choices and specifically on the functioning of housing systems. Susan Smith and colleagues have explored the ways in which health status is associated with people's housing options and choices and thus contributes to shaping this increasingly polarized spatial distribution of deprivation in the UK (Smith and Easterlow 2005; Smith *et al.* 2003; Smith *et al.* 1997). They identify and document three processes by which people's experiences of long-term illness result in a greater likelihood of living in neighbourhoods with higher levels of deprivation, including higher than average levels of long-term illness, and which are viewed in turn as unhealthy places.

First, the authors detail what they term *selective placement*. This comprises processes occurring once people have developed a long-term illness. As a result of this illness they then move into neighbourhoods that are more 'unhealthy' than their previous place of residence. Making this decision is largely concerned with affordability and availability of properties that meet particular needs. A scheme of Medical Priority Rehousing did enable some of those with long-term illness to be advantaged in relocation to more suitable housing for their particular needs (Smith *et al.* 1997). However, the wider political and economic context in the UK at the time had led to much of the stock of public housing being sold to private owners. The stock that remained available to buy at low price, or that was available for welfare-based relocation, was most often located in the less desirable, marginalized neighbourhoods.

Second, people who wish to move elsewhere become trapped after developing a long-term illness. They are unable to move, unlike the healthy residents of the neighbourhood. Three sets of factors influence this process of entrapment. Financial considerations are manifest through a combination of increased expenses incurred by people with long-term illness and depressed incomes. People may feel tied in or anchored to their residence by investments already made to accommodate their mobility needs. The importance of memory and emotional attachments to the house and wider neighbourhood is sometimes overlooked but can also act as a force for entrapment.

Third, processes of *selective displacement* operate where those who do live in healthier neighbourhoods feel pressure to move: almost half of those interviewed, in one study (Smith and Easterlow 2005). Thus the healthier neighbourhoods effectively push out those who are unhealthy through extra pressures on incomes and the context of housing costs (Smith and Easterlow 2005).

The particular importance drawn out from these studies is twofold. First, they demonstrate in detail some of the processes by which health and ill-health act as forces in determining residence and thereby the character of different neighbourhoods. Also more importantly, this set of studies argues that the extent that such processes of selectivity can operate depends on policy orientations and institutional practices and their interaction with people's own emotions and self-perceptions. This work illustrates well the danger of only seeing health as an outcome and failing to 'position the health divide as a marker of discrimination as well as an index of risk' (Smith and Easterlow 2005: 181).

This focus on emotion and self-image overlaps with work on the way in which different experiences of health may be associated with responses from other people not suffering from ill-health. People's future life chances often depend upon their social context and the stigma of ill-health can also have powerful impacts.

Stigmatization

All illnesses can be viewed as stigmatizing to some extent in that 'they represent potential or existing physical limitations; they are associated with particular negative images and myths, and therefore they take on symbolic meaning' (Fife and Wright 2000: 51). The ways in which a stigmatized illness can impact on communities and places can be explored at different scales. Processes experienced at the individual scale can be aggregated to inform our understanding of how social discrimination may build up into a map of spatial discrimination.

The seminal work on stigma at the individual scale comes from Goffman (1963). Goffman defines stigma as: 'the situation of the individual who is disqualified from full social acceptance' (1963: 9) and categorizes common stigmatized statuses into three groups – physical imperfection, character flaws, and membership of a negatively regarded group. Individuals are stigmatized through a process of discounting and discrediting by others, who redefine them as no longer wholly acceptable members of society, turning them into persons whose identities are spoiled and tainted. As the self can be seen as produced through processes of interaction with others and perceptions of others' assessments of self, stigmatization operates not only through the responses of others but also through internalized feelings of low self-worth and shame, resulting in withdrawal from social interaction (Fife and Wright 2000). The effects of stigma may include loss of social status; lessened life-chances and opportunities; reduced social interaction, employment opportunities and emotional well-being; and lowered self-esteem. An exploration of the multi-dimensional ways that illness may impact on perceptions of the self, comparing HIV/AIDS and cancer, concluded that the nature of the illnesses themselves had few direct effects on self-evaluation. What did impact on self-evaluation was the different stigma that the two diseases generated. The severity of the illness did have an indirect effect in that greater stigmatization was associated with greater severity;

nonetheless, the effects of stigma were significant over and above either the impact of functional health status or perception of the illness's severity (Fife and Wright 2000).

The pattern of HIV/AIDS in western society, associated with homosexuality and intravenous drug use, involves all three of Goffman's types of stigma. In the comparison of groups of people living with either HIV/AIDS or cancer, the stigma experienced by those with HIV/AIDS was, as predicted, much higher than those with cancer (Fife and Wright 2000). The experience of living with HIV/AIDS leads many to exercise major changes to their lifestyles including changes in residence. Amongst people living with HIV/AIDS in Australia, 15 per cent reported the current accommodation as unsuitable for their needs, whilst 44 per cent had already changed their living arrangements. Of these, 24 per cent said this was for financial reasons. Over half of the study participants were not in work and reported that the only positive aspect of not working was health benefits, whereas it negatively impacted on finances and enjoyment of life; three-quarters reported a fall in income since developing HIV/AIDS, including a third of those in full-time employment. Changes in living arrangements were not only mediated, however, by financial changes; 48 per cent reported the change was for lifestyle or social reasons. Highest amongst the social reasons were discrimination and abuse, and a sixth of all study participants explicitly reported experiences of HIV/AIDS-related discrimination and harassment resulting from their current residential location (Ezzy et al. 1998). Here again we can see the direct effect that living with a disease can have on residential options, in this case operating through the processes of stigmatization provoking selective displacement.

The effect of adult disease on the transfer of human capital to the next generation, discussed in the previous section, is also exercised through processes of stigmatization. The impact on children of an HIV-positive parent or carer may be exacerbated through the difficulties children experience in sharing their problems and seeking the support they need. Children in Scotland often became carers for their HIV-positive parents through episodes of increased illness, by carrying out housework, cooking, bathing the parents, cleaning the bed and caring for younger siblings. Whilst a few viewed school as a place of refuge, enjoyed school and were doing well, the majority experienced substantial educational difficulties at school with consequential impacts on future life-chances. Many missed substantial portions of the term from absenteeism whilst caring, or through tiredness when in the classroom, an effect further compounded by feeling isolated and lacking support. In particular, children did not want teachers or other children to know that their parent was HIV-positive. Moreover, the parents and the extended family asked the children to keep the illness a family secret. Children were aware that if they shared the secret with friends, they risked being ostracized, discrimination from their peers and anger and blame from their parent and other family members (Cree et al. 2006). The distribution of HIV/AIDS in the UK is already strongly spatially patterned with marked clustering in large urban centres. The study by Cree and colleagues was explicitly carried out in the three main centres for HIV/AIDS in Scotland: Edinburgh, Glasgow and Dundee. The effects of the illness on the next generation, mediated in part by the stigmatized nature of the disease, decreases these children's life-chances and opportunities and creates a vicious cycle reproducing conditions of deprivation. At worst it may initiate a vicious spiral downwards through inter-generational transfer of poverty and disadvantage in these areas.

Whilst the effects of stigma have resulted in great attention to anonymity and confidentiality issues in western society, Rotheram-Borus et al. (2005) argue that this outcome is unlikely to be the same in all contexts. In small communities in low income countries greater concerns about stigma may help increase the stigmatized nature of the disease and concomitant impacts on those living, or associated, with it. Here, a potentially misplaced concern with a sensitive response to a disease might well aggravate stigmatization and its associated negative consequences.

Work on the individual and on how stigmatization effects people and their life-chances, opportunities and interactions with communities and places has also been scaled up by geographers who have explored the nature of stigmatization in relation to places. Of particular interest here is the stigmatization places experience when they become associated with the production of poor health. Industrial cities were once viewed as centres of growth and prosperity but in a post-industrial age have experienced a shift in image to become unhealthy, 'tainted' places by dint of association with industrial pollution and environmental contamination. Drawing on the definitions and concepts outlined by Goffman, two studies, one in Teesside in the northeast of England (Bush *et al*. 2001) and one in Hamilton, Ontario, in Canada (Wakefield and McMullan 2005), demonstrate how places too may become stigmatized. Goffman (1963) stressed that the more visible the problem the more likely it was that stigmatization would occur; the highly visual nature of pollution from heavy industry creates powerful stigmatic symbols (Bush *et al*. 2001). In both cities, planners and politicians fear the unhealthy image of post-industrial era environmental contamination will discourage new investment, promoting deeper marginalization and decline. In both cities, various actions have been undertaken to make the environment healthier, including improvements in air and water quality. In both cities, the planners and politicians have initiated campaigns outside and within the city to challenge the hegemonic virtual image of unhealthiness by asserting a counter-image, the actual image of a clean, pollution-free city. Both studies demonstrate how the stigmatized characteristics of place are transcribed on to its residents; the polluted nature of the place signifies the polluted nature of the residents who are in turn stigmatized by the same criteria.

Residents in both Teesside and Hamilton have a mixed set of responses to the stigmatization of their city. Some resist the labelling. Respondents in Teesside object to being labelled by people outside the area as 'smogs' (Bush *et al*. 2001). Residents in Hamilton emphasize the health-affirming or maintaining characteristics of sites in their city. Personal qualities of the residents are highlighted, particularly in Hamilton, as a counter to the polluted image, but the authors warn this empowering discourse may bring its own costs. Valuing the image of toughness and blue-collar grit may affirm strength of character, but projecting an image of unassailable coping may reduce the outsiders' concern for the neighbourhood's well-being (Wakefield and McMullan 2005).

Such processes of renegotiation of stigmatized identities do not, however, constitute any real resistance or contestation of the stigmatization process. On the contrary, processes of stigmatization were re-expressed in a more localized manner that mirrored the 'processes of image creation and social exclusion occurring at the regional level' (Wakefield and McMullan 2005: 309). Residents, perceiving themselves as stigmatized by others, responded very much as Goffman had suggested, by attempting to 'normalize' themselves through disassociation with the characteristics of the stigma. In these cases, the characteristics of the stigma are associated with place, and thus the technique of disassociation involves a literal distancing. Residents in many areas of both Teesside and Hamilton make an explicit distinction between their neighbourhood, which is not polluted and is healthy, and those unhealthy neighbourhoods which are nearer to the original source of the perceived contamination (South Bank in Teesside; North End in Hamilton). These neighbourhoods, then, are doubly stigmatized: by outsiders stigmatizing the city as a whole, but also by a highly localized process within the city which results in deepening social exclusion and disadvantage for already deprived neighbourhoods. A counter-discourse to this highly local imaging of the cities was offered by the residents of South Bank in Teesside, who claimed the air pollution affected distant neighbourhoods just as much as theirs (Bush *et al.* 2001).

These processes of stigmatization of places illustrate two important considerations regarding the relationship between health, disease, communities and places. First, whilst the dominant image constructed of a place is always only partial with room for negotiation and potential change, this should not be overstated because the processes of negotiation and resistance are themselves highly partial. The result of local renegotiations of a city's stigmatized identity is a highly localized re-expression of stigma that contributes to the production and reproduction of neighbourhood inequalities. Second, the studies illustrate how powerful health is as a metaphor which can generate harmful processes, deepening disadvantage and deprivation. Indeed, Wakefield and McMullan explicitly contrast their study to the body of work within geography on therapeutic landscapes, the exploration of places associated with health and healing (Gesler 1998).

Healing places and spaces

The therapeutic landscape literature emphasizes reputations gained because of a perception of security, safety, identity and material and aesthetic support (Gesler 1998). Much of this research explores the therapeutic effect or the social construction in different contexts of exceptional places of healing, such as Lourdes (Gesler 1996; see also Chapter 15) or particular types of places. Again, less attention has perhaps been given to how health itself has affected those places. Of particular interest here is the commodification of places perceived to be healing, and the creation and marketing of healing locations.

The design of spaces for healing and health promotion reflects social values but also reinforces and reproduces these values. Research on the location and activities of mental asylums in the nineteenth century emphasizes the value given to fresh air, adequate daylight and free-draining soils (Gesler *et al.* 2004). The value given to the rural setting for healing reflects a perception of urban living as the cause of much disease, an ambivalence regarding urbanization and industrialization and a fear of loss of values and distance from what is natural (Smyth 2005; Tonnellier and Curtis 2005). Such ambivalence towards the urban and a romanticization of the rural persists and is reflected in current enthusiasms for outdoor leisure pursuits in areas perceived as natural and whose current form of naturalness is in turn protected. National parks in this context are clear examples of therapeutic landscapes. A number of studies of the formal locales of health provision explore the way in which these settings reflect and re-institute power relations and thus serve to reproduce various enactments of social inclusions and exclusions (Smyth 2005).

The structures, procedures and interactions of family planning services serve to support the control by experts through the manipulation of knowledge and technology which reproduces social norms of heterosexuality and able-bodiment (Gillespie 2002). These norms are also found in health-promoting settings such as gyms (Andrews *et al.* 2005). Political ideologies are reflected, enacted and promoted through health-related institutions. The perceived expansion of 'wellness tourism' represents a new expression of a resort or retreat but also reflects a new ideology towards health, with an emphasis on individual responsibility for well-being. The old specialized 'cure institution' of the spa is increasingly complemented by more general leisure-based hotels, which market themselves with facilities and services to promote well-being (Mueller and Kaufman 2000). Similarly, the design of new hospitals clearly reflects the neo–liberal agenda of the patient as client, offering choice and leisure activities, whilst at the same time reproducing the power of the expert and the hospital through explicit emphasis on the availability of state-of-the-art technologies (Kearns and Barnett 1999; 2000).

As a final consideration, the expansion of the Internet has made possible a whole range of new types of spaces and virtual places in which to seek or experience health and healing (see also Chapter 33). In these virtual spaces and places, it is strangely the disembodied nature of health-seeking that enables encounters that have a highly embodied relevance. From searching for information, to online medical consultations, to membership of support groups, the role of health and disease in taking people on a journey through the Internet's spaces and places may change not only the impact of their illness but also the nature of their social networks. Virtual healthy communities may subvert the construction of power hierarchies in society between expert and lay categories.

A study of pregnant women who had a drug-abuse history found the women were more likely to participate via an electronic voice bulletin board than in face-to-face meetings. Almost all the comments women left concerned exchanges of emotional support, and women reported that the more they participated, the more they felt a sense of solidarity with others participating (Alemi *et al.* 1996). Similar studies of users of Internet-based support groups for depression have reported considerable benefit in reducing feelings of social isolation (Houston *et al.* 2002), although very few studies have assessed the effects of peer interactions in isolation from other medical interventions (Eysenbach *et al.* 2004). Websites disseminating health information are estimated at more than 70,000, with 50 million people seeking health advice (Cline and Haynes 2001). The ready availability of health information online raises questions about availability and inequalities in searching and evaluating what is largely unregulated information (Eysenbach and Köhler 2002). Nonetheless, the potentially greater access to information for the general public may radically challenge the traditional relationship between the expert service provider and the lay user, a relationship recognized as already under pressure and being renegotiated through the actions of patient support networks (Rabeharisoa and Callon 2002). At the same time, differences in access to, and use of, the Internet mirror other inequalities in public access to, and provision of, health services. Whether global, national and sub-national inequalities in access to these new and emerging spaces of health care reflect existing health care inequalities, redistribute them, reduce them or polarize them still further are contemporary questions for geography.

Concluding comments

The chapter has provided four topics of health and disease through which to explore how contemporary health and disease issues may act as forces for change within communities and places. Health and disease clearly impact on the spatial patterning of inequalities. Processes by which this occurs are complex and likely to be highly contextually specified. Research summarized here identifies impacts on income, costs, social status and inter-generational transfers of impaired human capital as some of the mechanisms by which health and disease exert their force. The particular processes of stigmatization are given some prominence in their hidden role affecting choice of location, expressions of need and wider impacts through stigmatized places. The institutions through which health care or health promotion are sought not only afford an insight into the social and power relations of the society in which they are embedded but also provide places and spaces in which those relations are enacted, reproduced and reinforced or challenged and changed. There is a surprising lack of research regarding health and disease as a force for change at the micro-scale of everyday processes. This absence of research has been commented on by several authors. Barnett *et al.* (2001) decry an unwillingness amongst social scientists to engage in policy-relevant research. Smith and Easterlow (2005) highlight a lop-sided, unbalanced, 'strange' geography of health suffering from 'healthism' in its bias to research on health as an outcome. The research examples presented here all afford forces for change themselves and go some way in redressing this imbalance in the geographies of health.

Further reading

Barnett, T., Whiteside, A. and Desmond, C. (2001) The social and economic impact of HIV/AIDS in poor countries: a review of studies and lessons. *Progress in Development Studies* 1 (2), 151–70.

Bush, J., Moffatt, S. and Dunn, C. (2001) 'Even the birds round here cough': stigma, air pollution and health in Teesside. *Health and Place* 7, 47–56.

Curtis, S. (2004) *Health and Inequality.* London: Sage.

Davey Smith, G., Dorling, D. and Shaw, M. (2001) *Poverty, Inequality and Health: 1800–2000 – A Reader.* Bristol: Policy Press.

Harper, C., Marcus, R. and Moore, K. (2003) Enduring poverty and the conditions of childhood: lifecourse and intergenerational poverty transmissions. *World Development* 31 (3), 535–54.

Smith, S.J. and Easterlow, D. (2005) The strange geography of health inequalities. *Transactions of the Institute of British Geographers* 30, 173–90.

Smyth, F.S. (2005) Medical geography: therapeutic places, spaces and networks. *Progress in Human Geography* 29 (4), 488–95.

References

Alemi, F., Mosavel, M., Stephens, R.C., Ghadiri, A., Krishnaswamy, J. and Thakkar, H. (1996) Electronic self-help and support groups. *Medical Care* 34 (10), 32–44.

Andrews, G.J., Sudwell, M.I. and Sparkes, A.C. (2005) Towards a geography of fitness: an ethnographic case study of the gym in British bodybuilding. *Social Science and Medicine* 60, 877–91

Arndt, C. and Lewis, J.D. (2000) The macro implications of the HIV/AIDS pandemic: a preliminary assessment. *South African Journal of Economics* 58 (5), 856–87.

——(2001) The HIV/AIDS pandemic in South Africa: sectoral impacts and unemployment. *Journal of International Development* 13, 427–49.

Barnett, T., Whiteside, A. and Desmond, C. (2001) The social and economic impact of HIV/AIDS in poor countries: a review of studies and lessons. *Progress in Development Studies* 1 (2), 151–70.

Bush, J., Moffatt, S. and Dunn, C. (2001) 'Even the birds round here cough': stigma, air pollution and health in Teesside. *Health and Place* 7, 47–56.

Case, A. and Ardington, C. (2004) *The Impact of Parental Death on School Enrolment and Achievement: Longitudinal Evidence from South Africa* (Centre for Social Science Research Working Paper 97). Cape Town: University of Cape Town.

Cline, R.J.W. and Haynes, K.M. (2001) Consumer health information seeking on the Internet: the state of the art. *Health Education Research* 16 (6), 671–92.

Cree, V.E., Kay, H., Tisdall, E.K.M. and Wallace, J. (2006) Listening to children and young people affected by parental HIV: findings from a Scottish study. *AIDS care* 18 (1), 73–76.

Curtis, S. (2004) *Health and Inequality.* London: Sage.

Davey Smith, G., Dorling, D. and Shaw, M. (2001) *Poverty, Inequality and Health: 1800–2000 – A Reader.* Bristol: Policy Press.

Dorling, D. and Rees, P. (2003) A nation still dividing: the British census and social polarisation 1971–2001. *Environment and Planning A* 35, 1287–1313.

Eysenbach, C. and Köhler, C. (2002) How do consumers search for and appraise health information on the world wide web? Qualitative study using focus groups, usability tests, and in-depth interviews. *British Medical Journal* 324, 573–77.

Eysenbach, G., Powell, J., Englesakis, M., Rizo, C. and Stern, A. (2004) Health related virtual communities and electronic support groups: systematic review of the effects of online peer to peer interactions. *British Medical Journal* 328, 1166–72.

Ezzy, D., de Visser, R., Grubb, I. and McConachy, D. (1998) Employment, accommodation, finances and combination therapy: the social consequences of living with HIV/AIDS in Australia. *AIDS care* 10 (supplement 2), S189–99.

Fife, B.L. and Wright, E.R. (2000) The dimensionality of stigma: a comparison of its impact on the self of persons with HIV/AIDS and cancer. *Journal of Health and Social Behaviour* 41, 50–67.

Foster, G., Shakespeare, R., Chinemana, F., Jackson, H., Gregson, S., Marange, C. and Mashumba, S. (1995) Orphan prevalence and extended family care in a peri-urban community in Zimbabwe. *AIDS care* 7 (1), 3–18.

Gaffeo, E. (2003) The economics of HIV/AIDS: a survey. *Development Policy Review* 21 (1), 27–49.

Gesler, W. (1996) Lourdes: healing in a place of pilgrimage. *Health and Place* 2 (2), 95–105.

——(1998) Bath as a healing place. In R.A. Kearns and W.M. Gesler (eds) *Putting Health into Place*, pp. 17–35. Syracuse, New York: Syracuse University Press.

Gesler, W., Bell, M., Curtis, S., Hubbard, P. and Francis, S. (2004) Therapy by design: evaluating the UK hospital building program. *Health and Place* 10, 117–28.

Gillespie, R. (2002) Architecture and power: a family planning clinic as a case study. *Health and Place* 8, 211–20.

Goffman, E. (1963) *Stigma: Notes on the Management of Spoiled Identity.* Prentice-Hall: New York

Gordon, D., Shaw, M., Dorling, D. and Davey Smith, G. (eds) (1999) *Inequalities in Health: The Evidence.* Bristol: Policy Press

Harper, C., Marcus, R. and Moore, K. (2003) Enduring poverty and the conditions of childhood: lifecourse and intergenerational poverty transmissions. *World Development* 31 (3), 535–54.

Houston, T.K., Cooper, L.A. and Ford, D.E. (2002) Internet support groups for depression: a 1-year prospective cohort study. *American Journal of Psychiatry* 159, 2062–68.

Kamali, A., Seeley, J.A., Nunn, A.J., Kengeya-Kayondo, J.F., Ruberantwari, A. and Mulder, D.W. (1996) The orphan problem: experience of a sub-Saharan Africa rural population in the AIDS epidemic. *AIDS care* 8 (5), 509–15.

Kearns, R.A. and Barnett, J.R. (1999) To boldly go? Place, metaphor and marketing of Auckland's Starship hospital. *Environment and Planning D* 17, 201–26.

——(2000) 'Happy Meals' in the Starship Enterprise: interpreting a moral geography of health care consumption. *Health and Place* 6, 81–93.

Mitchell, R., Dorling, D. and Shaw, M. (2000) *Inequalities in Life and Death: What if Britain were More Equal?* Bristol: Policy Press.

Moore, K. (2001) *Frameworks for Understanding the Intergenerational Transmission of Poverty and Well-being in Developing Countries* (Chronic Poverty Research Centre Working Paper 8). Manchester: CPRC, University of Manchester.

Mueller, H. and Kaufman, E.L. (2000) Wellness tourism: market analysis of a special health tourism segment and implications for the hotel industry. *Journal of Vacation Marketing* 7, 5–17.

Norman, P., Boyle, P. and Rees, P.H. (2004) Selective migration, health and deprivation: a longitudinal analysis. *Social Science and Medicine* 60, 2755–71.

Nyamukapa, C. and Gregson, S. (2005) Extended family's and women's roles in safeguarding orphans: education in AIDS afflicted rural Zimbabwe. *Social Science and Medicine* 60, 2155–67.

Rabeharisoa, C. and Callon, M. (2002) The involvement of patients' associations in research. *International Social Science Journal* 54, 57–63.

Rotheram-Borus, M.J., Flannery, D., Rice, E. and Lester, P. (2005) Families living with HIV. *AIDS care* 17 (8), 978–87.

Sachs, J.D. (2004) Health in the developing world: achieving the Millennium Development Goals. *Bulletin of the World Health Organization* 82 (12), 947–49.

Smith, S.J. and Easterlow, D. (2005) The strange geography of health inequalities. *Transactions of the Institute of British Geographers* 30, 173–90.

Smith, S.J., Alexander, A. and Easterlow, D. (1997) Rehousing as health intervention: miracle or mirage? *Health and Place* 3 (4), 203–16.

Smith, S.J., Easterlow, D., Munro, M. and Turner, K.M. (2003) Housing as health capital: how health trajectories and housing paths are linked. *Journal of Social Issues* 59 (3), 501–25.

Smyth, F.S. (2005) Medical geography: therapeutic places, spaces and networks. *Progress in Human Geography* 29 (4), 488–95.

Thomas, R., Evans, S., Gately, C., Stordy, J., Huxley, P., Rogers, A. and Robson, B. (2002) State-event relations among indicators of susceptibility to mental distress in Wythenshawe in the UK. *Social Science and Medicine* 55, 921–35.

Tonnellier, F. and Curtis, S. (2005) Medicine, landscapes, symbols: *The Country Doctor* by Honoré de Balzac. *Health and Place* 11, 313–21.

UNAIDS/WHO (2005) *AIDS Epidemic Update.* Geneva: UNAIDS/WHO.

Urassa, M., Boerma, J.T., Isingo, R. Ngalula, J., Ng'weshemi, J., Mwaluko, G. and Zaba, B. (2001) The impact of HIV/AIDS mobility on mortality and household mobility in rural Tanzania. *AIDS* 15, 2017–23.

Wakefield, S. and McMullan, C. (2005) Healing in places of decline: (re)imagining everyday landscapes in Hamilton, Ontario. *Health and Place* 11, 299–312.

11

Development

Katie D. Willis

The existence of government departments or agencies such as the UK's Department for International Development (DFID), the United States Agency for International Development (USAID), the Canadian International Development Agency (CIDA) and the Japan International Cooperation Agency (JICA) highlights the way in which 'development' as a political goal has been incorporated into the state apparatus of countries in the Global North. Of course, these organizations and similar institutions elsewhere in the economically richer countries of the world are not neutral. The development projects they seek to support are founded on particular ideas about what 'development' is and where 'development' should be carried out.

In this chapter, the main trends in thinking about 'development' will be discussed, focusing on the post-Second World War period. This is not because 'development' did not exist before the 1940s; rather it reflects the fact that 'international development' as a concept has became much more institutionalized in government structures after the Second World War, particularly as countries in Africa, Asia and the Caribbean gained their independence.

A key theme of this chapter is the link between constructions of 'development' and development policies. Policies, whether they derive from governments, international agencies or community organizations, are based on certain understandings of what 'development' is. While certain approaches have gained prominence at particular periods, they have not been uncontested. This chapter will provide an overview of key approaches and how they have been implemented and experienced at a range of scales.

Development: measurement, scale and actors

How 'development' is defined will affect the way in which it is measured. Two of the most commonly used measures of 'development' are Gross Domestic Product per capita (GDP p.c.) or Gross National Product per capita (GNP p.c.). These are purely economic measures. GDP p.c. is the total value of all goods and service produced within a country divided by the total population, while GNP p.c. is the value of all goods and services claimed by residents of a particular country regardless of where that production took place divided by the total population. Such indicators are often used by organizations such as the World Bank and the International Monetary Fund (IMF) in assessing levels of economic development.

The use of purely economic measures has, however, been criticized. While higher levels of economic wealth per person may lead to higher levels of human welfare, this may not always be the case. To reflect this, in the 1980s the United Nations Development Programme (UNDP) devised the Human Development Index (HDI). Mahbub Ul Haq was particularly influential in this process, which resulted in a measure of development incorporating indicators of economic status (GDP p.c.), health (life expectancy at birth) and education (adult literacy rate for people over 15 and gross enrolment rates in primary, secondary and tertiary education). The idea was that 'development' should encompass health and education as well as economics. The resulting index falls between 0 and 1.

While there are clearly correlations between the economic measures and the HDI, not least because the HDI includes GDP p.c. as a component, the relationship is not always straightforward. Having a measure such as the HDI also stresses the need to look beyond economic dimensions when examining 'development' (See Table 11.1).

Economic indicators and the HDI are usually calculated on the basis of national data. This reflects both the way in which information is gathered and also the scale at which 'development' is discussed. As this chapter will outline, different development theories and policies will promote development interventions at different scales, some preferring national-level strategies, others advocating local-level activities, drawing on the expertise of people and communities at the grassroots. Thus, different development actors are implicated depending on the theory or approach adopted. These actors range from individuals and communities, through governments at a range of scales, non-governmental organizations (NGOs), private sector companies (sometimes referred to more generally as 'the market') and multilateral organizations such as the United Nations and the World Bank. This chapter will outline how different actors and scales fit into the main development theories and policies.

Development as economic modernization

'Development' as a specific set of activities and goals is often identified as dating from the immediate post-Second World War period. After the economic uncertainty of the 1930s Depression and the widespread death and destruction of the war, governments were seeking to ensure peace and stability in the future. This led to the creation of multilateral institutions, such as the World Bank, the International Monetary Fund and the United Nations, as well as

Table 11.1. Development indicators by region 2003

Region	GDP pc (US$ PPP)	HDI
Arab states	5,685	0.679
East Asia and Pacific	5,100	0.768
Latin America and Caribbean	7,404	0.797
South Asia	2,897	0.628
Sub-Saharan Africa	1,856	0.515
Central and Eastern Europe and CIS	7,939	0.802
OECD	25,915	0.892
World	8,229	0.741

Source: Adapted from UNDP (2005: Table 1).

bilateral agencies within individual countries. In his inaugural address as president of the United States, Harry Truman called on the richer countries of the world to use their technological expertise to help poorer countries. His speech is often viewed as the moment which ushered in the 'age of Development' (Escobar 1995).

The 'development' to which Truman referred was based on the experiences of the societies and economies of the Global North. The focus was therefore on wealth creation through greater use of mechanization in agriculture, industrialization and urbanization. The underlying premise was that greater economic wealth would translate to better living conditions for the population. By following the appropriate path, all countries could achieve success.

This idea of development as economic modernization and as unilinear was reflected in a number of models of economic change which are often classified as 'modernization theories'. The most well known of these was Walt Rostow's 1960 publication *The Stages of Economic Growth*, within which he used the experiences of a number of countries to describe the ways in which societies moved from 'Traditional' based on small-scale subsistence farming through three intermediate stages to a 'Period of High Mass Consumption' based on complex social hierarchies, centralized political control, high levels of savings and investment and industrialization. Rostow argued that in order to achieve 'Take-off' countries would usually require some external intervention such as colonialism. W. Arthur Lewis (1955) made similar arguments, although he represented economic change as a move from the 'traditional' to the 'modern'. He saw foreign investment as the key to economic development, arguing for 'industrialization by invitation'.

In the post-Second World War period, as more and more countries in the Global South gained their independence, the formal colonial links of the past were replaced with 'development assistance' or 'aid'. Projects which were funded tended to be large infrastructure projects, such as roads or dams, and often involved reliance on foreign technology rather than drawing on local knowledges and materials. This approach to development has often been termed 'top-down development' as it is based on the decisions of global and national elites, rather than local community members. The belief was that the benefits accruing from this top-down development would trickle down to the grassroots communities.

The 'Green Revolution' of the 1950s and 1960s is often used as an example of how such policies could benefit economically poorer parts of the world. The 'Green Revolution' describes processes of agricultural modernization through greater use of machinery, inorganic fertilizers, pesticides, irrigation and high-yielding variety (HYV) seeds, in particular of rice and wheat. Through the adoption of such policies, Pakistan became self-sufficient in wheat by 1968, while India's drive to self-sufficiency in all cereals was well advanced by the end of the 1960s (Borlaug 1970). These achievements should not be underestimated, although the Green Revolution has received significant criticism, not least because of the effects on the natural environment, the increased reliance on externally provided inputs and the tendency for inequalities between richer and poorer farmers to increase.

Structuralist, dependency and Marxist approaches

For modernization theorists and the policy makers who followed this analysis, interventions from outside a country were viewed as positive in the drive for economic development in the Global South. However, for other theorists it was this very relationship with the 'outside world', in particular the global capitalist system, which lay at the root of the South's development problems. Rather than presenting a route through which technology, expertise and capital could be channelled for beneficial purposes, external links were ways in which resources and profit could be removed.

These perspectives on development are often characterized as challenging the Eurocentrism of modernization theories because they grew out of the experiences of academics and policy makers in and of the South. The Latin American structuralists, associated with the UN ECLA (United Nations Economic Commission for Latin America, also known as CEPAL in Spanish), form one of the most well-known and influential groupings. ECLA was set up in 1947 with its headquarters in Santiago, Chile with Raúl Prebisch as the head from 1950–62. Under Prebisch, ECLA promoted economic development policies recognizing the different global economic landscape which faced the countries of Latin America, compared with that experienced by most countries in the Global North during their industrialization drive. Prebisch and his colleagues argued that Latin American economies should be protected from competition from European and American companies while they were becoming established. This led to the promotion of import-substitution industrialization policies (ISI) which included imposing tariffs and quotas on imported goods. The idea was not to cut Latin American countries off from the global economic system, but rather to try and level the playing field. These policies achieved some successes, but were hampered by limited local markets and domestic technology, among other factors.

ISI clearly involved government intervention into industrial development processes. This was also the case in agriculture, where the structuralists argued for land reform to try and address the vast inequalities in rural wealth between a few large land-holders and a largely impoverished peasantry. Such interventions were often controversial as they involved a redistribution of land away from domestic elites or foreign companies. The US government was very wary of such activities, fearing they indicated a move towards communism in the Americas, but under the Kennedy administration of the early 1960s some land reform projects were incorporated into the Alliance for Progress programmes. This was an aid scheme to support Latin American governments who were viewed as democratic and capitalist friendly. Thus geopolitical decisions, especially during the Cold War, were key in framing development interventions in the Global South.

Dependency theories also came largely out of Latin America. While structuralists tended to propose policies which would lead to economic development within a more regulated global economic system, dependency theorists argued that the state of 'underdevelopment' in the Global South was a direct result of exploitation by the countries of the Global North. André Gunder Frank (1967) used examples from Chile and Brazil to argue that there were chains of exploitation from Europe right down to the peasants in rural Latin America. Frank termed this the 'development of underdevelopment'. Walter Rodney made similar arguments in the African context, particularly in his 1972 book *How Europe Underdeveloped Africa*. For Frank, Rodney and the other dependency theorists, the only way 'development' could be achieved was through withdrawal from the global economic system.

Dependency theories have been criticized for not providing sufficient links to policy and being overly focused on external factors, while ignoring possible internal causes of economic development problems such as poor government. The focus on economic dimensions of development, rather than broader social and political elements, has also been highlighted.

In contrast to dependency theories, the adoption of Marxist-inspired policies in the South demonstrates how theories of development have been applied, although these experiments have had limited success. Karl Marx (1818–83) argued that societies and economies moved through stages, from pre-capitalism through capitalism to communism or socialism. As with Rostow's later discussions regarding linear stages, Marx viewed traditional subsistence agricultural societies as 'backward' and saw progress as industrialization, mechanization and urbanization. However, for Marx, capitalism as a means of organizing production was highly undesirable as it was based on the means of production (land, mineral resources, capital, for example) being owned by very few people who became rich by exploiting the work-force, who had to sell their labour to make a living. The inequalities which Marx saw as inherent in capitalism were also played out on a global scale, with richer parts of the world exploiting the economically poorer parts of the world (as the dependency theorists would later highlight). For Marx, capitalism was inherently unstable and eventually the system would collapse, being replaced by a communist system where the means of production were owned by the people and resources were distributed not according to wealth, but according to need.

In reality, Marxist-inspired policies have been the outcome not of a collapse of capitalism, but rather of a conscious implementation by governments. Following independence in the Global South, many governments chose to follow a communist-style path, with strong central government control over land, infrastructure and industry. They felt that this form of development intervention would provide for the neediest people in society, ensuring basic levels of healthcare, education and income. This also means that measures of income inequality tend to be lower in countries following this form of development strategy, rather than market-led ones.

In sub-Saharan Africa, a number of 'African socialist' experiments were implemented in the 1960s. This was an attempt to adapt Marxist ideas to an African context, thus transforming a European-derived theory to local conditions. Julius Nyerere's *Ujamaa* ('family-hood') programme in Tanzania is one of the most well known (Collier *et al.* 1986). It was based on Tanzania's predominantly rural and agricultural economy and traditional ideas of communal working and support. Nyerere's ideas were strongly influenced by Mao's rural-focused development strategies adopted in China after the 1949 revolution. A failure to increase productivity sufficiently, a lack of foreign investment and hostility from rural populations contributed to the abandonment of the policy in the 1980s.

Other attempts to adopt Marxist-inspired policies in the Global South also experienced severe problems, not least because of the reactions of the governments of the capitalist West who saw any move from a standard capitalist development route as a sign of communist sympathies. During the Cold War, development 'aid', including weapons, was provided to governments and opposition forces by the USA and the USSR as a way of garnering support in countries as diverse as Vietnam, Mozambique and Cuba. Thus, even when the countries of the Global South were attempting to follow an autonomous development path, they found themselves embroiled in wider geopolitical battles over which they had no control.

Neo-liberalism

In the 1970s, some theorists began to challenge the ways in which development assistance was provided from North to South. In particular, the role of the state was placed under particular scrutiny. While economic development in the form of increasing income per capita was still at the heart of how development was defined, the ways in which this economic growth was to occur were challenged. Neo-liberal theorists, such as Bela Balassa and

Deepak Lal, argued that government intervention often led to inefficiencies and that economic growth would be much more likely to occur if markets were left to allocate resources.

These arguments about reducing the role of the state in economic activity drew on the work of eighteenth- and nineteenth-century theorists such as Adam Smith and David Ricardo who promoted the benefits of a division of labour and free trade as the ways to maximize economic growth and therefore human well-being. Balassa, for example, used economic growth data from Latin America and East Asia in the 1950s and 1960s to argue that the economies which experienced the highest rates of growth (South Korea and Taiwan) were the ones with the least state interference in the economy (see Figure 11.1). These neo-liberal arguments were given additional support as countries following ISI policies were increasingly finding it difficult to sustain growth levels due to internal market and capital limits.

By the early 1980s, international institutions such as the World Bank, had adopted neo-liberalism as the key framework for developing policies. The move away from state-centred development solutions to market-led ones was being promoted not only in the Global South but also in the North, with Margaret Thatcher in the UK and Ronald Reagan in the USA being the most vocal advocates.

In 1982, the Mexican government defaulted on its debt payments, triggering the 'debt crisis' which spread throughout the Global South, providing an opportunity for neo-liberal policies to be introduced in most parts of the world. High levels of national debt were common in the 1960s and 1970s as governments borrowed to pay for industrialization programmes. However, with increasing oil prices in the 1970s and a slowing down in the global economy, governments found themselves unable to meet their repayments and were forced to default. As private banks were unwilling to continue lending in this situation,

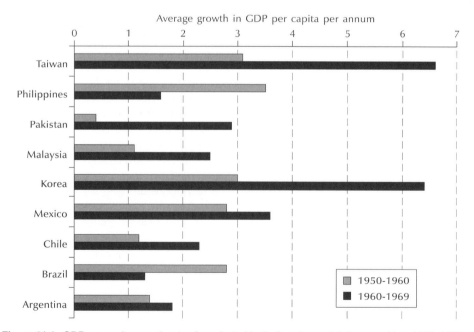

Figure 11.1. GDP per capita growth rates for selected Latin America and Asian countries, 1950–1969.
Source: Based on data from Balassa (1971: 180).

governments were forced to ask the World Bank and International Monetary Fund for help (see Chapter 54). Their proposed solution was the adoption of structural adjustment policies (SAPs).

SAPs included both a stabilization element and a restructuring element. Countries had to agree to adopt SAPs in order to receive further funding from the international financial institutions. SAPs were based on neo-liberal ideas, focusing on reducing the role of the state and increasing the role of the market, particularly through the opening up of the economy to foreign investment. The World Bank and the IMF, reflecting the opinions of the key Northern governments who hold the most power in these institutions, could set the development policy agenda, as most countries had no alternative but to accept the SAPs as a prerequisite for receiving future funding.

While SAPs achieved success in stabilizing economies, restructuring often had very severe effects on the welfare of the mass of the population. Reducing the role of the state usually meant cutting back on education and health spending, as well as reductions in subsidies for basic foodstuffs. Opening up the economy to foreign investment led to the creation of jobs in export-processing sectors but also increased competition for domestic firms, many of which went out of business, with the loss of thousands of jobs. SAPs are, therefore, often criticized for exacerbating levels of poverty and hurting not only the poor but the middle classes as well. Publications such as Cornia et al.'s (1987) *Adjustment with a Human Face* argued that adjustment policies needed to be accompanied by safety net policies to protect the most vulnerable.

Just as Balassa had used East Asian countries to promote ideas about the role of market-led development, so the World Bank used East Asia as an example of how market-led, open economies could flourish and provide both economic and social development. In its 1993 publication *The East Asian Miracle* the World Bank compared the experiences of East Asia with those of sub-Saharan Africa and Latin America in the period 1965–89, arguing that East Asia had achieved high levels of economic growth (over 4 per cent per annum average increase in GDP p.c.) while maintaining low levels of income inequality through the adoption of market-led policies. While such claims were challenged by many because in reality the East Asian governments had not been as passive as they were often presented in the book, the World Bank and many Northern governments continued to see East Asian policies as the key to development success. The Asian crisis of 1997 challenged that interpretation, as financial collapse across most of the region following the devaluation of the Thai baht revealed a rather more fragile situation. The World Bank explained the crisis by claiming that governments in the region had not been regulating the flow of financial capital as they should.

Neo-liberalism remains at the heart of development policies adopted by the key international financial institutions, although there have been some changes, for example by placing poverty reduction at the heart of agreements with aid and loan recipient governments and promoting wider participation in the development of these policies. These changes will be discussed in more detail below.

Sustainable development

Focusing on development as an increase in economic wealth has usually failed to recognize the environmental destruction which often accompanies economic growth. Thus, development for current populations may be at the expense of development for future generations.

175

Ideas of 'sustainable development' have become much more common since the report of the Brundtland Commission *Our Common Future* (WCED 1987) and the United Nations Environment Conference in Rio de Janeiro in 1992 (Elliott 1999). However, prior to this more widespread acceptance of the discourse of sustainable development, some theorists were paying attention to the problems of combining particular development trajectories with environmental protection.

In 1972 the Club of Rome published *The Limits to Growth* (Meadows *et al.* 1972) which used models of the relationships between population growth, economic growth and resources to stress the need for rapid change in development policies to prevent a Malthusian crisis whereby population would outstrip resources. Meadows *et al.* used different scenarios of population growth, non-renewable resource use, pollution, industrial output and food supply to predict future trends. Their conclusions were that if no major changes were made, disaster would strike before 2100. Their recommendations were focused mainly on the countries of the Global North, arguing that Northern governments and populations should take steps to limit consumption, rather than expecting poorer countries to make these sacrifices. For some, this suggested a backwards step in development progress and the findings were strongly contested, with opponents arguing that human ingenuity and technological advances would overcome these 'limits to growth'.

This contestation is also apparent in the ways in which 'sustainable development' has been understood and the ways in which associated policies have been implemented. For the Brundtland Commission (also known as the World Commission on Environment and Development, WCED), sustainable development is, 'development that meets the needs of the present without compromising the ability of future generations to meet their own needs' (1987: 33). In this report and at the Rio Conference, the tensions between 'development' and the environment were recognized, but proposed policy responses have varied greatly. Countries in the Global South felt that they should not be forced to restrict their economic development when countries of the Global North had industrialized and urbanized without controls in the past. These North–South debates were also reflected at the Rio + 10 Conference in Johannesburg in 2002. Development agencies, governments and NGOs have all taken on board the concept of 'sustainable development' but this does not mean that they all use it in the same way.

Responses to the sustainable development challenge can be characterized as being either technocentric, i.e. using technological advances to provide solutions, or ecocentric, i.e. focusing on the natural environment and choosing alternative, small-scale and decentralized solutions (Elliot 1999). For many multilateral agencies and Northern governments, it is technocratic solutions which hold the key because they are viewed as being much more compatible with continued economic growth and capitalism. For example, environmental pricing mechanisms and carbon trading have been introduced to use the market to promote 'environmentally friendly' policies.

An alternative approach to sustainable development is reflected in the work of Fritz Schumacher. In his 1973 book *Small is Beautiful*, Schumacher argued that economic progress could be achieved without the destruction of the natural environment or the denial of human agency. Rather than implementing 'development' using technologically advanced machinery that would only employ a few people, would create overdependence on external suppliers and could destroy the environment, Schumacher called for 'intermediate technology' to be adopted, drawing on the skills of local people and fitting in with local cultural practices and environmental characteristics. This was not a call to stop development or progress; instead it sought an appropriate route to development.

Grassroots development

The small-scale, local development interventions outlined previously in relation to sustainable development fit in with what has sometimes been termed 'grassroots development' or 'alternative development'. Unlike top-down development led by governments and international agencies, grassroots development is viewed as 'bottom-up' because it starts from particular environmental, social, cultural and economic circumstances and draws on the stated needs of local people. Grassroots development has become particularly popular since the 1980s, as the failure of large-scale projects to 'trickle-down' benefits to poor and marginal populations became increasingly apparent. Rather than assuming what poor people want, grassroots development is predicated on asking local communities about their priorities. This, it is argued, is not only more efficient in that projects are implemented successfully, but it also leads to greater participation and empowerment for marginal and excluded groups. 'Development' in such contexts is, therefore, a much broader concept than economic growth alone.

The key actors in grassroots development are local people, communities and, in particular, NGOs. NGOs vary greatly in size, from vast international organizations such as Oxfam and Save the Children, to very small-scale organizations working with communities on particular projects (see One World International Foundation 2006 for a range of NGOs). The role and number of NGOs in development has expanded rapidly since the 1980s. This is particularly associated with the shift towards neo-liberal policies. As the state has withdrawn from service provision, a void has been created which private sector companies are unwilling to fill, because of the lack of profit-making opportunities. NGOs have often been called upon to fill this gap and meet the needs of the very poorest. Thus, in many parts of the South, NGOs have taken over from the state in service provision in health, education and housing provision. The supposed efficiency and appropriateness of NGO activities in meeting the needs of the poor has meant that increasing amounts of multilateral and bilateral aid are channelled through NGOs, rather than going to governments in the Global South (Van Rooy 1998).

This focus on NGOs providing a 'magic bullet' able to solve all development problems was clearly overstated. While many NGOs have achieved great successes, there are limits to what NGOs can achieve, not least because they cannot cover all needy communities. In addition, NGOs, despite supposedly working for the needs of the poor communities, have other accountabilities, not least to donors. This has led to 'donor-led development' policies where project funding is channelled towards projects and sectors which are popular with donors, regardless of what local people require. In addition, NGOs are often forced to concentrate on projects which produce rapid tangible results, rather than focusing on longer-term, more sustainable and appropriate development (Edwards and Hulme 1995).

Grassroots development is also meant to give voice to the poor, leading to welfare improvements but also reducing feelings of marginalization and exclusion. There has been an increase in calls for greater participation in development by the poor, so leading to more appropriate development interventions and empowerment. However, the nature of this participation is often problematic. In its most radical sense, 'participation' should mean that the poorest set the agenda about what projects should be adopted and how they should be run. They should be at the heart of implementation and evaluation. In reality, 'participation' is often very superficial, involving brief consultations along with contributions of labour and money. There is no real attempt to challenge existing forms of power relations and unequal structures.

The World Bank and the development departments of Northern governments, such as those mentioned at the start of this chapter, have taken on notions of 'participation'. It can fit very neatly into neo-liberal ideas about decentralization and a growing role for non-state actors but, in being used by such organizations, it often loses its radical transformative potential. The contributors to Cooke and Kothari's 2001 book *Participation: The New Tyranny?* discussed this trend, claiming that the idea of 'participation' had become ubiquitous and had been co-opted by development actors unwilling to challenge existing power relations. However, this does not mean that 'participation' should be abandoned as a concept in development policy; as Hickey and Mohan's (2004) book on the topic argues, there are ways in which communities, working with NGOs, can achieve real transformations in their lives through participatory projects.

Post-development

The chapter so far has dealt with different conceptions of 'development' and the debates on how 'development' should be achieved. However, the concept of 'post-development' challenges the very notion of 'development', arguing that rather than debating how it should be achieved, development as a goal should be abandoned.

Arturo Escobar's book *Encountering Development: The Making and Unmaking of the Third World* (1995) is often regarded as a key text in the post-development field. Using examples from Colombia, Escobar highlighted the ways in which post-Second World War development interventions were based on identifying 'problems' which needed a technical fix through aid programmes. Escobar argued that the problems were identified by outsiders and based on Eurocentric ideas of progress and modernity rather than the perspectives and needs of the people directly affected. Similar arguments are made in *The Development Dictionary*, edited by Sachs (1992), where the power relations inherent in the construction and use of a range of development ideas, such as 'poverty', are discussed. For post-development theorists, 'development' is a Northern idea which has been imposed on Southern countries, peoples and environments with very serious negative consequences. Post-development theorists argue that small-scale, people-led, environmentally friendly change is what is required.

While post-development's arguments about the ways in which discourses of development come out of particular contexts and can be imposed by the more powerful on the least powerful have been welcomed, the approach has also received much criticism. The 'development' being criticized by theorists such as Escobar and Sachs is usually represented by the top-down modernization-style projects of the 1950s and 1960s, rather than the more diverse range of policies which are adopted today. Post-developmentists have also been criticized for being negative about 'development', without recognizing some of the positive outcomes from certain 'development' policies such as reduced infant mortality rates (see Chapter 9 and Corbridge 1998).

Development aid in the early twenty-first century

Despite the critiques of the 'development' project by post-developmentists and the promotion of 'bottom-up' strategies, 'development' interventions from the North to the South remain a key part of the global agenda at the start of the twenty-first century. However, 'development' has now become very focused on 'poverty reduction'. While reducing poverty was certainly implicit in development policies in the past and at global, national and local levels, it has now taken centre stage. This focus on poverty is justified because poverty is viewed as restricting people's life chances and inhibiting wider forms of economic and political change. This is reflected in the Millennium Development Goals (MDGs) which were agreed by the United Nations in 2000 (United Nations 2006). MDG number 1 is 'to eradicate extreme poverty and hunger' and the target which the UN members agreed to was 'between 1990 and 2015, [to] halve the proportion of people whose income is less than US $1 per day'. These MDGs now shape development interventions in many spheres, including the World Bank, the development agencies of Northern governments and some large NGOs.

According to the World Bank and Northern governments, the best route to poverty reduction is to follow neo-liberal policies. However, there have been some changes since the SAPs of the 1980s. In the 1990s, Poverty Reduction Strategy Papers (PRSPs) were introduced as part of the conditions for World Bank funding to national governments. PRSPs require governments to explain what steps they will take to address poverty issues in their country, and there has to be evidence of citizen participation in the discussion and writing of the PRSP. As outlined earlier, the nature of participation can vary a great deal.

Development assistance from multilateral agencies and Northern governments is not only dependent on appropriate PRSPs: there are also issues around what has been termed 'good governance', which includes factors such as 'democratization, the rule of law, human rights protection, transparency, participation and accountability' (Minogue 2002: 117). Great importance is placed on the involvement of a range of different development actors, most noticeably the state, the private sector and NGOs. Attaching political conditions to development assistance is supposed to make development aid more effective and efficient, as corruption and waste should be reduced and assistance should be directed to the people and communities who need it the most. While this clearly fits into the neo-liberal agenda, Minogue (2002) highlights the fact that political conditionality has become much more widespread following the end of the Cold War. Previously, Northern governments had been willing to overlook political irregularities in return for support from 'friendly' countries. The end of the Cold War changed the geopolitical landscape, but the 'good governance' agenda still seems to be selectively implemented, particularly within the context of the 'war on terror'. There are also debates around the Eurocentric nature of the 'good governance' agenda, with little or no recognition of the cultural specificity of ideas of individual human rights, for example.

If governments are viewed as following the good governance rules, development aid is sometimes forthcoming. In 2005 nearly US $77.5 billion of overseas development assistance (ODA) was provided to the poorer countries of the world, with over a quarter of this going to Africa (OECD 2006). This aid was a vital contributor to countries' economic status, particularly in sub-Saharan Africa in both 1990 and 2003 (see Figure 11.2). ODA also made up over a quarter of GDP in nine countries in 2003, of which only the Occupied Palestinian Territories and Timor-Leste were outside Africa (see Table 11.2).

The focus of much development attention on sub-Saharan Africa is not surprising given the prevalence of poverty in the region, but on a global scale more poor people (as measured by living on less than US $1 per day) are found in Asia. This is because of the poverty levels in China (16.6 per cent under US $1 per day in 2003) and India (34.7 per cent), both of which have populations of over one billion. There have been a number of high-profile attempts to address Africa's plight, both of which stress the capacity of Africans themselves to deal with many of the challenges facing the region. The first of these, the New Partnership for Africa's Development (NEPAD), was set up in 2001 and came out of cooperation between African governments. The Commission for Africa was set up by the UK Prime

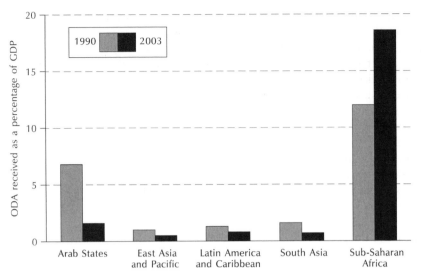

Figure 11.2. Net ODA received as percentage of GDP 1990 and 2003.
Source: Based on data from UNDP (2005: Table 19).

Table 11.2. Countries where over 25 per cent of GDP was derived from ODA in 2003

Country	%
Democratic Republic of Congo	94.9
São Tomé and Principe	63.3
Guinea–Bisssau	60.8
Timor-Leste	44.2
Eritrea	40.9
Burundi	37.6
Sierra Leone	37.5
Malawi	29.1
Occupied Palestinian Territories	28.1

Source: Adapted from UNDP (2005: Table 19).

Minister, Tony Blair, in 2004 to identify the challenges facing Africa and to provide recommendations to reduce poverty (Commission for Africa 2005: 2). It was made up of sixteen people, most of whom were African politicians, business people and civil servants, and reported in 2005.

In both cases, the call is for partnerships between African governments, African people (living in Africa and overseas) and external donors. While the focus is on neo-liberal economic policies and the importance of good governance, there are also calls for changes in the way the international system is operating. Rather than focusing either on factors internal to a country, as with 1970s neo-liberalism, or with exogenous factors, as with dependency theories, there is now an attempt to consider both elements in the drive for 'development'.

Considering structural factors of the global trading system is no longer the preserve of left-wing theorists and activists. Meetings of the World Trade Organization (WTO), since it was formed in 1995, have been increasingly characterized by pressures from Southern governments and NGOs to make the world trading system fairer. WTO trade talks have been increasingly breaking down as groups of governments within the South, most noticeably China, Brazil and India have been demanding changes in the way Northern governments organize trade. Southern governments complain that while they are expected to follow the rules on free trade, the European Union and USA protect their agricultural markets and provide subsidies to their farmers. Such demands are also being taken up by some NGOs as they take on an advocacy role, in addition to their activities as service providers.

So 'development' remains a goal for governments, individuals, organizations and communities across the world. While what 'development' is and how it should be achieved may vary widely, the idea that improvements in living standards, political participation and equity are desirable is widespread. Dominant debates about routes to development and the resources available to achieve development reflect existing power relations, not only on a global and national scale, but also within communities and households.

Further reading

Desai, V. and Potter, R. (eds) (2002) *The Companion to Development Studies*. London: Arnold.

Hickey, S. and Mohan, G. (eds) (2004) *Participation: From Tyranny to Transformation?* London: Zed Books.

Kothari, U. and Minogue, M. (eds) (2002) *Development Theory and Practice*. Basingstoke: Palgrave.

Power, M. (2003) *Rethinking Development Geographies*. London: Routledge.

Rahnema, M. with Bawtree, V. (eds) (1997) *The Post-Development Reader*. London: Zed Books.

Sen, A. (1999) *Development as Freedom*. Oxford: Oxford University Press.

Simon, D. (ed.) (2006) *Fifty Key Thinkers in Development*. London: Routledge.

Willis, K. (2005) *Theories and Practices of Development*. London: Routledge.

World Bank (2006) http://www.worldbank.org

References

Balassa, B. (1971) Trade policies in developing countries. *American Economic Review* 61, 178–87.

Borlaug, N. (1970) The Green Revolution: Peace and Humanity, speech on the occasion of the awarding of the Nobel Peace Prize. Available at http://nobelprize.org/peace/laureates/1970/borlaug-lecture.htm

Collier, P.S., Radhwan, S. and Wangwe, S. (1986) *Labour and Poverty in Rural Tanzania*. Oxford: Oxford University Press.

Commission for Africa (2005) *Our Common Interest: An Argument*. London: Penguin Books. (See also http://www.commissionforafrica.org)

Cooke, B. and Kothari, U. (eds) (2001) *Participation: The New Tyranny?* London: Zed Books.

Corbridge, S. (1998) Beneath the pavement only soil: the poverty of post-development. *Journal of Development Studies* 34 (6), 138–48.

Cornia, G.A., Jolly, R. and Stewart, F. (1987) *Adjustment with a Human Face*. Oxford: Oxford University Press.

Edwards, M. and Hulme, D. (eds) (1995) *Non-Governmental Organisations – Performance and Accountability: Beyond the Magic Bullet*. London: Earthscan.

Elliott, J.A. (1999) *An Introduction to Sustainable Development*, second edition. London: Routledge.

Escobar, A. (1995) *Encountering Development: The Making and Unmaking of the Third World*. Princeton: Princeton University Press.

Frank, A.G. (1967) *Capitalism and Underdevelopment in Latin America*. London: Monthly Review Press.

Lewis, W.A. (1955) *The Theory of Economic Growth*. London: Allen and Unwin.

Meadows, D.H., Meadows, D.L., Randers, J. and Behrens, W.W. III (1972) *The Limits to Growth*. London: Pan Books.

Minogue, M. (2002) Power to the people? Good governance and the reshaping of the state. In U. Kothari and M. Minogue (eds) *Development Theory and Practice*, pp. 117–35. Basingstoke: Palgrave.

One World International Foundation (2006) *Global Partner Database*. Available at http://www.one-world.net/section/partners

Organization for Economic Cooperation and Development (OECD) (2006) *Development Aid by Region 2005*. Available at http://www.oecd.org/dac/stats/regioncharts

Rodney, W. (1972) *How Europe Underdeveloped Africa*. London: Bogle-L'Ouverture Publications.

Rostow, W.W. (1960) *The Stages of Economic Growth: A Non-Communist Manifesto*. Cambridge: Cambridge University Press.

Sachs, W. (ed.) (1992) *The Development Dictionary: A Guide to Knowledge as Power*. London: Zed Books.

Schumacher, E.F. (1973) *Small is Beautiful*. London: Abacus.

United Nations (2006) *UN Millennium Development Goals*. Available at http://www.un.org/millenniumgoals/

United Nations Development Programme (UNDP) (2005) *Human Development Report 2005*. Oxford: Oxford University Press. (Also available at http://www.undp.org)

Van Rooy, A. (1998) *Civil Society and the Aid Industry*. London: Earthscan.

World Bank (1993) *The East Asian Miracle*. Oxford: Oxford University Press.

World Commission on Environment and Development (WCED) (1987) *Our Common Future*. Oxford: Oxford University Press.

12

Economic globalization

Philip Kelly

'Globalization' is a curious word. When it passes the lips of a political leader it is nearly always being used to refer to an external and irresistible set of forces that a country must respond to – a set of pressures to bear, or a competitive race to keep up with. When it is used in the popular media it often carries the same connotation but is also treated as something that isn't just 'outside the door' and threatening to come in, but as a factual transformation of life that defines our current epoch – it has 'arrived'. When it is used by 'anti-global' activists and protestors it is often as shorthand for a capitalist economic system that is exploitative, unfair and ecologically unsustainable. Hence the apparently contradictory placard being waved at the Seattle protests of 1999: 'Worldwide Struggle Against Globalization'. The problem with all of these interpretations is that they treat globalization as an external force and as a completed state of affairs. There is often very little sense that globalization is something that has been created out of a set of political choices, or that it ultimately boils down to a set of real processes of interconnection between places, or that it is a set of ongoing transforming tendencies rather than a completed transformation.

It is important, then, to unpack the word and the concept in order to understand both how it is used in political and popular debate, and what it refers to in terms of underlying processes of change. This chapter starts this process by examining the types of flows and connections that constitute contemporary globalization. We need to remind ourselves that global interconnections are nothing new, and have been emerging over at least the last 500 years. There is, however, fairly compelling evidence that there is something distinctive about contemporary economic globalization that sets it apart from its historical precedents, and our arguments move on to consider five criteria for assessing recent change: extensity, intensity, velocity, impact and institutionalization. In the final section we take a different angle and examine the ways in which globalization has become, as an idea, more than the sum of its parts – as a discourse it serves not just to describe the world, but also to make us think about it in a certain way.

What is economic globalization?

If we assume that there is something real 'out there' that is labelled globalization, then what are the dimensions of economic life in which we should search?

To address this question it is worth thinking about the three fundamental components of economic life: **capital** that is invested in the production of tangible goods or intangible services; **commodities** themselves, which may consist of tangible products such as food or computers, or intangible products such as television broadcasts or software that are traded and moved across space; and **people**, as both productive labour and consumers of commodities. An initial definition of economic globalization, then, could be based on the increasing movement of these three economic flows across global space.

It is important to note at the outset, then, that economic globalization is a *multi-stranded* set of flows. Although the word is often used to talk about the import and export of commodities (from cars and clothes, to olives and oil) and the global institutions and agreements that regulate them, we must also be mindful of the less tangible flows of services and knowledge that are also a form of trade, the financial flows that facilitate these trade flows, and flows of people as temporary or permanent migrants and tourists. Often these flows are connected together – for example, financial flows of investment from the US to Mexico create resorts that attract international tourists, or build factories that will generate exports. Or, in an even more convoluted manner, we could imagine German capital invested in an electronics factory in the Philippines, whose products are being supplied to an American assembly plant in Malaysia, and whose workers might save some of their income in order to finance an immigration application to Canada. The point, therefore, is that flows of capital, commodities and people are connected together (for more on this issue, see Sassen 1988).

A second point to make is that globalization is a not something 'out there', but is constituted by many repeated and increasing acts of interconnection. It is, therefore, nonsensical to talk about immigrant workers arriving 'because of globalization', or Chinese-made toys dominating markets in North America and Europe 'because of globalization'. These processes *are* globalization – globalization is, in reality if not grammatically, a verb not a noun. This also points to why it is important to see globalization not as an 'end-state' – a condition that we either have or haven't attained. Instead, it should be viewed as a set of 'globalizing tendencies' that are proceeding and in some cases intensifying with the variety of flows and connections that it comprises.

A final point to make in defining globalization is that it is not just about the movement of money, or things, or people, across global space: it is also concerned with the ways in which economic processes in particular places are becoming increasingly dependent upon processes happening or originating elsewhere. In other words, the world is not simply becoming more connected, it is also becoming more *integrated*.

Economic globalization can, then, be defined as the increasing linkages between places across the world through various interconnected economic flows, the deepening institutionalization of these linkages, and the process of intensifying interdependence that is created as a result. Many would argue, however, that this process is not a new one: indeed, it has been emerging for the last 500 years or longer. It is important, therefore, that we acknowledge the historical precedents for contemporary globalization before suggesting that something new is happening now.

Globalization in historical context

It is only in the last 10–15 years that globalization has become a ubiquitous buzzword to capture a sense that the integration of globally dispersed places is dramatically increasing. In the frenzy of hype and controversy over this concept, one could be forgiven for thinking that our predecessors led very insulated and disconnected lives. In the hyperlinked world of dis-counted air travel, email, and fresh fruit all the year round, it's hard to imagine how distant parts of the world could ever have been connected together without the technologies we now take for granted.

Yet global economic interconnection is far from being a novel process. It was 500 years ago that European ships reached the furthest corners of the Eurasian continent to trade in the exotic goods of the region. What they discovered, however, were extensive trade routes already established by Arab, Gujarati, Malay, Chinese and other peoples, stretching across virtually all of what we now call Asia (Wolf 1982; Reid 1993) (Figure 12.1).

As European societies flexed their military muscles around the world, they created trading empires, drawing raw materials such as sugar, spices, cotton and rubber into their burgeon-ing industrial economies. For 300 years until the 1850s, Spanish galleons plied the Pacific and Atlantic oceans, linking the Philippine islands with Acapulco, in what is now Mexico, and ultimately with Spain itself. For other colonial powers too (notably Britain, France, Portugal and the Netherlands) their overseas adventures were initially less about conquering territory and more about establishing control over trade routes – which usually meant control of port cities rather than extensive hinterlands. Thus from the sixteenth century onwards, some scholars identify an integrated capitalist world economy based on market exchange of raw materials, mostly agricultural crops or mineral resources (Wallerstein 1974). Economic life, has, from this point of view, been 'world-wide' since long before the notion of globalization was coined.

By the mid-nineteenth century, then, the world was very much knitted together by flows of capital and commodities, and a division of labour existed between the industrializing countries of the 'core' and the largely resource-based economies of the 'periphery'. Indeed,

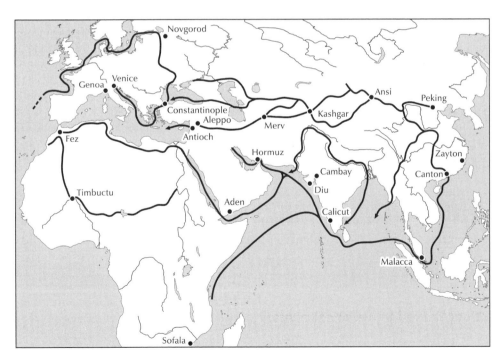

Figure 12.1. Map of Old World trade routes in AD 1400.
Source: Adapted from Wolf (1982: 28)

such was the density of these global strands of interconnection that European powers increasingly felt the need to control hinterlands and territories, as well as trading ports, in order to protect their access to raw materials and commodities from their competitors. Thus began the scramble to carve up Africa, South America and much of Asia into territorial colonies, all aimed at securing the supply of raw materials for the expanding industries of the European core. One could argue, in fact, that the world of the late nineteenth century was even more integrated than the world of today – after all, within colonial empires, the flows of capital and commodities had far fewer obstacles than they do in today's world of borders, customs and national currencies (Hirst and Thompson 1996). Writing these lines in 1848, Karl Marx and Friedrich Engels were not being prescient about the future of capitalism, but were simply describing what they saw happening at the time:

> Urged onward by the need for an ever-expanding market, the bourgeoisie invades every quarter of the globe. It occupies every corner; forms settlements and sets up means of communication here, there, and everywhere.
>
> By the exploitation of the world market, the bourgeoisie has given cosmopolitan character to production and consumption in every land. To the despair of the reactionaries, it has deprived industry of its national foundation. Of the old-established national industries, some have already been destroyed and others are day by day undergoing destruction. They are dislodged by new industries, whose introduction is becoming a matter of life and death for all civilised nations: by industries which no longer depend upon the homeland for their raw materials, but draw these from the remotest spots; and by industries whose products are consumed, not only in the country of manufacture, but the wide world over. Instead of the old wants, satisfied by the products of native industry, new wants appear, wants which can only be satisfied by the products of distant lands and unfamiliar climes. The old local and national self-sufficiency and isolation are replaced by a system of universal intercourse, of all-round interdependence of the nations. We see this in intellectual production no less than in material. The intellectual products of each nation are now the common property of all. National exclusiveness and particularism are fast becoming impossible. Out of the manifold national and local literatures, a world literature arises.
>
> By rapidly improving the means of production and by enormously facilitating communication, the bourgeoisie drags all the nations, even the most barbarian, into the orbit of civilisation. Cheap wares form the heavy artillery with which it batters down Chinese walls and compels the most obstinate of barbarians to overcome their hatred of the foreigner. It forces all the nations, under pain of extinction, to adopt the capitalist method of production; it constrains them to accept what is called civilisation, to become bourgeois themselves. In short, it creates a world after its own image.
>
> (Marx and Engels 1963: 28–31)

Putting aside the colourful language and the casual racism of the times, we have here a description of economic (as well as political and cultural) globalization 150 years ago that would not be out of place in relation to today's world economy. But it is also worth noting that trends towards integration have not moved solely in the direction of deepening global ties. While the late nineteenth century was a period of ever closer interconnection, at least *within empires*, most of the twentieth century saw decreasing levels of integration and growing economic nationalism and protectionism. In Western Europe and North America, much of the last century was a period of emphatically nationally based economic activities. Contemporary globalization must, therefore be understood both as a recurrence of previous trends, albeit in an intensified form and, potentially a reversible one.

What is different about economic globalization?

If the historical record of global economic integration reminds us that the process has a long lineage but one that is not immune to setbacks and reversals, we should also take note from Marx that the expansion of capitalist relations of production and exchange around the world is no mere outcome of the technological developments that make it possible. It is, rather, a fundamental imperative of capitalism as an economic system to constantly expand and innovate in search of new ways to increase profit. At the level of capitalism in general, then, there is little that is new about globalization. It simply represents an expansion of capitalism through the creation or incorporation of new spaces – a process that is as old as capitalism itself, but always appears in new and innovative guises (Harvey 1982).

If spatial expansion is inherent in capitalism, and if economic connectivity itself is not a new phenomenon, then what is it that distinguishes our times and makes globalization such a compelling characterization? Globalization was barely used as a concept prior to the 1990s – tap the word into any library catalogue or database and thousands of items will show up, but nearly all of them published since 1990. What has happened that has made the current period distinctive? We can address this question by examining five features of contemporary globalization and noting how they have created a new and distinctive context for economic life: extensity, intensity, velocity, impact and institutionalization. These are based on the analytical framework developed by Held *et al.* (1999), although their empirical investigation of the processes of globalization is exclusively focused upon developed industialized countries of the global North, what they term 'States in Advanced Capitalist Societies' (SIACS).

The geographical extensity of globalization

Economic globalization is, at its core, a spatial concept – it implies a stretching of economic relations to 'fill out' the planetary space occupied by human societies. Perhaps the most significant events in facilitating this completion of the spatial scale of the 'global' economy over the last three decades have been the collapse of the Soviet Union and its satellite states in Eastern Europe and their opening up to investment, trade and migration flows. Following the momentous events of 1989, the 'iron curtain' was lifted and flows of capital, commodities and people started to move between hitherto separate blocks of countries. Suddenly, there was no longer a bi-polar world divided between 'first world' capitalist and 'second world' communist societies.

While they were differently timed, and operated in different ways, other closed economies also increasingly opened themselves up over the 1980s and 1990s – including, for example, Deng Xiao Ping's 'open door' policy in China since 1978, and Vietnam's *Doi Moi* (or 'renovation') initiated in 1986. Both started the process of allowing market forces to encroach upon centrally planned socialist economies. At the same time, structural adjustment programmes imposed by the International Monetary Fund and World Bank in many parts of the developing world forced governments to liberalize their economies and dismantle barriers to trade and commodity flows as a condition for access to development loans. These changes greatly increased the scope of places connected into worldwide economic flows. Only following the dissolving of these barriers between the 'first', 'second' and 'third' worlds was it possible to talk of economic activities that were truly global in scope – hence the emergence of 'globalization' in common usage dating from about that time.

Not only have political and regulatory barriers been removed to economic flows, but technological advances in transport and communications (to be discussed below), and changes in production processes, have allowed the integration of far more places than ever in the creation of a single product or service. Even the simplest of commodities, such as a piece of fruit or a T-shirt, might involve contributions from a handful of countries. A more complex commodity, such as a car or a computer, might involve dozens of different sites. All are connected by transport and communications technologies that allow different parts of the production process to be separated across vast distances but coordinated globally. In this sense, globalization has become far more extensive than at any point in the past. While colonial trading networks tended to be bilateral linkages between resource-producing colonial territories and the industrialized metropolitan cores, contemporary networks of production are far more disparate and diverse.

Nevertheless, most of the flows that are commonly thought of as constituting globalization are actually between far fewer places than one might imagine. As Figure 12.2 shows for the cases of foreign direct investment flows, around 80 per cent of the world's stock of FDI originates in the US, EU and Japan. Figure 12.3 provides a similar picture for trade in manufactured goods – 81 per cent of world merchandise exports originate in the US, EU or East/Southeast Asia.

Just as there is an uneven geography to the process of incorporation into global flows, there is also an unevenness in the nature of that incorporation in different places. This is an important point as it highlights the dangers of conceiving a globalizing economic world as some sort of level playing field. In fact, just as during the colonial period, some places are incorporated into the global economy as resource producers, realizing very little of the value that will ultimately be added to their natural riches. Other places, such as business and financial hubs, are nodes for the highest value and most richly rewarded activities in the global economy – for every few hundred poorly paid labourers on a plantation, down a mine or in a factory, there is a lawyer, currency/commodity trader, accountant or management

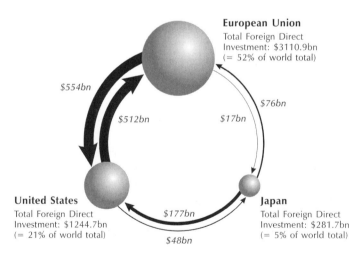

Figure 12.2. Global triad concentration of FDI flows.

Source: After Dicken (2003). Reprinted by permission of Sage Publications Ltd.

Copyright © Peter Dicken 2003.

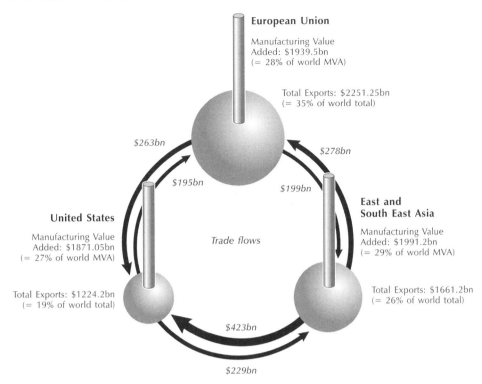

Figure 12.3. Global triad flows of manufacturing exports.

Source: After Dicken (2003). Reprinted by permission of Sage Publications Ltd.

Copyright © Peter Dicken 2003.

consultant who is richly rewarded. Similarly, when a European tourist visits a 'hill tribe' in northern Thailand they are both engaged in a globe-spanning form of economic activity, but clearly on very different terms. Thus we should be careful not to obscure the uneven terms of incorporation into a global economy with the demise of a language based on 'first', 'second' and 'third' worlds, or 'core' and 'periphery'.

The intensity of global interconnections

While the geographical extent of economic relations is an important criterion for assessing the realities of globalization, the presence of a connection is in itself not enough. During the Spanish colonial period in the Philippines, from the sixteenth until the nineteenth centuries, the colony was connected to the Americas and to the European core by trading links, but only one galleon a year was making the trip from Manila to Acapulco. The connection was there, but the intensity of the link was small. We also therefore need to consider the magnitude of global flows and their relative importance.

Between 1975 and 2000, the total number of recorded migrants around the world increased from 84.5 million to around 175 million (IOM 2005). This represented an increase from 2.2 per cent to 2.9 per cent of the world's population. The remittances sent home by those migrants are substantial contributions not just to their families and communities, but also to the national economies of sending countries (see also Chapters 9 and 59). Remittances sent

189

through formal channels alone (and the real amounts would be larger still) had increased from US $46 billion in 1990 to an estimated US $232 billion by 2005 (IOM 2005; Migration Policy Institute 2006). Table 12.1 shows the magnitude of remittances in 2001 for countries with the highest level of dependence on such flows. Ten countries around the world were dependent on migration remittances for more than 10 per cent of their total wealth.

The growing magnitude of other international flows tells the same story. Total world exports of merchandise in 1970 amounted to US $317 billion; by 1990 this had grown to just over US $3,493 billion, and by 2004 it stood at US $8,975 billion. Similarly, total Foreign Direct Investment outflows stood at US $14.1 billion in 1970, US $239 billion in 1990, and US $730 billion by 2004.

To put these figures in perspective, global trade in goods and services amounted to 18.8 per cent of global output (or GDP) in 1980, but accounted for 27.2 per cent by 2004. Corporate operations based on foreign direct investment – that is, companies producing outside of their home country – created 6.5 per cent of the world's goods and service in 1990, but 9.6 per cent in 2004 (UNCTAD 2005). In the space of just 14 years, we saw a very significant increase not just in the magnitude of foreign investment and trade flows, but also in their significance in the global economy. Across a variety of indicators, then, we see a growing intensity of global economic flows, and as a result of the increasing intensity of interconnection, the interdependence of places has also intensified.

The speed of interconnection

While global connectedness may have existed for centuries but intensified in recent years, the speed with which places can be connected through various forms of flows has taken

Table 12.1. Top fifteen countries with the highest total remittances received as a percentage of the GDP, 2001 (US$)

Country	Total remittances (in millions)	GDP (in millions)	Total population	Total remittances as percentage of GDP	Total remittances per capita
Lesotho	209.0	796.7	1,852,808	26.2	112.80
Vanuatu	53.3	212.8	192,910	25.0	276.14
Jordan	2,011.0	8,829.1	5,153,378	22.8	390.23
Bosnia and Herzegovina	860.1	4,769.1	3,922,205	18.0	219.29
Albania	699.0	4,113.7	3,510,484	17.0	199.12
Nicaragua	335.7	2,067.8	4,918,393	16.2	68.25
Yemen	1,436.9	9,177.2	17,479,206	15.7	82.21
Moldova (Republic of)	223.1	1,479.4	4,431,570	15.1	50.34
El Salvador	1,925.2	13,738.9	6,237,662	14.0	308.64
Jamaica	1,058.7	7,784.1	2,665,636	13.6	397.17
Dominican Republic	1,982.0	21,211.0	8,475,396	9.3	233.85
Philippines	6,366.0	71,437.7	81,369,751	8.9	78.24
Uganda	483.0	5,675.3	24,170,422	8.5	19.98
Honduras	541.0	6,385.8	6,357,941	8.5	85.09
Ecuador	1,420.0	17,982.4	13,183,978	7.9	107.71

Source: Migration Policy Institute (2003); http://www.migrationinformation.org/feature/display.cfm?ID=137

quantum leaps through various technological advances in recent decades. Technologies such as commercial jet aircraft for mass passenger travel, and containerization for relatively inexpensive freight movement, both of which emerged in the 1950s, have facilitated the speed and scale of physical flows and are evaluated in the next chapter. Communications, meanwhile, based on satellite linkages and optical fibre technology, allow instantaneous data transfer, making all sorts of activities much easier to coordinate and manage across global space (see Chapter 61). Thus what could be transported before can now be moved far more quickly and economically, and what could never have been transmitted in the past (for example, satellite television, webcasts and documents attached to emails) is now possible. What we have seen, then, is a process of time–space compression, in which the time needed to move people, things or information has been vastly reduced.

Nevertheless, as we have already noted, the possibilities created by technology aren't necessarily realized, for a variety of reasons. First, transportation systems still comprise hubs that aren't necessarily close and accessible to all. One might have to travel for several hours to reach an airport even if a flight itself covers a large distance in a small amount of time. The same is true for mobile phone coverage – in many parts of the world, access to global wireless communications are an exclusively urban phenomenon. This is particularly so in the case of satellite and optical fibre linkages. The bandwidth available for data transfer between continents, for example, is far higher into and out of North America than it is between any other continents (see Figure 12.4).

The realities of rapid global connectivity are often therefore experienced by nodal points in the global system, rather than uniformly across space. It might be more accurate, then, to

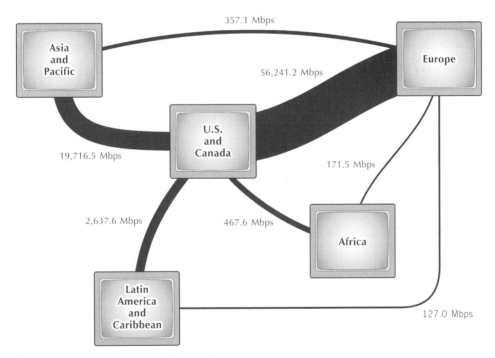

Figure 12.4. Interregional Internet bandwidth.

Source: After Dicken (2003). Reprinted by permission of Sage Publications Ltd.

Copyright © Peter Dicken 2003.

think about globalization as an intense degree of connectivity between nodes in a network, rather than the enveloping universality that the word implies.

A second point to note is that access to the technologies of rapid transport and communications is largely the preserve of the privileged few, and there is therefore a social as well as spatial unevenness to the technological possibilities of transport and communications. While internet access creates *possibilities* for instantaneous transfer of data and an unlimited marketplace, without access to a computer and reliable electrical power it is largely meaningless. In Africa, for example, it is estimated that 2.64 per cent of the population were internet users in 2004, and across all of Asia the figure was about 8.2 per cent. In the United Kingdom, however, the figure was close to 64 per cent (International Telecommunications Union 2005).

Related to this point about social unevenness of access to space-shrinking technology is a third point – technology is largely driven by *profitability* rather than *possibility*. Technology doesn't drive the globalization of capitalist economic activities, but is itself driven by the imperatives of capitalism. Technologies of connection are developed for instrumental purposes – they are developed where they will be used, and they are used by those who can pay for them. We should therefore avoid inferring that the privileges of global movement afforded to the few are actually accessible to the many.

The impact of globalization

We have established the increasing, but uneven, extensity, intensity and speed of global economic connections. These measures calibrate the magnitude and extent of global connections, but only implicitly acknowledge the impact of economic globalization. How, then, is globalization implicated in the lives of people who are caught up in dynamics of change at the global scale? For any given strand of global connectivity, there are countless ways of assessing its impact, and we have already noted the significance of remittances in particular in the lives of those receiving them.

A more dramatic, and negative, recent example of global integration impacting lives was during the Asian economic crisis of 1997–98. Since the 1980s, a number of developing Asian economies had been encouraged, and in some cases coerced, by international lenders to liberalize their economies and permit the free entry and exit of greater flows of investment capital – both direct investment in the bricks and mortar of factories, hotels, resorts, etc., and the even more mobile financial capital that sought profit from trading in stocks, bonds, currencies and debt. In countries such as Thailand, Indonesia and South Korea, capital flows fuelled booming economies and vastly inflated valuations of land and other assets. These inflated prices encouraged more lenders and investors to arrive, hoping to cash in on the boom. Money was lent to unprofitable and unproductive projects, often on the basis of political connections rather than economic viability.

However, with a booming economy comes inflation of prices, and this undermined the position of exporters in an increasingly competitive global economy. Eventually, currency traders noted this discrepancy and started selling their holdings of Thai baht, and then Indonesian rupiah and Korean wan, as well as other regional currencies. The value of these currencies crashed in the second half of 1997, leaving manufacturers unable even to buy the raw materials needed to fill their export orders. The response of the International Monetary Fund was to bail out affected economies, but only with conditions attached that forced drastic budget cutting upon national governments and the further opening of national economies to global flows of trade and investment.

The impact of this crisis was sudden and dramatic. As a result of these countries' integration into global flows of capital, decisions made in the trading offices of banks and investment houses in Tokyo, London, New York and elsewhere had a rapid effect on the livelihoods of millions. In Indonesia alone, during 1998, food prices rose 133 per cent, real wages went down by 35 per cent, and there was a 50 per cent increase in the number of people living below the poverty line (Silvey and Elmhirst 2003; Manning 2000).

This example highlights just how much global integration can affect the lives of workers and consumers everywhere. One could equally argue, of course, that the dramatic improvements in living standard in many countries of East and Southeast Asia were a result of the same openness to foreign investment and access to global markets, but the crisis of 1997–98 highlighted the vulnerabilities that come with such exposure.

The institutionalization of globalization

The novel dimensions of globalization that we have highlighted so far – extensity, intensity, velocity and impact – all relate to the flows that connect places together. A final dimension, perhaps most important of all, is the deepening institutionalization of such global flows through a variety of organizations that facilitate, foster and regulate them. The most important among these are states and supra-state organizations, private sector intermediaries and, most of all, transnational corporations.

States and globalization

We noted at the beginning of this chapter that political leaders often represent globalization as something external, something beyond their control – a force that has to be reckoned with, but cannot be resisted. What this rhetoric conceals is the extent to which states themselves are the authors and shapers of globalization. It has been the policy of more and more states to open their economies to global flows of capital, commodities, and (to a lesser extent) labour, that has allowed such global flows to exist.

In the trading of commodities, the lowering of tariff and other barriers within regional groupings such as the European Union or the North American Free Trade Agreement, has been supplemented through global institutions. Since 1995, the World Trade Organization has provided a framework for the free (or at least freer) movement of commodities between member states. The WTO and any other trade agreement, is, however, an agreement *between states*. Similarly, it is governments that decide on the conditions for capital investment within their jurisdictions, issue work or tourist visas to foreign nationals, permit the use of radio and television frequencies and so on.

States may also carve out parts of their territories where different regimes of mobility are applied to capital, commodities and people – for example in export processing zones. Thus it is governments that agree to create the conditions for globalization – it is not necessarily something beyond their control. That said, we should be careful not to homogenize the diversity of states participating in the global trading system. While some governments have the power to resist certain elements of integration (for example, several European governments, including Britain, have remained outside the Euro currency zone), others are almost forcibly integrated. As we saw in the example of the Asian economic crisis above, developing countries that have needed to turn for financial assistance to institutions such as the International Monetary Fund and the World Bank have usually been left with little choice but to open up their economies to imported goods and foreign investment.

States, then, are key actors in the processes of economic globalization – they are not the marginalized anachronisms often implied by enthusiasts of the 'borderless world'. What we have seen occurring over the last few decades, however, is a widespread delegation of *national* state powers over economic flows to supra-state organizations. Increasingly, the regulation of global capitalism is in the hands not of cooperating states but of state-mandated regulatory authorities – in this sense there has been an important shift from internationalism to globalism. The prime example of this process is the World Trade Organization, formed in 1995 as a culmination to nine years of negotiation under the General Agreement on Tariffs and Trade that had regulated trade flows in much of the world since the Second World War. At its founding the WTO included 124 countries, and it provides a framework for challenging 'unfair' trade barriers imposed by one country on another. The WTO is, however, only the most prominent of an array of global bodies that have taken on the management of international flows of goods, services and information (see Chapter 18). Other examples include those that are sector-specific (OPEC regulating oil exports from many producers, for example, or the now-defunct Multi-Fibre Arrangement that governed the textile trade from 1974 to 2004). The rise of such state-like regulatory organizations is part of a distinctively globalizing world economy and unlike anything that existed in previous eras of global connectedness.

Global private intermediaries

Besides formal intergovernmental frameworks for facilitating and regulating global flows, there are also increasing numbers of private institutions that shape and regulate the global economic system (Sassen 1996). Credit ratings agencies, for example, are entirely private companies and yet their evaluations of governments and firms can significantly affect creditworthiness and thus the flow of loan or investment capital that is available in different parts of the world. A rather different form of global intermediary is represented by the various organizations that inspect and certify agricultural crops and products on the basis of organic production techniques or fair trade practices. These organizations are not under the auspices of any state or group of states, but do influence the nature of trade in a marginal but increasingly important manner.

Transnational corporations

The institutional players that define globalization, at least in the popular consciousness, are transnational corporations (TNCs). A key transformation in recent decades has been the increasing number, scale and scope of firms that conduct their business on a global scale. Rather than simply trading with, or investing in, distant places, TNCs encompass multiple sites around the world within a unified and integrated management structure (see Chapter 22). While the other globalized institutions we have mentioned facilitate or regulate globalization (and, in their globality, are themselves a manifestation of globalization), it is TNCs that are the prime purveyors of global integration.

The manner in which this is done varies greatly depending on the firm and the sector involved. Some firms establish their global connections through networks of subcontractors – for example, from a clothing retailer in the US to a contractor in Hong Kong, and then to an array of subcontractors in China. Others actually own the facilities in which their products are made but may assemble components from various places around the world – Dell computers, for example, are assembled in just a few sites worldwide, but the components are drawn from suppliers in dozens of countries. These are just two examples drawn from diverse production networks that firms have constructed to take advantage of different costs, markets and incentives around the world (see Dicken 2003).

Imagined economies of globalization

We have thus far focused on the empirical realities of economic globalization, acknowledging that a set of transformational processes really are underway, but noting their unevenness and inequality. At the start of this chapter, however, we observed that globalization is not just a set of real changes underway 'out there', but is also a representation that is deployed in ways that are somewhat removed from the realities of the processes it actually describes. In this sense, globalization is a discourse – a vocabulary, idea and set of institutions that do not simply reflect the world, but also shape the way in which we understand it (Cameron and Palan 2004).

To *represent* contemporary economic change as 'globalization' has a number of implications. First of all, as we have noted throughout this chapter, it serves to erase the unevenness and inequality in the global economy by replacing spatial categories such as North and South, or developed and underdeveloped, with a universalizing sense of homogeneity. Second, globalization serves as a discursive tool with which to justify certain types of governmental policy while obscuring alternatives. When globalization is represented as the defining characteristic of our age, it marginalizes alternative ways of conceiving economic futures. The protection of livelihoods on a national scale gets represented as an anachronistic response when the rational thing to do is to 'ride the wave' of global integration. In other words, it precludes imagining economic life at other scales, such as the local, regional or national.

Are there alternative ways of reading globalization? Certainly there are progressive strategies for being a part of a globally integrated economy. Instead of seeing globalization as an external force that bears down upon localities, we could see globalization as the ultimate weaving together of a collective humanity – an approach that would imply a responsibility for the rights and needs of distant strangers (and environments). Movements to foster fair trade in products such as coffee, clothing and precious gems are examples of this kind of thinking.

In a more analytical way we can think about how globalization might be reconceived through metaphors and images that construct a more careful representation of the global economy. One approach is to emphasize the networked nature of the global economy, such that multiple places and people are linked together in complex and integrated processes (Dicken *et al.* 2001), but acknowledging in the process that these networks are uneven in their coverage. This is a useful approach, although we also need to stay aware of the power imbalances and inequalities that exist even for those who are enrolled in such networks (Sheppard 2002).

Another approach has been to view globalization not as a movement upwards of the scale at which economic lives are lived, but instead as a multiplication of scales. Therefore, economic processes must now be understood as being constituted by the intersection of forces that occupy local, regional, national and global scales (see Chapters 18–24 for illustrations of how these forces operate). None of these scales can be assumed to be necessarily more important nor more powerful than any of the others, but the ability to command larger scales is frequently a reflection of power. The production of scale is, therefore, a powerful tool in the contested struggle for livelihoods around the world (Kelly 1999; Herod and Wright 2002).

Conclusion

We have seen that dramatic changes have occurred in recent decades: the expansion of an integrated global economy to include formerly closed national territories; an intensification of the magnitude of flows of capital, commodities and people; the development of technologies to link together distant places through the transport of people, information and commodities; the growing impact of global connections on everyday life; and, the increasing numbers of economic institutions (states, supra-states, private intermediaries and transnational corporations) that organize themselves at a global scale. The result is a growing sense that the economic lives of places and people are increasingly integrated and interdependent. Moreover, the pace of change seems to have accelerated in the last two decades in particular.

We have, however, also noted a number of caveats that should serve to moderate our acceptance of globalization as the defining feature of our times. First, all of the trends we have identified are partial and ongoing tendencies – we live in a globalizing world, not a globalized one. Second, these tendencies are not without historical precedent and are the product of collective social arrangements at particular points in time. In this collective sense, we have created globalization; it is not an irresistible or inevitable force that has descended upon us. Finally, these tendencies are very unevenly developed, both across different places and across different social groups. Globalization is not a reality for everyone and in fact is a boon to the lives of relatively few. Much of what we consider to be the 'realities' of contemporary globalization is in fact a reflection of our positioning in urban centres of powerful countries, and it is we who reap the lion's share of the benefits.

Further reading

Cameron, A. and Palan, R. (2004) *The Imagined Economies of Globalization*. London: Sage.

Dicken, P. (2003) *Global Shift: Reshaping the Global Economic Map in the 21st Century*. London: Sage.

Dicken, P., Kelly, P., Olds, K. and Yeung, H (2001) Chains, networks, territories and scales: towards a relational framework for analyzing the global economy. *Global Networks* 1 (2), 89–112.

Held, D., McGrew, A., Goldblatt, D. and Perraton, J. (1999) *Global Transformations: Politics, Economics and Culture*. Cambridge: Polity Press.

Kelly, P. (1999) The geographies and politics of globalization. *Progress in Human Geography* 23: 379–400.

Stiglitz, J.E. (2002) *Globalization and its Discontents*. New York: Norton.

References

Cameron, A. and Palan, R. (2004) *The Imagined Economies of Globalization*. London: Sage.

Dicken, P. (2003) *Global Shift: Reshaping the Global Economic Map in the 21st Century*. London: Sage.

Harvey, D. (1982) *Limits to Capital*. Oxford: Blackwell.

Held, D., McGrew, A., Goldblatt, D. and Perraton, J. (1999) *Global Transformations: Politics, Economics and Culture*. Cambridge: Polity Press.

Herod, A. and Wright, M. (eds.) (2002) *Geographies of Power: Placing Scale*. Oxford: Blackwell.

Hirst, P. and Thompson, G. (1996) *Globalization in Question*. London: Polity Press.

International Telecommunications Union (2005) http://www.itu.int/ITU-D/ict/statistics/ (accessed 3 February 2006).

IOM (International Organization for Migration) (2005) *World Migration 2005: Costs and Benefits of International Migration*. New York: IOM.

Kelly, P. (1999) The geographies and politics of globalization. *Progress in Human Geography* 23, 379–400.

Manning, C. (2000) Labour market adjustment to Indonesia's economic crisis: context, trends, and implications. *Bulletin of Indonesian Economic Studies* 36 (1), 105–37.

Marx, K. and Engels, F. (1963) *The Communist Manifesto of Karl Marx and Friedrich Engels*, edited with an Introduction, Explanatory Notes and Appendices by D. Ryazanoff. New York: Russell and Russell. (Original work published 1848.)

Migration Policy Institute (2003) http://www.migrationinformation.org/feature/display.cfm?ID=137

——(2006) http://www.migrationpolicy.org/ (accessed 3 February 2006).

Reid, A. (1993) *Southeast Asian in the Age of Commerce: Volume II, Expansion and Crisis*. New Haven: Yale University Press.

Sassen, S. (1988) *The Mobility of Labor and Capital: A Study in International Investment and Labor Flow.* Cambridge: Cambridge University Press.

——(1996) *Losing Control? Sovereignty in an Age of Globalization*. New York: Columbia University Press.

Sheppard, E (2002) The spaces and times of globalization: place, scale, networks, and positionality. *Economic Geography* 78 (3), 307–30.

Silvey, R. and Elmhirst, R. (2003) Engendering social capital: women workers and rural–urban networks in Indonesia's crisis. *World Development* 31 (5), 865–79.

UNCTAD (2005) *World Investment Report 2005*. New York: UNCTAD.

Wallerstein, I. (1974) *The Modern World System*. New York: Academic Press.

Wolf, E. (1982) *Europe and the People Without History*. Berkeley: University of California Press.

13

Transport

The movement of goods and people

John Preston

Introduction

Transport geography may be defined simply as 'the study of transport systems and their spatial impacts' (Hoyle and Knowles 1992: 9). However, the authors of this definition would be the first to admit that this is somewhat simplistic. In particular, one can distinguish between the study of transport systems in and of themselves and the study of the inter-relationship between transport systems and socio-economic activity. This in turn has led to an increasing concern with social as well as spatial impacts. This chapter will focus both on transport systems themselves and their wider social impacts.

It was once fair to describe transport geography as a semi-moribund backwater. However, transport geography has undergone something of a revival in recent years, as reflected by the successful launch (in 1993) of the *Journal of Transport Geography* and a plethora of texts both in the UK (Hoyle and Knowles 1992; Tolley and Turton 1995) and North America (Black 2004; Taaffe *et al.* 1996; Hanson and Giuliano 2004), as well as the very influential *Transport Geography* on the web (now rebranded as *The Geography of Transport Systems* – Rodrigue *et al.* 2006). Similarly, in Germany, the Transport Research Group of the German Geographical Society has been increasingly active (Gather *et al.* 2001). A good example of the current state-of-the art at the global scale, albeit with an Anglo-American bias, is provided by the *Handbook of Transport Geography and Spatial Systems* (Hensher *et al.* 2004).

There are a number of reasons for this revival and this chapter will focus on a few of them. In part, it is caused by the broadening of the scope of transport geography alluded to in the opening paragraph. However, in this chapter six broad themes will be examined. First, the last 50 years have been characterized as an era of hypermobility (Adams 1999). One set of explanations relates this transition to hypermobility to the dual processes of technological innovation and income growth. Second, the last 50 years have seen a pattern of falling transport costs and this provides a second, economic, explanation of recent trends. Hypermobility has contributed to the persistence of the urban transport problem and this is the third issue that will be addressed by this chapter. Following on from this, the fourth issue to be examined will be the restructuring of inter-urban networks, particularly in air travel and container shipping. A fifth issue is the role of transport in creating new spaces and in place making. Lastly, these inter-related issues will be examined through the lens of the sustainability concept. It is concluded that transport is an important driver of change – one that shapes places as well as being shaped by them – and that transport's power to make or break places is not just confined to cities but extends to continental regions.

Trends in mobility

Mobility may be defined as the ease of moving and can be measured in either units of vehicle kms (intermediate demand) or in passenger kms/tonne kms (final demand). There has been a global explosion in the amount people and goods travel in the second half of the twentieth century (Whitelegg and Haq 2003). However, that is not to say that everyone and everywhere has experienced massive increases in mobility. The young, the elderly and those on low incomes, particularly in developing countries, may have missed out on the mobility explosion. With this important caveat, this section briefly reviews the aggregate trends in mobility over the last 50 years for the United Kingdom (UK), although these trends are broadly typical of many countries around the globe.

In 1952, the average person in the UK travelled around 4,300 km. By 2002, this had increased almost threefold to 12,700 km. As Figure 13.1 shows, this growth is entirely the result of car travel. Over this 50-year period, the use of all other modes decreased in total. In particular, the use of bus, pedal cycle and motorcycle decreased by up to one half. Data on walking is not readily available but what data there is suggests an absolute decline. The only other mode to have shown a substantive increase over this period is air travel, which has had explosive growth – with per capita travel increasing almost forty-fold. Rail has had

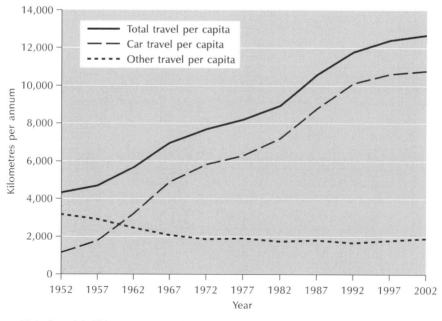

Figure 13.1. Growth in UK passenger travel per capita, 1952–2002.

fluctuating demand over the period but has been broadly stable, with an overall increase of travel per capita of less than 10 per cent over the whole period.

The relatively minor role of walking is a particular feature of advanced economies. In developing economies, walking and cycling are more important. Olvera *et al.* (2003) present some data that suggest walking per capita may have even increased in the rapidly growing city of Dar es Salaam (Tanzania).

The freight moved per person in the UK has increased from 1,700 tonne kms in 1952 to 4,200 tonne kms in 2002, an increase of close to 150 per cent. As Figure 13.2 shows, this is mainly the result of increases in road freight, although since the early 1970s the use of other modes has increased as growth in pipeline- and water-borne traffic (both largely related to the North Sea oil and gas industries) more than offset the reduced use of rail (down by one half). In terms of tonnes lifted, the growth is less dramatic, with around 45 per cent growth per capita. Nonetheless, it is growth which puts pay to the myth of dematerialization and other exaggerated claims for deindustrialization. Moreover, the statistics suggest large increases in length of haul, which have led to concerns over food miles and interest in the much travelled yoghurt pot.

These growth trends are not new. Grubler and Nakicenovic (1991 – cited by Haggett 2001) analysed data for France going back to 1800 and found that total personal mobility had grown a thousand-fold while population had only increased two-fold. A 500-fold increase in per capita mobility over the last 200 years is consistent with exponential growth of 3.2 per cent per annum. A three-fold increase in mobility over the last 50 years is consistent with an exponential growth of 2.2 per cent per annum. This is suggestive of a substantial reduction in mobility growth rates over time, and is confirmed by evidence of reducing rates of mobility growth, at least in advanced economies, from the literature on transport intensity (the ratio of mobility to GDP – see Tapio 2005).

The growth in mobility is related to the substitution of slow modes (walking, cycling, public transport) for fast modes (air, car) as incomes rise and hence enable the purchase of faster but more expensive travel. However, there have also been technological improvements to fast

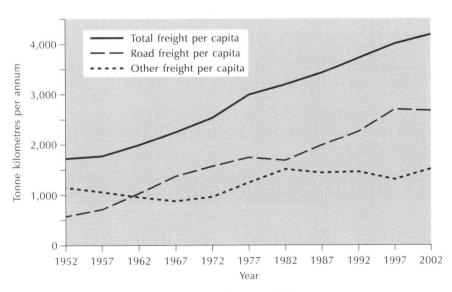

Figure 13.2. Growth in UK freight transport per capita, 1952–2002.

modes to increase their speeds, although here the dominant historic pattern has been rapid reductions in journey times, followed by gentler reductions. Examples include Haggett (2001) on transatlantic and United States transcontinental crossings or Thrift (1990) on the impact of the stage coach and the railways in Great Britain. There may thus be technological explanations for the periodic slowing down of mobility growth. Rodrigue *et al.* (2006) illustrate this technological determinism viewpoint by tracing the successive rapid growth and subsequent stabilization of the turnpike, canal, rail, trunk road and motorway networks in the UK (see Figure 13.3). It should be noted that the subsequent decline of these networks is not shown in this figure. For example, the national rail network in Great Britain peaked around 1928 at 32,565 route km. By 2003/4 this had reduced to 16,652 route km (Department for Transport 2005: Table 6.1). What this also suggests is that there have been differential phases of time–space compression, but within a pattern of broad convergence.

However, there are also behavioural explanations that complement the technological explanations given before. There is some evidence that on average the time per day individuals spend travelling is constant, although this relationship does not hold across life-cycle, location, income or car ownership (Metz 2004). Nonetheless, given this aggregate constancy, increased travel speeds may be expected to lead to increased travel distances. Schafer and Victor (2000) believe that this process results in an elasticity of transport demand with respect to income of around unity. Over the 50-year period since 1952, GDP per capita in the UK has grown by 195 per cent, while traffic units per capita (passenger kms plus freight tonne kms) increased by 179 per cent. This is clearly a close correspondence. It is consistent with the view that as incomes rise, people consume more of the goods they like.

Proponents of the 'mobility turn' in transport are extremely sceptical of meta-narratives based on grand theories such as unitary income elasticities or constant travel time budgets. They will point out that these exercises in empirics fail to identify a key point, that the automobile and other technologies have led not just to changes in mobility and hence

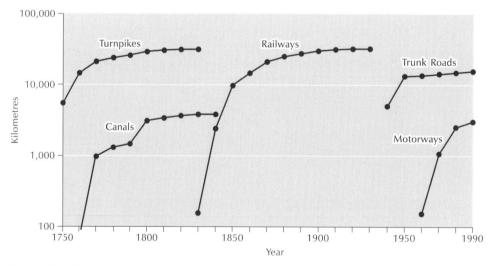

Figure 13.3. The development of the UK transport system, 1750–1900.
Source: After Rodrigue *et al.* (2006).
Reprinted with kind permission of Jean-Paul Rodrigue.

activities but also to changes in attitudes to mobility and movement, in particular the emergence of the culture of automobility (Featherstone *et al.* 2004). Proponents of the new mobilities paradigm (Urry 2004) posit that in postmodern society mobility is more highly valued than in traditional or modern societies. Tastes have changed and people like mobility more today than they ever did. They also question the assumption that transport and activities can be separated, and argue that travel is not dead time but with mobile technologies can be used to make a phone call, text a message, listen to a CD or iPod or watch a DVD, while travel can also be used for personal reflection and social interaction. In extremis, this viewpoint suggests that the intrinsic utility of travel has become more important than its derived utility.

This is contrary to the traditional view of transport as a derived demand. According to this viewpoint, transport itself is an economic bad, not an economic good, exhibiting intrinsic disutility, not utility. In the main people do not value mobility for its own sake but for the derived utility that comes from the quantity and quality of the socio-economic activities that can be accessed. This viewpoint would argue that increases in mobility over the past 50 years are likely to have been positively correlated with increased accessibility. Accessibility may be defined as the ease of reaching and can be measured by indices that reflect the range of opportunities that can be reached and the generalized costs incurred in reaching them. Aggregate indices can be traced back to Hansen (1959) and have clear links with gravity model formulations. More recently, more disaggregate accessibility indices based on composite utility measures have been developed. These log sum measures are derived from random utility models (particularly the pervasive logit formulation) and can be shown to be consistent with measures of total user benefit.

However, the relationship between mobity and accessibility might be expected to exhibit diminishing returns and even a turning point where increased mobility is associated with reduced accessibility, because of, for example, congestion, resource depletion and/or excessive centralization of facilities. An important research issue is where and when (if ever) this turning point is reached. It is the contention of proponents of the new realism that this turning point has been reached (Goodwin *et al.* 1991), while radical environmentalists argue that it has been passed (Hillman 2004). These views are illustrated by Figure 13.4. There are interesting parallels with the concept of the mobility transition (Zelinsky 1971) and in particular the projected Phase V in which non-economic travel becomes dominant and mobility becomes counter-productive (at least in economic, if not in social, terms).

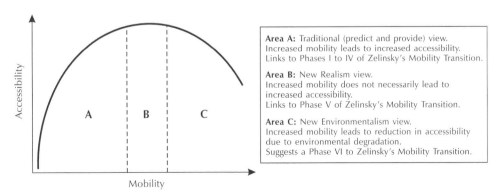

Figure 13.4. Relationships between mobility and accessibility.

Trends in costs

Another set of explanatory factors for the mobility increases of the twentieth century are related to falling transport costs. Rietveld and Vickerman (2004) illustrate the reductions in international and domestic transport costs using Dutch data. They show that between 1929 and 1998 world merchandise exports as a percentage of GDP have increased by 91 per cent, while the real costs of ocean shipping reduced by 47 per cent between 1930 and 1990 (although costs have been relatively static since 1960). They also present Dutch data on the costs of international transport which suggest that between 1950 and 1998 real costs per tonne km for rail and road have halved, for inland waterways they have reduced by 40 per cent and for air they have reduced by over 90 per cent. These trends might be expected to lead to the death of distance and the emergence of truly footloose activities. This does not appear to be the case. The reduced costs of transport as a factor of production means that its use as an input has increased, allowing the exploitation of economies of scale and new patterns of backward and forward linkages. Moreover, transaction costs remain correlated with distance and national boundaries. These trends have permitted the shift from national systems of just-in-case production to global systems of just-in-time production, the cosmopolitanization of consumption and the increased importance of logistics and supply chain management (Hesse and Rodrigue, 2004). Moreover, although the transportation cost component of bulk materials has continued to fall, there is evidence of an increase in this proportion for manufactured goods in effect because transport has substituted other inputs. The result of these trends is not a smoothing of production and consumption surfaces or a reduction in freight transport. Reports of the death of distance and the end of geography seem premature.

The urban transport problem

From Ancient Rome through Victorian London to present-day Bangkok, the city has been the locus of transport problems. This has been accentuated in the era of hypermobility where transport has both strengthened (through enforcing agglomeration economies) and weakened (through the promotion of sprawl) central cities. John Michael Thomson has identified seven enduring features of the urban transport problem (Thomson 1977). The first is the problem of traffic circulation and the rise in congestion as urban road space fails to keep up with the growth in the road vehicle population. For example, traffic speeds in inner London decreased by 20 per cent over 30 years (1968–1998), with average speeds in the morning and evening peaks at 12 miles per hour or less, the equivalent to the speed of horse-drawn carriages some 100 years earlier. The second is the problem of parking provision. The third relates to the difficulties faced by pedestrians (and other vulnerable road users, such as cyclists) as they compete for road space with motor vehicles. The fourth relates to the high level of accidents caused by the transport system, and the fifth relates to the high level of environmental damage, particularly in terms of air pollution and noise pollution and in carbon emissions. The sixth problem relates to congestion of public transport systems in the peak periods, particularly in monocentric conurbations with tidal flow patterns of movement. The seventh problem relates to the inadequacy of public transport in off-peak periods, restricted by radial route structures and low levels of demand (although this problem has been partially solved by differential pricing). There are a number of other aspects that could be added to this list. For example, much recent work has focused on the social inequities in urban transport systems, inequities that have increased as society polarizes and new social mosaics lead to what Ed Soja describes as fractal cities. With respect to urban transport, geographers have shown particular interest in its role in the dual processes of social exclusion and inclusion (see, for example, Rajé 2004).

Geographers have not, however, sought solely to problematize urban transport. They have also studied combinations of policy instruments that might provide solutions. A three-fold categorization of such instruments considers physical, economic and regulatory measures. Traditional emphasis has been on physical measures and in particular the construction of new infrastructure. This became known in the UK as the 'predict and provide' approach (Owens 1995). However, there has also been a realization, particularly in the developing world, that managing and maintaining existing infrastructure is just as important as constructing new infrastructure. In the developed world new technology, described variously as ITS (intelligent transport systems), transport telematics or informatics, offers prospects of making better use of existing infrastructure through tools such as advanced traveller information systems, intelligent speed adaptation, automatic guidance systems (ultimately leading to driverless cars) and new generations of traffic control made possible by pervasive computing technologies. Parallel to this are technological developments to improve the environmental performance of transport, through either improvements to existing technology such as the internal combustion engine (new generation vehicles), the development of emergent technologies such as hydrogen fuel cells, biofuels or battery electric vehicles, or hybrid combinations (as exemplified by the emblematic Toyota Prius). Another important development has been the move away from the 'hard' engineering of new roads towards the 'softer' engineering involved in traffic calming (with its origins in the Dutch *Woonerf* schemes of the 1970s) and planning for cyclists and pedestrians.

However, it is unlikely that physical measures, on their own, will solve the urban transport problem. Economic measures have long been a feature of transport systems, particularly in the shape of petrol and vehicle tax and subsidies to public transport. Since at least the 1960s transport economists have been arguing the case for a more sophisticated form of road pricing that better reflects the congestion and other external costs that motorists impose on society. Progress towards such pricing has been slow. Motorway tolling, which is relatively commonplace, is normally about raising funds for new investments rather than aligning prices with costs. The first big advance was the introduction of supplementary area licensing in Singapore in 1975, which subsequently migrated to an electronic road pricing system (1998). More recent advances include the introduction of congestion charging in central London (2003) and the introduction of nationwide lorry charging in countries such Germany using GPS technology (2005) The latter charging scheme is really about fiscal harmonization (ensuring that non-German road hauliers face similar taxation to German hauliers) but it is important in demonstrating that the technology is now available for sophisticated forms of road user charging. Another important area in terms of economic measures is with respect to workplace parking. Attempts have been made to reduce what are effective subsidies to employees by initiatives such as the still dormant workplace parking levy in the UK, while in the US cash-outs are employed so that non-car commuters are not unduly penalized.

The third raft of measures widely used in transport is regulatory – sometimes referred to as command and control. These may involve different forms of regulation. Regulation of safety is commonplace throughout advanced economies, and there has been a tendency to increase the scope of these regulations (particularly given post-9/11 concerns with security) and the enforcement of these regulations. Regulation of transport services and prices has decreased as liberalizing waves of deregulatory reforms have been enacted (see later). However, these reforms have often been accompanied by pro-competition regulations (referred to as anti-trust measures in the US) dealing with issues such as predatory behaviour, restrictive practices and mergers. The transport sector has seen deregulation, but with rules rather than an out-and-out competitive free-for-all. Increasingly, there are environmental regulations such as those concerning fuel content and the efficiency of petrol and diesel engines in the European Union and corporate average fuel efficiency standards and zero emission vehicle quotas in the US. Those of a more radical ecocentric perspective argue for a system of tradable carbon credits and mobility rationing. Although such measures seem to be a long way off at present, they have been given impetus in the UK by the target of a 60 per cent reduction in carbon emissions by 2050 and globally by the twin forces of rising oil prices and the increasing scientific evidence on anthropogenic-induced climate change. With respect to carbon, transport is a very poor performing sector, with transport's share of carbon emissions in the UK rising from one in eight to over one in four in a 30-year period (1970–2000) and transport accounting for over half of the country's oil consumption.

Traditionally, urban bus and rail operations were publicly owned and controlled. Governments regulated fares and service levels and in theory pursued social objectives rather than pure commercial objectives. However, critics (particularly those influenced by the Austrian and Chicago schools of economics) argued that governments were captured by operators (regulatory capture) and over-extended their powers (regulatory creep), and instead of increasing social benefits, subsidies were dissipated by higher operating costs (leakage) and inefficient business practices (x-inefficiencies). Britain took the lead in deregulating local transport, with the exception of London because public transport remains regulated in London and Northern Ireland. Buses were deregulated and privatized as a result of the 1985 Transport Act and railways being privatized and partially deregulated as a result of the 1993 Railways Act. Other countries have followed Britain's lead, most noticeably Chile and New Zealand, but most have been more circumspect. The evidence from Britain outside London is that on the road competition has reduced operating costs by up to 50 per cent but has failed to stem the tide of falling patronage (down 35 per cent between 1985/6 and 2001/2). By contrast, comprehensive tendering in London, a form of off-the-road competition, has achieved similar cost savings while also increasing bus usage (up 25 per cent between 1985/6 and 2001/2). As a result the London bus model (initiated in 1984) has been widely copied around the world, with the earliest and arguably best example being Copenhagen (1989). Other early pioneers include a number of French cities that have long traditions of management contracts and San Diego, which began tendering in 1979 (Preston 2005). The deregulation of bus and rail runs counter to other regulatory trends in urban transport but is more consistent with the neo-liberal approach adopted in inter-urban transport.

The inter-urban transport challenge

In many respects, long-distance inter-urban transport has been viewed as less of a problem than local urban (and indeed rural) transport. This is mainly because congestion is less of a factor in inter-urban transport (although not entirely absent) and, as a result, environmental and safety impacts are more limited as well as being more dispersed. Physical measures have tended to dominate inter-urban transport. Predict and provide road schemes continued on inter-urban routes long after major urban motorway schemes were abandoned, and the predict and provide philosophy still dominates the air sector, albeit with considerable lags (e.g. Heathrow Terminal 5). Many countries aspire to grandiose high speed rail schemes following the perceived success of the Shinkansen services in Japan and TGV Sud-Est in

France. The main stumbling block has been finance, and the key development here has been private finance initiatives – often in the form of public–private partnerships, based on either actual tolls (for example, in Brazil) or shadow tolls (for example, in the UK).

Aside from fuel and vehicle taxes (for private transport) and fares (for public transport), economic measures have been less prevalent than in urban transport – in part because inter-urban transport has much better prospects of making operating profits and hence is more likely to be viewed as a commercial activity.

The usual gamut of regulatory measures concerning safety, competition policy and environmental issues apply to inter-urban transport, albeit with added complications for international transport. Like urban transport, the sector has seen a strong trend towards the deregulation of prices and services. This was initiated in the US by the deregulation of the airline industry (1978) and the rail industry (as a result of the Staggers Act of 1980). In contrast to the big bang approach of the US, the European Union has adopted a more gradual, softly-softly approach. For example, internal air services were liberalized through the implementation of three reform packages, with the process beginning in 1987 and being completed in 1997. The results, in both the US and Europe, have been a major reconfiguring of services. In particular, in the airline industry networks have reconfigured to form hubs and spokes as major carriers seek to exploit advantages of vehicle size and market dominance (through computer reservation systems, code-sharing arrangements, frequent flyer programmes, etc.). Superimposed on this pattern has been the development of low-cost carriers, originating with Southwest Airlines in the US and Ryanair and easyJet in Europe.

Similar patterns are emerging in the shipping industry, although arguably here technological rather than regulatory changes are the driving force. In particular, containerization has been important, with the current (fifth) generation of container ships carrying 7,500 TEUs (Twenty-foot Equivalent Units – the standard measure of containers), with plans in the future for ships that can carry 12,500 TEUs. This has been supplemented by the replacement of the traditional liner conferences (a form of cartel) with more fluid shipping alliances. An example of the impact is given by Table 13.1. This shows that the North European container market doubled in a ten-year period, with an annual growth rate of 7.2 per cent. However, container transhipment has trebled, with an annual growth rate of 11.6 per cent.

This has led to the development of hub ports specializing in handling super container ships, in particular Rotterdam (at the mouth of the Rhine river system) and Hamburg (at the mouth of the Elbe river system), which in 2000 accounted for around 40 per cent of North European container throughput. Similar hubs have developed elsewhere particularly in East Asia (Singapore, Hong Kong) while brand new hubs are emerging, such as Gioia Tauro (Italy).

Table 13.1. Recent evolution of the North European container market

	1990		2000	
	Throughput ('000 tonnes)	Market share (%)	Throughput ('000 tonnes)	Market share (%)
DDS	7,079	46.0	13,830	45.0
CTS	2,177	14.1	6,504	21.1
DSS	6,136	39.9	10,432	33.9
Total	**15,392**		**30,766**	

Notes: DDS = Direct Deep Sea; CTS = Container Transhipment; DSS = Direct Short Sea.

Developments in shipping are not just restricted to the freight sector. Passenger cruises are enjoying something of a resurgence, originating in the USA but fast becoming a global phenomenon. For example, Southampton registered its record number of ocean liner passengers in 1956. Competition from the airlines initiated a long decline, but in recent years passenger numbers have been growing, in line with increasing incomes and the increasing taste for global mobility. This in turn has led to social, economic and environmental transformations of popular cruise destinations, particularly in the Caribbean.

These reconfigured air and sea networks are thus heavily implicated in the process of globalization and the stretching of economic and social relations – a process Anthony Giddens describes as distanciation. At a national level, the development of motorways and high speed rail networks has had a similar effect.

Spaces and places

We have seen that combinations of technological, economic and political changes have impacted on the transport sector but that this has not produced a uniform geographic space. Transport has played an important role in place building. Many of the world's great cities have their origins as seaports (for example, New York), as river crossings (Paris) or as stopping places on trade routes (Timbuktu). With industrialization came the emergence of canal towns (such as Stourport in the UK) and subsequently railway towns (such as Crewe or Swindon). Subsequently, there has been the emergence of cities associated with the motor industry (such as Detroit (US) and Birmingham (UK)). Latterly, edge cities have emerged that are partly associated with airports. For example, Tyson's Corner (Virginia) is associated with Washington Dulles International Airport.

There are those who advocate that motorization has led to the emergence of a geography of nowhere, a vast suburban landscape of bland uniformity (Kunstler 1993). There are those that also argue that automobility has led to a decrease in participation in civil society and the emergence of the 'bowling alone' phenomenon, although other technologies are implicated here, not least television. However, motorization has not necessarily led to the death of central cities, not least because public transport remains important in such locales. The cultural impact of urban transport systems has been considerable, as witnessed by the iconoclastic status of the London bus, the Paris metro, the Shanghai maglev or the Melbourne tram. Moreover, new rail systems have made important contributions to an urban renaissance, exemplified by light rail in Portland (Oregon), where smart growth has been heavily promoted, and heavy rail in Bilbao (Spain). Transport systems have been instrumental in developing urban networks, as witnessed by the role of railways in the Randstad (Netherlands) and Rhine–Ruhr (Germany) conurbations and the development of links along motorway corridors such as the M4 and M62 in England. In short, transport systems shape places just as places shape transport systems. Even if, as Manuel Castells advocates, we have moved from a network of places to a network of flows, transport remains responsible for many of these flows and these flows connect real places and real people. Information technology does not appear to have been a substitute for transport but a complement – increases in virtual mobility have been accompanied by increases in physical mobility. For example, jumbo jets are heavily implicated in the current dominance of a triad of truly global cities (London, New York, Tokyo) and their continental hinterlands, while offering only limited connections to other parts of the globe, such as much of Africa.

Sustainability

Sustainability has emerged as a useful concept through which transport geographers can examine the processes of economic, social and environmental change that the evolution of transport systems has produced and the impacts of such changes on transport systems themselves. A major challenge has been the development of workable definitions of a sustainable transport system. For example, Richardson (1999: 27) has defined such a system as:

> one in which fuel consumption, vehicle emissions, safety, congestion, and social and economic access are of such levels that they can be sustained into the indefinite future without compromising the ability of future generations of people throughout the world to meet their own transportation needs.

As an academic device, sustainability has a number of advantages. First, the literature on sustainable transport is relatively mature, is global in its coverage and is inclusive of transport geography (see, for example, Roberts 1992; Whitelegg 1993; Newman and Kenworthy 1999; Banister *et al.* 2000; Black and Nijkamp 2002). Second, there is an increasing amount of empirical evidence on the economic, social and environmental impacts of transport policy measures, encapsulated for example by the Victoria Transport Policy Institute (VTPI) Transportation Demand Management Encyclopaedia and the KONSULT database. Third, there is considerable institutional support for the concept of sustainable transport, particularly from supra-national bodies such as the World Bank (1996) and the European Conference of Ministers of Transport (ECMT) (2001). Fourth, as illustrated by Figure 13.5, sustainability,

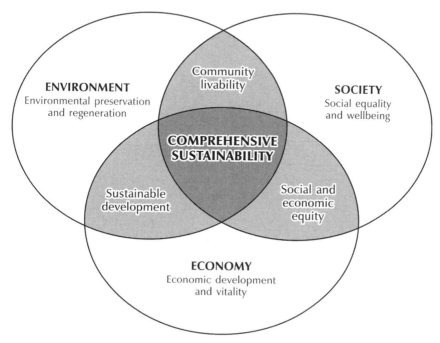

Figure 13.5. The three dimensions of sustainability.
Source: Adapted from http://www.cstctd.org/CSTmissionstatement.htm

by highlighting the inter-relationships between society, economy and the environment, provides an interdisciplinary core for transport studies/geography. Lastly, a triarchy of economy, society and environment provides a firmer base for integrated policy appraisal than the pentarchy of economy, safety, environment, accessibility and integration championed by the UK's New Approach to Appraisal (Price 1999).

However, the progress of sustainability has been hampered by the emphasis of the European Union (and others) on sustainable mobility (Banister *et al.* 2000). We have seen that the traditional view is that in the majority of cases mobility is not highly valued in and of itself. Moreover, as long as mobility is highly dependent on non-renewable fossil fuels, sustainable mobility is even more of an oxymoron than sustainable development. Sustainable accessibility has been put forward as a more promising and consistent policy goal (see, for example, Le Clercq and Bertolini 2003). The major challenge here is to operationalize and popularize an accessibility planning based approach, although some progress has been made here (e.g. Halden 2002, and the subsequent development of the Accession accessibility planning tool – Accession 2006). Weaknesses lie in the difficulties in representing the complete range of quantity and quality of attractions, in analysing individuals rather than zonal aggregates, and in incorporating the intrinsic as well as the derived utility of travel.

However, there other ways that the sustainability concept needs refining in a transport context. One is to include more explicitly a political dimension. Polices such as road pricing that are seen to be economically, socially and environmentally sustainable may not be politically sustainable. The second is to include issues surrounding technical feasibility and technological obsolescence. An example of work that has attempted to operationalize the sustainability concept in urban transport context (and with particular reference to Toronto, Canada) is that of Kennedy *et al.* (2005) who, building on ideas from the political and management sciences, have identified four pillars on which such a concept might be built, including top-down governance, bottom-up neighbourhood initiatives, funding policies and technology policies.

Conclusions

Modern industrial society has seen an explosion in mobility. Growth has continued into postmodernity only slightly tempered by rising oil prices and the emergence of rival information technologies. Positivist explanations see this growth rooted in technological advancements, rising incomes and falling transport times and costs. More humanistic approaches see these trends linked to changes in tastes, with mobility becoming more highly valued in more individualized, more atomistic societies. Structuralists see recent transport trends as manifestations of a process of the annihilation of space by time. Transport is implicated in both regimes of mass accumulation with their Fordist modes of regulation and in post-Fordist regimes of flexible accumulation. Post-structuralists focus on the role of transport in the production of space at a variety of scales from the local (such as the social impact of the redevelopment of Brussels Midi high speed rail station) to the global (such as the role of flag airlines in neo-imperialism). Such epistemological disputes, and related methodological controversies particularly concerning the interplay of quantitative and qualitative approaches, have also contributed to the revival of interest in transport geography. The key implications of the mobility explosions of the last 200 years are the continued (but also evolving) problematic nature of local transport and long distance transport's role in the stretching of economic, social and cultural relations over ever longer distances. Transport has continued in its historic role as the maker and breaker of cities (Clark 1957) but has also become the maker and breaker of entire regions too.

Further reading

Black, W.R. (2004) *Transportation: A Geographical Analysis*. New York: Guilford Press.

Goodwin, P.B., Hallett, S., Kenny, F. and Stokes, G. (1991) *Transport: The New Realism* (Reference 624, Transport Studies Unit). Oxford: Oxford University Press.

Hanson, S. and Giuliano, G. (eds) (2004) *The Geography of Urban Transportation*, third revised edition. New York: Guilford Press.

Hensher, D.A., Button, K.J., Haynes, K.E. and Stopher, P. (eds) (2004) *Handbook of Transport Geography and Spatial Systems*. Oxford: Elsevier.

Hillman, M. (2004) *How Can We Save the Planet?* Harmondsworth: Penguin.

Hoyle, B.S. and Knowles, R.D. (eds) (1998) *Modern Transport Geography*, second edition. Chichester: Wiley.

Rietveld, P. and Vickerman, R. (2004) Transport in regional science: the 'death of distance' is premature. *Papers in Regional Science* 83, 229–48.

Schafer, A. and Victor, D.G. (2000) The future mobility of the world population. *Transportation Research* 34 A, 171–206.

Tolley, R. and Turton, B. (1995) *Transport Systems, Policy and Planning: A Geographical Approach*. Harlow: Longman.

Victoria Transport Policy Institute (VTPI) *Transportation Demand Management Encyclopaedia*. Available at http://www.vtpi.org/tdm

References

Accession (2006) Accessibility Planning Software Version 1.4. Available at http://www.accessiongis.com

Adams, J. (1999) *The Social Implications of Hypermobility* (OECD Project on Environmentally Sustainable Transport). Paris: OECD.

Banister, D., Stead, D., Steen, P., Akerman, J., Dreborg, K., Nijkamp, P. and Schleicher-Tappeser, P. (2000). *European Transport Policy and Sustainable Mobility*. London: Spon.

Black, W.R. and Nijkamp, P. (2002). *Social Change and Sustainable Transport*. Indiana: Indiana University Press.

Clark, C. (1957) Transport: maker and breaker of cities. *Town Planning Review* 28, 237–50.

Department for Transport (2005) Transport Statistics Great Britain. Available at http://www.dft.gov.uk/stellent/groups/dft_transstats/documents/page/dft_transstats_041489.pdf

ECMT (2001) *Implementing Sustainable Urban Transport Policies*. Paris: OECD.

Featherstone, M., Thrift, N. and Urry, J.(eds) (2004) Special section on automobilities. *Theory, Culture and Society* 21, 4.

Gather, M., Kagermeier, A. and Lanzendorf, M. (eds) (2001) *Verkehrsentwicklung in den Neuen Bundeslandern* (Proceedings of the Annual Meeting of the Transport Research Group of the German Geographical Society). Erfurt: Erfurter Geograpische Studien.

Grubler, A, and Nakicenovic, N. (1991) *Evolution of Transport Systems*. Vienna: IIASA Laxenburg.

Haggett, P. (2001) *Geography. A Global Synthesis*. Harlow: Prentice Hall.

Halden, D. (2002) Using accessibility measures to integrate land use and transport policy in Edinburgh and the Lothians. *Transport Policy* 9 (4), 313–24.

Hansen, W.G. (1959) How accessibility shapes land use. *Journal of the American Institute for Planners* 25, 73–76.

Hanson, S. and Giuliano, G. (eds) (2004) *The Geography of Urban Transportation*, third revised edition. New York: Guilford Press.

Hesse, M. and Rodrigue, J.P. (2004) The transport geography of logistics and freight distribution. *Journal of Transport Geography* 12 (3), 171–84.

Hoyle, B.S. and Knowles, R.D. (eds) (1992) *Modern Transport Geography*. Chichester: Wiley.

Kennedy, C., Miller, E., Shalaby, A. and Coleman, J. (2005) The Four Pillars of Sustainable Urban Transportation. *Transport Reviews* 25 (4), 393–414.

Knowledgebase on Sustainable Urban Land Use and Transport (KonSULT) (2006) http://www.elseviersocialsciences.com/transport/konsult/index.html

Kunstler, J.H. (1993) *The Geography of Nowhere. The Rise and Decline of America's Man-made Landscape*. New York: Simon and Schuster.

Le Clercq, F. and Bertolini, L. (2003) Achieving sustainable accessibility: an evaluation of policy measures in the Amsterdam area. *Built Environment* 29 (1), 36–47.

Metz, D. (2004) Travel time constraints in transport policy. *Proceedings of the Institution of Civil Engineers: Transport* 157 (2), 99–105.

Newman, P. and Kenworthy, J. (1999) *Sustainability and Cities. Overcoming Automobile Dependence*. Washington: Island Press.

Olvera, L.D., Plat, D. and Pochet, P. (2003) Transportation conditions and access to services in a context of urban sprawl and deregulation. The case of Dar es Salaam. *Transport Policy* 10 (4), 287–98.

Owens, S. (1995) From 'predict and provide' to 'predict and prevent'? Pricing and planning in transport policy. *Transport Policy* 2 (1), 43–50.

Preston, J. (2005) Tendering of services. In D. Hensher and K. Button (eds) *Handbook of Transport Strategy, Policy and Institutions*. Amsterdam: Elsevier.

Price, M. (1999) A new approach to the appraisal of road projects. *Journal of Transport Economics and Policy* 33, 221–26.

Rajé, F. (2004) *Transport, Demand Management and Social inclusion. The Need for Ethnic Perspectives*. Aldershot: Ashgate.

Richardson, B. (1999) Towards a policy on a sustainable transportation system. *Transportation Research Record* 1670, 27–34.

Roberts, J. (ed.) (1992) *Travel Sickness: The Need for a Sustainable Transport Policy in Britain*. London: Lawrence and Wishart.

Rodrigue, J.P., Comtois, C. and Slack, B. (2006) *The Geography of Transport Systems*. Hofstra University, Department of Economics and Geography. Available at http://www.people.hofstra.edu/geotrans/

Taaffe, E.J., Gauthier, H.L. and O'Kelly, M.E. (1996) *Geography of Transportation*, second edition. Upper Saddle River, New Jersey: Prentice Hall.

Tapio, P. (2005) Towards a theory of decoupling in the EU and the case of road traffic in Finland between 1970 and 2001. *Transport Policy* 12 (2), 137–51.

Thomson, J.M. (1977) *Great Cities and Their Traffic*. London: Gollancz.

Thrift, N. (1990) Transport and communications, 1730–1914. In R. Dodgson and R.A. Butlin (eds) *An Historical Geography of England and Wales*. London: Academic Press.

Urry, J. (2004) The new mobilities paradigm. Paper presented to Workshop on Mobility and the Cosmopolitan Perspective, Reflexive Modernisation Research Centre, Munich.

Whitelegg, J. (1993) *Transport for a Sustainable Future. The Case for Europe*. London: Belhaven.

Whitelegg, J. and Haq, G. (2003) The global transport problem: same issue but a different place. In J. Whitelegg and G. Haq (eds) *The Earthscan Reader on World Transport Policy and Practice*. London: Earthscan.

World Bank (1996) Sustainable transport: priorities for policy reform. Available at http://www.worldbank.org/transport/pol_econ/tsr.htm

Zelinsky, W. (1971) The hypothesis of the mobility transition. *Geographical Review* 61 (2), 219–49.

14

Cultural change

Eric Pawson

Since the late 1980s, there has been what is often described as a 'cultural turn' in human geography and other social sciences. This phrase is used to denote a surge of interest in the difference that culture makes and in the distinctions that are encapsulated by the term 'culture' in an extended range of situations, e.g. French culture, black culture, student culture. But what exactly is meant by culture and how does it contribute to or drive change? These are not easy questions, but they deserve exploration at a time when the concept has gained widespread currency in everyday as well as in academic speech. This chapter proceeds by means of an opening anecdote, or story, which seeks to describe a particular intersection of cultural identities. Its purpose is to suggest that taken-for-granted ways of thinking, doing and being, when put in cross-cultural context, have a specificity that is revealed as being as exotic as those that by comparison seem strange and distant. Whoever we are, in other words, we have culture.

Story telling is a social device employed in many cultural contexts (see Chapter 34). It is a means of making things more immediate and easier to comprehend. The story related here is drawn from a moment in the encounter between the expansionary capitalist culture of eighteenth-century Britain (an earlier articulation of what is now commonly called globalization) and the indigenous peoples of the Pacific. It serves as a preface to the first part of the chapter, which is a discussion of the meanings of culture, and an exploration of what is involved when we talk of cultural change. The second half of the chapter turns to the ways in which geographers have dealt with such matters through their practices of cultural geography, before concluding with another encounter: the tensions between processes of contemporary globalization and the ever insistent yet shifting spaces of culture.

Encounters (1): discovering culture

Late in life, Horeta Te Taniwha, a Maori who had been a young boy when Captain Cook's ship *Endeavour* visited his part of northern New Zealand, remembered the encounter. It was 1769 and Horeta's people were astonished by the first Europeans they had ever seen. The old men said that the ship with its great sails was an atua, or a god. They saw the people on board as tupua, strange beings or 'goblins'. For them, this was confirmed when the Europeans rowed ashore:

'Yes, it is so: these people are goblins; their eyes are at the back of their heads; they pull on shore with their backs to the land to which they are going.' The Europeans gathered food and plants on and around the beach and, overcoming their surprise, the Maori gave them things, like stones and grass, in which they seemed to be interested. The Europeans uttered 'words of their language. Perhaps they were asking questions, and, as we did not know their language, we laughed, and these goblins also laughed, so we were pleased' (in Salmond 2003: 131–32).

Not all such encounters passed off without incident. On several occasions when Europeans offered goods to trade, Maori people went off seemingly without keeping their side of the bargain. Sometimes this ended in the sailors shooting at them, if the trade goods were thought valuable enough to be worth retaliation. The expectation of the sailors was one of immediate reciprocity rather than this apparent cheating, but the Maori had certain protocols to observe, with return gifts customarily delayed to be part of a subsequent show of chiefly generosity. Other encounters, however, were more serious, notably with cannibalism during Cook's second voyage to the Pacific.

In 1774, the consort ship the *Adventure*, separated during a storm from Cook's *Resolution*, put in to Queen Charlotte Sound at the northern edge of New Zealand's South Island (Plate 14.1). Cook had spent time in the Sound four years before. On this occasion, and apparently to settle scores after earlier misunderstandings, sailors on board the *Adventure's* cutter were attacked by Maori. They were then killed, dismembered and eaten. The *Adventure* left the

Plate 14.1. *View in Queen Charlotte's Sound, New Zealand*, by John Webber, RA. This is the scene of the trial of the cannibal dog. It is painted in oils, worked up from a sketch made on Cook's third voyage. It shows two astronomical observation tents on the beach, the British ships standing out to sea. Maori are fishing and drying fish. Alexander Turnbull Library, National Library of New Zealand, ref B-098-015.

Sound before Cook arrived in the *Resolution* some months later, and the truth of the situation was then withheld from him. But when on his third voyage in 1777 the *Resolution*, with the *Discovery,* returned to the Sound, his sailors expected Cook to avenge the attacks. So too, it seems, did the Maori, who were bemused by Cook's assurances of friendship in a situation in which they themselves anticipated the exacting of a harsh penalty for the insult of eating his kin.

Cook, however, was under orders from the Admiralty in London to treat indigenous peoples in as enlightened a manner as was possible. He seems therefore to have wished to extend benefit of the doubt, despite many of the sailors and some officers on the third voyage being witnesses to the aftermath of the earlier cannibal feast. Instead, the sailors on the *Discovery*, at a safe distance from their commanding officer, captured and took on board a Maori dog. There they tried it for cannibalism, and finding it guilty, cooked and ate it.

As Anne Salmond says in *The Trial of the Cannibal Dog*, such behaviour was not extra-ordinary in the cultural context of the time. Animal trials had a long history in Europe, where animals were often understood and treated as metonyms for their owners. To attack the animal was therefore to attack the person. In this case, in a carnivalesque atmosphere, the sailors were able to show how they felt about the fate of their comrades, whilst laughing at the horror of it, and indicating to their commanders, out of range, what they thought of the failure to take revenge. Eating the dog, however, did break a cultural norm for Europeans schooled in the belief that it was an unclean animal. But these were European sailors who had spent, in many cases, years in the Pacific, where dog was often a feast meat. '[F]ew were there of us,' wrote Cook, 'but what allowe'd that a South Sea Dog was next to an English lamb' (in Salmond 2003: 8).

What do such encounters tell us about the nature of 'culture'? Clearly, people who are differentiated by attributes such as ethnicity, class and age are embedded in cultural practices that are distinct from one other. They also tell us that we seek to understand others and interpret and evaluate what they do in relation to ourselves and to our own experiences. People who eat people may seem less than human to others, even if to themselves the act is a powerful way of 'biting the head' of their foes' ancestors, thereby compromising the capacity of those foes to act effectively. We have only our own frames of reference with which to make sense of the world. This chapter seeks to examine such frames of reference, and to assess how they change, by using historical, contemporary and cross-cultural perspectives in order to throw them into sharper focus.

Meanings of culture

'Culture' has been called as one of the complicated words in the English language (Williams 1976). It has been described variously as being complex to the point of defying 'the tasks of ordinary analysis', so overused as to be useless, and 'a deeply compromised idea' (Bennett 2005: 63). At the same time, it is an idea that we cannot do without. This is demonstrated by the huge number of new contexts in which it is now being used, to portray not just forms of difference between nations or peoples, but also within and across the relations between them. This multiplication of uses is directly related to the waning of the use of the term as a normative standard, in which it was synonymous with refinement (as in 'persons of culture'). The word is derived from the Latin *cultura*, referring to processes of cultivation of nature, as in caring or tending of plants. It is still in use in this sense, as agri-culture, viti-culture or horti-culture. A modern usage is 'tissue culture', which describes a particular method of artificial development of microscopic organisms, and plant and animal cells. Applied to people, culture therefore originally denoted individual growth and attainment. Thomas Hobbes wrote in Chapter 31 of *Leviathan* (1651) that 'the labour bestowed on the earth is called culture; and the education of children, a culture of their minds'.

A decisive change occurs in the meaning of 'culture' from the late eighteenth century, when it is increasingly applied not only to individual but also to social development. This reflects the diffusion of Enlightenment ideals of human wholeness or perfectability. It is a product of the realization that individuals cannot improve in isolation from beneficial social conditions (Eagleton 2000). It is also related to the impact of industrialization as well as of overseas exploration and colonization, all of which gave cause for reflection about what we would now describe as 'cultural' difference and change. At about the same time *Kultur*, the German equivalent, appears and the idea of *civilization* comes into use in French (Rampley 2005). In English however there soon emerges a tension between 'civilization' as indicative of a standard of material progress, and 'culture as the embodiment of a set of higher standards in whose name material civilization might be indicted for its shallowness, coarseness, or incompleteness' (Bennett 2005: 65). From this perspective, industrialization could be condemned for its failings and colonized societies for their 'wildness' or even 'savagery'.

Culture was then the means by which such apparent shortcomings could be overcome. It came to inform a set of practices which, through the development of social institutions such as public libraries, museums, concert halls and art galleries, sought to raise cultural standards. The face of the nineteenth-century city was transformed by this deployment of culture as a force for moral uplift. Gothic architecture, with its religious associations, and neo-classical styling, with its references to Rome and Greece, were widely employed to construct the new cultural edifices. In turn, they provided homes for the products of culture, such as literature, paintings and orchestral music. In the twentieth century, public broadcasting systems were an outcome of the same normative conception, with both programme content and presentational style being seen as matters in which a standard of universal applicability should be set. In recent decades, however, broadcasting has been one of the main arenas in which this definition of culture has been challenged, with the emergence of multiple yet fluidly segmented cultural markets, serviced by hosts of conventional and web-based radio and television stations seeking the attention of different age and ethnically based cultures.

Intellectually, the lessening of distinctions between high culture and 'the rest' owes much to the work of the cultural critic Raymond Williams, who showed that the supposedly universal standards associated with the normative view reflected those of ruling groups and classes. This insight opens up spaces in which a more democratic vision of what counts as 'culture' can be taken. Williams's own characterization of this was as 'a particular way of life, whether of a people, a period, a group, or humanity in general' (Williams 1976: 80). This rather open-ended definition can, however, be read in different ways. It can lead to a superorganic view of culture, as a possession floating free of social practice. It is also not inconsistent with a nineteenth-century perspective, in which it was common to divide societies according to their position on an upward continuum, rising from the 'savage' state, through the 'barbaric', to that of an 'improved' or cultured way of life (Pawson 1999). Such 'stages' of development are deeply sedimented in western ways of thinking. Hence to Eagleton 'the word culture traces a momentous historical transition', from hunting and gathering, through agriculture, to urban development, in which paradoxically the urban dwellers are cultivated and those who live by cultivating the soil are not (Eagleton 2000: 1–2).

Perhaps the main problem with the 'ways of life' conception of culture is that it implies that cultures are differentiated as fixed and separate entities. In an era of globalization and postmodern capitalism, the currents of cultural change seem both to coalesce and to differentiate with rapidity. This accounts for the emergence of terms such as 'transculturation' and 'cultural hybridity', which portray cultural traits and relations as fluid and impermanent. Bennett (2005: 68) summarizes the change in emphasis as a shift 'from speaking of different cultures to a stress on cultures in difference, with the implication that cultural activities are caught up in processes of differing rather than being simply different from the outset'. Just as the anecdote of the incident of the cannibal dog demonstrates how cultural encounters can generate change, there is now a much wider interest in exploring the processes of hybridity that characterize mundane as well as momentous encounters. Recent work on imperialism, for example, emphasizes not only how colonial sites such as the plantations of the West Indies were hybrids constructed by and of people, plants and ideas drawn from diverse sources, but the manner in which metropolitan societies and landscapes were also hybridized in complex and contradictory ways (Casid 2005; Thompson 2005).

Cultural change

It is clear that the various meanings of the term 'culture' are rooted in change. Since contemporary interpretations focus on the fluidity of cultural identities, it could be concluded that culture and change are virtually synonymous. In some senses this is true, although quite what is meant by 'change' depends on circumstance. For example, fashions concerning dress, drink and drugs that characterize popular cultures at particular times may shift from season to season and place to place. However, more deep-seated cultural attributes, such as foundational assumptions about how society is to be organized and how property is to be secured, alter very much more slowly. 'Property' is itself a cultural concept, and its meaning varies according to context. Collective ideals of property persist amongst indigenous peoples, despite long exposure in many cases to capitalist individualism, and that individualism is itself deeply rooted amongst the peoples of north-western Europe. Macfarlane (1987) traces this back to at least the late thirteenth century in England. Then there are matters for which the pace of change is intermediate, such as the relations between people and animals. Animal trials, like that of the 'cannibal dog', are probably unknown amongst Europeans today, but then the English, for example, have also only taken to pet-keeping in a general way within the last three to four centuries (Thomas 1983).

It may therefore be worthwhile to attempt a long-run view of cultural change in order to gain some perspective other than that which is grounded in the present. A common assumption about cultural change in Western thinking is that it is progressive, in the sense of 'irreversible changes in one direction only, and that this direction is towards improvement' (in Wright 2004: 3). This conception of material progress is no older than two to three hundred years and is clearly linked to the emergence of the terms 'culture' and 'civilization' in the eighteenth century. It became firmly established in mid to late Victorian times. Given the great changes of that era – industrialization, urban growth, imperial extension and trade – it is not difficult to see why this should have been so.

To those who were benefiting, progress seemed to be empirically self-evident, but it also gained credence simultaneously as an intellectual belief. This was because it appeared to be supported by parallel advances in scientific understanding. Of central significance in this respect was the application of Darwin's theory of evolution as a secular explanation of human development. In turn, the discovery by geologists of the great eons of time over which the Earth's development has taken place, created the context within which it was possible to make sense of evolution. This does not mean that sense was made everywhere in the same way. Livingstone (2005) has shown how local cultures read science differently according to context. In colonial New Zealand, the theory of evolution was co-opted to justify the naturalized imperialism that saw the vigorous establishment of northern hemisphere flora and fauna as a victory over apparently 'weaker' indigenous species. In contrast, in Charleston it was resisted as subverting the racial hierarchy, being seen at odds with beliefs in the American South about the separate origins of black people and white people (see also Chapter 34).

These readings, however, shared a focus on the attainments of the European present relative to those of both past times and of other peoples. Those attainments were therefore integral to a Eurocentric ethnocentrism that made little allowance for models of cultural change other than those that suited this way of understanding. One consequence of this was that peoples of other ethnic origins with whom Europeans came into contact were mapped on to the same, or a parallel, evolutionary ladder that they had drawn for themselves: the 'momentous historical transition', from hunting and gathering, through agriculture, to urban development. This made it very difficult to explain cultural attainments that seemed not to fit: how could Africans have built the city of Great Zimbabwe? How could the Mayans of central America have discovered mathematics and writing? And how could the small destitute population of Easter Island have possibly constructed such large statues? Such questions exposed anomalies that could not be explained within a Eurocentric frame of reference.

Answers to these questions are now being provided, in part because work which points the way, such as that of Flenley and Bahn (2003) on Easter Island, is more likely to be heard. Just as progressive interpretations of evolution were consistent with the cultural politics of the Victorian era, so too do more complex, less triumphal explanations suit the doubts and uncertainties of a postmodern age. This parallels the shift in understanding of culture itself from a normative value to a de-centred description of multiple practices. From this perspective, it is apparent that cultural change is not always forward moving in the Victorian sense. It has not always tracked in one direction only, nor has it always been towards improvement. For example, it is now widely accepted that the American hemisphere that Europeans referred to as 'the new world' was not relatively empty at the time they discovered it for themselves: it probably had an Indian population of over 50 million. Huge quantities of earth and stone were moved to create built environments. Not until New York City passed 30,000 people in 1775 did a European centre in North America exceed the largest Indian one, that of Cahokia near present-day East St Louis. But perhaps the most striking realization has been that by the late eighteenth century much of the Americas was more (not less) forested than it had been two hundred years before. The pace of regeneration varied, but it is agreed by many researchers that New England and the eastern seaboard saw extensive advance of forest frontiers during this period (Denevan 1992).

This is not what might be expected with the arrival of allegedly vigorous European pioneers. The most likely reason, however, was the abandonment of fields and reduction in burning as the consequence of a falling Indian population following the introduction of European diseases. All the same, the account does not fit with the standard progressive narrative in which indigenous peoples are supposed to be close to nature, lacking in agency, and not capable of widespread environmental change. It decentres European cultural experience. In the same way, it is now clear that there is no 'victory' of northern hemisphere plant and animal species over those native to New Zealand: there is only the usual hybridized outcome typical of colonial environments, in which continual effort is required to maintain that hybridity in a state that meets the needs of colonizers for grass and croplands. There are plenty of examples in the past where environments suitable for food production could not be sustained and the result was ecological and cultural collapse (Diamond 2005; see also Chapter 43).

Wright (2004) compares humans with other animals: like them we are highly specialized and adapted to specific ecological niches. But there is a crucial difference. 'Our specialization is the brain. The flexibility of the brain's interactions with nature, through culture, has been the key to our success' (p. 29). Cultural change can occur far more quickly than genetic adaptation. Yet it is very slow in respect of the wider cultural building blocks on which our understandings and practices are built. Albert Einstein, in his 'Telegram to prominent Americans', printed in the *New York Times* on 25 May 1946, summed up this state of affairs: 'The unleashed power of the atom has changed everything save our modes of thinking and we thus drift toward unparalleled catastrophe.' This succinct diagnosis is no less applicable sixty years on, but for a far wider range of reasons. The environmental outcomes of societal fixation with material progressiveness are becoming more and more clear, not least amongst them being enhanced global warming and loss of biodiversity. Einstein's judgement reflects the history of cultural change outlined in this section: our ability to reflect meaningfully on varying human circumstances is now far outstripped by our capacity to alter our material environments. It is now appropriate to turn to one evolving intellectual tradition that has tried to reflect meaningfully, that of cultural geography.

Cultural geographies

The different ways in which cultural geography has been practised reflect the broader changes in the definition of 'culture' and the democratization of the term, or its use to describe a much wider set of practices and performances than those of elites alone. There has been a sharp break between an older tradition of cultural geography that emerged in the United States early in the twentieth century, owing a certain amount to anthropology, and the more recent explorations of difference in the 'new cultural geography' produced by a younger generation of mainly British practitioners since the late 1980s (Johnston and Sidaway 2004). This newer tradition is more closely allied to cultural studies.

For many years, cultural geography was broadly understood to refer to the American tradition in the study of 'cultural landscapes', and textbooks using the term in that sense are still widely adopted in US universities. This tradition is associated with the so-called Berkeley school, which was named after the home institution of its intellectual leader, Carl Sauer. He taught at the University of California at Berkeley, on the eastern side of San Francisco Bay, between 1923 and 1957. The members of the school were particularly interested in the capacity of people to alter their environments, and in 'the differences in cultural conduct that distinguish one human group from another', and hence led to the production of different styles of landscape (Sauer 1956: 49; see also Chapter 2). Much of Sauer's research was historical in nature, and conducted in the field in Latin America or in the then sparsely populated American south-west. Amongst other interests, he sought to define the 'cultural hearths' from which various crops, such as peanuts, maize and sweet potato, diffused more widely across the landscape. His work was carried on by his students, including Andrew Hill Clark, who taught at another famous American geography department, that of the University of Wisconsin at Madison, between 1951 and 1975. One of his most notable books was on New Zealand, in which he explored its 'invasion', to quote from the title, from the time of Cook onwards, 'by people, plants and animals' (Clark 1949).

In many respects the American form of cultural geography was democratic, in as much as it was concerned with ordinary landscapes. It also focused on long-term cultural changes, consistent with the approach discussed in the preceding section of this chapter. However, the emphasis was more often on outcomes than it was on process or people, and some of Sauer's disciples distilled their study to one of objects, such as the regional occurrence of barns, bridges or fences of distinctive types. The practice of the Berkeley school came under criticism for a conception of culture that was static and 'superorganic' (Duncan 1980). By this was meant an essentializing and reifying tendency, reducing culture to some sort of homogenous possession, distinct and different between cultural groups from the outset. Shurmer-Smith dismisses Jordan and Rountree's Berkeley-inspired definition of culture as 'meaningless' when they describe 'it' unambiguously as 'a total way of life held in common by a group of people' (1982: 4). In response, she writes that she does not believe 'that there is any such *thing* as culture . . . culture is practised, not owned'. It is what we do, not what we have: it 'is the communicating, sense-making, sharing, evaluating, wondering, reinforcing, experimenting qualifier of what people *do*' (Shurmer-Smith 2002: 2–3).

The people in this definition fall broadly into two categories in the practice of new cultural geographies. First, and the focus of largely but by no means exclusively British geographers, are the 'cultures' and 'subcultures' of ethnicity, class, age and sexuality for which such terms are now used so widely (Crang 1998; Shurmer-Smith 2002). Second, and more the focus of geographers in countries like Canada, Australia and New Zealand, but again not exclusively, is the study of postcolonial conditions of indigenous peoples and their ongoing relations with dominant cultural traditions (Pawson and Cant 1992). In both categories of practice, there is the attempt to deal with cultural difference even-handedly, sometimes in both political and theoretical senses. Nature is seen as always in some sense cultural, in as much as different cultural groups attribute significance and meaning to their environments in particular ways. But then, as Eagleton puts it, 'cultures are built out of that ceaseless traffic with nature which we call labour. Cities are raised out of sand, wood, iron, stone, water and the like, and are thus quite as natural as rural idylls are cultural' (Eagleton 2000: 4). Hence David Harvey argues that there is nothing 'unnatural' about New York City, and doubts that indigenous peoples can be said to be 'closer to nature' than capitalist societies (Harvey 1996: 186–88).

Cultural geographers are however challenged by their own positionalities, whether their field site is, for example, suburban Paris or rural Nicaragua (Cupples 2002). Those who study in countries of colonial settlement with substantial indigenous populations have had to engage with the cultural politics of aboriginality. For Derek Gregory (1994), an awareness of his own cultural 'situatedness' occurred when he moved from the UK to Canada, although a primary source of his appreciation of this, as for many cultural geographers, is the writing of the literary theorist Edward Said. Said's classic text *Orientalism* (1978) argues that 'the Orient' was created as an imaginative geography as part of the Western imperial project. It had no prior existence, but was imagined as an 'other' – exotic, enticing, yet inferior – cultural realm in order to serve processes of colonial exploitation. In the same way Maori people in New Zealand, or Aboriginal people in Australia, did not name or distinguish themselves as a whole before their incorporation in the European realm. Rather, they were identified by lines of descent and family groupings, employing degrees of difference that eluded all but the more carefully observant European colonizers.

The concept of Australia as *terra nullius* is another example of an imperial imaginative geography. The literal meaning of this Latin term is 'empty land'. It was not empty to those who had lived there for 40,000 years before Europeans raised their flags a mere two hundred years or so ago. From a Eurocentric position, however, to imagine it as empty was to obvious advantage. Recent cultural geographies have revealed that it is rather a closely inscribed series of cultural landscapes, created and reproduced by Aboriginal peoples who, at time of contact, were speaking about 250 languages. Likewise, although European mapping was employed as a cultural weapon of dispossession, it is apparent that indigenous methods of mapping were and are still used to reproduce an intimate awareness of territory and detailed spatial knowledges (Turnbull 2000; see also Chapter 35). The mobilization of cultural identities, in terms of kin-based networks and of territorial belonging, has become both conspicuous and contested, both amongst indigenous peoples as well as between them and hegemonic cultures. Cultural geographies of belonging and resource use can contribute to processes of historical acknowledgement, contemporary social justice, and legal redress in recognition of Aboriginal title to land and water that was never voluntarily ceded.

Cultural geography in this tradition is postcolonial in as much as it represents part of a 'continuous engagement with the lasting effects of colonialism' (Pawson (1999: 26)). Such an engagement is likely to be theoretical as well as historical, and may be personal as well as academic. In *Dissident Geographies*, Blunt and Wills (2000: 168) call for geographers to:

> highlight the importance of representing people and places across different cultures, traditions and contexts but also point to the difficulties of such endeavours ... [P]ost-colonial studies challenge the production of knowledges that are exclusively western and ethnocentric by not only focusing on the world beyond 'the West' but also by destabilizing what is understood and taken for granted about 'the West'.

Encounters (2): global cultures?

An example of a belief taken for granted about the developed world (which must also include the wealthy countries of east Asia such as Japan and South Korea) is that it is the engine of processes of capitalist expansion and domination that are leading to widespread if not universal cultural homogenization. Popular reaction to this is often tinged with nostalgia about heritage and tradition. It marks a change of sentiment from a hundred years ago, when the western imperial project was broadly proclaimed, in both metropole and amongst colonizers, as civilizing and improving. Then the reproduction of a degree of sameness was the goal, informed by the normative conception of western or Eurocentric culture.

The change of sentiment can be traced back at least fifty years. In the long boom years following the Second World War, some writers began to formulate anxious theses about the ways in which the individual was being deprived of significant agency through involuntary compliance with the machinery of consumer capitalism. A notable example, popular with students in the 1960s, was Herbert Marcuse's *One Dimensional Man* (1964). It was not long before such ideas were extended into the geographical sphere. In *Place and Placelessness,* Edward Relph (1976) argued that place identity was being eroded by the standardization of landscapes through insensitivity to the significance of place. The tendency was and has remained pervasive in a range of contexts, including malls, suburbs, theme parks and tourist resorts. Far from becoming less popular over time, the citation of Relph's book by other writers was increasing towards the millennium. This suggests that its formulation retains appeal (Gold 2000).

The reason is not hide to find. Placelessness is now theorized in the context of political economy approaches to understanding postmodern capitalism, and specifically globalization. One of the characteristics of this form of capitalism is a radical restructuring of spatial relations since 1970, as capital has become more attuned to the qualities of places in the search for more profitable sites of accumulation. Political elites have often responded to this with programmes to enhance the cultural economy of places, driving a new wave of investment in cultural facilities that matches that undertaken in the nineteenth century. Prestige projects, such as new art galleries, museums, sports stadia, convention centres and revived waterfront districts, which play to contemporary styles of consumption, have been widely employed as means of interplace competition (see Chapter 30) (Plate 14.2). Along with the co-option of

Plate 14.2. The Spinnaker Tower, Portsmouth waterfront, opened October 2005. It is intended to form a focal point of difference for the waterfront regeneration, which otherwise contains all the elements of 'serial replication': bars, restaurants, shops, and apartments. Nonetheless, it echoes the form of the luxury Burj Al Arab Hotel on the coastline of Dubai. Image courtesy of LUSAS.

local tradition through the heritage industry, these spectacles are designed to retain or attract both capital and consumers. But the result is that 'places that seek to differentiate themselves end up creating a kind of serial replication of homogeneity' (Harvey 1993: 8). This is the consequence of the commodification of culture, in which few places stand out.

It would be a mistake, however, to paint a globalized world as formulaic and lacking differentiation. Even though it is commonplace to think of it as ever more closely intertwined in terms of economy, society and culture, globalization is no great leveller. It has rather led to increasing degrees of social and economic polarization, and cultural distinctiveness, within and between national territories. If ever it was possible to believe in monolithic national cultures, it is so no more. Markers as varied as class-based social protest on the one hand, and street landscapes of ethnic food industries on the other, make this clear. The immigrant transnational cultural faces of cities like Paris, Birmingham and Vancouver are postcolonial traces of imperial histories. Streets like Kilburn High Road in London have multiple identities, 'constructed out of a particular constellation of relations, articulated together at a particular locus' (Massey 1993: 66). Further, within such streets the experience of different groups varies enormously, with some being liberated by a sense of insertion into a globally articulated culture, and others being imprisoned by fear of difference and lack of mobility.

Political decolonization in the Third World and the collapse of the neo-imperial structures of the former Soviet bloc has led to the resurgence of nationalisms (see Chapter 19). Nationalism can be defined as 'the desire to bring cultural and territorial imperatives together', co-existing with and sometimes overriding differences such as those of class (Johnson 1995: 98). This rediscovery of place 'poses as many dangers as opportunities for the construction of any kind of progressive politics' (Harvey 1993: 27). The emergence of reactionary nationalisms is evident in much of the world. However, some places have successfully challenged earlier negative imaginaries. Ireland, for long the 'afterthought of Europe' (in James Joyce's phrase), now occupies a role as generator and exporter of cultural ideas in music, dance, literature and film. It is sufficiently similar to Britain and the US to be unthreatening, yet different enough to be intriguing. Hence the paradox of increasing profiles of cultural distinctiveness in a globalizing world can be explored in a number of ways. This realization has led to fundamental challenges to the everyday conception of globalization as something abstract, up and out there, in favour of a socially networked form of contemporary capitalism, emergent through everyday habitats, in which different expressions of culture are contesting with each other, effervescent and tentative, hybridizing to produce new forms (Flusty 2004). It is not the end of history, as was notoriously proclaimed at the end of the Cold War.

Conclusion

This chapter has sought to explore some of the meanings of culture and to chart some of the ways in which it contributes to change and is itself in change. A number of themes have been recurrent. The definition of culture is no longer normative, in the sense of specifying self or social improvement, although this is the root of the term. Rather, it has been democratized, and is used to describe specific but fluid ways of thinking, doing and being. Culture is now seen as performative rather than essentialized, and in this sense is implicated in constant processes of change. Hence the paradox that as the world grows smaller, connected by networks that are always both global and local, cultural difference becomes no less apparent. But if superficial elements of popular cultures change rapidly, more foundational attributes of difference, such as the Western belief in progressive change, are deeply sedimented. In this sense, an awareness of culture does something to reveal us to ourselves.

Further reading

Anderson, K. and Gale, F. (eds) (1999) *Cultural Geographies*. Melbourne: Addison Wesley Longman.
Bennett, T., Grossberg, L. and Morris, M. (eds) (2005) *New Keywords. A Revised Vocabulary of Culture and Society*. Malden, Mass.: Blackwell.
Shurmer-Smith, P. (ed) (2002) *Doing Cultural Geography*. London: Sage.
Turnbull, D. (2000) *Masons, Tricksters and Cartographers. Comparative Studies in the Sociology of Scientific and Indigenous Knowledge*. Amsterdam: Harwood Academic.
Wright, R. (2004) *A Short History of Progress*. Melbourne: The Text Publishing Company.

References

Bennett, T. (2005) Culture. In T. Bennett, L. Grossberg and M. Morris (eds) *New Keywords. A Revised Vocabulary of Culture and Society*, pp. 63–69. Malden, Mass.: Blackwell.
Blunt, A. and Wills, J. (2000) *Dissident Geographies. An Introduction to Radical Ideas and Practice*. Harlow: Longman.
Casid, J.H. (2005) *Sowing Empire. Landscape and Colonization*. Minneapolis: University of Minnesota Press.
Clark, A.H. (1949) *The Invasion of New Zealand by People, Plants and Animals: The South Island*. Brunswick, New Jersey: Rutgers University Press.
Crang, M. (1998) *Cultural Geography*. New York: Routledge.
Cupples, J. (2002) The field as a landscape of desire: sex and sexuality in geographical fieldwork. *Area* 34 (4), 382–90.
Denevan, W.M. (1992) The pristine myth: the landscape of the Americas in 1492. *Annals of the Association of American Geographers* 82 (3), 369–85.
Diamond, J. (2005) *Collapse. How Societies Choose to Fail or Survive*. London: Penguin Books.
Duncan, J.S. (1980) The superorganic in American cultural geography. *Annals of the Association of American Geographers* 70 (2), 181–98.
Eagleton, T. (2000) *The Idea of Culture*. Malden, Mass.: Blackwell.
Flenley, J. and Bahn, P. (2003) *The Enigmas of Easter Island: Island on the Edge*. Oxford: Oxford University Press.
Flusty, S. (2004) *De-Coca-Colonization. Making the Globe from the Inside Out*. London: Routledge.
Gold, J. R. (2000) Classics in human geography revisited. *Progress in Human Geography*, 24 (4), 613–15.
Gregory, D. (1994) *Geographical Imaginations*. Oxford: Blackwell.
Harvey, D. (1993) From space to place and back again. Reflections on the condition of postmodernity. In J. Bird, B. Curtis, T. Putnam, G. Robertson and L. Tickner (eds) *Mapping the Futures. Local Cultures, Global Change*, pp. 3–29. London: Routledge.
——(1996) *Justice, Nature and the Geography of Difference*. Cambridge, Mass.: Blackwell.
Johnson, N.C. (1995) The renaissance of nationalism. In R.J. Johnston, P.J. Taylor and M.J. Watts (eds) *Geographies of Global Change. Remapping the World in the Late Twentieth Century*, pp. 97–110. Oxford: Blackwell.
Johnston, R.J. and Sidaway, J.D. (2004) *Geography and Geographers. Anglo-American Human Geography since 1945*, sixth edition. London: Arnold.
Jordan, T. and Rountree, L. (1982) *The Human Mosaic. A Thematic Introduction to Cultural Geography*, third edition. New York: Harper and Row.
Livingstone, D.N. (2005) Science, text and space: thoughts on the geography of reading. *Transactions of the Institute of British Geographers* NS 30 (4), 391–401.

Macfarlane, A. (1987) *The Culture of Capitalism*. Oxford: Blackwell.

Marcuse, H. (1964) *One Dimensional Man*. London: Routledge and Kegan Paul.

Massey, D. (1993) Power-geometry and a progressive sense of place. In J. Bird, B. Curtis, T. Putnam, G. Robertson and L. Tickner (eds) *Mapping the Futures. Local Cultures, Global Change*, pp. 59–69. London: Routledge.

Pawson, E. (1999) Postcolonial New Zealand? In K. Anderson and F. Gale (eds) *Cultural Geographies*, pp. 25–50. Melbourne: Addison Wesley Longman.

Pawson, E. and Cant, G. (eds) (1992) Theme issue: indigenous land rights in Canada, Australia and New Zealand. *Applied Geography* 12 (2), 95–200.

Rampley, M. (2005) Visual culture and the meanings of culture. In M. Rampley (ed.) *Exploring Visual Culture. Definitions, Concepts, Contexts*, pp. 5–17. Edinburgh: Edinburgh University Press.

Relph, E. (1976) *Place and Placelessness*. London: Pion.

Said, E. (1978) *Orientalism*. London: Routledge and Kegan Paul.

Salmond, A. (2003) *The Trial of the Cannibal Dog. Captain Cook in the South Seas*. Auckland: Penguin Books.

Sauer, C. (1956) The agency of man on earth. In W.L. Thomas (ed.) *Man's Role in Changing the Face of the Earth*, pp. 49–69. Chicago: University of Chicago Press.

Shurmer-Smith, P. (ed.) (2002) *Doing Cultural Geography*. London: Sage.

Thomas, K. (1983) *Man and the Natural World. Changing Attitudes in England 1500–1800*. London: Allen Lane.

Thompson, A. (2005) *The Empire Strikes Back? The Impact of Imperialism on Britain from the Mid-Nineteenth Century*. Harlow: Pearson Longman.

Turnbull, D. (2000) *Masons, Tricksters and Cartographers. Comparative Studies in the Sociology of Scientific and Indigenous Knowledge*. Amsterdam: Harwood Academic.

Williams, R. (1976) *Keywords. A Vocabulary of Culture and Society*. London: Fontana/Croom Helm.

Wright, R. (2004) *A Short History of Progress*. Melbourne: The Text Publishing Company.

15

Ideological change
Belief, religion and place

Chris Perkins

It is widely recognized that during the last two centuries religion has come to play a less significant role in Western societies. Religious beliefs have not disappeared but the influence of churches in social and political life has declined, paralleling a decline in the number of churchgoers. In the West secular states and consumerist concerns have gained ground at the expense of a more spiritual outlook. Churches are being converted to new uses or become redundant. Western societies have grown increasingly profane and religion as a social force has increasingly become a matter of individual belief, rather than a collective concern. The Cold War was fought on grounds of ideological opposition that largely stemmed from materialist concerns. Soviet communism rejected religious belief as false consciousness and actively developed aggressive policies against organized religion, whilst the free world espoused a capitalist ethos that valued material prosperity rather than spiritual concerns, an ethos that has been exported around the globe under the guise of neo-liberal globalization.

But this image of steady decline is fundamentally flawed. Religious freedom is enshrined in article 18 of the UN Declaration of Human Rights and many national constitutions also affirm this right to teach, practise, worship and observe individual religious beliefs (Park 1994: 185); ideology continues to have a profound and often direct impact upon places as well as individuals. Even secular Western societies are imbued with religious practice, culture and histories. Moral and ethical values of secular societies, their architecture and institutions, as well as social practices and norms such as patriarchy, all can be traced to a religious social heritage. Ideological change is also fuelling powerful disagreements central to contemporary geopolitics: Fukuyama's (1992) view that history ended with the collapse of the Soviet Union has proved naïve and over-simplistic. Fundamentalist religious belief, whether from the neo-conservative moral majority in the USA or from resurgent Islam, is a powerful force in the new millennium, and other new religious beliefs are emerging in the secular West. These religions ideas and beliefs shape places.

The ways in which geographers have engaged with these issues have also reflected changing times. Traditional concerns concentrated upon describing distributions, charting the diffusion of religions and their relationships to development, population or places, e.g. Park (1994, 2005). Humanistic geographers sought to explore ways of life, including associations between religion and the cultural landscape, e.g. Tuan (1976). More recent approaches to religion and belief address the role of religion in modernity by interrogating notions of identity, community, sacred space and religious practice (Kong 2001), and have begun to incorporate new cultural understandings of place at scales ranging from the body up to international geopolitics (Holloway and Valins 2002). Some view religion as wrapped up with social and political issues; others argue for a more essential nature of sacredness; but there is generally a wider acceptance of complexity and of interplay between belief, embodied actions, social agency and structures.

This chapter negotiates a complex terrain between the material and spiritual, mapping out different ways of understanding the power of belief and charting the expression of these ideas at different spatial scales. We move from issues relating to the role of religion in global change through places and landscapes and their association with belief, to the scale of the community, before exploring the interplay between religion and individual identity. But first it is necessary to introduce the changing nature and significance of different faiths.

The religious world

Definitions of religion are fraught with difficulty. Park (1994: 33) brings together seven alternatives and argues for a pragmatic definition as 'a system of thought and behaviour expressing belief in God'. One useful classification might be to distinguish between universalizing religions that seek converts (such as Christianity or Islam) and ethnic religions that do not seek to diffuse through missionary zeal (such as Hinduism or Judaism). Of course, the nature of the belief varies between religions that are non-theistic (not believing in a being called God, such as animistic religions), through those that believe in one deity (such as Islam, Christianity and Judaism), to those that are polytheistic (such as Hinduism). To these might be added agnostic and atheist belief systems. The ways in which religious beliefs are expressed comprise ethical systems, representations such as art, rituals, doctrines, social experience, institutions, myths and narratives within myths (Smart 1989). The relationship between religion and governance is important. 'Established' religion associated with secular rule has declined in significance in Western democracies, but the resurgence of Islam has led to the rise of theocracies where Sharī'ah law is enshrined as a central part of governance. The geography of these belief systems is often in conflict, and their traces extend well beyond ceremonies and the architecture of worship.

Religious beliefs developed early in the cultural evolution of humanity, with prehistoric tombs providing clear evidence of organized and shared religious rituals. The major contemporary global religions grew from two different sources an 'IndoGangetic hearth' from which emerged Hinduism, Sikhism and Buddhism and a 'Semitic hearth' which spawned Judaism, Islam and Christianity (Park 2005). It is possible to chart subsequent processes by which these faiths diffused and fragmented. Figure 15.1 maps contemporary distribution of the most significant religious faiths at a global scale and Table 15.1 quantifies the numbers of adherents to these faiths. Many more detailed national exercises have also been carried out, often employing census data to chart variations in religious belief, e.g. Pacione (2005) for Scotland. These distributions reflect a constant ebb and flow of changing beliefs, in which the nature of belief and practice changes, and the number of adherents rises and falls as religions spread through migration or conversion. What remains certain in this process is that every society, however secular, relies upon ideology and myth (Claval 2001). The remainder of this article explores how religion and ideological concerns are mapped out at different

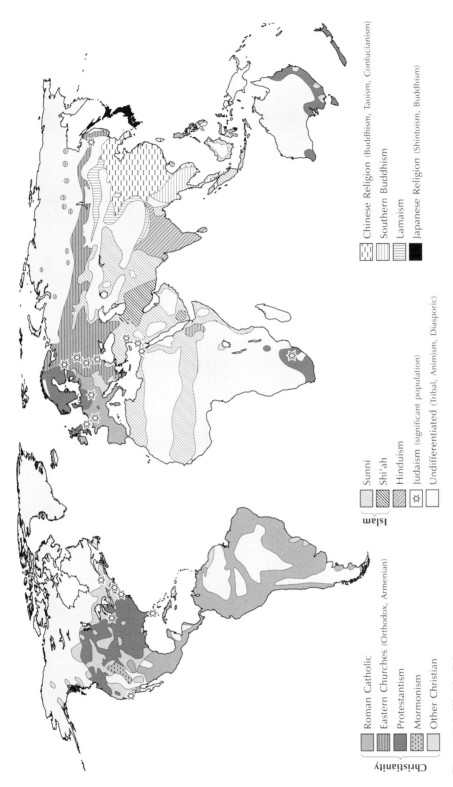

Figure 15.1. World religions.

Chinese Religion (Buddhism, Taoism, Confucianism)

Southern Buddhism

Lamaism

Japanese Religion (Shintoism, Buddhism)

Sunni

Shi'ah

Hinduism

Judaism (significant population)

Undifferentiated (Tribal, Animism, Diasporic)

Islam

Roman Catholic

Eastern Churches (Orthodox, Armenian)

Protestantism

Mormonism

Other Christian

Christianity

Table 15.1. The major religions of the world ranked by number of adherents

Christianity	2.1 billion split into Catholic, Protestant, Orthodox and other
Islam	1.3 billion split into Sunni and Shiite
Secular/non-religious/agnostic/atheist	1.1 billion
Hinduism	900 million
Chinese traditional religion	394 million
Buddhism	376 million
Primal-indigenous	300 million
African Traditional and diasporic	100 million
Sikhism	23 million
Juche	19 million
Spiritism	15 million
Judaism	14 million
Baha'i	7 million
Jainism	4.2 million
Shinto	4 million
Cao Dai	4 million
Zoroastrianism	2.6 million
Tenrikyo	2 million
Neo-Paganism	1 million
Unitarian-Universalism	800,000
Rastafarianism	600,000
Scientology	500,000

Source: Adapted from http://www.adherents.com/Religions_By_Adherents.html

scales and how these mythic elements underpinning everyday life are negotiated and prac-tised. We start by considering how religion is related to global change.

Globalization and belief systems

There are many possible interpretations of emerging social, cultural and economic power. Theorists who focus largely upon economic readings of globalization (addressed in Chapter 12), differ in their interpretations from those who emphasize more cultural associations implicit in colonialism and post-colonialism (see Chapter 14). It can be argued, however, that belief systems play a significant role in both of these frameworks, and perhaps more significantly are themselves powerful forces in the global geopolitics of the war on terror. Interactions between faith, place and politics are of course complex, as witnessed by the four following examples.

There has been a tendency to paint religions as stabilizing forces in society: rural areas are seen as places with most religious adherents; cities are where secular worldviews dominate. But contemporary religious faith also often grows from urban roots: inner-city evangelical missions and the role of Islamic clerics suggest religious change often comes from the cities. The nature of religion can also be increasingly radical and forward looking. The rise of radical militant Islam, of catholic liberation theology, of Solidarity in the overthrow of Soviet power in Poland illustrate that religion can often be a powerful force associated with global change, whilst acting as a conservative force elsewhere.

A second example concerns places and the ways religions imagine relations between the sacred and the profane, between this world and the next. Theologies posit particular relations with natural world that can justify secular action. Thus it has been argued that the Judaeo-Christian worldview situates people and culture above nature which exists for humankind to exploit (White 1967). According to this thesis, contemporary resource-depletion and environmental crisis stem ultimately from biblical edicts. In contrast, Buddhist worldviews see a much greater unity of all living things. In practice relations are much more complex, fractured and contested. In different contexts there are different outcomes. Christian notions of steward-ship and sustainability may outweigh any belief in a natural right to exploit nature, and Buddhist funeral practices may lead to forest degradation despite a veneration for living things (Park 1994).

A third illustration focuses around the supposed association between war and religious belief. Conflicts in the Middle East are cast as an inevitable consequence of a clash between Christianity and Islam, or between Judaism and Islam. A new 'clash of civilizations' is seen to have emerged after the end of the Cold War (Huntington 1993). American intervention in the Middle East becomes part of a new crusade by the forces of the democratic Christian West against an alien civilization. Global terrorist forces well beyond the usual Islamic ste-reotypes may be seen to stem from religious belief (Juergensmeyer 2003).

However, numerous studies cast doubt upon the central tenet of the Huntington thesis: there is no evidence that conflict is more likely between states that belong to different civi-lizations (e.g. Henderson and Tucker 2001). It is true that wars have often been prosecuted between different religious groups, but they are more likely to be between factions of the same faith. The conflict in Iraq after the overthrow of Saddam Hussein might be traced to the profound differences between Sunni and Shiite factions of Islam, but this conflict clearly also relates to more complex cultural and social associations articulated in the specific Iraqi context. Similarly, to paint international terrorism and *jihad* as inevitably Islamic mis-represents the rich cultural diversity of Islam and greatly underplays geopolitical tensions and international disparities of wealth. The world's religions also serve as powerful forces for peace: Aboriginal, Hindu, Buddhist, Confucian, Jewish, Muslim and Christian traditions all offer rich spiritual resources for non-violent resolution of conflicts (Coward and Smith 2004).

A final example relates to the ongoing links between genocide and belief in the twentieth century. It can be argued that the Holocaust was a direct outcome of anti-Semitic feeling, and that Armenian, Rwandan and Bosnian genocides reflected religious differences. But Bartov and Mack (2001) show that the intersection of state-organized murder and religion is best analysed not only as a force legitimizing atrocities, but also as a means of resisting and coming to terms with these traumatic events. The context, positioning and timing of events really matters.

These four examples suggest the most fruitful way forward may be to explore *how* belief systems are related to change at different scales. Park (1994) exemplifies associations between religion, demography, development and politics and provides a useful starting point for this process.

Belief systems are clearly associated with the different demographies described in Chapter 9, even though it is very hard to unpack the significance of religion, ethnicity or other cultural practices from socio-economic factors, and even harder to ascribe causal relations. Any crude analysis at a national scale is fraught with difficulty. For example, the populations of most Islamic states are growing faster than average, and tend to be characterized by higher birth rates and higher than average mortality. But this may also be associated with a young marriage age and relative economic disadvantage, rather than with cultural practices that can be more directly related to Islam. It is more fruitful to explore the links between belief and factors that more directly control fertility, mortality and migration. Religious edicts on family planning have clearly impacted on wider social issues that have produced hugely different geographies. Opposition from the Catholic Church to artificial birth control contributed to generally higher fertility amongst Catholic populations than those with Protestant traditions during the western European economic take-up in the nineteenth century. But inter-denominational differences are now much less significant. It can also be argued that the Chinese state's role in promoting fertility control stems from its materialist belief systems.

There are also clear links between the development process and belief systems. For example, Max Weber famously ascribed the rise of capitalism to the gradual triumph of dissenting religion over Catholic orthodoxy during the reformation (Weber 1930). Development in this view follows belief systems, rather than being governed by more structural or material concerns. The precise association may be very complex. In some contexts neo-liberal economic development is held back. For example, unequal gender roles may reduce labour flexibility and preserve traditional rural values: Hindu villagers in India may be unwilling to adapt to changing demands. Elsewhere, Islamic banks offer a much greater emphasis upon interest-free banking that leads to more redistributive economic policies (Park 1994: 178).

The development process also impacts upon the nature of belief. Berger (1999: back cover) is among many who argue that 'while modernization may have secularising effects it also provokes a reaction that more often strengthens religion'. By examining the local political context this relationship can be explored in greater detail. For example, in Singapore traditional Chinese rituals are being changed to fit with modern living (Kiong and Kong 2000).

States where religious practice is enshrined in jurisprudence often enact legislation and pursue national policies that are directly influenced by these belief systems, but which may also lead to more significant global change. The Islamic revolution in Iran led to a profound change in the basis of Iranian civil society and also strongly encouraged the global resurgence of fundamentalist Islamic politics. The Taliban regime in Afghanistan enacted very restrictive civil policies that severely limited women's capacity to act outside the domestic sphere, but partly as a consequence of its domestic policies also served as a focus for American foreign intervention in the aftermath of 9/11 (Gregory 2004). Elsewhere religious political parties may exert substantial influence upon national policies that can have a major impact on international relations, even when they receive little local support. Extreme religious parties in Israel, for example, have strenuously, and largely successfully, opposed significant concessions for Palestinians, strongly supported Zionist settlement policies and successfully mobilized the American Jewish lobby. Western responses to Middle Eastern political differences emerge in a process that justifies political action on 'affectual' grounds, where emotion and belief matter as much as rational realpolitik (Ó Tuathail 2003).

Religious impacts on international policy making are also mapped out in territorial partition on the ground, which continues to create international tension. Partition of the Indian subcontinent created India as a state with a Hindu majority and Pakistan as a state with a Muslim majority, leading to significant migration and to ongoing conflict over contested territories such as Kashmir. The Dayton accord remapped changed religious identities, but also reflected international power-politics, just as Israeli–Palestinian relations are played out on the West Bank, but also in the United Nations and Washington, DC.

Landscapes and sacred places

Religious belief may also be reflected in the nature of places. This section considers some of the ways in which landscapes as a whole are religious, explores material evidence of religious practice within these contexts and focuses on sacred places and pilgrimage sites.

Religious landscapes

Wider social and economic practice has been strongly influenced by religious beliefs that uniquely mark complete landscapes, through distinctive settlement patterns and agricultural practices. The study of these cultural landscapes has been a particular focus of the Berkeley School of cultural geography and it is the American cultural landscape that has seen the most intensive investigation.

Christian denominations have had significantly different landscape impacts during the historical geography of settlement of North America, that reflect their beliefs and the settlement history of an area. Chris Park (1994) brings together this diverse research field and the following section is closely derived from his work. Roman Catholics in Louisiana, Dutch Reformed Church Calvinists in parts of Michigan and Germanic Lutheran groups in Texas have left their mark on the landscape, creating unique folk architecture and very different ways of life that may survive to this day. Anabaptist landscapes in North America remain as testimonies to the faith and persistence of these Protestant traditions. Hutterite communities living on communal farms in the Canadian provinces of Manitoba, Alberta and Saskatchewan preserve traditions of communal living in which secular and religious communal life are clearly separated and in which a diverse agricultural landscape survives amid surrounding commercial agriculture. Close-knit Amish communities across the USA maintain a traditional agrarian lifestyle cut off from outside influences, farming the land without mechanized support, using sustainable methods that preserve the self-sufficient Amish lifestyle. Utopian Mormon settlement patterns around Salt Lake City in Utah reflect the separatist edicts of founder Joseph Smith. Urban settlement patterns are based on carefully planned grid-based development, each part sufficient to itself, with wide streets developing around central public structures (Sopher 1967 and Chapter 29). Meanwhile the Mormon edict of stewardship led to the development and persistence of small sustainably managed farms in the surrounding rural areas.

The administrative geography of most Christian European nations also reflects the power of the Church. Parish boundaries in the UK map out catchment areas for church membership and reflect the settlement geography of the area, but also delineate structures of governance in a social context where significant social power resided with the clergy (Pounds 2004). This legacy survives in rural areas as boundaries and parish institutions.

Kibbutzim in Israel are another example of a landscape associated with religious belief. These communal agricultural settlements reflect the central importance of land in Zionist ideology and their unique form contrasts strongly with Palestinian settlements on the West Bank (Kellerman 1996).

Indian villages and towns are a final example of the practical and symbolic significance of religion for landscape. They were traditionally designed with layouts that reflected Hindu principles, centred on a temple, with associated meeting halls and surrounding supporting land uses (Park 1994).

Sacred landscapes and religious landscape features

The landscape itself may be imbued with sacred qualities and the ways in which cultures relate to nature are closely associated with religious faith (Glacken 1967). Australian Aboriginal cosmologies evoke landscape associations between the tracks of the ancestors from the dreamtime that are left as topographic features in the landscape (Young 1993). Natural features may be venerated by religions: the River Ganges is seen as holy by Hindus, Mount Fuji has a spiritual significance for Japanese Shintoism, animistic religions venerate living things.

Eliade (1959) argues that sacred places become sacred through an irruption that is revealed to someone or to a group of people. The transcendent quality of the sacred then becomes ritualized through religious practice, such as feasting or fasting, the creation of religious symbology, ceremonial practices, religious narratives and folklore (Chidester and Linenthal 1995). For example, New Age alternative movements construct, perceive and sense the landscape around Glastonbury as sacred, as a result of belief in psychic and spiritual energy being concentrated in the landscape; because of the wealth of historical myth associated with the Tor and because of the number of like-minded people who congregate in the area, practising and enacting their beliefs (Holloway 2003).

The process of sacrification may also be symbolic. For example, the Zionist revival is articulated around a geographical imaginary that confers particular associations on the land of Israel and upon sites identified in the scriptures (Azaryahu and Kellerman-Barrett 1999).

More detailed elements in these landscapes may also be explained in relation to particular cultural norms or sets of religious beliefs. Landscapes of worship are the most obvious reflection of this approach. Places of worship themselves clearly leave a prominent stamp: churches, temples and mosques are often some of the largest and most permanent built structures and can themselves act as foci around which development occurs. Other direct traces of religion on the landscape include places of burial or commemoration or symbolic sites such as shrines. Park (1994) charts features such as domestic altars, roadside shrines and chapels.

The architectural form of these places of worship is itself often governed by religious principles: orientation, shape and location reflect symbolic values (Tuan 1977). Thus Buddhist temples in the Kyoto area of Japan differ in their form, location and garden layouts according to their founding dates (Tanaka 1977). The distinctive and complex form of the Hindu temple also reflects a process of change and accommodation with secular life (Park 1994). The history, form and siting of Christian churches reflects the power of the denomination and its beliefs, but has always included an altar facing east, whilst the mosque stands pre-eminent in the Islamic city, its status guaranteed in Sharī'ah law.

Complete settlements may serve largely religious functions or attain symbolic significance that prompts profound social movements, such as the many Christian crusades to capture Jerusalem or the regular annual pilgrimage to Mecca. And religious institutions have been and still are powerful landowners, exerting huge influence well beyond the place of worship itself.

Whereas orthodox treatments in this tradition focused on description of built forms, an increasing emphasis is being placed upon more critical structural explanations, such as David Harvey's (1979) analysis of the powerful discourses underpinning the struggle over the construction of the Sacré Cœur in Paris. Just as religious identity is increasingly studied as part of a wider and more critical social theory, so are more complex and ambiguous readings of religious landscapes becoming more significant. For example, symbolic readings of religious landscapes as texts imbued with cultural and powerful meanings are becoming much more significant. James Duncan's (1990) historical geography of the city of Kandy, where building design at once reflected a cosmological orthodoxy mapped out in sacred texts but also legitimated rule, was an early and influential example of this trend. Other more recent work in this area traces links between religious landscapes and tourist practices (Poria et al. 2003); regional (Raivo 2002) and national (Palmer 2002) identity; and colonialism and post-colonial literatures (Scott and Simpson-Houseley 2001).

The impact of the rituals of death on landscapes has been a particular focus for study, with the cemetery forming a particular focus for attention. Studies have focused on cemetery location, landscape, architecture, morphology and even social and ethnic segregation within cemeteries e.g. Francaviglia (1971). Just as the emphasis has shifted towards social process in the analysis of places of worship, so has a consideration of the cemetery increasingly moved away from static and ideographic emphases towards a focus on process and meaning (e.g. Pitte 2004). The emphasis has shifted away from a narrow obsession with largely apolitical cultural explanations to interrogate more symbolic and political aspects of commemoration and the marks it leaves behind. For example, Mandy Morris (1997) charts the ambiguities of preservation in which an imperial landscape of commemoration is maintained in Commonwealth military cemeteries. The iconography of these sites celebrates individual sacrifice but also evokes the British establishment, with a presumption of Christian faith, and an assertion of the power of the regiment. The context for this commemoration also evokes national values, through carefully orchestrated and regulated planting regimes emulating the English country garden often adrift in an alien landscape.

Pilgrimage

Faith involves movement as well as a fixed relation to place. Pilgrimage plays an important part in contemporary religious practice and is performed by Muslims, Christians, Buddhists, Sikhs, Hindus, Jews, Taoists, Confucianists and Shintoists. It comprises very heterogeneous actions and places but typically involves a journey to a sacred place, in search of healing, to fulfil a religious duty, or as an act of purgatory. These sacred places often have long histories, but pilgrimage may be fluid and changing. Buddhist pilgrimage circuits in Japan documented by Tanaka (1977) change over time and the sanctity of sites themselves is not fixed.

A descriptive and structural emphasis in academic work on pilgrimage has shifted towards more ethnographic perspectives, and increasingly it is recognized that pilgrimage is a complex phenomenon, closely intertwined with practices of tourism and changing in response to globalization (Eades and Salnow 1991).

The scale, nature, significance and impacts of pilgrimage vary. The risks for pilgrims may be great. During the *hajj* in Saudi Arabia in the last decade, crowd pressure has led to significant numbers of pilgrims dying. In Baghdad pilgrimage to the shrine of Imam Moussa Qadim, the eighth-century Shia saint, is once again permitted after the overthrow of Saddam Hussein. An estimated 1 million pilgrims paraded through the streets on 31 August 2005, panic set in on the Aima Bridge over the Tigris and an estimated 965 people died (Fisk 2005).

Pilgrimage is a global phenomenon involving a very large number of places. In Western Europe Nolan and Nolan (1989) identify 6,150 Christian pilgrimage sites, visited by an estimated 70–100 million people a year. Most of these sites are in Catholic nations. The best-known and most popular destination is Lourdes in the French Pyrenees, which attracts around 5 million pilgrim visits a year to a town with around just 18,000 permanent inhabitants (Park 2005). The factors that have contributed to Lourdes' attraction as a place of healing include the religious pilgrimage tradition; its central role in political, economic, social and cultural changes in France; and belief in miraculous cures (Gesler 1996). Numbers of pilgrims have grown since the establishment of the grotto where the vision took place, reflecting increasing mobility.

Economic impacts of the larger pilgrimages can be very significant: the *hajj* in Mecca forms the third most significant part of the Saudi economy after oil income and oil company-related expenditure (Park 1994). Around 2 million pilgrims from more than 100 countries travel to the holy city of Mecca in the twelfth month of every Muslim lunar year to re-enact rituals that Muslims have been performing for centuries (Bianchi 2004). *Hajj* numbers have fluctuated according to the geopolitical situation in the Middle East, but there has been a doubling in participation since the 1970s. It has been argued that, geographically and culturally, today's *hajj* is nearly universal (Bianchi 2004). The highest rates of participation in the *hajj* are in countries closest to Mecca, but air travel allows Muslims throughout the world to travel with increasing frequency, and wealth correlates more closely with participation rates than the distance from Mecca or the proportion of a country's population that is Islamic. The growth in participation has been accompanied by a steady rise in the proportion of women pilgrims, to about 45 per cent of the overall total in 2004, despite large disparities in female pilgrimage in the more fundamentalist traditions. The *hajj* community is increasingly female, educated, youthful, urban and non-Middle Eastern.

Hindu pilgrimage reflects the pantheistic nature of the faith, with many diverse sites visited. Increasing disposable income is leading to a much more mobile pilgrim population, some of whom verge on being tourists. But increased access is also allowing a greater number of more devout pilgrims to participate, in what has been described as an increasingly 'curious blend of secularisation and sacrilisation' (Park 1994: 275).

Larger pilgrimages are more than religious festivals, they become significant political events. The *hajj*, for example, is regulated by national governments and the Organization of the Islamic Conference. It is, however, argued that:

> no authority – secular or religious, national or international – can really control the hajj. Pilgrims believe that they are entitled to travel freely to Mecca as 'Guests of God' – not as guests of any nation or organization that might wish to restrict or profit from their efforts to fulfil a fundamental religious obligation.
>
> (Bianchi 2004: 1)

Journeys to shrines also leave a whole series of traces – pilgrim routes are increasingly mapped out with infrastructures supporting the quest. Traces may be artefactual (for example, long-distance footpaths such as the Camino to Santiago, or new airports such as Knock in Ireland); spiritual and performative (for example, new places of worship such as the Basilica at Lourdes, or the tightly prescribed seven days of rituals in the *hajj*); or representational (such as imagery like the sea shell of Santiago, or modes of pilgrim dress, etc.). And these traces are increasingly contested. For example, the roads to Santiago de Compostela have very different meanings for individual pilgrims as against those managing the 'heritage attraction' of the pilgrimage site (Graham and Murray 1997). However, despite often intense political argument, individual pilgrims may sustain a shared sense of identity in the face of apparently overwhelming external pressures. Jurkovich and Gesler (1997), for example, describe pilgrims visiting Medjugorje, a Catholic pilgrimage site, during the height of the Bosnian conflict. Shared beliefs, rituals, myths and othering allowed them to sustain a sense of a devout, non-materialistic rural community despite the all-pervasive Bosnian conflict in the area around the site. Where pilgrimage sites are shared between faiths, tensions between religions may sometimes erupt into violence, for example in Jerusalem, between Jews, various Christian denominations and local Palestinian people. The poetical power of pilgrimage to such places outweighs risks and politics.

Identity and belief

A conventional view has been that belief may be associated more with spirituality than with politics. According to this view, the recognition of what is sacred is a matter of consciousness. People develop attachments to religious places, such as places of worship like a mosque or temple, and a shared religious community constitutes an important part of people's sense of place. Most research until the 1990s idealized the nature of this shared experience, without interrogating the often complex and negotiated identities, behaviours and practices associated with religious community and identities constituted around religion (Kong 2001). Geographers also tended to focus upon the sacred place alone (see previous section), rather than on wider social concerns and the contribution that belief might bring to social identity or action.

More recently research around religious identity has come to emphasize the complexities of place and to move away from considering only the sacred. This kind of research examines associations between religion and everyday behaviour, as well as focusing upon rituals, institutions and technologies. Practices as diverse as family relations, children's education, expenditure patterns, eating and drinking, dress, the use of cosmetics, and sexual behaviour, for example, have been linked to religious beliefs (Poria *et al.* 2003). Social and political views are also clearly linked to religion.

Taking Judaism as an example illustrates the complexity of everyday associations. Donin (1991) is probably the most influential guide to everyday Jewish practices. He introduces the Jewish creed and relates this to laws and taboos relating to everyday life. The central importance of observing the sabbath is considered, and the significance of a kosher diet, family life and love and reverence is stressed. The synagogue is introduced, festivals described and Jewish practices around, birth, bar mitzvah, divorce and death introduced. Being a Jew is about much more than belief: it encompasses a lifestyle and identity which profoundly shapes places.

This process is often closely affected by technologies of communication: the media through which religious experience and identity are shared may be crucial. In the USA the rise of right-wing evangelical Christianity is in part associated with the development of religious television channels; these offer platforms for particular strands of belief to be disseminated and encourage particular kinds of political action, such as opposition to abortion (Hendershot 2004). Similarly, the role of the Internet is changing the nature of community and simultaneously allowing greater access to global messages, whilst also fostering new kinds of local association between people of similar beliefs. Khatib (2003) shows, for example, how cyberspace enables Islamic fundamentalist groups to communicate, safeguard and strengthen their multiple identities.

Social institutions well beyond sacred places or places of worship also play important roles in constituting and reinforcing religious identities. Religious schools continue to play an important role and serve to defend religious identities, as well as encouraging the segregation of communities (Valins 2003). The nature of teaching in religious schools also affects the secular world outside. For example, the rising significance of madrassah-based Islamic education has been demonized as a factor perhaps associated with the tragedy of 9/11 (Sikand 2005). Arguments over the teaching of creationist ideas in the American educational system also clearly illustrate the strongly contested significance of religious education.

The nature and practices of prayer and worship can also be seen as social and spatial, as well as being concerned with individual spiritual encounters. For example, a micropolitics of worship emerges from ethnographic work in Presbyterian churches, where pews, decor and church design reinforce but also partly constitute practices of worship (MacDonald 2002). Talmudic conceptions of space in orthodox Jewish culture can also be understood as negotiated and bounded, with the recent growth of *eruvim* a reflection of the Jewish diaspora but also of relations between private and public space and between ethnic identity and orthodox religious practice (Vincent and Warf 2002).

The politics of religious identity are complex. Dwyer (1999) recognizes that young British Muslim women construct identities that may be simultaneously global and local but also simultaneously empowering and constraining. Her study shows that membership of a local community offers support through shared practices, but at the same time is constructed as Asian and juxtaposed to other British identities. The local community offers security, shared beliefs and day-to-day experiences, but also carefully monitors and regulates behaviour, constraining individual freedom. Gender roles and age may be as significant as religious affiliation for this group and power is crucial. Membership of the global Muslim community, the *umma*, is also contested. In the aftermath of 9/11 and the 7 July bombings in London, an increase in anti-Muslim feeling led to a greater sense of global Muslim unity in the face of perceived oppression, but at the same time revealed the very great diversity and differences of opinion within the broader Islamic religious identity (Afshar *et al.* 2005). Muslim women choosing to wear the *hejaab* can be seen to be making an active political decision that may be strongly contrasted with more combative male political Islamism, but which may also bring women or girls into conflict with secular social norms, for example in the French school bans of 2004 over wearing the veil at school.

Indeed, the use of clothing, fashion and bodily appearance serves as an important marker for religious identity (Arthur 1999). Tensions between individual bodies and socio-religious communities are often played out in how believers look or dress and are often strongly gendered. Leaders of communities in many Christian traditions are marked by their ceremonial dress, with the ecclesiastical hierarchy clearly identified in dress codes. Religious orders identify themselves through their clothing; monks and nuns become metaphorically and visibly separated from the rest of society as well as being literally separated by their habit. Sikh and orthodox Jewish men grow their beards; prayer in the mosque requires that outside shoes should not be worn. Bodily deportment in space is also associated with religious practice and identity. Christian services involve kneeling, sitting and standing together in a congregation. Praying in Islam involves facing Mecca.

Dietary prescriptions also play important roles as marking religious boundaries: Muslim and Jewish prescriptions over eating unclean meat; the Islamic rejection of alcohol; Hindus not eating meat, eggs or fish; Buddhists being unwilling to raise stock for meat or wool, etc. (Simoons 1994). These dietary practices identify the faithful and also impact upon the landscapes in which religious groups live. Halal butchers in the urban landscape in Bradford and the lack of vineyards in the eastern Mediterranean stem directly from religious norms.

Conclusions

To understand the complex ways in which religion is associated with change requires more than traditional approaches to the geography of religion. Religions move people as well as making places. So making sense of the links between place and the power of belief necessarily has to involve a social as well as a spiritual approach, and has to integrate material with ideological forces. Only through an analysis at different scales can we begin to understand the significance of religions in changing the world.

Further reading

Holloway, J. and Valins, O. (2002) Editorial: placing religion in geography. *Social and Cultural Geography* 3 (1), 5–9.

Kong, L. (1990) Geography and religion: trends and prospects. *Progress in Human Geography* 14, 355–71.

——(2001) Mapping 'new' geographies of religion: politics and poetics in modernity. *Progress in Human Geography* 25 (2), 211–33.

Ley, D. (2000) Religion. In R.J. Johnston, D. Gregory, G. Pratt and M. Watts (eds) *The Dictionary of Human Geography*, pp. 697–99. London: Blackwell.

Park, C.C. (1994) *Sacred Worlds: An Introduction to Geography and Religion*. London: Routledge.

Sikand, Y. (2005) The Indian madrassahs and the agenda of reform. *Journal of Muslim Minority Affairs* 25 (2), 219–48.

References

Afshar, H. Aitken, R. and Franks, M. (2005) Feminisms, Islamophobia and identities. *Political Studies* 53 (2), 262–83.

Arthur, L.B. (1999) *Religion, Dress and the Body*. New York: Berg.

Azaryahu, M. and Kellerman-Barrett, A. (1999) Symbolic places of national history and revival: a study in Zionist mythical geography. *Transactions of the Institute of British Geographers* 24 (1), 109–23.

Bartov, O. and Mack, P. (eds) (2001) *In God's Name: Genocide and Religion in the Twentieth Century*. New York: Berghahn Books.

Berger, P.L. (ed.) (1999) *The Desecularization of the World: Resurgent Religion and World Politics*. Grand Rapids, Michigan: Eerdmans.

Bianchi, R.R. (2004) *Guests of God*. Oxford: Oxford Scholarship Online Monographs.

Chidester, D. and Linenthal, E.T. (eds) (1995) *American Sacred Space*. Bloomington, Indiana: Indiana University Press.

Claval, P. (2001) The geographical study of myths. *Norsk Geografisk Tidsskrift* 55 (3), 138–51.

Coward H. and Smith, G.S. (2004) *Religion and Peacebuilding*. New York: SUNY Press.

Donin, H.H. (1991) *To Be a Jew: A Guide to Jewish Observance in Contemporary Life*. New York: Basic Books.

Duncan, J. (1990) *The City as Text: The Politics of Landscape Interpretation in the Kandayan Kingdom*. Cambridge: Cambridge University Press.

Dwyer, C. (1999) Contradictions of community: questions of identity for young British Muslim women. *Environment and Planning A* 31, 53–68.

Eades, J. and Salnow, M.J. (eds) (1991) *Contesting the Sacred: The Anthropology of Christian Pilgrimage*. London: Routledge.

Eliade, M. (1959) *The Sacred and the Profane: The Nature of Religion*. San Diego: Harcourt Brace Jovanovich.

Fisk, R. (2005) In Iraq, a man-made disaster: one thousand feared dead after Shia pilgrims are caught in stampede. *Independent*, 1 September 2005. Available at http://news.independent.co.uk/world/fisk/article309465.ece

Francaviglia, R.V. (1971) The cemetery as an evolving cultural landscape. *Annals of the Association of American Geographers* 61 (3), 501–9.

Fukuyama, F. (1992) *The End of History and the Last Man*. New York: Free Press.

Gesler, W. (1996) Lourdes: healing in a place of pilgrimage. *Health and Place* 2 (2, June), 95–105.

Glacken, C. (1967) *Traces on the Rhodian Shore*. Berkeley: University of California

Graham, B. and Murray, M. (1997) The spiritual and the profane: the pilgrimage to Santiago de Compostela. *Ecumene* 4, 389–409.

Gregory, D.J. (2004) *The Colonial Present*. London: Blackwell.

Harvey, D. (1979) Monument and myth. *Annals of the Association of American Geographers* 69, 362–81.

Hendershot, H. (2004) *Shaking the World for Jesus: Media and Conservative Evangelical Culture*. Chicago: University of Chicago Press.

Henderson, E.A. and Tucker, R. (2001) Clear and present strangers: the clash of civilizations and international conflict. *International Studies Quarterly* 45 (2) 317–38.

Holloway, J. (2003) Spiritual embodiment and sacred rural landscapes. In P. Cloke (ed.) *Country Visions*, pp. 158–77. London: Pearson.

Holloway, J. and Valins, O. (2002) Editorial: placing religion in geography. *Social and Cultural Geography* 3 (1) 5–9.

Huntington, S. (1993) The clash of civilizations? *Foreign Affairs* 72, 22–49.

Juergensmeyer, M. (2003) *Terror in the Mind of God: The Global Rise of Religious Violence*. Berkeley: UCLA Press.

Jurkovich, J.M. and Gesler, W.M. (1997) Medjugorje: finding peace at the heart of conflict. *Geographical Review* (87), 447–67.

Kellerman, A. (1996) *Society and Settlement: The Jewish Land of Israel in the Twentieth Century*. New York: SUNY Press.

Khatib, L. (2003) Communicating Islamic fundamentalism as global citizenship. *Journal of Communication Inquiry* 27 (4), 389–409.

Kiong, T.C. and Kong, L. (2000) Religion and modernity: ritual transformations and the reconstruction of space and time. *Social and Cultural Geography* 1 (1), 29–44.

Kong, L. (2001) Mapping 'new' geographies of religion: politics and poetics in modernity. *Progress in Human Geography* 25 (2), 211–33.

MacDonald, F. (2002) Towards a spatial theory of worship: some observations from Presbyterian Scotland. *Social and Cultural Geography* 3 (1), 61–80.

Morris, M. (1997) 'Gardens 'for ever England': landscape, identity and the 1st World War cemeteries on the Western Front. *Ecumene* 4 (4), 410–34.

Nolan, M.L. and Nolan, S. (1989) *Religious Pilgrimage in Modern Western Europe*. Chapel Hill: University of North Carolina Press.

Ó Tuathail, G. (2003) 'Just out looking for a fight': American affect and the invasion of Iraq. *Antipode* 35 (5), 856–70

Pacione, M. (2005) The geography of religious affiliation in Scotland. *Professional Geographer* 57 (2), 235–55.

Palmer, C. (2002) Christianity, Englishness and the southern English countryside: a study of the work of H.J. Massingham. *Social and Cultural Geography* 3 (1) 25–38.

Park, C.C. (1994) *Sacred Worlds: An Introduction to Geography and Religion*. London: Routledge.

——(2005) Religion and geography. In J. Hinnells (ed.) *Routledge Companion to the Study of Religion*. London: Routledge.

Pitte, J.-R. (2004) A short cultural geography of death and the dead. *GeoJournal* 60 (4), 345–51.

Poria, Y., Butler, R. and Airey, D. (2003) Tourism, religion and religiosity: a holy mess. *Current Issues in Tourism* 6, 4.

Pounds, N.J.G. (2004) *A History of the English Parish: The Culture of Religion from Augustine to Victoria*. Cambridge: Cambridge University Press.

Raivo, P.J. (2002) The peculiar touch of the East: reading the post-war landscapes of the Finnish Orthodox Church. *Social and Cultural Geography* 3 (1), 11–24.

Scott, J.S. and Simpson-Houseley, P. (2001) *Mapping the Sacred: Geography and Postcolonial Literature*. Amsterdam: Rodopi.

Simoons, F.J. (1994) *Eat Not this Flesh: Food Avoidance in the Old World*, second edition. Madison: University of Wisconsin Press.

Smart, N. (1989) *The World's Religions: Old Traditions and Modern Transformations*. London: Cambridge University Press.

Sopher, D.E. (1967) *Geography of Religion*. New York: Prentice Hall.

Tanaka, H. (1977) Geographic expression of Buddhist pilgrim places in Shikoku Island, Japan. *Canadian Geographer* 21, 111–32.

Tuan, Y.F. (1976) Humanistic geography. *Annals of the Association of American Geographers* 66, 266–76.

——(1977) *Space and Place*. Minneapolis: University of Minnesota Press

Valins, O. (2003) Defending identities or segregating communities? Faith-based schooling and the UK Jewish community. *Geoforum* 34 (2), 235–47.

Vincent, P. and Warf, B. (2002) Eruvim: Talmudic places in a postmodern world. *Transactions of the Institute of British Geographers* 27 (1), 30–51.

Weber, M. (1930) *The Protestant Ethic and the Spirit of Capitalism*. London: Allen and Unwin.

White, L. (1967) Historical roots of our ecological crisis. *Science* 155, 1203–7.

Young, E. (1993) Hunter-gatherer concepts of land and its ownership in remote Australia and North America. In K. Anderson and F. Gale (eds) *Inventing Places: Studies in Cultural Geography*, pp. 255–72. Harlow: Longman.

16

Information technology

Michael Batty

Information technologies (IT) change the way we see places and experience separation and distance. The application of different processing, storage, communications and display technologies in the second half of the twentieth century encouraged a shift to a global economy operating around the processing of information. Remote sensing and surveillance, personal and distributed computing, the Internet, mobile technologies, global positioning systems and electronic mail have changed every aspect of life and profoundly altered geographies.

This chapter describes the changing nature of these technologies and discusses direct and indirect implications of their increasing significance. We begin by outlining the evolution of IT over the last 50 years, emphasizing how the miniaturization of computer hardware and the development of more and more generalized and user-friendly software have merged with communications and digital network technologies. Computation has thus moved primarily from scientific and data processing applications to ways of communicating information within business and society at large. We then show how IT has been used to fashion new tools which help us understand a range of different geographies in deeper ways. These are based on spatial analysis and simulation using statistical theory, but more recently geographic information systems, new tools for mapping and the collection of new data sets through remote imagery, have come to dominate this scene. In complementary fashion, just as IT is providing new tools, it is also changing the very geographies that these tools are designed to address. We thus show how IT is entering space as infrastructure and changing behaviour in work and production through the marketplace. Moreover, IT is embedding itself into the very fabric of our physical society making our routine behaviour more intelligent. We conclude by showing the continuing power of this medium and the current focus on computing across networks, the dramatic rise in digital information, and the emphasis on searching for information quickly and efficiently. This is leading to many visual map systems in 2D and 3D being established in the public domain as freeware and promises to change the nature of how we use IT in geography as radically as anything we have seen so far in the history of the discipline.

The origins of digital computers

The development of modern computing as we now know it has taken place over the last 50 years since the end of the last world war (Agar 2001). The crucial insight that led to the development of the digital computer was the notion that numbers could be represented in their most elemental 'binary' form as 0s and 1s, and that this representation could be associated quite unambiguously with signals flowing across an electrical network. This meant that various kinds of mathematical processing could be reduced to addition and subtraction at this elemental level, and opened the way to a very wide range of information processing. Right from the beginning, computers were hailed as universal machines in that any information that could be reduced to binary form could be processed, manipulated, stored and ultimately communicated in a plethora of ways. Although it took over 30 years for words and pictures as well as numbers to be routinely regarded as being computable, this possibility was evident from the start and, as we shall see in this chapter, the revolution is by no means over yet: indeed, we are probably only at the beginning.

It is important to note immediately that the foundations of digital computing and computers lie in logic and philosophy, not in engineering *per se*, and that these logics were rapidly developed in the 1920s and 1930s by some of the great minds of the twentieth century, namely Turing, Godel and von Neumann (Davies 2000). Universal machines were established using pencil and paper well before the hardware emerged. What makes the IT revolution so intriguing is that the universality of a medium where everything that can be reduced to 0s and 1s is able to be manipulated and stored, was anticipated long before its hardware was developed. The extent to which a phenomenon is computable is thus only limited by our own ingenuity in representing it in binary form. But besides universal computation, two other features have dominated the development of computers. I would not be writing this chapter using word processing software on my laptop were it not for the massive miniaturization that has occurred with respect to the hardware that digital computation requires. The first machines were dinosaurs compared to what we have today and, as is well known, the amount of memory on a computer chip which contains the guts of the digital processing has doubled every 18 months for at least the last 30 years. This is Moore's Law, after Gordon Moore, one of the founders of the world's largest computer chip company, Intel (Tuomi 2002). Consequent upon this increase in memory, the speed of processing has also increased by the same order, and thus computational devices are now embedded in virtual every appliance we use: digital computation has thus become universal and all-pervasive.

The second feature involves communication. Fifty years ago, it was never anticipated that telecommunications would converge and merge with computation, but as computer systems grew in size, computation became distributed over networks, and networks themselves moved from taking analogue signals to digital, the example *par excellence* being the phone system. Chapter 62 describes some of the consequences of this shift in more detail. Moving data across networks and computing information in remote places is the basis, of course, of the World Wide Web and the Internet, and the growth in capacity of such networks and speed of access has been even faster than the growth in memory. We thus stand at a threshold where the world is fast becoming entirely computable in terms of the material environment, while our ability to communicate digitally is opening up dramatic possibilities for changing the way we interact and behave on a routine basis. This has very profound implications for geography. Indeed, the subtitle of this encyclopedia, 'From Local to Global', is as much a consequence of our newfound power to compute and communicate as it is of any of the other issues raised in the chapters of this book.

A good definition of information technology is that set of technologies which embrace hardware, software, data and the organizational structures used in computation and communication. This chapter begins by sketching how computers and communications – IT – have developed over the last 50 years. It emphasizes the notion that layer upon layer of technology characterizes the computer revolution, with each layer adding new uses and new value to what has gone before. We will then outline information technology as it stands at the beginning of the twenty-first century, with the network dominating and with massive convergence occurring between computation, communication, consumption and production. The chapter then explores two sides of the IT coin: the use of IT as a method exemplified by tools such as GIS helping us to do better geography; and second, how IT is affecting the very development of the material and cultural spaces that geographers study as computers become ever more embedded into the material world and even into ourselves. Finally, this chapter sketches an emerging paradigm based on a world of infinite computability where our behaviours are altering as new patterns of using computers take hold in everyday life.

The evolution of IT

For the first 20 years, until about 1970, IT was dominated by hardware. Computers were located in remote places, behind closed doors. Users wrote programs that were submitted manually and fed into computers as punched cards and/or paper tape, where the focus was mainly on numerical processing based on scientific or data applications. In the 1970s, this began to change as users were linked to computer centres using teletypes and visual display units, locally in spoke–hub formation. However, it was the invention of the microprocessor in 1971 and its subsequent use at the heart of the microcomputer that really changed all this. Microcomputers, now called personal computers or PCs, emerged in the mid 1970s, and the massive dissemination that subsequently occurred led to standard software programs that could be run on any such machine. By the mid to late 1980s, these had converged on two systems, IBM PCs and Apple Macintoshes. In fact, software as a term did not really emerge until the late 1970s when two 'killer applications' – word processing and spreadsheets – were invented. The PC, of course, spawned the graphics revolution, because for the first time computer screens could be used to generate pictures, spurred on by the development of computer games.

Parallel to the dissemination of computers on to the desktop and into the home came developments in networking from the most local to the global. Local area networks based on stringing computers together began to dominate office environments, with specialization based on the client–server model emerging by the early 1990s. In terms of traditional hardware, as early as the 1960s machines in remote centres across continents and oceans had been linked together over telephone lines for military purposes, and this led to the development of rudimentary email. By the late 1980s, such networking linking university computer centres was writ large, with PCs also being connected up. Then quite suddenly, the emergent Internet as it was being called, became much more user-friendly with the invention of the World Wide Web. Graphical browsers were developed through which web pages displaying all manner of information became available, and the prospect of delivering very diverse information across the web came into view. Electronic commerce emerged in the late 1990s during the dot.com boom and at last the prospect of computers as universal machines no longer appeared quite so fanciful.

In this 50-year history, computation has been embedded into ever smaller devices and it is currently drifting into the network environment. Layer upon layer of software is now being built and integrated. No longer is it necessary to program computers in low-level languages to achieve very dramatic results, while software is gradually merging with ideas about how to build new organizations in business and government – orgware, as it has been called. Data are now as important as software, while hardware has become ever more trivial in terms of cost. In fact, there is now the prospect of the most routine software being effectively free, with costs being increasingly associated with value added by new layers of applications mostly associated with spin-offs such as advertising and commerce. This nexus of computation and communication and its generalization into private and public life is now widely referred to as 'cyberspace' and its terrain is beginning to be charted by geographers such as Dodge and Kitchin (2001).

From the vantage point of the early twenty-first century, IT and computing comprise a very different set of activities from that associated with its early years. First, it is now all-pervasive with the most recent developments being at the very small scale as computation becomes central to handheld devices, phones, palmtop computers, TVs, gaming consoles and music players, which are all merging and converging. Second, computation is increasingly about networks linking hardware whose form is almost irrelevant and whose function is largely storage and basic processing. Third, the dominant applications involve new patterns of work, the marketplace and entertainment rather than scientific analysis, whence IT sprang. There is every prospect that IT will be one part of a wider grid embracing all communication devices in a form that enables one to 'plug into the wall' or 'tune into the ether' to get computer power any time, anywhere. But we are getting ahead of ourselves, and to put some flesh on this skeleton in terms of geography let us now return to specific applications, beginning with a brief summary of some of the computer tools that geographers are using to better understand their world.

IT tools for understanding geographies

Computers used in exploring geography first made an impact in the 1950s when researchers began to store and process geographical data digitally. Simulation using computers paralleled these developments, but as the computer revolution broadened and gathered pace, the number of distinct applications mushroomed and diversified. It is thus convenient to discuss these applications under three distinct themes, identifying trends but also focusing on human (rather than physical) applications which tend to dominate geographical applications. These themes involve data, analysis and simulation.

The early development of computers in geography was almost entirely focused on the development of tools for a better understanding of geographical systems (Sui and Morrill 2004). Although IT tools are largely associated with quantitative geography, IT in general has also tended to respond to the major theoretical paradigms dominating geography, particularly in the social world that has loosely moved from classical scientific analogies to political economy and thence to cultural issues. The first use of computers involved statistical analysis and data and paralleled the quantitative revolution which began in the 1950s in North America. Databases were modest in size but did not reflect geometry at different scales. Interaction between places was coded as relational data and the focus was largely on measuring the strength of relations between different places using basic correlation (and auto-correlation) analysis. A particularly good statement of these early applications, almost all of which were aided by computer applications, is contained in the book *Spatial Analysis* (Berry and Marble 1968). Although statistical geography provided the first applications of computers, in recent years computers have become less central, although remaining basic to such analysis. The focus is now much more on exploring new theoretical ideas about how geographic phenomena are correlated in space and time and how they may be visualized and modelled: for the first time geographers are beginning to make important contributions to statistical theory *per se*. That all of this is being accomplished in a digital environment based on exploratory data analysis and GIS is now largely taken for granted (Anselin 2005).

Paralleling the development of statistical geography, efforts were also being made to develop methods of simulation. In many senses, when computers were first developed simulation was the prime focus in science, rather than data storage, communication or analysis. From the late 1950s, a succession of simulations involving geographical systems as diverse as land use and transport to hydrological systems such as river networks through to climate models were developed, and these have continued apace to the present day. The focus of these simulations has only changed insofar as the methods for simulation have changed. Models have become more temporally dynamic. The scale of resolution, particularly in the social sciences, where simulation began with aggregate quantities – entire populations – has got finer in that agents and particles can now represent the basic elements used in simulating how geographies emerge and develop from the ground up. A good summary of the state of the art in geographical modelling using computers is contained in the recent book *GIS, Spatial Analysis, and Modeling* (Maguire *et al.* 2005).

Of course, the most dramatic impact of computers and IT in geography in recent years has not been in simulation but in representation and in graphics. It was not until the late 1970s that computer graphics came of age in computing, and this was largely because ways of representing pictures in computer memory and displaying them on widely available devices had to await the microcomputer with its dramatically expanded memory and its display screen (Maguire 1989). Prior to that, computer maps were developed but these were extremely specialist in focus, produced on elaborate line plotters or on oscilloscopes, and this dramatically restricted their availability. But once computer graphics began in earnest, computer cartography quickly developed, and this was followed almost immediately by geographic information systems (GIS) and subsequently by an increasing interest in geovisualization (Dykes *et al.* 2005). Chapter 36 explores the diverse nature of mapping and other scientific visualizations.

Contemporary GIS in fact is a fusion of three key ideas with a strong focus on representing spatial/geographical systems in consistent two-dimensional map form. The three ideas that have come together are based on ways of representing the geometry of the Earth's surface in consistent relational form as spatial data, the notion of tagging such geometry with attributes which are often pictured as map layers, and the notion of developing rapid search techniques for accessing spatial data with respect to particular attributes and particular places. This has meant that GIS has developed for both routine/tactical and strategic applications, being used for real time query and control as well as less immediate professional management and policy-making.

GIS is very much data-driven, with the data within such systems undoubtedly configured with certain paradigms or world views in mind. The quest in GIS has thus been to represent the world in a way that makes it graphically accessible to a very wide range of users, using all the contemporary means of communicating this information that we have at our disposal, from hand-held devices to super-computers. Closely associated with these developments have been new ways of acquiring geographic information based on three key developments.

The first two of these are based on remote sensing technologies at opposite ends of the scale. Satellite imagery is now routine in that devices are positioned in orbit to provide a range of information at different resolutions and with respect to different spectra, from which a variety of physical information ranging from urban development to climate change can be inferred, as we show in Figure 16.1(a). Much of this data can only be unlocked using GIS, and the provision of such data in large pixel grids or rasters has led to the development of specific kinds of GIS (Batty 1999). In contrast, at the small scale, devices also based on geo-positioning from satellite technologies are being used to acquire data. For example Figure 16.1(b) shows tracks made by schoolchildren from their schools to their homes and has been generated by providing the children with wristwatch-size GPS devices. This kind of technology is likely to become much more widely deployed to generate spatial information at the smallest scale. CCTV coverage too is part of these developments, while (car) navigation systems, web cameras and the like are providing new insights into geographical organization at the smallest scales.

Data which are collected by more conventional means, such as by census or from online systems involving transactions processing and subsequent association with specific populations, are being rapidly made available across the Internet. For example, the UK population census is by and large online. Academic geographers are now able to download such data at a variety of administrative scales, from local authority to small areas such as census collection

Figure 16.1a. Remotely sensed, thematic maps and multimedia within GIS. Satellite imagery layered across London from different sources in Google Earth.

districts. Fine scale geodemographic data from the commercial sector is also being made available at the smallest of scales based on seven-digit postcodes or zipcodes. These data are rather different from those collected by remote sensors but still require GIS to unlock them, and much more elaborate geometric representation is needed in the way spatial units are displayed and accessed. An example of this sort of information is pictured in Figure 16.1(c).

With the emergence of graphical user interfaces to multiple sources of information held on computers around the world, the nature of geographical analysis and inquiry is rapidly changing. Until about ten years ago, geographers dealing with digital information and analysis tended to be experts in the storage, retrieval and representation of such information, and often in its subsequent use in simulation and even policy-making. But as access to information has become more user-friendly through the web and as digital information is accessible through ever simpler software, the audience for such information has become wider and more diffuse. For example, much information is now textual as well as graphical and the geographical focus has been supplemented by data that does not require the accuracy and

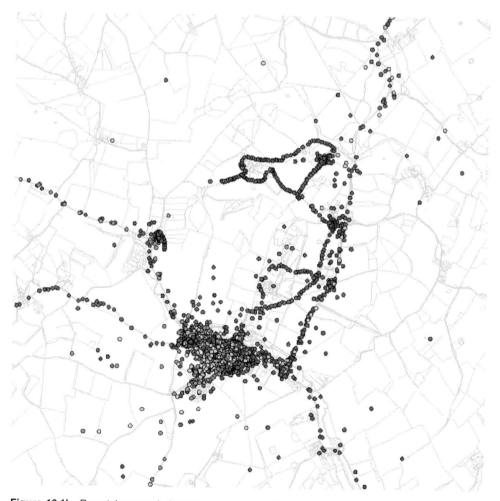

Figure 16.1b. Remotely sensed, thematic maps and multimedia within GIS. Tracks made by children between home and school in Hertfordshire, UK, 2005, using GPS.

249

precision of that used in GIS. Multimedia information is becoming all important, as we show in Figure 16.1(d), where panoramas linked to maps are available so that users can learn about a specific locale through the web (see also Chapter 40). Of course, to undertake more detailed analysis, this would have to be supplemented with the sorts of information shown in Figures 16.1(a) to (c). In some respects, the opening up of geographic information makes this chapter as open-ended as any in this encyclopedia, for it is not clear as to how geography will change as new information such as this and new high-level user-friendly tools are fashioned for less expert users. This is for a future that appears to be changing as rapidly as anything that we have seen so far.

Perhaps the greatest changes in geographical analysis that IT is likely to bring in the next decade involve the analysis of really large data sets. For the first time, we are getting access to data sets with millions of observations, but our tools are still in the comparative Stone Age in that they are really equipped to deal with little more than hundreds of distinct objects or observations. Although we have made progress in visualizing comparatively modest data sets so that we can get a handle on their form, we have yet to broach the problem of how to explore, analyse and model really huge data sets. But we are now able to access geodemographic data which contains detailed information on entire populations, geometric data consisting of millions of points captured remotely, and observations of physical changes over space recorded in real time over very long durations. In the recent past, progress has been

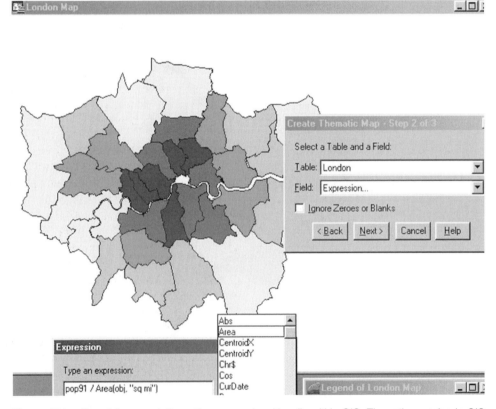

Figure 16.1c. Remotely sensed, thematic maps and multimedia within GIS. Thematic mapping in GIS population density in Greater London 1991.

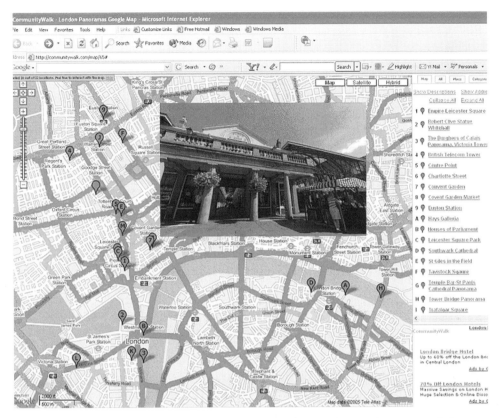

Figure 16.1d. Remotely sensed, thematic maps and multimedia within GIS. Open source GIS panoramas in Google Maps.

made by visualizing the complexity of such data sets on standard display units, but these are restricted to no more than a few thousand points at best. In the next few years, entirely new statistical and visual methods will be invented in which IT will be central so that we can deal with such richness and variety.

IT generating new geographies

The dissemination of tools and methods for understanding geographies merges almost imperceptibly into the new digital infrastructure which is changing geography. In one sense, this is part and parcel of the shaping of the social world through technology, paraphrasing Winston Churchill's famous quote that 'We shape our buildings; thereafter they shape us' (Brand 1995). The personal and institutional use of computers clearly changes the world around us, and this is most evident in the evolution of networks that enables us to communicate digitally and thereby embed computational power in the form of hardware and software into our physical and social environment. We noted earlier that the first physical infrastructure based on computers were spoke and hub formations, in which users were linked by dumb terminals to mainframe machines. With the advent of the microcomputer, local area networks were established in small-scale office and factory environments where servers moved information to clients and vice versa. On a less local scale, mainframes and then PCs were knitted together, first across military networks which then morphed to become the Internet, while accessibility to distributed computers was massively improved with the invention of the World Wide Web. This constituted the most basic infrastructure of the information society, defining itself as the rudiments of cyberspace which has evolved a geography, indeed many geographies of its own (see Chapter 33 for an exploration of these worlds).

This geography continues to evolve rapidly and it is unlike any of the physical or Euclidean geographies that form the traditional focus of the discipline. Maps of cyberspace, although containing some notions of distance, are much more subtle blends of relations based on topologies and speed of access, and the kinds of distortions that have emerged provide a glimpse of the kind of complexity that the IT revolution has added to contemporary society. In Figure 16.2(a) and Figure 16.2(b), we provide a glimpse of this infrastructure in two maps of part of the network of relations between major world-wide web clusters, taken from Martin Dodge's Cyber-Geography Research site (http://www.cybergeography.org/). This says more about the way this infrastructure has developed organically without any top-down plan than about its geographical form. In fact, the Internet is one of the most fashionable

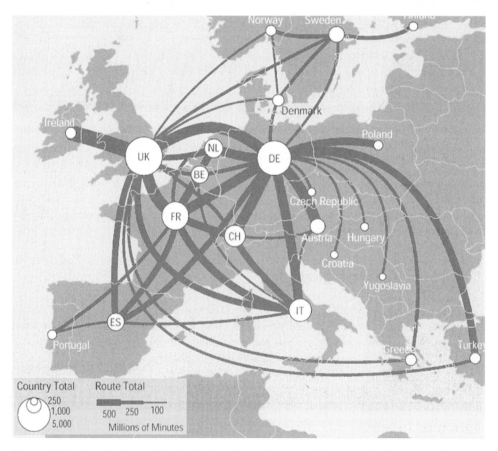

Figure 16.2a. Visualizations of InterNetwork traffic and topology. Telephone traffic between European countries 2000 (http://www.telegeography.com/).

examples of the way computing has decentralized work and leisure and of rapid bottom–up growth in economies and societies.

Yet, in one sense, this infrastructure is no more than new communication lines being established in a different material form from the traditional technologies used to underpin physical transport using automobiles, trains and planes and described in Chapter 13. The key difference, of course, is that digital communication is interactive and comparatively invisible and that those taking part can change the nature of the communication at either ends of the channel. In fact, as digital access is orders of magnitude faster than traditional communication

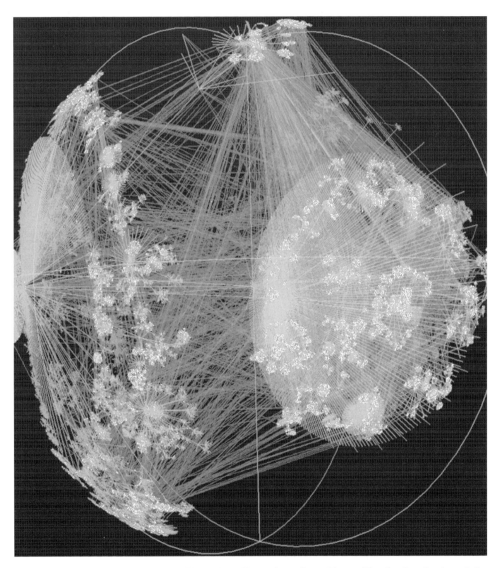

Figure 16.2b. Visualizations of InterNetwork traffic and topology. Young Hyun's visualization of the Internet 2001, based on 535,000-odd Internet nodes and over 600,000 links. The nodes, represented by light dots, are a large sample of computers across the whole range of Internet addresses (http://www.caida.org/~youngh/).

technologies, the effects on Euclidean distance, and the traditional fall-off in interaction with such distance, is quite dramatic. There have been various pronouncements about the 'death of distance' (and the accompanying death of geography) based on the notion that all physical transactions which involve moving people will be substituted for ethereal electronic transactions where individuals do not need to move (Cairncross 2001), but this is never likely to occur. What the IT revolution has in fact done is to make considerably more complex the role of interactions in society; face-to-face communications are not declining – far from it, if anything they are intensifying and being complemented by new electronic communications. In one sense, this is part of globalization and the increasing complexity of contemporary society.

As soon as this kind of electronic infrastructure began to appear and converge with other forms of telecommunications, ideas about intelligent cities, virtual cities, the information city, and the computable city appeared, with the prospect that city infrastructures would become intelligent enough to renew themselves, move people automatically and safely from place to place, and to provide an environment where information was immediately accessible (Batty 1997; Aurigi 2005). Many of these visions remain optimistic, notwithstanding the dark side of such technologies that continue to be represented in the genre of punk science fiction and movies such as *The Matrix*. However, this kind of infrastructure only represents the bare bones of how the geographies of contemporary societies are changing; it is the activities that are communicated across such networks and the ways these are changing behaviour that constitute the way IT is changing the geographies that we study (Graham 2004). As we noted earlier, this concerns how production and consumption are changing through the way electronic communication is being tempered and blended with traditional material communications.

What we have been discussing, albeit rather briefly, is the way hardware and software have entered the physical environment as infrastructure. But what is changing geography most and creating new geographies is the way this hardware and software are being used to generate new behaviours and activities whose signatures and imprints can be understood through spatial patterns. These patterns relate to the way individuals, groups, firms and governments mould space consciously or unconsciously to their ends. Let us begin with domestic consumption which, in geographic systems, is largely composed of many individuals or small groups expending their incomes on various goods which 'optimize', in some way, the qualities of their lives. With the development of computer networks, sellers are being rapidly linked to buyers, specifically where the purchase of goods can be quite routine with little difference in quality with respect to any transaction. Buying books, travel, hotel accommodation, computers and other electronics, sometimes automobiles and white goods, have all been revolutionized by the appearance of the Internet and online retailing. For a much vaster range of products, the Internet is providing instant information about their price, quality and availability. This instant information is changing the nature of product distribution. Already you can see patterns of retailing in cities beginning to respond to such changes, most notably in changes in the book and travel industry. Furthermore, the net generates many more indirect locational effects, for it enables individuals to buy over much longer distances and in more remote places than hitherto. It enables users to search for the cheapest and best within limits and thus to make purchases in the global marketplace in a way that links commercial transactions in a manner barely anticipated a decade or more ago.

The way this is impacting on the spatial pattern of retailing is rather unclear, for it is obfuscated by many other trends such as out-of-town shopping, the emergence of niche 24-hour convenience outlets in places like stations and airports, shopping abroad and so on, all amidst a general swell in retail consumption as the world gets richer, as it surely and inexorably is doing. Town centres are increasingly less attractive for general purpose shopping, but they are changing into leisure hubs. Neighbourhood centres are also suffering, but much of this is the result of a general diffusion of retailing habits caused by the Internet as well as the increased availability of retail outlets in unconventional locations across urban areas. If we can say all this for personal consumption, it is writ large for business consumption – *b* to *b*, as it is sometimes called. Multiple business services in a world that is largely based on the tertiary sector are now delivered over the net. So too are government services, where electronic procurement of services and their electronic delivery to citizens is a major short-term goal of many Western states.

When we turn to production, and in one sense, *b* to *b* is production, then the impact of IT has been profound. This is part of a long process of technological innovation which shows itself through automation where the production process is characterized by machines replacing human workers and highly skilled replacing the less skilled (Zuboff 1988). This is part and parcel of the drive to globalization as firms seek to minimize costs and maximize efficiency. A recent example is in the growth of IT skills in India based on the preparation of PowerPoint presentations for American executives in US firms in real time but overnight, an activity that is made possible not only by the time difference but also by the fact that the skill base for preparing such executive presentations is so much better quality in India than in the US, reportedly. In the era of machine automation which reached its zenith in the mid-twentieth century, vertical integration of the production process took place with the creation of ever larger firms producing better but more homogeneous products. In the last 50 years, this has begun to change. IT is gradually making production possible in smaller units based on a much greater diversification of products, which incorporate much higher skill bases and cater for niche markets. IT is thus widening choice in what is produced as well as reducing overall labour costs, and this is occurring globally. The old patterns of industrial location based on the balance between supply locations – traditionally primary resource centres – and demand at the market are beginning to break down in a world where these linkages are mainly informational and electronic and where physical movement of goods plays an increasingly small part in the overall production process. Of course, we are nowhere near the world of William Gibson (1984) in his novel *Neuromancer*, which introduced the term 'cyberspace' and that genre of the cyberpunk sci-fi, for most of our final demands still have to be satisfied physically, but the proportion of our daily activities affected by IT is increasing rapidly, as is clearly manifested throughout this encyclopedia.

IT in the geographies of the twenty-first century

The last section of this chapter could easily have been illustrated with images of web pages from sites where you can buy books, travel or computers, but this is no longer a novelty and this final section instead concentrates on the merger of new IT tools for understanding geography with the very activities of selling and searching which are creating these new geographies. In short, our tools are themselves beginning to fashion these new geographies, while these new geographies are beginning to fashion our tools. Once again we see the IT revolution advancing by building layer upon layer of new software usage, a key characteristic not only of the information or post-industrial society but also of our contemporary society more generally, perhaps of the evolution of society through all time.

The dominant use of IT now involves global networks (generically the Internet) which are fast becoming the dominant means of access to software and data. Increasingly, software processing is being embedded within and linked to the net. Most short-term predictions up to around 2015 anticipate that the majority of data processing, search and transmission will be web-based by then. Indeed, for vast amounts of past and most current word and image documentation which is either being converted to or is directly produced in digital form, search is fast becoming the dominant activity in IT (Battelle 2005), and much scientific computation is being enabled by search. The prospect of drawing any kind of software and data from places which are remote but which are instantly accessible across the web using new forms of 'grid' technology is focusing the cutting edge on web browser technology, and this is likely to become the interface to new forms of operating system that are no longer desktop-based but network-based. These portents are everywhere. At the time of writing, Amazon.com's 'Search Inside the Book' facility is simply the tip of the iceberg, while Google's book-scanning project is exciting a level of interest and concern in copyright that threatens to blow apart our traditional assumptions as to who owns what when it comes to digital information and its continued dissemination. The resolution of the

Figure 16.3a. Web pages displaying search, entertainment, and commerce. A search result for the term 'geography' in GoogleScholar.

Napster case, which concerned the right to copy music across the web, is simply the beginning of a long battle over the ownership of information in the digital domain (Lessig 2003). Searching for information, of course, is related to commercial consumption, and this is revolutionizing the advertising industry and hence the way the marketplace is structured. Chapter 62 explores these themes in greater detail. Niche search and download is becoming standard as we see in systems such as iTunes from Apple, Google Scholar and such like. Local search engines combined with maps are about to end the idea of Yellow Pages and related directories. An array of these kinds of information search facilities is pictured in browser form in Figures 16.3(a–d).

Perhaps the most exciting feature of how IT is being fashioned by geography at the present time is in the adoption of mapping systems as tools for very general data organization and search by the most routine and user-friendly web browsers. These ideas were highlighted almost a decade ago by then US Vice President Al Gore, who proposed a Digital Earth prototype (Goodchild 2000). Systems for keying in locations to online maps fashioned for straight navigation or tourist usage have been around for several years, but recently this kind

Figure 16.3b. Web pages displaying search, entertainment, and commerce. iTunes Music Shop from Apple where you can download tunes for 99c a pop.

of geography has been elevated into open source software which is letting other users add free content across the whole range of multimedia. Google Maps, for example, is like most other free online map systems except that users can add any content they like to locations and routes. In Figure 16.4, we show how end users have configured these maps to display information about the recent 2005 Hurricane Katrina which devastated New Orleans and the US Gulf Coast. In one sense, we can add layer upon layer of information of any kind to this interface and thus build up and customize a publicly available GIS which anyone can use. Of course, one of the key uses is to add information associated with routine search, bringing together buyers and sellers. Google have gone even further in their Google Earth product where the entire interface is global, where you can zoom in on any area of the planet and layer any area with new information. This information can even be displayed in 3D, as we show in Figure 16.5 for central London once again. This provides the prospect that users will adapt this infrastructure not only to routine high-level usage such as tourism and business but also to professional usage such as planning and design. GIS merges into CAD (computer-aided design) but now this can be in the public domain. What is the betting that within five years, if not tomorrow, geography students will all be using systems like Google Earth to learn not only about GIS – geographical tools – but about the geography itself?

Figure 16.3c. Web pages displaying search, entertainment, and commerce. Search Inside the Book: previewing the product prior to purchase in Amazon.com.

What is more, with many of these new open-source softwares, any user can add them into their own software, into their own programs and web pages. It has been argued that this kind of 'Mapping Hack' adds to the democratic potential offered by GIS (Schuyler *et al.* 2005). This is yet another example of how the IT revolution builds and adds value, layer by layer, with earlier layers becoming ever deeper within the infrastructure, meaning that both new IT professionals and users simply accept what has gone before and thus hone their skills on what are the most recent and most topical software applications. There is a very important message here. The IT revolution represents one of the most rapid but classic examples of how society builds on its achievements. You do not have to understand how computers work or how networks work, how software is written or how data is structured to make use of GIS. It helps, of course, but it is no longer essential, although the principles of GIS functionality – spatial analysis – are usually required. But once GIS is loaded into information infrastructure such as Google Earth (and similar products being launched, such as Microsoft's Virtual Earth and ESRI's ArcExplorer), then a much wider range of users is enfranchised, users who do not have to know the detailed principles because the software is increasingly user-friendly in ways that those less skilled in geography understand. All of this is being developed too on a range of devices at different scales. Everything we have introduced in this

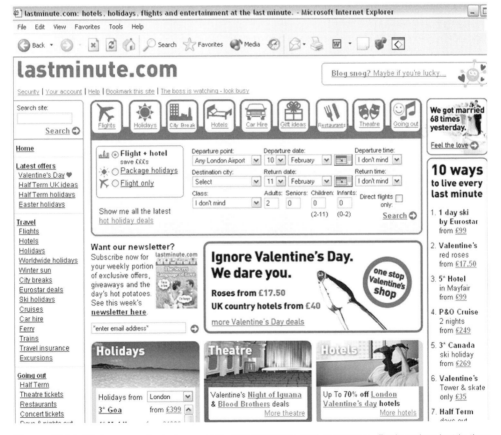

Figure 16.3d. Web pages displaying search, entertainment, and commerce. Buying trips: just-in-time purchasing from lastminute.com

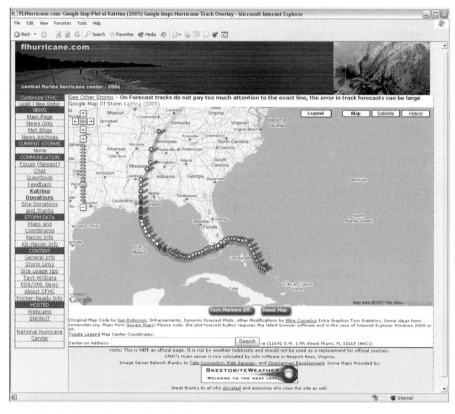

Figure 16.4. Hurricane Katrina in Google Maps.

Figure 16.5. Visualizing Central London in 3D in Google Earth with multiple map layers.

chapter will be possible on any IT device within a generation, and on devices that we cannot even imagine which will be produced within the next 25 years.

It is tempting to conclude this chapter by telling you that by the time you read it, there will have been yet another twist in the IT story. The entire history of the last 50 years has been dominated by those involved in the current generation of IT not being able to anticipate the immediate future: back in 1943, Thomas J. Watson Sr, the founder of IBM, told the world, 'I think there is a world market for maybe five computers' (quoted in Surowiecki 2004, 32–33). In 1977, Ken Olson, the founder of the world's largest workstation company, DEC, pronounced that there would never be any need for personal computers in the home, while in the early 1990s Bill Gates went on record as saying that the development of the Internet was a mere distraction from the desktop. Nobody anticipated the rise of Google and the importance of search, while the ability to merge every kind of information we need on one device cannot be far away. A recent advert from Nokia was marketing a phone that had the Google homepage shown large on the screen. How long before geographers are able to access all they need on their handheld devices, whether they are doing GIS, or learning about a place, or writing an essay, or . . . ?

Acknowledgements

The author thanks Andy Hudson-Smith of CASA, UCL for Figures 16.1(d), 16.4 and 16.5, Martin Dodge of the University of Manchester for Figures 16.2(a) and (b), and Kay Kitazawa of CASA, UCL for Figure 16.1(b). The web pages illustrated are credited as annotated.

Further reading

Battelle, J. (2005) *The Search: How Google and its Rivals Rewrote the Rules of Business and Transformed Our Culture.* London: Nicholas Brealey Publishing.

Brunn, S.D., Cutter, S.L. and Harrington, J.W. (eds) (2004) *Geography and Technology.* Boston, MA: Kluwer Academic Publishers.

Dodge, M. (2005) *Cyber-Geography Research.* Available at http://www.cybergeography.org/ (accessed 25 October 2005).

Graham, S. (ed.) (2004) *The CyberCities Reader.* London: Routledge.

Lessig, L. (2003) *The Future of Ideas.* New York: Random House.

Maguire, D. (1989) *Computers in Geography.* London: Longman.

Maguire, D., Batty, M. and Goodchild, M. (eds) (2005) *GIS, Spatial Analysis, and Modeling.* Redlands, CA: ESRI Press.

References

Agar, J. (2001) *Turing and the Universal Machine: The Making of the Modern Computer.* London: Icon Books.

Anselin, L. (2005) Spatial statistical modeling in a GIS environment. In D. Maguire, M. Batty and M. Goodchild (eds) *GIS, Spatial Analysis, and Modeling,* pp. 93–111. Redlands, CA: ESRI Press.

Aurigi, A. (2005) *Making the Digital City: The Early Shaping of Urban Internet Space.* Aldershot, UK: Ashgate.

Battelle, J. (2005) *The Search: How Google and its Rivals Rewrote the Rules of Business and Transformed Our Culture.* London: Nicholas Brealey Publishing.

Batty, M. (1997) The computable city. *International Journal of Planning Studies* 2, 155–73.

——(1999) New technology and GIS. In P.A. Longley, M.F. Goodchild, D.J. Maguire and D.W. Rhind (eds) *Geographical Information Systems: Principles and Technical Issues: Volume 1*, pp. 309–16. New York, NY: John Wiley and Sons.

Berry, B.J.L. and Marble, D. (eds) (1968) *Spatial Analysis*. Englewood Cliffs, NJ: Prentice Hall.

Brand, S. (1995) *How Buildings Learn: What Happens After They're Built*. New York, NY: Penguin Books.

Cairncross, F.C. (2001) *The Death of Distance: How the Communications Revolution Is Changing our Lives*. Cambridge, MA: Harvard Business School Press.

Davies, M. (2000) *The Universal Computer: The Road from Leibniz to Turing*. New York: Norton.

Dodge, M. and Kitchin, R. (2001) *Atlas of Cyberspace*. Harlow, UK: Addison-Wesley.

Dykes, J., MacEachren, A.M. and Kraak, M.-J. (2005) *Exploring Geovisualization*. New York: Elsevier for the International Cartographic Association.

Gibson, W. (1984, 2004) *Neuromancer*. New York: Ace Books.

Goodchild, M.F. (2000) Communicating geographic information in a digital age. *Annals of the Association of American Geographers* 90 (2), 344–55.

Graham, S. (ed) (2004) *The CyberCities Reader*. London: Routledge.

Lessig, L. (2003) *The Future of Ideas*. New York: Random House.

Maguire, D., Batty, M. and Goodchild, M. (eds) (2005) *GIS, Spatial Analysis, and Modeling*. Redlands, CA: ESRI Press.

Schuyler, E., Gibson, R. and Walsh, J. (2005) *Mapping Hacks*. Sebastopol, CA: O'Reilly.

Sui, D. and Morrill, R.E. (2004) Computers and geography: from automated geography to digital earth. In S.D. Brunn, S.L. Cutter, and J.W. Harrington (eds) *Geography and Technology*, pp. 81–108. Boston, MA: Kluwer Academic Publishers.

Surowiecki, J. (2004) *The Wisdom of Crowds: How the Many are Smarter than the Few*. New York: Little, Brown.

Tuomi, I. (2002) The lives and deaths of Moore's Law. *First Monday* 7 (11, November). Available at http://firstmonday.org/issues/issue7_11/tuomi/index.html

Zuboff, S. (1988) *In the Age of the Smart Machine: The Future of Work and Power*. New York: Basic Books.

17

Biotechnology

A.M. Mannion

Biotechnology is the manipulation of living organisms and their components, including genes, to undertake specific tasks which in principle are beneficial to society. It also marks another of several thresholds in the domestication of carbon by humans, as discussed by Mannion (2006). The shift from scavenging to active hunting as well as gathering, often associated with the harnessing of fire, more than 2 million years ago, marked the emergence of humans as engineers of their environment and thus as biotechnologists. The domestication of plants and animals and the emergence of agriculture, beginning *c.*12,000 years ago, marked another turning point in people–environment relationships; this biotechnology, as agriculture can be defined, facilitated socio-economic and large-scale environmental change (see Bellwood 2004). The manipulation of microorganisms such as yeasts and fungi also has a long history for brewing and baking. Further advances in agricultural biotechnology have been made down the centuries through crop and animal breeding which increased yields and have contributed to the industrialization of agriculture. These developments involved the manipulation of whole organisms. However, the discovery by Watson and Crick in the early 1950s (Watson and Crick 1953) of the molecular structure of deoxyribonucleic acid (DNA), a major component of genes, opened up new opportunities for manipulating organisms at the micro level. This new science of genetic engineering has blossomed since the 1980s; it represents another threshold in the relationship between people and other organisms and thus between people and environment. It also opens up possibilities of exploiting characteristics which confer advantage from the Earth's biodiversity, not only for food crops but for many organic substances such as fragrances and substances of medicinal value. Today, several genetically modified (GM) crops are available and despite controversy GM cotton, canola, soybean and maize are widely grown in the Americas and Asia, though not in Europe. Such developments are changing the geography of agriculture and possibly rural geography worldwide. New developments are also beginning in forestry. Further aspects of biotechnology include the harnessing of organisms for resource capture and recycling, pollution abatement and the provision of renewable energy. All are emerging fields with considerable potential for the improvement of environmental quality. There are, however, disadvantages: applications may cause environmental impairment, and the lack of technology transfer may disadvantage poor nations who cannot afford to develop or purchase capacity.

Biotechnology in agriculture

Modern biotechnology builds on the plant and animal breeding which has taken place since the initial domestication, itself a selection of organisms with natural advantages for human use. Cloning, for example, facilitates the mass production of identical plants from individuals which have been traditionally bred for their advantages or genetically modified. This exploits the capacity of plants to regenerate from individual or groups of cells, a characteristic known as totipotency; it facilitates cloning via tissue culture whereby plant tissue is nurtured *in vitro*, i.e. in a growth medium, to produce seedlings. Thus crop plants with high production potential can be rapidly produced and distributed. Genetic modification (methods are described by Skinner *et al.* 2004; Slater *et al.* 2003; Curtis 2004) allows traditional breeding to be short circuited; once individual genes or their components have been isolated as controllers of specific characteristics they can be manipulated to heighten or dampen that characteristic in the plant, or the component can be transferred into other species which will then express the desired characteristic; such products of genetic modification are sometimes referred to as designer or bespoke crops. This approach to crop breeding also maximizes energy and nutrient flows insofar as the output of desired product is greater than with non-engineered crops. It shifts the emphasis from modifying the environment to increase productivity to modifying the crop. It also broadens the resource base from which new or improved crops can be developed because the genes or their components can derive not only from unrelated plants but also from bacteria, fungi, animals, insects, etc. Indeed, commercial preparations of some species of these groups are already part of the bio-technological tool kit of agriculture, notably the use of biopesticides such as *Bacillus thuringiensis,* a bacterium with the capacity to kill insect pests such as the cotton bollworm. There are five areas of agronomy which can be addressed more efficiently and rapidly by this technology than by traditional plant breeding: improved productivity, disease (e.g. viruses, fungi) and pest (e.g. insect) resistance, plant architecture, herbicide resistance, and environmental stress (e.g. drought, frost, salinity, heavy metals). Ultimately, it may even prove possible to overcome nitrogen deficiency in soils, a major factor limiting growth and a large energy-consuming factor in agriculture because of the widespread use of artificial fertilizers, by engineering crops to fix their own nitrogen as do various strains of bacteria. As is discussed later, some of these possibilities have come to fruition and others are on the verge of realization. However, none of these developments has escaped criticism. As with any technology, biotechnology has advantages and disadvantages both for the environment and for society, the realities and possibilities of which are examined later.

Developments to 2005

Many developments associated with the industrialization of agriculture occurred after, the Second World War, including a rapid increase in artificial nitrogen fertilizer use and the invention and deployment of many new pesticides and animal health products. Against this backdrop of intensification modern biotechnology began to emerge as a world player in the 1960s, beginning with the large-scale development of biopesticides and followed by the marketing of the first GM crop, the Flavr Savr tomato, in 1994 and the adoption of GM cotton, canola, maize and soybean in the late 1990s.

Biopesticides

Biopesticides fall into two categories: biochemical pesticides are naturally occurring substances which control pests and which are often used as templates for the artificial production

Table 17.1. Some microbial biopesticides and their targets

Biopesticide type	Target
Fungal biopesticides	
Entomophaga praxibulli	Grasshoppers
Entomophthora plutellae	Plutella (a moth)
Neozygites floridana	Cassava green mite
Metarhizium anisopliae	Various insects e.g. aphids, locusts, whitefly, froghoppers
Beauveria bassiana and B. brogniarti	Colorado potato beetle
Verticillium lecanii	Aphids, whitefly, rust fungi
Bacterial biopesticides	
Varieties of Bacillus thuringiensis	See text
Agrobacterium radiobacter	Crown gall disease of fruits, ornamental trees and shrubs
Burkholderia cepacia	Nematodes, some soil fungi

of chemical pesticides, while microbial pesticides comprise commercial preparations of specific microorganisms which cause mortality to certain pests. The latter are components of the biotechnology arsenal and most commonly include preparations of fungi and bacteria. The best known and most widely used biopesticide is that based on *Bacillus thuringiensis* (Bt), the history and applications of which have been documented by Metz (2003). This is a naturally occurring bacterium found in soils, on insects and on plant foliage. According to Agrow (2001) Bt's pathogenicity toward flour moths was discovered in 1911 in Germany; by the late 1930s *B. thuringiensis* var *kurstaki* was available commercially in France and in the USA by the 1950s to combat lepidopteran (butterflies and moths) pests. This variety remains important today. Further research led to the discovery of additional pathogenic varieties, e.g. *B.t.* var *israelensis*, which extended the use of Bt pesticides against other insects including coleoptera (beetles) and diptera (small flies, mosquitoes) and *B.t.* var *aizawai*, another variety effective against Lepidoptera. The market for such pesticides expanded in the 1980s. The main targets of these biopesticides are cotton bollworm and other lepidopteran pests and Colorado beetle in potatoes; there is also a human health aspect insofar as mosquitoes and blackflies (the latter cause river blindness) can be controlled. Bt toxins are effective only when ingested by the target. In 2000 the biopesticide market was valued at $160 million, of which 90 per cent was the result of Bt products (Agrow 2001) though this is only *c.*1 per cent of the worldwide agrochemical market (i.e. fungicides, herbicides and insecticides). Bt pesticides are marketed as powders containing bacterium spores and crystals of the toxin itself, which are effective when applied by sprays to above-ground crop parts. Other microbial biopesticides and their targets are listed in Table 17.1, which gives an idea of the range of species harnessed to combat a wide variety of targets, notably insects. All have been developed in the last 30 years and, along with Bt pesticides, they are often used as components of integrated pest management strategies wherein a variety of crop protection strategies are used, including conventional agrochemicals.

Genetically modified crops

The commercial debutant of genetic modification was the Flavr Savr tomato, developed by the Californian company Calgene; it was approved for general sale by the US Food and

Drug Administration (FDA) in 1994 (see Martineau 2001 for a review). The tomato was engineered to alter the ripening process, and thus increase the length of time the fruits could remain on the vine, in order to produce a more intense flavour before being picked for shipping to supermarkets. This contrasts with established practice of harvesting fruit while still green to retain firmness and then ripening with ethylene while in transit. The Flavr Savr received a mixed welcome; the horticulture and food industries generally welcomed this new addition to a large and versatile tomato market while groups concerned about, and outrightly opposed to, crop-GM voiced concerns about potential adverse health effects of such 'franken foods'. The Flavr Savr tomato enjoyed limited success with no repercussions for human health but proved ephemeral and was withdrawn in 1997.

However, new developments in the genetic modification of major crops were occurring by this time; GM was beginning to 'come of age'. The first GM crops were planted in 1995; a decade later, 81 million ha were planted with GM crops.

Table 17.2 gives data on 14 so-called mega-countries, i.e. those countries growing GM crops on more than 50,000 ha. Other countries which grow GM crops are Germany and Honduras, which both grow GM maize, and Colombia, which grows GM cotton. The USA grows more than half the world's GM crops and produces all four of the major types; according to the Pew Charitable Trusts (2005) 81,000 acres, 74,000 acres and 13,947 acres were planted with GM maize, soybean and cotton respectively, representing 45 per cent, 85 per cent and 76 per cent of the total US acreage, in 2004. James (2004) points out that whilst most GM crops are produced in the developed world, developing countries are beginning to adopt GM crops rapidly; they already produce c.33 per cent of GM crops and experienced a higher growth rate at 7.2 million ha than developed countries at 6.1 million ha from 2003 to 2004. Moreover c.90 per cent of those adopting GM crops in 2004 were resource-poor farmers in developing countries. Table 17.2 gives details of the most commercially significant GM crops grown; many others are grown on smaller scales, e.g. potatoes, sugar beet and others; those being grown or developed for developing countries are listed in the BioDeC database of the Food and Agriculture Organization (FAO 2005).

Table 17.2. Countries with more than 50,000 ha of GM crops

Country	Extent (10^6 ha)	Major crops
Canada	5.4	Canola, maize, soybean
USA	47.6	Soybean, maize, canola, cotton
Mexico	0.1	Cotton, soybean
Spain	0.1	Maize
Romania	0.1	Soybean
India	0.5	Cotton
China	3.7	Cotton
Philippines	0.1	Maize
Australia	0.2	Cotton
Brazil	5.0	Soybean
South Africa	0.5	Maize, soybean, cotton
Paraguay	1.2	Soybean
Uruguay	0.3	Soybean maize
Argentina	16.2	Soybean, maize, cotton
World total	81.0	Canola, maize, soybean, cotton

Source: Adapted from James (2004).

Skinner *et al.* (2004) state that:

> The great majority of transgenic crops currently grown in the field are derived from the 'magic bullet' type of transformation. That is, a single gene has been inserted into the crop species; the product of that gene causes a demonstrable change in phenotype of the plants.

This is the observable characteristics of an organism which reflect both its genetic constitution and environmental factors. The dominant traits which have been so engineered are herbicide resistance and insect resistance. For some crops, so-called stacked genes have been inserted so that the plant develops both types of resistance. For example, 'Herculex I' maize exhibits resistance to gluphosinate (glyphosate) herbicides and to some lepidopteran species. There are GM varieties of cotton with similar characteristics, and 'New Leaf Plus' potatoes have been modified to show insect resistance and virus resistance. There are many possibilities for crop improvement using genetic engineering, with a recent development, that of 'Golden Rice', just entering the market place. In this case, the metabolic pathways of rice have been altered using genes from the daffodil and a bacterium to encourage the production of beta-carotene which can be readily converted into vitamin A in the human body (Potrykus 2001); it is anticipated that the crop will contribute to combating the disease known as vitamin A deficiency, which causes blindness. Herbicide-resistant rice has also been produced and there is the possibility of engineering other traits such as salt tolerance (see review by Oard and Jiang 2004). Canola has been engineered to alter the fatty acid content of its seeds; for example to increase the oleic acid content, a beneficial unsaturated fat, and to reduce the saturated linolenic acid content. The latter has also been genetically engineered in soybean.

The insect resistance engineered in the crops listed in Table 17.2 (and others) is based on the insertion of a gene from *Bacillus thuringiensis* (see section on *Biopesticides*). This enables the crop plants to produce their own endotoxin which kills the insect predators. Developed in 1989, this trait confers several advantages, not least being a substantial reduction in conventional pesticides with reduced costs, fewer accidents and reduced impact on the wider environment. The GM cotton appears to have been well received. Surveys of resource-poor farmer satisfaction in India indicate increased yields, reduced costs and improved human health. For example, Nielsen (quoted in Council for Biotechnology Information, 2004) notes that in India profits increased 78 per cent, on average, when compared with the profits of farmers who planted traditional varieties, that yields increased *c.*29 per cent and pesticide use declined by 60 per cent. In China Bt cotton was introduced in 1999; immediate increases in yields of *c.*25 per cent and a considerable reduction in the volume of conventional pesticides ensued, with a bonus that the natural predators of insect pests in cotton increased by *c.*25 per cent (reported in Chrispeels and Sadava 2003). In South Africa, smallholder farmers first planted Bt cotton during 1998–99; a preliminary survey of this and the subsequent season reported by Ismael *et al.* (2001) and Bennett *et al.* (2003) shows benefits similar to those of India and China. The latter also noted a drop in hospital admissions due to pesticide poisonings which they attribute, at least in part, to reduced pesticide applications; this also reduced the time necessary for tending crops leaving farmers free for other activities. Wu-Jun (2004) notes that in China the use of Bt cotton has resulted in a 70–80 per cent decrease in the use of chemical pesticides and an increase in arthropod diversity and population sizes which has reduced predator aphid populations. Large-scale cotton producers have also benefited from the adoption of GM cotton, though not as significantly as small producers. For example, in the USA, where there had been *c.*80 per cent adoption of GM cotton by 2004 (James 2004), at least a 5 per cent increase in productivity has been achieved with a decrease in costs of between $25 and $65 per acre as a result of reductions in chemical pesticide use. In Spain, one of few European countries to adopt Bt crops, Bt maize cultivation on 25,000 ha between 1998 and 2003 has resulted in a saving of €15.5 million, with 66 per cent going to farmers and 34 per cent to the seed industry (Demont and Tollens 2004). Other advantages as well as disadvantages of GM crops are discussed below.

Engineered herbicide resistance in major crop plants such as maize, canola and soybean is a desired trait because it allows specific herbicides to be used without impairment of the crop. Thus plant competitors are reduced or eliminated and so competition for soil nutrients, light and water is reduced, as is the hand or mechanized labour of weeding. Research on soybean metabolism by Padgette *et al.* (1996) demonstrated that a gene from the soil bacterium *Agrobacterium tumefaciens* inserted into crop plants conferred resistance to the glyphosate herbicide known as Roundup. Crop plants with this gene are now known as Roundup Ready and are marketed as a package of GM seeds and herbicide. GM crop plants resistant to other herbicides have also been developed, e.g. gene transfer from the fungus *Streptomyces viridochromogenes* confers resistance to the herbicide bialaphos (also known as Basta). Gianessi (2005) has reviewed the economic impacts of glyphosate-resistant crops in the USA. He notes that *c.*80 per cent of soybean and *c.*70 per cent of cotton-growing areas are now planted with such crops, which has saved farmers $1.2 billion because of the reduced need for weeding, herbicide applications etc. The latter has been reduced by 37.5 million lbs. Gianessi also notes that there is a potential saving of *c.*$93 million if glyphosate-resistant sugarbeets replace conventional sugarbeet. Certainly, the Food and Agriculture Organization (FAO) anticipate that the role of biotechnology in world agriculture will increase in the coming decades as new methods of increasing production to feed growing populations are developed (Bruinsma 2003).

Other realities and possibilities

Genetic modification offers many possibilities in agriculture and horticulture, both directly and indirectly. Much research is ongoing on the potato, which is an important crop worldwide but especially in developing countries. The International Potato Institute (Centro Internacional de la Papa 2005) documents collaborative efforts with the Belgian Agency for Development and Co-operation to develop potatoes with resistance to the potato tuber moth (*Phthorimaea operculella*) which is the single most important insect pest on potatoes in developing countries. It causes damage primarily in storage but also in the field. Table 17.3 gives details of GM potato varieties with resistance to this moth which have been developed

Table 17.3. GM potato varieties with Bt genes

Region or country	Potato variety
Central Africa	Mabondo, Sangema, Murca and Cruza 148
Andean region	Tomasa Condemayta, Costanera, Achirana INTA, María Tambeña and Revolución
Colombia	Pardo Pastusa
Costa Rica	Atzimba
North Africa	Desiree
Southern South America	Desiree

Source: Based on Centro Internacional de la Papa (2005).

using Bt genes for a number of developing countries. Prospects are also good for the development of GM sweet potatoes with Bt resistance to sweetpotato weevils. Other possibilities for potato improvement include resistance to various viruses, nematodes, bacterial wilt and potato late blight (caused by the fungus *Phytophthora infestans* which was responsible for the Irish potato famine of the mid-1840s).

Improving marketability is one goal of genetic modification, as exemplified by the marketing of flowers. According to the database of Agbios (2005), the carnation has been successfully engineered to increase shelf life and to alter the flower colour as well as to exhibit herbicide resistance. The economic advantages are obvious. Another example is a reduction in the nicotine content of tobacco, which could have health benefits. Table 17.4 lists a number of other GM crops which are already available. As this shows, the dominant traits so far engineered are those which facilitate defence against competitors and thus reduce the flow of resources away from the crop.

Efforts are also underway to engineer traits which enhance human health and other traits which allow crops to withstand adverse environmental conditions such as drought, frost or flooding (see review by Grevich and Daniell 2005). In relation to human health (see review by Kirk and Webb 2005), it is possible that crop plants could be engineered to express foreign proteins which act as vaccines; experimental work is underway on tomato, tobacco, potato, banana and maize. Amongst the potential vaccines are anti-rabies, the blocking of HIV transmission and protection against diarrhoea, hepatitis B, tuberculosis and dental caries. The expression of such vaccines in crop plants would make their distribution and administration much easier and cheaper than conventional vaccines, especially in developing countries, and there would be considerable savings for health services worldwide with implications for the geography of health. There is also considerable potential for animal health vaccines, e.g. to combat anthrax and foot-and-mouth disease; cost and application would be vastly improved (see review by Santos and Maria José Wigdorovitz 2005). The capacity of plants to generate 'useful' substances for human health (note the comments previously re: golden rice) need not be confined to vaccines; other therapeutic products include hormones, antigens, enzymes, peptides, etc., as discussed by Teli and Timko (2004).

The possibility of engineering crop plants to suit particular environments is also under investigation, following the successful production of several cereals with some form of tolerance to an environmental stress through conventional breeding. The possibilities of combating drought, waterlogging, frost and high heavy metal concentrations are attractive in terms of additional food production from land which is damaged or unsuitable for the cultivation of

Table 17.4. Examples of other GM crops and their traits

Crop	Trait
Cantaloupe	Delayed ripening
Chicory (Radicchio)	Herbicide resistance
Flax	Herbicide resistance
Papaya	Viral resistance
Squash	Viral resistance
Tomato	Delayed ripening, insect resistance
Creeping bent grass	Herbicide resistance
Lentil	Herbicide resistance
Sunflower	Herbicide resistance
Tobacco	Herbicide resistance, reduced nicotine

Source: Based on Council for Biotechnology Information (2005) and Agbios (2005).

available varieties. Raised salinity concentrations in soils and waterlogging, often due to injudicious irrigation, cause declines in crop productivity and sometimes land abandonment, so tolerant crops could reclaim the land and restore productivity. Tolerant varieties of rice, sorghum and wheat would be especially beneficial for many developing countries and research is underway to produce all three. Similarly, the expression or enhanced expression of therapeutic substances in plants could help combat certain diseases and nutrient deficiencies. Various possibilities are outlined by Grevich and Daniell (2005). In the long term, genetic modification might be brought to bear on the fundamental process of photosynthesis to improve productivity, and on the fixation of nitrogen within non-leguminous crop plants to overcome nitrogen deficiency in soils and thus render the use of artificial nitrate fertilizers, a major input of fossil-fuel energy in agriculture and a cause of pollution, unnecessary.

There are also possibilities for animal husbandry. Direct genetic modification of animals is becoming a reality and could lead to the enhancement of desired traits, such as meat, milk, or wool quality. The success of recent cloning experiments, notably the production of 'Dolly' the sheep, may make the reproduction of animals with desired traits commercial in the future. Current research and developments are documented by Animal Biotechnology (2005). Many applications of plant modification could also benefit animals, such as the production of therapeutic substances (see section on other realities and possibilities) and the manipulation of protein, amino acid, etc., content in fodder crops to improve secondary productivity in the animals themselves. Some of these possibilities have been discussed by Sun and Liu (2004).

Advantages and disadvantages of biotechnology in agriculture

As with all technologies, agricultural biotechnology has advantages and disadvantages. Some of these are summarized in Figure 17.1 and there are discussions in Wesseler (2005). It is axiomatic that the main advantages are improved productivity and marketability which enhance food security. There are also environmental and ecological advantages, not least of which is that less land is required to increase or maintain productivity. Thus pressure to clear further areas of natural ecosystems is diminished and their ecological integrity and capacity to perform vital services, such as biogeochemical cycling, is preserved. Inherently conservational, this also means that potential for generating new 'goods' from the biosphere for future generations is less compromised. In this respect, agricultural biotechnology may be judged an important tool for achieving sustainable development. It also offers possibilities for producing slow-growing crops, e.g. oil palms, with enhanced traits more rapidly than is possible with traditional breeding, and could thus increase the plantation productivity of many nations in the developing world, including small island nations. Moreover, if reduced volumes of pesticides and herbicides are required, as in the case of Bt and herbicide-resistant crops (see previous sections), then fossil-fuel and petrochemical inputs are also reduced, thus contributing to reduced carbon emissions and general energy efficiency in agriculture. A major breakthrough in this context would be the elimination of artificial nitrate fertilizer use, though there are no immediate possibilities for direct crop plant nitrogen capture. The improvement of pasture and fodder crops could also improve the secondary productivity of animal herds and reduce costs.

The disadvantages of biotechnology are also economic and environmental. Economic disadvantages include the possibility of laboratory production of specialized products such as vanilla, which would threaten the livelihoods of poor farmers in Madagascar, Mexico, Tahiti and several other island nations. The coupled production and sale of herbicides and the seeds of herbicide-resistant crops could lead to a spiral of dependency and control by agrochemical/biotechnology companies. Similarly, there is much concern about intellectual property rights. First, if useful genes are discovered in a wild or cultivated plant, who can exploit them and under what circumstances? This is a matter of co-operation and balance, though injustices may ensue. Plant resources ownership, with many new discoveries coming from the rich biodiversity of developing countries, must be recognized, as must the vast resources provided by agrochemical/biotechnology companies, usually in the developed world, to turn the plant and/or its genes into a viable product. This is important in the case of new agro-chemicals or pharmaceuticals which may result or in the case of improved crops through genetic modification. Having provided the resource, developing countries must then not be deprived of its benefits because of its costs; this 'genetic imperialism' must be eschewed through adequate provision to protect the interests of all parties. Related to this is the development of GM crops (or other commodities) which would benefit the poorest nations most but which are beyond their financial reach; technology transfer could be effected through aid and development packages.

The potential environmental disadvantages of GM crops mirror the environmental advantages outlined above. One possibility is the development of crop plants with the capacity to tolerate environments which would otherwise be hostile. This could lead to further encroachment into natural ecosystems where clearance would emit yet more carbon dioxide into the atmosphere and accelerate rates of species extinction. Even GM crops with Bt or herbicide-resistant traits may encourage the spread of cultivation because of the potential of enhanced profits. For example, soybean cultivation in Brazil, prompted by worldwide

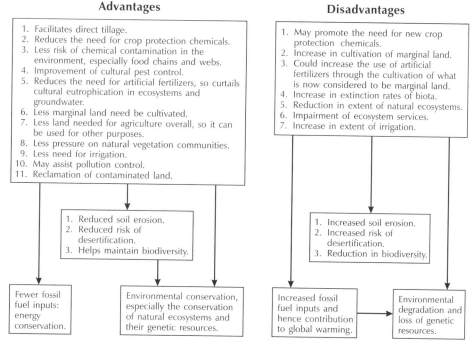

Figure 17.1. The advantages and disadvantages of crop biotechnology.
Source: After Mannion (2006).

© A.M. Mannion.

271

demand, has increased substantially in savannah regions and is encroaching into tropical forest regions; both the growing and infrastructure for export exacerbate ecosystem destruction (see Hecht 2005 and Fearnside 2005); the prospect of increased profits through GM varieties may exacerbate an already problematic situation. Ecological problems specific to individual traits may also occur, as Owen and Zelaya (2005) have discussed in relation to herbicide-resistant crops and the development of herbicide resistance in weeds of cultivation. They note that some herbicide-resistant crop plants may themselves become weeds of other herbicide-resistant crops, and that some weeds are decreasing as others increase because the latter can combat the tillage and herbicide regime best. Consequently, and because of the possibility of the spread of herbicide resistance through interbreeding with wild relatives of cultivated species, weeds (sometimes referred to as super weeds) which necessitate new management strategies may develop. This begs the question as to where next farmers and agrochemical scientists will find the answers to improved weed control. Similar problems obtain in relation to the use of Bt pesticides and Bt crops. Insects have a remarkable ability to develop resistance to conventional pesticides and there is already concern that resistance to Bt pesticides is developing. It is entirely likely that target insects will eventually develop resistance to Bt crops, probably within as short a time span as ten years, prompting questions as to how crop protection from insect pests will be achieved beyond 2015.

Other disadvantages of GM crops are not as well founded scientifically. For example, acceptance in Europe has been marginal. This is partly because agriculture in Europe is depressed due to external competition and partly because of food scares such as BSE, the so-called mad cow disease (Bovine Spongiform Encephalopathy), and its human counterpart Jacob Creutzfeld disease. This disease is thought (it remains unproven) to have entered the food chain because of the feeding of imperfectly treated animal protein to herbivorous cattle which were then consumed by humans. Whilst the primary use of Bt cotton is for its fibre, the cottonseed residue is fed to farm animals and thus enters the food chain. No adverse reactions have yet to be documented, but such concerns are justified and require proactive screening programmes by government agencies. Other concerns may yet materialize.

Biotechnology in forestry

Traditional plant breeding has been employed to improve such characteristics as insect resistance and wood quality, but the process is slow because of the amount of cross-breeding necessary, the imprecise nature of the exercise as progeny may not always exhibit the desired traits, and the long life-cycles of trees which involve as long as a decade before they reach sexual maturity. The techniques of genetic modification offer many possibilities for the relatively rapid generation of forest species with desired traits to suit specific objectives, as in the case of plantation species for fruit, nut and oil production. As in the case of genetically modified crops, GM trees represent an element of the industrialization of forestry and all the potential problems of contamination of the wider environment apply equally. Safeguards are thus essential to conserve the gene pools of natural and semi-natural woods/forests and the use of GM trees should be confined to planted forests surrounded by a buffer zone. Genetic engineering may itself assist in this protection by facilitating the production of sterile species which do not flower and so do not produce pollen. Alternatively, GM species with no wild relatives within range could be grown.

The possibilities of forest biotechnology have been outlined by Cambell *et al.* (2003). Apart from the issue of sterility, they highlight possibilities of altering the lignin content of wood to facilitate processing, as well as the engineering of virus, insect and herbicide resistance. They report two significant developments: an engineered decrease in the lignin content of poplars, an advantage for pulp and paper production through reducing lignin waste which causes pollution of effluent or requires extraction, and the engineering of papaya with resistance to papaya ringspot virus. The latter is now grown in commercial papaya plantations. Other possibilities include the engineering of insect and herbicide resistance. White and black poplars, European larch and white spruce have all been engineered with insect resistance through the insertion of Bt genes. In experimental plots, this results in considerably less damage to leaves and increased productivity. Resistance to several herbicides, including the environmentally benign glyphosate, has been engineered in poplars; the advantage is reduced costs of weed control. Other possibilities include tolerance to specific pollutants and heavy metals so that trees can be used in bioremediation programmes on contaminated land (see next section), and the potential of using forest trees as chemical 'factories' (see Carson *et al.* 2004 for a review).

Biotechnology in resource recovery, recycling, pollution abatement and bioremediation

The capacity of certain types of organisms to tolerate, and/or concentrate, or degrade various chemicals can be harnessed to recover and recycle useful substances and to render harmless molecules which might cause impairment of environment and/or human health. Such a capacity may also prove useful for reclaiming contaminated land and water in a process known as bioremediation. Many organisms are known to be able to undertake such tasks and are already being used to improve environmental quality and to recover valuable resources. Identification of the genetic basis of this ability could ultimately lead to the engineering of the capacity in other organisms which might be particularly beneficial: for example, the enhanced capacity of several plant species to tolerate heavy metal concentrations would be an asset for the reclamation of some types of mine-damaged land.

Organisms involved in resource recovery include various bacteria, notably chemolithotrophs which extract energy for their metabolism by breaking down specific compounds such as sulphides. This ability can be harnessed to facilitate biomining, i.e. the release of metals such as copper, nickel, gold, silver and uranium from ore deposits. The bacteria effect microbial leaching as water in which they are contained percolates through sulphide-bearing rocks. This produces sulphates which are more soluble than sulphides and from which the metals can be extracted. The most important bacteria which can undertake this process are *Thiobacillus ferrooxidans*, *T. thiooxidans*, *Leptospirillium ferrooxidans* and several *Sulfolobus* spp. which can operate under conditions of low pH and often at high temperatures. Various applications are reviewed by Rawlings *et al.* (2003) and Biobasics (2005). The latter observes that about 25 per cent of world copper production is obtained through biomining, which is generally acclaimed as a more sustainable and environmentally friendly method of ore extraction than traditional techniques. The acquisition of gold through biomining, for example, avoids the use of cyanide, which contaminates the environment and is a hazard to human health. Microbial leaching also facilitates metal extraction of low-grade ores. In relation to GM microbes for metal extraction, Biobasics (2005) states that 'because genetically engineered microorganisms need careful control and monitoring, they will not likely be available for commercial use for several years to come, and then only for controlled processes, like those possible in reactors'.

The extraction of heavy metals and other harmful substances from water and soils by bacteria is one tool of bioremediation, a form of reclamation which harnesses various organisms. The United States Geological Survey (USGS 1997) lists numerous examples of bioremediation (see also Singh and Ward 2004), including the biodegradation of pesticide, gasoline, creosote and sewage spills. Indeed, sewage treatment worldwide relies on the capacity of organisms to break down organic matter. Many organisms also have the ability to concentrate chemicals within their tissues, especially metals. As well as the bacteria, algae and fungi which have this capability, many higher plants can also concentrate heavy metals which accumulate in their tissues. This ability can be exploited to recycle useful and/or valuable metals, including uranium and gold. For example, Keim and Farina (2005) have examined the capacity of the bacterium *Magnetotactic cocci* to concentrate gold and silver and refer to several other bacteria with a similar capacity. Higher plants with the ability to cope with high concentrations of heavy metals can be used to revegetate contaminated areas, a form of phytoremediation (see Singh and Ward 2004). For example, Mkandawire *et al.* (2004) have discussed the potential of duckweed for removing arsenic and uranium from mine waters in eastern Germany and so reducing downstream contamination; Chang *et al.* (2005) have demonstrated that poplar (*Populus davidiana*) trees could be used to revegetate the tailings from an abandoned gold mine in South Korea because of their ability to tolerate high concentrations of lead and arsenic which are often present in gold ores.

The genetic modification of organisms, such as those referred to previously, to enhance their capacity for recycling and/or bioremediation would be advantageous to counteract pollution and shortages of useful metals. It could lead to 'bespoke' organisms for specific problems and ultimately result in less land and water degradation.

Biotechnology and renewable energy resources

Biomass has always been a source of fuel and food, but in the last 50 years modern biotechnology has been applied to produce fuel and food energy in novel ways. Moreover, interest in alternative energies to those derived from fossil fuels has recently increased prompting new developments. Food energy provision other than that derived from conventionally grown crops has also increased in recent years, notably the production of single-cell proteins such as Quorn®.

A well-known example of biomass energy is that of ethanol. It is widely used in Brazil, where it is made from sugar cane and molasses and where it accounts for about 40 per cent of total fuel consumption; Brazil is also exporting ethanol to Japan. Ethanol can be produced by distillation from many sources including wood pulp, maize, sugar beet, wheat and barley; it can be used to fuel vehicles directly, sometimes in combination with gasoline, as in Brazil, where it is also used to generate electricity; but most is used as industrial alcohol. In Europe, rapeseed oil (a form of biodiesel) has been developed for vehicular use but has been adopted only on a limited basis. Crops for the production of biomass fuel are an alternative to crops for food in Europe and other developed countries where agriculture is becoming uneconomic and set-aside policies are encouraging alternative land uses. However, they require inputs of fossil fuels through fertilizer use and mechanization and produce carbon dioxide; thus they are not free of environmental costs. Other sources of biomass fuels are: wood bark and logging residues, crop residues, rotation coppice, wood-bark mill residues, manures from livestock, seaweed, waterweed and algae (see Burdon 2005 for further details and the Alternative Fuels Data Center 2005), as well as methane from land fills and livestock. Genetic modification could enhance the energy-producing capacity of crops used to produce biomass fuels.

Single-cell proteins (S-CPs) offer an entirely new method of producing food in fermenters rather than the field. Energy and nutrients, e.g. carbon dioxide, methanol, ethanol, sugars and carbohydrates, are combined to stimulate the growth of micro-organisms such as yeasts, algae, bacteria and fungi to produce cellular protein. This can be produced for animal and/or human consumption. Some algal products are marketed as health foods. However, the chief economic S-CPs are Pruteen[R] and Quorn[R]. The former was a pioneering product of ICI in the 1970s for animal feed. Its production involved the growth of the bacterium *Methylophilous methylotrophus* in methanol as the energy source and ammonia as the nitrogen source. The resulting biomass comprised about 80 per cent protein with a high vitamin content. Despite its food value, Pruteen[R] was never commercially viable because other animal feeds, such as soybean, were being produced more cheaply, but its production represented groundbreaking technology. Quorn[R], in contrast, was developed in the 1980s following the discovery of the fungus in 1967 and has proved to be a commercial success. This is a mycoprotein, i.e. based on fungal biomass, namely that of *Fusarium graminearum*. The mycelial threads of the fungus can be produced industrially via fermentation in a mixture of glucose and ammonia. Its fibrous mass can be variously flavoured and it has the advantage of a high protein and low fat and calorie content (see Quorn 2005 for details of products, etc.). One measure of its success is Quorn's statement that '400,000 Quorn meals are now eaten every day in the UK'. It has now been introduced into the USA. Genetic modification of other microorganisms with high food value could provide a new generation of fermented foods in the long term.

Conclusion

Modern biotechnology is becoming a major force on agricultural landscapes, especially in North and South America. Almost a decade after the first GM crops were planted the acceptance of such crops has increased, though less so in Europe than elsewhere, possibly because agriculture is economically weak and there is no shortage of food. There is little evidence for adverse impacts and some evidence for social and environmental benefits. This should not lead to complacency. For all GM organisms, proactive screening should be a strict requirement prior to use in the field in order to prevent hybridization which may produce organisms with detrimental effects. Moreover, the introduction of genes and/or gene products, e.g. those of Bt, into food chains should be carefully monitored. In economic terms, the transference of technology to nations most in need, especially sub-Saharan Africa, would be beneficial for development and the alleviation of poverty. The products of agricultural biotechnology and the agents of bioremediation offer considerable potential for environmental and economic improvement if used judiciously.

Further reading

Burdon, I. (2005) Biomass power generation. In C.A. Hempstead and W.E. Worthington Jr (eds) *Encyclopedia of 20th-Century Technology*, pp. 74–76. London: Routledge.

Chrispeels, M.J. and Sadava, D.E. (2003) *Plants, Genes, and Crop Biotechnology*, second edition. Sudbury, Mass.: Jones and Bartlett.

Council for Biotechnology Information (2005) http://www.whybiotech.com.

National Centre for Biotechnology Education (2005) http://www.ncbe.reading.ac.uk.

Pew Charitable Trusts (2005) *Genetically Modified Crops in the United States* (Factsheet). Available at http://www.pewagbiotech.org.

Pringle, P. (2003) *Food, Inc.: Mendel to Monsanto: The Promises and Perils of the Biotech Harvest.* London: Simon and Schuster.

References

Agbios (2005) *Global Status of Approved Genetically Modified Plants.* Available at http://www.agbios.com.

Agrow (2001) *Biopesticides: Trends and Opportunities.* Available at http://www.pjbpubs.com.

Alternative Fuels Data Center (2005) *Alternative Fuels.* Available at http://www.eere.energy.gov/afdc/.

Animal Biotechnology (2005) *Genetically Engineered Animals.* Available at http://www.animalbio-technology.org.

Bellwood, P. (2004) *The First Farmers.* Oxford: Blackwell..

Bennett, R., Buthelezi, T.J., Ismael, Y. and Morse, S. (2003) Bt cotton, pesticides, labour and health: a case study of smallholder farmers in the Makhathini Flats, Republic of South Africa. *Outlook on Agriculture* 32, 123–28.

Biobasics (2005) *Biomining.* Available at http://www.biobasics.gc.ca.

Bruinsma, J. (2003) *World Agriculture: Towards 2015/2030. An FAO Perspective.* London: Earthscan.

Cambell, M.M., Brunner, A.M., Jones, H.M. and Strauss, S.H. (2003) Forestry's fertile crescent: the application of biotechnology to forest trees. *Plant Biotechnology Journal* 1, 141–54.

Carson, M., Walter, C. and Carson, S. (2004) The future of forest biotechnology. In R. Kellison, S. McCord, and K.M.A. Garland (eds) *Forest Biotechnology in Latin America.* North Carolina: Institute of Forest Biotechnology. (Available at www.forestbiotech.org).

Centro Internacional de la Papa (2005) *The Bt Potatoes.* Available at http://www.cipotao.org.

Chang, P., Ju-Yong, K. and Kyoung-Woong, K. (2005) Concentrations of arsenic and heavy metals in vegetation at two abandoned mine tailings in South Korea. *Environmental Geochemistry and Health* 27, 109–19.

Council for Biotechnology Information. (2004) *Bt Cotton Creates Three Times the Earnings for Indian Farmer.* Available at http://www.whybiotech.com.

Curtis, I.S. (ed.) (2004) *Transgenic Crops of the World.* Berlin: Springer.

Demont, M. and Tollens, E. (2004) First impact of biotechnology in the EU: Bt maize adoption in Spain. *Annals Applied Biology* 145, 197–207.

Fearnside, P.M. (2005) Deforestation in Brazilian Amazonia: history, rates, and consequences. *Conservation Biology* 19, 680–88.

Food and Agriculture Organization BioDeC. (2005) *Biotechnologies in Developing Countries.* Available at http://www.fao.org.

Gianessi, L.P. (2005) Economic and herbicide use impacts of glyphosate-resistant crops. *Pest Management Science* 61, 241–45.

Grevich, J. and Daniell, H. (2005) Chloroplast genetic engineering: recent advances and future perspectives. *Critical Reviews in Plant Sciences* 24, 83–107.

Hecht, S.B. (2005) Soybeans, development and conservation on the Amazon frontier. *Development and Change* 36, 375–404.

Ismael, Y., Bennett, R. and Morse, S. (2001) Farm level impact of Bt cotton in South Africa. *Biotechnology and Development Monitor* 48, 15–19.

James, C. (2004) *Global Status of Commercialized Biotech/GM Crops: 2004* (ISAAA Briefs No. 32). New York: International Service for the Acquisition of Agri-Biotech Applications (ISAAA).

Keim, C. and Farina, M. (2005) Gold and silver trapping by uncultured *Magnetotactic cocci.* *Geomicrobiology Journal* 22, 55–63.

Kirk, D.D. and Webb, S.R. (2005) The next 15 years: taking plant-made vaccines beyond proof of concept. *Immunology and Cell Biology* 83, 248–56.

Mannion, A.M. (2006) *Carbon and Its Domestication.* Dordrecht: Springer.

Martineau, B. (2001) *First Fruit: The Creation of the Flavr Savr Tomato and the Birth of Biotech Food.* New York: Schaum.

Metz, M. (ed.) (2003) *Bacillus thuringiensis: A Cornerstone of Modern Agriculture.* Binghampton, New York: Hawthorn Press.

Mkandawire, M., Taubert, B and Dudel, E. (2004) Capacity of *Lemna gibba* L. (Duckweed) for uranium and arsenic phytoremediation in mine tailing waters. *International Journal of Phytoremediation,* 6, 347–62.

Oard, J. and Jiang, J. (2004) Rice transformation: current progress and future prospects. In G.H. Liang, and D.Z. Skinner (eds) *Genetically Modified Crops. Their Development, Uses, and Risks,* pp. 235–45. New York: Food Products Press.

Owen, M.D.K. and Zelaya, I. (2005) Herbicide-resistant crops and weed resistance to herbicides. *Pest Management Science* 61, 301–11.

Padgette, S.R., Re, D.B., Barry, G.F., Eichholtz, D.A., Delannay, X., Fuchs, R.L., Kishore, G.M. and Farley, R.T. (1996) New weed control opportunities: development of soybeans with Roundup Ready™ gene. In S.O. Duke (ed.) *Herbicide-Resistance Crops: Agricultural, Economic, Environmental, Regulatory and Technological Aspects,* pp. 53–84. Boca-Raton: CRC Press.

Potrykus, I. (2001) Golden rice and beyond. *Plant Physiology* 125, 1157–61.

Quorn (2005) *Quorn.* Available at http://www.quorn.co.uk

Rawlings, D.E., Dew, D. and du Plessis, C. (2003) Biomineralization of metal-containing ores and concentrates. *Trends in Biotechnology* 21, 38–44.

Santos, D. and Maria José Wigdorovitz, A. (2005) Transgenic plants for the production of veterinary vaccines. *Immunology and Cell Biology* 83, 229–38.

Singh, A. and Ward, P. (eds) (2004) *Biodegradation and Bioremediation.* Berlin: Springer.

Skinner, D.Z., Muthukrishnan, S. and Liang, G.H. (2004) Transformation: a powerful tool for crop improvement. In G.H. Liang, and D.Z. Skinner (eds) *Genetically Modified Crops. Their Development, Uses, and Risks,* pp. 1–16. New York: Food Products Press.

Slater, A., Scott, N. and Fowler, M. (2003) *Plant Biotechnology: The Genetic Manipulation of Plants.* Oxford: Oxford University Press.

Sun, S.S.M. and Liu, Q. (2004) Transgenic approaches to improve the nutritional quality of plant proteins. *In Vitro Cellular and Development Biology – Plant* 40, 155–62.

Teli, N. and Timko, M. (2004) Recent developments in the use of transgenic plants for the production of human therapeutics and biopharmaceuticals. *Plant Cell, Tissue and Organ Culture* 79, 125–45.

United States Geological Survey (USGS) (1997) *Bioremediation: Nature's Way to a Cleaner Environment.* Available at http://www.water.usgs.gov.

Watson, J.P. and Crick, F.H.C. (1953) Molecular structure of nucleic acids. *Nature* 171, 737–38.

Wesseler, J. (ed.) (2005) *Environmental Costs and benefits of Transgenic Crops.* Berlin: Springer.

Wu-Jun, J. (2004) The international debate on the biosafety of genetically modified crops: scientific review of several cases of debate. *Chinese Journal of Agricultural Biotechnology* 1, 3–8.

Part III

Actors in the process

Chris Perkins

The driving forces described earlier in this book do not operate in a political or institutional vacuum. Change is enacted at different scales. And the nature of the agencies with power over place matters. This block of chapters explores the ways in which organizations operating at an international scale impact upon national policies. It contrasts regional initiatives with the governance of cities and discusses the significance of the firm, household and individual.

A characteristic of our age is the extent to which global institutions and international agreements allow an international order to be preserved and to develop. Formal organizations with a global reach encompass some national governments, a plethora of NGOs, and privately owned multinational corporations. In Chapter 18 Klaus Dodds charts the significance of these different agencies and explores some of the processes by which agreements are reached, illustrating these wider issues by focusing on world trade and global finance. Examples illustrate the complex operation of these shadowy but hugely powerful bodies.

The nation-state grew as an idea in early modern Europe, coalescing around imagined national communities that came to be embodied in legal and political frameworks. These states have played and continue to play a significant role in geographical change. They articulate shared cultural and economic goals, impacting upon identities and landscapes however, at the same time their diverse legislative processes hide often contested and diverse geographies. In Chapter 19 Marcus Power explores the changing significance and powers of the nation-state in the face of global change.

The scale and nature of political organization affect changes within nation-states and in trans-border regions. In many contexts, there are significant contrasts between central state power and regional agendas being advanced at provincial or local state levels. In highly federal nations provincial authorities may direct policy in almost every field with the exception of foreign policy areas. In contrast a highly centralized nation devolves little power down from the level of the national state. The nature of subsidiarity clearly influences both individual lives and regional geographies. Chapter 20 by Martin Jones explores these diverse forms of subsidiarity, through a detailed consideration of the institutions involved in regional governance in Britain.

People live in settlements governed by interests that may significantly change lives and geographies. Planning legislation may help to explain the form of cities or rural areas but also reflects the interests of those in control of the city. Trends towards increased entrepreneurialism are apparent in many Western urban contexts, where concerns focus upon selling the city, preservation of heritage, regenerating brownfield areas and attracting inward investment. In contrast cities experiencing more unregulated growth often suffer severe environmental impacts, which urban policy is much less able to control or mitigate. Kevin Ward focuses upon these aspects of the urban scale in Chapter 21. He explores trends in governance, focusing in particular on the links between the built fabric of the city, governance and theory.

Privately owned companies are the driving force behind the development of capitalism, but despite globalization the nature of the firm varies very greatly according to local culture. In Chapter 22 Henry Yeung explores how the cultural political economy of the firm shapes change and discusses the significance of the firm to the contemporary global economy. He explains the differing scales at which firms operate, and examines sectoral variation and the spatial and social networks linking companies and other agents.

Chapter 23 shifts attention from work to home as a scale of analysis. Here Helen Jarvis explores the significance of the fact that in almost all cultures people continue to live their lives in households, sharing their living space with a small number of other individuals, often bound together by family relationships. The social relations enacted and reified in households, from gender or sexuality roles to notions of class, age or disability are, however, significant well beyond the spatial bounds of the house. The household supports and responds to change and facilitates participation in the labour market and in the construction of identity. This chapter explores the diverse nature of household geographies and their coping strategies when faced with change.

In the last decade many social theorists have returned to approaches that focus upon individuals, how they relate to places and how the local context constructs identity. Such approaches focusing on the role of the body increasingly recognize that individuals themselves also have the power to shape place, whilst exercising identities formed through the social process *in* places. In Chapter 24 Vera Chouinard discusses the ways in which such an embodied geography might be mapped out, charting the significance of context and the negotiation of power relations, with particular attention being given to feminist geographical theories.

18

International order

Klaus Dodds

Introduction

If you watched or participated in Live8 week (July 2005) then it is likely that you care about the international order. Even if you might not use that term, you might feel passionately that the current 'order of things' seems unfair and profoundly unjust. A great deal of attention focused on the artists and performers who entertained crowds in London, Edinburgh, Berlin, Paris, New York and Johannesburg. High-profile celebrities and campaigners such as Bono and Bob Geldof used this publicity to remind world leaders such as President George W. Bush and Prime Minister Tony Blair to transmogrify global public opinion, that lives are lost needlessly in Africa and elsewhere due to poverty and hardship. This is the kind of message that many of those Live8 campaigners wanted to bring to bear on the leaders of the G8 (Canada, France, Germany, Italy, Japan, Russia, the United Kingdom and the United States) as they gathered to discuss world economic and environmental issues at Gleneagles in Scotland between 6 and 8 July 2005. However, it also might be the case that the G8 is part of the problem, and this in turn tells us something about how powerful countries can shape the international order, for better and or for worse. Their capacity to fund aid programmes is only one part of the equation. Agenda setting is a significant component of the practical manifestation of international order.

The purpose of this chapter is not to encourage a sense of despair and hopelessness. While there are no easy answers to global issues such as climate change, poverty and terrorism or AIDS, we need at the very least to understand how the prevailing system of international governance operates. One way into this complicated subject is to consider the slippery term 'international order' and how it might relate to these (aforementioned) issues. According to some academic writers such as Hedley Bull, the two are inextricably linked (Bull 1995; Rengger 2000). It is slippery in the sense that academics, campaigners and policy makers do not agree with one another over the use and significance of the term. International order matters because it signifies not only the operational basis of the prevailing global political system but also an opportunity to consider how the 'order of things' might be changed. Some campaigners whether or not they are concerned with humanitarian suffering or trade subsidies, for example, would wish to question the privileged role of the state and the principles associated with sovereignty and national borders.

The first part of this chapter situates this discussion of international order within the literature of critical geopolitics (see also Chapter 56). Thereafter, the analysis considers the prevailing international order in the post-1945 era, including the creation of the United Nations and some of the ways international law attempts to address equality and justice. Thereafter, the ending of the Cold War in 1989–90 and the emergence of the so-called *new world order* is considered. The chapter concludes with consideration of some of the contemporary challenges to international order, which embrace *inter alia* trans-national terror networks, anti-globalization and climate change. These arguments encapsulate material that needs to be read in relation to Chapters 11, 12, 15, 19 and 20 elsewhere in this book.

This contribution aims to evaluate some of the claims made by political leaders apropos changing the world for the better. If nothing else, we need to be vigilant and ask ourselves: what are we seeking to change and who will benefit from such changes? The answers to these questions vary depending on who the 'we' is referring to. There should be no doubt as to the importance of these kinds of questions given the challenges facing all of us. As Tim Flannery concluded in the *New York Review of Books* in relation to long-term climate change:

> Ever since 1986, we have been running the environmental equivalent of a budget deficit, which can only be sustained by plundering the capital made available by the natural world ... the inevitable conclusion is that our species has entered a crisis that will last for much of the twenty first century.
>
> (Flannery 2005: 26).

Great powers and international neo-liberal order: geopolitical perspectives

The emerging literature of critical geopolitics alongside other scholarly literatures in human geography and International Relations (IR) explores how political and economic geographies of international order are created and reproduced (for example, Agnew and Corbridge 1995; Taylor and Flint 1999; Agnew 2003; Dicken 2003). This set of writings calls into question existing structures of power and knowledge, which shape global political life. It exposes the cultural and political assumptions that lie embedded within concepts and terms such as 'new world order' (Williams 1993; Dalby 1996; Ó Tuathail 1996; Dijkink 1996; Shapiro 1997; Ó Tuathail and Dalby 1998; Dodds 2005). This is all the more important in a world characterized by extremes of poverty and wealth.

The international system of governance operates geographically and John Agnew and Stuart Corbridge have explored how this might be so:

> [Orders] have necessarily geographical characteristics. These include the relative degree of centrality of state territoriality to social and economic activities, the nature of the hierarchy of states (dominated by one or a number of states, the degree of state equality), the spatial scope of the activities of different states and other actors such as international organizations and businesses, the spatial connectedness of disconnectedness between various actors, the conditioning effects of informational and military technologies upon spatial interaction, and the ranking of world regions and particular states by dominant states in terms of 'threats' to their military and economic 'security'.
>
> (Agnew and Corbridge 1995: 15)

Although this is a detailed list and while we cannot consider all the items cited in the aforementioned quote, it is worthwhile noting that the ensuing experiences of international order vary and always depend on a range of flows and processes such as the movement of people, ideas, capital and technologies (Herod *et al.* 1998).

An international order is thus a system of governance, which involves *inter alia* state power, diplomacy, international law and conflict. The role of powerful states such as the United States in the post-1945 era has been instrumental in securing a particular type of international order. There is nothing inevitable or natural about the prevailing architecture of post-1945 world politics. Two areas of concern are worth highlighting at this stage. First, consideration has to be been given to how the United States has consolidated practices and rules of conduct about world politics. This is particularly germane in the contemporary era when the United States government of President George W. Bush stands accused of setting aside international conventions such as the Geneva Convention on Prisoners of War. As the sole remaining superpower, the United States not only maintains rules and codes of conduct but also persuades others to respect central tenets of international law and justice. However, since the events following the 11 September 2001 attacks on New York and Washington, the United States stands accused of bypassing the United Nations Security Council and causing a crisis of international legitimacy. As the veteran critic of American foreign policy Noam Chomsky has claimed:

> The National Security Strategy (NSS) announced in September 2002, and its immediate implementation in Iraq, have been widely regarded as a watershed in international affairs . . . It undermines the seventeenth century Westphalian system of international order, and or course the UN Charter and international law.
>
> (Chomsky 2005: 17)

The NSS reserved the right of the United States to undertake pre-emptive military strikes against groups and states deemed to pose a military threat. This overturns a key element of the UN Charter relating to conflict resolution and the non-use of pre-emptive military action.

This matters greatly because it confirms that international order is geographically varied and that the United States reserves the right to pursue its own sense of international order. It has, as critics contend, used its military and political power to subvert other organizations such as the International Criminal Court (ICC) by refusing to support it. The ICC is designed to promote a more universal mechanism for international justice. Other countries (often poor ones in the former Communist regimes of the Soviet Union and Eastern Europe as well as the Global South) have been pressurized into agreeing never to place American service personnel serving in those countries before the authority of the ICC. The United States' decision to pursue a strategy of prevention and pre-emption with regard to their self-declared Global War on Terror also overturns a whole series of United Nations norms and international law (Ó Tuathail 2003; Spence 2005) (see also Plate 18.1). This matters because it effectively militarizes global political space and creates a world, as Agnew and Corbridge (1995) note, of states and regions identified as 'threats' to the 'security' of the United States. In turn, these 'global threats' are then used to create and sustain claims to 'homeland security' within the United States (see also Campbell 1992: Kaplan 2003).

Second, the world order constructed in the aftermath of 1945 has an economic dimension. Principles of free trade and open access to markets were closely connected to an American post-war vision of a new world order. International institutions such as the

Plate 18.1. *Of course there will be a role for the UN.*
© Steve Bell. Published in the *Guardian* 4 April 2003.

International Monetary Fund and the World Bank were an essential element in this (Harvey 2003; Steger 2003). These kinds of liberal economic ideals served as a model to be emulated by the rest of the world. In order to ensure their diffusion, the United States was willing to deploy military force in an attempt to secure a particular global form of capitalism. With the presence of an ideological adversary in the form of the Soviet Union, wars, interventions or coups were launched after 1945 on economic and ideological grounds (Harvey 2003; Roberts *et al.* 2003). The United States has long been accused of intervening during the Cold War for the purpose of extending its economic influence and the power of American-owned corporations. All of this was carried out under a general banner of ridding the world of communism and promoting instead global capitalism. So if we are to understand the geographies of international order, we need to appreciate the changing geopolitics of capitalism.

American Cold War geopolitical strategy was, therefore, predicated on not only containing communism but also promoting the practices and rules of conduct (for example, removing trade barriers) associated with global capitalism. Unsurprisingly, the American invasion of Iraq in 2003 has been widely interpreted by critics as the latest example of the United States' desire to secure economic advantage, in this case preferential access to oil resources in a strategically significant region. The United States economy is oil based, and corporations such as Halliburton have benefited from this particular exercise of military force. But how do military interventions in places such as Iraq square with a world described as a borderless, free and fair and open to all forms of competition? One answer to this question would be to argue that the military power of the United States is essential to secure the functioning of the international economic and political order. Hence some people's rights and opportunities to access markets and trade possibilities apparently become more significant than others. The creation of the World Trade Organization in 1995 was supposed to address such inequalities, but subsidies and trade barriers remain and continue to favour North American and European states.

284

This chapter suggests, therefore, that the international order created after 1945 is far from being liberal/Liberal. While some areas of international life have been liberalized in the form of trade access, service provision and investment, others have been curtailed and constrained domestically and internationally. Despite the high-minded intentions of the United Nations and a corpus of international law associated with human rights, the geographies of international order have consistently favoured powerful states and multinational corporate interests. Violent interventions by the United States in places such as Kosovo, Iraq and Afghanistan in the last decade have only consolidated this impression. What has changed arguably is that the new meta-narrative of geopolitics is the 'Global War on Terror' as opposed to the 'War against Communism' (Taylor 1990; Williams 1993; Johnston *et al.* 2002).

International order and the post-1945 era

Consider the following sonorous preamble:

We the Peoples of the United Nations Determined

to save succeeding generations from the scourge of war, which twice in our lifetime has brought untold sorrow to mankind, and

to reaffirm faith in fundamental human rights, in the dignity and worth of the human person, in the equal rights of men and women and of nations large and small, and

to establish conditions under which justice and respect for the obligations arising from treaties and other sources of international law can be maintained, and

to promote social progress and better standards of life in larger freedom,

And for these Ends

to practice tolerance and live together in peace with one another as good neighbors, and

to unite in our strength to maintain international peace and security, and

to ensure by the acceptance of principles and the institution of methods, that armed force shall not be used, save in the common interest, and

to employ international machinery for the promotion of the economic and social advancement of all peoples,

Have Resolved to Combine our Efforts to Accomplish these Aims

Accordingly, our respective Governments, through representatives assembled in the city of San Francisco, who have exhibited their full powers found to be in good and due form, have agreed to the present Charter of the United Nations and do hereby establish an international organization to be known as the United Nations.

(United Nations 1945)

The extract is taken from the preamble of the United Nations Charter, which was signed in the city of San Francisco in June 1945 and entered into force in October of that year. The attending signatories were mindful of creating an international political order robust enough to avoid the horrors of another global conflict (Taylor 1990). With assistance from the United States and other major world powers such as Britain, France, Russia and China, the United Nations was expected to provide an international forum for the peaceful resolution of disputes. It was also intended to provide a framework for establishing and reinforcing basic 'rules' governing international political intercourse via bodies such as the United Nations General Assembly and Security Council.

For scholars such as Hedley Bull (1995), the study of international order was an essential element in understanding how states exist within a so-called 'anarchical society'. He used the term 'anarchical' in order to draw attention to the fact that there was no world government capable of controlling the behaviour of states. States saw the importance of preserving an international community based on mutual recognition, the preservation of peace and the acknowledgement that states were independent. He also suggested that great powers such as the United States had a responsibility to help manage international order and this in turn contributed to a balance of power. During the Cold War, the United States and the Soviet Union managed to maintain some semblance of international order even when relations between the two countries were highly strained (McMahon 2003: 6–10). In the aftermath of the dangerously divisive Cuban Missile Crisis, which nearly precipitated a Third World War between the two superpowers, a partial prohibition on nuclear testing in 1963 illustrates this fragile global stability.

The post-1945 international order contained a number of essential ingredients. The key political agent was the state and its accompanying government. Membership of the United Nations continues to this day to be open only to recognized states; other forms of political organization such as regional bodies, non-governmental organizations and non-recognized states and governments such as the Turkish Republic of Northern Cyprus are not members. In 2004, there were 185 members. Second, the principle of sovereignty is acknowledged as paramount. In other words, states enjoy complete jurisdiction over their national territories. Some states such as Switzerland choose not to join the United Nations because they wish to protect long-established positions of neutrality. Third, national borders were considered inviolable and states deemed internally hegemonic and should not be subject to interference from others. Finally, the International Court of Justice (ICJ) based in The Hague, inaugurated in April 1946, provides a mechanism to resolve disputes peacefully and in accordance with international law. The ICJ replaced the Permanent Court of International Justice, which was created in 1922.

These principles were considered essential in the aftermath of a global conflict precipitated by the German invasion of Poland in September 1939 and the Japanese attack on the United States in December 1941. Earlier acts of violence during the 1930s, such as the Japanese invasion of Manchuria and the German–Italian bombing of Republican Spain, had also consolidated a widely held view that states had to be protected from aggressive acts. The Charter of the United Nations spelt out clearly the norms and values which member states acknowledged when seeking membership and now provide a blueprint for the normalization of international political relations. Existing practices such as diplomacy helped consolidate that vision of nations co-existing in a world where there was no greater authority than the state. The appointment of an ambassador, for example, illustrates the significance of recognizing other states and their sovereign authority, and recalling an ambassador signalled displeasure at the behaviour of another state. This was not uncommon during the Cold War, as countries complained about standards of behaviour such as fears that ambassadorial buildings were being 'bugged' by the host government.

On a more mundane level, anyone who travels internationally is accustomed to the ritual of passport control and customs clearance. The passport allows us to travel as national citizens but also provides the basis for other states to check and control people's movements (Torpey 2000). We all recognize the sovereignties of different countries whenever we pass through these controls. Even those engaged in people-smuggling, and other forms of migration not sanctioned by states, are forced to recognize these controls and procedures – hence their determination to avoid checkpoints associated with airports, railway stations and seaports. During the Cold War, Soviet citizens and others such as Eastern Europeans often faced restrictions on their freedom to travel. Participating in sport and the arts provided opportunities for movement, and some sports and ballet stars such as Rudolf Nureyev and Martina Navratilova, from the Soviet Union and Czechoslovakia respectively, defected in the 1960s and 1970s.

If prevailing understandings of 'international order' acknowledged the state and its borders, the founding participants of the United Nations recognized that there might have to be some kind of limit on this absolute authority to organize national affairs. The generation haunted by memories of the Holocaust had to respond to the suffering of others, even when this occurred beyond national boundaries. The 1948 Convention on the Prevention and Punishment of the Crime of Genocide introduced an important restriction on state sovereignty. As it noted:

Article 3
The following acts shall be punishable:

- (a) Genocide;
- (b) Conspiracy to commit genocide;
- (c) Direct and public incitement to commit genocide;
- (d) Attempt to commit genocide;
- (e) Complicity in genocide.

Article 4
Persons committing genocide or any of the other acts enumerated in Article 3 shall be punished, whether they are constitutionally responsible rulers, public officials or private individuals.

Article 7
Genocide and the other acts enumerated in Article 3 shall not be considered as political crimes for the purpose of extradition.

The Contracting Parties pledge themselves in such cases to grant extradition in accordance with their laws and treaties in force.

Article 8
Any Contracting Party may call upon the competent organs of the United Nations to take such action under the Charter of the United Nations, as they consider appropriate for the prevention and suppression of acts of genocide or any of the other acts enumerated in Article 3 (UN 1948).

Article 8 of the 1948 Convention clearly stipulates a restriction on practices associated with sovereignty and national borders. United Nations members, under the Convention, have a clear obligation to call upon the organization to confront genocide and or the attempt to commit genocide. Alongside other important international conventions such as the Geneva Conventions (1925 and 1949), these kinds of international legal instruments attempt to establish 'ground rules' for political life. In the case of the Geneva Conventions, they stipulate how states should treat prisoners of war, for example. This is important because it signified a determination to ensure that states could not expect to remain members of the United Nations if they did not abide by certain common standards. Moreover, if states attempt to commit genocide then they should expect other members of the United Nations to respond and if necessary violate the sovereignty of any party guilty of causing extreme human suffering.

Had those principles and legal instruments been used in the manner envisaged by their creators then it is possible much suffering could have been diminished or perhaps avoided altogether. Unfortunately for the victims of war and other hostilities, the attempt to establish a new international order was not quite so straightforward. For example, other forms of international intervention such as the United Nations Universal Declaration on Human Rights (1948) were not universally accepted and or welcomed. Despite the good intentions of the Committee responsible for the Declaration, some parties found the focus on individual rights an anathema. The Soviet Union favoured a far stronger focus on collective rights. Others worried that the Declaration could be used by outside parties to interfere with their internal cultural and religious composition. States such as Saudi Arabia resented the inclusion of the right to freedom of worship. The white minority regime of South Africa did not wish to acknowledge the equal rights of its Asian, Coloured and Black African citizens. It took another forty years before all South Africans were able to participate in social and political life in an equitable manner.

Perhaps the biggest obstacle to the realization of this form of post-1945 international order was the onset of the Cold War. The United Nations and its vision of international order would only be implemented and respected if the largest parties (in terms of political and military influence) worked with one another. The Security Council of the United Nations, as the major decision-making body, depended on the so-called permanent five (P5) Britain, China, France, the Soviet Union and the United States to co-operate closely because every member enjoyed the power of a permanent veto. Each of these parties had within its power the capacity to frustrate United Nations activity.

The United States and the Soviet Union were the most significant members and held fundamentally different senses of international order. For the United States, international order was best secured by promoting economic recovery, international financial stability, anti-communism and freedom in the broadest sense (Sharp 2000). For the Soviet Union, prospects for a socialist international order would be enhanced if the Soviets and their allies were able to develop a sense of territorial and economic security, thus limiting American domination. The Soviets, like the Americans, were eager to export their sense of vision to the wider world. Despite their ideological disagreements, both agreed that European imperialism had no place in the post-1945 period. They were determinedly anti-colonial and eager to end European domination of the so-called Third World. These rival ideologies also had implications for the citizens of the United States and the Soviet Union, who were expected to support imposed visions of international order. Dissidents in the Soviet Union were sent to brutal labour camps in Siberia and pro-communist sympathizers in the United States could be publicly disgraced and jailed.

As the intensity of the Cold War spread from a dispute over access and control of continental Europe to encompass other parts of the world, so the capacity of the United Nations to help shape international order diminished. Both sides routinely blocked the UN and its capacity to implement resolutions requiring parties to act on behalf of others. As a consequence, violations of international law such as the illegal invasion of other countries by the Soviet Union and the United States went unchallenged. In the period between 1945 and 1989, the United States invaded Guatemala, the Dominican Republic and undermined governments in Iran and Chile. The Soviet Union invaded Hungary, Czechoslovakia and Afghanistan and, like the Americans, supported local allies in conflicts throughout Southern Africa, the Middle East, South East Asia and Central America. For many states in the Global South, the principles of sovereignty and the inviolability of national borders meant very little in practice.

These kinds of interventions significantly undermined the kind of international order envisioned by the creators of the United Nations. Political geographers such as John Agnew and Stuart Corbridge (1995) have drawn our attention to the geographical consequences of that order. The Cold War was not just a struggle for ideological mastery (US-led capitalism and liberal democracy versus Soviet-led communism and state socialism): it was also a very real and bloody struggle for territorial influence. Millions of lives were lost on battlefields, but also in the cities and countryside of many regions in the Global South. It mattered greatly how the United States and the Soviet Union represented particular regions as strategic and or non-strategic. Regions were ranked by importance; in the 1960s, the Middle East and South East Asia were judged to be highly significant. So, the prevailing international order was of considerable consequence in the 1960s to the people of Vietnam and in early 1970s to the inhabitants of Angola and Mozambique.

If we were to extend this discussion beyond the geopolitics of the Cold War, we would also have to acknowledge the role of an international economic order, which over the course of the Cold War had established global capitalism as the dominant economic model for the international community of states. Institutions such as the International Monetary Fund (IMF) and the World Bank (WB) created in 1944 (under the Bretton Woods Agreement) have alongside the United Nations played their part in shaping the international financial order. They are responsible for stabilizing the international financial system (IMF) and determining international lending (WB) especially if directed towards long-term infrastructural projects such as dams and transport (Steger 2003: 37–55). This international management was supplemented in 1948 by the entry into force of the General Agreement on Tariffs and Trade (GATT), which sought to promote global trade with a minimum of trading barriers. This was replaced by the WTO in 1995.

As with the United Nations more generally, the IMF, GATT and WB can be hugely significant in supporting a particular vision of international order. Many countries in the Global South have found, from the 1970s onwards, that borrowing money and securing broader international financial confidence depends greatly on economic assessments carried out by these international bodies. States can find it very hard to act in a sovereign manner. Heavily indebted countries or those accused of government corruption have found their capacity to borrow sharply circumscribed. Without an adequate money supply, governments may not be able to pay their employees and may be unable and or unwilling to support essential services such as education, medical care and welfare. Children, the elderly and women often suffer disproportionately. In many countries in sub-Saharan Africa, Structural Adjustment Programmes in the 1980s and 1990s led to sweeping cuts in state spending as national governments were forced to display financial savings and 'good governance' (Simon et al. 1995).

Throughout the Cold War, the prevailing international order based on the UN Charter and other international bodies such as the IMF and the WB contributed to an unequal 'order of things'. The Global South bore the brunt of this inequality. States were routinely invaded, destabilized and/or financially weakened. The United States and the Soviet Union resisted all attempts to interfere with their sovereign authority and weaker states found that there was no effective world government to appeal to. Despite attempts to promote a New International Economic Order (NIEO) in the 1970s alongside the campaigning work of the Non-Aligned Movement (NAM), Third World critics found it difficult to persuade the richer North to consider an international order based on equity, justice and genuine intellectual exchange (Young 2003: 16–17). Despite their growing presence following decolonization and national independence, Third World states found that the United Nations as an international forum could not act as a world authority. Any attempt to prevent injustice required more powerful states to collaborate. The so-called Permanent Five on the Security Council rarely acted in unison during the Cold War. International order was as a consequence variable on the ground. Location mattered.

The ending of the Cold War and a birth of a new world order?

With the destruction of the Berlin Wall in November 1989, one of the seemingly permanent and evocative reminders of the Cold War disappeared. Many analysts recognized the opportunity to pursue a different kind of agenda. If the United Nations was paralysed during the Cold War because of the dispute between the United States and the Soviet Union, then surely new opportunities abounded with the dismantling of former Communist regimes in East and Central Europe. Within months of the Berlin Wall being pulled down by German protestors, Saddam Hussein's Iraq invaded Kuwait over disputed oilfields. Stung by this apparently blatant violation of international law, the United States used the United Nations to condemn this invasion as illegal. Iraq was ordered to leave Kuwait. President George Bush Senior recognized that a new mood of opportunism (and danger) now existed. As he noted in a speech in September 1990:

> We stand today at a unique and extraordinary moment. The crisis in the Persian Gulf, as grave as it is, also offers a rare opportunity to move toward an historic period of cooperation. Out of these troubled times, our fifth objective – a new world order – can emerge: a new era – freer from the threat of terror, stronger in the pursuit of justice, and more secure in the quest for peace. An era in which the nations of the world, East and West, North and South, can prosper and live in harmony. A hundred generations have searched for this elusive path to peace, while a thousand wars raged across the span of human endeavor. Today that new world is struggling to be born, a world quite different from the one we've known. A world where the rule of law supplants the rule of the jungle. A world in which nations recognize the shared responsibility for freedom and justice. A world where the strong respect the rights of the weak. This is the vision that I shared with President Gorbachev in Helsinki. He and other leaders from Europe, the Gulf, and around the world understand that how we manage this crisis today could shape the future for generations to come.
>
> Once again, Americans have stepped forward to share a tearful goodbye with their families before leaving for a strange and distant shore. At this very moment, they serve together with Arabs, Europeans, Asians, and Africans in defense of principle and the dream of a new world order. That's why they sweat and toil in the sand and the heat and the sun. If they can come together under such adversity, if old adversaries like the Soviet Union and the United States can work in common cause, then surely we who are so fortunate to be in this great Chamber – Democrats, Republicans, liberals,

conservatives – can come together to fulfill our responsibilities here. Thank you. Good night. And God bless the United States of America.

(Bush 1990)

The term 'new world order' is used several times in the speech and it is clear that President Bush's vision of order revolved around the rights and responsibilities of states and their representatives. It also paved the way for an understanding of the United States as a quasi 'global policeman'. President Bush foresaw a role for the United States as a global enforcer. By September 1990 the future of the Soviet Union was in jeopardy as economic crisis combined with nationalistic movements demanding independence. As the sole remaining superpower, the country had the military and diplomatic capacity to enforce United Nations resolutions. Given the strategic and resource importance of Iraq, the United States acted quickly to establish a coalition of willing states to ensure that any actions against Iraq were with the blessing of the United Nations. United Nations Resolution 678 authorized the use of force if Iraq failed to leave Kuwait. The eventual war against Iraq was brief and brutal in terms of human and environmental impact (Barnaby 1991; Luke 1991; Leaver 1992). Many thousands of Iraqis died in the face of the overwhelming American-led military force. Iraq was vanquished but Saddam Hussein was *not* removed from power. Despite encouraging groups within Iraq to overthrow the regime, the US and its allies offered no help to resistance movements in the aftermath of the Kuwaiti occupation. The American administration argued that they did not possess explicit UN authorization for the removal of the Iraqi leader.

For a short period of time, United States commentators speculated that a new world order was being initiated. Collective security, the revival of the United Nations and the promotion of multi-lateral co-operation were celebrated as the values of this NWO. Some writers such as Francis Fukuyama claimed that the 'End of History' was being initiated (Fukuyama 1992, 2004). History in this sense referred to the struggle over ideas, and Fukuyama claimed that ideas associated with liberal democracy and capitalism had prevailed decisively over other ideologies such as socialism and communism. His argument seemed reasonable – people in Latin America, Central and Eastern Europe alongside sub-Saharan Africa were embracing democracy in the 1990s. A new international order based on the triumph of these ideas would prevail in due course. The prospects for long-term peace appeared positive. Others, however, were less optimistic. Samuel Huntington, writing in the American journal *Foreign Affairs*, warned of a rather different international order. Rather than a new world order based on democracy and market economies, he foretold of a 'clash of civilizations'. The United States and the West more generally would face new religious-cultural challenges from China and the Islamic worlds. Processes associated with globalization would only heighten such conflict as ideas, people and technology such as the Internet brought these civilizations into sharper contact with one another (Huntington 1993, 1996).

Subsequent events have called into question optimistic interpretations for the ending of the Cold War and a New World Order. A botched attempt to deliver humanitarian assistance to Somalia in 1992 dented American confidence. Television pictures of dead American ser-vicemen being dragged around the streets of Mogadishu had a severe effect on US foreign policy confidence. President Clinton was elected in the 1992 presidential election on a platform which concentrated on domestic economic issues. American attempts subsequently to promote a more cautious foreign policy strategy were called into question by the genocide in Rwanda in 1994. Approximately 1 million people perished as the wider international community failed to assist (Dallaire 2004). Alongside the persistent failure to prevent mass killings in the former Yugoslavia between 1992–95, attempts to secure a new post-Cold War order were exposed as inept. The UN failed to prevent the massacre of 8,000 Bosnian men and children in the town of Srebrenica in July 1995 despite the presence of Dutch peace-keepers. The United Nations stood accused of being useless and great powers were labelled indifferent and cowardly in their reluctance to intervene to relieve human suffering (Campbell 1998; Ó Tuathail 2000, 2002; Simms 2002).

The international system and its prevailing norms seemed ill-equipped to cope with post-Cold War era wars *within* states, acts of genocide, and the upsurge in stateless and displaced peoples in regions such as South East Europe, Central Africa and Southern Africa (Hyndman 2000; Moorehead 2005; Ogata 2005). In Bosnia, for example, 1.3 million people were internally displaced and over 700,000 were dispersed around the European continent. International obligations such as the 1951 Geneva Convention dealing with stateless peoples and refugees are an important element in shaping the obligations of other states and governments. One might argue that we can tell a great deal about the prevailing nature of international order by the way these kinds of conventions are adhered to by recipient states. States often spend a great deal of resources trying to restrict the number of people successfully applying for asylum or preventing stateless persons and refugees from leaving their country of origin. More generally, this desire to control movement can be seen as sitting somewhat uneasily with the liberal trans-national optimism of the United Nations in the late 1940s and 1950s. As Caroline Moorehead has noted, 'people today face formidable barriers if they try to cross from one country to another' (Moorehead 2005: 80). For the refugee and the stateless person, a few feet can be the difference between life and death. And yet even the crossing of a border does not guarantee safety, as many found to their cost in West and Central Africa and South East Europe in the 1990s.

The United Nations depends on member states to provide the resources and political leadership to decisively intervene in the affairs of other states. The 1948 UN Declaration on Human Rights alongside the 1951 Genocide Convention depends upon a sense of collective determination to implement where appropriate. However, UN conventions resolutions dealing with human suffering are applied in an ad hoc manner. Intervention in some places is more likely than others even if the scale of human suffering is equivalent. At present there is no proposal to use United Nations resources to intervene decisively in countries such as India (Kashmir), Russia (Chechnya) and Sudan (Darfur), which have been accused of carrying out violent anti-terror campaigns against their own citizens. But other countries such as Serbia were attacked in March 1999, as a result of fears that the then government had embarked on a murderous campaign against Albanian Kosovars. The forces of the North Atlantic Treaty Organization (NATO, created in 1949) were used (without the approbation of the UNSC) for the first time against an adversary. These double standards have led to accusations that the prevailing 'international order' is inherently unfair. As Edward Said concluded:

> What concerns me most, though, as an American and a citizen, is what the Kosovo Crisis portends for the future of the world order. 'Safe' or 'Clean' wars, in which American military personnel and their equipment are almost totally invulnerable to enemy retaliation or attack, are profoundly troubling to think about ... Such wars share the same structures as torture, with the investigator-torturer having all the power to choose and then employ whatever method he wishes; the victim, who has none, consequently is left to the whim of his persecutor.
>
> (Said 2000: 342–43).

His words have considerable prescience in the light of events post-11 September.

11 September and the Global War on Terror: unilateral order?

The 11 September 2001 attacks on the World Trade Center and the Pentagon resulted in the deaths of nearly 3,000 people. A fourth plane, possibly intended for the White House, crashed in a field in Pennsylvania, killing all occupants. The events of that day were clearly shocking and President George W. Bush swiftly declared a 'War on Terror' as it became clear that self-confessed Islamic militants were responsible for the suicidal attacks. The Al-Qaeda terror network was held responsible for the planning and execution of the attacks. Within weeks, the United States armed forces, alongside a group of countries dubbed the 'coalition of the willing', attacked and overthrew the Taliban regime in Afghanistan and pursued the Saudi extremist Osama bin Laden. A number of countries including Britain, Australia, Italy and Spain promised and delivered political and military support to the United States administration. Within 18 months of the attacks, the US government launched an attack on Saddam Hussein's Iraq in response to fears that his regime possessed Weapons of Mass Destruction (WMD) capability and a possible link to the Al-Qaeda network.

As a consequence of these actions and others such as the use of its military base in Guantanamo Bay as an interrogation centre, the United States has been accused of behaving in a dangerous and unilateral manner. Despite the support of a limited number of governments, many others feel that the Bush administration is placing international norms in jeopardy. Concern has been raised about the manner in which the United States planned and executed the invasion of Iraq in 2003 without the imprimatur of the Security Council. The destruction of Iraq's infrastructure was considerable, as was the loss of civilian life. American service personnel searching for so-called militants and terrorists have been estimated, at the time of writing, to have killed 25–30,000. Moreover, there has been a worry that the treatment of prisoners of war has not been in keeping with the Geneva Conventions (Rose 2004). Airbases and military camps have been used to imprison and abuse such prisoners including the infamous Abu Ghraib prison in Baghdad. The US military have also flown other prisoners to countries such as Egypt, Jordan and Syria where it is alleged prisoners were tortured and denied basic human rights for the sake of extracting information about terror networks.

For critics of American foreign policy practices, this kind of behaviour undermines international order. The United States as the largest military power has a responsibility to behave in a restrained manner and help the United Nations to protect international norms regarding, for example, the treatment of prisoners of war. As Peter Singer noted:

> Rather than ensure that the nation he [President George W. Bush] leads is a good global citizen, Bush has spurned the global institutions for global co-operation and set back the task of making the rule of law, rather than force, the determining factor in world affairs.
>
> (Singer 2003: 224; see also Kennedy 2004)

By ignoring United Nations Security Council reservations about the assault on Iraq, critics warned that extremists such as Osama bin Laden would use this apparent by-passing of the United Nations to further legitimize his campaign against the United States. Bin Laden has claimed that the Middle East and Islamic world is imperilled by Western cultural, political and economic dominations. He has also directed attention to the plight of Palestinians and contended that the international community is not prepared to support their struggle against the Jewish state of Israel. Like Samuel Huntington, but with very a different kind of endpoint, bin Laden believes in a 'clash of civilizations' and wants to undermine existing international order. The late Palestinian-American writer Edward Said warned of a 'clash of ignorance' and urged all parties to resist the temptation (especially in the aftermath of an outrage such as 11 September) to simplify cultural and political complexities.

Even if we are mindful of the warning to respect complexity, the behaviour of the United States in the aftermath of 11 September has concerned many American citizens and the wider world. The Bush administration stands accused of undermining the norms and practices of international order. The rejection of the Kyoto Protocol process and unwillingness to support the International Criminal Court (ICC) are two examples (see Plate 18.2). In March 2005, a National Defense Strategy paper warned that the United States should avoid being restricted by international forums and judicial processes such as the ICC and be resolute in projecting and defending their vital national interests. As the paper noted under the category of 'Our vulnerabilities':

Nevertheless, we have vulnerabilities:

- Our capacity to address global security challenges alone will be insufficient.
- Some allies and partners will decide not to act with us or will lack the capacity to act with us.
- Our leading position in world affairs will continue to breed unease, a degree of resentment, and resistance.
- *Our strength as a nation state will continue to be challenged by those who employ a strategy of the weak using international fora, judicial processes, and terrorism.*
- We and our allies will be the principal targets of extremism and terrorism.
        (Department of Defense 2005, emphasis added by author)

It is striking that the present administration of the United States views 'international fora and judicial processes' as strategies of the 'weak'. International order depends on such components, and even military powers the size of the United States rely on these processes and

Plate 18.2.
© Steve Bell. Published in the *Guardian* 30 March 2001.

conventions, including those sponsored by the United Nations (*The Times* 2005). As the Nigerian Nobel Prizewinner for Literature, Wole Soyinka wisely concluded:

> Unilateral action, or the appropriation of a global duty of response, by any one nation, serves only to diminish the United Nations. That the culprit in this respect should be one of such powerful achievements as the United States, and that it is the host to that organization physically, on its own soil, only denoted an enervation of the global vision ... What the United States lacks is philosophical leadership, despite its formidable reserves of original thinkers.
>
> (Soyinka 2004: 132)

Conclusions

Writing this conclusion in the aftermath of the 7 July 2005 terrorist attacks on London, it is difficult to avoid commenting on the continuing impact of the so-called Global War on Terror. While we should be outraged and distressed by the loss of life in London, such acts are a daily reality for the citizens of Iraq (see Plate 18.3). The lack of domestic order, let alone international order, is a daily reality here rather than an occasional outrage. Such events (however deadly and outrageous) should not distract us from thinking about the processes which lead hundreds to die needlessly in other less apparently dramatic ways. Far more children die of preventable diseases every day than do victims of terror (see Chapter 10). If all human life is precious, then we should be equally shocked and appalled by these losses.

International order matters because it provides a framework for the operations of states and their governments and a context, which other groups and interests occasionally resist or overturn. The destruction of the Berlin Wall in November 1989 is a salient example. But

Plate 18.3. *Ongoing two minutes silence Baghdad.*
© Steve Bell. Published in the *Guardian* 15 July 2005.

issues such as climate change and poverty are harder to confront because they go to the apparent heart of an international system based on states, borders and global forms of capitalism. While we have stressed the role of the United States in shaping post-1945 international order, we should be in no doubt that, as the present century unfolds, other economic powers such as China and India will demand greater recognition of their values and interests.

If there is no international order and agreement over common procedures and norms, then progress towards distributive justice (i.e. economic equity, human rights protection and global environmental standards) becomes well-nigh impossible. The George W. Bush administration's disregard of such norms is not sustainable as it creates new enemies and alienates existing allies. Order is fundamental to the tenure of justice. If order involves developing a sense of humankind as a whole and not just an international order of nation-states, then issues such as global climate change, let alone global terrorism, require a more generous sense of justice.

Acknowledgements

I would like to thank Chris Perkins and Francis Robinson for their very helpful comments on an earlier draft. Steve Bell kindly gave his permission for three cartoons to be reproduced in this chapter.

Further reading

Bull, H. (1995) *The Anarchical Society*. London: Macmillan.
Dalby, S. (2002) *Environmental Security*. Minneapolis: University of Minnesota Press.
Dijkink, G. (1996) *National Identity and Geopolitical Visions*. London: Routledge.
Dobson, A. and Marsh, S. (2001) *US Foreign Policy since 1945*. London: Routledge.
Gregory, D. (2004) *The Colonial Present*. Oxford: Blackwell.
Harvey, D. (2003) *The New Imperialism*. Oxford: Oxford University Press.
Halper, S. and Clarke, J. (2004) *America Alone*. Cambridge: Cambridge University Press.
Held, D. (1995) *Democracy and the Global Order*. Stanford: Stanford University Press.
Huntington, S. (1996) *The Clash of Civilizations and the Remaking of World Order*. New York: Simon and Schuster
Klare, M. (2001) *Resource Wars*. New York: Hill and Wang.
Mittleman, J. (ed.) (1996) *Globalisation; Critical Reflections*. Boulder: Lynne Rienner.
Ó Tuathail, G. (2000) The post-modern geopolitical condition: states, statecraft and security at the millennium. *Annals of the Association of American Geographers* 90, 166–78.
Said, E. (2001) The clash of ignorance. *The Nation* 22 October, 9–12.
Shapiro, M. (1997) *Violent Cartographies*. Minneapolis: University of Minnesota Press.
Torpey, J.C. (2000) *The Invention of the Passport: Surveillance, Citizenship and the State*. Cambridge: Cambridge University Press.

Relevant websites

http://www.g8.gov.uk
http://www.hrweb.org/legal/genocide.html
http://www.makepovertyhistory.org

http://www.un.org/aboutun/charter/
http://www.un.org/Overview/rights.html

References

Agnew, J. (2003) *Geopolitics*. London: Routledge.

Agnew, J. and Corbridge, S. (1995) *Mastering Space*. London: Routledge.

Amnesty International (2005) *Guantanamo and Beyond: The Continuing Pursuit of Unchecked Executive Power*. Available at http://www.amnesty.org (accessed 2 July 2005).

Barnaby, F. (1991) The environmental impact of the Gulf War. *The Ecologist* 21, 166–72.

Bull, H. (1995) *The Anarchical Society*, second edition. London: Macmillan.

Bush, G. (1990) *Address to the Joint Session of Congress on 11th September 1990*. Available at http://www.sweetliberty.org/issues/war/bushsr.html

Campbell, D. (1992) *Writing Security*. Manchester: Manchester University Press.

——(1998) *National Deconstruction: Violence, Identity and Justice in Bosnia*. Minneapolis: University of Minnesota Press.

Chomsky, N. (2005) *Doctrines and Visions*. Harmondsworth: Penguin.

Dalby, S. (1996) The environment as geopolitical threat: reading Robert Kaplan's *Coming Anarchy*. *Ecumene* 3, 472–96.

Dallaire, R. (2004) *Shake Hands with the Devil*. New York: Carroll and Graf.

Department of Defense (2005) *National Defense Strategy*. Washington: Department of Defense. Available at http://www.globalsecurity.org/military/library/policy/dod/nds-usa_mar20005-ib.htm

Dicken, P. (2003) *Global Shift*. London: Sage.

Dijkink, G. (1996) *National Identity and Geopolitical Visions*. London: Routledge.

Dodds, K. (2005) *Global Geopolitics: A Critical Introduction*. Harlow: Pearson Education.

Flannery, T. (2005) Endgame. *New York Review of Books* 11 August, 26–29.

Fukuyama, F. (1992) *The End of History and the Last Man*. New York: Free Press.

——(2004) *State Building*. London: Profile Books.

Harvey, D. (2003) *The New Imperialism*. Oxford: Oxford University Press.

Herod, A., Ó Tuathail, G. and Roberts, S. (eds) (1998) *An Unruly World?* London: Routledge.

Huntington, S. (1993) The clash of civilizations? *Foreign Affairs* 72, 22–49.

Hyndman, J. (2000) *Managing Displacement: Refugees and the Politics of Humanitarianism*. Minneapolis: University of Minnesota Press.

Johnston, R., Taylor, P. and Watts, M. (eds) (2002) *Geographies of Global Change*. Oxford: Blackwell.

Kaplan, A. (2003) Homeland insecurities. *Radical History Review* 85, 82–93.

Kennedy, D. (2004) *The Dark Side of Virtue*. Princeton: Princeton University Press.

Leaver, R. (1992) The Gulf War and the new world order. *Australian Journal of Political Science* 27, 242–57.

Luke, T. (1991) The discipline of security studies and the codes of containment: learning from Kuwait. *Alternatives* 16, 315–44.

McMahon, R. (2003) *The Cold War*. Oxford: Oxford University Press.

Moorehead, C. (2005) *Human Cargo*. New York: Henry Holt.

Ogata, S. (2005) *The Turbulent Decade*. New York: Norton.

Ó Tuathail, G. (1996) *Critical Geopolitics*. London: Routledge.

——(2002) Theorising practical geopolitical reasoning: the case of US Bosnia Policy in 1992. *Political Geography* 21, 601–28.

——(2003) Just out looking for a fight: American affect and the invasion of Iraq. *Antipode* 35, 856–70.

Ó Tuathail, G. and Dalby, S. (eds) (1998) *Rethinking Geopolitics*. London: Routledge.

Rengger, N. (2000) *International Relations, Political Theory and the Problem of Order*. London: Routledge.

Roberts, S., Secor, A. and Sparke, M. (2003) Neo-liberal geopolitics. *Antipode* 35, 886–97.

Rose, D. (2004) *Guantanamo: America's Assault on Human Rights*. London: Faber and Faber.

Said, E. (2000) The treason of intellectuals. In T. Ali (ed.) *Masters of the Universe?* pp. 341–44. London: Verso.

Shapiro, M. (1997) *Violent Cartographies*. Minneapolis: University of Minnesota Press.

Sharp, J. (2000) *Condensing the Cold War*. Minneapolis: University of Minnesota Press.

Simms, B. (2002) *Unfinest Hour: Britain and the Destruction of Bosnia*. London: Allen Lane.

Simon, D., van Spengen, W., Dixon, C. and Närman, A. (eds) (1995) *Structurally-Adjusted Africa*. London: Pluto.

Singer, P. (2003) *The President of Good and Evil*. London: Granta Books.

Soyinka, W. (2004) *The Climate of Fear*. London: Profile Books.

Spence, K. (2005) World risk society and war against terror. *Political Studies* 53, 284–302.

Steger, M. (2003) *Globalization*. Oxford: Oxford University Press.

Taylor, P. (1990) *Britain and the Cold War: 1945 as Geopolitical Transition*. London: Belhaven.

Taylor, P. and Flint, C. (1999) *Political Geography*. London: Longman.

The Times (2005) Bush overrides objections and installs Bolton as UN envoy, 2 August 2005.

United Nations (1945) *United Nations Charter*. New York: United Nations.

——(1948) *Convention on the Prevention and Punishment of the Crime of Genocide*. New York: United Nations.

Williams, C. (ed.) (1993) *The Political Geography of the New World Order*. London: Belhaven.

Young, R. (2003) *Post-Colonialism*. Oxford: Oxford University Press.

19

National states

Marcus Power

Whilst there are an enormous number of different definitions of national states traditionally, states are regarded as a space or *territory* (of land or water) which has relatively well-defined political boundaries that are recognized internationally. A geographical perspective is crucial to any understanding of nations and states and it is important not to conflate the two. Nations are defined on the basis of culture, ethnicity, religion or language whereas states are political units, of which there are approximately 200 in the world today (Braden and Shelley 2000). Nations contain people who share a sense of independent political identity, common cultural traits and a sense of difference from other groups of people living outside the national territory. States, on the other hand, are defined principally by their boundaries, which are drawn in order to separate and distinguish states and to delimit the territorial authority of each state (which in turn has to be recognized by the international community). Recognition of these territorial rights by the international community is known as sovereignty, a concept that implies that in terms of international law, the government of a state has jurisdiction over its territory. As Anderson (1983: 7) has argued, 'nations dream of being free' and as such 'the gage and emblem of this freedom is the sovereign state'.

The boundaries of many states are consistent with the territories inhabited by particular nations, but there are also many states that contain more than one nation within their boundaries. Indeed, territory is central to the formation of both nations and states. Thus it is necessary to examine how international political relations and the states that have resulted from these relations have been *geographically produced*. Rather than assuming a fully formed state system and uncontested state-delimited territories, it is important to examine the power struggles within and between different societies over the right to speak sovereignly about geography, space and territory (Ó Tuathail 1996: 11). In the contemporary world, many commentators have argued that processes of globalization (in the form of increasingly transnational flows of capital and through the growth of global and regional forms of government) are challenging the ability of the nation-state to effectively practise its claim to a sovereign monopoly over a bounded space and to protect its citizens from external political, cultural or economic change. Although national-states take many forms and are today very different from the states of two or three hundred years ago, they continue to be very significant forces and the national-state context continues to matter to the workings of the global political system and the global economy.

So this chapter starts by charting the historical geography of state formation, before considering the changing roles of national institutions and impacts on notions of what it means to be a citizen. Only then can we evaluate the continuing significance of the state in a globalizing world.

An historical geography of state formation

In order to understand how national states are constituted and come to operate, it is necessary to think *historically* as well as geographically. The nation-state has long been a major focus for both geographers and historians, yet whilst the claims made for and on behalf of states clearly deserve critical attention, this is not an easy task since to discuss nations, states and nationalism is to enter a terminological maze in which one easily and soon becomes lost (Akzin 1964; Grundy-Warr and Sidaway 2005). In many ways the history of statehood has often been more complicated than dominant accounts in the social sciences have made it appear (Agnew 2002), whilst historical understandings of what states are and how they work have changed over the years. Increasingly there has been a growing awareness of the need to be sensitive to the limits as well as the strengths of state power, and a widening recognition that states have rarely (if ever) had the exclusive monopoly on the means of violence that much political theory might lead one to expect (Thomson 1994). Consequently, it is crucial to understand that the world contains a variety of state forms that cannot be reduced to a single model of statehood. This is important because many accounts have tended first to focus on European forms of statehood and political organization and then to view all other states as variations on a European meta-narrative, as variants of a kind of master story or plot that governs all others. In other words there has been a tendency (given the age of many European states) to focus on ideal-type cases (typically France or England) and to see all other states as imitators of these European prototypes (Agnew 2002).

In such analyses, the historical evolution of the (European) nation-state is often traced through four broad phases: pre-agrarian, agrarian, industrial and post-industrial (Johnston *et al.* 2000). In the pre-agrarian phase 'tribal' loyalties are seen to have predominated with hunting and gathering bands viewed as too isolated and small scale to permit the existence of an independent political institution. The emergence of literacy and a specialized class of clergymen in the agrarian phase is argued to have made possible the centralized organization and storage of records, rules and culture (although again communities remained isolated and the power of the clergy was very much localized territorially; Johnston *et al.* 2000). A crucial phase of transition in this somewhat conventional sequence is seen to be the emergence of the absolutist state, where a single monarchy displaced prior (decentralized) feudal arrangements, laying the foundations of modern nation-states by introducing, for example, uniform taxation structures, standing armies and bureaucracies. With the beginnings of industrial society, a centralized state agency takes on key roles of education and authority and seeks to rationalize these functions throughout the national territory.

Only with the rise of the modern territorial state in sixteenth-century Europe did a close affiliation between political community and territory begin to emerge, and only since then have citizenship and territory been conjoined (Agnew 2002). In other words, the clear bounding of states is one of the main differences between modern European-style political organization and the types of polity that prevailed in feudal, absolutist, clan, imperial and nomadic societies around the world in the past (Agnew 2002: 113). As noted earlier, there is a profound territorial link between the nation and the state because the state claims to be a sovereign expression of the nation, to be bound to it in ways which have territorial limits. Thus each nation-state has a geography 'which is charted, demarcated, mapped and represented to the "national population" in their school atlas and geography lessons' (Grundy-Warr and Sidaway 2005: 431). In tracing the historical roots of statehood it is important to consider different conceptions of sovereignty that have existed in the past, from medieval Europe to parts of the pre-colonial world. During medieval times in Europe much smaller communities and political units existed than those we know today, and thus sovereignty was much less territorial than with most modern states in that it was shared between a wide variety of secular and religious institutions and different levels of authority: 'feudal knights and barons, kings and princes, guilds and cities, bishops, abbots and the papacy' (Anderson 1995: 70). Far from having fixed and well-defined borders, the territories of medieval European states were discontinuous, with ill-defined and fluid frontier zones (Anderson 1995). There was thus no single original and foundational ideal-type case scenario of statehood and seeing all other states as simply mimicking a prototype is deeply problematic. The main point here is that not all nation-states necessarily develop as a consequence of particular models, prescribed stages or exclusively according to some larger overarching history of Europe. Different patterns of nation-state evolution have been, for example, observed in the military/authoritarian states of South America or amongst the states of South and South East Asia (Johnston *et al.* 2000; Grundy-Warr and Sidaway 2005).

The contemporary system of states, in which all of the land surface of the Earth is divided into state units, is something that is fairly new (Grundy-Warr and Sidaway 2005), given that earlier in the twentieth century the borders between many of today's states were only vaguely defined and more recently large areas of the world were ruled by colonial empires or dynastic realms (e.g. the Ch'ing Empire in China). Thus the concept of nation-statehood simply did not form part of the political vocabulary in many parts of the world where an imperial order rather than a defined nation had predominated (Grundy-Warr and Sidaway 2005). Between 1800 and 1878, European imperial rule, including former colonies in North and South America, was significantly expanded, increasing from 35 per cent to 67 per cent of the Earth's land surface, adding another 18 per cent between 1875 and 1914, the period of 'formal colonialism' (Hoogevelt 1997: 18). In the last three decades of the nineteenth century, European states thus added 10 million square miles of territory and 150 million people to their areas of control or 'one fifth of the earth's land surface and one tenth of its people' (Peet with Hartwick 1999: 105). Figures 19.1(a) and (b) charts this changing significance of the nation-state, contrasting the situation at the peak of European empires with contemporary national boundaries.

The number of sovereign states on the world political map today has increased steadily since the Second World War as a result of the collapse of European empires and the resulting decolonization of former European colonies in Africa, Asia and Latin America. Decolonization is the long, tortuous and often violent process by which colonies achieved political independence from the colonial metropolitan power – a process that was highly uneven in its history and geography. Today few formal colonies and no large-scale dynastic empires remain, and so territories that once formed part of an empire (e.g. Portuguese or Japanese) are now divided into self-avowed and recognized sovereign states with the same apparatus of statehood as the former imperial powers had (e.g. United Nations representation, leaders, flags, national anthems, capital cities and so on). The key point then is to recognize the historical and geographical *variability* of states (Grundy-Warr and Sidaway 2005) and that the global map of states is continually changing – some states have recently disappeared as separate entities (as in the former East Germany and South Yemen) whilst others have split into

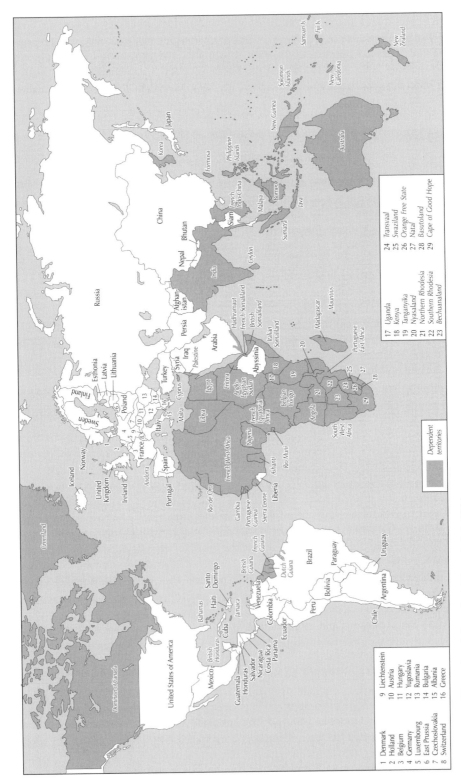

Figure 19.1a. The nation-state: colonial boundaries, 1924.

1 Denmark	9 Liechtenstein
2 Holland	10 Austria
3 Belgium	11 Hungary
4 Germany	12 Yugoslavia
5 Luxembourg	13 Rumania
6 East Prussia	14 Bulgaria
7 Czechoslovakia	15 Albania
8 Switzerland	16 Greece

17 Uganda	24 Transvaal
18 Kenya	25 Swaziland
19 Tanganyika	26 Orange Free State
20 Nyasaland	27 Natal
21 Northern Rhodesia	28 Basutoland
22 Southern Rhodesia	29 Cape of Good Hope
23 Bechuanaland	

Dependent territories

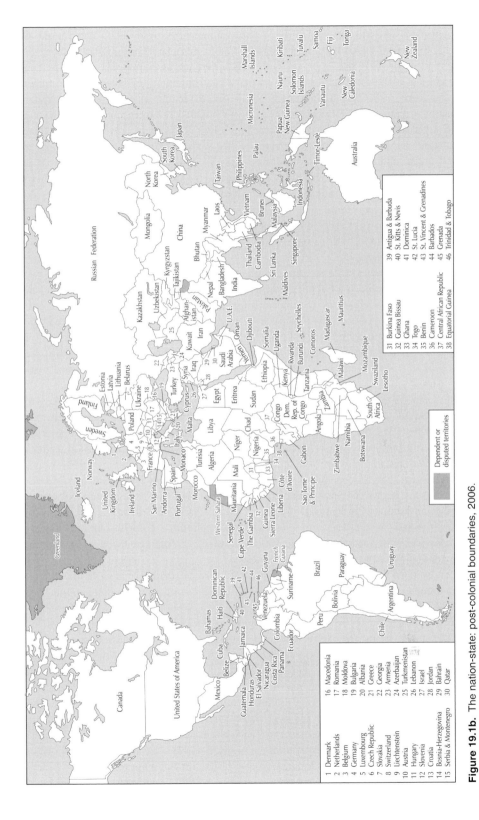

Figure 19.1b. The nation-state: post-colonial boundaries, 2006.

1 Denmark	16 Macedonia	31 Burkina Faso	39 Antigua & Barbuda
2 Netherlands	17 Romania	32 Guinea Bissau	40 St. Kitts & Nevis
3 Belgium	18 Moldova	33 Ghana	41 Dominica
4 Germany	19 Bulgaria	34 Togo	42 St. Lucia
5 Luxembourg	20 Albania	35 Benin	43 St. Vincent & Grenadines
6 Czech Republic	21 Greece	36 Cameroon	44 Barbados
7 Slovakia	22 Georgia	37 Central African Republic	45 Grenada
8 Switzerland	23 Armenia	38 Equatorial Guinea	46 Trinidad & Tobago
9 Liechtenstein	24 Azerbaijan		
10 Austria	25 Turkmenistan		
11 Hungary	26 Lebanon		
12 Slovenia	27 Israel		
13 Croatia	28 Jordan		
14 Bosnia-Herzegovina	29 Bahrain		
15 Serbia & Montenegro	30 Qatar		

Dependent or disputed territories

component parts (like the former USSR, Yugoslavia and Czechoslovakia). This should also remind us that, as Grundy-Warr and Sidaway (2005: 424) have noted 'states, like other communities, particularly the "nations" with which they are associated, are not to be taken at face value'. It is therefore important to recognize the ambiguity of states as social institutions (Low 2005: 465). To put it another way, a certain degree of unity, individuality and functionality is often falsely ascribed to states in ways which fail to recognize that states are also partly *symbolic systems*, mythicized abstractions and a complex of representations. Terms like 'the state' are thus made real in certain words, texts (e.g. maps) and deeds – in and through language and action. The symbolism of the state must continually be re-enacted and re-imagined (Grundy-Warr and Sidaway 2005) whilst the power of the state is celebrated through symbolic events like military parades, national holidays, state celebrations and ceremonies that serve to legitimize the authority of the state (e.g. 4 July in the USA). As Grundy-Warr and Sidaway (2005) have argued, symbolic systems like these are used to make states seem important and 'real' to us (e.g. through the bureaucratic acts of state such as the action of showing a passport).

During the late nineteenth and early twentieth centuries, the European colonial powers sought to integrate subjects of their colonies into their European-centred economies and European notions of 'civilization'. European languages, economic activities, industries, educational systems and political institutions were thus superimposed and transplanted upon local cultures (Braden and Shelley 2000). In the nineteenth century, a large number of new states emerged in the Americas in uprisings and revolts against the Spanish and Portuguese empires, which in many ways provided examples to other nationalists in the colonial world. Most of Africa and Asia escaped from colonial domination in the twentieth century, often through violent national 'liberation' struggles against colonial powers and white colonial settler populations. After the decolonization of these colonies (which in Africa took place roughly between 1945 and 1975) members of different national groups were divided in their political loyalties, and each state consisted of a diverse set of national groups which made the project of building national unity very difficult and produced many conflicts and tensions in the 'post-colonial' period. To varying degrees cultures are always heterogeneous and contested across different social relations like age, gender and class, and multiple sub-cultures can exist within any supposedly 'national' society (Grundy-Warr and Sidaway 2005). All of this had made the task of building and consolidating statehood a complicated one in many former colonies and has led to the articulation of a variety of complex and competing claims and demands by the citizens of these new states.

In many parts of the non-western world and in Africa in particular there has been a lack of correspondence between national territories and state boundaries as a direct result of the colonial history of these regions. Boundaries between colonies were drawn at conference tables in European capitals by officials and diplomats with little if any knowledge of local conditions, and so boundaries were drawn to suit the needs and interests of the European imperial states. Many of these boundaries clearly cut across and are overlaid upon pre-existing cultural and ecological boundaries, creating artificial distinctions that ignored cultural similarities and notions of pre-existing nations. In some instances nationalist ideologies have recognized that the state itself may be multinational (as in the United States, Britain, Switzerland, Nigeria and South Africa) and have claimed a goal of an 'inclusive national identity' that supposedly unites disparate 'sub-nations' and communities (Grundy-Warr and Sidaway 2005). When a dominant nationalist ideology is asserted within a territory this can, however, involve the suppression of, or conflict with, other claims on the same territory (as with the emergence of the state of Israel). In this respect we need to understand that nations are contested systems of cultural representation that have consequences for people's access to the resources of the nation-state. Thus many claims to statehood are suppressed and denied (as in Burma, which has witnessed over fifty years of political struggle between various movements seeking greater political autonomy or complete independence from the 'Union of Myanmar', as the country is currently named by the ruling military junta). It is important then to recognize that there are many self-identified nations without their own state (e.g. the Kurds) and that frequently smaller nations within a multi-national state (such as Quebec in Canada) claim that they should enjoy full statehood, articulating claims which are often resisted by the national state (as in Northern Ireland, where many Catholics (Republicans) wish to see the province united with the rest of Ireland – a claim rejected by the national state in the UK).

National state agencies and the uneven development of citizenship

In a study of the legacies of late colonialism in Africa, Mamdani (1996) argues that colonization was fundamentally about differentiating between peoples of the colony at the national level, where administrators and settlers were given the status of citizens and the indigenous peoples were seen as subjects with no rights. This raises the question of the extent to which colonial state machineries were decolonized, reworked and transformed after independence. The colonial state had rested on force for its legitimacy, a legitimacy which was thus highly superficial. Colonial states also had a role in creating political and economic communities, defining the rules of politics and the boundaries of community whilst creating power structures to dominate them. The colonial state was also the dominant economic actor, creating a currency, levying taxes, introducing crops, developing markets, controlling labour and production. Above all colonial state administrations sought the integration of the colonial economy into the wider economies of empire, to make linkages with the metropole and to establish flows of peoples and resources. After the formal end of colonialism, new states have had to formulate alternative methods of garnering legitimacy for their authority (i.e. other than the use of force preferred by the colonists). In this way, the institutional segregation preferred by the colonial state was, according to Mamdani, in many cases later reproduced in post-colonial times. Interestingly, Mamdani argues that it is necessary to break away from the entrapment of Africa within 'history by analogy' which either exoticizes Africa or represents the continent's history as part of larger European stories of the past or meta-narratives. The African state today takes hybrid forms – with European roots and beginnings but with a variety of African 'inflections' and complexions (Ahluwalia 2001).

This question of the state's relations with its citizens has also been marked by some eurocentrism in the ways in which differences between political and cultural traditions in 'Western' societies and those of non-Western societies are ignored or downplayed. Many western governments and international institutions seem keen to universalize their understandings of citizenship in ways which fail to recognize the variability of states and models of political membership and different notions of state–society relationships (Low 2005). The term 'citizenship' refers to 'a status as a member of a particular, usually geographically demarcated, community that allows claims to be made on its state organizations' (Low 2005: 443). From birth each individual is born into a world already divided into mutually exclusive territorial compartments, each with their own state organizations, which has major consequences in that states can differ markedly from others in their capacity for and methods of intervention to shape a society and in their responsiveness to popular needs and demands. These inherited state structures are hard to replace and radically reshape, whilst immigration legislation makes

305

it very difficult for people to move to a different territorial compartment in search of less oppressive or more responsive state institutions (Low 2005). What we need to consider here, then, is the extent to which people recognize the right of the political institutions responsible in a particular territorial state to make laws, raise taxes, to deal with other states on their behalf and to regulate economic and social institutions like firms or families. This legitimacy and authority to devise laws and policies is important here, but this is not unambiguous and not without contestation. Thus state activities are subject to sometimes fierce contestation by groups of society that question this authority and legitimacy or do not feel that there is adequate space within society to express their identities. Similarly, where visible opposition to states is seemingly more absent this does not automatically mean that states have a solid grounding in popular consent, since many people are not always fully aware of state activities or are too preoccupied with survival to express an interest either way in what 'their' states are doing (Low 2005).

Nationalism, particularly through the twentieth century, became one of the most dominant and widespread influences on world politics and is a term used to describe the feeling of belonging to an imagined national community (Anderson 1983) but also the corresponding political ideology which holds that a particular national community has a right to and a claim over a specified territorial unit. The ideology of nationalism can, however, be used to make states and their borders seem natural and justifiable and provides the basis on which many states claim to 'embody' and represent particular national communities. Such claims need to be problematized as 'society' is not a phenomenon purely defined by national state boundaries and neither should it always be assumed that states as we know them are the 'natural' units of politics (Agnew and Corbridge 1995). This comes back to our earlier point that states should not always be taken at face value and that states do not always 'fit' the labels that are attached to them or the analyses that are used to understand them. In sub-Saharan Africa, for example, states have been variously labelled in the academic literature as 'failed' or 'collapsed', as 'patrimonial' or 'clientelist', 'kleptocratic' or 'predatory', 'extractive' and even 'vampire-like' (Power 2003). The notion of a 'vampire-like' state dramatically illustrates the idea of the state as fundamentally extractive, draining away the very lifeblood of the nation and its people. To attach a simplistic label to a state, however, is to ignore the variations of ideas and opinions that can exist within the state apparatus: there are often conflicts within the state and opposition to corrupt practices, for example (Power 2004).

Some citizenship rights, such as the right to vote or to free speech and assembly, connect states and citizens in ways which are designed to make politics seem more legitimate, but others are designed to erect barriers between citizens and states by specifying what states cannot do to their citizens (such as arrest them without proper legal justification) (Low 2005). Historically, states have been organizations that have specialized in violence, and in very basic terms being a citizen involves being a part of the apparatus that provides (or sometimes fails to provide) protection from supposed internal and external 'threats'. The geographies of citizenship vary across the globe and within countries, and because states operate simultaneously at a variety of spatial scales (from local to global) these geographies are rarely confined simply to the domestic sphere and must be considered as relational. Nonetheless, within the territorially defined compartments that are nation-states, citizenship promises a chance to influence and shape the personnel and policies of state organizations in exchange for a recognition by citizens that they have responsibilities (e.g. to pay taxes, to fund state activity and to respect and obey the laws of the state). Citizenship also helps to guarantee the provision by states of benefits and services and gives citizens a vested interest in continuing and respecting established political arrangements (Low 2005). As the nature of states is itself so varied, it is difficult to generalize about the kinds of state agencies that exist in the world, which is also partly a consequence of the particular ideology adopted by each state. Typically, the state apparatus (or set of institutions and organizations through which state power is exercised) is quite varied, with a number of sub-apparatuses (see Table 19.1).

It is also worth remembering that the relationship between local and national state organizations varies considerably – in some states (where sovereignty is divided) such as in the United States, sovereignty is shared between fifty states and the federal level. In other, more 'unitary' states, sovereignty is typically held by a central national parliament (e.g. France and the UK) although newer, more regional forms of governance (such as those emanating from the European Union) have complicated this scenario somewhat (Taylor and Flint 2000). The internal territorial structure of states (especially the division of powers between local and national states) also has implications for the uneven geographies of citizenship in that the activities of 'local' states vary according to the regional problems experienced by their local citizens and the different levels of resources available to provide citizenship benefits. Chapters 20 and 21 explore these associations in greater detail. As Murray Low has argued, however, the development of citizenship has been historically as well as geographically uneven in that it has not always simultaneously been about civil, political *and* social citizenship and takes forms which vary enormously through time and between different geographical scales.

Some models of the historical evolution of citizenship argue that civil citizenship (legal and civil rights, such as access to the courts) came first and were later followed by political citizenship (rights to free speech and to vote) and then social citizenship (rights to state guarantees of socio-economic well-being). Although it is very difficult to model the historical and geographical evolution of citizenship there has been a massive expansion of state activities in the fields of social and economic policy in the twentieth century (albeit unevenly). As Low (2005: 449) has put it: 'Large scale efforts at poverty relief, the provision of income for unemployed people, minimum wages for workers and health services and education at a range of levels are largely twentieth century phenomena.' In many poor countries of the Global South the conditions needed to guarantee the establishment of social and economic

Table 19.1. The typical sub-apparatuses of the state

State function	Explanation of principal activities
Political	The set of political parties, elections, governments and constitutions
Legal	Including mechanisms for conflict resolution between competing social groups
Health/education and welfare	Basic services for the well-being of the population like schools, hospitals and unemployment benefits
Information, communications and media	Organizations seeking to allow the state to disseminate information and to oversee telecommunications and media output
Administrative	A sub-apparatus that co-ordinates and ensures compatibility between all the various other sub-apparatuses
Repressive	The mechanisms for internal and external enforcement of state power through civilian police and the armed forces
Production	Overseeing state-manufactured and state-distributed goods
Financial	Organizations that oversee fiscal and monetary arrangements and regulate economic relations
Regulatory	Organizing state interventions into non-state activities, including family and industrial relations

Source: Adapted from Johnston *et al.* (2000: 791–2).

citizenship benefits simply do not exist, and therefore attempts to create indigenous versions of European welfare systems have faced many difficulties. The uneven process of the development of citizenship is also gendered in that access to state benefits has often been based on the assumption that men are the most economically productive members of the household and therefore should be the principal recipients of state benefits like unemployment benefits and pensions. Welfare states have also therefore often been anything but gender-neutral (Low 2005). In practice, citizenship rights such as the right to vote or access to welfare benefits are not universal and access to them has been highly unequal for both men and women. In addition to gender, 'race' and nationality are also important issues here, in that states today are far more actively engaged in regulating admission to the communities within their borders; this means that citizenship benefits have been narrowed by some states through the use of immigration legislation which can be used to deny citizenship rights to migrants, for example, who are excluded on the basis of their place of birth, nationality, kinship relations with existing residents and so on (Low 2005).

Thus it is important to recognize the extent to which states 'become sites of contention' (Low 2005: 453) where citizens have increasingly come to put pressure on them to transform their activities. Some of the activities that are often considered a basic prerequisite of statehood (such as tax collection and military conscription) have therefore often been sites of intense and occasionally violent struggle, and contestation and these contexts for resistance are explored in greater detail in Chapter 57. Indeed, many of the twentieth-century citizenship benefits and rights discussed above are themselves often the product of protracted periods of struggle – struggles over the distribution of state resources (e.g. welfare benefits) or over the expression of a particular social or cultural identity (e.g. the struggles of ethnic minorities). In many ways it is precisely these struggles and relations between states and societies that enable us to better understand the roles and activities of particular states in the world today.

Globalization and the spatiality of statehood

There have been a bewildering array of theories of the state, many of which (in seeking to understand why states act in the ways they do) focus on the relations, conflicts and struggles between interest groups and social classes. In general, current analyses of the state typically distinguish between *state apparatus* (the mechanisms through which state functions are operationalized), *state form* (how a specific state structure takes different forms in different types of society, such as capitalist or socialist) and *state function* (those activities undertaken in the name of the state; Johnston *et al.* 2000). The apparatus, the form and the function of the state all matter a great deal when we think about the implications of globalization for nation-statehood. In recent years many commentators have discerned or predicted the demise or decline of the state, particularly in the context of debates about 'globalization'. In particular there is a sense that nation-states are being 'hollowed out', with power being dispersed to localities, independent organizations, and supra-national bodies (like the North American Free Trade Agreement (NAFTA) or the European Union). The implication here is that the power of the state is being subverted, eroded and superseded as a consequence of the scale and power of globalization and the transnational flows of capital, people, ideas, technologies and so on that this involves. Chapter 18 develops these arguments in greater detail. According to this viewpoint power is redistributed away from 'national states' which are now supposedly being bypassed or undermined as the principal organizers of political life as we move towards something of a 'post-national' world. Allied to this is the assumption that new spaces of governance are emerging which complicate nation-statehood by introducing new spatial scales at which governance operates. As Goodwin (2005) has argued, in the UK, for example, debates over devolution indicate that the material spaces of government and the immaterial spaces of identity both seem to be moving away from the established order of the nation-state in two directions. They are moving downwards, to a regional or sub-regional space, and upwards, to a supra-national space. Government by the United Kingdom Parliament, and a sense of British identity, is being replaced by government from Edinburgh, Cardiff or Brussels and an identity which draws on notions of being Welsh, Scottish or European (Goodwin 2005). A citizen of Edinburgh (for example) can vote in the city elections as a citizen of the city; he or she can vote in the Scottish election as a citizen of Scotland; he or she can vote in the UK elections as a citizen of the UK; he or she can vote in the European elections as a citizen of Europe and, if that is not enough, he or she can engage in any number of international non-government organizations (NGOs) campaigning on issues like the environment, human rights and so on. This is a world of multi-level politics and power and of multi-layered citizenship – at least in part (Held and McGrew 2003). The nature of state sovereignty is thus clearly changing.

In addition to the new spatial *scales* at which governance now operates, it has been argued that new *forms* of governance are starting to emerge which have implications for state–society relations. What is being suggested here is that in some states traditional government is being replaced by new forms of governance – where states have devolved power (sometimes only temporarily) to 'partnerships' between parts of the state and private actors or to non-governmental organizations (NGOs). The conclusions that follow from these debates about the new scales and forms of governance generally assume that states no longer have the same power they once had to command politics, society and economics within their own boundaries. In some ways, however, the supposed 'death' of the nation-state has been exaggerated greatly (Anderson 1995) and its pronunciation has been somewhat premature. Arguably the use of the term 'globalization' in recent years has often suggested that this a new and novel process in which states are no longer the primary units of decision-making and that it is *only now* that states are finding themselves located in something called the 'world market'. Yet this is clearly far too simplistic, in that many countries have been connected to world markets for centuries, in many cases by colonial experiences. Non-Western cultures and economies have thus been intertwined with these processes of globalization *throughout* the twentieth century rather than just at its culmination (Power 2003).

Nevertheless, new information, communication, transport and manufacturing technologies have allowed production, commerce and finance to be planned and organized on a global scale. Transnational corporations or TNCs are seen to traverse national boundaries and borders in a way that eclipses national state institutions and their capacity to 'broker' political, economic or social change within national territory. The apparent hypermobility of migrants, exiles and refugees, plus old and new identities, associations, networks and affiliations that are other than 'national', has been taken to mean that the idea of the nation-state is being challenged from all directions (Grundy-Warr and Sidaway 2005). We must, however, reject the myth of states as powerless (particularly those in the so-called 'third world') and incapacitated by the transnational forces of globalization where states are viewed as monolithic, with the state seen to have abdicated entirely its power to the world market-place in this somewhat Orwellian language of globalization. States continue to wield significant regulatory power and they still enact laws about such things as trade unions, property, business and so on. As Grundy-Warr and Sidaway (2005: 439) have put it: 'Everywhere buying a property or land or setting up a legal business require some kind of registration with the state. No amount of globalization has ended this.' Often quite sweeping generalizations have also been made about the impacts of globalization in the Global South, and so it is important to remember that this process is highly spatially uneven and differentiated and that not all places have been affected in the same way by the same transnational forces. Neither should we assume that particular regions, spaces and places simply passively accept globalization, since this precludes the possibility that there will be reactions to and even backlashes against globalization at the local level.

In some ways, then, it is important to be wary of the myth that the nation-state is nowadays some kind of 'paper tiger', whereby its roles in the world have been replaced by other actors and agents such as transnational corporations. Nonetheless, as Beck (2001) has argued, the nature of one important role of the state, to oversee national security, *has* changed markedly following the terrorist attacks on the US in 2001, such that it is no longer simply a matter of *national* security. Whilst there have always been alliances between states around security issues the crucial difference today, however, is that global alliances are necessary not just for *external* security but also for *internal* security. In other words, foreign and domestic policy, national security and international co-operation are today very much enmeshed. Thus for Beck (2001: 3):

> The distinctions between internal and external, police and army, crime and war, war and peace, which underlie our conception of the world have gone and have to be renegotiated and re-established ... the category of the nation state thereby becomes a zombie category.

Although the notion of the nation-state being some kind of moribund, 'zombie category' is highly debatable, the point Beck is trying to make is that in the face of the menace of global terrorism (but also of climate change, of migration, of organized crime, etc.) the only path to national security is by way of transnational co-operation. Paradoxically, he argues, states must *de*-nationalize and *trans*nationalize themselves for the sake of their own national interest: that is, relinquish sovereignty, in order, in a globalized world, to deal with their national problems. In the global 'war on terrorism' led by the US that has followed the 2001 terrorist attacks, the domestic, foreign and defence policies of Germany, France, Pakistan, Great Britain, Russia and many other states besides have become ever more closely interwoven (Beck 2001).

Nonetheless, the state continues to be a powerful stratifying force in the world, and if we accept that global economic integration has distributive consequences both within and outside of nation-states (where some people gain and others lose) then it becomes clear that states still matter (Held and McGrew 2003). Despite the often celebrated political and economic integration that globalization is seen to have produced in the last thirty years (in regions such as Europe or North America), there are still very different welfare state regimes in existence, which have different distributional outcomes that continue to have important implications for people and places. When we examine the variegated impacts of globalization (e.g. on economic growth, on inequality within or between nation-states) it is very difficult to conclude that national politics are no longer important. States can, in their territorial spaces, still make a significant difference to levels of poverty and inequality; they still have the capacity to empower citizens, to increase national economic competitiveness and to ameliorate the worst consequences of exposure to the world economic market (Held and McGrew 2003).

The crucial point to recognize here, then, is that we live in a world where politics is now multi-level and multi-layered, where political power is being significantly reconfigured. Powerful states, such as the US state, still have a distinctive capacity to make and break rule systems with coercive consequences as seen in the US response to terrorist attacks on US territory. This is not to cling to some outdated notion that the nation-state remains the only political container that still matters, since it remains one of many important political containers. The decisions that a powerful state like the US chooses to take or not to take have important global consequences for multilateralism (the notion that states should work together toward common goals through organizations such as the United Nations) for the possibility of global trade reform, international poverty eradication, the global environment and so on. Thus the asymmetries of power between the US and other less influential states still continue to impact in important ways upon a number of major global issues such as terrorism, global warming or international trade and development (Held and McGrew 2003). Large and powerful states, such as the US and China, are still the primary loci of decisions about war and peace and still hold vast arsenals of nuclear, chemical and conventional weapons. The G8 organization is a good example of these asymmetrical power relations in action in that the G8 is a group made up of the world's wealthiest countries including the UK, the US, Russia, France, Canada, Italy, Germany and Japan. At recent G8 meetings (such as the summit held in Gleneagles, Scotland in July 2005) there has been an enormous amount of hype about the capacity of just eight men (the leaders of the world's 'most powerful' states) to 'make poverty history' and to take far-reaching decisions which supposedly will change the course of world history (through decisions about trade, debt, climate change and so on; see also Chapter 18). Although the G8's capacity to effect global change on issues like trade, debt and poverty has often been overstated, there remains a popular concern that the G8 leaders have almost too much power and influence and a strong belief in the need to harness this concentrated power and influence for progressive ends, such as the cancellation of the debts owed by the world's poorest countries. Only time will tell if the leaders of just eight states can truly 'make poverty history' or if a more long-term solution requires a much wider degree of collaboration and participation as well as a new kind of multilateralism.

Further reading

Agnew, J. (2002) *Making Political Geography*. London: Arnold.

Anderson, J. (1995) The exaggerated death of the nation-state. In J. Anderson, C. Brook and A. Cochrane (eds) (1995) *A Global World? Re-ordering Political Space*, pp. 65–112. Oxford: Oxford University Press and the Open University.

Braden, K.E. and Shelley, F.M. (2000) *Engaging Geopolitics*. London: Pearson.

Goodwin, M. (2005) Citizenship and governance. In P. Cloke, P. Crang and M. Goodwin (eds) *Introducing Human Geographies*, pp. 189–98. London: Arnold.

Grundy-Warr, C. and Sidaway, J.D. (2005) The place of the nation-state. In P. Daniels, M. Bradshaw, D. Shaw and J.D. Sidaway (eds) *An Introduction to Human Geography: Issues for the Twenty-first Century*, pp. 422–41. London: Pearson.

Low, M. (2005) States, citizenship and collective action. In P. Daniels, M. Bradshaw, D. Shaw and J.D. Sidaway (eds) *An Introduction to Human Geography: Issues for the Twenty-first Century*, pp. 443–65. London: Pearson.

Mann, M. (1993) *The Sources of Social Power, Volume II: The Rise of Classes and Nation-States, 1760–1914*. Cambridge: Cambridge University Press.

Power, M. (2003) *Rethinking Development Geographies*. London: Routledge.

Taylor, P.J. and Flint, C. (2000) *Political Geography: World-Economy, Nation-State, Locality*, fourth edition. Prentice Hall: London.

References

Agnew, J. (2002) *Making Political Geography*. London: Arnold.

Agnew, J. and Corbridge, S. (1995) *Mastering Space: Hegemony, Territory and International Political Economy*. London: Routledge.

Ahluwalia, P. (2001) *Politics and Post-colonial Theory: African Inflections*. London: Routledge.

Akzin, B. (1964) *State and Nation*. London: Hutchinson.

Anderson, B. (1983) *Imagined Communities: Reflections on the Origin and Spread of Nationalism*. London: Verso.

Anderson, J. (1995) The exaggerated death of the nation–state. In J. Anderson, C. Brook and A. Cochrane (eds) *A Global World? Re-ordering Political Space*, pp. 65–112. Oxford: Oxford University Press and the Open University.

Beck, U. (2001) The cosmopolitan state: towards a realistic utopia. *Eurozine*, 12 May. Available at http://www.eurozine.com/article/2001-12-05-beck-en.html (accessed 12 August 2005).

Braden, K.E. and Shelley, F.M. (2000) *Engaging Geopolitics*. London: Pearson.

Goodwin, M. (2005) Citizenship and governance. In P. Cloke, P. Crang and M. Goodwin (eds) *Introducing Human Geographies*, pp. 189–98. London: Arnold.

Grundy-Warr, C. and Sidaway, J.D. (2005) The place of the nation-state. In P. Daniels, M. Bradshaw, D. Shaw and J.D. Sidaway (eds) *An Introduction to Human Geography: Issues for the Twenty-first Century*, pp. 422–41. London: Pearson.

Held, D. and McGrew, A. (eds) (2003) *The Global Transformations Reader*. London: Polity Press.

Hoogevelt, A. (1997) *Globalisation and Postcolonialism*. London: Macmillan.

Johnston, R.J., Gregory, D., Pratt, G. and Watts, M. (eds) (2000) *The Dictionary of Human Geography*. London: Blackwell.

Low, M. (2005) States, citizenship and collective action. In P. Daniels, M. Bradshaw, D. Shaw and J.D. Sidaway (eds) *An Introduction to Human Geography: Issues for the Twenty-first Century*, pp. 443–65. London: Pearson.

Mamdani, M. (1996) *Citizen and Subject*. Princeton: Princeton University Press.

Ó Tuathail, G. (1996) *Critical Geopolitics: The Politics of Writing Global Space*. London: Routledge.

Peet, R. with Hartwick, E. (1999) *Theories of Development*. London: Guilford.

Power, M. (2003) *Rethinking Development Geographies*. London: Routledge.

——(2004) Geographies of governance and regional politics. In D. Potts and T. Bowyer-Bower (eds) *Eastern and Southern Africa: Development Challenges in a Volatile Region*, pp. 255–94. London: Pearson.

Taylor, P.J. and Flint, C. (2000) *Political Geography: World-Economy, Nation-State, Locality*, fourth edition. London: Prentice Hall.

Thomson, J.E. (1994) *Mercenaries, Pirates and Sovereigns: State-building and Extra-Territorial Violence in Early Modern Europe*. Princeton: Princeton University Press.

20

Regional initiatives and responses

Martin Jones

Geographers have always had a fascination with the shifting territorial contours of the state. Words such as 'devolution', 'federalism' and 'region' are central to the geographer's lexicon and mark the boundaries of this discipline. The 'regional concept' (Dickinson 1976), for instance, has been highly relevant for the construction of theory, the formulation of public policy, and for the delivery of a geography relevant for both academic and lay audiences. This 'regional appeal' is set to continue, with geographers arguing for new ways of looking at regions (Amin 2004; Paasi 1996) and with politicians and policy-makers mobilizing regions as preferred scales for socio-economic development (HM Treasury, DTI and ODPM 2003; Katz 2000).

In thinking about these topics, Charles Fawcett showed the way forward in his book *Provinces of England: A Study of Some Geographical Aspects of Devolution* (Fawcett 1919). This academic and political text of unique scholarship aimed to distinguish and delimit 'regions of everyday life' – a timely endeavour given calls for devolution in relation to the 'Irish Question'. Fawcett used his twin interests, the geography of England and political geography more broadly, to review the potential and practicalities for administrative devolution. The book was, however, more than just about England. Its text is perhaps more relevant today than at the time of publication, for the early twenty-first century will be known as the era of devolution and constitutional change – with major rounds of state restructuring taking place across the globe, producing new relationships between central state power and regional agendas (Rodríguez-Pose and Gill 2003). The eminent geographer Michael Storper (1997) has even suggested that we are now living in a 'regional world', where regional economies are the building blocks for a networked, interconnected and global state of being. This chapter is concerned with exploring this 'region world' but, in contrast to Storper's focus on the geographies of firms and regions, I am more interested in how the scale and nature of political organization constitutes our economies.

New regional agendas: geography and states

As we saw in the previous chapter, the inter-state system initially instituted by the Treaty of Westphalia in 1648 – whereby nation-states commanded a monopoly of legitimate power within their self-enclosed and mutually exclusive borders, and with this constructed national citizens as political subjects – has been fundamentally challenged by organizations and processes lying within and outside the boundaries of the state. In short, and demonstrated throughout this chapter, the national state system position as a shaper of economic and political processes, and the anchor for social and cultural identities, is being fundamentally challenged through a series of 'new regionalist' territorial developments (Brenner *et al.* 2003). This is not to say that these scales are now dominant and/or did not play a role previously within the construction of a national state space. They are instead involved in the intense process of jockeying for an increased role in the instillation of new territorial governance.

This process is working itself out differently in different national (and post-national) geographical contexts. Scholars frequently highlight two contrasting models, with each allowing a different mode of subsidiarity, but in both cases foreign policy and key aspects of fiscal policy are retained by the centre as devolution rarely gives away the kernel of state power (see Harvie 1994; Keating 1998). In federal nations – such as Germany and the United States – provincial authorities formulate and deliver policy across a wide range of public policies. By contrast, more centralized nations – such as the United Kingdom, until the late 1990s – retain power at the centre and devolve less power down through regional and local scales.

Rather than provide a global survey of this spectrum, which would ultimately gloss over the complex and interrelated links between politics and geography, this chapter draws on developments in Britain to explore different regional initiatives and responses co-existing in the same sovereign political space. The British state has been undergoing major structural and strategic changes, with a unitary system of government being gradually replaced by a quasi-federal system, and this provides a global window on key political geographical processes in motion (Goodwin *et al.* 2005). To illustrate this, the remainder of the chapter discusses regional responses and initiatives in the field of economic governance, thus connecting with discussions in Chapters 12 and 30. This concern for geographical specificity provides a link back to the work of Fawcett (1919) and the chapter also seeks to demonstrate the relevance of regional studies in a global world. This latter concern is particularly evident in the following quotation.

> We are all localists now. Centralism has come to be synonymous with bureaucracy, rigidity and control freakery. These vices are contrasted with the virtues of local and regional diversity, creativity and innovativeness. The beauty of devolved government is that it *can do things differently.*
>
> (Walker 2002: 5, emphasis added)

The above quotation from the British journalist and social commentator David Walker sums up many of the concerns of this chapter. The territories of Scotland, Wales, Northern Ireland and England – armed with a Parliament (Scotland), Elected Assemblies (Wales, Northern Ireland, and London), Regional Development Agencies and strengthened Government Offices for the Regions (England) – provide the basis for doing things differently. The New Labour Party, elected in 1997 and under the leadership of Tony Blair, sees devolution and constitutional change as furthering modernization to safeguard the socio-economic and political future of this United Kingdom. Devolution represents a considerable and irreversible shake-up to the British and UK state apparatus. In the words of Vernon Bogdanor, we are witnessing 'the most radical constitutional change this country has seen since the Great Reform Act of 1832' (Bogdanor 1999: 1). This Act set in motion a modern democratic state.

One way of exploring regional responses and initiatives triggered by this is to focus on 'economic governance' – the term that captures the ongoing interactions between markets, policies, institutions and networks, with our attention focused on frameworks and mechanisms of: infrastructure and site provision; capital formation and investment regimes; fiscal regimes and financial management; innovation, entrepreneurship and technology policy; labour markets, pay and skill formation. The question of economic governance, then, refers to the mobilization of available institutional and productive resources to develop a coherent overall sense of economic identity. The complex interrelationships between economic governance and devolution and vice versa are important questions for researchers and practitioners of human geography, and I can only touch on some of these here.

Academic writings in recent years have drawn our attention to different 'varieties' of capitalism and economic governance, such as neocorporatist, neo-statist, neo-Schumpeterian, and neoliberal approaches (Jessop 2002). In the last case, the optimal mechanism for practising economic governance is one with open, competitive and unregulated markets – liberated from most forms of state interference. Of course, over the past century there have been no states in the West that have fully aimed at suppressing markets: they have always, and in a variety of ways, aimed at organizing them. In contrast, there have been, and there can be, no markets that do not rely on some rules they cannot themselves set. The key point is rather that there are always both a plurality of modes of economic governance and a variety of forms of state. Late twentieth-century UK was characterized by neoliberal economic governance and its ongoing weaknesses played a large part in the Conservative Party's fall from power. The ascendancy of the New Labour Party is based around a 'third way' alternative; with faith being placed in the spatial and territorial reorganization of the national state apparatus to deliver public policy and *revive* state, economy and civil society (Giddens 2002).

Devolution – the relative transfer of power and responsibility from the nation-state downwards to other units of government and governance – follows from this philosophy, is an increasingly prevalent global phenomenon, and better economic governance is frequently cited as a justification of devolution. Decentralized approaches tailored to sub-national, regional and local circumstances are considered better able to address the continuing problems caused by entrenched territorial inequalities in growth, income and employment. Additionally, decentralized structures are expected to deliver an enhanced, democratized, political settlement that renders economic development institutions more open and accountable to local, regional and sub-national territorial circumstances. These processes, however, do not operate in a spatial vacuum: territories are never empty but are filled with pre-existing policies and their legacies. Devolution thus has profound implications for the nature and practice of economic governance: it provides political space for adjusting and altering existing trajectories of economic governance. In turn, the 'success' of economic governance has consequences for further rounds of devolution, set within the limits of constitutional change. In short, devolution and economic governance are opposite sides of the same coin.

Devolution, constitutional change and economic governance

The chapter will now provide an overview of the major changes that have occurred to the institutions of economic governance across the UK following devolution. The text should be read in conjunction with Figures 20.1–20.4, which are based on research undertaken with colleagues (see Goodwin *et al.* 2005) and provide institutional maps of the post-devolution

315

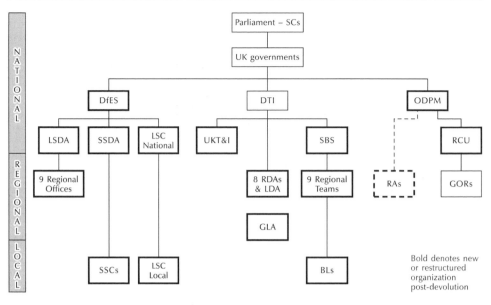

Figure 20.1. Post-devolution administrative structures in England.

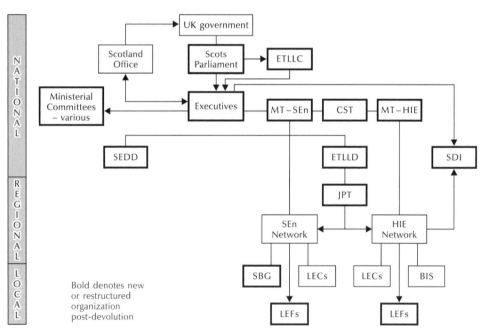

Figure 20.2. Post-devolution administrative structures in Scotland.

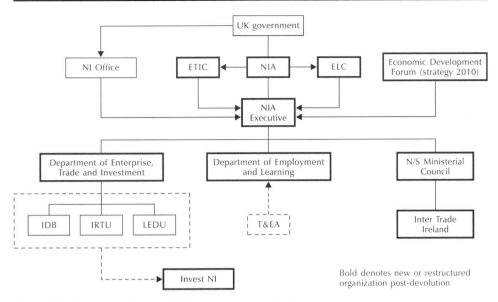

Figure 20.3. Post-devolution administrative structures in Northern Ireland.

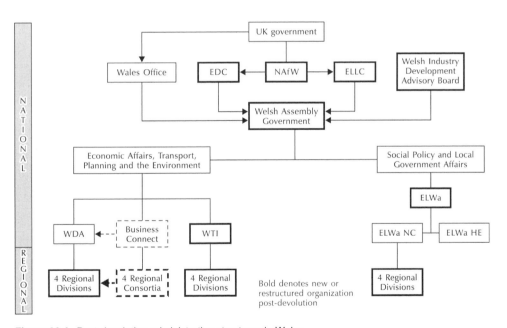

Figure 20.4. Post-devolution administrative structures in Wales.

structures of economic governance in each devolved territory. These illustrate clearly that different regional initiatives and responses have been implemented since 1997. Key questions are how and why this has happened, and if this is important for the future of the national state.

As suggested previously, the devolution settlement established new state structures in the form of a Scottish Parliament, Elected Assemblies for Wales, Northern Ireland and London, and Regional Development Agencies within the English regions. In some senses this process provided each territory with an outline of a new form of the state, the precise shape and contents of which would depend on social and political forces acting within Northern Ireland, Scotland, Wales and England. Significantly, economic development was one of the policy areas devolved to these new institutions and these actors could, of course, have left the structures of economic governance untouched; there was no necessary reason why state restructuring should have proceeded any further. The new Parliament in Edinburgh and Assemblies in Belfast, Cardiff and London could have simply taken charge of the existing structures. However, research has revealed the considerable political pressures that emerged in each territory as the newly devolved administrations sought to place their own stamp on policy development – pressures which resulted in a completely new configuration of economic governance. But before discussing events after 1997, the pre-existing institutional and political scene in the four territories is briefly considered, as the processes and relations of devolution inevitably built on these legacies. Geography matters.

Economic governance pre-devolution

England is renowned as an 'enigma' within the territorial politics of a devolved UK. Nowhere is this more apparent than in the context of economic governance. At one level, the economic development of England is often conflated with broader policies relevant to the whole of the UK. In contrast, economic development is further devolved to regional bodies such as the Government Offices for the Regions. As a result, many of the key institutions involved in economic development before 1997 in England were based either at a unitary UK scale or at a more regional scale. The consequence of this is that there was little territorial integrity for economic development at the scale of England, and indeed no discrete economic development strategy for England as a territorial entity.

Scotland possesses a relatively long history in a UK context of economic development initiatives and institutional development, which can be partially related to its distinct institutional settlement (a Scottish Office being created in 1885, with functional responsibilities from the 1960s) and its diverse economic history (Keating 2005). In the post-war period, the performance of the Scottish economy was below that of the UK mean, and following agitation from the left and the Scottish trades union movement, a number of regional policy initiatives were instigated by central government as a means of redressing the problem. In response to further economic decline and long-standing agitation from trade unions, and later Scottish nationalists, the government created the Scottish Development Agency (SDA) in 1975, as a means of enhancing economic development within Scotland. However, the Thatcherite UK government favoured an 'enterprise culture' and Highlands and Islands Enterprise and Scottish Enterprise were created to formulate and deliver training and enterprise policy. This relatively long institutional legacy in Scotland with regard to economic development demonstrates clearly issues of path dependency in the evolution of new institutions within the overall framework of devolution. Geography again matters.

There has been a long-standing recognition of *Northern Ireland* as a separate administrative entity within the UK state. A parliament existed here between partition in 1921 and the installation, because of civic unrest, of 'direct rule' in 1972. At this point, the Office of the Secretary of State (NIO) was formed, with overall responsibility for the government of the territory. The NIO dealt with a broad range of responsibilities from this period onwards, including: economic and social policy; constitutional and security issues, including law and order; political affairs; and policing and criminal justice. The Northern Ireland Assembly (NIA), then, has a considerably wider scope for action when compared with the National Assembly for Wales (NAfW). Perhaps as a result of the longer legacy of administrative devolution in Northern Ireland, the NIA possesses the ability to legislate on matters reserved for Westminster, subject to approval by the Secretary of State and Parliamentary controls.

Wales has a relatively short history of administrative devolution when compared to Scotland and Northern Ireland, if not England (Cooke and Clifton 2005). The Welsh Office (WO), the specific government office concerned with the territory of Wales, was formed in 1965. As in Scotland, a Development Agency was created during the 1970s, following internal pressure from left-wing and nationalist causes. The relatively narrow policy remit of the WO, especially when compared to the NIO, has had some impact on the later responsibilities devolved to the NAfW. The NAfW has responsibility for health, education and training, transport, planning, economic development and local government and social policy, but possesses only a secondary legislative capability. Economic policy pre-devolution was based on a number of institutions. At the head of the apex lay the WO and the Secretary of State for Wales, and the primary implementation bodies were the Welsh Development Agency (WDA), the Development Board for Rural Wales (DBRW) covering mid-Wales, and the Land Authority for Wales (LAW). Broadly speaking, the WDA and DBRW possessed the responsibility for capital investments and area-based regeneration. The WDA alone dealt with inward investment whilst the LAW was concerned with land acquisition, assembly and site infrastructure. The other main strand of economic policy was centred on the role of the four Training and Enterprise Councils (TECs) and their role in promoting vocational training within the business community.

Economic governance post-devolution

As might be expected of new institutions seeking to make a political mark, significant changes were made to the political and administrative structures operating at an Assembly and Parliamentary level. New regional initiatives and responses have emerged, with their geographies shaped by social and political forces operating in and through the state at new territorial scales.

In Northern Ireland, for instance, the Training and Employment Agency (T&EA), formerly under the remit of the Department for Economic Development (DED), was immediately absorbed into a new Department of Employment and Learning (DEL). As part of this 'making a difference', the new Assembly established a Department of Enterprise, Trade and Investment (DETI) alongside the Department of Employment and Learning together with their respective Committees (see Figure 20.3). Taking over the majority of functions of the previous DED (other than training) DETI is concerned with providing an appropriate framework for strengthening economic development across Northern Ireland. DEL has responsibility for higher and further education, vocational training employment services, labour relations and training grants. Again there was a political motive suggested for this re-organization, as new forces were gaining access to the new scales of the state.

The Scottish Executive also shows how political pressures can stimulate organizational change. Commentators characterized the pre-devolution situation as one of 'benign neglect', where the institutions of economic governance received written guidance from a minister operating as part of a UK government, but were then left to 'develop their own strategies'. In contrast to this, the Scottish Parliament established a new department and committee structure to oversee economic development (see Figure 20.2; Parry and Jones 2000). The Enterprise and Lifelong Learning Department, along with an Enterprise and Lifelong Learning Committee, took over most of the responsibilities of the business and industry policy functions of the former Scottish Office, together with responsibilities for Lifelong Learning and Further and Higher Education policy. More responsibilities followed in 2003 with the formation of the Enterprise, Transport and Lifelong Learning Department (expanding the remit of ELLD). Other key developments within the Scottish Executive include the formation of Ministerial Taskforces, including one launched to give greater ministerial oversight at a national level of the operation of Local Economic Forums (a post-devolution development in economic governance networking – see later) and the creation of the Joint Performance Teams to set 'stretching' targets for the delivery agencies of Highlands and Islands Enterprise and Scottish Enterprise.

In Wales, the National Assembly has also established new departments and committees in order to oversee economic governance (see Figure 20.4). Again, there was a political desire by those who now had access to the levers of power, that these should be used to facilitate a coordinated strategy, which would suit the new territorial scale of governance. Thus instead of being seen as effectively the regional office of London (Whitehall), there was a deliberate move to focus the activities of economic governance on the key goals of the National Assembly's strategic plan for Wales. Accordingly, the Assembly set up a Ministry and Committee for Economic Development, covering national economic matters, including indigenous and inward investment, European economic policy (including structural funds), industrial policy and business support, tourism and urban development and regeneration. For much of the life of the Assembly, the First Minister has also held the economic development portfolio, illustrating its political importance. It also established a new Ministry and Committee of Education and Lifelong Learning. The portfolio for this ministry involves the delivery of all publicly funded education, training, and skills development policy.

England remains an 'enigma' within the territorial politics of a devolved UK. Despite devolution, there remain no dedicated economic governance structures at the scale of England as a whole. England is sandwiched between the government's various UK-wide policies and the activities of regional scale institutions such as the Government Offices and the Regional Development Agencies. The DTI and ODPM, however, are widely recognized as being almost exclusively English departments, but confusion exists over whether/how they should incorporate the 'devolved territories', and vice versa. With the exception of activists campaigning in the North East and South West for regional autonomy, England has not been subject to the same kinds of territorial cultural-political pressures felt within Northern Ireland, Scotland and Wales to reform its institutions of economic governance. The main driving force has instead been the politically driven restructuring of a number of Whitehall ministries – some in the aftermath of New Labour's second election victory in 2001, and some as the result of Westminster political reshuffling in the middle of 2002. Although this restructuring has occurred at a UK level, these changes are impacting on the character of England's economic governance.

First, in June 2001 the Department for Education and Employment was restructured and its functions transferred to a Department for Education and Skills and the Department for Work and Pensions (previously the Department of Social Security). Second, the Department of Transport, Local Government and the Regions (DTLR) was also restructured. In May

2002, a separate Department of Transport was (re)created, and responsibility for local government and the regions was given to the newly created Office of the Deputy Prime Minister (ODPM) at the same time – although the Department of Trade and Industry (DTI)
took over from the DTLR as the sponsoring department for the RDAs. Thus, three UK
government departments have significant responsibility for regional economic development
within England – the DfES, DTI and ODPM – although on-the-ground actors feel there is
confusion over policy responsibilities (see Goodwin *et al.* 2005).

Implementation: new regional responses

These strategic-political changes at Assembly and Parliamentary levels have been accompanied by varying degrees of state restructuring on the ground, where policies are implemented. There is no necessary or *a priori* reason why this should have happened under
devolution. These changes are being driven by political developments that are fuelling the
creation of new strategies and associated policies. Geography again matters.

   As might be expected, England has shown the least changes as a direct result of
devolution – outside of establishing 'strategic' Regional Development Agencies, accompanying Regional Chambers (also known as unelected Regional Assemblies), and regional-
scale administrative structures for its UK ministries (see Figure 20.1). Learning and Skills
Councils (LSCs) were established in April 2001 but were planned before devolution; they
followed Labour's review of skills policy. They are responsible for the planning, funding, and
management of post-sixteen education and training outside the higher education sector.
Significantly, below a national LSC, there is a network of 47 local LSCs which have taken
over the funding of colleges and other institutions in the FE sector, the work-based training
tasks of the Training and Enterprise Councils, the funding of school sixth forms and the
responsibility for adult and community learning – previously based with the Local Education
Authorities. In tandem with the RDAs, the LSCs are at the front of the government's drive
to secure effective economic development by harnessing the benefits of a 'knowledge-driven
economy'. This has, however, resulted in a complex series of differently scaled institutions on
the ground in England with a remit of economic governance. Spatial tensions were inherent
when researchers examined the issues of collaboration and competition between different
agencies (see Jones *et al.* 2004).

   The other three territories have witnessed more significant post-devolution changes at an
implementation level, but somewhat ironically these have been driven by a desire to impart
the kind of territorial co-ordination that seems a problem in England. Northern Ireland, for
instance, has witnessed an almost complete change in the institutions that deliver economic
development policy (see Figure 20.3). *Strategy 2010*, commissioned before devolution,
argued that economic development in Northern Ireland should be addressed by one lead
agency. This was subsequently accepted and acted upon by the new Assembly (see special
edition of *Local Economy* (2001)). Part of this acceptance was again linked to the political
forces now able to operate through the state in Northern Ireland following devolution.

   Invest Northern Ireland (INI) was accordingly established in April 2002 to operate as a
Non-Departmental Public Body sponsored by the DETI, and took on the functions of
almost all the other institutions previously concerned with aspects of economic development
in Northern Ireland. These include the Local Enterprise Development Unit, the Industrial
Development Board and the Industrial Research and Technology Unit. In addition, this new
agency incorporates the role of the Company Development Programme (formerly with the
Training and Employment Agency) and the business development functions of the Northern

Ireland Tourist Board. As noted previously, the Training and Employment Agency, formerly within the remit of the Department of Economic Development, has now been transferred to the Department of Employment and Learning. This is a reflection of political reality – the need to create enough government departments for the four political parties operating within a power-sharing structure.

This is to be contrasted with Scotland, where economic governance is being driven by the *integration* of strategy, policy and delivery through the Scottish Parliament and Scottish Executive – particularly via FDSS (the Framework for Economic Development in Scotland) and SSS (Smart, Successful Scotland). The first strategy sets the debate, vision and parameters of economic governance, whereas the second is a detailed implementation framework for driving, amongst other things, the enterprise network. As Figure 20.2 indicates, fewer new institutions have been formed in Scotland to implement and deliver economic development policies at a local level (see also Keating 2005). Social policy and regeneration, however, has witnessed the creation of Communities Scotland, Careers Scotland and Future Skills Scotland. A lighter touch, though, has occurred in economic governance, by taking ownership of existing structures and networks.

The only new implementation structures of economic governance in Scotland are the Local Economic Forums (LEFs), formed to facilitate cohesion and counter the congestion, confusion, overlap and duplication that was said to exist with regard to local economic development prior to devolution. Following a review in 2004, LEFs were flagged as local delivery mechanisms for lifelong learning, improvements to labour market co-ordination, and community planning (Audit Scotland 2004). Another post-devolution change relates to the Local Enterprise Companies (LECs). Originally created as a means of delivering the enterprise and employment projects, the Executive changed the constitution of LECs from private sector companies limited by guarantee to being public bodies. LECs are now subsidiaries of SE and HIE, and as such their staff are employees of these core organizations, to make the LECs more accountable to the new territorial scale of governance and bring them within the legislative framework of the new Parliament. Finally, the institutions concerned with Scotland's international linkages have been merged in 2001. Locate in Scotland, the institution concerned with attracting foreign investment into Scotland, and Scottish Trade International, concerned with encouraging the trade of Scottish goods abroad, have merged into one institution, Scottish Development International. This single institution has taken on the functions of both its predecessors and may demonstrate a more holistic attitude to Scotland's overseas linkages, post-devolution.

In Wales, the National Assembly initially operated through a mixture of new and pre-existing delivery institutions (see Figure 20.4). The Welsh Development Agency assumed the functions of the Development Board for Rural Wales and the Land Authority for Wales in 1998, combining responsibility for capital investments and area-based regeneration with rural development and land acquisition to form a new 'Powerhouse' agency (Morgan and Mungham 2000). The WDA also added the business support functions of Business Connect to its remit, and took over responsibility for Wales Trade International designed to promote the export of Welsh products and services. A key new institution post-devolution was Education and Learning Wales (ELWa). This was formed under the Learning and Skills Act 2000, which also formed LSCs in England, to deal with all aspects of post-sixteen education and training in Wales. As such, ELWa took over the training responsibilities of the TECs, and also incorporated the responsibilities of the Higher Education Funding Council for Wales and the Further Education Council for Wales within its remit. However, in 2004 it was proposed that the operations of ELWa and the WDA be taken back into relevant divisions of the Welsh Assembly under the infamous 'bonfire of the quangos' (see *Western Mail* 15 July 2004). This transfers political power back to the Assembly – although economic governance is still limited by budgets and the lack of fiscal powers – and illustrates the complex nature of governance after devolution.

An important policy experiment in Wales post-devolution has been to regionalize the governance of economic development. This formed a strong contrast with practice in Scotland, where the Scottish Executive has continued to act through two regional agencies covering Highland and Lowland Scotland, and with practice in Northern Ireland, where the Northern Ireland Assembly operates largely through agencies covering the whole province. Building mainly on the work of the Regional Economic Development Fora, and the National Assembly Committee areas, four regions have become key spaces in the political and economic geographies of Wales: North Wales, Mid Wales, South West Wales and South East Wales. Much of the operation of both the WDA and ELWa was based on this emerging regional structure. This is especially the case with ELWa, which had four regional offices, with only a small central corporate national team. Regionalization seems to demonstrate a spatial rather than a sectoral approach towards the delivery of economic development. The drive to regionalization within Wales can be partly explained by the political sensitivities towards devolution within the territory and a corresponding wariness of efforts to centralize activities in Cardiff, given the abolition of LAW and DBRW (Morgan and Mungham 2000), and the desire to divide Wales into management territorial units for 'sustainable spatial development' is also important (Welsh Assembly Government 2004).

Conclusions

This chapter has used Britain as a window through which to view new regional agendas and initiatives that are emerging as part of constitutional change, devolution and economic governance. It has looked at each UK territory in turn, but it is useful to draw these arguments together so as to summarize the overall significance of these changes.

At a basic level, devolution in the UK has certainly been followed by a remaking, and indeed a rescaling, of the institutions responsible for formulating and implementing economic policy. These changes, though, have not just been the result of any simple transfer of power and functions from the UK scale to each individual territory, altering in the process the pathways of subsidiarity. What we are witnessing is a very complex rescaling of governance, both vertically, between scales, and horizontally, between institutions operating over the same territory. This is partly because the asymmetrical devolution witnessed within the UK has meant that these new spatial divisions are themselves *uneven* across the four devolved territories. Attempts at rationalization have occurred, both at a formal governmental level, and at a more local scales where policies are delivered. But these have proceeded very differently in each territory, influenced by the political forces able to formulate and articulate different regional agendas.

Given that the institutional forms within any territory affect its ability to 'pin down' or 'embed' global processes of economic development (see Chapter 22), this institutional unevenness – caused by the precise parameters and delineations of the different regional agendas – also possesses the potential to create uneven capacities to act and uneven patterns of economic success and/or failure. If this is the case, then the changing patterns of economic governance within the UK after devolution may well have implications far wider than economic development alone. They could influence the perceived success or failure of the devolution project as a whole. Concordats do exist between territories and central government over certain policy areas, but are not particularly significant for agencies concerned with economic development in the four territories (cf. Trench 2001).

Asymmetrical devolution, then, can contribute to significant *economic* tensions by creating uneven capacities within institutions of the various devolved territories. Warning signs of such uneven capacities are evident and there are emerging tensions, associated *inter alia* with: frustrations for not being able to fully control funding flowing through English regions (Morgan 2002); arguments for loosening the leash on the 'red dragon' by giving more economic autonomy to the Welsh Assembly (for discussions, see Richard Commission 2004); claims for 'full fiscal autonomy' in Scotland beyond its current devolved economic governance settlement (*Scottish Affairs* 2002); the return of debates on differential territorial funding in relation to the Barnett formula (Heald and McLeod 2005); and ongoing concerns that devolution is creating increased inter-territorial economic competition (McGregor and Swales 2005). It is important for human geography and regional studies to investigate how these issues are resolved. Research will help determine the future of this (devolved) Union but will also contribute to understanding the national and global significance of other regional initiatives and responses.

Acknowlegements

This chapter draws on research undertaken as part of a wider project entitled 'Constitutional Change and Governance: Territories and Institutions', which was funded by the Economic and Social Research Council (Grant L219252013). I would also like to thank my colleagues on this project, Mark Goodwin and Rhys Jones, for allowing me to draw on our collective research.

Further reading

Amin, A. (2004) Regions unbound: towards a new politics of place. *Geografiska Annaler* 86, 33–44.

Brenner, N., Jessop, B., Jones, M. and MacLeod, G. (eds) (2003) *State/Space: A Reader.* Oxford: Blackwell.

Goodwin, M., Jones, M. and Jones, R. (2005) Devolution, constitutional change and economic development: explaining and understanding the new institutional geographies of the British state. *Regional Studies* 39, 421–36.

HM Treasury, DTI and ODPM (2003) *A Modern Regional Policy for the United Kingdom.* London: HMSO.

Rodríguez-Pose, A. and Gill, N. (2003) The global trend towards devolution and its implications. *Environment and Planning A* 21, 333–51.

References

Amin, A (2004) Regions unbound: towards a new politics of place. *Geografiska Annaler* 86, 33–44.

Audit Scotland (2004) Questions raised about the future of local economic forum. Press release 10 June, Audit Scotland, Edinburgh.

Bogdanor, V. (1999) *Devolution in the United Kingdom.* Oxford: Oxford University Press.

Brenner, N., Jessop, B., Jones, M. and MacLeod, G. (eds) (2003) *State/Space: A Reader.* Oxford: Blackwell.

Cooke, P. and Clifton, N. (2005) Visionary, precautionary and constrained 'varieties of devolution' in the economic governance of the devolved UK territories. *Regional Studies* 39, 437–51.

Dickinson, R. (1976) *Regional Concept: Anglo-American Leaders*. London: Routledge and Kegan Paul.

Fawcett, C.B. (1919) *Provinces of England: A Study of Some Geographical Aspects of Devolution*. London: Hutchinson.

Giddens, A. (2002) *Where Now for New Labour?* Cambridge: Polity.

Goodwin, M., Jones, M. and Jones, R. (2005) Devolution, constitutional change and economic development: explaining and understanding the new institutional geographies of the British state. *Regional Studies* 39, 421–36.

Harvie, C. (1994) *The Rise of Regional Europe*. London: Routledge.

Heald, D. and McLeod, A. (2005) Embeddedness and UK devolution finance within the public expenditure system. *Regional Studies* 39, 495–518.

HM Treasury, DTI and ODPM (2003) *A Modern Regional Policy for the United Kingdom*. London: HMSO.

Jessop, B. (2002) *The Future of the Capitalist State*. Cambridge: Polity.

Jones, R., Goodwin, M., Jones, R. and Pett, K. (2004) Devolution, state personnel, and the production of new territories of governance in the United Kingdom. *Environment and Planning A* 36, 89–109.

Katz, B. (ed.) (2000) *Reflections on Regionalism*. Washington DC: Brookings Institution.

Keating, M. (1998) *The New Regionalism in Western Europe*. Cheltenham: Elgar.

——(2005) *The Government of Scotland*. Edinburgh: Edinburgh University Press.

Local Economy (2001) Special issue: economic development in Northern Ireland. *Local Economy* 16, 2–71.

McGregor, A. and Swales, K. (2005) Economics of devolution/decentralisation in the UK: some questions and answers. *Regional Studies* 39, 477–94.

Morgan, K. (2002) The English question: regional perspectives on a fractured nation. *Regional Studies* 36, 797–810.

Morgan, K. and Mungham, G. (2000) *Redesigning Democracy*. Bridgend: Seren.

Paasi, A. (1996) *Territories, Boundaries and Consciousness: The Changing Geographies of the Finnish–Russian Border*. Chichester: Wiley.

Parry, R. and Jones, A. (2000) The transition from the Scottish Office to the Scottish Executive. *Public Policy and Administration* 15, 53–66.

Richard Commission (2004) *Report of the Richard Commission on the Powers and Electoral Arrangements of the National Assembly for Wales*. Cardiff: National Assembly for Wales.

Rodríguez-Pose, A. and Gill, N. (2003) The global trend towards devolution and its implications. *Environment and Planning A* 21, 333–51.

Scottish Affairs (2002) Special issue on fiscal autonomy. *Scottish Affairs* 41.

Storper, M. (1997) *The Regional World: Territorial Development in a Global Economy* New York: Guilford.

Trench, A. (ed.) (2001) *The State of the Nations 2001: The Second Year of Devolution in the United Kingdom*. Exeter: Imprint Academic.

Walker, D. (2002) *In Praise of Centralism: A Critique of the New Localism*. London: Catalyst.

Welsh Assembly Government (2004) *People, Places, Futures – The Wales Spatial Plan*. Cardiff: Welsh Assembly Government.

21

Urban policy and politics

Kevin Ward

Introduction

From my office I can see the top of the cranes that dominate the landscape of Manchester's downtown. It is hard not to be impressed by their number and by the way they dwarf existing buildings. On a grey day – and there are many in Manchester during the winter (and some years, even during the summer) – they inject a sprinkling of colour into the skyline. Orange, red, yellow. I know from looking out of my window that cranes come in a range of different colours. These large machines, moving through the otherwise dull and overcast sky, draw you towards them. There is graciousness to how they swing through the air. Once stationary, they hang over the narrow streets that run through the centre of the city and which remind its residents, and those that visit it, of Manchester's industrial past. This sense of becoming, of being a work in progress, sums up the recent history of Manchester's downtown. Apparently Graham Stringer, the former leader of Manchester City Council – the UK tier of local government – often counted the cranes from his office, producing a sort of 'crane index'. The more cranes on the skyline, the more he judged his governance of the city as successful. And Manchester remains, quite literally, a city 'on the up'. Five skyscrapers are in the process of being completed, the most visible being the 47-storey Hilton Tower on the south west of the city centre.

Of course, the leader of Manchester City Council was not the first urban politician to talk in these terms. The last two decades have seen many Western cities experiencing massive reinvestment, of which the presence of cranes on the skyline is but one indicator. And urban political leaders of all political stripes have not been slow at talking up their successes. Apartments and penthouses have been manufactured out of derelict and under-used offices and warehouses. New flat and housing complexes have been built. And it is not just residential development. Café bars, cinemas, gyms, hotels, museums, nightclubs, restaurants: walk around your nearest city. What do you see? It is likely that there will be plenty of evidence of this flowing of capital back in the city centres and the downtowns, of the rebuilding of the consumption infrastructure.

Perhaps nowhere did cranes taken on such a symbolic importance as in post-unified Berlin. The tearing down and rebuilding work mirrored the change in the political conditions under which this was performed, as communism, it seemed almost overnight, was replaced by capitalism. The dismantling of the Berlin Wall in 1989 heralded a series of reconstruction projects. Elected officials here too pointed to the puncturing of the city's skyline with cranes as testament to the slow realization of the new post-unification vision for Berlin (Cochrane and Jonas 1999). As the architect Peter Davey (1999: 6) wrote some ten years after the wall came down, 'if you stand on the platform of the S-Bahn at the Lehrter Bahnhof and look south, the sky is filled with tower cranes to the horizon'.

More recently, however, the size and the speed of this redevelopment has been eclipsed by the urban (re)construction of China's cities. Amazing though it might sound, in 2004 half of the concrete used in construction around the world was poured into China's cities! Nowhere is the extent of this urban redevelopment clearer than in Beijing, which is the host city for the 2008 Olympic Games. Described as experiencing an 'orgy of construction', the city is 'changing before people's eyes, with each new building battling the next for attention' (http://news.bbc.co.uk/2/hi/asia-pacific/3701581.stm).

And the urbanization of Chinese society is not a one-off; elsewhere outside the Western world, societies are experiencing urbanization as never before. According to the United Nations (2003) 2007 will see for the first time more than 50 per cent of the world's population living in 'urban settlements'. Already the world's urban population is over 3 billion, more than the population of the world in 1960, and it is expected to double in 38 years. The urbanization is particularly pronounced in those countries the report terms 'less developed', where the growth rate per annum is 2.3 per cent, compared to a 1 per cent growth rate for the world's population as a whole. For those of you without a head for figures, this means that between 2000 and 2030 it is predicted that the urban population of the world's previously poorest countries will be increasing at twice the rate of growth experienced by the world's total population. This growth will see new cities emerge and existing ones get larger. For example, in 1950 there were 86 cities in the world with a population over 1 million; today there are 400, and by 2015 there will be at least 550 (Davis 2004). 'China [will] cease to be the predominantly rural country it has been for millennia' (Mengkui 2003: 8), but the reducing of the global countryside will happen across the world and will happen quickly and with profound implications, both for those living in cities and for how we understand their governance.

Accompanying this massive physical renewal of many existing cities, and the emergence of new ones, has been a significant change in the meaning of, and the participants in, the urban politics of redevelopment. While details differ from one city and from one country to another, we can identify two general patterns.

The first is the growing emphasis placed on the marketing or selling of cities, and their assets (Philo and Kearns 1993). Cities and those that govern them have become more adept at producing and massaging images – of architecture, buildings, peoples and public spaces. And greater care is now paid to varying the images, and the text in which they are embedded, depending on the target audiences. A look on the websites of cities will probably reveal the sophisticated manner in which most cities now sell themselves. 'Before' and 'after' photographs, ringing endorsements from local celebrities and reference to league tables are likely to dominate. Most attractive place to live, to work, to play, to invest, to retire, to be ill, to be healthy; first city to host an open-air concert, to develop a million-pound apartment, to marry a same-sex couple. Or a visit to a nearby tourist office is likely to reveal quite how many glossy brochures and promotional campaigns are available. Selective histories, partial walking tours and retail listings are sure to be pinned on walls and stacked on tables. If you want to take a sample, though, bring a large bag! These strategies constitute an emphasis on the supply-side of urban redevelopment. Alternatives, particularly on the demand side, continued to be pursued, but often play second fiddle to the more high-profile and attention-grabbing activities.

The second discernible pattern is the change in who is involved in the urban politics of redevelopment. Once local redevelopment was something performed primarily by local government, and was often a relatively low priority behind the other services it delivered, such as education, health and transport. Meeting the demands citizens placed on these collectively consumed services was often as much as local government could do. Those who led and staffed local governments did not do much more in this area beyond performing legislative responsibilities in the form of drawing up and regulating planning and zoning acts. In some cases the absence of political activity around urban redevelopment was caused by the particular relationships that existed between central and local government within a country. In the UK, for example, it was central government that was understood to lead on redevelopment matters, in the form of, for example, urban and regional policy, and other forms of spatially-targeted programmes (see Chapter 20). Local government delivered central government services locally. While there were examples of some local governments doing things a little differently, such as partnering local businesses or launching promotional campaigns, these were the exception, not the norm. In the US, in contrast, civic boosterism – the promotion of places – has a longer history. In some cities and regions it dates back to the competitions that occurred over the extension of the railroads. One place would compete with another, courting investors to secure a station on the train-line. Additionally, in the US, local governments in the different states have greater political autonomy in the country's governmental architecture. In other parts of the world, while there are clearly differences between what is meant by urban redevelopment and those that participate, there are also noticeable similarities. So work on cities in China (Xu and Yeh 2005; Wu 2005), Nigeria (Oluwu 1993), Russia (Kudrin 1997) and South Africa (Maharaj and Ramballi 1998; Robinson 2005; Rogerson 1997) has revealed the extent of the change in the role of local government in a range of geographical contexts. Above all, regardless of their political persuasions and the wider international and national networks of which they are part, local governments around the world have to one degree or another had their roles in urban redevelopment remade. This not only matters empirically, and perhaps politically, but it also matters conceptually. In the context of different geographical scales being involved in constituting 'the urban', we can think of the global in the urban (and vice versa), the national in the urban (and vice versa), the neighbourhood in the urban (and vice versa), and so on. And in thinking about the example of entrepreneurial 'urban' policy and politics, we are forced to re-think our understandings and usages of terms such as 'global' or 'urban'. This is the point that Massey (1991) made many years, and which more recently, through his own work on urban politics, McCann (2002, 2004) has considered.

The conceptual complexities of thinking about the urban as bounded and clearly delimited should become clear as you read on through this chapter, as should the issues involved in thinking about the relationships that exist between such taken-for-granted categories as the 'urban' and the 'global'. Perhaps, more fundamentally, the changes in the nature of urban policy and politics that I outline in this chapter speak to wider discussions elsewhere in human geography and beyond, over 'glocalization' (Swyngedouw 1997) or 'glurbanization' (Jessop and Sum 2000), both terms striving to capture the complicated scalar shifts underway in the organization of the contemporary state, transformations with implications for how we understand and study entrepreneurial urbanism (Brenner 1999; Ward 2003).

I begin this chapter with an attempt to step back from the details of the different empirical accounts of change in the politics of urban redevelopment, and briefly contend with some conceptual issues raised by these studies. I detail what is meant by entrepreneurial urbanism and how this approach might capture some of the generic tendencies in the restructuring of the politics of urban redevelopment, whether they occur outside my window or yours. I then document some of the different types of strategies cities have pursued as part of the 'entrepreneurial turn' performed by cities and those now involved in their governance. Finally, I consider some of the conceptual limits to entrepreneurial urbanism, and also some of the policy limits, as in some cases cities struggle to manage the consequences, environmental, housing and so on, of 'overheating' economies.

Entrepreneurial urbanism

> Above all, the city has to appear as an innovative, exciting, creative, and safe place to live or visit, to play and consume in.
>
> (Harvey 1989: 9)

So what is meant by entrepreneurial urbanism? Well, we can understand it as a process of change in the very meaning of urban redevelopment and of those involved in doing and evaluating it. Of course, entrepreneurial urbanism might look and feel different in different parts of the world. You might know of types of urban redevelopment that, once you've read and thought about this chapter, don't appear to be examples of entrepreneurial urbanism. There are probably plenty of these, some perhaps even in the city in which you live. The shift has not been a complete and total one, nor can it ever really be. It is rather something to which those who govern cities aspire, to be fully entrepreneurial. Old and new ways of governing are likely to co-exist, a messy compromise that reflects the outcome of local bargaining and negotiation. Nevertheless, as I pointed to at the beginning of this chapter, we can see some similarities in how cities, whether Eastern European, North American or South East Asian, are going about redevelopment. If we step back from the details of one or two cases and look across national boundaries we can identify some common patterns of change (Hall and Hubbard 1996; Harvey 1989; Jessop and Sum 2000; Ward 2003).

Entrepreneurial urbanism is the *consensus* that exists amongst city governments of one political persuasion or another over the positive benefits that can be wrought from the restructuring of its activities. Of course, as those of you who have read Marx will know, none of us make history under conditions of our own making. Local political leaders, and those from the other walks of life they partner, such as local business representatives, are pursuing their strategies in a world in which many factors are beyond their control. Those in charge of cities are speculating, are taking risks in the name of improving economic competitiveness. And, like any risks, some come off and others don't. Again, if you sit and think for a minute, you might know examples of unsuccessful redevelopment schemes: industrial parks that have remained half full, museums or galleries in which the attendance figures have been below those projected, or residential new builds in which supply has exceeded demand and outside which 'for sale' or 'for rent' signs are seemingly permanent fixtures.

Returning to the conceptual issues, Harvey (1989), drawing on his observations on Baltimore in the US during the 1980s, highlights three defining characteristics of entrepreneurial urbanism. First, underpinning it is the notion of public–private partnership: that is, the formation of alliances or coalitions of elected politicians, policy-makers, business owners and executives and others to design, deliver and evaluate urban development strategies. In some cities and countries this has marked a radical break from past practices. In the UK, for example, the emergence of the modern welfare state in the 1940s involved local government taking charge for what urban redevelopment was performed (Cochrane 1993). Other interests, such as business and community representatives, were only involved insofar as local councillors represented their needs and wants. In the US, however, the representatives of business have always been more involved in the politics of urban redevelopment, in part because of what Cox and Mair (1988) term 'local dependence': that is, the senses of attachment to a particular locale felt by businesses, governments and others. The factors behind this attachment or dependence are many. Think about local government: it is relatively immobile. It is only given meaning in and through the local services it delivers to local people or manages. It is not possible for local government to relocate elsewhere, which is an option business faces. But businesses can also be 'locally dependent'. Materials might be sourced in a particular place, making relocation expensive. More generally, owners or managers regardless of their institutional affiliations or loyalties might feel a sense of attachment to a place, the result of a particular set of emotions and histories. In the US Cox and Wood (1997) used the example of local utilities – such as gas and electricity companies – to argue that some types of businesses, by way of their products, are more prone than others to be locally dependent.

The other aspect of public–private partnership – over and above why business gets involved – is what their formation means for local government. It is possible to think about this in two ways. First is about where government stops and starts. Or, put another way, to ask the question: where are the edges of local government? This is a *quantitative* issue, about the size – in terms of staff employed, money spent, functions delivered and geographical area governed. Some have argued that in recent years we have witnessed the general rise in lean urbanization (Merrifield 2002), the shrinking in size of local governments as they form partnerships to deliver services or contract out some functions to the private sector. The other aspect of what entrepreneurial urbanism and the formation of public–private partnerships has meant for local government is a *qualitative* restructuring of its operations. By this I mean a change in what local government does, how it does it, and how what it does is audited or evaluated. Or, put another way, how is the *power* to govern – not as a thing but as something that is produced through social relations – affected by these changes and, in turn, how does the exercising of power affect the nature of the changes? So *within* local government new ways of working have been introduced, often drawing on practices from the private sector. The performance of local government staff, and of the departments and the units they are part of, is now subject to regular evaluation against a range of performance indicators, the origins of which, again, often lie within the private sector.

Second, the activities pursued by public–private partnerships are entrepreneurial and involve the taking of risk. Local government leaders, with their counterparts from the private sector, speculate on the future development of the city, investing public finances in so-called 'flagship' or 'mega-project' schemes. The emphasis is on taking risks in the name of maintaining and improving the city's performance as *judged* against various economic and social indicators. As part of this restructuring we have also seen the expansion of the indicators that governments and the media – and perhaps even you and me – use to judge a city's success. Think about the publishing of regular league tables – the best cities in which to perform a range of activities (McCann 2004). For public sector workers, such as architects and planners, this has involved some changes in their job remits. In addition to performing their statutory requirements, deciding on planning and zoning issues and so on, these professionals have been involved in new ways of working with customers. Planning departments have, in some case, been merged with other departments. Individuals have found themselves working in new area-based teams consisting of economists, engineers and planners. Work is no longer always organized according to professional demarcations but, rather, often through units, on a project-by-project basis. Decision-making has been speeded up and new ways of reaching decisions have been designed, often circumventing formal committees, and, some have claimed, the democratic decision-making process (Kitchen 1997).

Third, entrepreneurial urbanism, as conceived of by Harvey (1989), emphasizes place over territory. What does this distinction mean, though, in this case? Well, by focusing on territory we mean pursuing policies and programmes where those whose benefit live within the boundaries of the territory, such as a city. We might think of education and housing projects producing benefits to those who live and study in the city. Others might also stand to gain from the pursuit of these territorial projects, but those who are to gain by design through the investment are those for whom the city is their home. However, the construction of place, in the form of a new waterfront development, or the focusing on conditions within a place, such as the recent relaxing of the licensing laws in the UK, can have impacts beyond the specific territory. Both examples involve in-place policies that, while having consequences for those who live and work in the city, are designed to appeal to other interested parties. The new waterfront development is targeted at investors, whether property developers and multi-national retailers who build and occupy it, or tourists who visit and consume the retail and entertainment experiences. In some cases this might involve different local groups being involved in the building, staffing and usage of the waterfront, although this is often understood as a small part of a bigger picture of attracting in capital from elsewhere. And, of course, at times there will be some decisions to be made over how to spend resources – money and time – on the pursuit of different strategies, the benefits of which will accrue to different groups, raising issues of spatial justice. How is it possible to make absolute judgements over which types of redevelopment are better or worse for the residents of a city? What about who gains more or less within the different neighbourhoods within a city? These decisions and lots of others are faced and resolved daily in city halls and other decision-making arenas. This does not make them any less important, though, to those of us, including you as the reader, who are challenged to reflect on what the pursuit of this type of urban redevelopment means in practice, on the ground, in the schools, at the homes, in the shops and in the offices, those places of everyday life.

If we now know what is meant by entrepreneurial urbanism, we can also think about this process of restructuring as consisting of three interlocking aspects that run through the general definitions that Harvey (1989) spelt out. It is against these that we might be able to make judgements about the degree to which cities are or are not entrepreneurial (Jessop 1997, 1998) although, as I hope you are beginning to appreciate, making these absolute judgements is less than straightforward. The first aspect is whether the city has in place a set of agencies and institutions to support entrepreneurial activities. This we can think of as the structural status. The second is whether the city has achieved the capacity to act as an entrepreneur: that is, whether there are enough of the agencies and institutions working together, presenting a unified position on strategies and a common approach to redevelopment. This we can think of as the strategic status. The third and final aspect is the ways in which those in charge of the city describe and present it. This we can think of as the discursive status. Although these are presented here as three discrete aspects, they are introduced at the beginning of this section as interlocking because how they fit together says something about a particular city's pursuit of entrepreneurial urbanism. Having established what is meant by entrepreneurial urbanism and its three different characteristics, in the next section I turn to examine some of the types of strategies cities have actually pursued in the last three decades.

Entrepreneurial strategies

In this section I want to explore four types of entrepreneurial strategies. The first are those strategies to improve the image of a city. If you are a student then you are likely to have looked at university brochures when choosing where to study. In recent years more and more cities have produced similar types of documents with the aim of selling the city. From the 1970s a number of cities in different parts of the world have turned their attention to branding. New York City's 'I♡NY', followed by the 1983 'Glasgow's miles better' – these are widely understood to be the first two campaigns that put the re-imaging of the city at the centre of a wider redevelopment programme. Efforts to market the city have taken place in many cities around the world over the centuries. However, as part of this emergence of entrepreneurial urbanism more cities are now turning to marketing themselves – often with the creation of a new marketing partnership or a refocusing of the efforts of existing agencies.

And, of course, as more cities spend time and money on advertising and marketing campaigns, so not to pursue these strategies is regarded as losing ground on your rivals. As a leader of a local government, or a city mayor in the US, the question seems to be not whether or not to market your city but, rather, how. The campaigns tend to draw on past images and meanings, sometimes to build on and manipulate these, in other cases to distant the city from them. In most cases these strategies seek to tread a careful line between, on the one hand, making use of those aspects of the city that have some wider positive currency and, on the other, sidestepping mention of places or use of images that are understood, in the terms used, 'to pollute the brand'. A good example of this can be found in the efforts to market Manchester, the city from which I write this chapter. Although these have not been without their problems (Ward 2000a, 2000b), strategies to market the city have successful blended images from Manchester's past with appeals to a more cosmopolitan future. Images from the city's past include the turn-of-the-twentieth-century warehouses, which have been gentrified in the last two decades, but don't include the 1970s downtown developments that puncture much of the urban built environment. Other campaigns are similarly – and perhaps necessarily – partial. In the campaigns run by rustbelt cities such as Detroit and Pittsburgh, for example, little mention is made of their industrial heritage, except in the context of talking about future development plans and the possibility of expanding the consumption base. In addition to using images from the past, these campaigns also seek to invoke certain meaning through their choice of slogans. The phrases may be used to place the city, as for example in the case of Durban, on the east coast of South Africa, which during the 1990s marketed itself as 'the Kingdom of the Zulu', or Birmingham, in the UK, which emphasized its geographical location through its 'Europe's meeting place' campaign.

The second type of strategies that have been pursued are those we might think about as event-based spectacles. These can last a day or a month, involve the production of 'urban spectacle' in one shape or form, and consist of fairs, festivals, markets, parades and other similar events. Intense periods – days or weeks – of activity around one or more theme take place as a means of promoting the host city to a wider geographical audience. The city region in which I live and work is illustrative. Greater Manchester – Manchester and the other nine boroughs that make up this wider 'city region' (Deas and Ward 2002) – is narrated as 'a great place for living life to the full; relaxing, experiencing the wide variety of spectacle on offer all year round, and being thoroughly entertained' (http://www.investinmanchester.com).

Historically, world expositions and fairs have served to promote a host city. The first of these, the Great Exhibition of the Works of Industry of All Nations, took place in London in

1851. Subsequently other cities, such as Paris, have hosted expos and fairs to promote the economic and cultural aspects of their cities and the nations they are part of, the most recent of which took place in 2005 in Aichi in Japan. Examples of these include high-profile spectacles around sport, such as Olympic Games and football World Cups, ethnicity, religion and sexuality, such as the carnivals/parades in Notting Hill, Seville, New York, San Francisco and Manchester. Through all these there is a mobilization of emotions, of hope and joy, of pain and suffering. Invoking or drawing upon how people feel about a particular place and a specific issue is a widely used strategy by urban politicians in the hosting of events. Think of the range of emotions we feel watching – live or via television – or even participating in events of this nature. They are highly charged spectacles, and an integral aspect to these strategies is to use the different types of affect to positive ends for the city in question.

Inward investment is the third type of strategy pursued by cities. Unlike the first two, where the emphasis is on the producing and manipulation of both material and affective aspects of the city, these strategies are more overtly economic. The focus is on increasing both the level and the quality of the investment into a city. The first of these is fairly straightforward. In recent years a number of new agencies or institutions have been established with the singular brief of increasing quantitatively the amount of investment taking place in a city. An example is the Manchester Inward Investment and Development Agency Service (MIDAS). This was created by a number of local governments, who together with existing coalitions of the public and private sectors felt that it was necessary to create a new agency with the responsibility of co-ordinating attempts to cajole, encourage and lobby businesses to invest into Manchester and the surrounding region. We have seen similar institutions – in terms of who is involved and the activities they pursue – emerge in other cities, in Africa, Asia, Europe, Latin and South America and North America. The World Bank's Urban Unit website contains a range of case-studies from around the world, documenting the different ways in which institution-building goes hand-in-hand with achieving sustainable urban development (http://www.worldbank.org/urban). The qualitative element, to improve the nature of inward investment, is harder to define. For most cities it is enough in and of itself to the increase the level of investment. For others, however, inward investment agencies claim that their strategy is about attracting 'high end' investment, by which they normally mean either the most important activities of a business, such as research and development, or from a particular sector, such as banking and finance. In both of these cases, the city's agencies are able to make more of the investment in terms of place marketing and promotion. They tell a story or a narrative about the city, positioning it as a centre of the 'new economy', or as home to members of what Florida (2002) terms 'the creative class'.

The fourth types of strategies are those on the urban landscape. New industrial parks, public spaces and residential developments: all are physical outcomes of the politics of urban redevelopment, which are the outcome of the urbanization of capitalism. Recent rounds of investment, the speculation that Harvey (1982) wrote about as the second circuit of capital, will leave its mark on the built environment, as past investments have and future investments will. The city is made up of layers, forming a *palimpsest*, what Harvey (1996: 417) describes as 'a composite landscape made up of different built forms superimposed upon each other with the passing of time'. In cities around the globe new investment has taken place in the built environment, from convention centres to shopping malls, new office blocks to waterfront features, residential apartments to sports complexes. The use of new build as a means of raising the profile of the city is perhaps the most obvious and visible reflection of the pursuit of entrepreneurial urbanism.

Entrepreneurial urbanism: some limits

This chapter has argued that entrepreneurial urbanism is a useful means of capturing and detailing the generic features of the changing role of local governments in the politics surrounding urban development. However, the concept and practice is not without its limits. In this short penultimate section I want to focus on two, its conceptual and its political limits.

Conceptually, there are three issues of which we need to be aware. First, in the most influential work on entrepreneurial urbanism, Harvey (1989) is talking about a transition from a managerial to an entrepreneurial mode of governance. He writes of a 'reorientation of attitudes' (p. 4). And yet, while he is not suggesting an overnight or geographically even transformation, he is nevertheless depicting a consensus around the replacement of one mode with another. This distinction is a useful way of looking at general tendencies. Beyond that, however, and the complexities of everyday life tend to get in the way. The two modes might co-exist, even within one local government, never mind a single city. In economic development there might be evidence of entrepreneurial urbanism, while in education and transport we might still see the imprint of managerial urbanism. In fact, what subsequent work has explored is entrepreneurial urbanism as a *qualitative process* of the restructuring of government. This emphasis allows us to separate out entrepreneurial urbanism in theory and in practice, the latter acknowledging the contingent, uneven and often partial transformation of the *modus operandi* of local government. The general point that this work is trying to convey is the ways in which local government has been qualitatively reoriented to meeting the needs of business, to improving what those in the redevelopment industry refer to as the 'business climate'. The second issue we need to consider is whether, in some cities, and nations, local government was ever managerial in the way Harvey (1989) and others described. It's been argued that this is an important assumption and one that, if not right, undermines the claims of a transition. Cox and Townsend (2005) argue against this means of capturing the politics of urban development. Instead they claim that even in the two countries that Harvey (1989) talks of in his original piece – the US and the UK – the evidence is not conclusive. While local government in the UK might once have been managerial as Harvey claims (Pahl 1970), in the US the picture is less clear cut. US local governments have historically possessed tax-raising and collecting powers, worked with the private sector and constructed a positive image of their cities through marketing activities. This, at the very least, means that beyond the very general claims that have been made about the emergence of entrepreneurial urbanism (Hall and Hubbard 1996), there needs to be an attention to context and to positionality. Third, and finally, assessing general patterns runs the risk of missing the range of other types of urban redevelopment politics and to see coherence and similarities where none exist.

In terms of political limits, managing the consequences of the 'entrepreneurial turn' can in some cases be as difficult as its achievement. There are now numerous examples of cities, the leaders of whom have struggled to manage the implications of the very growth they encouraged through entrepreneurial strategies (Low *et al.* 2000; While *et al.* 2004). In some cases the consequences are environmental. Worsening air pollution, increasing travel-to-work times and decaying infrastructure, such as failing railways and roads, speak to the often unforeseen and hidden outcomes of producing what might narrowly be understood as a 'successful' local economy. And quite how a distinct urban politics of nature and environment of cities might speak to the politics around economic development is not yet obvious. It is clear, though, that this has become in the last few years a pressing issue in cities of both the global south and the north – and that the implications for, and fate of, each are related.

Conceptually, moreover, it is a challenge to thinking through how our existing under-standings of entrepreneurial urbanism make sense of the rise of environmental concerns.

Of course, it is not just struggles over nature and the environment that appear to be absent from entrepreneurial urbanism accounts. There are other consequences of the pursuit of entrepreneurial urbanism, over which there is an actual politics. Long waiting lists for pre-school childcare, irregular public transport, long working hours: all perhaps suggest a city where the ability to live and to work is out of kilter (Jarvis 2005; McDowell *et al.* 2006). Issues of work–life balance, of ensuring that many of the socially reproductive tasks still performed by women are valued, often but not always tend to get forgotten in the specta-cular claims that accompany the pursuit of one entrepreneurial strategy or another. The emphasis on urban redevelopment occurs in many cases without an appreciation or under-standing of what it means for those who live and work in cities.

Conclusion

Fancy a coffee? Perhaps you would like a beer? Or maybe a workout in a gym followed by a viewing of some French *nouvelle vague*? While the city centres or downtowns of the past might have been found lacking if these were your wants, there is a better than good chance that your local city might now be able to meet your consumptive needs. Work out, eat out, slob out, so to speak. This chapter has been about the general processes behind the creation of the built environment we can see as we walk around a growing number of city centres around the world. It has explained what is meant by entrepreneurial urbanism and its conceptual limits, and documented some of the types of entrepreneurial strategies performed in recent years. I hope some of these are familiar, and that in reading through this account you might be able to see links within and between cities that might otherwise remain un-made.

Although this chapter has focused on the fate of local government in the doing of urban redevelopment, and the emergence of entrepreneurial urbanism, these changes have not occurred in a vacuum. Cities are embedded in regions and nations, and are part of relations that stretch across space. Ideas, money, people, policies: all are moved across space through networks, some of which are trans-urban, some trans-national. Recent efforts in geography to think about cities as open and porous, as constituted in place through relations that stretch one from place to another, whether cities or nations, means that in thinking about entre-preneurial urbanism it is important not to lose sight of what is behind the observable chan-ges. For they are not part of some natural order, but are rather the result of a number of wider economic and political trends. And behind trends are people, producing numbers and writing reports. This perhaps trivial point raises the possibility of imaging and realizing an alternative urban world, in which entrepreneurial urbanism is but one of many political outcomes (Robinson 2005).

Further reading

Brenner, N. (1999) Globalization as reterritorialization: the re-scaling of urban governance in the European Union. *Urban Studies* 36, 431–51.

Deas, I. and Ward, K. (2002) Metropolitan manoeuvres: making Greater Manchester. In J. Peck and K. Ward (eds) *City of Revolution: Restructuring Manchester*, pp. 116–32. Manchester University Press: Manchester.

Hall, T. and Hubbard, P. (1996) The entrepreneurial city: new urban politics, new urban geographies. *Progress in Human Geography* 20, 153–74.

Harvey, D. (1989) From managerialism to entrepreneurialism: the transformation of urban politics in late capitalism. *Geografiska Annaler* 71B, 3–18.

Massey, D. (1991) The political place of locality studies. *Environment and Planning A* 23, 267–81.

Mengkui. K. (2003) quoted in the *Financial Times* 16 December, 8.

Robinson, J. (2005) *Ordinary Cities: Between Modernity and Development*. Routledge: London.

Ward, K. (2003) Neo-liberal 'turns', entrepreneurial urbanism and the limits to contemporary urban re-development. *City* 7, 201–11.

References

Brenner, N. (1999) Globalization as reterritorialization: the re-scaling of urban governance in the European Union. *Urban Studies* 36, 431–51.

Cochrane, A.D. (1993) *Whatever Happened to Local Government?* Open University Press: Buckingham.

Cochrane, A.D. and Jonas, A.E.G. (1999) Reimagining Berlin: World City, National Capital or Ordinary Place? *European Urban and Regional Studies* 6, 145–64.

Cox, K.R. and Mair, A.J. (1988) Locality and community in the politics of local economic development. *Annals of the Association of American Geographers* 78, 307–25.

Cox, K.R. and Townsend, A. (2005) The English politics of local economic development and the American model. *Regional Studies* 39, 541–53.

Cox, K.R. and Wood, A. (1997) Competition and change in mediating the global: the case of local economic development. *Competition and Change* 2, 65–94.

Davey, P. (1999) Building Berlin: construction projects in Berlin, Germany. *The Architectural Review*, January, 4–6.

Davis, M. (2004) Planet of slums: urban involution and the informal proletariat. *New Left Review* 26, 5–34.

Florida, R. (2002) *The Rise of the Creative Class: And How It's Transforming Work, Leisure, Community and Everyday Life*. Basic Books: New York.

Hall, T. and Hubbard, P. (1996) The entrepreneurial city: new urban politics, new urban geographies. *Progress in Human Geography* 20, 153–74.

Harvey, D. (1982) *The Limits to Capital*. Chicago: The University of Chicago Press.

——(1989) From managerialism to entrepreneurialism: the transformation of urban politics in late capitalism. *Geografiska Annaler* 71B, 3–18.

——(1996) *Justice, Nature and the Geography of Difference*. Oxford: Blackwell.

Jarvis, H. (2005) *Work–Life City Limits: Comparative Household Perspectives*. Basingstoke: Palgrave, Macmillan.

Jessop, B. (1997) The entrepreneurial city: re-imaging localities, redesigning economic governance, or restructuring capital? In N. Jewson and S. MacGregor (eds) *Transforming Cities: Contested Governance and New Spatial Divisions*, pp. 28–41. Routledge: London.

——(1998) The narrative of enterprise and the enterprise of narrative: place marketing and the entrepreneurial city. In T. Hall and P. Hubbard P (eds) *The Entrepreneurial City: Geographies of Politics, Regime and Representation*, pp. 77–102. Chichester: John Wiley and Sons.

Jessop, B. and Sum, N.L. (2000) An entrepreneurial city in action: Hong Kong's emerging strategies in and for (inter) urban competition. *Urban Studies* 12, 2287–2313.

Kitchen, T. (1997) *People, Politics, Policies and Plans: The City Planning Process in Contemporary Britain*. London: Paul Chapman.

Kudrin, A. (1997) St Petersburg's progress towards the market. *International Journal of Urban and Regional Research* 21, 406–24.

Low, N., Gleeson, B., Elander, I. and Lidskog, R. (eds) (2000) *Consuming Cities: The Urban Environment in the Global Economy after the Rio Declaration*. London: Routledge.

McCann, E. (2002) The urban as an object of study in global cities literatures: representational practices and conceptions of place and scale. In A. Herod and M. Wright (eds) *Geographies of Power: Placing Scale*, pp. 61–85. Oxford: Blackwell.

——(2004) 'Best places': inter-urban competition, quality of life and popular media discourse. *Urban Studies* 41, 1909–29.

McDowell, L., Ward, K., Fagan, C., Perrons, D. and Ray, K. (2006) Connecting time and space: the signification of transformations in women's work in the city. *International Journal of Urban and Regional Research* 30, 159–71.

Maharaj, B. and Ramballi, K. (1998) Local economic development strategies in an emerging democracy: the case of Durban in South Africa. *Urban Studies* 35, 131–48.

Merrifield, A. (2002) *Dialectical Urbanism: Social Struggles in the Capitalist City*. New York: Monthly Review Press.

Oluwu, D. (1993) Local institutions and development: the Nigerian experience. In A. Goetz and S.E. Clarke (eds.) *The New Localism: Comparative Urban Politics in a Global Age*, pp. 34–56. London: Sage.

Pahl, R. (1970) *Whose City? And Other Essays on Sociology and Planning*. London: Longman.

Philo, C. and Kearns, G. (eds.) (1993) *Selling Places: The City as Cultural Capital*. Oxford: Pergamon Press.

Robinson, J. (2005) *Ordinary Cities: Between Modernity and Development*. London: Routledge.

Rogerson, C.M. (1997) Local economic development and post-apartheid reconstruction in South Africa. *Singapore Journal of Tropical Geography* 18, 175–95.

Swyngedouw, E. (1997) Neither global nor local: 'glocalization' and the politics of scale. In K.R. Cox. (ed.) *Spaces of Globalization: Reasserting the Power of the Local*, pp. 137–66. New York: Guilford Press.

United Nations (2003) *World Urbanization Prospects: The 2003 Revisions*. Geneva: United Nations.

Ward, K. (2000a) State licence, local settlements and the politics of 'branding' the city. *Environment and Planning C: Government and Policy* 18, 285–300.

——(2000b) From rentiers to rantiers: 'active entrepreneurs', 'structural speculators' and the politics of marketing the city. *Urban Studies* 37, 1101–15.

——(2003) Neo-liberal 'turns', entrepreneurial urbanism and the limits to contemporary urban re-development. *City* 7, 201–11.

While, A., Jonas, A.E.G. and Gibbs, D. (2004) The environment and the entrepreneurial city: searching for the urban 'sustainability' 'fix' in Manchester and Leeds. *International Journal of Urban and Regional Research* 28, 549–69.

Wu, F. (2005) The city of transition and the transition of cities. *Urban Geography* 26, 100–6.

Xu, J. and Yeh, A.G.O (2005) City repositioning and competitiveness building in regional development: new development strategies in Guangzhou, China. *International Journal of Urban and Regional Research* 29, 283–308.

22

Firms

Henry Wai-chung Yeung

Introduction: same firms, different firms

What have Ford, BMW and Toyota got in common? They are all transnational automobile firms and amongst some of the best known brand names in the world. In 2004, their sales and revenues exceeded the GDP figures of most national economies. Ford, the largest among the three of them, achieved a massive US $171.6 billion turnover in 2004. Trailing closely was Toyota's US $154.2 billion net revenues in 2004. BMW, the luxury carmaker, raked in US $53.5 billion in sales in the same year. For these multi-billion dollar automobile giants, everything seems to be *global* – from product presence and production locations to workforce and shareholders. All three transnational firms have their automobiles distributed worldwide – from Alaska to Russia and from South Africa to New Zealand. These cars are assembled all over the world in dedicated plants while their parts and components are sourced globally. In some cases (e.g. Ford's Mondeo) the end product is a truly global product, engineered and manufactured by some of the best talents and workers in the US and Europe, and sold to the entire global market. Needless to say, these firms rely on global financial markets for investment capital far greater than firms in other business sectors. Their shares are listed and sold in major stock markets located in international financial centres. All these facts point to the *natural* convergence of these three global firms. We would think therefore that global competition in the automobile industry should have driven these 'global' firms to behave in similar ways and to converge in their corporate practices, production activity and international business culture. Indeed, Toyota announced in April 2002 its Global Vision 2010. One of its four key themes is to be 'a truly global company that is trusted and respected by all peoples around the world' (Toyota 2005).

Upon a closer look, however, these firms are far from being global corporations that bear no resemblance to their country of origin. All three transnational corporations (TNCs) started off as family businesses – Henry Ford and his family in the US, the Quandt family in Bavaria, Germany, and the Toyoda family in Japan. Today, family members continue to be involved in all three companies. In 2005, two members of the Ford family sat on Ford's board of directors (Edsel B. Ford II and William Clay Ford, Jr.), one of the Quandt family members was the deputy chairman of BMW's supervisory board (Stefan Quandt), and two of the Toyoda family members were involved in Toyota's board of directors and senior management (Shoichiro Toyoda and Akio Toyoda). Most of Ford's board of directors were Americans; virtually all of BMW's supervisory board and board of management were Germans; and all of Toyota's board of directors and senior management were Japanese.

Clearly, these firms are really global only in terms of the market reach of their products and, perhaps, component sourcing. By virtue of their different origins, historical developments, and management structures, they remain *national* firms that carry with them distinctive cultural traits and behavioural patterns. This is where they diverge in their corporate practice and management processes. Geography matters here as the country of origin or the so-called 'home country effect' shapes their heterogeneous approaches to inter-firm and intra-firm relationships. These firm- and national-level differences can be summarized by the concept *economic culture*. Culture is a complex concept and refers to a wide range of shared beliefs and norms. So do Ford, BMW and Toyota have different economic cultures? Embodying the American culture of market-based price competition, Ford's adversarial approach to its suppliers differs sharply from its Japanese competitor, Toyota, which seeks cooperative relationships with its business network members (Womack *et al.* 1990). Reflecting its continental European culture, BMW sits somewhere in between these two distinctive corporate cultures of adversarial competition and cooperative partnership. Within intra-firm relationships, their approaches to transnational management vary significantly as well. While Ford is much more amenable to hiring international executives to manage its worldwide operations – no doubt a reflection of its American style of management – Toyota remains highly Japanese in its international operations, let alone its domestic business in Japan. Its presidents for sales and manufacturing in North America are 'company men' sent from Japan.

These fine differences in both national and corporate cultures among the three auto giants tell us something important about *the geography of firms*. This chapter focuses on the firm as a scale of our inquiry into the role of actors in geographical processes of change. The next section offers a critical review of how the firm is analysed in economics and economic geography. By unpacking the typical firm, I show how diverse actors and interest groups govern firms differently in different geographical contexts. The analysis also yields important insights into how social relations and corporate conventions shape firm behaviour in different places and discursive contexts. The penultimate section sheds some light on the differing geographical scales at which firms operate and examines how different networks link firms and other actors in society and space. Taken together, this chapter shows how capitalist firms and their global networks bring together diverse localities in an era of global change and adjustments.

Nature of the firm in economics and economic geography

As Alfred Marshall's characterization of the representative firm, the theory of the firm has fascinated generations of economists and, more recently, other social scientists. As Williamson (1990: 1) notes, the theory of the firm is 'one of the two key analytical constructs on which microeconomic theory rests (the other being the theory of consumer behavior)'. Classical and neoclassical economics views the firm as simply a set of production units responding to competitive initiatives in accordance with the law of diminishing returns. While the market is regarded as the most efficient means of organizing economic activities, the firm is simply seen as 'a black box which responds directly to changes in costs and the pressures of the market' (Hodgson 1988: x). The firm converts inputs into outputs according to its production function and market demand. As neoclassical economics is primarily concerned with issues of price equilibrium and optimal distribution of resources, the firm does not occupy an important position in its research agenda.

More recent behavioural and managerial theories of the firm, however, have attempted to unpack the firm as a collection of productive resources (Penrose 1995) and alternative governance structures (Williamson 1999) organized by managers with different expectations, bounded rationalities and information matrices. The emergence of such a quasi-contractual approach has seriously challenged the neoclassical 'black box' conception of the firm. In this transaction costs approach, the firm is necessarily seen as 'a nexus of treaties' made up of numerous contractual and non-contractual governance structures. The firm becomes an alternative governance structure to the market. The approach is less concerned with the firm as a productive force in the global economy. Instead, the firm is mostly seen as an organizing entity in the economy.

Reflecting these general theoretical developments in economics, the firm has become a contested analytical category in economic geography (Dicken and Thrift 1992; Taylor and Asheim 2001; Yeung 2005a). Much neoclassical economic geography takes the firm as a self-contained and homogenous 'black box' capable of producing economic outcomes in space. This conception of the firm is clearly evident in the 'geography of enterprise' approach that was preoccupied with the locational and behavioural patterns of the firm in space. This approach viewed the firm as an unproblematic category. The emergence of a radical approach in the 1970s and 1980s led to a major theoretical and empirical reorientation of research in industrial (economic) geography. This radical literature subsumed the firm under dominant capitalist class relations such that capital's logic explains the spatial behaviour of the firm (see a review in Scott 2000). Put in their historical contexts, these different perspectives on the firm have served the purposes of economic geography well by analysing the spatial organization of the firm.

The recent emergence of 'new economic geographies', however, has challenged these pre-existing conceptions (see Thrift and Olds 1996; Yeung 2005b). Influenced by a more contingent and relational interpretation of the 'economic', new economic geographers have drawn insights from network theories and post-structural management theory to develop alternative conceptions of the nature and organization of the firm. The firm becomes an analytical category in new economic geographies because the mechanistic and atomized view of the firm in neoclassical and transaction costs economics is unacceptable. The assumption that the firm is an efficient way to coordinate economic activities tends to underestimate the importance of the firm as a social organization that brings together diverse actors for productive activities. Although other economists have attempted to incorporate social relations in their analyses of the firm (e.g. role positions and role sets) the problem remains unsolved as the social contexts of these positions and sets are often taken away, resulting in what sociologist Granovetter (1985) calls 'undersocialized' analysis of the firm.

This undersocialized understanding of the firm in economics has made it extremely difficult to account for the phenomenon that opens this chapter. If the firm is merely a transaction-cost economizing device in a typical production function, then there should be no difference among the three transnational automobile firms (Ford, BMW and Toyota). After all, they are merely carmakers that bring together different component suppliers and assemble these components into automobiles for sales in consumer markets throughout the world. These three firms can only be different if they represent more than just economic agents of capitalism. To explain this non-economic dimension of the firm, we need to bring into our analysis the role of *social actors* and their *relational networks* (Yeung 2005a; Grabher 2006). As a means of organizing social life, this relational perspective conceptualizes the firm as a constellation

341

of network relations governed by social actors. Instead of being a mechanistic production function or an abstract capitalist imperative, it is a contested site for material and discursive constructions at different organizational and spatial scales. The firm is necessarily a site of power relations and power struggle among actors; it is a socio-spatial construction embedded in broader discourses and practices. The firm, in short, is a legal organizational entity arising from relational constructions of social networks and actors embedded in these networks. The firm is not a static 'point' or 'black box' as identified by most economists. It is indeed a dynamic and evolving organization constructed through ongoing social relations and discursive struggles among social actors in different localities and places.

Cognizant of parallel developments in economic sociology (see Peck 2005; Grabher 2006) this relational perspective draws upon insights from new economic geographies for an organizational analysis of the firm. It affords significant analytical importance to *social actors* because they make or break a particular firm. Highly corporatized supermarket chains, for example, are often run differently from neighbourhood family-managed stores. Even among what most consumers consider as similar retail giants such as Wal-Mart and Costco in the US, there are significant differences in the ways they treat their employees and customers (Herbst 2005). The world of transnational retail giants is clearly made up of drastically different firms that range from Wal-Mart to Tesco and Carrefour (Wrigley *et al.* 2005). This emphasis on social actors is important because, even in evolutionary economics, social actors have no distinguishable role in the firm. As proclaimed by one of its influential proponents:

> firms are the key actors, not individual human beings. Of course (implicitly) firms must provide sufficient inducements to attract and hold the individuals that staff them. But within these [evolutionary economics] models, individuals are viewed as interchangeable and their actions determined by the firms they are in.
>
> (Nelson 1995: 68)

This way of seeing social actors as 'interchangeable' and thus perfectly 'substitutable' has no doubt reduced each individual to an 'atom' in the economic system, allowing for nothing other than economic rationality and profit maximization to drive firm behaviour. This economistic conception of the firm has abstracted away human diversity and discursive practices that come to constitute firms in different localities and places.

In reality, however, the firm is about how the everyday life of actors is conducted in the process of engaging production, exchange and transactions. The firm provides a setting for organizing social relations in different places and at different spatial scales. Its very composition is made up of socio-spatial relations that define the core of the firm. To paraphrase Gibson-Graham (1996: 15), the firm does not have an 'invariant "inside"'. It is constituted contingently through ongoing social relations at different organizational and spatial scales. This conceptualization of the firm extends Penrose's (1995: 9) theory of the growth of the firm in which she argues that the firm is 'a complex institution, impinging on economic and social life in many directions, comprising numerous and diverse activities, making a large variety of significant decisions, influenced by miscellaneous and unpredictable human whims, yet generally directed in the light of human action'. To her, the firm is both an administrative unit and a collection of productive resources with certain boundaries (p. 24). The growth of the firm is significantly dependent on its existing repertoire of resources and managerial competence. The relational perspective on the firm in economic geography, however, goes beyond the growth of the firm *per se* and investigates its organization and socio-spatial constitution. By taking into account all those 'miscellaneous and unpredictable human whims' in corporate decisions and behaviour, we can understand why Ford, BMW and Toyota are such *different* organizational entities embedded in different corporate cultures and geographical contexts.

Such a relational view of the firm clearly stresses interconnectedness, hybridities and possibilities, just as broader notions of place as network described in Chapter 5 stress the relation rather than the entity. Its intellectual origin can be traced back to the 'substantivist' school (social organization approach) in economic sociology after Max Weber and Karl Polanyi (see Peck 2005; Grabher 2006). To the substantivists, the economy does not have a separate status from everyday social life as claimed by classical and subsequently neoclassical economists. Instead, the substantivists regard the economy as an instituted process to produce a structure with a definite function in society. Such modern organizations as the firm, therefore, are seen as an outcome not merely of economic rationality, but also of social rationality. This view of modern organizations has given rise to the notion of the socially constructed nature of modern organizations. It is one thing to view the firm as a social construct; it is yet another thing to clarify exactly what this social construction of the firm is about. A relational approach to the firm argues that the firm is an organizational unit bringing together diverse social relations in which actors in the firm are embedded. These relations may be inter-personal relationships, family linkages or simply social ties. Through the interpenetration of these relations, the firm is constituted not by individual actors who are seen as rational and self-interested in neoclassical economics. Rather, the firm is constituted through the broader relations of these individual actors that also define the boundary of the firm. For example, the firm in Chinese business can be both an economic device and a social organization for the advancement of the family and its immediate network actors (Yeung 2004).

Though the firm is bounded by certain contractual obligations – a phenomenon well explained in transaction costs economics – these obligations are effectively carried out through specific social relations among actors within the extended boundaries of the firm. As such, the activities of the firm (e.g. production, exchange and transactions) are the collective outcome of realizing social relations and obligations by these actors. The firm exists because it serves to provide an organizational framework for the coordination of these social relations by specific actors. Its existence is not predicated on the minimization of transaction costs *per se*. For example, the success of Benetton as a firm is explained with reference to its embeddedness in a geographically specific set of social relations (e.g. complex family business and subcontracting relations in Italy) that allow Benetton to innovate and exploit the advantages of flexibility in production and organization:

The Benetton we see is quite different if we look only at the focal firm or if we look more broadly at the social relations in which it is embedded. What makes Benetton possible, in part, is 'a sophisticated application of "telematics" [computer applications in design, production and distribution] to enable a far more flexible manufacturing system than an older, labour-intensive organization could have achieved' (Clegg 1990: 124).

This relational view of the firm as embedded in complex production networks therefore explicitly acknowledges the important role of social actors and their embedded relations in *governing* the firm – a theoretical approach explicitly developed in the global production network perspective in economic geography (see Henderson *et al.* 2002; Coe *et al.* 2004).

Geographies of firms

Closely related to the issue of organizational loci is the importance of territoriality and geography in constructing the firm. If networks are social structures and relational processes

343

constituted by intentional actors and are causal mechanisms capable of effecting empirical changes, they must be recognized as having distinctive time–space specificity in their workings such that no regular conjunctions of events and outcomes can be fully predicted by network formation. We can expect networks to create a variety of different spatial configurations in economic life. Some networks are relatively more localized because they are dependent on the traded and untraded interdependencies of geographical agglomeration achieved through territorial embeddedness (see Storper 1997). Other 'global' networks, however, are controlled 'at a distance' when the key actors are spatially distanciated from the sites where empirical events happen (see Dicken *et al.* 2001). In all cases, however, a specific spatial configuration is created and connected to other configurations at lower and higher geographical scales. Territoriality and scale matter because they shape the constitution of the firm through their geographical effects on social actors and their network relations. Understanding the territoriality of actor networks helps us to understand the nature and behaviour of the firm at different organizational and geographical scales.

For example, think of the relationship between the child labour employed by a Nike subcontractor in Indonesia and the executive board of Nike in the US. This subcontractor is strongly embedded locally in Indonesia through extra-firm networks with state officials, thereby being able to circumvent local labour laws. This child labour abuse by the subcontractor, however, may be discovered by some NGOs or media reporters from outside Indonesia and popularized unfavourably in the US. This local event in Indonesia may trigger the Nike board in the US to reconsider its relationships with all its subcontractors that result in tightening of its suppliers' code of conducts. This change in Nike's corporate practice may come voluntarily as a reflexive reaction from top management. The board may also be forced by the bad publicity generated by the NGOs to declare the end to the use of child labour by its subcontractors. The Indonesian subcontractor may be finally dismissed from Nike's global production networks. What appears to be a local phenomenon may be represented by institutions at another geographical scale. The outcome may become global when Nike forbids all its worldwide subcontractors to employ child labour for the manufacturing of all Nike products.

The Nike example shows that by virtue of its flows in different spheres (i.e. capital, labour, goods and services) the firm is a *de facto* territorial device for organizing social life. Headquartered in Beaverton, Oregon, Nike specializes in the design, R&D and marketing of its sports products. Its production in Asia is entirely handled by developed partners in Hong Kong, Taiwan and South Korea. These partners have established production facilities throughout Asia, e.g. in Bangladesh, China, Indonesia, Malaysia, Sri Lanka, Thailand and Vietnam. A Japanese trading company handles the financial and logistical aspects of Nike's production in Asia. Nike's subcontractors in South America (e.g. in Brazil, El Salvador, Ecuador and Mexico) and Eastern Europe (e.g. in Bulgaria, Turkey, Tunisia) are managed respectively by its international buying offices in the US and Europe. As of 1 April 2005, Nike had contracted over 700 such factories throughout the world. Its 124 active contract factories in China alone employed over 200,000 workers and its 34 active contract factories in Vietnam employed another 84,000 workers. As a consequence of intense criticisms from social and labour movements on the working conditions in its subcontractors' factories, Nike has attempted to develop extensive subcontractor monitoring and assessment systems. Through its partnership in the Global Alliance for Workers and Communities, it aims to give greater voice to its contract factory workers through regular field studies and focused interviews. It remains unclear if this partnership will dramatically improve the conditions of factory workers.

344

The actors and networks that constitute a firm such as Nike are territorially embedded. Emphasizing this general issue of territorial embeddedness in the firm and its networks is important because it sidesteps a potential weakness in emphasizing the networked nature of economic activity. Moving away from the 'topological presupposition' (Thrift and Olds 1996) of the 'bounded region' runs the risk of losing sight altogether of profound geographical variations across localities and regions. More significant, however, is the tendency to denigrate the role of the territorial state in shaping the governance of the firm. While some approaches in economic geography successfully incorporate the state as an actor, the state as a *territorial* entity is less well recognized (see Chapter 19 for a wider discussion of the role of the nation-state). A network link that crosses international borders is not just another example of 'acting at a distance'. It may also represent a *qualitative disjuncture* between different regulatory and cultural environments. Although networks crosscut national borders, the integrity of the latter can be maintained because networks themselves are often compelled to 'localize' differently within specific national territories. National regimes of regulation continue to create a pattern of 'bounded regions'. Networks of social actors and their economic activities are not simply superimposed upon this mosaic; nor is the state just another actor in these firm-specific networks.

The regulatory environment created by different states is still an immensely formative influence on the firm and its network development. Even firms operating in highly internationalized sectors (e.g. finance and electronics) still tend to retain distinct organizational forms and practices that largely reflect the regulatory environment of their home country (see Christopherson 1999; Dicken 2003). At the same time, however, the very fact that production networks coordinated by firms cross nation-state boundaries means that territories (at all scales) are, in effect, 'inserted' into firm-specific networks whose coordinative and control mechanisms may lie elsewhere. This has implications beyond that of the old debates on the 'external control' of local economies. A relational perspective on the firm encourages us to address the direct and indirect connections between firms and economic activities stretched across geographical space, but embedded in particular places. We have a mutually constitutive process: while social actors and their firm-specific networks are often embedded within territories, territories are also embedded in these networks. As space is socially constructed through culturally mediated processes, the spatiality of social relations has to be negotiated by social actors, and this process may be intertwined with how actors make sense and construct their corporate reality. Understood as such, different territorial configurations of regions and industrial ensembles may be closely linked to corporate constructions and both may thus mutually influence each other (see Dicken and Malmberg 2001; Coe *et al.* 2004).

To sum up this relational perspective on the firm in new economic geographies, we need to start by identifying both social actors and their firm-specific networks because the firm is constituted by 'spaces of network relations'. Social actors in the firm can be represented by different operating units, business divisions, labour unions, subcontractors and other organizational forms. We then need to understand the intentions and motives of these social actors and the bargaining power in their network relationships. These relationships are embedded in particular spaces. This, of course, does not mean that all social actors in each network must be bound together in exactly the same territory. Rather, there are distinct 'spaces' for social actors to engage in network relationships. These 'spaces' can include localized spaces (e.g. financial districts in global cities) and inter-urban spaces (e.g. webs of financial institutions and the business media that bind together global cities). The firm is made up of social actors engaged in relational networks within a variety of 'spaces'. The analytical lens we

345

adopt can thus vary widely. It may be geographical, sectoral or organizational, or some combination of these. The key point is to recognize the fundamental interrelatedness of all of these phenomena, not in some abstract sense as shown in neoclassical economics, but in seriously grounded forms.

Spaces of firms

One such space that makes a difference to economic change and outcomes lies at the *intra-firm* scale. Different corporate cultures and conventions may exist in the same space of a single firm. The failure to understand these divergent corporate cultures and conventions has been argued by some economic geographers to represent 'the cultural crisis of the firm' (Schoenberger 1997). This crisis has led to irrational corporate strategies that subsume major industrial players to unexpected business failures. The stakes of understanding corporate cultures and conventions and appreciating their geographical specificity become very high. What then exactly is corporate culture? How do conventions come into the picture? Corporate culture can be viewed at the following four levels:

- *Ways of thinking*: This refers to the mental level that ranges from ideas and meanings to processes of interpretation and the construction of knowledge. These ideas and meanings can be top-down in the sense that the top management imposes them on employees. They can also be bottom-up in a more cooperative context. Different ways of thinking can persist even in the same firm, let alone different firms. We can think of 'subcultures' co-existing in the firm. For example, employees in the finance department are often much more prudent and thrifty than their colleagues in the marketing department. Engineers have very different worldviews from accountants, salespeople and clerical workers. This difference in ways of thinking can be translated into the next level, when different actors in the firm behave differently in their everyday practice.

- *Material practices*: At the action level, corporate culture is about what we do and how we go about doing it. It thus entails a wide range of everyday practices such as conversations, meetings, work tasks, divisions of labour, making products, delivering services, and so on. Over time, many of these material practices become routinized such that employees will perform them almost as a matter of fact. The need to write minutes of meetings may be so routinized in some firms that the appropriate personnel will do so 'naturally'. In other firms, there are routines on how to dispose of used papers, whether coffee breaks are held indoor/outdoor, and what kind of taboos can be discussed openly. Different employees may understand and conduct these practices routinely. In doing so, they contribute to the formation and perpetuation of specific corporate cultures. Employees in other firms may not buy into certain material practices. Their understandings are also mediated by a whole variety of other factors such as personal feelings and institutional constraints (e.g. in professional business such as law and accountancy where secrecy and confidentiality prevail). Their everyday practices may therefore subvert dominant corporate cultures.

- *Social relationships*: Everyday practice is both a material and a social activity. We need rooms to hold meetings and assembly platforms to make cars – the material aspect of practice. But equally important are the social relationships that bring different people together in a room or an assembly platform. Friendship, partnership and team spirits are particularly important as the social glue that facilitates how the job is done. Social relationships thus become the organizing framework through which work is distributed, obligation is met, order is followed through, strategy is executed, and so on. These social relationships are about behavioural norms and standards among peers: some firms have very hostile working relations among co-workers, whereas cooperation and mutual help may be common in other firms. Once institutionalized and shared, they become *conventions* that are taken for granted in everyday social interaction within the firm. For example, few employees in McDonald's fast food outlets will question the routinized social relationships between the cashier and the burger maker. The former needs to complete an order and a transaction with the customer and the latter depends on the former in order to make to order. Both of them must cooperate or else the entire service chain will break down.

■ *Power relations*: This idea of a chain within firms is further evident in a hierarchical and vertical sense when social relations are embedded in differential power and control among different employees. These power relations can be expressed in the form of dress codes (formal vs informal), greeting styles (last name vs first name), reporting procedures (hierarchical vs lateral), decision processes (centralized vs consensual), and so on. Not all firms have highly hierarchical command chains – some prefer to adopt a more flexible and flattened reporting system so that the negative effects of unequal power relations (e.g. employee dissatisfaction) can be mitigated. This difference in vertical power relations can occur in firms from within the same country of origin and between different home countries.

Taken together, corporate cultures and conventions can exert very powerful *stabilizing* effect on the behaviour and practice of actors in specific firms. This is where interesting economic-geographical questions might be asked: how do corporate cultures evolve in specific places, and how they exhibit tendencies of path dependency – a process whereby past behaviour guides present and future decisions such that similar behavioural outcomes emerge? To answer these two questions, I draw upon a well-known geographical study of international competition by Erica Schoenberger (1997). Her study was primarily concerned with how large and powerful corporations, once dominant leaders in their respective industries and markets for decades, can suddenly become uncompetitive. Two of the examples she used are Xerox, the American giant in the copying and imaging business, and Canon, its Japanese challenger. Her main puzzle is that Xerox, as the first company to introduce and market the xerographic machine in 1949 and a billion-dollar US firm by the 1960s, was on the verge of collapse by the early 1980s. Its market share in copier machines dwindled from over 90 per cent in the early 1970s to just under 15 per cent at the end of the decade. Xerox's market share loss was taken over by Japanese entrants such as Canon, Ricoh and Sharp. As early as 1970, Canon developed its own first plain-paper copier, the NP-1100, by avoiding Xerox patents in copier technology. In 1971, Xerox did approach Canon with the idea of licensing Canon's copier technology. But Xerox's technologists, presumably the most 'knowing' people in the organization, condemned the approach as selling out to juniors.

In these two cases, spaces of economic cultures worked out rather differently in terms of their competitive outcomes. At the time when these Japanese entrants were focusing on developing small, low-volume, simple, cheap but reliable copiers, Xerox was paying its attention exclusively to its American rivals, Kodak and IBM. As Schoenberger (1997: 195) writes, 'this segment of the market had been written off as uninteresting. The dominant culture [in Xerox] valued large, fast, technically elegant, and high-margin [machines] and, in the absence of any viable alternatives in the market, these commitments were unchallenge-able'. The central command in Xerox was so focused on its archrival American competitors and their familiar style of competition that it failed to recognize or respond to a new kind of competition from 'outsiders'. To Xerox, the Japanese competition simply didn't matter, not because it did not exist, but because it was invisible and it came from the 'wrong place' – Japan – that clearly fell outside the known world of competition. The corporate culture in Xerox was so blindfolded by its instantaneous success in the US and its excessive focus on American counterparts. This reflects a corporate culture of what counts (competition from Kodak and IBM) and what does not (the likes of Canon, Ricoh and Sharp). The end result is clear – Xerox was almost forced out of the very industry it helped to create.

The case of Xerox clearly shows how corporate culture can stabilize the competitive environment as much as immobilize the ability of the firm to change in response to this competitive environment. The relegation of the Japanese competition by Xerox headquarters as 'localized' and 'unthinkable' had profound effects on the competitive outcome in this industry; it heralded the change of fortune in favour of Japanese manufacturers throughout the 1980s and the 1990s. The key economic-geographical lesson, then, is that spatial change in competitive dynamics is not necessarily an outcome of economic factors (e.g. price, cost, technology and investment) but also of cultural factors within certain firm spaces (e.g. ignorance and a superiority complex) that significantly influence the effectiveness of these economic forces.

Conclusion

This chapter has shown not just the enormous variety of firms as the core economic insti-tutions of capitalism. More importantly, it has unravelled the socio-spatial nature of con-temporary capitalist firms from a relational perspective. In doing so, the chapter has enabled us to go beyond conventional economistic understanding of the firm as merely a cost-efficient organizational device in the event of market failure. Indeed, we can appreciate better the complex interrelationships of different actors that constitute and drive the firm. We can also see how these interrelationships can be organized in the form of networks that span different territorial formations. There are thus 'places' even within the same firm as its corporate cultures vary in different geographical contexts. These firm-specific 'places' can exert a powerful influence on change and continuity in different locations in which the firm oper-ates. The cases of Xerox and Nike have offered useful evidence to make apparent these 'places' and their importance in shaping firm behaviour.

This co-existence of different 'places' is much more likely among *different* firms, particu-larly those from different countries of origin. In the case of the three automobile giants, they have drastically different organizational networks to facilitate their productive activities. They also exhibit very different corporate cultures and behaviour, leading to divergent responses to change in the global economy. The contemporary landscape of capitalist firms is thus char-acterized not by the same firms everywhere, but by a mosaic of different firms even at the time when their globalization efforts are stepping up. In doing so, they articulate different places into their corporate networks and exert profound influence on these places. And yet, these firms are becoming more embedded in these places via social relations developed over time. As argued strongly in Dicken (2000), this intertwined relationship between firms and places represents perhaps one of the most significant insights in a relational perspective on the firm in economic geography.

Further reading

Dicken, P. and Malmberg, A. (2001) Firms in territories: a relational perspective. *Economic Geography* 77 (4), 345–63.

Dicken, P., Kelly, P.F., Olds, K. and Yeung, H.W.C. (2001) Chains and networks, territories and scales: towards an analytical framework for the global economy. *Global Networks* 1 (2), 89–112.

Schoenberger, E. (1997) *The Cultural Crisis of the Firm*. Oxford: Blackwell.

Taylor, M. and Asheim, B. T. (2001) The concept of the firm in economic geography. *Economic Geography* 77 (4), 315–28.

Yeung, H.W.C. (2005a) The firm as social networks. *Growth and Change* 36 (3), 307–28.

References

Christopherson, S. (1999) Rules as resources: how market governance regimes influence firm networks, in T.J. Barnes and M.S. Gertler (eds) *The New Industrial Geography: Regions, Regulation and Institutions*, pp. 155–75. London: Routledge.

Clegg, S.R. (1990) *Modern Organization: Organization Studies in the Postmodern World*, London: Sage.

Coe, N., Hess, M., Yeung, H.W.C., Dicken, P. and Henderson, J. (2004) Globalizing' regional development: a global production networks perspective. *Transactions of the Institute of British Geographers*, New Series 29 (4), 468–84.

Dicken, P. (2000) Places and flows: situating international investment. In G.L. Clark, M.A. Feldman and M.S. Gertler (eds) *The Oxford Handbook of Economic Geography*, pp. 275–91. Oxford: Oxford University Press.

——(2003) 'Placing' firms: grounding the debate on the 'global' corporation. In J. Peck and H.W.C. Yeung (eds) *Remaking the Global Economy: Economic-Geographical Perspectives*, pp. 27–44. London: Sage.

Dicken, P. and Malmberg, A. (2001) Firms in territories: a relational perspective. *Economic Geography* 77 (4), 345–63.

Dicken, P. and Thrift, N. (1992) The organization of production and the production of organization. *Transactions, Institute of British Geographers* 17, 279–91.

Dicken, P., Kelly, P.F., Olds, K. and Yeung, H.W.C. (2001) Chains and networks, territories and scales: towards an analytical framework for the global economy. *Global Networks* 1 (2), 89–112.

Gibson-Graham, J.K. (1996) *The End of Capitalism (As We Knew It): A Feminist Critique of Political Economy*. Oxford: Blackwell.

Grabher, G. (2006) Trading routes, bypasses, and risky intersections: mapping the travels of 'networks' between economic sociology and economic geography. *Progress in Human Geography* 30, 163–89.

Granovetter, M. (1985) Economic action, and social structure: the problem of embeddedness. *American Journal of Sociology* 91, 481–510.

Henderson, J., Dicken, P., Hess, M., Coe, N. and Yeung, H.W.C. (2002) Global production networks and the analysis of economic development. *Review of International Political Economy* 9 (3), 436–64.

Herbst, M. (2005) *The Costco Challenge: An Alternative to Wal-Martization?* Available at http://www.laborresearch.org/print.php?id = 391 (accessed on 15 August 2005).

Hodgson, G.M. (1988) *Economics and Institutions: A Manifesto for a Modern Institutional Economics*. Cambridge: Polity Press.

Nelson, R.R. (1995) Recent evolutionary theorizing about economic change. *Journal of Economic Literature* 33 (1), 48–90.

Peck, J.A. (2005) Economic sociologies in space. *Economic Geography* 81 (2), 129–75.

Penrose, E. (1995) *The Theory of the Growth of the Firm*, revised edition. Oxford: Oxford University Press.

Schoenberger, E. (1997) *The Cultural Crisis of the Firm*. Oxford: Blackwell.

Scott, A. J. (2000) Economic geography: the great half-century. *Cambridge Journal of Economics* 24 (4), 483–504.

Storper, M. (1997) *The Regional World: Territorial Development in a Global Economy.* New York: Guilford Press.

Taylor, M. and Asheim, B.T. (2001) The concept of the firm in economic geography. *Economic Geography* 77 (4), 315–28.

Thrift, N. and Olds, K. (1996) Refiguring the economic in economic geography. *Progress in Human Geography* 20 (3), 311–37.

Toyota (2005) http://www.toyota.co.jp/en/about_toyota/message (accessed 18 July 2005).

Williamson, O.E. (1990) The firm as a nexus of treaties: an introduction, in M. Aoki, B. Gustafsson and O.E. Williamson (eds) *The Firm as a Nexus of Treaties*, pp. 1–25. London: Sage.

——(1999) Strategy research: governance and competence perspectives. *Strategic Management Journal* 20, 1087–1108.

Womack, J.P., Jones, D.T. and Roos, D. (1990) *The Machines that Changed the World.* New York: Rawson Associates.

Wrigley, N., Coe, N.M. and Currah, A. (2005) Globalizing retail: conceptualizing the distribution-based transnational corporation (TNC). *Progress in Human Geography* 29 (4), 437–57.

Yeung, H.W.C. (2004) *Chinese Capitalism in a Global Era.* London: Routledge.

——(2005a) The firm as social networks. *Growth and Change* 36 (3), 307–28.

——(2005b) Rethinking relational economic geography. *Transactions of the Institute of British Geographers* 30 (1), 37–51.

23

Households

Helen Jarvis

Introduction

The notion of a household as a co-resident group 'eating out of a common pot' is identifiable in every society across the globe (Robertson 1984; Crehan 1992). Arguably the household is fundamental to geographic understanding on three levels: as a barometer of social and demographic change; as a tool (site and scale) of geographic analysis; and as a major welfare provider. The household is the foremost realm of non-capitalist economic production (Gibson-Graham 1996) – and of all the social (re)production work necessary for individuals and families to 'go on' from one day to the next (Jarvis *et al.* 2001). There has nevertheless been a tendency for the *dynamic nature* of households, as 'little welfare states' (Folbre 2001: 202), to be neglected. In orthodox economic theory, for instance, the household is typically denied any internal workings. The process of decision-making is a 'black box' and decisions are assumed to be made either by a 'benevolent dictator' or as a 'small factory' about which 'the household' meets as a committee to agree a shared course of action (Becker 1981).

A sustained critique of the caricature of 'rational economic man' behaviour distinguishes contemporary human geography, especially where the discipline draws on a legacy of anthropological accounts of kinship to highlight divisions *within* as well as *between* household collectives (Malinowski 1913; Creighton and Omari 1995; Kabeer 1997; Beall and Kanji 1999). Indeed, the household can be said to have 'come of age' in substantive and methodological terms in the 1990s, largely as a result of feminist contributions to labour market research and the awareness this raised of the wider implications (for housing, migration, transport, child-care, consumption and more) of women's increased participation in paid employment outside the home. Growth in women's employment combined with new patterns of marriage, cohabitation and divorce, longer life expectancy and falling fertility rates to produce a 'wider palette of family and domestic situations' (Buzar *et al.* 2005: 414). In the developed world these trends are associated with a reduced working age population and a situation in which the rate of growth in the number of households (and concomitant pressures on land for housing and associated infrastructure) exceeds that for total population. This is because more households only accommodate one person – each typically occupying a larger family dwelling.

This chapter is organized into four sections. The first considers the household as a barometer of socio-demographic change. It traces a shift in interest from the individual to the household and identifies household processes driving residential mobility and migration. The second section traces a similar shift in the way households are conceived, epistemologically, from that of a closed, consensual 'unit' to that of a multi-faceted 'lens' receiving and transmitting the preferences, decisions, structural constraints and unintended consequences of everyday routines and practices. A third section considers the socially and geographically situated constitution of the household as a complex institution (and *de facto* welfare provider) in 'multiple' economies and local, regional and trans-national circuits of consumption, production and social-(re)production. The concluding section summarizes the main arguments for a broad and deep understanding of the 'household-as-process'.

The household as a barometer of socio-demographic change

There is a tendency in the social science literature to use the terms 'household' and 'family' interchangeably as a shorthand for 'a group of people who live together, share resources (even if that sharing is not equitable or fair), and who (at least at some level) make efforts to co-ordinate their activities' (Nelson and Smith 1999: 5). Yet there are good reasons for differentiating families and households. By definition, a family comprises a group of two or more people who live together and are related by birth, marriage, cohabitation or adoption. One person living alone does not constitute a family and one person living without permanent shelter is not a household. While, historically, most definitions rest with kinship and co-residence, there is evidence that the co-determinacy of 'family' and 'household' and 'home' and 'household' are being eroded by new varieties of household composition (Buzar *et al.* 2005: 416). Some sense of this transformation is evident in the proliferation of 'blended' or step-families, where two families are 'blended' through marriage, resulting in a fragile web of domestic and parenting arrangements (Smart and Neale 1999). It is similarly evident in the term 'fictive kin', used to indicate the emotional significance of friendships in situations of dislocation and isolation, where new migrants replace absent kin with close-knit social networks and cultivate within them the kind of mutual trust and support conventionally associated with bonds of blood and marriage (Stack 1983).

Complexity is also illustrated in relation to decisions made in dual-career households, such as those contributing to new patterns of 'dual location' living. Some couples find it either not possible, or not necessary, to maintain a close partnership through 'cohabitation' in the strictest sense, but instead 'live apart together' (LAT) in two households with two residences (Gross 1980; Green *et al.* 1999). Others live in one household but have a 'commuter marriage' involving one shared home and a second apartment for use by one partner who works away from home on a regular basis (Winfield 1985). One French study found that 6 per cent of the adult population of Paris were living in LAT relationships in the mid 1990s (Caradec 1996), while in Sweden it is estimated that 2 per cent of all couples maintain a close relationship across two residences (Levin and Trost 1999). Before turning to consider the implications of this new diversity of household types and living arrangements, it is worth putting the headline trends into historical and geographic context.

The shrinking household

After the two world wars, the 'nuclear family' of mother, father and children became the 'norm' for the English-speaking advanced world, while the 'extended family' of three generations characterized much of the developing world. Arguably, both these trends are being eroded by social and economic changes attributed to processes of globalization (Bongaarts 2001; see also Chapter 12). In the 1950s more than 70 per cent of American families maintained a 'traditional' employment structure comprising a male breadwinner and an economically inactive wife. By 1980 this figure had fallen to 15 per cent (Rowbotham 1977: 455). The new norm in 'couple families' is for both parents to be employed outside the home, often for long hours.

Across the world we find a trend of shrinking household size. In 1990, average household size in developed and developing countries was 2.7 and 4.8 persons respectively. By 2050, it is projected that the range may be as little as 2.6 to 3.4 (O'Neill *et al.* 2000, in UNFPA 2001: 80). Multi family households are rare in the UK and USA, but this household type is common in the developing world and an important source of welfare in old age. In India, the proportion of single-person households currently stands at just 4 per cent, while in urban areas 35.6 per cent of households comprise 3–4 members (28.9 per cent in rural areas) and 20.8 per cent comprise 7 or more members (26.4 per cent in rural areas) (Census of India 2001). There is nevertheless evidence of a shift towards nuclear families and more non-family households in rapidly developing countries: extended family arrangements are being undermined by pressures of rural to urban and international migration (see Chapter 59), the emergence of a new middle-class urban elite and a cultural shift towards individual achievement over collective welfare.

In 2001, the British household averaged 2.4 people in size (compared with an average of 2.6 in the USA). Table 23.1 illustrates the dominant trends of change in household composition over the period 1961 to 2001. This shows that one-person households accounted for 30 per cent of the population in 2001, up from 12 per cent in 1961. Single-family households accounted for just 56 per cent of all households in 2001 compared to 74 per cent in 1961 (ONS 2003). In the USA, 81 per cent of all households were families in 1970, but by 2003 this proportion had dropped to 68 per cent (USCB 2004b). Similarly, in 1961 lone parents accounted for just 6 per cent of households in Britain (2 per cent with children under age 18) but by 2001 they accounted for 11 per cent of all households. The USA has seen less dramatic growth in one-person households (19 per cent in 2003) but a rising proportion of lone-parent households. This type accounted for 16 per cent of all households in 2003 and, of this, 35 per cent of all African American households (USCB 2004b: Table 1).

Table 23.1. The changing profile of household composition: decennial census data for England and Wales 1961–2001

	1961	1971	1981	1991	2001
One person					
under pensionable age	4	6	8	11	13
over pensionable age	8	12	14	16	17
Two or more unrelated adults	5	4	5	3	2
Single-family households couple					
no children	26	27	26	27	27
one or more dependent children	38	35	30	25	23
adult offspring only	10	8	8	8	6
Lone parent					
one or more dependent children	2	3	5	6	7
adult offspring only	4	4	3	3	4
Multi-family households	3	1	1	1	1

Source: ONS (2003).

This trend of households shrinking in size has potentially damaging and far-reaching consequences. Smaller households pose a threat to the natural environment because economies of scale are lost with respect to land use and energy consumption for housing, transport and utilities (UNFPA 2001). Social divisions are also made worse by the concentration of employment characteristics (such as permanent, insecure and low wage) within particular household structures. Because most adults in couple households are from the same occupational class, the population is increasingly divided between affluent 'work-rich' dual-career households, 'multiple-job' low-income households and 'employment deprived' no-earner households (McRae 1986; Jarvis 1997). Children in lone-mother households in the USA are five times more likely to grow up in poverty than children in households with two adults of working age (USCB 2004a: Table C8), and because of the concentration of this household type within spatially segregated black and minority ethnic neighbourhoods, poor households are further disadvantaged by limited scope for support from the wider community.

Migration and mobility

There is keen interest among academics, policy makers and planners to scrutinize the wider social, cultural and economic influences, and *implications*, of change in the profile and composition of households, such as with respect to connections between housing, employment, migration and mobility. As Randolph (1991: 37) observes 'it is households who consume housing, but individuals who participate in the labour market'. Close attention has been paid to the relationship between household structure and relative mobility because long-distance relocation entails the coordination or sacrifice of individual attachments to a job, place or social network.

According to Mincer (1978) the economically inactive wife in a male breadwinner household is a 'tied mover' who moves for the sake of her husband's career. In dual-breadwinner couples it is recognized that the wife's financial contribution from paid employment may inhibit such a move, making the husband a 'tied stayer' (Smits et al. 2003: 603). There is speculation as to whether women have gained 'decision power' alongside greater labour market participation (Bielby and Bielby 1989; Bonney and Love 1991; Breugel 1996; Cooke 2003). The general view is that the normalization of two earners in couple households contributes to both inertia and persistent gender inequalities, whereby 'wives are more likely to be tied movers in migrating families while husbands, if they are tied at all, are more likely to be tied stayers than tied movers' (Mincer 1978: 754). Hardill (2002: 8) observes that women in dual-career households, even childless women, are more likely to be the 'trailing spouse'.

Hall et al. (1997) associate household transition (a change in household status) with geographic mobility as a major impetus to the segregation of communities by age, class, race and sexuality. Moves ranging from a young person leaving the parental home, through family formation, household dissolution, the 'empty nest' and various stages of retirement and ageing, each function through segmented housing markets. Some places attract particular households and lifestyles because of their climate, landscape or reputation for cultural diversity. This has long been observed with respect to the concentration of 'snow bird' retirees in the US 'sun belt' (Frey et al. 2000; Williams et al. 1997). It is similarly observed in clusters of same-sex households in cosmopolitan cities and neighbourhoods (such as San Francisco's Castro district) boasting a liberal politics and openness to diversity (Knopp 1995; Florida 2002; Black et al. 2000). In Britain, Duncan and Smith (2001: 484) find a correspondence between places known to provide an escape from the 'rat race' and people forming 'alternative' family arrangements. From this they argue that geographies of partnering and parenting do not rest with individual 'choice' but are instead informed by social relations in geographically situated households as part of neighbourhoods and community networks.

The household as a tool of analysis: from unit to lens

It is easy to see how, as a barometer of social and demographic change, the household provides a useful 'unit' for projecting future demand for housing, schools, shops and age-related services, as well as modelling residential segregation and uneven development by migration flows and life-course related settlement patterns. Yet it is with respect to the way households are assumed to think and behave that scholarship becomes ideologically divided. Those working within a neoclassical paradigm view household behaviour as something to be 'read off' from the assumption that household members seek to 'maximise utility on the basis of a set of shared preferences represented by an aggregate utility function and a common budget constraint' (Agarwal 1997: 2). By contrast, a behavioural approach recognizes that households sharing similar characteristics often respond differently to the same stimulus. This latter approach emphasizes the need to open up the household to look at changing divisions of labour, gender roles, conflict resolution and bargaining power.

Orthodox departures

According to orthodox theory, households choose a home location by 'trading off' housing costs, which tend to fall with distance from a central place, against transport costs, which tend to increase with distance (Evans 1985: 14). The limitations of this approach are severe: individuals and households are assumed to be featureless and interchangeable; consumers are assumed to hold perfect information; choices are apparently made in a vacuum; and little or no recognition is afforded to the role of legal and socio-economic institutional constraint.

Orthodox understanding would also have it that gender roles and divisions follow a pattern of specialization or 'competency' based on the relative earning potential of each member. This notion of spouse 'bargaining' emerged with the 'new home economics' (NHE) of Nobel Prizewinning economist Gary Becker (Becker 1965, 1981). The NHE provided a framework for analysing the allocation of time by married couples based on the concept of joint utility maximization (Becker 1965). For instance, Manser and Brown (1980: 31) applied this framework to a two-person co-operative 'game' to explain decisions concerning marriage, fertility, labour supplies and the unequal distribution of resources (such as food and leisure time) within families. While the NHE posits 'social explanations based entirely on trade between rational individuals' (Gardiner 1997: 150), Marxist theory also characterizes household relationships by consensus rather than conflict (Folbre 1986: 254). Critics of both neo-classical and Marxist approaches reject a unitary conception and instead theorize households as social collectives in which gender and power relations need to be examined (Beall and Kanji 1999: 3).

Scholars such as Zelizer (2005: 235) maintain that 'income catalyses relational work' such that power in decision-making can be determined on the basis of breadwinning, and on this basis alone dual-earner households are understood to be fundamentally more democratic than sole-breadwinner households. A model of bargaining in which decision-power is imputed from different combinations of spouse employment is illustrated in Table 23.2. The nine permutations shown here reinforce the pattern of household employment noted previously. In the United States nearly 60 per cent of these couples with children comprise two working parents.

Table 23.2. Inference of gender role 'bargaining power' from spouse paid employment

	Female Employment Status:		
	Employed	*Unemployed*	*Inactive*
Male Employment Status:			
Employed	**59.86%** Dual earner: Egalitarian	**2.21%**	**21.83%** Male Breadwinner: traditional gender roles
Unemployed	**2.05%**	**0.37%** Income assumed to be from state welfare alone	**0.80%**
Inactive	**3.51%** Role-reversal is rare	**0.22%**	**1.74%** Assumed retirement/ income from pension

Source: USDC (2003).

In just 20 per cent a 'traditional' male breadwinner supports an economically inactive spouse as home-maker. The reverse of this scenario, a mother in full-time employment together with a full-time house-husband, is notably rare, with less than 4 per cent identified in this category.

Critics of this approach argue that paid employment varies enormously in terms of status as well as income, and economically inactive mothers can establish a non-economic bargaining position by adopting a moral voice, speaking on behalf of dependent children and the wider family. Within the dual-earner category, for instance, employment combinations vary both with hours worked and autonomy (see, for instance, Jarvis 2002); and a house move which would facilitate male breadwinner promotion (generating increased household income) can be vetoed by non-monetary considerations such as local social and kin networks or children who 'refuse to leave'. Moreover, women appear not to have gained as much leverage in domestic decisions as is assumed on the basis of increased earning. Despite the normalization of a dual-breadwinner arrangement, there is little evidence of equal parenting and it is widely expected that employed mothers undertake a 'second shift' of unpaid domestic labour (Hochschild 1989; Somerville 2000: 6). Those who argue that income contributions do not adequately explain spatial divisions of household gender relations have been instrumental in highlighting the role of localized cultures and social networks in shaping household behaviour.

Methodological innovations

The household has emerged as a significant site of concern in both quantitative and qualitative analysis. While the profile of a population of households is typically drawn from aggregate cross-sectional census data, actual household structures (such as dual career, same sex, multi-generation) can be examined through the manipulation of micro-data, such as with the British Sample of Anonymised Records (SAR) and the US Public Use Microdata

(PUMS) (Jarvis 1997; Boyle *et al.* 1999). Different types of dual-earner household can be differentiated by hours worked and spouse occupation for each spouse. In this way Dorling (1995) observed that half of all British men working more than 60 hours a week lived in families with young dependent children. Longitudinal panel surveys, such as the British Household Panel Survey (BHPS), can be used to explore people's transitions through particular household types and the relationships of these to transitions into and out of poverty, owner occupation and the like (Berthoud and Gershuny 2000; Bond and Sale 2001). Perhaps the most exciting research involves multiple methods, such as the combination of household biographies with geographic information systems (GIS) to build up a detailed time–space landscape of household activities, resources and movements (see, for instance, Kwan 1999; Pavlovskaya 2004).

There remain serious limitations to all forms of secondary data analysis, not least that observation is limited to decisions which are 'revealed' by action (such as migration). Neglected are within-household conflicts which result in non-action or other manifestations of compromise. Consequently there is a strong case for primary qualitative research involving diaries, biographies and narrative analysis. The suggestion is that household behaviour reflects 'structures of feeling' negotiated over time as part of an integrated and shared biography. A biographical approach such as that illustrated in Box 23.1 highlights the way individual and household preferences evolve as a function of 'linked lives' and the intersection of housing, employment, gender and generation (Bailey *et al.* 2004). Intimacy and repetition create a high degree of stability, whereby each member might anticipate the other's view or action in a given situation.

Welfare and livelihood: within and beyond the household

In many respects NHE marked the beginning of a household 'renaissance', both by suggesting the possibility of scrutinizing unequal gender relations within the household and by stimulating a wholesale critique of 'rational economic agency' (see for instance Ferber and Nelson 1993). This changed the research aim from one representing a scale of analysis to one which accounted for the 'household as process', as a set of dynamic interactions (Wallman 1984: 53).

Box 23.1. Preference, biography, entitlement

Sharon and Jamie Fuller* live to the east of San Francisco in Alameda County. They describe their housing situation as the anchor point to their current way of living, including how they organize child-care for their six-year-old daughter. Although both parents earn an income from professional employment (Sharon as a part-time solicitor and Jamie as a self-employed photographer) their household income is insufficient to secure a mortgage on a single-family home in the high-cost Bay Area. For several years now they have lived with Sharon's mother in the house she owns. They present the arrangement as being mutually beneficial whereby Sharon's mother 'helps somewhat with child-care when we get in a pinch – the fall-back is Grandma' and she is helped in turn by them '(taking) her shopping and to her doctor's appointments'. As Sharon explains: 'The house(hold) is actually three things: it's that we have this on-site support system; then there's my mother's situation – she's actually told us she wouldn't stay (on) in the house if we didn't live with her because there's always a danger that she could fall; and then the other thing is the housing market – we can't afford to buy in this area.'

(Jarvis 2005: 138–9)

*One case from a sample of 100 household biographies: pseudonyms used to preserve anonymity.

It heightened awareness of the household as a site of conflict and negotiation (of gender roles, labour divisions), within which men and women (and adults and children) at times hold antagonistic interests and priorities (Sen 1990; Burgoyne 1990). The significance of this renaissance should not be underestimated. It raised awareness of the prevailing partial and patriarchal systems of accounting which measure gross domestic product (GDP) and recognize as 'development' only those activities attributed a monetary value. As Linda McDowell (2004: 146) argues, this system overlooks all those resources that are outside the market – goods and services and labour exchanged voluntarily or for love, in households and the community, without which the formal capital economy would collapse. By contrast, a holistic (or pluralist) approach recognizes formal and informal (cash-in-hand) work, remittance economies, domestic food production and self-provisioning, reciprocity and the 'economy of regard' state benefits and redistributive economies and, crucially, care work (Jarvis 1997). It is within a 'whole economy' perspective that attention turns to social (re)production as an expression of 'the diverse conditions and organizational relations which allow human beings to survive in various social contexts and groups. In this sense it is synonymous with 'livelihood' or 'survival strategies' (Mingione 1991: 124).

Diverse coping strategies

The concept of household 'strategies' provides a useful means of unpicking the locally situated response of households to periodic economic crises, family life-cycle events and changes in the norms and values of household members and their social milieu. Evidence of a whole range of coping strategies indicate the extent to which each household relies on a web of networks together with multiple economic relationships to maintain or adapt its livelihood when external conditions change (Gullestad 1984; Petterson 1996: 238).

Strategy types include those described as personal strategies (Yeandle 1984); work strategies (which operate interdependently with the gender roles and divisions of labour which they support) (Pahl 1984); strategies of financial management and domestic organization (Pahl 1989) and livelihood strategies (Ellegård and de Pater 1999; Hapke 2001). Most argue that income provides inadequate evidence of household resource capability because survival and upward social mobility depend more crucially on social and kin networks and access to knowledge and favours, as the practical means by which to fix home repairs, care for children, and journey from place to place (Nelson 2004).

Household members engage in 'multiple economies' in order to secure income and domestic reproduction, raise children, and care for the disabled, frail and sick (Pavlovskaya 2004). They work formally and informally, in many economic spaces outside and inside their homes, do paid and unpaid work, produce and exchange goods, services and emotional care. Extreme creativity can be observed in the way they stitch together a patchwork of arrangements to ensure young children, disabled and frail elderly relatives are cared for round-the-clock and all are clothed and fed (Skinner 2003). Pettersen (1996: 238) claims that while resources vary by household circumstance, the extent to which households consciously 'choose' between different strategies should not be overestimated: options are limited by both external circumstances and internal dynamics, including the taken-for-granted aspects of family life. Strategies are therefore complex, varied and subject to change.

Household chains of exploitation

An emphasis on household strategies of behaviour highlights the unequal distribution of a whole range of resources, beyond income and property, especially in relation to uneven development. Moreover, it shows how the burden of social (re)production work has increased as a direct consequence of the rolling back of state welfare functions and a climate of increasingly ruthless competition. The cost of privately undertaking once public or collective welfare services disproportionately falls to women and is especially high for ethnic minority women. There is growing awareness that exchanges between households, especially those shaped by international migration (such as with low wage and unprotected domestic workers), is often exploitative. This is illustrated in Box 23.2 in relation to what Ehrenreich and Hochschild (2003) describe as the 'global care chain' borne out of unequally resourced household coping strategies. The growing commodification of care is viewed as the female underside to globalization, whereby 'in the absence of help from male partners, many First World women have succeeded in tough "male world" careers only by turning over the care of their children, elderly parents and home to women from the Third World' (Ehrenreich and Hochschild 2003: 2) (see also Mattingly 2001: 370).

Household networks and geographies

Alongside greater understanding of intra-household dynamics has grown concern to examine 'the extra-household socio-economic and legal institutions within which households are embedded, and how these institutions might themselves be subject to change' (Agarwal 1997: 2). Households do not function on the head of a pin or in a social vacuum. In this way, Wheelock and Oughton (1996: 156) identify the household 'as a node in a multilayered web or the locus for a number of networks of relations: economic, social and technological' which stretches through communities, social and kin networks and a multiplicity of formal and informal economic opportunities. Similarly Jarvis (1999a: 226) argues that the household needs to be understood as part of a wider social and material infrastructure where processes of household decision-making are represented over time and space 'within a web of networks: of social and kin relations; of resource provision; and of information, knowledge and learning'. In short, household members participate in spheres of activity inside and beyond the nominal boundaries of the household (the 'home sphere') – through employment, trade union or political activity, by escorting children to school and entering into reciprocal exchanges with other households or extended family. These activities and social interactions

---

Box 23.2. Care chains

In San Francisco, as with many other 'successful' cities, 'work-rich' two-wage households do not represent a monolithic demographic, universally advantaged group. Well-paid, high-status professional working parents required to work long hours and travel on business at short notice increasingly demand '24-hour' markets such as those for routine day-care, emergency child- and elderly respite-care, grocery delivery and 'lifestyle management' concierge services. Low-wage service providers (typically Mexican and Filipina migrants) are drawn into these new markets only to experience increasingly exploitative 'non-standard' contracts and shift-work. At both ends of the income scale, working parents experience difficulties combining jobs, 'balancing' home and work, and co-ordinating care-work and the paid or unpaid services of others engaged as care-givers. Social divisions combine with uneven development in the geographies of everyday co-ordination. In San Francisco, a new generation of 'loft dweller' lives, but rarely works, in the city. The cleaners and day-care providers employed by these households, on the other hand, work in the city while travelling back each night to homes far out on the East Bay. The metropolitan area is witnessing the rise of a new occupational stratification, one defined by (and defining) household lived experience.

(Jarvis 2005: 150)

both shape and are shaped by household ideology through the mediation of a multiplicity of overlapping institutions (including race, class and gender).

Summary

Arguably the household functions as a key site (and process) of analysis in questions of housing choice and residential mobility, transport, leisure, consumption, child-care and gender relations – forces which shape the ecological footprint and quality of life of cities throughout the developed world. Moreover, the household functions as a useful barometer of social and demographic change within and between advanced and developing economies.

It has been observed that households are both shrinking in size and becoming more fluid in a life-course made up of increasingly complex household transitions. These changes in household structure have profound implications for land use and urban planning. This is illustrated in the paradox that households which have theoretically gained income from the normalization of a two-income structure often struggle to afford a home near to where they work. In the most 'successful' towns and cities it now takes more than one good income to enter the housing market or simply maintain living standards. At the same time, household research shows that dual-career households are less residentially mobile than the traditional male-breadwinner household and more likely to pursue job mobility from a fixed place of residence by extending their daily journeys to work (Jarvis 1999a: 1036; Smits *et al.* 2003). Consequently, one of the unintended consequences of the proliferation of two-income and dual-career households, as well as growing numbers of households overall, is greater congestion on the roads and a growing spatial mismatch between where people live and where they work, shop and drive their offspring to school.

Geographic scholarship has only recently begun to penetrate the inner workings of the household as a dynamic institution and welfare provider. There is a long tradition in regional and economic geography of a unitary, utility-maximizing, household. Yet it is only by looking more closely at divisions of labour within the household that we can begin to understand how social divisions associated with uneven development are reproduced between households through exploitative local-to-global chains. At the same time that people are observed to make sense of their lives at a level which is perceived to be 'local', within social networks of 'sense-making, unravelling the complexities of colliding worlds; gender, generation, uncertainty and change' (Kvale 1996: 52–8) they are also linked to distant places and communities 'virtually', through the global media and new information and communications technology (ICT), and by migration and mobility (Wellman 2001). In short, greater understanding of the diversity of household geographies sheds light on the social implications, local contexts and deep contradictions of global restructuring.

Further reading

Buzar, S., Ogden, P.E. and Hall, R. (2005) Households matter: the quiet demography of urban transformation. *Progress in Human Geography* 29 (4), 413–36.

Dunne, G. (1997) *Lesbian Lifestyles: Women's Work and the Politics of Sexuality.* Basingstoke: Macmillan.

Fraad, H., Resnick, S. and Wolff, R. (1994) *Bringing It All Back Home: Class, Gender and Power in the Modern Household.* London: Pluto.

Folbre, N. (1994) *Who Pays for the Kids? Gender and the Structures of Constraint.* London: Routledge.

——(2001) *The Invisible Heart: Economics and Family Values*. New York: The New Press.

Friedlander, D., Okun, B.S. and Segal, S. (1999) The demographic transition then and now: processes, perspectives and analyses. *Journal of Family History* 24, 493–533.

Hanson, S. and Pratt, G. (1995) *Gender, Work and Space*. London: Routledge.

Hardill, I. (2002) *Gender, Migration and the Dual Career Household*. London: Routledge.

Himmelweit, S. (2000) *Inside the Household: From Labour to Care*. Basingstoke: Macmillan.

Jarvis, H. (2005) *Work/Life City Limits: Comparative Household Perspectives*. Basingstoke: Palgrave.

Little, S.E. (2000) Networks and neighbours: households, communities and sovereignty in the global economy. *Urban Studies*, 37 (1), 1813–25.

Mattingly, D. (2001) The home and the world: domestic service and international networks of caring labor. *Annals of the Association of American Geographers*, 91 (2), 370–86.

Mitchell, K., Marston, S.A. and Katz, C. (eds) (2004) *Life's Work: Geographies of Social Reproduction*. Oxford: Blackwell.

Nelson, M.K. and Smith, J. (1999) *Working Hard and Making Do: Surviving in Small Town America*. Berkeley: University of California Press.

Rakodi, C. and Lloyd-Jones, T. (2002) *Urban Livelihoods: A People Centred Approach to Reducing Poverty*. London: Earthscan.

Wallace, C. (2002) Household strategies: their conceptual relevance and analytical scope in social research. *Sociology*, 36 (2), 275–92.

Useful web portals

British Household Panel Survey (BHPS) http://www.iser.essex.ac.uk/ulsc/bhps/
Center for Ethnography of Everyday Life (CEEL) http://ceel.psc.isr.umich.edu/
Families and Work Institute (FWI) http://www.familiesandwork.org/

References

Agarwal, B. (1997) 'Bargaining' and gender relations: within and beyond the household. *Feminist Economics* 3 (1), 1–51.

Bailey, A.J., Blake, M.K. and Cooke, T.J. (2004) Migration, care and the linked lives of dual-earner households. *Environment and Planning A* 36, 1617–32.

Beall, J. and Kanji, N. (1999) *Households, Livelihoods and Urban Poverty* (Urban Governance Partnership and Poverty Theme Paper 3). Birmingham: University of Birmingham, UK. Available at http://www.idd.bham.ac.uk/research/Projects/urban-governance/resource_papers/theme_papers/3_households_livelihoods.pdf

Becker, G. (1965) A theory of the allocation of time. *Economic Journal*, 75 (299), 493–517.

——(1981) *A Treatise on the Family*. London: Harvard University Press.

Berthoud, R. and Gershuny, J. (eds) (2000) *Seven Years in the Lives of British Families: Evidence on the Dynamics of Social Change from the British Household Panel Survey*. Bristol: Policy Press.

Bielby, W. and Bielby, D. (1989) Family ties: balancing commitments to work and family in dual earner households. *American Sociological Review* 54, 776–89.

Black, D., Gates, G., Sanders, S. and Taylor, L. (2000) Demographics of the gay and lesbian population in the United States: evidence from available systematic data sources. *Demography* 37 (2), 139–54.

Bond, S. and Sales, J. (2001) Household work in the UK: an analysis of the British Household Panel Survey 1994. *Work Employment and Society* 15 (2), 233–50.

Bongaarts, J. (2001) Household size and complexity in the developing world in the 1990s. *Population Studies* 55, 263–79.

Bonney, N. and Love, J. (1991) Gender and migration: geographical mobility and the wife's sacrifice. *Sociological Review* 39, 335–48.

361

Boyle, P., Cooke, T. Halfacree, K., and Smith, D. (1999) Integrating GB and US Census microdata for migration analysis: a study of the effects of family migration on partnered women's employment status. *International Journal of Population Geography* 5, 157–78.

Breugel, I. (1996) The trailing wife: a declining breed? Careers, geographical mobility and household conflict in Britain 1970–89. In R. Crompton, R. Gallie and L. Purcell (eds) *Changing Forms of Employment: Organisations, Skills and Gender*, pp. 235–58. London: Routledge.

Burgoyne, C.B. (1990) Money in marriage: how patterns of allocation both reflect and conceal power. *Sociological Review* 38, 634–65.

Buzar, S., Ogden, P.E. and Hall, R. (2005) Households matter: the quiet demography of urban transformation. *Progress in Human Geography* 29 (4), 413–36.

Caradec, V. (1996) Les Formes de la vie conjugale des 'jeunes' couple 'âgés'. *Population* 51, 897–928.

Census of India (2001) Census of India Household Tables. Available at http://www.censusindia.net/results/HH-series-tables-2001.html

Cooke, T.J. (2003) Family migration and the relative earnings of husbands and wives. *Annals of the Association of American Geographers*, 93 (2), 353–78.

Crehan, K. (1992) Rural households: survival and change. In H. Bernstein, B. Crow and H. Johnson (eds) *Rural Livelihoods: Crises and Responses*, pp. 87–113. Oxford: Oxford University Press in association with the Open University.

Creighton, C. and Omari, C.K. (1995) *Gender, Family and the Household in Tanzania*. Avebury: Aldershot.

Dorling, D. (1995) Visualising changing social structure from a census. *Environment and Planning A*, 27 (2), 353–78.

Duncan, S.S. and Smith, D. (2001) Geographies of family formations: spatial differences and gender cultures in Britain. *Transactions of the Institute of British Geographers* NS 27 (4), 471–94.

Ehrenreich, B. and Hochschild, A.R. (eds) (2003) *Global Woman: Nannies, Maids and Sex Workers in the New Economy*. London: Granta.

Ellegård, K. and de Pater, B. (1999) The complex tapestry of everyday life (Introduction to special issue). *GeoJournal* 48, 149–53.

Evans, A.W. (1985) *Urban Economics: An Introduction*. Oxford: Blackwell.

Ferber, M.A. and Nelson, J.A. (eds) (1993) *Beyond Economic Man – Feminist Theory and Economics*. London: University of Chicago Press.

Florida, R. (2002) *The Rise of the Creative Class – and How It's Transforming Work, Leisure, Community and Everyday Life*. New York: Basic Books.

Folbre, N. (1986) Hearts and spades: paradigms of household economics. *World Development* 14 (2), 245–55.

Frey, W.H., Liau, K.-L. and Lin, G. (2000) State magnets for different elderly migrant types in the United States. *International Journal of Population Geography* 6 (1), 21–44.

Gardiner, J. (1997) *Gender, Care and Economics*. Basingstoke: Macmillan.

Gibson-Graham, J.K. (1996) *The End of Capitalism (As We Knew It): A Feminist Critique of Political Economy*. Oxford: Blackwell.

Green, A.E., Hogarth, T. and Shackleton, R. (1999) *Long-distance Living: Dual Location Households*. Bristol: Policy Press.

Gross, H. (1980) Dual career couples who live apart: two types. *Journal of Marriage and Family* August, 567–76.

Gullestad, M. (1984) *Kitchen-Table Society: Case Study of the Family Life and Friendships of Your Working-Class Mothers in Norway*. Oslo: Universitetsforlaget. US distribution, New York: Colombia University Press.

Hall, R., Ogden, P.E. and Hill, C. (1997) The pattern and structure of one-person households in England and Wales and France. *International Journal of Population Geography* 3, 161–81.

Hapke, H. (2001) Gender, work and household survival in South Indian fishing communities: a preliminary analysis. *The Professional Geographer* 53 (3), 313–31.

Hardill, I. (2002) *Gender, Migration and the Dual Career Household*. London: Routledge.

Hochschild, A.R. (1989) *The Second Shift*. New York: Avon Books.

Jarvis, H. (1997) Housing, labour markets and household structure: questioning the role of secondary data analysis in sustaining the polarization debate. *Regional Studies* 31 (5), 521–31.

——(1999a) The tangled webs we weave: household strategies to co-ordinate home and work. *Work, Employment and Society* 13 (2), 225–47.

——(1999b) Identifying the relative mobility prospects of a variety of household structures, 1981–99. *Environment and Planning A*, 31, 1031–46.

——(2002) 'Lunch is for wimps': what drives parents to work long hours in 'successful' British and US cities. *Area* 34 (4), 340–53.

——(2005) *Work/Life City Limits: Comparative Household Perspectives*. Basingstoke: Palgrave.

Jarvis, H., Pratt, A.C. and Wu, P.C.C. (2001) *The Secret Life of Cities: The Social Reproduction of Everyday Life*. Harlow: Prentice Hall.

Kabeer, N. (1997) Women, wages and intra-household power relations in urban Bangladesh. *Development and Change*, 28 (2), 261–302.

Knopp, L. (1995) Sexuality and urban space: a framework for analysis. In D. Bell and G. Valentine (eds) *Mapping Desire: Geographies of Sexualities*, pp. 149–61. London: Routledge.

Kvale, S. (1996) *InterViews: An Introduction to Qualitative Research Interviewing*. London: Sage.

Kwan, M.P. (1999) Gender, the home–work link, and space–time patterns of non-employment activities. *Economic Geography* 75, 370–94.

Levin, I. and Trost, J. (1999) Living apart together. *Community, Work and Family* 3, 279–94.

McDowell, L. (2004) Work, workfare, work/life balance and an ethic of care. *Progress in Human Geography* 28 (2), 145–63.

McRae, S. (1986) *Cross-Class Families: A Study of Wives' Occupational Superiority*. Oxford: Clarendon Press.

Malinowski, B. (1913) *The Family among the Australian Aborigines*. London: University of London Press.

Manser, M. and Brown, M. (1980) Marriage and household decision-making: a bargaining analysis. *International Economic Review*, 21 (1), 31–44.

Mattingly, D. (2001) The home and the world: domestic service and international networks of caring labor. *Annals of the Association of American Geographers* 91 (2), 370–86.

Mincer, J. (1978) Family migration decisions. *Journal of Political Economy* 86, 749–73.

Mingione, E. (1991) *Fragmented Societies: A Sociology of Economic Life Beyond the Market Paradigm*. Oxford: Blackwell.

Nelson, M.K. (2004) How men matter: housework and self-provisioning among rural single-mother and married-couple families in Vermont, US. *Feminist Economics* 10 (2), 9–36.

Nelson, M.K. and Smith, J. (1999) *Working Hard and Making Do: Surviving in Small Town America*. Berkeley: University of California Press.

O'Neill, B.C., MacKellar, F.L., and Lutz, W. (2000) *Population and Climate Change*. Cambridge: Cambridge University Press.

ONS (2003) Social Trends 34. London: The Stationery Office. (Available at http://www.statistics.gov.uk/pdfdir/sot0104.pdf)

Pahl, J. (1989) *Money and Marriage*. London: Macmillan.

Pahl, R.E. (1984) *Divisions of Labour*. Oxford: Blackwell.

Pavlovskaya, M. (2004) Other transitions: multiple economies of Moscow households in the 1990s. *Annals of the Association of American Geographers* 94 (2), 329–51.

Petterson, L.T. (1996) Crisis management and household strategies in Lofoten: a question of sustainable development. *Sociologia Ruralis* 36: 236–48.

Randolph, B. (1991) Housing markets, labour markets and discontinuity theory. In J. Allen and C. Hamnett (eds) *Housing and Labour Markets: Building the Connections*, pp. 16–47. London: Unwin Hyman.

Robertson, C. (1984) *Sharing the Same Bowl: A Socio-economic History of Women and Class in Accra, Ghana*. Bloomington: Indiana University Press.

Rowbotham, S. (1997) *A Century of Women: The History of Women in Britain and the United States*. London: Penguin.

Sen, A. (1990) Gender and co-operative conflict. In I. Tinker (ed.) *Persistent Inequalities: Women and World Development*, pp. 123–50. New York: Oxford University Press.

Skinner, C. (2003) *Running Around in Circles: Coordinating Childcare, Education and Work*. York: Joseph Rowntree Foundation/Policy Press.

Smart, C. and Neale, B. (1999) *Family Fragments?* Cambridge: Polity Press.

Smits, J., Mulder, C.H. and Hooimeijer, P. (2003) Changing gender roles, shifting power balance and long-distance migration of couples. *Urban Studies* 40 (3), 603–13.

Somerville, J. (2000) *Feminism and the Family: Politics and Society in the UK and USA*. Basingstoke: Macmillan.

Stack, C. (1983) *All Our Kin: Strategies for Survival in Black Community*. New York: Basic Books.

UNFPA (2001) *State of the World Population. Footprints and Milestones: Population and Environmental Change*. New York: United Nations Population Fund.

United States Census Bureau (USCB) (2001) *Households and Families 2000: Census 2000 Brief*. Washington DC: US Department of Commerce.

——(2004a) *Current Population Survey Reports, Table C.8*. Available at http://www.census.gov/population/ www/socdemo/hh-fam.hh4.pdf

——(2004b) *America's Families and Living Arrangements: 2003. Populations Characteristics*. Issued November. Available at http://www.census.gov/prod/2004pubs/p20–553.pdf (page 2 and Table 1, page 3).

Wallman, S. (1984) *Eight London Households*. London: Tavistock.

Wellman, B. (2001) Physical place and cyber place: the rise of networked individualism. *International Journal of Urban and Regional Research* 25, 227–52.

Wheelock, J. and Oughton, E. (1996) The household as a focus for research. *Journal of Economic Issues* 30 (1), 143–59.

Williams, A.M., King, R. and Warnes, T. (1997) A place in the sun: international retirement from Northern to Southern Europe. *European Urban and Regional Studies* 4 (2), 115–34.

Winfield, F.E. (1985) *Commuter Marriage; Living Together, Apart*. New York: Columbia University Press.

Yeandle, S (1984) *Women's Working Lives: Patterns and Strategies*. London: Tavistock.

Zelizer, V.A. (2005) *The Purchase of Intimacy*. Princeton and Oxford: Princeton University Press.

24

Individuals

Vera Chouinard

Introduction: placing individuals in geography

Human geographers, like other social scientists, have long been concerned with understanding why individuals interact with the world around them in particular ways. What they have disagreed about, often vehemently, are the causes and consequences of this process. For behavioural geographers, individuals interact with their environments through a series of individual decision-making processes. Finding a home in the city, for example, involves decisions about a number of trade-offs: distance to paid work, children's needs, amenities in different locations and expenditure on housing. The outcome of this decision-making process is the purchase of a home in a particular urban neighbourhood. Taken in aggregate, such individual decision-making processes explain why and how cities and regions change. Similarly, geographers using micro-economic models of urban and regional change see individual decision-making as the cause of phenomena such as gentrification of inner-city neighbourhoods and the growth of urban fringe areas. Individuals are regarded as universally utility-maximizing agents whose decisions drive processes of change in cities and regions. Geographers using more phenomenological approaches, in contrast, stress processes of assigning complex meanings to places and landscapes as central to understanding why and how individuals relate to the world around them. Still other geographers have used 'critical social' approaches to understand individuals' places in the world; those perspectives informed by critical social theories which see individuals as both subject to and agents of relations of power which shape where and how they can interact with the world around them and share the critical political goal of working toward more just societies. Marxist and feminist geography are two examples of such critical social approaches.

In short, human geographers disagree about how to explain individuals' roles in changing the world around them! Subtle differences surface even within particular traditions – social geographers, for instance, use different critical social theories to understand individuals' places in the world.

In this chapter, I focus on recent critical social approaches. In many ways, these approaches have rocked the explanatory foundations of human geography and contributed to long-term epistemological and ontological changes. I begin by discussing the origins of critical social geographical approaches – the rise of radical and feminist geography from the late 1960s (see also Chapter 62). This is followed by a discussion of contemporary critical social geographic perspectives on individuals' places in the world. The chapter concludes by considering how far we've come in advancing our understanding of 'individuals' in human geography and in particular focuses upon newly emerging embodied and emotional geographies.

Re-placing individuals: radical and feminist geography

The late 1960s marked the beginnings of significant intellectual and political movements in human geography. A new generation of human geographers began to search for ways of understanding the world that addressed issues of power and oppression, social relevance and social justice. They were inspired not only by a restless dissatisfaction with existing approaches to understanding the world but also by developments in the world around them: anti-war and civil rights movements, urban riots, student unrest and an emerging women's movement. Phenomena such as these cried out for geographic explanations that addressed how and why power was distributed in society and space, what this meant in terms of who was empowered and who was not, and shed light on ways in which people could work towards more just societies and spaces of life.

With its establishment in 1969 under the editorship of Richard Peet at Clarke University, *Antipode* became a key forum in which human geographers explored radical alternatives to the positivistic approaches that dominated the discipline. Articles explored the implications of anarchism, Marxism and even feminism for geographic explanation and political action. As the 1970s progressed, Marxist theory and explanation became increasingly influential in radical circles with David Harvey's (1973) *Social Justice and the City* a key impetus.

Throughout the 1970s and 1980s, an increasingly theoretically and empirically sophisticated Marxist geography rocked the foundations of the discipline. What was revolutionary, in an explanatory sense, about this approach was the focus on the role of power in urban and regional change. Individuals were not the autonomous and free agents imagined in liberal conceptions of society and space – exercising the capacity to freely choose where or how to live and work, for instance – but were caught up in prevailing relations of power, in particular class relations, which profoundly influenced where and how they could live and how the cities and regions in which they lived changed.

Marxist geographers' work revealed a great deal about how class power and oppression was implicated in urban and regional change: the redlining of poor inner-city neighbourhoods by powerful financial corporations (Harvey and Chatterjee 1974), the movements of property capital which fuelled inner-city gentrification and displaced the poor (Smith 1979), the role of class conflict and struggles to discipline labour in workplaces (Walker 1981), the struggles between corporate capital, the local state and citizens around urban renewal in the transformation of particular urban built environments (Fincher 1981) and the contested role of the capitalist state in struggles to increase access to affordable housing (Chouinard 1989), to mention only a few. What these and many other studies did was to differentially locate individuals within class relations of power in capitalist societies as, for example, members of the capitalist or working class, with unequal capacities to shape the world around them. Individuals were not passive subjects of the class relations of power in which they were embedded but were also agents who struggled, individually and collectively, to transform those relations and their conditions of life in particular places (e.g. by withholding labour power from capitalists through strike action). Or as Marx so famously put it, 'Men [*sic*] make their own history, but not under circumstances they themselves have chosen but under the given and inherited circumstances with which they are directly confronted' (Marx 1974: 146).

From the late 1970s, another stream of radical thought and political action gained increasing influence in human geography: the second-wave feminist movement. Critical not only of the lack of representation of women in the discipline of geography but also the lack of attention to gender differences in spatial behaviour and in access to resources and opportunities in society and space, feminist geographers began to challenge human geographers to 'include the other half of the human' in human geography (Monk and Hanson 1982; Women and Geography Study Group 1984). Initially they emphasized that phenomena such as urbanization and suburbanization could not be explained without attention to women's lives and activities. Later feminist geographers, under the particular influence of socialist feminism, increasingly tackled the challenges of using feminist theories of patriarchy and gendered relations of power in class-divided societies to explain geographic phenomena such as industrialization and transformations in domestic economies (e.g. Mackenzie and Rose 1983).

In what ways did this early feminist geographic work challenge prevailing ways of understanding individuals' places in the world? It certainly challenged most human geographers' implicit assumption that individuals or subjects were universally male. It also challenged malestream radical geographers' emphasis upon class power. But, as feminist geographers such as McDowell (1999) have stressed, feminist geography's project was more fundamental than simply adding in women to existing theoretical and empirical approaches. It was nothing less than to build on feminist knowledge in ways that revolutionized approaches to geography and contributed to feminist politics that challenged the oppressions women faced in society and space.

Throughout the 1980s, feminist geographers' work shed light on many facets of the role of gendered relations of power in urban and regional change: in transformations in the spatial form of cities (e.g. McDowell 1983); in the way that suburbs were planned in order to sustain traditional 'womanly activities' such as shopping and the gendered divisions of labour on which this was based (Bowlby 1984); in the role of changing class and gender relations in the socio-spatial dynamics of industrial restructuring (Massey 1983); and in the links between transformations in class and gender locations in paid work associated with processes of economic restructuring and phenomena such as gentrification (Rose 1989). Feminist geographers were engaged in a project not only of advancing a sophisticated critical understanding how and why women came to be situated in society and space, too often in oppressive and marginalizing ways, but of beginning to imagine ways of politically challenging these locations and the relations of power that sustained them.

While the feminist geography of the 1980s was not without its lively debates, it was in the 1990s that feminist geography itself was dramatically re-envisioned and re-mapped. Building on critiques of the Western feminist movement as predominantly white and middle class, and on related scholarly critiques of categories such as 'woman' and 'gender' as unified entities and universal bases of women's political interests, feminist geographers began to embrace differences other than those of gender and class as fundamental to understanding women and men's places in the world. Increasingly, differences such as age and places in the life course (Katz and Monk 1993), race (Kobayashi and Peake 1994), sexuality (e.g. Valentine 1996), ability (Chouinard and Grant 1995), and locations in transnational relationships of power (e.g. Pratt 1998) began to figure prominently in explanations of how individuals were located in socio-spatial relations of power and what this meant in particular locales and regions.

At the same time, postmodern and poststructural theories of society and space were encouraging feminist geographers to think about categories such as gender in less unified and stable ways. To this was added the so-called cultural shift in social geography. Increasing concerns with discourse, representation and issues of identity in the critical social sciences encouraged feminist geographers to turn their attention to topics such as the construction of women in the imaginary of the nation-state (e.g. Radcliffe 1996), performances of diverse sexualities on urban streets (Bell and Valentine 1995), performances of masculine identities in corporate financial workplaces (McDowell and Court 1994) and socio-spatial constructions of race and place in the urban landscape of the United States (Kobayashi and Peake 2000). Reflecting influential developments in feminist theory, such as Butler's (1990) theory of gender performativity, feminist geographers were also paying growing attention to how diverse bodies, and processes of embodiment, were implicated in oppression and resistance. While such developments might be seen as a return to more individualistic ways of understanding our changing world, in fact they reflected concerns to probe how diverse people perform and resist particular identities and in so doing help to perpetuate and challenge prevailing relations of power.

Although feminist geographers' contributions to understanding people's changing places in the world are still too often ignored in malestream subdisciplinary areas of inquiry such as political geography (see Staehli and Kofman 2004), there is no question that their work has fundamentally altered our understanding of how women and men are situated in society and space, and of the kinds of oppressions we need to challenge in the twenty-first century. In particular, their work has demonstrated the multiple axes of power and difference (including sex, gender, race, sexuality, ability and geographic location) in which individuals are situated, and has explored the many ways in which struggles to negotiate these relations shape lives and places.

Contested places: perspectives on individuals in contemporary critical social geography

From the 1970s onwards, the work of Marxist and feminist geographers revolutionized our understanding of how individuals are placed in the world and why this matters. No longer could individuals be understood without considering power relations. Gone were the days of imagining atomistic and 'free' individuals: power and oppression had moved to centre-stage.

Throughout the 1990s and into the twenty-first century, critical social and feminist geographers have built on these foundations by exploring theoretical perspectives that have further enriched our understanding of individuals as firmly situated within complex socio-spatial relations of power: through postmodern and poststructural theories, postcolonial and queer theory, psychoanalytic and critical race theory. Accompanying these developments has been a 'cultural turn' through which matters of discourse and text, representation, difference, identity and subjectivity as mediums of power, oppression and resistance have been brought to the fore. This has also been a time of questioning our knowledge of the world around us: of learning to recognize partiality, uncertainty, situatedness, contradiction and incompleteness.

In this section, I illustrate some of the important ways in which these developments have transformed our understanding of individuals' places in the world. I begin with a brief discussion of what we might understand a critical social geography to be, before turning to important intellectual and political 'streams' within this rapidly evolving movement. I will not, in this brief chapter, cover all facets of this work, but seek rather to illustrate some of the important ways in which individuals' places in the world, and the collective possibilities for challenging prevailing relations of power and oppression in which we are all enmeshed, are being geographically re-imagined.

Critical social or human geography comprises a large international body of research that seeks to build on the radical traditions of the past three decades. Critical geographers encompass researchers who work from increasingly sophisticated political economy perspectives that, although still concerned with class, now also attend to differences such as race and gender as bases of oppression and resistance. They also encompass work by feminist geographers, although the extent to which critical social geography can or does so in practice has been open for debate (see, for example, Bondi 1990). And they refer to work being conducted by geographers who are particularly influenced by critical social theoretical and political positions such as postmodernism and postcolonialism, through which researchers strive to understand the social world in ways that are less determinate and more unsettling and more attentive to how power is deployed and resisted through identities, discourse, cultural representation and practice.

Critical social geography is about transgressing borders, metaphorical and real, both intellectually and politically. But it is also about 'doing geography' in intellectually and politically progressive ways that can help to challenge social and spatial inequalities.

It is important, therefore to keep in mind that the 'streams' of change in understanding individuals' places in the world that I describe are in practice neither discrete nor being travelled in identical ways during the ongoing transnational critical geography project. A related caveat, as Harvey (2000) reminds us, is that it would be incorrect to assume that all critical social geographers have left their radical Marxian or feminist roots behind to pursue one or more 'post' types of geography. As always, the story is rather more complicated: geographers have opted for a whole range of permutations of radical thought and practice.

Postmodern influences

One important stream in critical social geography of the late twentieth and early twenty-first century has been that of postmodernism. A slippery term, postmodernism refers to an intellectual and practical movement that is manifest in different ways in areas of inquiry and practice as diverse as architecture and aesthetics, critical literary and cultural studies, and the philosophy of knowledge. Common threads in this movement are the sense that the era of high modernity is behind us, and that intellectual and political practices must respond to the 'postmodern' condition in which we live.

At the inevitable risk of oversimplifying, there are two principal ways in which postmodernism has influenced geographers' understanding of individuals' places in the world. The first is conceptual or theoretical and involves considering postmodernity as marking some kind of epochal shift in urban and regional change. The second is to explore postmodernism's emphasis on incompleteness, uncertainty, partiality, fragmentation and difference in knowledge and how geographers go about trying to understand the world. I deal briefly with each of these in turn.

David Harvey (1989), following Jameson (1998), provided an historical materialist interpretation of postmodernity as complex political and cultural changes associated with the underlying dynamics of global capitalism. He argued that processes such as accelerating time–space convergence, the peripheralization of labour and the erosion of traditional forms of political power within the working class (see Chapter 55) were contributing to a fragmentation of identities which diminished possibilities for a coherent class-based politics. At the same time, the dizzying pace at which capital transformed cities and regions, for example through proliferating spectacular sites and images of consumption, left individuals understandably off balance, divided from one another and overwhelmed.

Edward Soja's work on postmodern geographies of urban and regional change is another influential example of this stream of work. Building on Lefebvre (1991) he argues for an understanding of transformations in cities and regions as material, political-economic outcomes of forces of change intrinsic to global capitalism, such as the peripheralization of growing segments of the labour force, and as lived and representational spaces in which the rapidly changing landscapes are apt to conceal and distort as much as they reveal. Soja (1996), for example, reminds us that global cities, in particular Los Angeles, are places in which histories of urban struggle are simultaneously but partially erased and reconstituted into fantastic 'others', and in which images of urban life, of Los Angeles as the quintessential city of 'dreams' for instance, belie material realities such as military might and surveillance. While Soja's approach shares Harvey's emphasis on how our lives are caught up in political economic forces of late capitalism, he also encourages us to think about people's journeys through urban and regional landscapes as simultaneously cultural and imaginary. The meaning of these places distorts and disguises the realities of power, history and the forces of change in places as well as revealing these.

Michael Dear (2000) encourages geographers to embrace the postmodern challenge to break with existing meta-narratives (such as historical materialism) about urban change, and to recognize fundamental shifts in the forces shaping people's lives in cities. He argues that phenomena such as edge cities as command centres of urban economies and the polarization of life between privileged gated communities of the cyberbourgeoisie and deprived 'in-beyond' places of life for 'protosurps' mark fundamental and postmodern shifts in the dynamics of urban change. While Dear's typology of urban form is provocative, his efforts to explain these developments fails to take us much beyond an understanding of individuals' changing places in cities as the outcome of political-economic and cultural forces of differencing in late capitalism.

Despite Ley's (2003) contention that the postmodern influence has passed in the social sciences and geography, there are two ways in which the effect of this movement persists. One is in encouraging greater attention to image and representation as fundamental to the dynamics of urban and regional change. This can be seen, for example, in Hudson's (2000) call to explore 'offshoreness' as part of processes of fundamental change in relations and practices of sovereignty within the global economy, and in Crang and Travlou's (1999) arguments for accounts of memory in urban landscapes. Individuals' places in the world, according to such accounts, are subject to forces of change which include complex juxtapositions of material and virtual reality and of language and image that we are only just beginning to recognize.

The second way in which postmodernism continues to influence geographic thought is through openness to contradictions, differences, uncertainties and silences in our understanding of urban and regional change and the role of individuals. Sometimes termed a 'sceptical realism' (e.g. Hannah 1999) this epistemological stance encourages us to recognize and embrace incompleteness, difference and uncertainty in a way that enlightenment epistemologies did not.

Re-placing individuals through cultural and other 'turns' in critical social geography

If political economy and feminist geographies of the 1970s and 1980s firmly located individuals within relationships of power and oppression, then developments in the critical social geography from the 1990s have broadened and in some ways deepened our understanding of subjectivity and resistance as contested geographical processes. In this section, I discuss some of the key ways in which developments in critical social geography in the late twentieth and early twenty-first centuries have altered our understanding of how individuals are situated in the world, and why this matters.

One much-remarked development in the social sciences has been that of the so-called cultural 'turn'. In part, this reflects the ongoing legacy of poststructural and postmodern philosophy and theory – concerns with partiality, uncertainty and differences in knowledge, with the roles of identity, discourse, text and language in our lived experiences of the world, and with connections and tensions between images and material, lived realities of day-to-day existence in places. It also reflects renewed and vigorous interest in problematizing individuals' relations to society and space as dynamic and subjective processes of identity formation that cannot simply be derived from their location within class and gender divisions of power, or the political-economic dynamics of late capitalist societies. Barnett (1998: 380) summarizes the cultural turn in geography in the following way:

> The cultural turn has many manifestations. Even as a summary, the following list is hardly exhaustive: a revivification of traditional areas of interest in cultural geography under the influence of new theoretical ideas; the 'textualization' of subfields such as political geography; the revival of interest in the historiography of geography under the influence of theories of colonial discourse and postcolonialism; a concern for the 'cultural' embeddedness of economic processes; an interest in examining the mobilization of culture as an accumulation strategy; greater concern for examining relations between identity and consumption; an ever-greater sophistication in understandings of the construction of social relations of gender and race as well as class; a focus upon cultural constructions of environment and nature. Perhaps one common thread connecting these and other myriad projects is a commitment to epistemologies, often loosely labelled 'poststructural', that emphasise the contingency of knowledge claims and recognize the close relationship among language, power, and knowledge. Both epistemologically and in the construction of new empirical research objects, the cultural turn is probably best characterized by a heightened reflexivity toward the role of language, meaning, and representations in the constitution of 'reality' and knowledge of reality.

It is difficult, from the vantage point of 2006, to think of any realm of critical social geography that has not been touched by this cultural turn. Geographers building on Marxian political economy approaches have, however grudgingly at times, taken up questions of identity formation, media representation and political cultures of resistance (e.g. Harvey 1993) and considered the role of discourse in social and material constructions of ethnic difference in urban built-environments (e.g. Fincher and Costello 2005). They have called for a critical cultural political economy (Sayer 2001), and argued for a poststructuralist understanding of class as a multiplicity of performances producing, appropriating and distributing surplus labour in which individuals are engaged – performances that are further complicated by other identities such as those relating to gender differences (e.g. Gibson 1998), for example. Feminist geographers have taken up what Kobayashi (1997) refers to as processes of differencing in society and space. They focus on why and how individuals, groups and places of life are constructed as negatively 'other' than hegemonic norms or ideals (e.g. white, heterosexual, masculine, able or suburban) and explored the implications of these processes for identity formation, oppression and resistance in society and space (e.g. Kobayashi and Peake 2000; Chouinard 1999; Valentine 1999). This work has helped to problematize and unsettle our understanding of individuals' places in the world. Their subjective experiences of those places can no longer be reduced to a singular aspect of location within prevailing relationships of power, such as class. Instead, it insists that individuals and groups are subject to multiple forces of differencing and are both subjects and agents of cultural and political-economic change. This has also challenged geographers to think about individuals' identities and/or subjectivities as far more complex over space and time than reductionist notions of 'identity politics' allowed.

It is clear that concerns with difference, identity and subjectivity have pervaded critical social geography in recent years. This has not meant, however, as Jacobs and Fincher (1998) stress, that this work has abandoned concerns with regimes of power and how individuals are enmeshed in and contribute to reproducing and resisting these. Rather, conceptions of these processes have become more nuanced, sophisticated and alert to the contingencies of difference, identity and subjectivity. Indeed, Jacobs and Fincher (1998) suggest that we think about these approaches as shedding light on a 'located politics of difference'. Power, and its deployment and opposition, has also come to be understood in less monolithic and more contradictory ways.

Some geographers have built on queer theory and studies to further our understanding of the complex social and spatial dynamics of heterosexist, heteronormative regimes of power and the constitution of identities and subjectivities that transgress and resist them in and through places. As Knopp and Brown (2003) explain, the aim of this work is also, in a postmodern and poststructuralist vein, to deconstruct and destabilize taken-for-granted concepts and categories through which we seek to 'know' the world and individuals' subjective experiences of places within it (such as lesbian and gay identities, sexuality, the closet, global capitalism and the state). In the same article, they use a deconstructed and malleable conception of the diffusion of gay identities, politics and culture to challenge notions such as that being 'closeted' is inevitably sexually, politically and culturally oppressive, and that it is only from metropolitan centres that the identities, knowledges and practices which transgress and resist heteronormative power diffuse. Concerns with understanding diversity in queer and not-so-queer lives – of how these lives and identities are shaped by people's locations within transecting relations and images of class, patriarchy, sexuality, race, gender, citizenship, motherhood, Western and non-Western places in the world – are central to the project of 'queering' geography (Nast 2002). Clearly this is not a concern with diversity for diversity's sake, but an effort to understand how individual lives and practices are shaped through people's investment in a complex and spatially shifting array of identities, images and ways of understanding places in the world. It also concerns practices of power that influence where they can and cannot go, how they live, and the extent to which they are privileged, oppressed or marginalized.

In recent years, geographers seeking a critical social understanding have also turned to postcolonialism and postcolonial theory. The former refers to an intellectual and political movement aimed at contesting and unsettling colonial and neocolonial forms of power and knowledge (Radcliffe 2005), while the latter can be described, very generally, as theoretical frameworks aimed at advancing our understanding of the discursive and material impacts and legacies of encounters between imperialists, colonizers and the 'colonized'. It is worth considering the ways in which geographers' encounters with postcolonial thought are changing our understanding of processes shaping individuals' lives and places. It is encouraging geographers to critically deconstruct persistent, modernist and hierarchical paradigms in imperialist and neocolonial knowledge – views, for example, of development and 'progress' as emanating inevitably from centres to peripheries, or of colonial settlement as proceeding on a fictional blank slate of wilderness devoid of human occupation. In doing so, it challenges received and particularly modernist Western ways of valuing and applying knowledge (see Slater 1998). Also, it is encouraging geographers to explore the complex ways in which individuals are caught up in, perpetuate and challenge discursive and material legacies of colonial and neocolonial encounters. So, for example, Nagar and Leitner (1998) examine how members of the Asian population in Dar es Salaam struggled after national independence along complex axes of difference (intra- and inter-racial, religious, class, caste and sect) to maintain distinctive spaces of life and identities rooted in colonial encounters. Questions about how identities have been shaped by senses of belonging to places, nations, indigenous and transnational communities and diasporas are also being raised. Gelder and Jacobs (1995), for example, examine how Aboriginal discourses about land claims based on the 'sacred' have helped to disrupt and unsettle non-Aboriginal senses of authority, possession and belonging in place and, in so doing, have given rise to a contradictory postcolonial racism in Australia.

It is worth stressing that geographers working with postcolonial thought are, of course, not the first to offer critical ways of thinking about people's lives and places in the world as situated within the context of transnational power, oppression, subjugation and resistance (nor undoubtedly will they be the last!). There is a long tradition of radical, political-economic accounts of colonialism and imperialism and uneven development (for a recent example see Harvey 2003). Scholars have rightly challenged us to attend as much to the material consequences of relations and processes of colonial and neocolonial domination as we do to its discursive and representational manifestations. In a more general vein, Neil Smith's (2000) call for critical geographers to once again attend closely to class as a salient axis of power, oppression, difference, subjectivity and struggle is a welcome reminder of how productive explanations of socio-spatial change might be which creatively criss-cross intellectual borders, for example between political economy and postcolonial explanations.

There are, of course, many other currents of change in critical social understandings of the individual and places. Concerns with identity, subjectivity, oppression, belonging and differencing have given rise to research on a wide range of topics. Ableness as a regime of power and processes of disablement, once barely discernable on geographers' radars, are, for example, now clearly on the intellectual and political agenda (see for example Chouinard and Crooks 2003). So too is whiteness and the racialization of identities, places and practices it sustains. Critical geographers are also drawing creatively on other intellectual and theoretical traditions, for example psychoanalytic theory, to help advance our understanding of our places in the world (Callard 1998). Such work is helping us to explore possible connections between the individual psyche and socio-spatial practices that help to mark out people and places as different, and in so doing enmesh us all in complex struggles over material and subjective places in the world (see, for example, Nast 2000 and Wilton 2003 on potential ways in which Freudian and Lacanian psychoanalysis can be deployed to advance our understanding of why able-bodied people so often react negatively to disabled people).

Feminist geographers have then in many ways been at the forefront not only of creatively and critically negotiating these intellectual and political currents of change, but also of putting new facets of people's lives on the geographic agenda. It is to these contributions that I now turn.

Developments in contemporary feminist geography

If early feminist geography focused on making women's lives and gender relations of power more visible in urban and regional change, and in a discipline predominantly 'gender-blind'

(Monk and Hanson 1982; Women and Geography Study Group 1984; Mackenzie and Rose 1983; Massey 1983), then more recent work has concentrated on advancing our understanding of how women's and men's lives and places in the world are shaped by multiple axes of power, difference, positionality and identity. This shift does not, unfortunately, mean that feminist scholars are now less marginalized in geography (witness, for example, Massey 1991; Bondi 1990). To the contrary, geographers still do have a great deal to learn from this substantial body of work. What it does reflect is feminist geographers' willingness to unsettle categories such as 'woman' and 'man', and critical knowledge itself, in increasingly sophisticated ways.

We have moved from binary conceptions of identities, subjectivities and power relations and from narrow conceptions of the spaces in which oppression, struggle and change occur, to what Fincher (2004) terms 'multiplicities'. So, for example, women and men are now understood to be located within and actively negotiating multiple relations of power and oppression as they go about their lives in particular places: class, gender, race, sexuality, ability, age, locations within transnational processes of neocolonialism, migration, development and the encounter between ethnically and religiously diverse groups, must be considered. Similarly, feminist geographers have increasingly challenged binary conceptions of where particular processes occur, demonstrating, for example, that political struggles over gendered and other identities, relations and processes of differencing are not confined to spaces in the public sphere such as legislatures, but that these also unfold *across* a multiplicity of spatial boundaries and territories: between private spaces such as the workplace and home, communal spaces organized around ethnicity and religion, the local state and civil society and so on (e.g. Fincher 2004).

These developments have meant that feminist geographers have in many ways remained at the forefront of rethinking individuals' places in the world, and of how identities and practices are implicated in the socio-spatial construction and reconstruction of identities across multiple geographic scales described in the chapters in this section of this book. Limited space precludes discussing many substantive areas of research through which feminist geographers are pushing the boundaries of geographers' wider thinking in these contexts (but see, for example, Blunt and Rose, 1994; Jones, Nast and Roberts 1997; Staehli *et al.* 2004; and Nelson and Seager 2005). I will focus the rest of this section on two important themes in this work: the body and embodiment, and what has come to be known as 'emotional geographies'.

Feminist geographers have played a pivotal role in demonstrating that the body, and processes of material and representational embodiment through which our bodies become personal and collective sites of making meaning and individuals and resisting oppression, is essential to understanding how identities are placed in the world. An embodied geography allows us to challenge oppressive social relations and practices which keep many people in highly marginalized, disempowering places. Building on the work of feminist scholars such as Butler (1990, 1993), they have examined how bodily performances that transgress gendered and sexualized boundaries are used to claim space for marginalized ways of being in places. Johnson (1996), for example, looked at how women body-builders struggle to claim space in gyms traditionally the exclusive preserve of men. Bell and Valentine (1995) examined how bodily performances, such as dressing in drag, were used to challenge the normative coding of places such as urban streets as exclusively heterosexualized, and in so doing asserted rights to transgress.

Understanding the differences that being situated within particular kinds of bodies makes to where we can and cannot be (and on whose terms), where we do and don't belong, whether we are valued or devalued, and even to appreciating capacities to engage in practices that challenge processes of differencing and oppression across multiple scales, has been central to feminist geographers' efforts to bring the body back into geographic imagination. Longhurst (1996, 2001) explores the differences that being situated within a pregnant body makes to where women are and are not allowed to be, and their subjection to social practices that influence experiences of places such as shopping malls. Chouinard (1999) examines how disabled women engaged in activism have found themselves out of place and excluded in spaces of women's organizing and the disability movement because of their disability and gender respectively, and considers tensions and divisions arising amongst disabled women activists along axes of difference such as sexuality. She argues that socio-spatial barriers to activism faced by disabled women must be understood as arising from multiple practices and processes of negative differencing to which they are subject, but also the material consequences such as marginalized class locations and tenuous relationships to paid labour that give rise to conditions of life such as low incomes. Others, such as Dyck (1995), examine how being situated within a chronically ill body alters women's lifespaces and ways of negotiating places such as the paid workplace. Valentine (1999) shows how experiences of being disabled and degrees of belonging in particular places are complicated by negotiations of identities and spaces coded as working class, masculine and feminine. Butler (1999) shows how ableist ways of expressing desire can work to marginalize non-able bodied lesbian women in lesbian-safe spaces.

It is important to emphasize that feminist geographers' analyses have neither individualized nor localized the differences that bodies and embodiment make to understanding our places in the world. By this I mean that bodies (including minds) are understood as simultaneously personal and relational – as sites through which we experience and relate to the world and through which others relate to us – where social meanings and practices of inclusion and exclusion are inscribed, negotiated and contested. It follows that embodiment is not something that happens exclusively to individuals but is part of the processes of differencing, through which individuals and collectivities (from dominant and marginalized groups, to nations, transnational and even global communities) are constituted across geographic scales. This multi-scalar nature of embodied life can be seen, for example, in feminist studies dealing with the challenges of being a foreign woman researcher (Nast 1998); in the othering and oppression of migrant Filipina domestic workers in Canadian homes (Pratt 1998); and in the disempowered locations of women in refugee camps arising from transnational gendered, racialized and cultural processes of differencing (Hyndman 1998).

An emerging direction in cultural and social geography, is what has been termed 'emotional geographies'. As Laurier and Parr (2000) note, this can be seen as related to efforts to bring the body back into geographic research. Western enlightenment thinking about individuals banished their bodies and embodiment from explanations of why and how people interact with the world around them (whilst privileging the mind) and also ignored the roles of emotions in the construction of knowledge and in our social lives. Feminist geographers are playing a key role in exploring the differences that emotions make in how we conduct research, interpret and use our findings and understand people and places (Koskela 2000; Widdowfield 2000; Laurier and Parr 2000; Smith 2000; Anderson and Smith 2001; Valentine 2003).

Widdowfield (2000) discusses her powerful emotions as a researcher examining the allocation of council housing in a deprived area of Newcastle, UK, and how her strong senses of injustice, anger and fear led her initially to read people's lives in that place in overly negative terms. Laurier and Parr (2000) argue that our understanding of partial and situated knowledges about people's health and disability can be enriched by attending to the emotions involved in research encounters. They note, for example, how feelings of anxiety associated with interviewing a man with schizophrenia whose leg was shaking were linked to interpretations of his behaviour as triggered by illness, rather than (as was the case) medication and the stress of the interview. They argue, further, that researchers need to acknowledge ethical dilemmas associated with recognizing emotions as central to interactions between researchers and those they 'research': from questions about how we write about emotions to whether or not there are types of emotions that should remain confidential. Valentine (2003) notes growing concern with how emotions ought to inform health and disability research and in so doing enable disabled people.

There is also a small but growing literature concerned with the role of emotions in situating individuals in relation to social and spatial change. Koskela (2000), for example, examines how video-surveillance elicits emotional reactions to urban spaces in highly gendered ways, arguing that women predominate in places such as shopping malls whilst men tend to be the ones behind the camera and its gaze. In a different vein, Smith (2000) examines the heightened emotions associated with spaces of musical performance, in terms of the experiences of both musicians and listeners.

These newly emerging research agendas around emotional geographies pose interesting challenges. In addition to difficult ethical dilemmas such as those noted previously, there are, as Anderson and Smith (2001) point out, crucial theoretical and empirical challenges in explaining individual roles in social and spatial change. These include struggling to overcome masculinized ways of treating emotions as irrelevant to explaining phenomena or policy-making. Activities and spatial spheres often tend to be labelled as public and therefore rational and emotionless realms of life. But emotions are centrally important to how, for example, we negotiate social relationships at work. They help to determine our effectiveness at work, levels of absenteeism, and the constitution of emotional lives that are enacted in 'private' spheres such as the home and also at the office or factory. They call on geographers to stretch their imaginations about the difference that emotions might make to our lives.

Conclusions: locating individuals in a complex world

Since the late 1960s, critical social and feminist geographers have made remarkable strides in advancing our understanding of why and how people are situated within relational, dynamic and multi-scalar processes of change in society and space. In so doing, they have forever altered the ways in which we understand individual lives, struggles over relationships of power and oppression, and ways of experiencing and negotiating diverse identities, social relations and places in the world. In a fundamental and very exciting sense, we have moved from understanding individuals to understanding individuals as complexly located with processes that are simultaneously local and global, personal and collective. We can look forward to many further advances as geographers continue to build on this vital legacy.

Further reading

Cope, M. (2004) Placing gendered political acts. In L.A. Staehli, E. Kofman and L.J. Peake (eds) *Mapping Women, Making Politics: Feminist Perspectives on Political Geography*, pp. 71–86. New York and London: Routledge.

Dyck, I. (1995) Hidden geographies: the changing lifeworlds of women with multiple sclerosis. *Social Science and Medicine* 40, 307–20.

McDowell, L. (1986) Beyond patriarchy: a class-based explanation of women's subordination. *Antipode* 18, 311–21.

——(1989a) Editorial: equal opportunities in geography. *Area* 21 (4), 323–32.

——(1989b) Towards an understanding of the gendered division of urban space. *Environment and Planning D: Society and Space* 1, 59–72.

Nagar, R. and Leitner, H. (1998) Contesting social relations in communal places: identity politics among Asian communities in Dar es Salaam. In R. Fincher and J.M. Jacobs (eds) *Cities of Difference*, pp. 226–51. New York: Guilford Press.

Nelson, L. and Seager, J. (2005) *A Companion to Feminist Geography*. London: Blackwell.

Philo, C. and Parr, H. (2003) Introducing psychoanalytic geographies. *Social and Cultural Geography* 4 (3), 284–93.

Pratt, G. (with the Philippine Women Centre, Vancouver, Canada) (1998) Inscribing domestic work on Filipina bodies. In S. Pile and H.J. Nast (eds) *Places through the Body*, pp. 283–304. London and New York: Routledge.

Smith, N. (2002) What happened to class? *Environment and Planning A*, 10–32.

Staehli, L.A., Kofman, E. and Peake, L.J. (eds) (2004) *Mapping Women, Making Politics: Feminist Perspectives on Political Geography*. New York and London: Routledge.

Valentine, G. (1999) What it means to be a man: the body, masculinities and disability. In Ruth Butler and H. Parr (eds) *Mind and Body Spaces: Geographies of Disability, Illness and Impairment*, pp. 167–80. London: Routledge.

Wilton, R.D. (2003) Locating physical disability in Freudian and Lacanian psychoanalysis: problems and prospects. *Social and Cultural Geography* 4 (3), 369–89.

References

Anderson, K. and Smith, S.J. (2001) Editorial: emotional geographies. *Transactions Institute of British Geographers* 26, 7–10.

Barnett, C. (1998) The cultural turn: fashion or progress in human geography? *Antipode* 30 (4), 379–94.

Bell, D. and Valentine, G. (1995) The sexed self: strategies of performance, sites of resistance. In S. Pile and N. Thrift (eds) *Mapping the Subject*. London: Routledge.

Blunt, A. and Rose, G. (eds) (1994) *Writing Women and Space: Colonial and Postcolonial Geographies*. New York and London: Guilford Press.

Bondi, L., (1990) Feminism, postmodernism and geography: space for women?. *Antipode* 22, 156–67.

Bowlby, S. (1984) Planning for women to shop in postwar Britain. *Environment and Planning D: Society and Space* 2, 179–199.

Butler, J. (1990) *Gender Trouble: Feminism and the Subversion of Identity*. London and New York: Routledge.

——(1993) *Bodies that Matter*. New York and London: Routledge.

Butler, R. (1999) Double the trouble and twice the fun? Disabled bodies in the gay community. In R. Butler and H. Parr (eds) *Mind and Body Spaces: Geographies of Illness, Impairment and Disability*, pp. 203–20. London: and New York: Routledge.

Callard, F.J. (1998) The body in theory. *Environment and Planning D: Society and Space* 16, 383–400.

——(2003) The taming of psychoanalysis in geography. *Social and Cultural Geography* 4 (3), 296–312.

Chouinard, Vera (1989) Explaining local experiences of state formation: the case of cooperative housing in Toronto. *Environment and Planning D: Society and Space* 7, 51–68.

——(1999) Body politics: disabled women's activism in Canada and beyond. In H. Parr and R. Butler (eds) *Mind and Body Spaces*, pp. 269–94. London: Routledge.

Chouinard, V. and Crooks, V.A. (eds) (2003) Disability in society and space. Thematic special issue of *The Canadian Geographer* 47 (4), 383–508.

Chouinard, V. and Grant, A. (1995) On not being anywhere near 'the project': ways of putting ourselves in the picture. *Antipode* 27, 137–66.

Crang, M. and Travlou, P.S. (1999) The city and topologies of memory. *Environment and Planning D: Society and Space* 19, 161–77.

Dear, M.J. (2000) *The Postmodern Urban Condition*. London: Blackwell.

Dyck, I. (1995) Hidden geographies: the changing lifeworlds of women with multiple sclerosis. *Social Science and Medicine* 40, 307–20.

Fincher, R. (1981) Local implementation strategies in the urban built-environment. *Environment and Planning A* 13 (10), 335–39.

——(2004) From dualisms to multiplicities: gendered political practices. In Lynn A. Staehli, Eleonore Kofman and Linda J. Peake (eds) *Mapping Women, Making Politics: Feminist Perspectives on Political Geography*, pp. 49–70. New York and London: Routledge.

Fincher, R. and Costello, L. (2005) Narratives of high-rise housing: placing the ethnicized newcomer in inner Melbourne. *Social and Cultural Geography* 6 (2), 201–17.

Gelder, K. and Jacobs, J.M. (1995) Talking out of place – authorizing the Aboriginal sacred in post-colonial Australia. *Cultural Studies* 9 (1), 150–60.

Gibson, K. (1998) Social polarization and the politics of difference: discourses in collision or collusion? In R. Fincher and J.M. Jacobs (eds) *Cities of Difference*, pp. 301–16. New York and London: Guilford Press.

Hannah, M. (1999) Skeptical realism: from either/or to both–and. *Environment and Planning D: Society and Space* 17, 17–34.

Harvey, D. (1973) *Social Justice and the City*. Oxford: Blackwell.

——(1989) *The Condition of Postmodernity*. Oxford: Blackwell.

——(1993) Class relations, social justice and the politics of difference. In M. Keith and S. Pile (eds) *Place and the Politics of Identity*, pp. 41–66. London and New York: Routledge.

——(2000) The difference a generation makes. In *Spaces of Hope*, Chapter 1, pp. 3–20. Berkeley and Los Angeles: University of California Press.

——(2003) *The New Imperialism*. Oxford University Press.

Harvey, D. and Chatterjee, L. (1974) Absolute rent and the structuring of space by government and financial institutions. *Antipode* 6 (1), 22–36.

Hudson, A. (2000) Offshoreness, globalization and sovereignty: a postmodern geo-political economy? *Transactions Institute of British Geography* 25, 269–83.

Hyndman, J. (1998) Managing difference: gender and culture in humanitarian emergencies. *Gender, Place and Culture* 5 (3), 241–60.

Jacobs, J.M. and Fincher, R. (1998) Introduction. In Ruth Fincher and Jane M. Jacobs (eds) *Cities of Difference*, pp. 1–25. New York and London: Guilford Press.

Jameson, F. (1998) *The Cultural Turn: Selected Writings on the Postmodern 1983–1998*. London and New York: Verso.

Johnston, L. (1996) Pumped up politics: female body builders refiguring the body. *Gender, Place and Culture: A Journal of Feminist Geography* 3, 327–40.

Jones, J.P., Nast, H.J. and Roberts, S. (eds) (1997) *Thresholds in Feminist Geography: Difference, Methodology, Representation*. Lanham, MD: Rowman and Littlefield,

Katz, C. and Monk, J. (eds) (1993) *Full Circles: Geographies of Women over the Life Course*. New York: Routledge.

Knopp, L. and Brown, M. (2003) Queer diffusions. *Environment and Planning D: Society and Space* 21, 409–24.

Kobayashi, A. (1997) The paradox of difference and diversity (or, why the thresholds keep moving). In J.P. Jones, H.J. Nast and S. Roberts (eds) *Thresholds in Feminist Geography: Difference, Methodology, Representation*, pp. 3–10. Lanham, MD: Rowman and Littlefield.

Kobayashi, A. and Peake, L. (1994) Unnatural discourse: 'race' and gender in geography. *Gender, Place and Culture* 1 (2), 225–43.

——(2000) Racism out of place: thoughts on whiteness and an antiracist geography in the new millennium. *Annals of the Association of American Geographers* 90, 392–403.

Koskela, H. (2000) 'The gaze without the eyes': video-surveillance and the changing nature of urban space. *Progress in Human Geography* 24 (2), 243–65.

Laurier, E. and Parr, H. (2000) Emotions and interviewing in health and disability research. *Social and Cultural Geography* 3, 98–102.

Lefebvre, H. (1991) *The Production of Space*. Oxford: Blackwell.

Ley, D. (2003) Forgetting postmodernism? Recuperating a social history of local knowledge. *Progress in Human Geography* 27 (5), 537–60.

Longhurst, R. (1996) Refocusing groups: pregnant women's experiences of Hamilton, New Zealand/Aotearoa. *Area* 28 (2), 143–9.

——(2001) Pregnant bodies in public spaces. In *Bodies: Exploring Fluid Boundaries*, Chapter 3, pp. 33–65. London and New York: Routledge.

McDowell, L. (1983) Towards an understanding of the gendered division of urban space. *Environment and Planning D: Society and Space* 1, 59–72.

——(1999) *Gender, Identity and Place: Understanding Feminist Geography*. Cambridge: Polity Press in association with Blackwell.

McDowell, L. and Court, G. (1994) Performing work: bodily representations in merchant banks. *Environment and Planning D: Society and Space* 12 (6), 727–50.

Mackenzie, S. and Rose, D. (1983) Industrial change, the domestic economy and home life. In J. Anderson, S. Duncan and R. Hudson (eds) *Redundant Spaces? Studies in Industrial Decline and Social Change*, pp. 155–99. London: Academic Press.

Marx, K. (1974) The Eighteenth Brumaire of Louis Bonaparte. In D. Fernbach (ed.) *Karl Marx: Surveys from Exile: Political Writings Volume II*. New York: Vintage Books.

Massey, D. (1983) Industrial restructuring as class restructuring: production decentralisation and local uniqueness. *Regional Studies* 17, 73–89.

——(1991) Flexible sexism. *Environment and Planning D: Society and Space* 9, 31–58.

Monk, Janice and Hanson, Susan (1982) On not excluding half of the human in human geography. *The Professional Geographer* 34, 11–23.

Nagar, R. and Leitner, H. (1998) Contesting social relations in communal places: identity politics among Asian communities in Dar es Salaam. In R. Fincher and J. M. Jacobs (eds) *Cities of Difference*, pp. 226–51. New York: Guilford Press.

Nast, H.J. (1998) The body as 'place': reflexivity and fieldwork in Kano, Nigeria. In S. Pile and H.J. Nast (eds) *Places through the Body*, pp. 93–116. London and New York: Routledge.

——(2000) Mapping the 'unconscious': racism and the oedipal family. *Annals of the Association of American Geographers* 90 (2), 215–55.

——(2002) Prologue: crosscurrents. *Antipode* (special issue, Queer Patriarchies, Queer Racisms, International) 34 (5), 835–44.

Pratt, G. (with the Philippine Women Centre, Vancouver, Canada) (1998), Inscribing domestic work on Filipina bodies. In S. Pile and H.J. Nast (eds) *Places through the Body*, pp. 283–304. London and New York: Routledge.

Radcliffe, S. (1996) Gendered nations: nostalgia, development and territory in Ecuador. *Gender, Place and Culture* 3, 5–21.

——(2005) Development and geography: towards a postcolonial development geography? *Progress in Human Geography* 29, 291–8.

Rose, D. (1989) A feminist perspective on employment restructuring and gentrification: the case of Montreal. In J. Wolch and M. Dear (eds) *The Power of Geography: How Territory Shapes Social Life*, pp. 118–38. London and Boston: Allen and Unwin.

Sayer, A. (2001) For a critical cultural political economy. *Antipode* 33 (4), 687–708.

Slater, D. (1998) Postcolonial questions for global times. *Review of International Political Economy* 5 (4), 647–78.

Smith, N. (1979) Toward a theory of gentrification: a back to the city movement by capital not people. *Journal of the American Planning Association* 45, 538–48.

——(2002) What happened to class? *Environment and Planning A,* 32, 1011–32.

Smith, S.J. (2000) Performing the (sound) world. *Environment and Planning D: Society and Space* 18 (5), 615–47.

Soja, E.W. (1996) *Thirdspace: Journeys to Los Angeles and Other Real and Imagined Places*. Malden, Mass.: Blackwell.

Staehli, L.A. and Kofman, E. (2004) Mapping gender, making politics: toward feminist political geographies. In L.A. Staehli, and L. Peake (eds) *Mapping Women, Making Politics: Feminist Perspectives on Political Geography*, pp. 1–14. New York and Abingdon, Oxon: Routledge.

Valentine, G. (1993) (Hetero)sexing space: lesbian perceptions and experiences of everyday spaces. *Environment and Planning D: Society and Space* 11, 395–413.

——(1996) (Re)negotiating the 'heterosexual street': lesbian productions of space. In N. Duncan (ed.) *Body Space: Destabilizing Geographies of Gender and Sexuality*, pp. 146–55. New York and London: Routledge.

——(1999) What it means to be a man: the body, masculinities and disability. In R. Butler and H. Parr (eds) *Mind and Body Spaces: Geographies of Disability, Illness and Impairment*, pp. 167–80. London: Routledge.

——(2003) Geography and ethics: in pursuit of social justice – ethics and emotions in geographies of health and disability research. *Progress in Human Geography* 27 (3), 375–80.

Walker, R. (1981) A theory of suburbanization: capitalism and the construction of urban space in the United States. In M. Dear and A. Scott (eds) *Urbanization and Urban Planning in Advanced Capitalist Societies*, pp. 383–430. New York: Methuen.

Widdowfield, R. (2000) The place of emotions in academic research. *Area* 32 (2), 199–208.

Wilton, R.D. (2003) Locating physical disability in Freudian and Lacanian psychoanalysis: problems and prospects. *Social and Cultural Geography* 4 (3), 369–89.

Women and Geography Study Group (1984) *Geography and Gender: An Introduction to Feminist Geography*. London: Hutchinson.

Part IV

Nature, rate, and direction of change

Examples

Ian Douglas

Previous sections of this encyclopedia have emphasized the changing nature of places and landscapes. But change and the effects of time impact differentially on the surface of the Earth. At critical locations, such as along rapidly eroding shorelines, where cliffs recede during storms, or on the fringes of booming cities, where new suburbs are built to accommodate thousands of in-migrants every month (as in Las Vegas and Phoenix), change is rapid and the local landscape may alter overnight. Elsewhere change is almost imperceptible, perhaps because natural processes are operating extremely slowly, or because the social and economic drivers of change are not having visible effects on particular places. Understanding place involves knowing about the rate and impacts of change, but also the extent to which things stay the same, appear to stay the same, or are made (or hoped) to stay the same. In Chapter 25, Chris Gibson argues that spatial fixity is the antonym of mobility, fluidity and flux, and although all the latter rightly underpin a vast proportion of the research in contemporary social science, they should not prevent analysis of the extent to which, in some places and at some times, continuity and stability prevail. He reviews the many processes that work to retain the character of places. One of them is the constancy of Aboriginal attachments to country and ways of managing the environment that have since been central elements in the successful political battles to win back rights over parts of Australia wrongly annexed after the 1788 European invasion.

Some places are deliberately preserved to retain their character. Preservation of buildings and the natural environment is driven by many motives that Lily Kong explores in Chapter 26. Whole sections of towns and cities may be managed as 'conservation areas' with regulations inhibiting changes that other drivers would seek to make. However, heritage today is not only about the elite, great heroes and the spectacular: it also emphasizes the vernacular, the recent, living memories and such intangible folkways as language and poetry. At the same time, both built and natural environments are conserved, not the least by the UNESCO World Heritage Site and Biosphere Reserve programmes. Although, some places appear simply to stand still for decades or centuries. Small rural towns in America and Australia retain much of the character of their first settlement a hundred years ago. Many mining settlements had a few decades of active growth and then declined. Similarly, the 'rust-belts' of the world, such as the declining industrial areas of Europe and the USA, are places of stagnation that have particular social and environmental problems. Stagnation is not necessarily bad: it enables wise use of resources to continue, as Jim Walmsley argues in Chapter 27. Development and change may not be normal for the human species: it may be a product of our present technological ability to consume and to reduce death rates.

At the other extreme from the unchanging rural areas are the rapidly growing manufacturing cities to which thousands of people are migrating every week. Perhaps the most dramatic contemporary change is the transformation, in twenty-five years, of the Pearl River Delta rice fields in Guangdong Province, China, into the 'new workshop of the world'. As Victor Sit shows in Chapter 28, in addition to huge export-oriented manufacturing, the Pearl River Delta region produces machinery for the China Mainland domestic market so that by 2000 it made 78.8 per cent of China's telephones, 60.2 per cent of its printers, 88 per cent of its electric fans, 80 per cent of its sound systems, 79 per cent of its rice-cookers, 72 per cent of its microwave ovens and 56 per cent of its fax machines. This was accompanied by the development of infrastructure transforming the delta into a major metropolitan region.

Some rapid transformations also occur through the deliberate creation of new towns to fulfil a single purpose by creating a specific image. Federal capitals such as Washington DC, Canberra, Brasilia, Dodoma and Abuja are good examples of designed symbols of political relationships and power placed either at junctions between rival power groups or to symbolize a shift from colonial coastal centres to the development of the national interior. As Howard Gillette shows in Chapter 29, most of these capitals have symbolic monumental buildings and avenues, but Dodoma in Tanzania was planned to reflect egalitarian values associated with the Garden City tradition. Although plans called for a mall, neither it nor its associated government structures were intended to be monumental. While some prominent government structures ultimately found elevated locations and began to assume monumental proportions, they did so in violation of stated expectations. The result, though different in appearance from other manufactured capitals, was a similarly mixed message, confirming that even the most consistent ideals cannot always be translated into physical form.

In other areas, changing places involved finding new uses for old structures and creating new homes and opportunities. In Chapter 30, Brian Robson shows that formerly derelict places may develop a completely new appearance as a result of active regeneration policies. British regeneration policies have brought successful changes to parts of former industrial cities but left outstanding problems for others. Regeneration of city centres by the building of apartments for young professionals is also one of the forms of reconcentration in large urban areas discussed by Ian Douglas in Chapter 31. The effect of decreasing rural employment on movement to urban areas is illustrated with a case study of Rosario, Argentina, while the way in which refugees from war and civil conflict move to urban areas shows a contrast between those who become a hidden part of the urban economy and those who survive in peripheral refugee camps.

This reconcentration is small compared with the trend of developing 'edge cities', new nodes of commercial activity and employment on peripheral ring roads and freeways, as part of the pattern of urban expansion that is now occurring in China as well as North America and Europe. Although large-scale urban dispersal has been widely condemned and its management (and even its reversal) has been made the object of a large number of policy (often referred to as 'smart growth') initiatives, dispersion continues and even accelerates in many places. As Peter Gordon explains in Chapter 32, settlement change never stops and there are always winners and losers. At the same time, there are push and pull forces at work. Giant hub airports (such as Chicago and Dallas) are the foci of intense urban activity, replacing the clusters once present around major shipping and rail transport interchanges. Just as cars and ubiquitous access replaced transit hubs, widely available personal air travel may one day diminish the role of the giant airport hubs. When that day comes, counter-urbanization forces may have received another boost.

Many everyday activities and social interactions nowadays, however, take place in virtual places – places that are dependent on networked computing infrastructure for their existence. And important virtual spaces are also increasingly produced in the material world through the embedding of information and communications technologies (ICTs) into the fabric of our settlements. In Chapter 33 Martin Dodge and Rob Kitchin explore these virtual worlds, developing a typology of cyberspace, and illustrating the significance of these apparently 'placeless' alternative communities through a case study of AlphaWorld. They also explore the intersections between the virtual and the real, charting the blending of virtual and real in phenomena such as electronic payment, traffic management and video-surveillance.

The responses to drivers of change differ widely. Despite trends towards a global similarity reflected in parts of cities looking the same around the world, there is still as much diversity in the urban landscape as there is in natural landforms and ecosystems. The geography of places loses none of its fascination, dynamism and interest even in the face of global change.

25

Unchanging places

Chris Gibson

Introduction

There is a Theravada Buddhist saying that 'no experience, no state of mind, no physical object, lasts'. The core of this Buddhist principle (known as 'annica') is *impermanence* – it emphasizes the constant flux in both physical matter and human culture, and warns against dogma, cherishing talismans or holding on to rigid opinions. It is a teaching about our perceptions (and misperceptions) of change: no event, landscape, person or idea remains the same, despite the appearance of constancy or the wish to preserve. What may look permanent may not be so enduring when conceptualized in a different manner, when observed over a longer timeframe or at a wider geographical scale.

This chapter is not about Buddhist culture or teachings, but it is about the tension so neatly encapsulated in the above saying – a tension between the appearance of constancy and the reality of change. Some places change little over decades or centuries. Villages in central China look as though they have not altered for 300 years. Small rural towns in America and Australia retain much of the character of their first establishment over 100 years ago. Many natural landscapes appear to be unchanging, unsullied by people where preserved as 'wilderness', while deep divisions and differentiations within cities appear to persist through subsequent generations.

But constancy may be deceptive, and even the most static places may be revealed as metamorphosing over a longer time period, or when interpreted at different geographical scales. This chapter discusses 'unchanging' places, whether real or perceived – those locations and landscapes that aren't apparently in flux, in contrast to the tumultuous and uncertain world around them. It is intended as a kind of counterpoint to many of the other chapters in this collection, which emphasize the dynamism of human geography and the increasing pace of social and environmental change. Amidst all the instability, some things change very slowly, or not at all.

This chapter begins with an overview of the different ways we can think ~~~
unchanging, drawing attention briefly to the importance of conceptual~~~
graphical scale. Both temporality and spatiality play an enormous role i~~~
of 'unchanging places' as sites of continuity, of flux, of more or less grad~~~

then moves through discussions of some selected examples of human and natural landscapes that appear constant, permanent or preserved, or which for various reasons humans might wish to see remain static. At various points I illustrate how there is a political dimension to 'unchanging places', one that can be interpreted as either radical or regressive, depending on one's perspective. In various ways perceptions of constancy come uncoupled from the reality of change.

Theorizing 'time' and 'scale'

It is crucial not to underestimate the temporal dimension in the study of places. Just as we can move beyond Cartesian understandings of physical space towards seeing places as produced, contested, metaphorical and relational (see Chapters 3, 4 and 5), we can also move beyond a simplistic chronological or rational view of time to understand how varying perceptions of it infuse our ways of interpreting the world. Indeed, the interrelations of time and space have provided fruitful topics for deeper philosophical debate. In physics, Einstein's theory of relativity changed perceptions of Cartesian space and time, when he revealed how they were not absolute but relative both to the observer and to the thing being observed. In human geography, debates about time and space have centrally concerned how social life and meanings are structured and negotiated (Hagerstrand 1970; Pred 1981; Thrift 1983; Harvey 1989; Gregory 1994), while for earth scientists, defining timeframes as well as geographical scales is a basic requirement for accurate understandings of process and change (evidenced particularly in climate change research).

Scale of analysis is important, because the same phenomenon can appear unchanging or tumultuous, depending on how perception of it is framed. Human bodies appear to age quite slowly, but when seen at the microscopic scale are in fact made up of trillions upon trillions of cells and inhabited by similarly huge numbers of bacteria, all busily undertaking specific tasks, reproducing themselves, dying and growing *en masse*. Cities look like bustling, changing places too – but, at a certain scale and timeframe, are more constant than they might appear (see discussion later).

In a straightforward manner, there are also profound differences between a geological and an 'everyday' or 'social' view of time that influence how we perceive continuity or change in places. Human society appears to change more rapidly and regularly than the non-human 'natural' world, with complete transformation in cities and economies sometimes occurring within mere decades or even years (as with the transitions in Asian 'Tiger' countries such as Singapore and Korea in the 1980s and 1990s). Meanwhile, the geological and biophysical landscapes upon which human societies are based often appear by comparison fixed, even timeless. Of course, physical scientists would strongly challenge the latter assumption, arguing that geological landscapes and ecosystems do indeed change, only that the timeframes vary. Some changes are only visible when measured in millions of years rather than decades or generations. Also, many 'natural' landscapes that seem timeless or unchanging are in fact the way they appear only because they are the product of human interventions such as conservation initiatives or resource management decisions, or because humans choose to see them that way (see discussion below). Other seemingly stable 'natural' landscapes may be changing more rapidly than we might assume, because of anthropogenic influences such as deforestation, climate change, the introduction of exogenous species, and various forms of industrial and urban pollution.

When we think of ancient landscapes and long timelines, we often presume that it is only physical geographical phenomena that change so slowly, perceiving 'natural' processes as gradual and 'human' change as fast-paced. But there is also some truth in the converse. Change in climate, ecosystems, evolutionary adaption and even geology can occur in brief time periods (Houghton *et al.* 2001), while social practices and geographies may have extensive timeframes. Both biophysical and social worlds can change rapidly, and simultaneously, because of extreme events such as the massive Indian Ocean tsunami of 26 December 2004. It profoundly changed the physical coastlines of many countries – including Indonesia, Thailand, Sri Lanka – and wreaked havoc on domestic fishing and tourism industries, killing many thousands of people and destroying infrastructure, all in the space of a few minutes (see Chapter 41). But just because so much can alter so quickly and dramatically is no reason to ignore or downplay the extent to which places, peoples, cultures and landscapes have largely evaded change.

Although major forces are reshaping world geography – capitalism, globalization, technological advances, environmental change – acknowledging the importance of these is not the same as suggesting that all places have been changed in equally profound ways. Some places are dynamic and ever-changing – even defined by their capacity to reinvent themselves – while others are not. In a place like Las Vegas, it is not unusual for major buildings less than 30 years old to be demolished to make way for new casinos, hotels and resorts – it is a city that physically re-shapes itself on a regular basis. But, in contrast, many places have retained fairly similar populations, characters, ecosystems, locally unique economic activities and built environments to those of many generations ago. That this is so does not require us to think of these places as 'static', as 'trapped in the past' or as museums of traditional societies, but more simply as places where, for one reason or another, the pace of change is slow.

Often such places are small and relatively isolated from transportation and technological advances, or are towns and parts of cities where economic stagnation has meant a lack of new investment or imperative to demolish and redevelop buildings. In seeking to re-theorize uneven global development, Manuel Castells (1996) talked of the emergence of a 'globally-disconnected fourth world' – a whole segment of the human population excluded from the global trading system, unable to reap benefits from circuits of investment and migration, and unlikely to 'keep up' with technological advances because of poverty, insufficient skills, poor biophysical environments or lack of infrastructure provision. Unlike previous eras of (inter)-dependency and exploitation (where one could talk of uneven and unfair, but nonetheless present relations between 'first' and 'third' worlds), Castells traces a bifurcation between parts of the world caught up in contemporary global changes, and other places (including wide parts of sub-Saharan Africa) where people are disengaged. Castells' theory suggests that some places are relatively unchanged because they do not participate equally in (or are excluded from) processes of trade, investment and technological diffusion.

While this might be true for many cases, the reasons why places change slowly may not be purely because populations are excluded from the global economy. Indeed, it would be wrong to assume that all local populations equally aspire to be caught up in rapid economic and cultural change. Many people instead hope to be able to negotiate the pace of change, to resist it, or to shape the manner in which they engage with processes of transformation. The clearest examples are where human cultures and places have deliberately sought to remain unchanged over very lengthy time periods, as in indigenous communities around the world, where ideas of 'traditional culture' and attachments to territory can be very strong. Elements of traditional cultural practices have survived in many places, despite the ravages of colonialism and capitalism. Sami communities in Norway, Finland and Sweden have been able to maintain elements of the traditional *siida* village systems, despite their physical presence within European nation-states who have sought to impose fixed borders and administrative jurisdictions, and who have authorized widespread dispossession of their traditional lands. Sami have unique social structures, fluid and overlapping sovereignties, customary rules for resource use and decision-making mechanisms centred around the practice of reindeer herding (Karppi 2001). In the Middle East, Bedouin communities have remained nomadic and upheld traditional customs, including the social organization of living space (with separate tents and camping spaces for men and women), dress, music and culture. In Australia, Aboriginal connections to country, spiritual beliefs and land management practices have in many parts remained consistent despite European colonization, and links can be drawn to social practices undertaken in similar ways for several thousands of years. Parallels exist within many diverse indigenous societies in the Americas, the Pacific and across Asia.

That numerous examples of very old cultural practices survive around the world demonstrates that there is a sense of continuity within human societies spanning much wider timeframes than we might first assume, though it is important to recognize that this is increasingly being constrained and challenged by governments, corporations and political pressures. Indigenous communities seeking to maintain traditions and strong connections to land face many common struggles including dispossession of territory, the imposition of central government policies, and demands for communities to adopt imposed languages, religious practices and customs. A good example is the combination of pressures facing the over 240 tribal peoples who inhabit West Papua (now controversially part of the nation-state of Indonesia). Since wresting control of the territory from the Dutch in the 1960s, Indonesia has repressed West Papuan resistance to colonialism through military force (killing an estimated 100,000 people since 1963), has targeted the province as a receiving location for its *transmigrasi* scheme (which encourages Javanese and other Indonesians from highly populated centres to decentralize to outer islands), and allowed foreign transnational companies to commence substantial mining and logging operations (Ondawame 2000; Elmslie 2003). Land has been seized for settlement of migrants from other parts of Indonesia, and West Papuans (whose traditional culture relates more to Melanesians in Papua New Guinea, Fiji and the Solomon Islands than to Javanese or other Indonesian groups) have been under substantial pressure to adopt Bahasa Indonesia, move away from distinct local cultures, and abandon claims to sovereignty.

Even where colonial conflict and violence have faded from memory, for many indigenous groups the exigencies of modern life compel them to seek cash incomes, avenues for employment in the capitalist economy, and state provision of modern infrastructure. In Sami lands, just as with native American tribes in the United States and Aboriginal nations in the north of Australia, the sheer loss of lands under indigenous control means that it is becoming more difficult (and in some instances near impossible) to sustain a viable 'traditional' economy. There is rarely enough food, water or shelter for local populations left on the parcels of land not encroached upon by colonial governments (as with reservations in North America) or won back through land rights struggles (as in Australia). In the Middle East, Bedouins still live a nomadic life, but their capacity to survive is increasingly challenged by encroaching agriculture and urban settlements, and the desires of nation-states to achieve efficiency in the provision of infrastructure and services by encouraging more permanent settlements.

Although tradition remains important for many indigenous groups, it is now being modified by external cultural impacts and transitions resulting from contacts with Western lifestyles and social practices. Through work, through education and from cultural flows associated with the more widespread dissemination of televisions, radios and the Internet, indigenous societies have embraced change and outside influence but, for most, not yet at the expense of diminishing the importance of the traditional, the spiritual beliefs and social practices that underpin their indigenous identities and links with the past. Unchanging places are sites of struggle and compromise.

It would be difficult to claim the same kinds of cultural continuities (or physical continuities, in the case of built environments) in most Western societies. Although medieval villages still survive in Britain, and many Asian and European cities can boast built environments that are several centuries old, it is clear that most non-indigenous societies are utterly transformed in comparison with their own antecedent communities. It is hard to imagine ways in which the cultures, social practices, economic life or residential settings of a contemporary Brit resemble those of people living in the same locale a thousand years ago – or even much further back (as a comparison with Australian Aboriginal culture would require). It is true that some traditions and spaces have survived multiple revolutions and upheavals, from Christmas and Easter, which have pagan origins, to town centres, transport routes and sites of worship which have been features of the human landscape for thousands of years. However, the absolute degree of transformation in Western societies prohibits the possibility of making comprehensive evaluations about how places have remained the same. It therefore matters how we conceptualize the relative magnitude of time in our analysis of 'unchanging places'. If what we define as 'unchanging' is measured in smaller timeframes (say, across decades or generations rather than millennia), then much more of the social, cultural and economic life of contemporary places could be seen as stable or constant.

Unchanging built environments

In terms of architecture and built form, a good proportion of the physical landscapes of places are inherited from the past. Not many places undergo facelifts with the severity of Las Vegas, and even in quite dynamic 'world cities' the layout of streetscapes and road networks, public parklands, mass transit systems (such as the London Underground and New York subway) and the bulk of commercial and residential architecture are bestowed from previous generations. These basic consistencies in the built environment shape the character of places enormously and provide a direct, tangible link to the past. Even in places where urban redevelopments were radical and dramatic, they have in turn become lasting legacies ensuring a sense of permanence. One cannot imagine Paris without Haussmann's grand boulevards, bridges and public buildings, planned and constructed upon the remains of the demolished medieval city in the 1860s; one cannot picture cities like Sydney or San Francisco without their iconic bridges or opera houses, or Los Angeles without its freeways (all relatively recent accoutrements). Even London appears to have an enduring architectural or urban character, in spite of its many transformations – it was a city rebuilt anew by Christopher Wren after the Great Fire in 1666, then dramatically shaped by the industrial revolution, subsequently bombed during the Second World War (and then rebuilt), and now a city of intense regeneration linked to the global financial industry. Cataclysmic events, radical planning schemes or waves of investment and construction have fundamentally changed the physical appearance of places, but have also established the bases for future continuities.

As infrastructure and physical capital investment have a long shelf-life, they tend to influence and structure urban life in ways that remain remarkably consistent. The international movement of capital, capitalists and skills encouraged by lowered trade barriers has had dramatic effects on places from which manufacturing has shifted offshore and traditional industries have died, and drastic short-term effects on people's livelihoods (as in the 2001–2 Argentine financial crisis) where capital has left countries. Nonetheless, as David Harvey (1989) argued, capitalists still require locations in which to produce commodities, and much capital investment is fixed. Although the evidence overwhelmingly suggests that capitalists are willing to uproot production and move in search of cheap labour or lax environmental laws with scant regard to the communities affected, they still cannot constantly move. Some investment must remain rooted in places for certain periods of time. It is this sense of fixity of investment that leads city governments to build infrastructures like transport, port facilities, town centres and so on – and some sense of continuity and presence on the part of production is required to legitimize such public projects (lest they become 'white elephants').

In contrast, where places have experienced a level of economic stagnation (see Chapter 27), built environments have often evaded dramatic changes because of lack of investment or support for redevelopment. Given its central role in the industrial revolution (and because of the subsequent extent of de-industrialization), Britain has substantial amounts of industrial heritage that are testament to this, with whole sections of the built environments of many industrial towns from the 1800s and early 1900s largely intact (Stratton and Trinder 2000). Such heritage has now become a feature of tourism promotions, to such an extent that websites such as industrialheritage.org.uk and AboutBritain.com list over 350 important sites of industrial heritage in all regions of the country, from the woollen mills of Leeds and Bradford to potteries in Devon and collieries in Wales. Also in Britain, Victorian and Edwardian seaside towns such as Great Yarmouth and Gorleston (in the East Anglia region) have retained much of their architectural heritage (Plate 25.1), largely because those towns were not rebuilt in the 1970s or 1980s. These seaside towns were neglected when air travel became cheaper, encouraging mass charter flight tourism to warmer European holiday destinations in

Plate 25.1. The Pavilion Theatre, Gorleston, UK, 2003. Seaside towns such as Gorleston have evaded changes felt in other tourist destinations since the 1980s and have retained much of their architectural heritage. Photograph by Chris Gibson.

Spain, France, Italy and Greece, so fundamentally altering the geography and scale of European tourist mobility. In the stagnating older northern European resorts and destinations the waterfront promenades, architecture, music halls and early theme parks remained – not so much through efforts to preserve them for heritage value, but more simply because there is little or no demand to demolish and redevelop those sites for other uses.

Just as the timeframe of analysis matters in interpreting 'unchanging places', so too does geographical scale. In the examples already discussed, an understanding relies on a particular geographical scale of analysis – individual buildings, streetscapes, the 'character' of a whole city or town, the global distribution of investment – that situates the 'place' observed within a spatial and historical continuum. Places that may appear 'unchanging' at one scale may appear highly mutable when re-conceptualized at another. When industrial heritage becomes part of the tourist circuit, it is immediately embedded in new sets of economic, cultural and technological relations associated with that industry. The tourism industry in turn operates across and between geographical scales, linking local destinations with regional and national marketing campaigns, and encouraging flows of tourists from other regions, from neighbouring or distant countries. These latter processes are not 'unchanging' at all, and are bound up in complex transitions in mobility, communications, consumer tastes and fashions. Australian country towns or American rural villages might also appear unchanging, but they too are connected in various ways to wider scales and processes that are dynamic. These include rural gentrification, farm subsidy policies and agricultural restructuring, salinity and other environmental problems, the ageing of populations and loss of young people through rural–urban migration. In a very different circumstance, what appear to be instances of the maintenance of traditional Aboriginal cultures (when seen as highly localized practices and ideas) may seem much more contemporaneous when situated in the wider struggle for recognition of indigenous rights. To extend on this discussion of the ambivalence of time-frame and geographical scale, in the remainder of this chapter, I discuss three types of 'unchanging places' in more detail. These are: socio-spatial patterns within cities, 'wilderness' places, and places where changes are resisted in an overt manner by humans.

Unchanging cities? Patterns and divisions

In many parts of major cities there are close, enduring relationships between different human activities and between those activities and the built environment. Investments and infrastructures in cities create patterns of work and residence, and divisions and distinctions within cities that persist with the lifecycle of that infrastructure. Ports tend to be loci for industrial complexes, mills, wheat silos, warehousing facilities, transport and logistics companies. Movement of goods and people required large numbers of manual workers who lived in working-class communities (as historically was the case in London's East End and in the San Telmo district of Buenos Aires). Where ports were especially used in wartime by naval ships of home and allied forces, they also generated red light districts, with bars, clubs and prostitution. These districts have often survived beyond the war eras in which red light trade was generated, as in Sydney's Kings Cross or Bangkok's Patpong district. Other port cities with major historic (and still active) red light districts include Amsterdam, Hamburg and New Orleans.

At the metropolitan scale, processes such as international migration, gentrification, the building of new kinds of settlements (such as master-planned estates) and changing employment and occupations have all complicated old-fashioned understandings of social patterns and divisions within cities (Hamnett 1994; Smith, 1996; Amin and Thrift 2002). However, in many cities certain socio-economic patterns have altered little throughout generations, even if the citizens themselves come and go. The truism that 'the rich get richer, the poor get poorer' reflects a stubborn statistical reality that under capitalism, inequalities in wealth persist. These regularly have spatial dimensions.

Areas of wealth and poverty, or relative affluence and disadvantage, can remain consistent under governments of different political persuasions, and in spite of schemes attempting to redistribute resources more equitably. There are several reasons for this. Most immediately, private housing markets become polarized over time, as certain areas of cities become known as places of wealth or poverty, as districts of high or low amenity value, access or incon-venience, or as areas that become fashionable (or not so), through the accrual or absence of 'cultural capital' in particular neighbourhoods – the awareness of trends and discernment that enables social status (Bourdieu 1984).

In the Kansai region of Japan, social status has in part been linked to certain districts that through physical infrastructure and the historical construction and marketing of competing private railway lines have remained socially differentiated for nearly a century (Semple 2005). The Hanshin and Hankyu lines run in parallel over the Kansai plain from Osaka to Kobe, but have formed the basis of the production of quite different places, organized long-itudinally on either side of the 'tracks'. These two urban zones were originally marketed in the 1910s–1920s by entrepreneurs as conversely elite (Hanyku) and respectable working-class (Hanshin) development projects. The railway lines and stations were built at the same time as their respective residential quarters, retail districts and entertainment facilities, in light of these marketing visions. Differences in class orientation were reflected in the landscape through the size of residential quarters, the quality of building materials and opulence in retail outlets. Although many decades have passed since their original construction (and despite massive cultural changes in Japan in this time), the settlements and suburbs along the two railway lines are still seen as possessing similar social status to when they were originally established. Decisions of developers and planners many decades ago produced the physical settings that would continue to distinguish populations, and differentiate contemporary urban life.

In many cities, decisions made by planners and civic authorities early in their history determined socio-spatial patterns well beyond the lives of those in power at the time. Syd-ney's spatial patterns were established at the founding of the colonial city, when British governors and skilled tradespeople built mansions on the east side of the farm cove settle-ment. On the west side of the settlement ex-convicts, poor workers and traders huddled in slums, built in and around warehouses, finger wharves and unplanned, unregulated laneways. This early spatial division of wealth set in train an 'east vs west' socio-economic divide in Sydney that broadly continues to this day, even with the mobility and increasing complexity of the city's population (Birmingham 2000). East-side suburbs (particularly those on the beaches and on harbour foreshores) are the most expensive residential neighbourhoods in Australia. And although western Sydney has become much more diverse, densely populated and internally differentiated since the 1980s, within it are many of the country's least wealthy suburbs and stereotypes persist about Western Sydney as an 'other' place of disadvantage and social problems.

Elsewhere in Sydney, its Chinatown remains in an area that became Chinese over 100 years ago, when Australia experienced successive gold rushes and Chinese entrepreneurs flocked to the port city's southern fringes. Whilst the financial sector has recolonized the city after decades of decay, the Chinese business presence remains strong. Similarly in Bangkok, its Chinatown still exists today on a site to which the Chinese were moved in 1782 in order for the royal government to establish the new capital. Bangkok has grown enormously around the original 'old city' of Ko Ratanakosin (where the Chinese were evicted from their original settlement) and despite the obvious demographic and physical changes, a particular cultural presence remains. As Anderson (1987) argued, however, Chinatowns are more than just districts in which a particular ethnic group resides. They are as much products or inventions of the non-Chinese populations of those cities, whether created through government policies of exclusion, through marketing and tourism campaigns, and as racial categories imbued with spatial meaning.

On a different continent, and with an even more complicated colonial history, Dar es Salaam, Tanzania, exemplifies this sense of persistent urban differentiation. After decades of German occupation, British authorities divided up the city socially and spatially at the end of the First World War. The city was divided into three 'classes': the area to the east of the city, Usunguni, where the previous German colonists had laid out a botanical garden, was designated for Europeans and was promptly decked out with asphalt roads, shady trees and a hospital; the Uhindini area, which was reserved for Asian 'coolie' immigrants brought by the British to work on the construction of the new colony; and the Uswahilini district, to the west, which was reserved for Africans (see Figure 25.1). Although Africans were part of all three communities in different capacities, they were largely excluded from political power, and the 'Township Authority', which reigned over Dar es Salaam from 1919 until independence in 1961, was dominated by Europeans and Indians (see Burton 2002). This basic segregation pattern, though certainly not enforced since independence, still marks out the social divisions of the city. Uzunguni (as it is now known) remains a European quarter, and the beaches and suburbs stretching out from there to the north have continued to be the preserve of the city's wealthy, including some upwardly mobile Tanzanians, but overwhelmingly foreign diplomats, international schools, United Nations and NGO workers. Meanwhile Uhindini has remained the city's Asian district, and Uswahilini has become Kariakoo, a vibrant, and overwhelmingly Swahili, commercial market area, in which the standard of infrastructure and services is still very poor, a lag reflecting the under-provision of services by the British 90 years before (see Chakravorty 2000 for a parallel in Calcutta, another colonial city).

In American cities, despite globalization, gentrification, state housing projects and downtown urban renewal schemes, some remarkably stubborn geographical divisions persist between contiguous rich and poor neighbourhoods, between white and black (Sassen 1991; cf. Hamnett 1994), and between moneyed and marginal neighbourhoods. Chicago's non-Hispanic white population still lives within an almost exclusively 'white' residential zone to the north of the city centre along the banks of Lake Michigan, while its south side (richly depicted in the crime novels of Sara Paretsky) was the city's major industrial district, and has maintained a strong and large African-American working-class community (Abu-Lughod 1999). As with many northern cities, South Chicago has de-industrialized since the 1970s, and is thus bound up in the series of industrial and geographical transformations linked to globalization including the flight of manufacturing capital and centralization and rationalization of domestic industries (see Chapter 27). Although heavily affected by complex economic change, a metropolitan-scale division in the city's social fabric remains unchanged (Figures 25.2 and 25.3). Although both the population and the city grew over the 20-year period, the extent of segregation has remained constant. As Abu-Lughod (1999: 334–6) argued, 'changes in the racial and ethnic composition have contributed little to desegregation'.

Planning and zoning schemes and the state organization of land uses can influence divisions and patterns within a city in more subtle ways. Although poor 'ghettos' have been frequently redeveloped, remodelled and rebuilt in attempts to ameliorate poverty and social and health problems (as in the American 'projects' of the 1960s and 1970s, and slum clearances in London in successive centuries), well-built residential districts populated by wealthy classes are rarely touched; they tend not to be demolished to make way for industry, nor rezoned for other land-uses or more dense urban development (Chakravorty 2000). In some cities, official government policies to escalate population densities across the city have been resisted most successfully in wealthy municipal areas where residents have sought to hold on to detached, suburban homes, leafy environs and low building-height restrictions. Wealthy

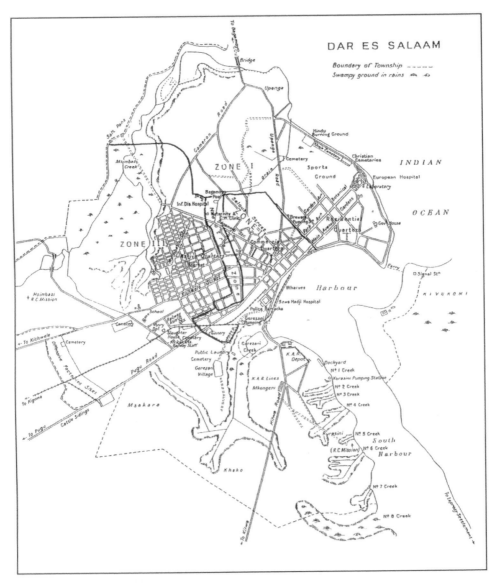

Figure 25.1. Dar es Salaam in 1925, showing the three segregated residential zones.
Source: Adapted from Burton (2002: 100).

residents tend to have access to time and monetary resources required to mount legal challenges to controversial planning decisions, and to capitalize on their own skills base in organizing campaigns. Invariably wealthy areas include professionals whose skills can be transferred to campaigns to fight redevelopment, such as lawyers, academics, advertisers and public relations experts. By contrast, many poor neighbourhoods lack the strategic resources needed to mount successful attempts to resist change.

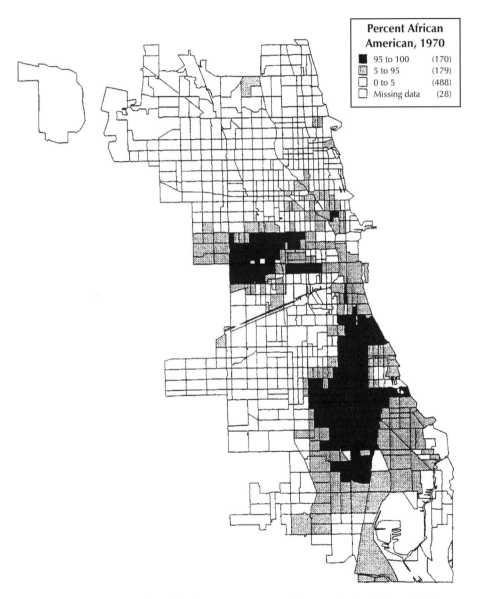

Figure 25.2. Distribution of African-Americans as percentage of census tracts, Chicago, 1970.
Source: After Abu-Lughod (1999: 336). Reprinted with kind permission of The University of Minnesota Press and Jeffrey Morenoff.

Cities have changed enormously (see Chapters 21, 28 and 30) and are complexes of networks of actors that are always remade continuously (Amin and Thrift 2002). Yet acknowledging this should not come at the expense of understanding how certain socio-spatial divisions and patterns persist, whether seen at the metropolitan (Sassen 1991) or neighbourhood scale (Short 1989). In conjunction with the physical structures established by planning and infrastructure provision, market forces reinforce enduring socio-spatial divisions as well as create tumult and change.

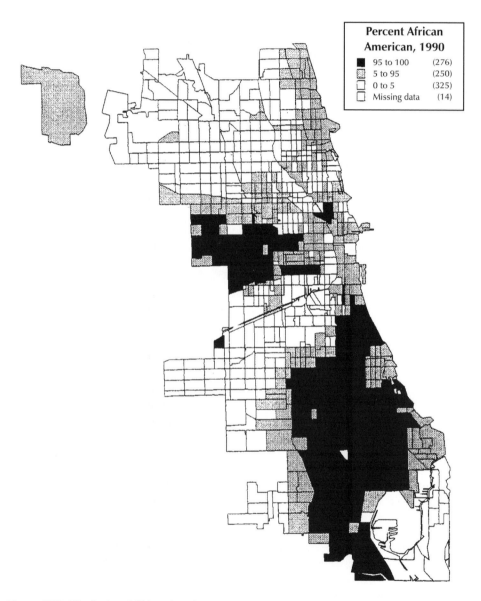

Figure 25.3. Distribution of African-Americans as percentage of census tracts, Chicago, 1990.
Source: After Abu-Lughod (1999: 337). Reprinted with kind permission of The University of Minnesota Press and Jeffrey Morenoff.

Unchanging nature? 'Wilderness' places

'Ministers come and go, even dictators die, but mountain ranges stand unperturbed'
(Spykman 1942: 41)

For all the places that appear unchanged, there are those that people wrongly assume are static, timeless or ancient. Increasingly common in many countries are the establishment of national parks and conservation areas, set aside for ecological or recreational goals. Such spaces are cherished by environmental movements, tourists and escaping urbanites, often seen 'as an island in the polluted sea of urban-industrial modernity, the one place we can turn for escape' (Cronon 1996: 69). However, the perception of 'natural' landscapes such as national parks and wilderness reserves as 'unchanging' – as beyond the influence of human alterations – falls prey to a deception. These landscapes are produced by decisions of humans to preserve, set aside and in some instances remove them from human influence (such as the land use and cultural practices of indigenous peoples, often evicted or excluded from preservation zones). Irrespective of conservation policies and the presence or absence of indigenous peoples, physical landscapes are in any case *always* dynamic, even if over a longer timeframe, while more controversially many ecosystems have been altered in much more profound ways than in previous millennia because of anthropogenic influence, whether through habitat destruction, urban development or agricultural expansion, or through 'indirect' impacts such as that of global warming on Arctic ice-caps, glacial fields and coral reefs.

That 'wilderness' creates the impression of perpetuity – of places remaining in a pre-human, and thus 'pristine' state – is hardly surprising. National parks, reserves and conservation zones are relatively recent human inventions (Cronon 1996) and reflect a changing meaning of the term that once denoted 'deserted' places that were 'desolate' or 'barren'. Instead, 'wilderness' has now come to be imbued with positive values, referring to places put aside to protect and cherish nature, places made in response to observations about the ills of industrial capitalism, habitat destruction and urban development.

That such spaces should be protected is in one sense a noble and justified sentiment given the rampant conversion of the world's habitat in a relatively short time for broad-acre farming, human settlements, industrial space, ports and other land uses (see Chapter 26). However, assumptions by visitors and promoters that these conservation areas are 'wilderness' – literally, uninhabited zones detached from human influence, in an unchanging, natural state – may be inaccurate. Such depictions are easily made and are very seductive, particularly for the tourism industry and its associated advertising, especially for guided tours and safaris (Waitt 1997). In the remote Kimberley region of Australia a combination of marketing, postcard imagery, constructions of tourist attractions and pre-existing understandings of desert Australia as 'timeless' have resulted in the portrayal of exactly this kind of 'wild' place (Waitt and Head 2002). Self-drive tourists in 2003 (Lane and Waitt, in press) argued that they were attracted to the place because of its 'ruggedness and remoteness', and its 'ancient nature', while the sense of stasis was vital: 'it's more untouched because they can't tame it. So we enjoyed it, to be somewhere where it still felt like it hadn't changed and where things are still untouched.' Even music reinforces this imagery: a CD of ambient music by Tony O'Connor (entitled *Windjana – Spirit of the Kimberley*), is marketed to tourists in this region as 'a tribute to one of the Earth's last untouched wilderness areas'. The CD is available in airports and souvenir shops, and alongside postcards and visual art both reinforces and taps into ideas of nature as eternal and separate from human influence.

397

Clearly, however, 'wilderness' is not untouched, untamed, empty or uninhabited. Australian national parks have often been created out of abandoned old pastoral stations, where Europeans once roamed cattle until unsustainable grazing practices made their fragile soil landscapes incapable of supporting viable enterprises. Their ecological characteristics are unlikely to be similar to that of pre-European colonization. Moreover, 'wilderness' areas are living human landscapes, even where built features like cities and towns are not present. They are invariably places where humans once lived – or still do, in the case of Aboriginal people residing in small communities in many national parks in Australia. To portray places like the Kimberley as 'timeless', 'empty' or 'untouched' has the effect of denying the important and continuing indigenous interests in those places.

In other countries, traditional peoples have been displaced or evicted by the creation of national parks and nature conservation areas, or their understandings of innate 'natural' features suppressed. In Alaska, scientists saw glaciers as inanimate nature, important records of weather, geomorphology, geology and landscape, and useful as a record of climate change. In contrast, an Aboriginal perspective – one mostly ignored or not taken seriously by scientists – saw glaciers not as inanimate geophysical phenomena, but as sentient, animate and quick to respond to human behaviour (Cruikshank 2005). In Australia, Aboriginal people are only since the 1990s being invited on to administration boards of national parks, being approached to sign co-management agreements, or starting to see their views being incorporated into operational plans for conservation areas. Although non-Aboriginal people may see national parks as 'wild' and 'unchanged', for many Aboriginal people these spaces look very different, and embody in the landscape a reminder of the effects of colonialism. 'Natural' spaces in Australian national parks look nothing like their pre-European precursors, because of earlier pastoralism and the removal of Aboriginal people and their land management practices. Prior to European occupation, Aboriginal people used fire and hunting practices in ways that influenced the landscape. National parks, created by Europeans under the guise of wilderness preservation, have removed that influence. They are generally more densely vegetated than they would have been before Europeans; they have hosted the re-colonization of invasive weed species or dominant fauna and flora from other parts of the country, and have seen particular species out-compete others because of the absence of consistent Aboriginal hunting and foraging (Low 2002).

In Tanzania, Maasai have been evicted from several national parks – including its most famous, the Serengeti – even though they have been traditional nomadic occupiers of these areas for many generations (Monbiot 2003). Maasai have been confined to areas less than a quarter of their original 200,000-square-kilometre territory – dispossessed by colonial invaders to make way for ranchers and farmers, and for wilderness conservation areas. In 1988 Maasai were evicted from the Mkomazi Game Reserve on the northern border with Kenya, on the grounds that the presence of Maasai was irreparably damaging the area's flora and fauna. Traditionally pastoralists, the Maasai were blamed for plummeting numbers of elephants and rhinos, two key species that were at the brink of extinction in the area. The area's 150 rhinos had been massacred and all but eleven elephants killed – largely by poachers for the ivory and rhino tusk trade. Given the severity of the situation, the eviction of humans from the area appeared initially justified, and indeed, numbers have slowly improved since, although it is not clear that it was the Maasai who were indeed responsible for the poaching in the first place. (An alternative and credible theory is that poaching largely occurred across the border in neighbouring Kenya, where the animals could migrate within the same habitat – and that numbers have only increased since the 1989 international moratorium on ivory trade and more aggressive policing of poachers in Kenya.) This highly controversial eviction (heavily criticized by human rights groups) created friction between Maasai and conservationists, and has created environmental and social problems at the edges of the game reserve, where Maasai now live in much higher population densities than pre-eviction. What this case demonstrates is how the perception of wilderness areas such as national parks and game reserves as spaces of 'unchanging' or 'pristine' nature could hardly be further from the truth. The removal of human influence – arguably necessary for the short-term management of serious environmental problems – has artificially altered ecosystems and created new kinds of highly *changed* places.

What complicates the story, and what adds complexity to this story of 'unchanging places', is that partly because of dispossession, Maasai have much more strongly than other African tribes resisted cultural change and retained aspects of traditional material and expressive culture (dress, body adornment, music, ceremony) in the face of change. The *shuka* (a red or purple cloth tied over one shoulder) is still worn; ears are still pierced and stretched; and men are regularly seen around Tanzanian cities and towns with traditional spears and clubs. They have not abandoned the pastoral way of life, have resisted forced-settlement attempts by colonial powers, and still adhere to cultural traditions such as the initiation of men into a *morani* warrior class (though aspects of that initiation, such as the hunting of lions, have caused legal conflicts with the Tanzanian government). The tension between continuity and change is no better exemplified in the contrasting and conflicting notions of 'wilderness' and culture as 'unchanging'.

Resisting change

There are many instances where people make overt attempts to keep places the same, despite external pressures or in the face of local desires for transformation. Many of these efforts to thwart change are contradictory – some appeal to a sense of spatial fixity in order to fight injustice or retain the character of a place in the face of destruction by powerful interests, while others more nostalgically or regressively draw upon the idea of places remaining static in order to further conservative or discriminatory agendas.

Heritage movements have sought to retain elements of human settlement patterns within cities and in rural landscapes through legislative mechanisms (preservation orders, zoning restrictions, site-specific historic listings). While preservation efforts have tended to focus on buildings, since the 1980s authorities have begun to adopt a more lateral and cultural understanding of heritage which recognizes the everyday social uses of buildings (as well as their physical features), the importance of heritage to different cultural groups, and the significance of industrial and environmental heritages. (See the following chapter for in-depth discussion of heritage and preservation movements.) In Sydney, Australia, a major political conflict occurred in the 1970s over proposed plans to demolish vast swathes of the old Victorian inner-city to make way for public housing, commercial office space and freeway projects. Unions objected to the forced displacement of the poor communities living in these quarters (who were often older port and warehouse workers, newly arrived ethnic groups and the unemployed), while middle-class environmentalists denounced the loss of the city's history. 'Green bans' (so called because of the solidarity between the union and environmental movements behind the heritage campaign) were placed on the developments (Mundey 1981; Burgmann and Burgmann 1998). Workers in the construction industry refused to work on the demolition of old residential terraces and prevented redevelopment occurring, though not without physical conflict. Primarily a dispute over heritage and the built environment, the Sydney 'green bans' were also a fight about deeper issues of the nature and pace of change in the city. Rapid redevelopment was deemed unfair and unjust, and pre-servation of the built environment was seen in contrast as a means to retain community and, at least in certain parts of the city, keep and sense of continuity about place and culture.

An ironic twist in the tale is that although Sydney's inner-city was spared widespread demolition, those districts would later undergo substantial gentrification, often based around the purchase and refurbishment of Victorian terraces saved by the green bans (Bridge 2001; Shaw 2004). Although some public housing was created in protected areas (which has meant the retention of pockets of working-class populations and culture), much of Sydney's inner-city has changed dramatically: older populations have sold up terraces and moved to other areas of the city (or in beach-side resorts on the coast), more vulnerable residents have been displaced by rising rents, while new younger couples ('yuppies', 'double-income, no kids' or DINKs) have moved in, often tied to the growth in employment in the finance sector in Sydney's central business district. An intention to 'fix' place ironically produced the condi-tions for subsequent change.

In numerous countries, indigenous people have emphasized that consistency in their social practices does not equate to their cultures being 'static' (Langton 1993). All cultures are inherently dynamic, and Aboriginal cultures, like those of other indigenous groups, have absorbed outside influences and changed over time in response to new ideas, changing environments and human desires. But in Australia a relative stability of Aboriginal people's sovereign ownership of country, and sustainability in land management practices, has indeed been achieved through the years by subsequent generations refining sophisticated systems of spirituality, hunting and foraging rights, fire management (fire being an important element of Aboriginal life, land management and farming practices), kinship structures and social obli-gations (Howitt 2001). The constancy of Aboriginal attachments to country and ways of managing the environment have since been central elements of political battles for land rights within the contemporary Australian nation-state. A sense of spatial 'fixity' underpinning Aboriginal claims has been successful in winning back rights over parts of the country that were wrongly annexed by Europeans since invasion in 1788 (Gibson 1999). The phrase that 'Aboriginal people have owned Australia for at least 40,000 years prior to European colo-nization' is one that has permeated popular consciousness, has underpinned landmark court victories for Aboriginal people, has provided the basis for recognition of native title rights, and has even been included as lyrics in popular rock songs, such as Midnight Oil's chart-topping pro-land rights anthem, 'The Dead Heart' (1987):

> We carry in our hearts the true country
> And that cannot be stolen
> We follow in the steps of our ancestry
> And that cannot be broken . . .
> 40,000 years makes a difference to the state of things

Although such discourses risk reinforcing the idea that Aboriginal cultures are 'stagnant' (something Aboriginal people themselves constantly negotiate), this sense of unchanging places has a clear political power.

That political power can, however, feed into rather different agendas. Spatial fixity – the desire to keep things the same, to prevent change – is a correlate of a set of much nastier sorts of racisms and exclusionary practices. As Massey (1994: 168) argued, spatial fixity can constitute a fundamentally conservative impulse, in which place is perceived as having a fixed identity or character (or one to which people should aspire) as a way of closing the place to outsiders, an identity 'defined by counterposition against the Other who is outside'. This sense of 'freezing' places and excluding people can be seen in numerous ways, and in numerous places, from the subtle to obvious, from the relatively mundane to the catastrophic. Examples include the enforcing of strict door policies by nightclubs (intended to keep that space 'the same', in terms of the people allowed in, the dress standards, and correct appearance, but which can produce sexism, racism and ageism); strong racism in particular parts of cities (articulated as a desire to 'keep out unwanted types') and nationalism itself – a sense of 'unchanging places' at a larger geographical scale, which is in essence an attempt to invent and uphold a common set of ideals, appearances, behaviours and customs (Anderson 1991), no matter the reality of diversity and globalization shaping and re-shaping places. At its most extreme, desires of the state to freeze place and people fold into biological determinism, in the manner of Nazi Germany, where claims were made to a 'pure', 'unchanging' biological inheritance – a superiority and national character, bred through generations, which laid the foundations for territorial expansion and became the trigger for the Holocaust and its array of inexcusable horrors. Any appeal to 'unchanging places' as a political maxim must be treated with extreme caution.

Conclusion

What this chapter highlights is that understanding place is not just about analysing the velocity and impacts of change, but the extent to which things stay the same, appear to stay the same, or are made (or hoped) to stay the same. Spatial fixity is the antonym of mobility, fluidity and flux, and although all the latter rightly underpin a vast proportion of the research in contemporary social science, they should not prevent analysis of the extent to which in some places and times, continuity and stability prevail.

The inclusion of Spykman's quote earlier in this chapter hints at how, for many people, geography itself is seen as something unchanging. Spykman wrote in an era where geography's claim to the immutable wielded a particular power and distinctiveness for the discipline: that amidst the tumult and change of world politics, economics and technology, geography connects us to more permanent landscapes and places. As Ó Tuathail (1996: 51) described in his critique of Spykman, 'geography is [seen as] a permanent, self-evident realm of necessity that is present to itself; it is a durable, immanent force … geography is literally beneath the world of the social, political and ideological'. But, of course, it isn't. This chapter has tried to show that geography – both human and physical – is bound up in the social, political and ideological. Thinking about different types of 'unchanging places' provides us one means to explore this complexity.

Further reading

Cronon, W. (1996) The trouble with wilderness, or getting back to the wrong nature. In W. Cronon (ed.) *Uncommon Ground: Rethinking the Human Place in Nature*, pp. 69–90. New York: W.W. Norton.

Harvey, D. (1989) *The Condition of Postmodernity*. Oxford: Blackwell.

Massey, D. (1994) *Space, Place and Gender*. Cambridge: Polity Press.

Pred, A. (1981) Social reproduction and the time-geography of everyday life. *Geografiska Annaler* 63B, 5–22.

Short, J.R. (1989) Yuppies, yuffies and the new urban order. *Transaction of the Institute of British Geographers* 26, 173–88.

Thrift, N. (1983) On the determination of social action in space and time. *Environment and Planning D: Society and Space* 1, 23–57.

References

Abu-Lughod, J.L. (1999) *New York, Chicago, Los Angeles: America's Global Cities.* Minneapolis: University of Minnesota Press.

Amin, A. and Thrift, N. (2002) *Cities: Reimagining the Urban.* Cambridge: Polity Press.

Anderson, B. (1991) *Imagined Communities, Reflections on the Origin and Spread of Nationalism.* London: New Left Books.

Anderson, K. (1987) The idea of Chinatown: the power of place and institutional practice in the making of a racial category. *Annals of the Association of American Geographers* 77, 580–98.

Birmingham, J. (2000) *Leviathan: An Unauthorised Biography of Sydney.* Sydney: Vintage.

Bourdieu, P. (1984) *Distinction: A Social Critique of the Judgement of Taste.* London: Routledge.

Bridge, G. (2001) Estate agents as interpreters of economic and cultural capital: the gentrification premium in the Sydney housing market. *International Journal of Urban and Regional Research* 25, 87–101.

Burgmann, M. and Burgmann, V. (1998) *Green Bans, Red Union: Environmental Activism and the New South Wales Builders Labourer's Federation.* Sydney: UNSW Press.

Burton, A. (2002) Adjutants, agents, intermediaries: the Native Administration in Dar es Salaam township, 1919–61. In A. Burton (ed.) *The Urban Experience in Eastern Africa c. 1750–2000,* pp. 98–118. Nairobi: The British Institute in East Africa.

Castells, M. (1996) *The Rise of Network Society.* Oxford: Blackwell.

Chakravorty, S. (2000) From colonial city to globalizing city? The far-from-complete spatial transformation of Calcutta. In F. Marcuse and R. van Kempen (eds) *Globalizing Cities: A New Spatial Order?,* pp. 56–77. Oxford: Blackwell.

Cronon, W. (1996) The trouble with wilderness, or getting back to the wrong nature. In W. Cronon (ed.) *Uncommon Ground: Rethinking the Human Place in Nature,* pp. 69–90. New York: W.W. Norton.

Cruikshank, J. (2005) *Do Glaciers Listen? Local Knowledge, Colonial Encounters, and Social Imagination.* Seattle: University of Washington Press.

Elmslie, J. (2003) *Irian Jaya Under the Gun: Indonesian Economic Development versus West Papuan Nationalism.* Honolulu: University of Hawai'i Press.

Gibson, C. (1999) Cartographies of the colonial and capitalist state: a geopolitics of indigenous self-determination in Australia. *Antipode* 31, 45–79.

Gregory, D. (1994) *Geographical Imaginations.* Oxford: Blackwell.

Hägerstrand, T. (1970) What about people in regional science? *Papers and Proceedings of the Regional Science Association* 24, 7–24.

Hamnett, C. (1994) Social polarisation in global cities: theory and evidence. *Urban Studies* 30, 401–24.

Houghton, J.T., Ding, Y., Griggs, D.J., Noguer, M., van der Hinden P.J., Dai, X., Maskell, K. and Johnson, C.A. (eds) (2001) *Climate Change 2001: The Scientific Basis.* Cambridge: Cambridge University Press.

Howitt, R. (2001) *Rethinking Resource Management: Justice, Sustainability and Indigenous Peoples.* London and New York: Routledge.

Karppi, K. (2001) Encountering different territorialities: political fragmentation of the Sami homeland. *Tijdschrift voor Economische en Sociale Geografie* 92, 394–404.

Lane, R. and Waitt, G. (in press) Inalienable places: self-drive tourists in north west Australia. *Annals of Tourism Research.*

Langton, M. (1993) *'Well I Heard it on the Radio and I Saw it on the Television . . . ': An Essay for the Australian Film Commission on the Politics and Aesthetics of Filmmaking by and about Aboriginal People and Things.* Sydney: Australian Film Commission.

Low, T. (2002) *The New Nature: Winners and Losers in Wild Australia.* Melbourne: Viking.

Massey, D. (1994) *Space, Place and Gender.* Cambridge: Polity Press.

Monbiot, G. (2003) *No Man's Land*, London: Picador.

Mundey, J. (1981) *Green bans and beyond*, London: Angus and Robertson.

Ondawame, O. (2000) Indonesian state terrorism: the case of West Papua. In S. Dinnen and A. Ley (eds) *Reflections on Violence in Melanesia*, pp. 277–89. Canberra: Asia-Pacific Press.

Pred, A. (1981) Social reproduction and the time-geography of everyday life. *Geografiska Annaler* 63B, 5–22.

Sassen, S. (1991) *The Global City: New York, London, Tokyo.* Princeton, NJ: Princeton University Press.

Semple, A. (2005) Urban form, agency and social differentiation in Kansai, Japan. Paper presented at the Institute of British Geographers Annual Conference, London.

Shaw, W. (2004) The good (old) days of whiteness: gentrification and heritage in Sydney, Australia. In R. Atkinson and G. Bridge (eds) *The New Urban Colonialism: Gentrification in a Global Context.* London: Routledge.

Smith, N. (1996) *The New Urban Frontier: Gentrification and the Revanchist City.* London and New York: Routledge.

Spykman, N. (1942) *America's Strategy in World Politics: The United States and the Balance of Power.* New York: Harcourt, Brace.

Stratton, M. and Trinder, B. (2000) *Twentieth Century Industrial Archaeology.* London: Spon.

Ó Tuathail, G. (1996) *Critical Geopolitics: The Politics of Writing Global Space.* London and New York: Routledge.

Thrift, N. (1983) On the determination of social action in space and time. *Environment and Planning D: Society and Space* 1, 23–57.

Waitt, G. (1997) Selling paradise and adventure: representations of landscape in the tourist advertising of Australia. *Australian Geographical Studies* 35, 47–60.

Waitt, G. and Head, L. (2002) Postcards and frontier mythologies: sustaining 'views' of the Kimberley as 'timeless'. *Environment and Planning D: Society and Space* 20, 319–44.

26

Preserved and conserved places

Lily Kong

Introduction

For centuries, people have sought to preserve and protect buildings, and now whole sections of towns and cities may be managed through planning processes and regulations inhibiting changes. Whole sectors of cities and complexes of buildings may be preserved, perhaps to commemorate individuals or celebrate past events. Meanwhile natural areas are given a variety of protection for their landscape, ecological or biodiversity status.

Interest in heritage, preservation and conservation worldwide is evident in the existence of a large number of international organizations, such as the International Council of Museums (ICOM), the International Council on Monuments and Sites (ICOMOS), the International Centre for the Study of the Preservation and the Restoration of Cultural Property (ICCROM), the International Institute for Conservation of Historic and Architectural Works (IIC), and the World Heritage Convention, to name but a few. This global concern also finds expression in many individual countries, albeit to different degrees. Britain, for example, has been so deeply engaged in the heritage industry for so long that the entire country has been described as one large museum (Hewison 1987). Among its array of agencies dealing with heritage are government departments such as the Historic Buildings and Monuments Commission (or English Heritage), the Royal Commission on Historical Monuments, and the National Heritage Memorial Fund, as well as independent voluntary organizations such as the National Trust. In other countries, however, interest in heritage only surfaced in more recent years. Singapore's National Heritage Board, for example, was established barely more than a decade ago in 1993, and the country has not witnessed as yet the growth in a wide range of heritage bodies as in Britain.

Overall, though, it may be said that 'heritage' has found a place not only in many official agendas, but also as part of civil society concern and as expressions of personal history and individual identity. This is perhaps particularly the case in the late twentieth and early twenty-first centuries.

This chapter introduces the nature of these conserved and preserved places. It explores exactly what constitutes the heritage that is conserved or preserved and explains why interest in conservation and preservation has grown apace in our age. There are many different approaches that underpin the creation and maintenance of heritage. Different meanings have come to be attached to processes of conservation and preservation, and these acts themselves become contested and dissonant. I conclude by arguing that conserved and preserved places fix and reify particular social values and operate as much more than a neutral series of old buildings or places.

What constitutes heritage, preservation and conservation?

What exactly constitute the heritage that governments, interest groups, businesses and/or individuals seek to recognize and valorize? Heritage may be conceived at the level of the individual, referring to personal inheritance or a bequest, or it may operate at the level of the social, referring to a collective heritage that links a group to a shared inheritance (Johnson 1999: 259). Heritage may also be conceived of as tangible or intangible. UNESCO defines tangible heritage as that 'involving sites that bear witness to multiple cultural identities, are representative of minority cultural heritages, are of founding significance or are in imminent danger of destruction' (UNESCO website). Intangible heritage is more clearly defined by the Convention for the Safeguarding of the Intangible Cultural Heritage as the 'practices, representations, expressions, as well as the knowledge and skills that communities, groups and, in some cases, individuals recognize as part of their cultural heritage' (UNESCO website). So conserved places reflect more than just a built fabric preserved in aspic. They may also include oral traditions and expressions, including language; performing arts; social practices, rituals and festive events; knowledge and practices concerning nature and the universe; and traditional craftsmanship. This heritage is:

> transmitted from generation to generation, and is constantly recreated by communities and groups in response to their environment, their interaction with nature and their historical conditions of existence. It provides people with a sense of identity and continuity, and its safeguarding promotes, sustains and develops cultural diversity and human creativity.
>
> (UNESCO website)

Whether individual or social, tangible or intangible, heritage is an inherently spatial phenomenon (Graham *et al.* 2000: 4), since it is grounded in location (bound, as it is, to specific places), displays distributional patterns, and exists within a hierarchy of spatial scales, at the level of the individual, societal, national, regional and international.

Heritage may also be conceived of in terms of 'high cultures' or 'everyday cultures'. The former is linked to a conservative notion of 'heritage' as comprising ideas and artefacts that are majestic and monumental, such as palaces, stately homes, national symbols and civic buildings. The latter is linked to a more 'radical' concept of heritage, which focuses on reclaiming the lived landscapes of common people, such as the homes of the labouring classes, neighbourhood streets and alleys, factories and workplaces, and community structures. This perspective of heritage has been introduced by those who advocate 'more cogent, credible, realist alternative views [of the past], centred on the lived experiences of a wider spectrum of the populace' (Butlin 1987: 37). In this sense, heritage is not an 'innocent' assemblage of cultural traditions and artefacts, but is a value-laden concept, 'embracing (and often obscuring) differences of interpretation that are dependent on ... class, gender and locality', and 'locked into wider frameworks of dominant and subversive ideologies' (Hardy

1988: 333). This issue will be explored more fully in a later section in terms of whose heritage is privileged and who defines this heritage.

For now, suffice it to say that heritage can be drawn from historical events, personalities, folk memories, mythologies, literary associations and surviving physical relics, all turned into products and places through interpretation, and often concretized in the built environment. Nevertheless, it is important to remember that heritage is *not* only about the built environment, but embraces the natural environment as well. One key means of protecting the natural environment is via protected areas (PA), defined as 'area[s] of land and/or sea especially dedicated to the protection and maintenance of biological diversity and of natural and associated cultural resources, managed through legal or other effective means' (UNEP website). Three main organizations are involved in defining and categorizing protected areas: the United Nations Environment Programme World Conservation Monitoring Centre (UNEP-WCMC), the World Commission on Protected Areas, and the IUCN (World Conservation Union) Programme on Protected Areas. Not unlike the built environment, natural environments are invested with a range of intangible meanings and values, characterized by the World Commission of Protected Areas as including recreational, spiritual, cultural, identity, existence, artistic, aesthetic, educational, research, peace and therapeutic values (Putney 2003: 7–8). These PAs are recognized as a means of livelihood, providing rural people with food, fuel, medicines, construction materials, soil nutrient recycling and protection, fodder, mulch and so forth. They are also sources of raw material and energy. The biodiversity and genetic stores serve as important inputs for pharmaceuticals. They are also sites of exceptional endowment of rare species and spectacular scenery, which attract tourists seeking aesthetic and spiritual experiences (Edroma 2003). Together, in all these various ways and reflecting the range of values invested in natural areas, natural landscapes are rendered sites worthy of preservation.

While some efforts have been made in the academic literature to distinguish between preservation and conservation, the two concepts are often used interchangeably and with some ambiguity. Nevertheless, preservation, in narrow terms, refers to the suspension or reversal of the natural processes of decay, such that the heritage object, building or landscape is maintained in a condition defined by its historic context (Hewison 1987). Conservation, on the other hand, is 'part of the process of change' (Lowenthal 1985: 275–87), where the very act of conservation goes beyond material preservation and involves reshaping, improving, modernizing and even fabricating the past according to current-day expectations. Fowler (1987: 181) draws attention to how conservation transcends the older, narrower meaning of preservation: whereas preservation connotes the prevention of further deterioration, conservation 'demands rather than allows change ... but always in the interest of that which is being conserved'. Fundamental to the concept of conservation is a 'recognition that most historic buildings and areas have changed with each generation, and must continue to change to survive' (Drury 1994: 197).

Why the growing concern for heritage?

It is possible to advance many different reasons for growing numbers of preserved and conserved places and increasing interest in heritage. The first is because globalization intensifies trends towards localization. While some have argued that globalization leads to homogenization (Featherstone 1993: 170), others have argued that with increasing trends towards globalization, we are in fact made more aware of 'the finitude and boundedness of the planet and humanity', and simultaneously become familiar with the range of local cultures that exist

(Featherstone 1993: 169). Indeed, others go further and argue that beyond familiarizing us with such local cultures, globalization 'produc[es] or perpetuat[es] distinctive cultural practices and differentiated identities' (Schiller 1994: 1). Massey (1993) discusses this production and perpetuation in terms of a search for a 'global sense of place', involving 'the search after the "real" meanings of place' and 'the unearthing of heritages', a 'response to [a] desire for fixity and for security of identity in the middle of all the movement and change' (Massey 1993: 236). In this regard, Larkham (1996) argues that conserved areas fulfil a psychological need, providing a sense of orientation and serving as symbols of stability. Lowenthal (1985) elaborates on how heritage projects create identities. The antiquity of heritage helps to connect the present to the past in an unbroken trajectory. The past validates the present by conveying an idea of timeless values and unbroken lineages, and restores lost or subverted values. The past is integral to individual and communal representations of identity and its connotations convey meaning, purpose and value. Preserved places serve as a visual confirmation of the past. This echoes Harvey's (1989) contention that locality only matters *because* of globalization and that the uniqueness and identity of place has become important as a result of the need for security in a shifting, uncertain age.

It is not difficult, however, to imagine how this assertion of the local amidst global forces may easily become a reactionary response, involving 'certain forms of nationalism' and 'sentimentalized recovering of sanitized "heritages"' (Massey 1993: 232). In other words, heritage could become a political project, a kind of arsenal for states in their nation-building efforts and engagement in 'cultural prestige competitions' (Smith 1990). The use of heritage in such instances serves political ends. At the same time, the political use of heritage may not just be to assert national identity; projects to preserve places may also be motivated by internal politics. They may be employed to earn the support of increasingly sophisticated voters in advanced societies where the delivery of economic success alone will no longer suffice, and for whom a respect for culture and history serves as important evidence of an enlightened leadership. This political impetus may be entirely negative, and the past rendered through heritage may be used to promote the 'burdens of history, the atrocities, errors and crimes of the past which are called upon to legitimate the atrocities of the present' (Graham *et al.* 2000: 19). The clearest example of this is the way in which Israel has appropriated Holocaust victimization and turned it into national heritage. This victimization and heritage of atrocity, in turn, becomes capital for Israel – 'global capital of victim-goodwill' (Graham *et al.* 2000: 70) – which is used to sanction its behaviour in the Middle East.

Third, Larkham (1996) draws attention to the didactic imperative in heritage projects. This is anchored in a moral duty to preserve and conserve heritage, as a means to remember and pass on the accomplishments of the past to future generations.

A fourth reason for the increasing importance of conservation and preservation is economic rather than cultural-social, psychological, political or moral. As more and more people travel for pleasure, the leisure and tourism services sectors have expanded, and heritage sites and events have found their places on tour itineraries as people search for the 'exotic' and the 'unknown'. Walsh (1992: 117) has highlighted the fact that heritage-based tourism has become more important since the 1980s. In Britain, tourism and heritage are officially recognized as being crucial to the country's economic success (Hewison 1987). Preserving the past, in these scenarios, commodifies heritage. It creates art, museums and landscapes protected by agencies such as the UK's several National Trusts, and turns these into theatres for the re-enactment of the past.

Intangible benefits may also be reaped through preservation and conservation that contribute to the wider economic regeneration of areas. Heritage provides a 'stage or background for other profit-seeking enterprises, contributing psychic stability and aesthetic satisfaction to people but also, by extension, to the cohesion and sense of well-being of communities in which they live' (Graham *et al.* 2000: 170). Urban conservation also adds to the liveliness of streets:

> liveliness that becomes a spectacle in itself. Visitors act as both performers and audience in public space, and while this is not usually an important economic function, the process increases the 'footfall' of visitors, their length of stay and perhaps also their disposition to spend.
>
> (Graham *et al.* 2000: 171)

However, from another perspective the economic logic behind heritage may be read as essentially a capitalist strategy. In this argument, heritage is not something that a society needs or wants, but the result of 'an artificial desire imposed on society by capital' (Walsh 1992: 116). In other words, the only reason why places are conserved or preserved in any society is because people are persuaded by capitalists that they wish to pay to experience them.

Cities have also used their heritage to differentiate themselves. Cities striving for global standing increasingly adopt this strategy and thus compete to attract talent to a place that not only operates efficiently and comfortably, but which also has a distinct identity and character. This motivation finds expression in lifestyles bound up with visiting heritage sites and celebrating the past, and in using restored buildings for prestige corporate offices. These are in effect strategies that places use to establish themselves as global in an increasingly competitive world.

Approaches underpinning preservation and conservation of heritage

Understanding the growing interest in heritage involves being aware of how preservation and conservation have been achieved. Approaches to preservation and conservation are framed by several considerations. The first is that of scale. In many countries, preservation is focused on buildings. However, whereas conservation began as a concern with buildings as individual entities, with little attention paid to the relationship between buildings, this has evolved over time. In Britain, for example, there was for a long time little interest in streets and plots. Instead, conservation emphasized the detailed architectural control of outstanding historic buildings. This focus evolved slowly from the late 1960s onwards, towards an appreciation of the townscape as a complete ensemble, with increasing interest in considerations like the grouping of buildings along street frontages and street furniture (Slater 1984: 332). While a building conservation policy had existed since the middle of the nineteenth century, a specific area policy only developed in 1967 (Wilde 1981: 16). A similar development is apparent in Canada, where pioneer schemes in area conservation date only from the early 1970s, as opposed to a much earlier awareness of the importance of building conservation. Encouraged by the independent heritage body, Heritage Canada, there is now a movement that firmly favours the retention of 'integrated environments' (Tunbridge 1981: 118). This is also true for Singapore, where policies first sought to preserve buildings in the 1980s, but where the focus in the mid-1980s turned to conservation of historic districts and ethnic areas, for example Chinatown, Singapore River and Little India (see Perry *et al.* 1996).

409

A second consideration that frames discussions about preservation is the extent of restoration to be undertaken. In general, there are two views on this subject, generally at odds with each other. In one view, the purpose of repair is to:

> restrain the process of decay, without damaging the character of buildings or monuments, altering the features which give them their historic or architectural importance, or unnecessarily disturbing or destroying [the] historic fabric. Repair work should be kept to a minimum necessary to stabilize and conserve buildings and monuments, with the aim of achieving a sufficiently sound structural condition to ensure their long-term survival.
>
> (Drury 1994: 200)

A second view argues that restoration should be based on historic value (authenticity of form), contemporary value (authenticity of function) and age value (authenticity of matter) (Hladik 2003: 259). Preserving original materials may contradict the conservation of original form, because allowing natural degradation means that the building becomes progressively destroyed. However, 'historical value' privileges authenticity of form but sacrifices authenticity of matter (Hladik 2003: 259). Restoration thus entails balancing different values. An example of this dilemma is the restoration of Munich after the First World War (Rosenfeld 2000). Whilst some argued for the restoration of damaged buildings to their original form, others recognized the need to display the workings of time and decay, viewing this as authenticity, and thus argued for a restoration of the buildings based on their post-war condition. In different periods of Munich's history, different views prevailed. In Japan both approaches are appreciated, stemming from a recognition of the aesthetic value in weather-worn materials and the aging look, as well as the appreciation of newness. This, in turn, has roots in the positive attitude that Japanese have towards aging and their Buddhist-influenced idea of cyclical time (Hladik 2003: 259). In Singapore, a compromise between the two approaches is struck through the classification of primary and secondary conservation areas. Buildings located in primary conservation areas are legally required to be restored to their original character, including the use of the exact type of original materials (whenever available). In contrast, there is greater flexibility for the restoration of buildings located in the secondary areas. The front façade of the buildings is to be conserved, whereas the rear portion can be redeveloped and intensified to meet the needs of the respective owner.

A third related consideration in the approach to preservation and conservation is the question of what constitutes authenticity and how that guides possible outcomes of the heritage process. Places are made up of both the material built environment and the activities and lifestyles of inhabitants. Often, conservation is recommended on the grounds of the former, such as the architectural merit, aesthetic value or historical significance of the built environment. Far less attention is given to the continuance of people's activities and lifestyles, a fact that is criticized in various preservation and conservation projects (see, for example, Yeoh and Kong 1994, writing about Singapore's Chinatown). Yet Lowenthal (1985: 214–25) has argued that it is impossible to recover the totality of any past place and event because total recovery would necessarily include a recovery of the intangibles, a preservation of past lifestyles that is not feasible or compatible with modernization. Indeed, any insistence that lifestyles be preserved may cause them to be out of context with the neighbouring areas, a lack of integration that, Drury (1994: 198) argues, renders them ironically inauthentic.

The preservation and conservation of natural environments has also changed over time, as the management of PAs shows. Edroma (2003) has outlined several ways in which PAs are managed for sustainability. First, historically, fortress conservation has been a commonly adopted strategy, where PAs are set aside, excluding people as residents and other uses to minimize human impact. This has not been successful, despite attempts to modify it ('new fortress conservation', see van Schaik and Kramer 1997) because it causes frustration, suspicion, resentment and conflict between the local communities and the PA management authorities. As a counter to fortress conservation, a second strategy of community conservation has been used, involving local residents in the management and conservation of natural areas by which they reside. Successful community conservation strategies involve stakeholders at all stages of the process, thus creating a sense of ownership and responsibility. Usually, this approach entails a collaborative management philosophy, which draws together local communities and the conservation authority for negotiated access to the natural resources of the PA. Third, a conservation-by-commercialization strategy has been adopted, whereby the heritage PA is expected to generate income, which is then distributed to the local communities so that they can initiate their own economic activities that in turn generate income without harvesting the natural resources of the PA. One example of this is investing in wildlife-related activities of the heritage properties, in recognition that local communities are more likely to protect them if biodiversity is valued as an asset and provides them the means of livelihood. However, in reality, this approach has not been very successful because sufficient revenue has not often been generated to support local populations. Fourth, integrated conservation development projects have been attempted which entail zoning a PA for protection, tourism and controlled human use, and at the same time designating a wildlife extension area, a zone outside a PA which would not be under the jurisdiction of the PA authority but where the PA authority would liaise with the appropriate local institutions and community structures to carry out various programmes to ensure its sustainability. Fifth, decentralized natural resource management has also been attempted, and has offered a more effective management option than a centralized system of management. For it to succeed, though, the resources must be valued in order to attract investment to manage them. The local people and the management authority must also 'have the capacity to manage the resources in the face of external actors and outside users' (Edroma 2003: 40).

The most successful of these various approaches to protecting natural heritage is likely to recognize the natural, social, cultural, historical and economic value of the environment. One example of this is the Mid-Wales Festival of the Countryside – an attempt at sustainable environmentally sensitive tourism development and marketing in an area of 7700 sq km. The Festival is a region-wide programme of tourism and recreational events involving a wide range of organizations including rural development agencies, conservation bodies, tourism organizations and local community groups. The aim is to provide environmental education and enjoyment of the countryside, and boost socio-economic development. Programmes are organized under the following themes: nature and wildlife (nature reserve visits), walks and guides, rural rides (white water rafting, trekking, biking, etc.), history and industry, arts and craft, and eating out (regional cuisine) (Taylor 1994: 220–4).

However, initiatives around protecting the natural heritage are not always so balanced: they often overly privilege recreational and tourism needs. Yet the extent to which divergent motivations for preservation and conservation can be balanced is ultimately what determines the success of efforts.

The dissonances of heritage

Commemorative activity is by definition social and political, for it involves the coordination of individual and group memories. Outcomes may appear consensual when they are in fact the product of processes of intense contest, struggle and, in some instances, annihilation (Gillis 1994: 5). As Graham *et al.* (2000: 34) succinctly put it, the nature and shaping of heritage is intimately related to the exercise of power. Preservation is a process of defining the criteria of social inclusion and exclusion. It is 'deeply implicated in the construction and legitimation of collective constructs of identity, such as class, gender, ethnicity and nationalism' (Graham *et al.* 2000: 40). Such constructions are neither monolithic nor consensual. As a consequence, 'dissonance' and contestation of meanings characterize heritage (Graham *et al.* 2000: 24), often emerging between those who subscribe to and embrace what the place represents and those who feel disinherited and excluded. These differences may emerge, for example, between elite and vernacular groups, between majorities and minorities, between males and females, tourists and locals, and so forth. Divergences emerge because of different ideologies (e.g. dominant heterosexual ideology *vis-à-vis* homosexual ideology) and motivations (e.g. economic impetus *vis-à-vis* a moral one). The following discussion will examine some key axes of divergence.

The creation of conserved or preserved places, it is argued, often stems from the actions of a social elite, whose own buildings and artefacts – often grand and spectacular – are designated 'heritage'. In fact, the making of heritage through legitimation by this elite may be interpreted as a means of perpetuating elitist control and power (Graham *et al.* 2000: 42). This vesting of power in the elite to define what constitutes heritage is not uncontested. According to Lowenthal (1985: 388), in the West, conservation efforts formerly reserved for 'features of renown and widely venerated monuments' are now more generally extended to the 'everyday neighbourhoods of purely local import'. This reflects a growing recognition of the value of the vernacular, in turn made possible by the increasing democratization of heritage-making processes.

In postcolonial societies, the question of whose heritage warrants conservation is further complicated by questions as to how far colonial impacts on the landscape should be retained *vis-à-vis* indigenous structures. Societies emerging from colonialism have to decide how far to divest the landscape of colonial associations by removing its stock of colonial structures, and to what extent they should accept colonial legacy as part and parcel of the socio-cultural baggage of the newly-independent state. Western (1985: 344), however, notes that, in practice, postcolonial societies often 'do not have the capability to rewrite forthwith a new image in their cities' as 'other priorities clamor' and colonial structures are often appropriated for new purposes and re-invested with new meanings.

Gender constitutes another factor in the unequal powers of preserving and conserving places. Melosh (1994) highlights how modernity and its heritage is largely conceptualized in masculine, middle-class, urban and Eurocentric terms, whereas women are equated with the pre-modern, with qualities of 'artificiality and decadence, irrationality and desire. Romanticism also placed the pre-modern woman within the realm of the home and family, being more linked to nature through her reproductive capacity' (Nash 1999: 21). This denigration of femininity has meant that women are largely missing in monumental representations of noteworthy past lives. This is evident in much of the former British Empire, for instance, where women are largely absent in heritage constructions, save for Queen Victoria (Graham *et al.* 2000: 45) and mainly appear as anonymized, generic categories such as mothers and nurses (Warner 1985). There are exceptions, for example, where women challenge the patriarchal and unrepresentative nature of a society's heritage, and where homosexuality is commemorated in the face of heterosexual dominance. One instance of the former is evident in Savannah, Georgia, where women were prominent in the city's original efforts in preservation (leading ladies of the city set up the Historic Savannah Foundation in 1955 as a reaction against demolition) and have since dominated conservation efforts (Ashworth and Tunbridge 1990: 220). An illustration of the latter is Amsterdam's construction of a homosexual monument and an associated tourism trail (Graham *et al.* 2000: 45), foregrounding an otherwise marginal(ized) ideology and lifestyle. Nevertheless, for the most part, commemoration in the nineteenth century largely took the form of national commemoration; the preserve of elite males who imagined themselves at the cutting edge of progress and felt the loss of the past and insisted on it being restored (Gillis 1994: 11). Despite the rise of feminism, individualism and various civic and social movements in the twentieth century, these ideologies have failed to have much of an impact on the commemoration agenda.

The underlying motivations for preservation and conservation, and their attendant influence on the approach adopted, have received a lot of attention. Debates are anchored in the question of who are the target of heritage preservation – locals or tourists. Numerous studies have shown how conservation can completely displace residents, as 'alien community interests' take over. These alien community interests may take the form of economic enterprises and this, as Tunbridge (1981: 121) pointed out, almost inevitably involves some trade-off between the 'physical and community fabric'. Singapore's conserved Chinatown illustrates this condition. Conservation of Chinatown is built on three planks: architectural splendour, economic vibrancy and viability, and the idea of an 'aesthetic' as opposed to a 'social' community. While distinctive shop-houses were conserved, the Urban Redevelopment Authority's underlying philosophy stressed that market forces should be left to decide what types of trades exist in conservation areas. This is because of the fundamental belief that successful purchasers of conserved buildings have to make economic returns in order to continue to restore and maintain them (*The Straits Times* 23 October 1991). Thus, while meticulous attention was paid to preserving buildings and other structures 'for the past they represent', lifestyles and trades were left to the vagaries of free competition (*The Straits Times* 23 October 1991). The result is that Chinatown's conservation, motivated by a recognition of its economic value, obscures tensions and contradictions. These include memory and history being reduced to architecture, an uneven competition between new commercial joints and older activities, and the wiping out of a local sense of community constituted by individual and social biographies, affective ties, local referents and daily routines. Preservation and conservation may in fact destroy the locus of memories and rewrite history as 'alien' commercial interests take over.

In more extreme situations, heritage industry planning has in fact led to the razing of the historic fabric of cities and the construction of heritage tourist destinations that purportedly preserve the past, but in effect essentialize a place, its history and people, presenting and marketing a static and overly antiquated image of the past. To that extent, heritage is a 'contemporary commodity purposefully created to satisfy contemporary consumption' (Ashworth and Larkham 1994: 16). In short, heritage in these contexts comes to be defined by consumers. Johnson's (1999: 265–8) elaboration of the case of Dublin makes the point. In 1987, the Irish National Heritage Park in County Wexford, a purpose-built heritage park, was opened. It presents examples of field monuments from the Mesolithic (700 BC) to the Anglo-Norman (*c.* AD 1200–1500) periods. Johnson criticizes the park as inauthentic and designed for a collective gaze, and for failing to offer a history of settlement in Ireland over thousands of years. While it attempts to convey the 'everyday life' of earlier peoples, 'the focus on material culture alone creates a static experience of life in the past'. The cut-off point in the sixteenth century also suggests that the Irish nation has produced little of value since then, suggesting that nationhood began in the island's early antiquities. Yet historians largely locate the emergence of nationhood to the last two centuries.

413

Who preservation is directed at, and how that guides action in heritage areas, must also be considered in relation to natural environments. Often, approaches to their preservation have to address tensions between preserving natural beauty, scientific value and cultural value, and responding to recreational and tourist demands. At different points and in different places, different priorities have been privileged. Often, natural environments have been preserved in order that visitors can enjoy them. Ironically, this has often led to a deterioration of the environment. The examples of Hua Shan, the sacred Taoist mountains in Shanxi Province and Qingcheng Shan in Sichuan, China, illustrate this well. Increasing tourist numbers have pressured the authorities to build hotels, chair lifts and even helicopter pads. In 1996, the World Wide Fund for Nature Alliance of Religions and Conservation warned of the need to ensure culturally sustained protection of the sacred mountains which espouse Taoist philosophical esteem for the natural world, with their intricate networks of paths and staircases on both mountains (see Chapter 13). The report warned that management responsibilities should be shared appropriately among provincial management bureaus, temple committees and the national Chinese Taoist Association, underscoring the importance of coordination across agencies in preservation efforts.

Another key tension that often arises is between the pull to preserve heritage and the need for a city to undergo urban development for pragmatic reasons, which may include meeting the social needs of housing, transport and other amenities, and meeting safety standards. The case of Kyoto illustrates this well. Kyoto heavily regulates the preservation and building of *machiya* (traditional low-rise wooden town-houses) on the grounds of fire and structural considerations, and this has left unsatisfactory the preservation of the historic districts. The realization that historic Kyoto had the potential to reap economic values via tourism led to the passing of an ordinance declaring Kyoto an International Cultural and Sightseeing City in 1950. Ironically, landuse policies and building regulations that followed brought about the destruction of historic Kyoto, with the traditional townscape and scenic surroundings dotted with obtrusive large buildings. Equally ironic was the requirement that *machiya* owners pay inheritance tax, which led many families to either develop their property, sell or relinquish them to the government (Ryoichi 2003: 367–84). Further, fire safety precautions have also erased the intimate atmosphere of narrow roads, with stipulations that a building should be set two metres back from the centre of the road where the road is narrower than four metres. The regulations not only posed difficulties in preserving the historic districts, but threatened to erase existing historic places such as Ponto-cho along the Kamo River (Masafumi and Waley 2003: 347–66).

Arguments over the meanings of preservation and conservation also extend to the financial management of heritage sites and the question of how the site should be accounted for (Hooper *et al.* 2005). Heritage items do not satisfy the concept of 'assets' because they are usually public goods: that is, they are for the benefit of the public and are not for sale (Barton 2000). Often, though not invariably, services of public heritage assets are provided free and are open to all citizens. For many involved with heritage collections, the problem is that by assigning a monetary value to the collections, the emphasis tends to be on the commercial value of these assets rather than their artistic, scientific, cultural or historical significance (Glazer and Jaenicke 1991). In this regard, Barton (2000: 220) argued that '[p]ublic heritage facilities/assets should be regarded as assets of the nation, which are managed by government as a trustee for the benefit of society; and that, as trust assets, they should be accounted for separately from administrative assets of government'. Similarly, Pallot (1990) concluded that heritage assets should be kept separate, and recommended a compromise position by calling them 'community assets'.

However, Rowles (1991) and Micallef and Peirson (1997) believe that heritage assets are commercially quantifiable even though they may not be for sale. Although the argument that 'collections cannot be measured in financial terms because they do not have financial attributes' has merit, the same argument could equally apply to most types of asset, for example land.

With this variety in opinion as to whether or not heritage assets *can* be properly accounted for, whether or not they *should* be accounted for, and indeed *how* any accounting for heritage assets might be achieved, most countries have not moved to adopt standards requiring accounting for heritage assets.

Conclusion

It has been argued that increasing interest in heritage in contemporary society reflects the trauma of loss and change, and fears of a menacing future (Lowenthal 2004). Mass migration, technophobic gloom and modern media magnify the past's remoteness. At the same time, the desire to assert identity and resist homogenization, the strategy of winning votes, the attractions of economic gain, and the aspiration to pass on the accomplishments of ancestors, all contribute to preservation of the past.

Heritage today is not only about the elite, the great heroes and the spectacular; it also emphasizes the vernacular, the recent (living memory as opposed to century-old antiques), and intangible folkways like language, poetry, kinship and music (as opposed to material culture). At the same time, both built and natural environments are conserved.

Approaches to preservation and conservation of heritage are similarly multifold, ranging in scale from a focus on buildings to street spaces anchored in area policies. Those in charge struggle with issues like the extent of restoration, balancing between maintaining authentic functions, materials and forms. How much of the activities and lifestyles of inhabitants can realistically be retained is a question that conservationists need to address. There are similar dilemmas for those engaged in managing natural environments as they seek to balance the roles of the local community, conservation authorities and other relevant groups such as religious bodies.

In preservation and conservation, particular versions of collective memory are inevitably privileged while erasing other versions of the past from present consciousness. Whose past is preserved and who defines what constitutes heritage are real sources of dissonance, which emerge along various axes: class, gender, the colonial–postcolonial divide, local tourist targets, and so forth. Preservation and conservation are often contested processes, as heritage is interpreted in different quarters with different sectoral and communal interests. In short, heritage is not just an assemblage of traditions and artefacts but is value-laden, with interpretations mediated by social factors and ideologies. Often, by objectifying heritage in concrete, visual form, values and ideologies are reified and fixed, and made much less transparent.

Further reading

Ashworth, G.J. and Tunbridge, J.E. (1990) *The Tourist-Historic City.* London: Belhaven.
Graham, B., Ashworth, G. J. and Tunbridge, J.E. (2000) *A Geography of Heritage: Power, Culture and Economy.* London: Arnold; New York: Bookpoint.

Hewison, R. (1987) *The Heritage Industry: Britain in a Climate of Decline*. London: Methuen.

Kramer, K., van Schaik, C. and Johnson, J.J. (1997) (eds) *Last Stand. Protected Areas and the Defence of Tropical Biodiversity*. Oxford: Oxford University Press

Larkham, P.J. (1996) *Conservation and the City*. London: Routledge.

Lowenthal, D. (1985) *The Past is a Foreign Country*. Cambridge: Cambridge University Press.

UNESCO (2003) *Linking Universal and Local Values: Managing a Sustainable Future for World Heritage* (UNESCO World Heritage Papers 13). Paris: UNESCO.

References

Ashworth, G.J. and Larkham, P.J (1994) From history to heritage – from heritage to identity: in search of concepts and models. In G.J. Ashworth and P.J. Larkham (eds) *Building a New Heritage: Tourism, Culture and Identity in the New Europe*, pp. 13–30. London: Routledge.

Ashworth. G.J. and Tunbridge, J.E. (1990) *The Tourist-Historic City*. London: Belhaven.

Barton, A.D. (2000) Accounting for public heritage facilities – assets or liabilities of the government? *Accounting, Auditing and Accountability Journal* 13 (2), 219–35.

Butlin, R.A. (1987) Theory and methodology in historical geography. In M. Pacione (ed.) *Historical Geography: Progress and Prospect*, pp. 16–45. London: Croom Helm.

Drury, P. (1994) Conservation techniques: the built environment. In R. Harrison (ed.) *Manual of Heritage Management*, pp. 196–201. Oxford: Butterworth-Heinemann.

Edroma, E.L. (2003) Linking universal and local values for the sustainable management of World Heritage Sites. In *Linking Universal and Local Values: Managing a Sustainable Future for World Heritage* (UNESCO World Heritage Papers 13), pp. 36–42. Paris: UNESCO.

Featherstone, M. (1993) Global and local cultures. In J. Bird, B. Curtis, T. Putnam, G. Robertson and L. Tickner (eds) *Mapping the Futures: Local Cultures, Global Change*, pp. 169–87. London and New York: Routledge.

Fowler, P.J. (1987) The contemporary past. In J.M. Wagstaff (ed.) *Landscape and Culture: Geographical and Archaeological Perspectives*, pp. 173–91. Oxford: Blackwell.

Gillis, J.R. (1994) *Commemorations: The Politics of National Identity*. New Jersey: Princeton University Press.

Glazer, A.S. and Jaenicke, M.R. (1991) The conceptual framework, museum collections and user-orientated financial statements. *Accounting Horizons* 5 (4), 28–43.

Graham, B., Ashworth, G. J., Tunbridge, J.E. (2000) *A Geography of Heritage: Power, Culture and Economy*. London: Arnold; New York: Bookpoint.

Hardy, D. (1988) Historical geography and heritage studies. *Area* 20 (4), 333–8.

Harvey, D. (1989) *The Condition of Postmodernity*. Oxford: Blackwell.

Hewison, R. (1987) *The Heritage Industry: Britain in a Climate of Decline*. London: Methuen.

Hladik, M. (2003) Time perception, on ineluctable aging of material in architecture. In N. Fiévé and P. Waley (eds) *Japanese Capitals in Historical Perspective: Place, Power and Memory in Kyoto, Edo and Tokyo*, pp. 257–79. London: Routledge-Curzon.

Hooper, K., Kearins, K. and Green, R. (2005), Knowing 'the price of everything and the value of nothing': accounting for heritage assets. *Accounting, Auditing and Accountability Journal* 18 (3), 410 – 433.

Johnson, N.C. (1999) Historical geographies of the present. In B. Graham and C. Nash (eds) *Modern Historical Geographies*, pp. 251–72. Harlow: Prentice Hall.

Larkham, P.J. (1996) *Conservation and the City*. London: Routledge.

Lowenthal, D. (1985) *The Past is a Foreign Country*. Cambridge: Cambridge University Press.

——(2004) The heritage crusade and its contradictions. In Max Page and Randall Mason (eds) *Giving Preservation a History: Histories of Historic Preservation in the United States*, pp. 19–44. New York: Routledge.

Masafumi, Y and Waley, P (2003) Kyoto and the preservation of urban landscapes. In N. Fiévé and P. Waley (eds) *Japanese Capitals in Historical Perspective: Place, Power and Memory in Kyoto, Edo and Tokyo*, pp. 347–66. London: Routledge-Curzon.

416

Massey, D. (1993) A global sense of place. In A. Gray and J. McGuigan (eds) *Studying Culture*, pp. 232–40. London: Edward Arnold.

Melosh. B. (1994) Introduction. *Gender and History* 6, 315–19.

Micallef, F. and Peirson, G. (1997), Financial reporting of cultural, heritage and scientific collections. *Australian Accounting Review* 7, 31–7.

Nash, C. (1999) Historical geographies of modernity. In B. Graham and C. Nash (eds) *Modern Historical Geographies*, pp. 13–40. Harlow: Prentice Hall.

Pallot, J. (1990) The nature of public sector assets: a reply to Mautz. *Accounting Horizons* 42, 79–85.

Perry, M., Kong, L. and Yeoh, B. (1996) *Singapore: A Developmental City State*. Chichester: John Wiley.

Putney, A.D. (2003) Perspectives on the values of Protected Areas. In D. Harmon and A.D. Putney (eds) *The Full Value of Parks: From Economics to the Intangible*, pp. 3–11. Lanham: Rowman and Littlefield.

Rosenfeld, G.D. (2000) *Munich and Memory: Architecture, Monuments, and the Legacy of the Third Reich.* Berkeley and London: University of California Press.

Rowles, T. (1991) Infrastructure and heritage asset accounting. *Australian Accountant* 61 (6), 69–74.

Ryoichi, K. (2003) Preservation and revitalization of machiya in Kyoto. In N. Fiévé and P. Waley (eds) *Japanese Capitals in Historical Perspective: Place, Power and Memory in Kyoto, Edo and Tokyo*, pp. 367–84. London: Routledge Curzon.

Schiller, N.G. (1994) Introducing identities: global studies in culture and power. *Identities* 1, 1–6.

Slater, T.R. (1984) Preservation, conservation and planning in historic towns. *Geographical Journal* 150, 322–34.

Smith, A.S. (1990) Towards a global culture? In M. Featherstone (ed.) *Global Culture: Nationalism, Globalization and Modernity*, pp. 171–92. London, Newbury Park and New Delhi: Sage.

The Straits Times, Singapore, various issues.

Taylor, G. (1994) Working with other interests: the natural heritage. In R. Harrison (ed.) *Manual of Heritage Management*, pp. 220–4. Oxford: Butterworth-Heinemann.

Tunbridge, J.E. (1981) Conservation trusts as geographic agents: their impact upon landscape, townscape and land use. *Transactions Institute of British Geographers* 6, 103–25.

UNEP website http://www.unep-wcmc.org/index.html?http://www.unep-wcmc.org/protected_areas/~main (downloaded on 9 October 2005)

UNESCO website http://portal.unesco.org/culture/en/ev.php-URL_ID=2225&URL_DO=DO_TOPIC&URL_SECTION=201.html (downloaded on 3 October 2005).

van Schaik, C. and Kramer, R. (1997) Towards a new protection paradigm. In K. Kramer, C. van Schaik and J.J. Johnson (eds) *Last Stand. Protected Areas and the Defence of Tropical Biodiversity*, pp. 212–30. Oxford: Oxford University Press.

Walsh, K. (1992) *The Representation of the Past: Museums and Heritage in the Post-modern World*. London and New York: Routledge.

Warner, M. (1985) *Monuments and Maidens: The Allegory of the Female Form*. London: Weidenfeld and Nicolson.

Western, J. (1985) Undoing the colonial city? *Geographical Review* 75, 335–57.

Wilde, M.G.R. (1981) Conservation areas: the British experience and its relevance for Singapore. *Planews* 8 (1), 16–24.

Yeoh, B.S.A. and Kong, L. (1994) Reading landscape meanings: state constructions and lived experiences in Singapore's Chinatown. *Habitat International* 18 (4), 17–35.

27

Stagnation

Jim Walmsley

Much work in geography and throughout the natural and social sciences in the last fifty years has been preoccupied with the notion of growth. The same is true of contemporary politics where the success or otherwise of governments has often been judged, by the electorate, in terms of the growth which they have been able to deliver. Discussion of economic growth commonly dominates election campaigns. Stagnation is the very opposite of growth. A fixation on growth in contemporary society has meant that relatively little attention has been paid to stagnation. Where it has been considered, it has invariably been treated as a problem and as a failure to develop.

Development versus stagnation

There is an entire literature, extending over many years, devoted to 'development', invariably defined in terms of economic growth. Forty years ago, Rostow (1965) identified what he claimed were stages of national economic growth, progressing – almost ineluctably – from 'traditional society', through 'the preconditions for take-off' and 'take-off' itself, to 'the drive to maturity' and, eventually, 'the age of mass consumption'. Other writers, at about the same time, chose to focus on the causes of 'under-development' and wrote of vicious circles of investment and subsequent development in which 'nothing succeeds like success', leading to a world where the gap between rich nations and poor nations widens (Myrdal 1957). Since 1945, writing about the state of the world has focused on growth – not surprisingly, for, in 1944, when the Allies were poised for victory in World War II, political leaders from Western Europe and North America met at Bretton Woods in the USA to plan post-war reconstruction. Among the initiatives adopted was a policy of fixing the value of the US dollar relative to the value of gold and then setting the value of all other currencies relative to the value of the US dollar. Despite occasions on which individual currencies were devalued or revalued relative to the US dollar, the Bretton Woods agreement heralded a period of stability in international trade arrangements which went a long way towards fostering economic growth. The 'Long Boom' period from 1945 to 1973 was an unprecedented time of sustained growth in the advanced economies, notwithstanding short setback periods in individual countries. The boom only came to an end in 1973–4 when the Organization of Petroleum Exporting

Countries (OPEC) quadrupled the price of oil, thereby triggering recession in advanced economies which had become reliant on oil. This prompted associated recession in those countries dependent on trade with advanced economies. In short, for almost three decades after the Second World War, growth was high on national political agendas. Stagnation was not.

A fixation on growth is not, of course, restricted to economies as a whole. The same fascination with growth is evident in consideration of the stock market. News bulletins record daily the fluctuations in various indices such as the FTSE (a battery of London stock market indicators compiled by the *Financial Times*), the Dow Jones and the NASDAQ Composite (New York indicators for the stock market generally and for hi-tech shares in particular, the latter being an acronym for the National Association of Securities Dealers Automated Quotations) and the Hang Seng (an indicator of stock market performance in Hong Kong). There is almost an expectation that the value of stocks and shares will rise in value. The same growth mentality is seen in consideration of the labour force, with politicians under pressure to ensure sufficient growth to accommodate new entrants to the labour force and to reduce unemployment rates.

Global population growth has alarmed many since 1945, prompting the Club of Rome to worry about exhaustion of the Earth's resources. The Club predicted that the rates of economic and population growth evident in the early 1970s could not be sustained for more than a few decades, thus extending the dire 'limits to growth' projections made by Thomas Malthus almost two centuries before (Meadows *et al.* 1972). Only late in the twentieth century did many advanced nations begin to realize that demographic trends, notably the ageing of populations at the same time that birth rates were dropping below replacement levels, would lead to decline rather than growth in population numbers. Until then, population pressure on resources had been the centre of attention both at the global scale and at the scale of individual regions. In particular, the growth of big cities spawned 'new town' or 'overspill' settlements and ill-fated initiatives such as 'green belts' which failed when growth and expansion simply leapt over the areas in question, fuelling suburban sprawl facilitated by the widespread use of the private car (Pacione 2005).

In short, the mindset underlying geography has, for the lifetime of most teachers and researchers working today, been one that centred on growth and emphasized upward trajectories for Gross Domestic Product (GDP), population, employment, trade, wealth and investment. Embedded within this overall goal of growth has been a battery of tools and techniques for either stimulating or measuring growth. In the realm of planning and policy-making, for instance, the emphasis has often been on concepts like the multiplier effect and benefit–cost analysis. Investment and spending were seen to 'multiply' through the area in which they were undertaken, as employees and the suppliers of other inputs spent their earnings locally, eventually trickling down to more distant areas. In such a mindset, 'stagnation' was rarely considered. Growth was what mattered, as shown by the absence of the word 'stagnation' from the indices of nearly all geography books. There had certainly been no consideration of a 'divider' effect whereby the withdrawal of jobs and services might reverberate through local economies, triggering a cycle of decline. In principle, a multiplier effect could be negative, implying contraction, but this was seen as little more than an aberrant case.

Stagnation as aberration

Where stagnation did become the centre of attention in the last fifty years, it was usually seen as a temporary aberration, a pause in an almost unremitting growth trajectory. For example, in the 1960s and 1970s, there was talk of 'stagflation', a term coined to describe the presence of inflation and the absence of growth in advanced economies. The political challenge was seen as one of overcoming stagflation and resuming growth. Where stagnation occurred outside advanced economies, as in so-called 'backward' parts of the Third World, the condition was also seen as a transitory one that would disappear once the alleged benefits of development percolated to the areas in question.

Dictionary definitions of stagnation, and the verb 'to stagnate', speak of making no progress, thereby being dull and sluggish. In this sense, stagnation signifies the absence of growth. Stagnation, from this perspective, may well be the precursor to actual decline. Indeed, the term often has pejorative overtones, almost implying a moral judgement that something which is stagnating is not doing as well as it should. The corollary is that something or someone is to blame. Stagnation is in fact often conflated with decline. To say that a place or an industry is stagnating can mean either that it is failing to grow (a state of relative decline) or it is actually going backwards (a state of absolute decline). Even where there is no implied critical judgement, the term stagnation conveys negative overtones, perhaps evoking sympathy. An area which is stagnating is often seen as backward and therefore worthy of government support.

Stagnation and economic restructuring

In geographical writing, the term stagnation is most commonly used in relation to economic performance and, especially, in relation to the outcome of the process of economic restructuring. It has therefore been an increasingly topical though still relatively ignored issue since about 1980. This time marks the approximate start of the era of globalization, a term which signifies the increasing integration of the national economies around the globe into a single economic entity (Waitt et al. 2000). In a sense, what is referred to as 'globalization' is simply the latest stage in the evolution of international trade links which began with the development of a 'world system'. The origins of the world system can probably be dated back to the sixteenth century (Wallerstein 1979). What is striking about the new world order is its universal reach, the speed at which change occurs, and the way in which social, cultural and political change is closely integrated with the economic change that is at the heart of new globalized relations. Major corporations are transnational in their reach and act out their corporate strategies on a global scale, deciding what to produce where (Fagan and Webber 1999). It is meaningful, therefore, to talk of a 'new international division of labour', but too simplistic to see Third World nations simply as sources of cheap labour and therefore attractive places for the relocation, from advanced economies, of labour-intensive activities such as the textile, clothing and footwear industries (Walmsley and Sorensen 1994). Any notion of a prosperous 'core' and a dependent 'periphery' (as illustrated in the relations between imperial powers and their colonies) has long since gone. The world today is highly complex, multi-layered and regionally diverse (Waitt et al. 2000).

Globalization has been made possible because of three fundamental changes. First, the emergence of transnational corporations, particularly during the Long Boom, fostered a diverse array of production and a global view of production, distribution and sales. Companies saw opportunities to produce all sorts of commodities and services in different locations around the globe and to trade these in a variety of places. This has resulted in a situation where more than two-thirds of the world trade in goods is undertaken by the top 500 TNCs. Motor vehicle manufacture is a good illustration of this. The concept of a 'world car' has been instrumental in encouraging uniformity in standards and alternative and inter-changeable international suppliers, even if the resultant vehicles have been superficially cus-tomized for local tastes, as in the use of different names for the same model and different marketing strategies. Second, advances in information technology, and especially, tele-communications, made possible the monitoring of production and distribution around the globe from a few key strategic locations (Graham and Marvin 1996). These locations can be thought of as command posts in the global economy. They are therefore commonly referred to as world cities (Pacione 2005). Computer-aided design (CAD) and computer-aided manufacturing (CAM) facilitated the servicing of niche markets at the same time that tele-communications facilitated a shift from the just-in-case system of production of the Fordist era to the just-in-time production system seen today (Waitt *et al.* 2000). 'World cities' are the nerve centres of global economy. They may not be centres for the manufacture of items which are then sent around the world, as at the height of the industrial era, but they house key personnel who make critically important decisions about what activity is undertaken where. Third, governments, for ideological reasons, have chosen to reduce protection (e.g. tariffs and other barriers to trade) and to pursue goals such as international competitiveness and international best practice (for example, floating national currencies and facilitating the international movement of money). This ideological position is linked to 'new right' think-ing and to the rise of what has variously been described as 'economic rationalism' and 'neoliberalism'. The essence of this ideological thinking emphasizes individualism and choice. It adopts the view that economic processes drive the contemporary world and that economic processes should therefore operate, as far as possible, without interference from governments. The free market is seen as the most efficient way of organizing the economic system (Robinson *et al.* 2000). Such ideologically driven thinking is justified by its suppor-ters on the grounds that global trade is possible (as a result of better physical communications and telecommunications) and, therefore, any business would be well served by focusing on global rather than national markets. Not only does this provide opportunities for economies of scale, it also avoids over-reliance on the vagaries of any one market.

Stagnation as inevitable

There have been many positive outcomes from the process of globalization. World cities have thrived. Some formerly marginal economies in the Third World have become inte-grated into the global economy and have benefited accordingly. However, as with every-thing, there are 'winners' and 'losers'. One of the negative outcomes of globalization has been a relatively rapid redistribution, on a global scale, of zones of 'stagnation'. Places in advanced economies which were once hives of industrial activity have become 'rust-belts'. Shipbuilding in the northeast of the United Kingdom and the steel industry in the northeast of the United States are examples. Areas in advanced economies that were dependent on the textile industry, on clothing and on footwear have similarly declined as manufacturing has been undertaken more cheaply elsewhere. Conversely, areas in lesser developed countries have become centres of growth. The case of the so-called 'East Asian tigers' (a popular description of Hong Kong, Singapore, South Korea and Taiwan) is probably the most out-standing example of rapid economic growth, but the phenomenon of growth has been evi-dent through southeast Asia with countries like Malaysia striving to become a developed nation by 2020 (Prime Minister's Department (Malaysia) 2005). Growth rates in China, Vietnam, Thailand and Indonesia are currently impressive. Locations in these countries which were areas of stagnation until the last one or two decades are now areas of growth. In a sense, this mirrors what is sometimes called the product life cycle. Over time, the demand for a commodity drops away as markets become saturated and as new commodities, which are either more competitively priced or of better quality, or of improved design and functionality, come on to the market. Much of the competition for manufacturing in advanced economies came not just from cheap labour locations but from innovation in the form of new machinery and technology which is much more productive than old and now outdated equipment. Just as there is something almost inevitable about the product life cycle, so there is something almost inevitable about stagnation afflicting an area which has depended on one or a few staple products and industries. Stagnating industries and stagnating regions are almost inevitable. Globalization has merely changed, quite rapidly, the nature and location of such stagnation.

Change in the pattern of stagnation is also evident at a more local scale. This is amply demonstrated in the cities of advanced nations. The process of de-industrialization in such places, which resulted from globalization and from manufacturing production booming in the newly industrializing countries, led to factory closure in many cities which had risen to prominence early in the industrial era. In many cases, the factories in question had been set up in the nineteenth century when cities were much smaller in geographical size. As a result, the factories were often in what are now inner suburbs, sometimes in cramped premises. The closure of these factories, and their subsequent decay through a lack of alternative use, produced a bleak landscape. Boarded-up facilities with 'Keep Out' signs are hardly conducive to civic pride. Unpleasant surroundings can lead to social incivility and to changes in the character of a place. Ports often faced a similarly depressing situation, sometimes compounding the problem because ports were often industrial centres. Containerization of sea trade meant that old port infrastructure, like bulk handling facilities, became obsolete as traffic switched to new custom-built entities which are better located with respect to road and rail interchange. Residential areas around such factories and ports also began to stagnate. The loss of local jobs, visual blight and out-migration to newer industrial and port areas all had a depressing impact on house prices. In some areas, however, this stagnation was rectified by a process of gentrification. As land and house prices declined, either relatively or absolutely, in formerly industrial inner suburbs, so the land became ripe for redevelopment. It was relatively cheap. At the same time, the changing nature of city centres and their surrounding areas (with growth of white-collar employment, cultural activity, and leisure and tourism facilities) saw the inner suburbs become attractive to middle-class residents who had lived hitherto in middle or outer suburbs. These individuals – the gentry – often bought and improved the inner suburban housing, giving rise to the term gentrification (Pacione 2005). Disused factories were turned into apartments or offices. Ports became marinas or tourist precincts. Once-thriving industrial areas, having experienced stagnation, then revived.

Stagnation as an enduring state

Gentrification suggests that stagnation can be a transitory state. Certainly, as society as a whole shifts its attention from production to consumption, there has been revitalization of many areas. Shopping, eating out, the arts, creative industries, tourism and leisure generally have all combined with tertiary and quaternary sector employment growth to help in revitalization. The London Docklands have changed dramatically in character in the last two decades. Sydney's Darling Harbour has gone from a railway shunting and storage area to an international playground and shopping hub, geared to tourism and leisure activities. However, not all places revitalize. Some fail to prosper as the nature of society and economy changes. Similarly, not all areas within the East Asian economies are prospering. Some places continue to languish. Some places, in other words, stagnate. It is wrong, therefore, to see stagnation as simply a temporary aberration from a growth trajectory and as something which will be either self-correcting (through land prices falling to the point where renewal becomes commercially viable) or something able to be fixed by government (through a publicly funded redevelopment scheme of one sort or another, as with the way in which development linked to the 2000 Olympic Games was used to rehabilitate a contaminated and abandoned industrial site in Sydney for subsequent use as a Games complex and village, and then private housing and office space). Some places face the prospect of long-term stagnation without the prospect of a reversal of economic fortunes.

There are many examples of mining settlements that are a shadow of their former selves. More generally, and taking a longer historical perspective, entire villages and even towns have been abandoned and have disappeared. Curiously, some of these places now have an afterlife as heritage items and therefore an attractiveness which they have not experienced for centuries. The deserted villages of the English Midlands, by way of illustration, attract tourists trying to trace the lineaments of long-gone buildings in residual earthworks. Ghost towns and mining centres are now so sought after that they are built along the lines of theme parks if they do not actually exist. Other places do not disappear but endure in a more or less steady state: they maintain their population levels and economic activity. From the point of view of ecological sustainability, this may be no bad thing. Perhaps a state of stagnation should be freed from its pejorative overtones and seen as a state of balance.

Adapting to turbulent environments

Balance is a relative term. It is difficult to ensure balance in a dynamic environment where many socio-economic and biophysical processes are at work. It is particularly difficult to ensure balance in what might be thought of as 'turbulent' environments where the degree and pace of change is without precedent and where, as a result, survival can only be assured on a trial-and-error basis, aimed at working out what is successful, and not on the basis of pre-planned strategies which may or may not be adaptive to the rapidly changing world (Emery and Trist 1973). This is a significant point because many features of the contemporary world have the hallmarks of turbulence (Walmsley 1980). The 'drivers' of turbulent change in the contemporary world are so varied that it is difficult to do justice to them, certainly within the space of a few pages. Nevertheless, some sense of these changes and of their far-reaching consequences can be obtained by highlighting two issues: climate change and demographic change.

Climate change is a critically important part of the turbulent environment in which all humans now live. The weight of scientific evidence suggests that the climate of the globe is getting warmer as a result of human-induced change, especially the production of greenhouse gases since the onset of the Industrial Revolution and particularly in the last century. Whether or not this change is superimposed on 'natural' fluctuations in temperature seems irrelevant when the short-term consequences, such as rising sea levels, demand fairly immediate action. The future of Pacific corals atolls is particularly uncertain. Unless coral can grow at a rate to compensate for the rise in sea level, some small island states will not so much stagnate as submerge (see Chapter 49).

Rising sea levels are not the only concern. Desertification is widespread as rainfall patterns shift. Overexploitation of marginal rainfall areas can lead to environmental degradation, which in turn can encourage the spread of deserts. The Saharan desert now covers settlements that existed in the past. Those areas of sub-Saharan Africa which experience drought also exhibit famine, often on a catastrophic scale. Altered fire regimes are another consequence of climate change. These can have far-reaching impacts, especially when accompanied by the spread of settlement into fire-prone areas. California and Portugal experienced devastating fires in 2004 and 2005. Indonesia, for different reasons, has suffered major fires, in its case related to land-clearing for farming. Storm frequency has changed too. In the Caribbean, 2005 was the worst hurricane season on record. Major damage in Florida was followed by even more severe flooding in New Orleans.

Sudden natural disasters like floods have an immediate negative impact on an area. However, in the longer term they may result in a net benefit as money and resources flow to the area and as investment in reconstruction peaks. It is difficult to describe a point of stagnation in this cycle of events. Presumably there is a point of sluggishness once the devastation has run its course and before rebuilding begins – but this is likely to be short-lived. More evident is the stagnation that can result from climatic natural disasters which are more insidious in their onset. Drought is one such example. It is not simply a lack of rainfall, but has to be defined in terms of the use made of that rainfall. Some farming practices are more demanding of water than others. Drought is, in many parts of the world, a natural event. In such cases, it should be possible to plan for it. For instance, if drought has occurred once in every five years in the past, it should be possible to design farm management strategies which will deliver profitable returns notwithstanding occasional bad years. All too often, though, farm practices can actually contribute to drought, through overstocking, the failure to build up fodder reserves, and the choice of inappropriate crops. The problems of drought are well demonstrated in the rangeland areas of Australia. Better scientific understanding of the biosphere might produce better climate forecasting, particularly if linked with better monitoring of existing conditions. Despite this, the future is very uncertain. On a global scale, the thawing of parts of the Siberian tundra in 2005 raised the very real threat of the release of massive amounts of methane and thus a significant contribution to greenhouse gases and global warming. The possible impact of the melting of polar caps on ocean currents is unknown.

Demographic change is another critically important part of the turbulent global environment. Demographic change can have a major impact on human well-being. Although the dire predictions of 'doomsters' from Thomas Malthus to the Club of Rome have not materialized, the Earth's population is growing quickly and putting pressure on resources (Cocks 1996). The US Bureau of Census (2005) has a 'clock' which estimates the world population from day to day. The pressure of population growth is most acute in some of the world's poorest nations where there is concern over basics like food supply, water quantity and quality, and timber for both heating and building. However, it is not just the number of people which is critical. As nations develop, consumption per capita tends to grow. One way of demonstrating this is to look at the so-called 'ecological footprint' of an individual (http://www.ecouncil.ac.cr/rio/focus/report/english/footprint/). This is an estimate of the amount of land which is needed to provide the goods and services required to support the lifestyle of the individual in question. For a subsistence farmer, the ecological footprint might be relatively small. For an affluent Westerner with a high level of consumption, a car, lots of travel, a big home and major energy requirements, the ecological footprint – for instance, 9.7 ha per person in the USA and 7.0 in Australia – is huge compared to footprints of 0.6 ha per person in many African countries such as Zambia (http://www.footprintnetwork.org/gfn_sub.php?content = footprint_hectares). It may be some time, if at all, before major centres of population like China (currently 1.6 ha per person) and India (currently 0.7 ha per person) approach the size of footprint common in the West, but increasing consumption by growing middle-class populations will bring more pressure on resources. To give a simple example, the demand for timber for construction, as well as for fuel, adds to the problems of deforestation and to the problems stemming from the rise in greenhouse gases.

The significance of climate change and demographic change is not so much in their direct impact on patterns of stagnation. Certainly, sea level rise, desertification and drought can all trigger economic and social problems, thereby causing areas that are directly affected to stagnate. Similarly, population pressure on resources can also lead to economic and social problems in affected areas, again manifesting as stagnation. However, the significance of both sets of changes lies also in the uncertainty which they create for the globe as a whole and the fact that the ramifications, in terms of stagnation, can be felt in areas other than those most directly affected. This poses problems for government policymakers.

Public policy responses to stagnation

In terms of understanding how stagnation is to be regarded and can be treated, it is important to recognize major changes to have occurred in the policy arena. Two areas stand out particularly: ideology and international relations.

Mention has already been made of the rise of neoliberalism and 'new right' thinking. This is related to the demise of the economic thinking associated with John Maynard Keynes and usually referred to as Keynesianism. In simple terms, Keynesian thinking saw a role for national governments in the economic policy arena as 'pullers of levers'. In particular, governments could, through a range of policy initiatives (e.g. interest rates control, public spending and welfare payments), stimulate demand within the economy generally (or dampen it, as the case may be). Replacement of Keynesian orthodoxy by a new neoliberal orthodoxy brought market forces to the fore and left government policy very much in the background. As a *laissez-faire* attitude came to permeate government circles around the world, so economic growth became paramount in public consciousness. A 'growth fetish' took over in the world of politics and in everyday life.

After a decrease in the hours worked by employees in advanced Western societies from the late nineteenth century onwards, workers began to work longer hours from about 1980. Commentators who had predicted that technological advances would mean that all the work which society needed could be done in a fraction of the time previously required, were proved wrong (Rifkin 1995). The much vaunted 'leisure society' failed to materialize. Similarly, the proponents of the view that jobs would shift from advanced economies to newly industrializing countries, with a result that work in advanced economies would become the preserve of the highly educated and leisure the curse of the less well educated, were proved wrong (Jenkins and Sherman 1981). Employees put in longer hours. The strain of this on relationships and health are well recognized, and many writers have commented at length on the work–life collision (Edgar 2005). Working longer and longer hours is, of course, essentially self-defeating in that the people who earn more and more money find themselves with less and less time to spend it. The obsession with growth and more and more money is rightly called a 'fetish' because there is evidence that, beyond a certain level (approximately US $10 000 per capita), human happiness has little correlation with income (Hamilton 2003).

The arena of international relations is interesting because the ideological commitment to neoliberalism and to the free movement of most factors of production (especially raw materials, investment capital, technology and management expertise) does not extend to labour. Indeed, border security has become a major concern of many advanced nations. In island states (like Australia), border security is much easier to ensure than in states with land borders (as in North America and Europe). In other words, the prevailing 'hands-off' ideology in much of the economically advanced world is blended with pragmatism and insularity. Nowhere is this seen more clearly than in treatment of refugees. The enormous world refugee problem involves 19 million people currently estimated to be stateless, refugees or asylum seekers (UNHCR 2005). Humanitarian urges to help these people fall prey to the self-interest of electors in affluent nations. This problem will grow as the number of environmental refugees grows: that is to say, those people displaced by natural disasters like rising sea level, drought and flooding. The failure of Western nations such as Australia and the USA to ratify the Kyoto Protocol on greenhouse gases by 2005 illustrates the power of self-interested lobby groups. The gap between rich and poor nations is growing despite the fine words expressed in the Millennium Development Goals. Aid to the Third World is inadequate given the scale of the problems to be confronted. Activities in the policy arena, both at the local level and internationally, seem to be serving to exacerbate inequality – and thereby increasing the gap between those regions which are prospering and those which are stagnating or declining. This situation becomes all the more regrettable when it is realized that activities in the policy arena, climate change and demographic change are all interrelated in complex and multi-layered ways.

Reconceptualizing stagnation

Climatic change, demographic change and political change all have important implications for the pattern of stagnation in the contemporary world. This importance can be appreciated by focusing on the core geographical concepts of distance and scale. The interrelatedness of the global politico-economic and biophysical environments means that the world should be viewed as a whole. Distance no longer insulates places from world events. Agricultural subsidies and surpluses in the European Union have a profound influence at the other side of the world, significantly affecting the well-being of farmers in Australia and New Zealand and poor farmers in Africa. Cyclone Katrina in 2005 caused damage to oil production facilities in the Gulf of Mexico, and this reverberated around the world in the form of increased oil prices, affecting car drivers everywhere. The corollary to this is that all areas are now potentially prone to stagnation. It is not enough to be confident that local conditions are favourable. In a globalized world, far-away events can have major ramifications at home. In addition, the interconnected nature of the global politico-economic and biophysical processes has developed in such a way that the pace of change has quickened. The Sudden Acute Respiratory Syndrome (SARS) outbreak was able to spread around the world, from east Asia to Canada particularly, in a short time. The same will be true of any influenza pandemic. The same is true of economic shocks. In short, stagnation might be sudden in onset. Uncertainty prevails.

This raises the question of what to do about stagnating areas. On the one hand, the prevailing *zeitgeist* of neoliberalism suggests that market forces can be left to operate. The location of disadvantage and stagnation, from this perspective, is a self-correcting process. Once the possibility of profit emerges from price differentials brought on by stagnation, entrepreneurs will step in with schemes which will lead to re-investment. On the other hand, the opposite end of the political spectrum are advocates of government intervention. Although no longer in the ascendancy, these people dominated political thinking throughout the Long Boom. They argue that governments can help relieve stagnation by investment in infrastructure and by training initiatives and introducing various inducements for venture capital.

Counter-posing these two positions implies that there is a range of alternatives between the two. This may be true, but it would be foolish to think that there is a certain formula for ridding an area of stagnation. What is currently viewed as stagnation, with all its associated pejorative overtones, might be better reconceptualized and viewed as a steady-state condition of development. The fact that stagnation demands attention is due to the privileging of the economic in the world today. If it is recognized that life extends well beyond the economic and that human happiness and well-being are dependent on a host of other considerations, then a state of stagnation, in terms of economic growth, may be nothing more than an opportunity to focus appropriate attention on the sort of non-economic changes which characterize communities everywhere and at any time: cultural shifts, changes in social attitudes, the development and use of social capital, and the fostering of care and concern. Of course, people tend to assess quality of life relative to others around them, not over time. In this way, a maintaining of quality of life can be seen as a decline in standards if others have more, notwithstanding the fact that more, in a material sense, does not mean more happiness. If the future is increasingly uncertain as a result of growing 'turbulence', then a reconceptualization of what is meant by stagnation may be warranted. If reversals of fortune can be sudden in onset and varied in location, a rethinking of stagnation as a negative might be called for. This will necessitate tackling two problems: educating affluent people to be satisfied with what they have; and fostering a more holistic and less economic view of life that does not privilege economic growth above all else.

Further reading

Cocks, D. (1996) *People Policy.* Sydney: University of New South Wales Press.
Dicken, P. (2004) Geographers and 'globalization': (yet) another missed boat? *Transactions of the Institute of British Geographers* 29, 5–26.
Eckersley, R. (ed.) (1998) *Measuring Progress: Is Life Getting Better?* Melbourne: CSIRO Publishing.
Martin, R. (2004) Geography: making a difference in a globalising world. *Transactions of the Institute of British Geographers* 29, 147–247.
Peck, J. (2002) American recession. *Transactions of the Institute of British Geography* 27, 131–5.
Sandler, T. (1997) *Global Challenges: An Approach to Environmental, Political, and Economic Problems.* Cambridge: Cambridge University Press.

References

Edgar, D. (2005) *The War over Work: The Future of Work and Family.* Melbourne: Melbourne University Press.
Emery, F.E. and Trist, E.L. (1973) *Towards a Social Ecology: Contextual Appreciation of the Future in the Present.* London: Plenum Press.
Fagan, R.H. and Webber, M. (1999) *Global Restructuring: The Australian Experience,* second edition. Melbourne: Oxford University Press.

Graham, S. and Marvin, S. (1996) *Telecommunications and the City: Electronic Spaces, Urban Places*. London: Routledge.

Hamilton, C. (2003) *Growth Fetish*. Sydney: Allen and Unwin.

Jenkins, C. and Sherman, B. (1981) *The Leisure Shock*. London: Methuen.

Meadows, D.H., Meadows, D.L., Randers, J. and Behrens, W.W. (1972) *The Limits to Growth: A Report for the Club of Rome's Project on the Predicament of Mankind*. London: Earth Island

Myrdal, G. (1957) *Economic Theory and Under-Developed Regions*. London: Methuen

Pacione, M. (2005) *Urban Geography: A Global Perspective*, second edition. London: Routledge.

Prime Minister's Department (Malaysia) (2005) *Eighth Malaysia Plan 2001–2005*. Available at http://www.epu.jpm.my/New%20Folder/development%20plan/RM8.htm

Rifkin, J. (1995) *The End of Work: The Decline of the Global Labour Force and the Dawn of the Post-Market Era*. New York: G.P. Putnam.

Robinson, G.M., Loughran, R.J. and Tranter, P.J. (2000) *Australia and New Zealand: Economy, Society and Environment*. London: Arnold.

Rostow, W.W. (1965) *The Stages of Economic Growth: A Non-Communist Manifesto*. Cambridge: Cambridge University Press.

United Nations High Commissioner for Refugees (UNHCR) (2005) *2004 Global Refugee Trends*. Geneva: UNHCR.

US Bureau of Census (2005) http://www.census.gov/ipc/www/popclockworld.html

Waitt, G., McGuirk, P., Dunn, K., Hartig, K. and Burnley, I. (2000) *Introducing Human Geography: Globalisation, Difference and Inequality*. Sydney: Longman.

Wallerstein, I. (1979) *The Capitalist World Economy*. Cambridge: Cambridge University Press.

Walmsley, D.J. (1980) Welfare delivery in post-industrial society. *Geografiska Annaler Series B* 62, 91–7.

Walmsley, D.J. and Sorensen, A.D. (1994) *Contemporary Australia: Explorations in Economy, Society and Geography*, second edition. Melbourne: Longman.

28

Rapid change

The Pearl River Delta under globalization

Victor F.S. Sit

Throughout history, some places have undergone rapid growth and expansion in a few decades, often because of new manufacturing and trading opportunities. Bruges in Belgium grew rapidly as a trading centre in the thirteenth century to a population of 40,000. Manchester expanded from 40,000 to nearly 500,000 in fifty years in the early nineteenth century. However, although there were tremendous environmental changes and human and social problems associated with these transformations, none of these historic urban expansions in any way matched the rapid transformations of contemporary urban areas. Just as England claimed in the nineteenth century to be the 'workshop of the world', exporting textile machinery and railway locomotives to every continent, so now can China, and especially the Pearl River Delta area, claim to be the manufacturing dynamo of world trade.

Recent Chinese urbanization and the Pearl River Delta case of rapid change

Under the central planning system of 1949–77, China's urbanization at the time may be characterized by a low growth rate, rigid government control and inland bias, and by being endogenous, i.e. foreign capital and global market stimuli were limited. Since 1978, with a new Open and Reform approach towards social and economic development, China has experienced an accelerated urbanization. The nation's level of urbanization was raised to 36 per cent by 2000. It had been the result of a relaxed official control over urban and economic growth, as well as the product of new policies that encouraged rapid growth of the coastal region and the promotion of external forces – especially foreign direct investment (FDI) – in the shaping of new economic and urban landscapes. These new dynamics have led to a new type of urban growth associated with the development and economic expansion of South China's coastal region, which has become a global export-processing and export-assembling platform (Zhang 2002; Sit 2001). As urban processes are inextricably tied to the development of the economy, and globalization in the form of FDI and the New International Division of Labour had gained significance in many less developed countries (LDCs), the relationship between transnational capital inflow and globalization of production and LDC urbanization has become intensified (Sit 1991; Gilbert 1993; King 1990; Lin 1994; Sit and Yang 1997). The case of the Pearl River Delta offers the opportunity for examining such a relationship in some detail. It is also the region of China that has astounded the world by its rapid structural and urban transformations since 1978, and is thus excellent for illustrating how global forces plus local reform have generated rapid urbanization and change in a formerly rural region of an LDC.

The Pearl River Delta (henceforth PRD or the Delta) lies to the southeast of the China Mainland, sharing a border with two former colonies (Hong Kong under the UK and Macau under Portugal) which are now Special Administrative Regions of China (Figure 28.1). The PRD was opened to foreign investors in 1979, earlier than other regions of China. Besides this, it has been most successful in utilizing foreign capital, taking advantage of (1) the post-Mao reforms and the spatially biased preferential open policies that have been implemented most vigorously in the area, and (2) the investment, support and entrepreneurship of its next-door neighbour, Hong Kong (Sit 1995; Zhang and Song, 2000). Since 1979, four types of special zones for attracting FDI have been established in the PRD – the Special Economic Zones (SEZ) of Shenzhen and Zhuhai; the Open Coastal City (OCC) of Guangzhou; the Economic and Technological Development Zones (ETDZ) in Guangzhou; and the Open Coastal Economic Area (OCEA), i.e. the Delta plus the two counties of Qingyuan and Guangning (Figure 28.1). They comprise the 28 cities and counties of the Delta. In the past 25 years, the Delta has been turned from an area having a low level of urbanization (27.4 per cent in 1980) into one of the most urbanized areas of all China, with an urbanization level of about 70 per cent in 2003. It now ranks as one of the three most urbanized regions of China, along with the Yangzi River Delta and the Beijing–Tianjin–Tangshan area (Sit and Cai 2003). The Delta is also the most advanced area with respect to foreign investment, economic growth, export-orientation and urban growth within the PRC (Table 28.1). The rapid change in the Delta has been breathtaking: by 2003 the Delta's GDP was about 30 per cent larger than that of Malaysia, a country with the same population as the Delta's but occupying eight times the Delta's land area. In the same year, the Delta's GDP was double that of Egypt, whose population and territory are about three times and twenty times those of the Delta; and its GDP is 10 per cent more than the whole of Thailand, though the Delta's population and territory are much smaller.

Sit and Yang (1997) have shown that economic globalization and transnational forces have shaped the nature and pattern of urbanization in the Delta in the post-1978 period and argue that a subset of urbanization has emerged there under their sway, i.e. a foreign-investment-induced urbanization, or exo-urbanization, as distinct from the endo(genous)-urbanization (or urbanization driven entirely by intranational or regional forces) which existed in the pre-1978 period in the PRC. This foreign-investment-induced urbanization is driven by a 'labour-intensive and assembly manufacturing' type of export-oriented industrialization based on inputs of large quantities of low-cost and low-skill labour and land. The short cycle of such investments and the quick returns they sought after led to the rapid multiplication of such investments and production in the Delta, resulting in a rapid transformation of the rural-based economy into an industry-based export-oriented economy over a large area. Owing to the big demand for cheap labour, the transformation had thus been accompanied by high rates of intra-provincial, intra-Delta rural–urban influx and a large-scale, inter-regional in-migration. Spatially, it has promoted the growth of small urban places and rural areas whose economies have been increasingly integrated into the world economic circuitry. This chapter will first chart the rapid changes induced by FDI in the Delta's economic

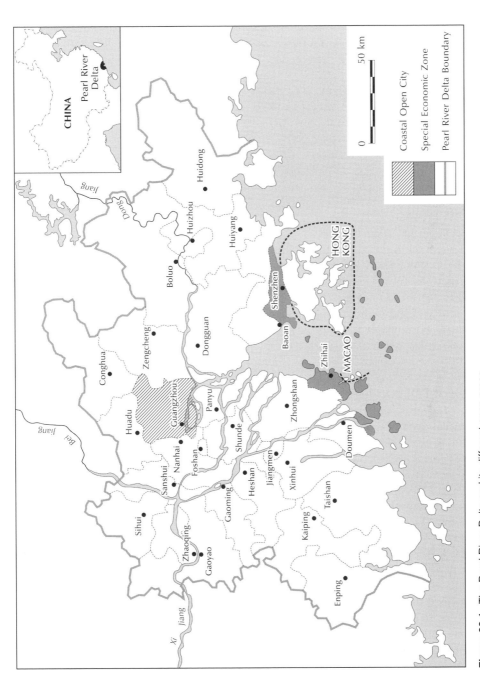

Figure 28.1. The Pearl River Delta and its different open areas.

Table 28.1. Major economic indicators of the Pearl River Delta, 1980–2003

	1980	1985	1990	1995	2000	2003
Year-end population (million)	16.3	17.6	19.3	21.4	23.1	25.8
GDP (RMB$ billion) at current price	11.9	30.4	87.2	389.9	737.9	1145.7
Per capita GDP (RMB$) at current price	731	1729	4524	18242	31983	44406
Composition of GDP (%)						
Primary industry	25.8	18.8	14.8	8.1	5.8	4.1
Secondary industry	28.9	32.2	38.8	41.7	44.6	45.5
Total gross output value of industry and agriculture (RMB$ billion)	19.1	41.8	112.4	617.3	1310.5	
Gross output value of industry (RMB$ billion)	15.2	36.4	104.8	587.8	1286.6	2210.3
Gross output value of agriculture (RMB$ billion)	3.9	5.4	7.5	29.5	40.8	
Exports (US$ billion)	0.6	1.6	8.1	46.1	84.7	145.3
Utilized FDI (US$ billion)	0.1	0.7	1.5	8.6	12.5	17.2

Source: Guangdong Statistical Bureau (various dates).

structure and population growth. It will then highlight the accompanying urban transformation. It will end with a discussion of the sustainability of the driving forces behind the Delta's growth as China has become much more open and developed, as symbolized by its accession to the WTO in 2004.

Influx of FDI and its impact on the Delta's economy since 1978

The recent trend of economic globalization and its impact on some LDC economies started roughly in the 1980s. Two developments have mutually reinforced each other and contributed to the development and integration of selected LDC economies with the global economy. The first is the emergence of the New International Division of Labour, made possible and necessary by advances in technologies of production, transportation and communication, as well as the changed labour market in the industrialized countries. The second is the wave of deregulation in international trade and investment by a host of LDCs that offered opportunities for global sourcing and global processing by MNCs. As one of the popular indicators of such a trend of economic globalization, FDI started to rise rapidly in some LDCs. In 1980–93, FDI inflow into LDCs increased annually at 15 per cent. In absolute terms, the amount had increased from US $13 billion to US $80 billion, or six-fold. Since 1993, China has become the largest FDI recipient among all LDCs. In 1990, FDI inflow into China represented 1.6 per cent of the world total. In 2000, it moved up to 3.2 per cent. Its cumulative FDI inflow in 1979–2001, i.e. US $385 billion, is about 1.8 times the total global inflow in 1990. The concentration of FDI in the Delta area of Guangdong Province has been a characteristic of the FDI inflow into China which is maintained up to the present (see Table 28.2). In 2003, China's FDI inflow was US $56 billion (8.8 per cent of the world), second only to the US (US $71 billion). That year the Delta accounted for 30.3 per cent of China's total intake. Its amount, US $17 billion, is 11 per cent of the total inflow

Table 28.2. FDI share by the Delta within China (US $100 million; %)

Year	Delta	Guangdong	Whole of China	PRD Share in	
				Guangdong	China
1980	1.0	2.1	–	47.6	–
1985	7.4	9.2	47.0	80.4	15.7
1990	17.0	20.0	103.0	85.0	16.5
1995	86.0	121.0	481.0	71.1	17.9
2000	125.0	146.0	594.0	85.6	21.0
2003	170.0	189.0	561.0	89.6	30.0

Source: *China Statistical Bureau* (various dates) and *Guangdong Statistical Bureau* (various dates).

Table 28.3. Non-local capital in fixed capital investment, 1980–94 (%)

Year	Guangdong	Shenzhen	Zhuhai	Delta
1980	0.53	7.77	13.42	0.83
1985	3.69	13.61	14.93	5.95
1990	5.88	18.01	17.73	11.14
1994	10.35	21.32	22.36	16.90

Source: Adapted from Shen *et al.* (2002).

received by all LDCs, larger than the total received by either Africa (US $13 billion) Southeast Asia (US $14.5 billion), Southeast Europe (US $13 billion) or South Asia (US $4.5 billion) (UNCTAD 2005).

In spite of the huge amount of FDI received and its continued increase, there have been comments that FDI (later termed as non-local investments, as Hong Kong and Macau investments are not regarded as 'foreign' after their return to Chinese sovereignty in 1997 and 1999) accounted for only a minor share of the Delta's total fixed capital investment (see Table 28.3). For example, it has been argued by Shen *et al.* (2002) that 'non-local' capital is not the main source of investments in the Delta. Rather, local capital, mainly in the form of loans and 'self-arranged capital', has been the predominant capital. Hence, Shen *et al.* argued that local capital is the main dynamic behind the Delta's hectic economic growth and urban change in the past three decades. As local authorities arranged most of the local capital for the infrastructural, utilities and residential housing construction which formed part of the hardware for wooing FDI, their role in development has been passive though supportive. In contrast, FDI into the Delta has always been dominated by investments in productive activities, particularly in export-processing and export-assembling. Some of these activities even took the forms of 'imported material processing for export' and 'compensation trade' that involved very little actual foreign investment or FDI inflow. However, the impacts on trade and local employment of these activities are large, though they have little effect on the FDI inflow. For example, in 1988, the Delta's receipt of processing fees amounted to US $381 million, while the total foreign capital it received that year was US $1391 billion (Sit 1995). As manufacturing value-added in the Delta is roughly 28 per cent, the amount of processing fees represented a 'real' FDI many times its size. To elaborate more on the significance of

435

FDI as the basic dynamic for the rapid economic and urban change in the Delta since 1978, we need to venture into more details of FDI in the Delta.

FDI: investment-bias in light and export-oriented manufacturing

The initial wave of FDI inflow in 1980–4 was concentrated largely in services which accounted for 87.2 per cent of the flow. Then, in 1985–9, manufacturing FDI suddenly went up to 77 per cent. Within the period, FDI-related industrial employment shot up to 3 million persons. By 1993, the share of foreign-invested enterprises (FIE) in the industrial output value of the Delta amounted to one quarter of the Delta's total. In Dongguan, industrial FIE accounted for 71.5 per cent of local employment, while it was 60 per cent in Shenzhen. As the inflow in 1980–4 was small, the aggregated record for 1980–93 indicated that FDI inflow had grown at an annual rate of 37.6 per cent, of which 70 per cent had gone into export-oriented manufacturing. Of the total FDI up to 2003 for the whole of Guangdong, manufacturing registered a share of 68 per cent. Available figures for the Delta in 1979–99 show the same trend as 65 per cent of the inflow of FDI that went to manufacturing while the flow to real estates investments accounted for only 11.3 per cent.

Hong Kong-bias in FDI sources

One of the critical factors for the Delta's success in wooing FDI is its geographical location next to Hong Kong, and the close blood and clan relations between its people and the Chinese entrepreneurs in Hong Kong. The sudden rush of manufacturing FDI from Hong Kong into the Delta since 1984 may also be related to the pull and push forces that operated in the FDI source and the host. The pull of the Delta had been the result of the new Open and Reform policies of the PRC, and initiatives of the Delta's local authorities in improving infrastructure and adopting new policies and measures to help investors in labour recruitment and management to obtain land and in factory construction. This also includes the granting of tax incentives to FIE and the cutting down of red tape in import and export. The push force in Hong Kong was created by local wage and land cost inflation, shortage of labour and increasing environmental charges. The close social and ethnic ties between Hong Kong entrepreneurs and local officials in the Delta have further smoothed the FDI flow from Hong Kong into the Delta. On top of these, Hong Kong's 100-year history of development in port infrastructure and its developed services in export and import, insurance and financing, as well as its post-war success in marketing and the production of light consumer products for the world, have equally contributed to the success in the hectic development and expansion of the Delta's FDI-induced export-industrial system (Sit 1995, 1998). In 1987–2003, Hong Kong-source FDI inflow into Guangdong amounted to US $106.5 billion. This accounted for 20.7 per cent of the China total, or about the total flow to the whole of Asia in 2003. In 2004, the FIEs of the province accounted for 65 per cent of its total industrial output and 64 per cent of its total exports.

Thus, Hong Kong's role is key to the rapid transformation of the Delta. As other regions of China are more distant from Hong Kong in physical and social terms, the Delta had outcompeted them in effectively maximizing Hong Kong's post-World War II experience in export industries and its logistics and financing hub functions, and had developed into China's and the world's largest light industrial production platform. In some respects, the Yangzi Delta subsequently copied some of the Delta's development strategy. Yet the key

Table 28.4. Exports and imports of Guangdong Province, 1990, 1995 (100 million US$)

Type	1990		1995	
	Export	Import	Export	Import
Processing and assembling with customers' materials	91.7	76.4	159.4	118.9
Compensation trade	1.3	1.0	1.0	0.2
Processing and assembling with imported materials	68.4	51.4	283.4	205.0
Processing equipment	–	7.4	–	11.7
FIE equipment	–	21.5	–	51.7
Others	10.8	39.1	140.1	80.9
Total	**222.2**	**196.8**	**563.9**	**473.8**

Table 28.5. Exports from the Delta, 1980–2003 (US$ billion/%)

Year	PRD	Guangdong	Nation	PRD share in	
				Guangdong	Nation
1980	0.6	2.2	18.1	28.2	3.4
1985	1.6	2.9	27.3	55.3	6.0
1990	8.1	22.2	62.1	36.5	13.0
1995	46.1	56.6	148.8	81.4	31.0
2000	84.7	91.9	249.2	92.2	34.0
2003	145.0	152.8	438.2	94.9	33.1

players there are more diversified, with Taiwanese, South Korean and Japanese FDI having a larger combined role.

Trade-creative and labour-intensive nature

Sit (1998) and Sit and Yang (1997) have detailed the characteristics of manufacturing FDI in the Delta. We may pinpoint its 'trade-creative' character by examining the changing trade statistics of Guangdong Province and the Delta in Tables 28.1, 28.4, and 28.5. Exports of Guangdong Province increased by 154 per cent in 1990–5, i.e. from US $22.2 to 56.4 billion, of which the amount involving out-processing had remained consistently high (at about 72 per cent). Indeed, the Delta's exports in 1980, when the drive of FDI-induced indus-trialization started, amounted only to US $0.6 billion (Table 28.1). The average annual increase from then to 1993 (US $200 billion) is 30.5 per cent, much higher than the overall growth rate of the GDP (18 per cent annual rate in 1980–93; 18.9 per cent in 1980–98). In 1980, FIE's contribution to exports was equally small, i.e. 17 per cent; while in 1993 it was raised to 62.2 per cent. Also, by 1993, 81.8 per cent of the Delta's exports by value were light industrial products. Not only did exports increase rapidly because of out-processing, but the increase in imports was equally linked directly to out-processing. The large volume of material flow so generated between Hong Kong and the Delta also boosted the cross-border vehicular flow. In 1990–2003, the total cross-border vehicular flow increased at an annual rate of 7.8 per cent. In 1990, 95.9 per cent of such flow was made up of cargo vehicles, while in 2003, though the flow of private cars had much increased, cargo vehicles still accounted for 79.5 per cent of the total (Yang 2004).

The trade-creative nature of FDI in the Delta had benefited Hong Kong directly in its transformation from a pre-1980 industrial economy into a post-1980 service economy. It is obviously linked to the predominant Hong Kong source of the industrial-FDI in the Delta and its out-processing nature. The resurgence of re-exports in Hong Kong and Hong Kong's increasing share in total China trade, i.e. from 13.5 per cent in 1980, to 30.5 per cent in 1990, and then 43.1 per cent in 2003, testified the expanding economic division of labour between Hong Kong and the Delta in the period, i.e. Hong Kong serviced as the 'front shop' in finance, project-management, logistics, marketing, export and import, etc., while the Delta served as the 'back factory' in processing and assembling (Sit and Yang 1997).

Transformation in the Delta's economy

In terms of per capita GDP, the transformation of the Delta is even more astonishing than its GDP growth. In 1980, it was ¥ 731, about 1.59 times the national average. In 1990, it rose to ¥ 4,524 (2.76 times the national level). By 2003, it was ¥ 34,295 (US $4,142), or 4.19 times the national level. The average rate of increase in the period of 1980–95 was 9.5 times for China as a whole and 15.9 times for Guangdong, but it was a hefty 24 times for the Delta. Thus, the Delta has drawn away from the rest of China as a rapidly developing region. By 2003, using the permanent (or registered) population as the consistent basis, the Delta had already entered the stage of the middle range of a medium-income society. Between 1980 and 2003, the composition of the primary, secondary and tertiary sectors in its GDP had also drastically changed. The share of the primary sector dropped from 25.8 per cent in 1980 to 18.8 per cent in 1990, and 4.1 per cent in 2003 (Table 28.1). The secondary sector increased its respective shares from 45.3 per cent to 46.4 per cent and then 52.4 per cent, while the figures for the tertiary sector are 28.9 per cent, 38.8 per cent and 43.5 per cent respectively. Thus, in about 2.5 decades, the Delta had been transformed from a rural economy into an industrial economy. As most of the industrial output was generated by FIE, FDI had thus driven the rapid growth of the Delta's economy and its structural transformation.

The nature of such an industrial economy has been further defined by features of the Hong Kong-source FDI; they are as follows:

1. mainly small and medium enterprises;
2. invested in labour-intensive and low-skill processing and assembling;
3. oriented to locations of cheap land close to Hong Kong;
4. tied to Hong Kong as they depend on Hong Kong for management, logistic links with the global supply chain, and other service support;
5. 'guerrilla' in style, i.e. in pursuit of quick returns and haphazard in nature (Sit and Yang 1997).

In 2002, the Delta's gross industrial output value was US $170.4 billion. Yet the average value-added of all its industries was only 26 per cent. Although there had been a change from the predominance of textiles, garments and plastics to newer industries, as the former 'traditional' branches only accounted for US $21 billion of the gross industrial output value in 2002 and the top two branches, i.e. electronic and telecommunication equipment (US $449.6 billion), and electrical equipment and machinery (US $417.8 billion) are 'new' industries, the value-added of the new industries remained less than 30 per cent. Thus, the nature of industrialization in the Delta has remained one of low-tech, low-skill and assembling in essence.

Population change and urbanization

Hectic urban growth

Using a consistent geographical area of the Delta (Figure 28.1) and based on the registered or permanent population, the level of urbanization of the Delta before 1980 was low. The rate of urbanization in 1949–78 was 0.75 per cent per annum, lower than the national figure of 0.89 per cent. Yet in 1980–93, the pace of urbanization rose to a high of 5 per cent per annum (Sit and Yang 1997). This raised the level of urbanization of 26.6 per cent in 1980 to 44.4 per cent in 1993 and then to 64.0 per cent in 2003 (Table 28.6).

In absolute size, the urban population was only 4.69 million in 1980, about half of which was concentrated in the primate city of Guangzhou, while the urbanization level was 75.6 per cent. The two other urbanized areas were the small cities of Foshan (203,000) and Jiangmen (135,000), which attained an urbanization level of 73.8 per cent and 64.7 per cent respectively. At this time, the 'temporary' or 'floating' population was low as both the related official policy and FDI-induced urbanization had only just begun. Based on the registered population, the urban population of the Delta roughly doubled between 1980 and 1993 to 8.66 million. It then further doubled from 1993 to 2003 to 15.35 million (Table 28.6). Such a record of growth over a time-span of 23 years, and over a wide territory of 40,165 sq km, is an astounding experience. Yet these figures do not adequately reveal the actual urbanization process that took place there, as a substantial proportion of the urban population increase was not officially acknowledged. This fact is due mainly to the time lag between the household registration or *hukou* system and the new reform policies. Since 1978, China has instigated the 'household responsibility system' in the countryside, and policies on 'town and village enterprises' (TVE) and on encouraging foreign joint ventures and out-processing. Hence, farmers were allowed much more freedom in farming decisions, and agricultural productivity greatly increased. At the same time, excess rural labour grew and was allowed to move into small towns and cities to take up non-farm employment in privately or collectively run TVEs and in FIEs.

These new developments were buttressed by new administrative measures in 1985 and 1986 that cancelled the earlier rural administrative organization – the Commune – and turned it into the township. In 1983, there were only 38 townships in the Delta, but their number was suddenly increased to 344 in 1986. These new townships differed from the old ones, as most of them administer several smaller villages. As a result, the township population increased from 1.1 to 7.8 million in 1983–6, and the non-agricultural population within them from 1 to 2.4 million. The 1986 administrative measures expanded the jurisdiction of cities to their neighbouring counties, e.g. Jiangmen was extended from 127 sq km to 7,296 sq km. The interplay of these dynamics within the rural parts of the Delta had led to a rapid decline of agriculture in 1978–93. Its share in the rural production fell from 68.4 per cent to 27.8 per cent, and share in rural employment fell from 89.5 per cent to 59.6 per cent. Sit and Yang (1997) alleged that of the 'officially' recognized increase in urban population of the Delta of about 4.2 million in 1980–93, natural growth accounted for only 17.2 per cent, while migration (both local, intra-provincial and inter-provincial) accounted for 50.2 per cent, and boundary change for 31.7 per cent.

Temporary population

Yet the picture of urban growth, or exo-urbanization, in the Delta is not complete if the 'temporary' or 'floating' population is left out. According to the 2000 census, the Delta's

439

Table 28.6. Population change in major PRD areas

	Area (km²)	Population in 10,000 persons												
		1980			1993			2003			2000c			
		P	T	U	P	T	U	P	T	U	Total pop.	P	U
Guangzhou[a]	1,252	303		229	370	91	304	429	189	524	618	416	596
Panyu	1,313	66		13	82	30	40	97		42	163	93	119
Shenzhen	1,983	8		3	88	207	52	151	550	122	701	122	648
Zhuhai[a]	728	13		4	58	33	14	82	42	51	124	75	83
Shunde	805	79		20	98	30	29	112		66	169	108	118
Nanhai	1,151	81		15	100	44	26	107		36	214	108	153
Dongguan	2,465	113		20	139	100	34	159		58	645	154	387
Zhongshan	1,831	101		19	122	77	33	138		59	236	134	143
Rest of Delta	28,637	999		146	999	92	334	1,123		577	1,507	1,242	673
Delta total	40,165	1,763		469	2,056	700	866	2,398		1,535	4,377	2,344	2,920

Notes:
[a] This only includes the urban districts of respective municipalities; for Zhuhai, it includes the whole municipality since 1993. P = permanent or registered population; T = temporary or floating population; U = non-agricultural or urban population.

[b] There was almost no reported temporary population in 1980. In 1982, the figure for the whole Delta was 11,000; the largest number, 8,000, was in Guangzhou. 2000c = 2000 Census, including temporary population.

total population based on registered population was only 23.4 million (Table 28.6). That is to say, the official population figure was only 53.5 per cent of the 'real' population. An analysis of the 3 million temporary population (of which the Delta accounted for 2.8 million) in Guangdong in 1990, which was one sixth of all temporary population netted out by the 1990 census in China, reveals a few interesting points: (1) 73.5 per cent were engaged in the secondary sector and only 17.9 per cent in services; (2) within the Delta, they accounted for 37.5 per cent of the total labour force in the secondary sector and 15 per cent in services; (3) their labour participation rate is 84.7 per cent; (4) of the men, 49.6 per cent were employed in manufacturing and 18.6 per cent in construction; and of the women, 77.1 per cent in manufacturing (in Dongguan 89.6 per cent, Shunde 83.7 per cent); (5) 72 per cent of them had migrated from rural areas.

This *de facto* urban population, though unrecognized by the governments, is estimated to be 12.3 million in 2003, or equal to 72.7 per cent of the 'official' urban population. Thus, researchers such as Shen *et al.* (2002) argued that there have been two streams of urban population growth in the Delta: the 'state-sponsored' and the 'spontaneous', or temporary, population, many of whom worked in TVEs. Figures for 1978–97 for the province of Guangdong indicate that TVE employment increased from 2 to 10 million in the period, and their output value increased from ¥ 4.3 to 608 billion, while 70.4 per cent of its TVEs were concentrated in the Delta. This has led to another alleged urbanization characteristic of the Delta, i.e. it has been due to 'rural-industrialization' (Lin 1997).

As previously stated, the 'temporary' population represents a lag in the household registration system in face of the new economic and migration reforms. A case study by Shen *et al.* (1999) on Shenzhen illustrated that the temporary population is closely controlled by the municipal government under detailed planning and a management system that embraces recruitment, documentation, controls and fee charges. First of all, the intake of migrants is divided into permanent and temporary. Skilled migrants for management and technologist posts may be granted permanent household registration, while unskilled labour for out-processing and other TVE employment would only be given a temporary resident status. A few of the key workers, like foremen, who have been in Shenzhen for some years, may be transferred to a 'blue-stamp' visa. The housing and education needs of the latter and their dependents are included in municipal planning. Besides, the newly accepted in-migrants of permanent resident status have to pay an annual municipal fee of ¥ 10,000 per person. Members of the temporary population are subject to a special regulation. Each is identified by a special temporary 'work permit', and is charged ¥3 00 per year as a management fee. In addition to this, the employment of temporary workers has to be approved by the municipal government. Often, FIE or TVEs approached local autho-rities, who organized the recruitment of temporary labour at their request from outside provinces or remote counties of Guangdong. Thus, although not included in official statis-tical yearbooks of respective local governments, the temporary population is effec-tively controlled and managed by the 'local state'. From such a perspective, the temporary population represents yet another proactive government action for wooing FDI and in furthering local economic growth through plugging in to economic globalization.

If the urban portion of the 'floating' population (as in the 2000 census data) is added to the non-agricultural or urban population, then the Delta had achieved an urbanization level of 66.7 per cent as early as 2000. By such logic, in 2003 it was likely to be an urbanized community with an urbanization level of over 70 per cent. It is estimated that 60 per cent of the actual urban population belonged to the category of temporary population, and the 'omission' indicated by Table 28.6 in the urban population of 2003 is likely to be more than 13.9 million!

From primacy to a matured urban system

In China, urban status is bestowed on to a local area by the central government. With an urban status, the settlement enjoys certain administrative responsibility and economic and judicial privileges. There are four levels of cities in China with corresponding administrative and economic jurisdictions: (1) provincial level, i.e. the centrally administered municipalities (total number: four) such as Beijing and Shanghai, which enjoy provincial administrative power and economic decision rights; (2) ε·' provincial (fifteen in number), e.g. Guangzhou and Shenzhen, which enjoy provincial-level economic rights; (3) prefecture-level, e.g. Zhuhai and Jiangmen, which enjoy sub-provincial economic power; and (4) county-level, e.g. Panyu and Fadu. In 2005, there were two sub-provincial cities, seven prefectural cities and eight county cities in the Delta. Of course, the situation at 2005 is the product of the growth of some earlier rural settlements and townships (Table 28.7) as well as administrative changes, as previously mentioned. In 1978, there were only three cities, i.e. the primate city of Guangzhou and the two small county cities of Foshan and Shunde. The rest of the identifiable urban settlements were townships of less than 200,000 persons (Figure 28.2). By 1984, the number of cities increased to twenty-five and the townships to 392. In 2005, there were seventeen cities and thirty-one city-administered districts. The latter are formerly separate cities or city-administered counties which still possess their individual characteristics as separate urban entities, therefore the actual number of cities was forty-eight.

Based on their 1980 boundaries we have traced the growth and change of the twenty-eight largest settlements in 1980–2000 in Tables 28.6 and 28.7 and in Figure 28.2. As there was almost no temporary population in 1980, and the 2000 census included all the people on the ground, these two figures more closely represent the real situation than the available figures for 1982 and 2003. Population growth in Shenzhen, Dongguan, Nanhai, Shunde and Zhuhai was the most spectacular. As a result of the emergence of these former small cities or townships into millionaire cities, the primacy situation of the Delta has changed towards a rank–size distribution, and the one-city primacy index of Guangzhou dropped from 10.98 to 0.92. In 2000, based on urban population, Guangzhou had been marginally overtaken by Shenzhen as the most populous settlement. The latter had grown from a small settlement of 30,000 into a metropolis of 6.48 million that rivals the two largest metropolises of Guangzhou (5.96 million) and Hong Kong (6.8 million). Therefore, by 2000, a dual-core situation was obvious within the Delta. The rise of Shenzhen and Dongguan also represents the attraction of Hong Kong as the main FDI source and tertiary services support-base in the industrialization drive of the Delta in the final quarter of the last century. Thus the urban change induced by exo-urbanization in the Delta is not just a rapid pace of urbanization, it has also led to a shift from primacy towards the rank-size rule in the urban system structure, and a better spatial spread of urban settlements compared to the data of 1980 (Figure 28.3). Underlying this change is the improved infrastructure of the Delta, particularly of transport, electricity, and telecommunications, which has allowed FDI to spread to a large number of formerly small cities and townships to enhance their growth and urban transformation. The large average annual increases for the extra-large cities and medium cities shown in Table 28.7 for 1980–2000, i.e. 11.89 per cent and 16.37 per cent respectively, correspond well with their increase in number, i.e. from one to seven and from one to thirteen. This indicates that most of the increases of the total urban population in these two categories of cities was due to rapid urban growth of former small settlements.

442

Table 28.7. Change of urban hierarchy in the Delta, 1980–2003

Year	Extra large city (over 1 million)		Large city (0.5–1 million)		Medium city (0.2–0.5 million)		Small city (less than 200,000)		Township[a] (less than 100,000)	
	Number	Urban population	Number	Urban population	Number	Urban population	Number	Urban population	Number	Urban population
1980	1	229 (48.7%)	0	0	1	20 (4.2%)	10[b]	146 (31.1%)	16	75 (16.0%)
1993	1	304 (33.3%)	1	52 (5.7%)	10	297 (32.5%)	13	196 (21.5%)	2	16 (1.8%)
2003	2	551.4 (39.1%)	5	320.1 (22.7%)	12	402.8 (28.6%)	9	135.3 (9.6%)	0	0
2000c	7	2165 (74.1%)	4	271 (9.3%)	13	415 (14.2%)	4	69 (2.4%)	0	0
Annual average increase (%)										
1980–93		2.20		–		23.06		2.29		–11.20
1993–2003		6.14		19.93		3.09		–3.64		–
1980–2000		11.89		–		16.37		–3.68		–

Notes:
[a] Includes only those that became cities after 1984.
[b] Only one of these is a designated city.

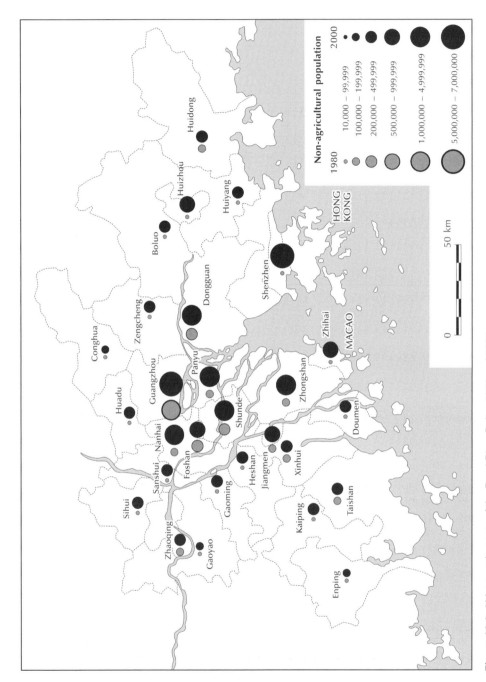

Figure 28.2. Urban settlements of the Pearl River Delta, 1980 and 2000.

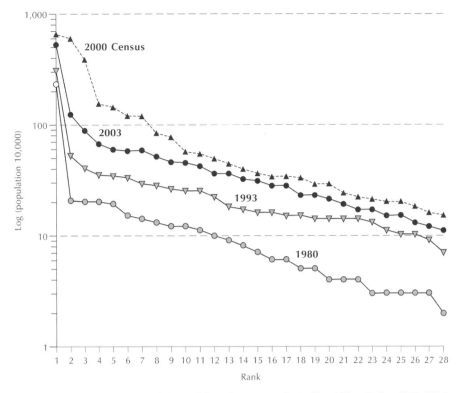

Figure 28.3. Changing rank–size relations of the urban system in the Pearl River Delta, 1980–2003.

Conclusion: is Hong Kong-led exo-urbanization sustainable?

This chapter has charted the inflow of the industrial FDI into the Delta since 1980, driven both by China's spatial-bias towards the coastal areas in the early phase of its Open and Reform, and by the pent-up demand for quantitative and spatial expansion of Hong Kong's successful export-oriented phase-one industries. We need to add further stress on the actions of local governments in the Delta and Guangdong Province, which have not only responded quickly to the new opportunities in formulating and implementing relevant policies and incentives but have also been proactive in improving the local infrastructure. For example, in electricity supply, in the early 1980s the demand of Guangdong exceeded supply by 48 per cent, while by 1996 the supply had exceeded demand. In postal and telecommunications, investments had increased by 680-fold. By 1998, the province registered 9.6 million fixed telephone lines, and 3.63 million mobile phone users. The highways had increased from 12,921 to 27,471 km in 1980–90, and new expressways of 784 km total length were added in 1989–98. The total railway length was doubled to 2,028 km in 1978–98, and new port capacities were added to Guangzhou, Shenzhen and Zhuhai which enabled them to handle large volumes of bulk cargo and modern containers. The close relationship between proactive government planning and construction of infrastructure by utilizing both local and non-local capital is a lesson to be learned by other regions of LDCs wanting to exploit global forces in development. Besides, local governments have been active in improving services,

445

and in attending to providing an adequate supply of labour at reasonable wages and its effective management, to enhance local security and stable shop-floor productivity.

We must also reiterate the importance of geographical and social/ethnic proximity between the Delta and Hong Kong as an important factor for the rapid change there since 1980. These have explained the effectiveness and high productivity of out-processing in the Delta and its hectic expansion from Hong Kong into the Delta. In the process, the Delta and Hong Kong (plus Macau) have also been welded economically into an extended metropolitan region (EMR) (Sit and Cai 2003). The division of labour between the core city – Hong Kong – and the periphery – the Delta – has generated a new urban economic region, or a global city-region, with economic globalization centred on its major international airports and container ports and the financial hub. This provides a lesson for the formulation of development strategies in the growing mega-city regions in East Asia. Besides, it points to the trend of global competition in the form of city-regions around major international trading and logistics infrastructure.

This chapter, however, has not touched on other aspects of rapid change which are of equal consequence of the Delta's integration with the global economy through FDI-induced industrialization. For example, the built-up area of many cities has drastically increased: Guangzhou's built-up area expanded from 72 to 207 sq km in 1980–93. The fastest growth in the period was reported in Shenzhen and Sanshui, which increased by 750 per cent and 710 per cent respectively. Within these major cities, a Western-style central business district (CBD) has appeared in the city core, with skyscraper banking and finance, offices and hotel buildings. There are also concentrated clusters of branches of national and foreign department stores. Correspondingly, the Delta experienced a drop in cultivated land. The acreage moved down from 14.51 million mu (Chinese acre) in 1980 to 9.55 million mu in 2000, i.e. a drop of 34.2 per cent. The issue of sustainability of continued rapid urban growth driven by low-tech and low-value-added industrialization has been raised. Added to these, the huge number of 'second-class' citizens in the temporary population who are spatially and socio-economically distinct and separated from the permanent (or largely local) population posed social problems as well as concerns for the security and stability of the Delta. Environmental aspects, such as noise, air and water pollution and problems of urban solid waste disposal, are other logical areas for concern and have been treated by other authors (Pun 2001; Sun 1996; Lin 2000).

It must also be pointed out that in the quarter-century of growth, experience in industrial activities and the improved infrastructure in the Delta have been made use of in the parallel development of import-substitute production for the domestic market in the China Mainland by local entrepreneurs. Remarkable growth of these 'local' industries in the production of colour TVs, light bulbs, washing machines and air-conditioners, sometimes with important equipment and technology and joint-ventured with multinational corporations (MNCs), have changed the Delta's over-reliance on export-oriented industrialization. Such a development has been dubbed as the 'Shunde model', 'Zhongshan model' and 'Nanhai model', based on the product clusters they have developed and the original ownership structure of the enterprises (Wang 2001). In 2000, the Delta produced 78.8 per cent of China's telephones, 60.2 per cent of its printers, 88 per cent of its electric fans, 80 per cent of its sound systems, 35 per cent of its colour TVs, 37.5 per cent of its air-conditioners, 79 per cent of its rice-cookers, 72 per cent of its microwave ovens, and 56 per cent of its fax machines, and so on (Guangdong Statistical Bureau 2001). Their large demands for raw materials and intermediate inputs have also generated the urge for the deepening of industrialization into iron and steel, oil refining and petro-chemical industries. In the latter development, the primate city Guangzhou has been taking the lead since the mid-1990s. On the eastern flank of the Delta, in Huizhou, the construction of huge plants for these industries is taking place. In short, the Delta is set for a second industrialization with new features of higher technology, higher skill and greater capital intensity, directed to both the foreign and the domestic markets. The rise of modern airports and international sea ports in the Delta, e.g. the new Baiyuan Airport in Guangzhou and modern container terminals in Shenzhen, have started to add pressure on Hong Kong's efficient, though high-cost, services. They underline the possibility of yet another phase of rapid change. Hong Kong's role may not be critical in this new round and its economic specialization vis-à-vis the Delta may not be the same as before.

Further reading

Asian Geographer (1989) Special issue – spatial development in the Pearl River Delta. *Asian Geographer* 8 (1 and 2). Hong Kong: Hong Kong Geographical Association.

Lin, Feng (2000) Towards a sustainable environment in the Pearl River Delta. In J.Y.S. Cheng (ed.) *Guangdong in the Twenty-First Century*, pp. 391–9. Hong Kong: City University of Hong Kong Press.

Shen, J. (2002) Urban and regional development in post-reform China: the case of the Zhujiang Delta. *Progress in Planning* 57, 91–140.

Sit, V.F.S (2001) Globalization, foreign direct investment, and urbanization in developing countries. In S. Yusuf, S. Evenett and W. Wu (eds) *Facets of Globalization: International and Local Dimensions of Development*, pp. 11–46. Washington DC: World Bank.

Sit, V.F.S. and Yang, C. (1997) Foreign-investment-induced exo-urbanization in the Pearl River Delta, China. *Urban Studies* 34, 647–77.

References

Gilbert, A. (1993) Third World cities: the changing national settlement system. *Urban Studies* 30, 721–40.

Guangdong Statistical Bureau (various dates) *Guangdong Statistical Yearbook*. Guangzhou: Guangdong Statistical Bureau. (Available at http://www.tdctrade.com/mktprof).

King, A.D. (1990) *Urbanism, Colonialism, and the World-economy: Cultural and Spatial Foundations of the World Urban System*. London: Routledge.

Lin, G.C.S.(1994) Changing theoretical perspectives on urbanization in Asian developing countries. *Third World Planning Review* 16, 1–23.

——(1997) *Red Capitalism in South China*. Vancouver: University of British Columbia Press.

National Statistical Bureau of China (various dates) *China Statistical Yearbook*. Beijing: National Statistical Bureau.

Pun, Ngai (2001) Cultural construction of labour politics: gender, kinship and ethnicity in a zhen workplace. In C.Y. So, N. Lin and D. Poston (eds) *The Chinese Triangle of Mainland China, Taiwan and Hong Kong: Comparative Institutional Analyses*, pp. 103–16. Westport: Greenwood Press.

Shen, J., Chu, D.K.Y. and Wong, K.Y. (1999) The Shenzhen model: factors of development and future direction of a mainland city near Hong Kong. In S. Ye, C. Gu and Y. Niu (eds) *Studies on the Regional Integration under the Model of 'One Country Two Systems'*. Beijing: Science Press (Chinese text).

Shen, J., Wong, K.Y. and Feng (2002) State-sponsored and spontaneous urbanization in the Pearl River Delta of South China, 1980–98. *Urban Geography* 23, 674–94.

Sit, V.F.S. (1991) Transnational capital flows and urbanization in the Pearl River Delta, China. *Southeast Asian Journal of Social Science* 19, 154–79.

——(1995) Industrial transformation of Hong Kong. In R.Y. Kwok and A.Y. So (eds) *The Hong Kong–Guangdong Link*, pp. 163–86. New York: M.E. Sharpe.

——(1998) Hong Kong's 'transferred' industrialization and industrial geography. *Asian Survey* 38 (9), 880–904.

Sit, V.F.S. and Cai, J.M. (2003) Formation and development strategies of China's extended metropolitan regions. *Geographical Research* 22 (5), 531–40.

Sit, V.F.S. and Yang, C. (1997) Foreign-investment-induced exo-urbanization in the Pearl River Delta, China. *Urban Studies* 34, 647–77.

Sun, D.Z. (1996) Resources, environment and sustainability in development of the Pearl River Delta. *Economy of the Pearl River Delta* 1, 4–6 (Chinese text).

UNCTAD (2005) *World Investment Report, 2005*. New York: UNCTAD.

Wang, J. (2001) *Innovative Space*. Beijing: Beijing University Press (Chinese text).

Yang, Chun (2004) From market-led to institution-based economic integration: the case of the Pearl River Delta and Hong Kong. *Issues and Studies* 40 (2), 79–118.

Zhang, K.H. (2002) What explains China's rising urbanization in the reform era. *Urban Studies* 39 (12), 2301–15.

Zhang, K.H. and Song, S. (2000) Promoting exports: the role of inward FDI in China. *China Economic Review* 11 (4), 385–96.

29

Manufactured places

Howard Gillette

The geographer Wilbur Zelinsky once described Washington DC as 'the first totally synthetic capital city'. Seizing on that description in the mid-1990s, even as the Walt Disney Corporation planned a US history theme park in nearby Manassas, Virginia, a writer for the *New York Times* suggested the entertainment company needn't bother. Washington was already its own theme park, Michael Wines claimed. 'More than any place except perhaps Hollywood, Washington creates its own identity.' Having no history of its own, the American capital had been manufactured out of whole cloth (Wines 1994: 1).

Wines overstated his position, and yet his criticism is suggestive. Not just in Washington either; in a number of places designers have attempted to jump-start totally new communities. This chapter explores how these monumental and planned urban creations have reflected different ideologies, times and places. It charts the historical development of diverse planned settlements in North America and juxtaposes these to the utopian garden-city ideal of Ebenezer Howard. Canberra's democratic classicism is contrasted with the centralist and Stalinist creation of new urban places in the Soviet Union. The imperial motivations underpinning architecture in New Delhi are described. The triumph of modernist style in Chandigarh and Brasilia is introduced and its influence explored in the context of a number of 'new' capitals forged to instil postcolonial identities in Africa. The Western New Towns movement is juxtaposed to the postmodern creation of theme parks and shopping malls evoking notions of hyper-reality.

Convinced that the past has inhibited the good life, better alternatives have been conceived and sought after. Utopian in some instances, authoritarian in others, these places, however short they have fallen of their goals, serve as visible signs of aspiration and ambition. As such, they reveal much about the values of those who would build new monuments to their age.

American dreams

There is a long history of the creation of new places as the means of extending centralized control, reaching as far back as Greek expansion in the eighth century BC, through the Roman Empire and later expansion of European states (Barth 1988). A new phase emerged

449

as a result of New World exploration where all manner of communities developed under the Law of the Indes in South America and according to mercantilist principles in North America. Both systems served the goals of empire and favourable trade balances for European colonizers. It was Washington DC, however, that was conceived especially as a break with past tradition, as both an emblem for a new nation and a new form of government. Rather than drawing from the Versailles where he grew up, as has been suggested by some (Mumford 1961, Dougherty 1974), Pierre Charles L'Enfant invested his 1791 plan for the city the symbolic language of republicanism. The city's broad avenues were arranged not just in geographic terms from north to south but also according to the different states' roles in the nation-building process. Pennsylvania, which had witnessed both the Declaration of Independence and the signing of the Constitution, thus was represented by the city's chief avenue passing from the president's house to the Capitol. Massachusetts and Virginia Avenues gained similar prominence, while Delaware and New Jersey, representing states with key roles in the ratification of the Constitution, gained secondary but visible roles in connecting to the Capitol. At key intersections of the state avenues with the underlying urban gird, L'Enfant envisioned squares where each state would be represented, thus giving pride of place not just to the executive and legislative branches but to the federal system itself (Scott 1991).

For several generations, L'Enfant's overly optimistic belief that a city of multiple focal points, well sited to take advantage of trade to the west, would grow quickly and grandly provoked only derision. It would take several more generations before Washington conceived and executed a monumental core that could adequately represent both its aspirations to world power and its growth among the ranks of major American cities. Today, Washington might be singled out as a place that willed itself to prominence, but it was hardly alone in its aspirations in nineteenth-century America.

America's relatively undeveloped land offered virtually unlimited opportunities to manufacture new towns. As pioneers spread west, no opportunity was lost to envision a new phoenix rising from the wilderness. Cities, not just the lonely frontiersman, were the engines of western expansion, and at key crossroads and tributaries, new communities emerged, virtually overnight. Pittsburgh, Cincinnati, St Louis, Louisville and Lexington led the way. Chicago, Cleveland and Detroit quickly followed, while a number of others that would join their company in the race for regional dominance failed to do much more than get off the drawing board. These 'instant cities,' as Gunther Barth (1988) has labelled them, conveyed in their early years a raw determination not matched by development, but their aspirations for recognition brought about quickly enough the institutions worthy of respect: schools, public buildings and institutions of culture and refinement.

The east witnessed its own version of the manufactured city. During the early years of the republican experiment, many Americans remained wary of urban forms associated with the expansion of Europe's industrial centres. Thomas Jefferson advised his countrymen to leave manufacturing to Europe. He could tolerate the country town on a river that might afford enough power to run a small mill, and even the importation of the power loom from England allowing the congregation of larger numbers of workers did not seem immediately alarming. Then the Boston Manufacturing Company broke entirely new ground when it determined to concentrate investment at the falls of the Merrimack River in what overnight became at Lowell Massachusetts' second largest city. As a result of a shortage of labour, company officials provided housing and other amenities such as planned recreation in the effort to attract women workers from New England farms. Buoyed by the chance to earn wages for a dowry and not bound to stay at work as a permanent proletariat, Lowell's workers appeared to escape the degradation Jefferson had predicted would be their fate (Bender 1975).

The idyllic conditions frequently cited at Lowell proved temporary, however, as growing competition induced owners to cut costs by substituting cheap immigrant labour for farm women, leaving them to provide their own food and board on limited wages. By the end of the Civil War, owners abandoned their paternalism, leaving workers to do the best they could to house their families on meagre wages. Soon conditions were not that much different than those Americans had previously decried in industrialized areas abroad. The ideal of the company town that would blunt the division between capital and labour did not disappear, however. Fearing that cities which concentrated manufacturing workers were inherently combustible, some corporations attempted to manufacture their own communities in rural locations. At Verdergrift, Pennsylvania, the Apollo Steel Company enlisted the famous landscape architect Frederick Law Olmsted to lay out a picturesque village. The corporation advertised the town as the 'workingman's paradise', but it reserved the resulting homes only for skilled workers and professionals, forcing immigrant workers to find alternative locations. One result was the outpost Rising Sun, a rundown area on the other side of the railroad tracks (Crawford 1995: 38, 52).

George Pullman was willing to extend the experiment of worker control further. Believing that both the provision of housing and its supervision would help retain and discipline his work force, Pullman required his workers constructing luxury passenger cars to live in the town he manufactured and named for himself outside Chicago. Placing considerable faith in the uplifting effect of beauty, he hired the architects who had completed work on his own properties to design a compact community built of red brick in Queen Anne style. Homes lining paved streets named after pioneers of the industrial age (Morse, Watt, Whitney, Bessemer, Stephenson and Fulton) included modern conveniences not commonly available to hourly workers, such as gas, water, indoor plumbing, sewerage and regular garbage disposal (Smith 1995: 181). Pullman broke the standard urban grid with monumental structures that served both the town and provided focal points for sociability. He shielded the company's huge industrial buildings at the edge of town with an artificial lake and a park through which a winding drive invited Sunday outings (see Plate 29.1). Described 'as handsome as any wealthy suburban area', the town proved not the ideal place Pullman envisioned despite the unprecedented control he exercised over his employees in private as well as public spaces. When the panic of 1893 induced Pullman to raise rents without adjusting wages, workers struck. A bloody clash with militia called in to terminate the strike killed the prospect of harmony and, with it, Pullman's experiment. By 1898, Pullman had begun to physically dismantle the town he had created (Crawford 1995: 38–9, 43).

The decentralized Garden City

A quite different motivation lay behind a contemporary effort to create garden cities in England. The chief figure in the movement was Ebenezer Howard, a stenographer and civil servant whose contact with American utopian reformers Henry George and Edward Bellamy helped motivate him to envision cooperative communities as alternatives to the greed and inequalities he associated with unregulated industrialism. Wary of the authoritarian powers that Howard believed would follow from Bellamy's centralized national state, he concluded that the best hope for founding a cooperative civilization lay in small, decentralized communities. To visualize the challenge, he conceived the image of three magnets. The town magnet historically had drawn residents through the promise of employment, but had burdened workers with high prices and terrible living conditions. The country's obvious amenities of

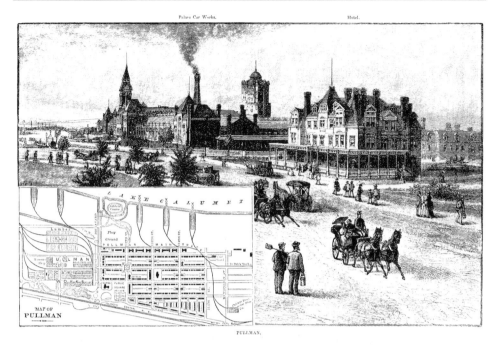

Plate 29.1. Pullman, from Richard T. Ely, 'Pullman: a social study', *Harper's Magazine* 70 (February 1885), 452–66, from the website organized by John Reps, http://www.library.cornell.edu/Reps/Docs/pullman.htm.

health and beauty were countered by backwardness. The task for the planner, then, was to create the new town–country magnet as a community that would offer high wages, low rents, the beauty of nature, bright homes and gardens, and freedom and cooperation. In Howard's words, 'all the advantages of the most energetic and active town life, with all the beauty and delight of the country' (Fishman 1977: 50).

Central to Howard's goal of obtaining desirable social ends was the creation of a completely planned environment. He called his approach to community organization 'social individualism', suggesting a good deal of flexibility for the evolution of personal relations. Overall, however, every detail of his ideal spelled cooperation, and in its physical details the Garden City revealed an unwavering commitment to substituting communitarian for previously competitive values. Absolute symmetry dominated the design of his ideal community. No household would be privileged under this arrangement. Each was assured access to adequate space for living, enhanced both by abundance of light and a small garden as well as easy access to the open space represented by the continuous greenbelt surrounding the town. Such housing arrangements, buttressed by centrally located common facilities – a museum, library, theatre, concert hall and hospital – seemed to assure easy mixing among residents and thus provided the civic underpinnings for the larger commitment to the common good. In line with his commitment to small communities, Howard set a fixed limit of 32,000 people living on 1,000 acres of land surrounded by a greenbelt (see Plate 29.2). As the first demonstration town filled up, he theorized, a new one would spontaneously sprout up nearby. Over time, a planned amalgamation would form, with each Garden City offering a range of jobs and services, but each connected to the others by rail. This larger Social City, as he called it, constituted the true Third Magnet as he originally envisioned it (Hall 1996: 93).

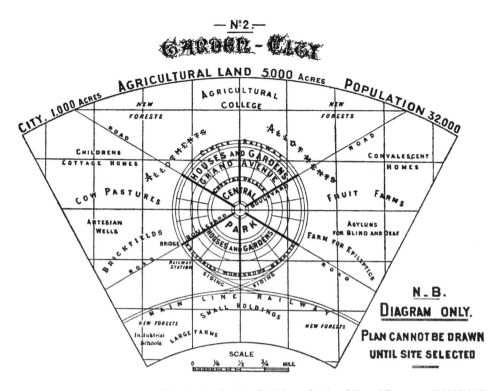

Plate 29.2. Ebezener Howard, 'Plan for the Garden City', from *Garden Cities of Tomorrow* (1902/1946), London: Faber and Faber.

Howard was disappointed not to secure the financial backing he expected from the working class. Finding he had to rely on businessmen for the investment necessary to bring his ideas to fruition, some of the more radical social thinking behind his effort was modified. In the hands of architects Raymond Unwin and Barry Parker the first Garden City built, Letchworth, dispensed with Howard's rigid geometric form of town planning. The physical elements of the new town, located 35 miles north of London, retained, however, the same self-conscious effort to enhance community functions through design. Unwin's proposal to organize the new city cooperatively around 'quadrangles' of homes in which three sides would be devoted to private apartments and the fourth to a common dining room, recreation room and nursery, never materialized, the victim of financial restraints (Fishman 1977: 70–1). Other elements spelling cooperation remained, however, not just in common access to open space but in the location of a symmetrical group of municipal and cultural buildings strategically located along a mile-long axis leading to the railway station. Although the town grew more slowly from its origin in 1904 than anticipated, by 1910 the practicality of Howard's vision had been realized. As Robert Fishman reports:

> The new town of Letchworth was a clean, healthy, and well-planned environment; it had shown its capacity to attract industry and residents; and the First Garden City Ltd., though still financially pressed, was beginning to reap the rewards of its investment and declare its first dividend.
>
> (Fishman 1977: 75)

453

For more than a decade Howard sought to start a second Garden City, settling finally in 1919 on a 2,400-acre site some 20 miles outside London at what would become Welwyn Garden City. Intended for 38,000 people, the town's development lagged both in population, which reached only 13,500 by 1938, and in attracting industry. Despite such disappointments, the town nonetheless gained the central elements of the Garden City scheme: a civic centre organized as a semicircle flanked by parkland, a separate industrial area with working-class housing adjacent, and a commercial centre formed as a grid divided by a broad avenue, Howardsgate, passing from the future site of the railway station to another broad avenue, the Parkway. Although the town offered no immediate innovation, it still appealed to planners, especially in the United States, as a superior alternative to unplanned suburban growth (Buder 1990: 126–7).

The Garden City ideal found adherents on both sides of the Atlantic, but the immediate direction of manufactured communities followed more the paternalist direction suggested in George Pullman's company town than the cooperative commonwealth envisioned by Howard. Here Washington DC's potential as a relatively clean slate played an important role in providing direction for the new century.

Critics of urban development looked not just to workers' poor conditions, but to the congestion that followed from unplanned development. The wholly manufactured creation of the Chicago World's Fair of 1893 – popularly referred to as the White City – established a vision for a planned urban environment that contrasted vividly with current conditions as both beautiful and efficient. Under the direction of architect Daniel Burnham, a corpus of buildings was carefully sited for displays around a grand lagoon. No less socially progressive critics than Henry Demerest Lloyd and William Dean Howells declared the fair a model for the ideal city. Burnham tried to convince the Chicago Commercial Club to fund permanent improvements at Lake Michigan's shorefront, even as the temporary buildings at the fair grounds were being dismantled. The depression of 1893 discouraged such investment, however, and it was not until 1900, when Congress named him to a commission formed to commemorate the national capital's centennial, that Burnham found a patron for his grand schemes. Aware of America's entry on to the world stage in the aftermath of the Spanish–American war, the commission sought to give the city a physical presence that could finally compare it favourably to other world capitals. By creating a uniform and monumental presence at the city's core, the Burnham plan elevated the visual presence of federal power and projected an identity 'worthy of the nation' in a time of national expansion (Gillette 1995). It would take a quarter-century to fully complete the new vision for Washington, but the power of this 'City Beautiful' plan had immediate effect elsewhere in the world, in such widely divergent places as Australia, Russia and India.

Antipodean democratic classicism

Canberra emerged as a result of an international competition to design a capital for the new Commonwealth of Australia formed in 1901 as a federation of six previously independent colonies. Struck as many reformers in England and America were with the chaotic development of cities, the Congress formed to conduct the competition was determined to create an ideal city of grand public buildings, homogeneous townscapes, distinguished residences, noble boulevards, parks and parkways. The winning entry, in 1912, from Chicago landscape architect Walter Burley Griffin in collaboration with his wife Helen, was heavily influenced by the City Beautiful movement closely associated with Burnham, especially the 1893

Columbian Exposition, which Walter had visited as a teenager, and Burnham's 1909 plan for Chicago. Plans for residential areas followed Garden City principles with the creation of picturesque neighbourhoods. The core of their proposal, however, consisted of a formal group of uniformly scaled buildings set around a water court having a 'connected park or garden frontage ... as in the case of the Mall at Washington' (Freestone 2000: 40). This 'parliamentary triangle' was cited on a series of terraces, with government buildings organized in a horizontal order and vertical hierarchy culminating with the Capitol. Serving as a ceremonial and archival centre rather than the actual seat of government, the Capitol nonetheless stood symbolically as the emblem of Australian achievements (Irving 1981: 86). Described by Walter Griffin as analogous to a theatre visible from the north central district of the city, the arrangement of public buildings, like Washington, was to be built on parallel lines in order that 'they will work together into one simple pattern into which the other groups must merge subordinately to maintain the fundamental simplicity' (Griffin 1955). Griffin's plan responded effectively to informed Australian opinion that the design should utilize advances in the science of town planning pioneered in England to capture 'the majesty of the powers' which the nation was seeking to embody symbolically in its new capital (Griffin 1911). The Federal Capital Advisory Commission responsible for implementing the vision remained cautious in pursuing its implementation, however, and when it put the plan on hold in 1921, Griffin abandoned years of effort to see it effected. His legacy in Canberra today is limited to the axial geometry of the central parliamentary triangle (Freestone 2000: 42).

Imperial power

The vocabulary of architecture could contain imperial as well as republican implications, even through the same style. In Russia, as in Australia, the Garden City ideal had to compete with revivalist interest in classicism and monumentality. A Society of Garden Cities formed in 1913, made up largely of professionals drawn from the capital at Petrograd, and several experiments in planned country communities followed (Starr 1976). With the Bolshevik revolution of 1917 and the shift of the capital to Moscow, however, other values predominated. Under the socialist regime, central, not dispersed, cities ruled as Moscow was designated the proper model for the nation. After a period of utopian experimentation, in 1935 the state made official its preference by issuing a plan to centralize industry in Moscow, expanding the city's boundaries from 111 to 219 square miles in order to accommodate worker housing. Although the plan incorporated a 6-mile greenbelt intended to contain future growth and conceived each district as a self-contained neighbourhood unit, the very emphasis on centralization made the realization of such Garden City-inspired goals difficult to realize. Even as wide avenues fashioned in baroque style radiated from the pseudo-classical administrative buildings located near the Kremlin, the state found it difficult either to limit population or to adequately service residential needs. Neighbourhoods originally intended to stabilize at between 5,000 and 12,000 people housed in three-storey structures gave way to much larger concentrations in nine-storey buildings. Service activities such as schools and recreational facilities designed to serve each district were overwhelmed. Instead of exemplifying the balance between work and residence, the state and its citizens, then, the Moscow of the Stalinist era was sharply divided between grand bureaucratic edifices and modern but crowded and poorly served residential quarters (Frolic 1975).

Over time the Russian experience demonstrated that the same architectural vocabulary could embrace imperial as well as republican implications. If classicism in Washington and

Canberra harked back to ancient democracies, in India the same idiom could be relied on to convey the power associated with empire. Such was the case when King George V declared, in a visit in 1912, that the capital of the British Raj would move from Calcutta to the more central and historically strategic former capital of Delhi. Left for years in a state of decay, Delhi's transformation, as a British planning journal affirmed in 1913, was intended 'to captivate the imagination of the Indians with the glories of architectural display'. Clearly influenced by the Washington plan of 1901, the proposal for New Delhi formed around a central axis running from the acropolis on the heights of Raisina to the ancient capital of Indapat, symbolizing, as the planning report suggested, 'the keystone of the rule of the Empire over India'. A cross radial joined the new Anglican cathedral on the south and the railway station in the north. The huge Viceregal House and the Secretariat buildings, designed by the planners Edward Luytens and Herbert Baker respectively, dominated the processional way. As the chief influence on the plan, Luytens was deeply versed in the Garden City and City Beautiful traditions. Despite a nod to the former, it was Beaux Arts formalism that dominated, offering, as Robert Irving writes, 'to British eyes, a symbolic contrast with the heterogeneous confusion and narrow, twisted byways of the existing city' (Irving 1981: 89). The British *Town Planning Review*, while considering the scheme 'boldly conceived', complained that 'the enthusiasm of the authors for the attainment of fine architectural effects precluded planners from giving much study to the problems of the individual and to the growth of the city as an organization of social units' (*Town Planning Review* 1913). Indeed, even as the arrangement of residential areas conformed to complicated formulas of race, rank and status, they failed to embrace the amenities associated with the Garden City movement (Hall 1996: 187–8).

Le Corbusier and the modern aesthetic

The British Empire spawned a number of manufactured cities, each determined, as in New Delhi, both to impress natives with the physical presence of grand government buildings and, through them, to direct affairs as the home country dictated. By the 1930s, the British had found in the plan for the Punjab at Chandigarh a new model, this time imported from France in the vision of Le Corbusier. Born Charles-Edouard Jeanneret, the French proponent of modernism for the machine age placed unwavering confidence in architecture's capacity to redefine each social function if applied properly. In this spirit he conceived new units of habitation as the means to transform society, by forming collective associations and personal habits to replace those individualized patterns he considered destructive. Instead of just office space, then, he located huge collective apartment buildings, known as unités, at the city's core. Each unit assured residents the necessary minimum for existence, while functions traditionally found in the home were centralized for collective use. The exceedingly high concentration of population left plenty of land for parks and recreation outdoors. Inside the apartment complexes considerable space was devoted to communal services, including dining and laundry services. Everything was uniform and standardized, according to what Le Corbusier considered the ideal city for the Machine Age

Le Corbusier never realized his ideal for Paris, and Chandigarh was poised at the outset to pursue quite a different plan modelled along the lines set by Barry and Unwin in the British Garden Cities. When Le Corbusier was asked to give expression to the plan, however, he changed its spirit entirely, directing it away from the solution of local problems and towards a preoccupation with visual form, symbolism, imagery and aesthetics (Hall 1996: 214).

Although use of the automobile was limited, wide avenues such as those envisioned for Paris dominated the plan. Government buildings, as was the tradition of the British Raj, gained prominence, but in ways only Le Corbusier could have envisioned (see Plate 29.3). Dominating the whole, despite Le Corbusier's bow to egalitarian residential patterns, was a 220-acre enclave, 'an acropolis of monuments', separated from the city by a canal and a wide approach boulevard that assured the capital complex visual as well as political dominance (Vale 1992: 109).

Le Corbusier's influence extended to one other manufactured city, Brasilia. Although he did not plan the new Brazilian capital himself, Le Corbusier's ideas lived on through the Congres Internationaux d'Architecture Moderne (CIAM), which adapted his belief that the proper plan could deliver workers from the 'tragic denaturing of human labour' produced in and by the cities of industrialized society (Holston 1989: 41). Although Brazil had long considered a new capital in the interior, it was not until the mid-1950s that President Juccelino Kubit-schek de Oliveira committed the government to carry out the plan. Significantly, he sought not just to relieve the congested port capital of Rio de Janeiro, but to use the new capital to transform the nation's social structure. Building on a theory of development promoted throughout Latin America during the 1950s that state-directed industrialization was the means by which underdeveloped countries could achieve rapid economic growth, Kubit-schek believed Brasilia would become a 'pole of development' for the nation, 'a stone cast to create waves of progress' (Holston 1989: 18).

Such bold ambitions were not immediately evident in the winning plan offered by architect Lucio Costa in 1957. Merely sketched on five medium-sized cards, Costa's proposal provided no economic analysis or land-use projections. His concept of a monumental axis for prin-cipal public buildings crossed by a huge central traffic spine lined with uniform residential

Plate 29.3. Le Corbusier and Chandigarh 1950.
Source: Federation Le Corbusier, available at http://www.fondationlecorbusier.asso.fr/urbchan.htm

457

apartments along lines suggested by Le Corbusier's 1933 *La Ville radieuse* plan for Paris was nonetheless praised for its grandeur. And, given reign to build an entirely new city, Costa and the city's principal architect, Oscar Niemeyer, set about the task of social reconstruction in ways that exceeded even Le Corbusier's utopian vision. In line with the aspiration for modernity, Niemeyer cast the government complex grouped along a grand mall in the emergent International Style. Affirming the equal status of each branch of government, he gave the legislative branch equal pride of place with the president in Plaza of Three Powers, although in reality it was the chief executive who held real power. Other elements in the plan were also idealized, not least the central residential district, which was planned in a sequence of superblocks, each marked by buildings of uniform height flanking the motor axis. Determined to eliminate historically manifest differences of social class, the architects standardized every living unit, making them equally accessible to public services. As James Holston puts it, 'As an attempt to preclude the stratified distribution of rights to the city associated with capitalism, the Master Plan's most encompassing intention [was] to create the foundations of an egalitarian urban organization' (Holston 1989: 79–80). Despite its egalitarian spirit, the new city was no more adept than the authoritarian Chandigarh in incorporating native poor into the new city. During construction, a squatter town emerged. Authorities tried to disperse it but, that failing, provided minimal streets and services. By the mid-1960s, as much as a third of the new capital's population was living in this 'sub-habitation' area. Ultimately, the two areas were forced to coexist, the sanitized home of bureaucrats visibly reminded of the past the new capital was supposed to extinguish in the nearby collection of sordid structures known officially as Taguatinga. Rising prices in the preferred government sector forced even the lower ranks of civil servants to locate in satellite cities (Vale 1992: 120).

Despite the considerable accomplishment of its completion in record time, Brasilia remained controversial for what it promised, not just for what it represented. The sociologist Gilberto Freyre has objected that the city, in eschewing the wellsprings of indigenous culture, stands as a monumental abstraction more compatible with the 'ingenuous bourgeois of the United States and the simplistic dictators of the Soviet Union'. Architectural historian Norma Evenson dissents, comparing modern Brazil's aspirations to the work of thirteen bankrupt former British colonies establishing a capital 'so grandiose in its outlines as to provoke derisive comment for at least fifty years after its founding' (Evenson 1973: 211). If the building of cities, she asserts:

> has been bound to power and ambition, to waste and extravagance and symbols of worldly vanity, it has also embodied the highest and most enduring ideals of collective life. As our urban inheritance reminds us of the lives and hopes and follies of our ancestors, so Brasilia takes its place as a visible witness to the flawed, aspiring human spirit.
>
> (Evenson 1973: 213)

Uniting the new nations

Brasilia is not the only manufactured modern capital. From the experiments of Chandigarh, Lawrence Vale reports (1992), a number of successors followed, two of which deserve attention for the ways in which aspirations for using physical design as a means of advancing national unity achieved mixed results. In Nigeria, the decision to create the new capital of Abuja in the interior as a replacement for the port city of Lagos was intended to overcome intense ethnic rivalries. Claiming to represent Nigerian tradition, the plan of 1979 none-theless reflected many of the elements of Washington DC. Government buildings lining a mall overtly copied from Washington suggested, as in the United States, equal branches of government through the creation of the 'Three Arms Zone', each branch given equal pro-minence in the whole. Like Washington, the government complex was set apart from resi-dential quarters, both physically and in its contrasting monumental proportions. Although this overtly postcolonial capital determined to assert the equality of its peoples, separate road systems carrying government workers to civic structures while workers made their way to industry by a separate inner highway cemented social differences, all rhetoric to the contrary.

In Tanzania, a similar effort to assert unity through a new inland capital carried with it socialist values not present at Abuja. Conscious of the dominance of agriculture in the country, the master plan for Dodoma published in 1976 avoided monumental government structures, privileging instead residences vested with the physical amenities as well as egalitarian values associated with Garden City tradition. Although plans called for a mall, neither it nor its associated government structures were intended to be monumental. While some prominent government structures ultimately found elevated locations and began to assume monumental proportions, they did so in violation of stated expectations. The result, though different in appearance from other manufactured capitals, was a similarly mixed message, confirming that even the most consistent ideals cannot always be translated into physical form (see Plate 29.4).

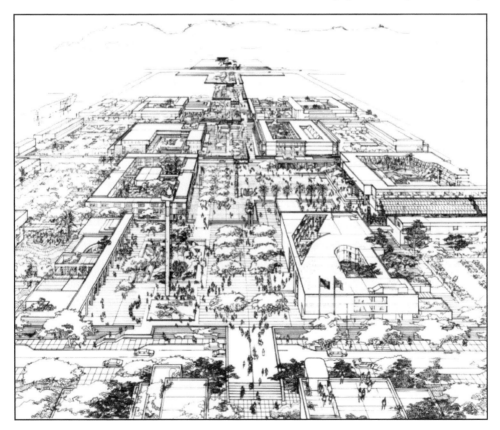

Plate 29.4. Dodoma master plan.
Source: http://www.jamesrossant.com/dodoma.html

The re-birth of the model city

Even as the Corbusian model gained some credence worldwide, the alternative vision of the Garden City remained, both with the construction of new model cities in England and in experimental efforts to propagate Howard's egalitarian vision in America. There, primary promoters of the Garden City ideal were a small group of architects and critics, which formed under the pretentious name of the Regional Planning Association of America (RPAA) in the early 1920s. Building on the short-lived model of towns constructed to produce ships during the First World War, RPAA members Henry Wright and Clarence Stein experimented first in Queens at Sunnyside Gardens and subsequently on open land at Fairlawn, New Jersey, 16 miles from New York City, in the effort to construct housing that was economically accessible to working people as well as designed to enhance community spirit. In Sunnyside Gardens, the architects concentrated 1,200 family units on 75 acres in such a fashion along the outside of superblocks extending twice the normal length of standard divisions so that open space at the interior could be reserved for common use. Houses fronted the common courtyards, but each had a private garden in the rear. Three-and-a-half acres was further set aside as a recreational park (Christensen 1986: 58–9). At Radburn, where they had the advantage of working on open land, the architects turned the homes away from the street towards open land, to assure both the healthy effects of nature and access to common space. Although the town lacked the protective greenbelt Howard had insisted on in the Garden City plan, the open square became, in the eyes of Stein and Wright, a foundation of the community, both by supporting recreation and by providing a common meeting ground (Christensen 1986: 68). The careful separation of pedestrian from motorized traffic added to the town's amenity and established the importance, as Stein put it, as a 'town for the motor age' (Stein 1957: 41, 46).

The Depression prevented Radburn from becoming, as had been hoped, a self-sufficient city. The ideal was recovered, however, in the New Deal's Resettlement Administration's New Towns programme. Directed by the progressive economist on leave from Columbia University, Rexford Tugwell, there were to be as many as 100 planned new towns, decentralized so as to take advantage of rural amenities while at the same time sufficiently supported to create nearby work. Conservative antagonism to the 'socialistic' aspects of new town communitarism limited construction, however, to only three such new cities. All were relatively small and lacking in the employment opportunities that could have made them self-sufficient (Arnold 1971). The use of principles drawn from the Garden City ideal, notably the integration of recreational and open space with housing design and the central location of common facilities, remained to inspire another generation of new town development.

The widest use of the Garden City idea took hold in Europe after the war, where governments used the idea to rebuild and decentralize older urban centres. Seeking to rationalize old patterns of development, planners embraced the use of specialized zones of housing, work, recreation and civic functions. In concert with prevailing fashion, they adopted the modernist architectural idiom, typified by the British new towns of Runcorn and Harlow and Tapiola in Finland (Bloom 2001: 20).

By contrast, in the United States government avoided the business of building new cities itself. The largest building experiments created in the post-Second World War era fell to private developers, and these efforts took three directions. The revival of the new town movement at Reston, Virginia, and at Columbia, Maryland, not far from the 1930s new town of Greenbelt, attracted considerable public attention, but they were the exception. Initially, the greatest breakthrough came from Arthur Levitt, who pioneered the use of mass production to produce affordable housing with sufficient amenities to satisfy a consumer-conscious middle class. On Long Island and in underdeveloped areas of Pennsylvania and New Jersey, he created three virtually instant communities. Started in 1947, the first Levittown, on Long Island, reached 60,000 by 1950, the largest community built by a single developer to date (Christensen 1986: 96). Specialized labour, prefabricated parts, tight schedules and identical house plans kept costs down. Although the third project, in New Jersey, offered several choices of design for the first time, the efficiencies of scale remained. Like the Greenbelt towns before them, Levitt's communities offered some strategically located community facilities grouped around 'Village Greens', including neighbourhood shops, a playground and a swimming pool. They never aspired to be economically self-sufficient and, as such, remained commuter suburbs, albeit built at an unprecedented scale. Despite the uniformity of construction that begged for caricature, such instant communities proved satisfactory to the great majority of new owners (Gans 1967). As alternatives to crowded cities, these homes, many occupied by the first in their families to become owners, appeared ideal for the primary domestic business of the 1950s, raising a family.

Almost coincidentally, another form of manufactured city appeared directed at the other end of the life cycle. In 1960, the first in a new cycle of retirement communities opened at Sun City, Arizona. Built around a golf course that with its green grass assured prospective buyers the community would stand out from the surrounding desert, the town reached a population of 45,000 concentrated on 9,000 acres by 1980. Offering a superior environment and plentiful cultural amenities for a leisure-oriented lifestyle, Sun City set off a boom in age-segregated communities. Tightly controlled by corporate rules for behaviour as well as design, such communities were bolstered by studies that claimed the elderly benefited from a protective environment that was both isolated from surrounding areas and fully predictable (Findlay 1992: 160, 171).

Reston, just a short drive from downtown Washington, was intended to be 'America's first full-scale satellite city'. Developed under the direction of Robert E. Simon with backing of the Gulf Oil Corporation, the new town encompassed seven villages, each with a projected population of 10,000. With densely built corridors of townhouses and a compact town centre located on the border of a lake, Reston was intended as an alternative both to cities and to the ugliness associated with contemporary suburban subdivisions. Not entirely immune to European trends, the town centre embraced a modernist aesthetic. Neighbour-hoods following more closely the lead of Radburn, where Simon's father had played a role in development, replaced individual yards and alleys with landscaped common spaces behind houses as part of an effort to enhance a sense of local community. Simon added a new twist to the concept of residential living, arguing that each neighbourhood should embrace a particular leisure activity. Queen Anne village, as the first to be developed, was to become a sailing and fishing town, its town centre modelled after the Italian fishing village of Portofino. Hunters Woods was to adopt appropriate equestrian recreational facilities and signage (Bloom 2001). While the purity of Simon's ideas were compromised over time, they nonetheless introduced the importance of theming to constructing and marketing new communities.

Simon took the unusual step of hiring a group of social scientists to evaluate and act upon preferences drawn from surveys of potential buyers. In Columbia, launched two years after Reston in 1963, mortgage banker and shopping centre developer James Rouse went even further in using experts to advise him how to design a city for modern living. The results were equally conscious plans for neighbourhoods designed along Garden City lines, each with its own primary school, localized commercial establishments and community meeting places. Appropriately enough, a regional shopping centre was located at the new town's core, confirming Rouse's belief that such places offered necessary opportunities for social and civic as well as commercial exchange. In a further commitment to relieve the concentration of minorities in nearby Baltimore, Rouse embraced an open housing stance not yet tried in other new towns and one that was only partially successful (Gillette 1999).

Magic kingdoms

Some reports have credited Disneyland, which Rouse described in 1963 as 'the greatest piece of urban design in the United States today', as a key influence in his effort to manufacture a new city (Findlay 1992: 53; see also Gindroz 2002: 3) In fact, as John Findley argues, Disney's 'Magic Kingdom' was highly influential among designers who despaired about the ill-effects of traffic and congestion in cities and suburbs alike. Disneyland, which opened for business in rural Orange County, California, in 1955, was no less an artificial creation than previous worlds fairs, which had themselves become models for urban visionaries (Sorkin 1992: 210). But as a completely planned environment that artfully directed millions through its attractions daily, it appeared to be everything nearby Los Angeles and the modern city was not. High standards of cleanliness compared well with urban disorder. Efficient monorail service contrasted with the delays associated with congested freeways. Enforced standards of politeness for the staff eclipsed negative standards of service found elsewhere.

Disneyland harkened back to an earlier, imagined time when everything appeared to be in its place. As suburban sprawl became ever more evident and standards for design permissive, it was virtually predictable that someone would generate alternative standards for places to live and not just to visit. Indeed, it was a slide presentation of a consumer study presented in a Disney office building in the late 1980s that alerted Miami-based architect Andres Duany to the possibilities of linking the values of security and responsibility associated with the 1950s to the individual freedoms and personal choice favoured by the 'Me Generation' of the 1970s (Ross 1999: 27). Using the term 'neotraditional' to describe their style, Duany and his wife, Elizabeth Plater-Zyberk, designed a small resort community on the Florida panhandle, which they christened Seaside. Intended to embody qualities of the small, pre-Second World War town, Seaside featured strategically located public buildings and civic spaces, convenient walking accommodations, homes built on small lots in order to encourage neighbourliness, and an effort to minimize the effect of parked cars by eliminating street-fronting lots. Like their Garden City predecessors, Seaside's creators believed, as one reporter put it, that architecture could induce neighbourliness and that 'social change can be brought about through architecture and planning' (Boxer 1998). Bolstered by the praise that came their way, Duany and Plater-Zyberk launched a movement, dubbed the New Urbanism, which applied similar principles to inner-city reconstruction as well as to new suburban development. The charter for the Congress for New Urbanism, issued in 1996, reiterated the goals manifest at Seaside, asserting, 'We recognize that physical solutions by themselves will not solve social and economic problems, but neither can economic vitality, community stability, and environmental health be sustained without a coherent and supportive physical framework' (Calthorpe and Fulton 2001: 282).

The Disney Corporation offered its own contribution to the new urbanism movement by building the neo-traditional community Celebration on excess land carved out from its Disney World holdings in Orlando, Florida. Disney officials met with Dunay and with

Rouse in the planning process, but the commission went to New York architect and neo-traditional enthusiast Robert A.M. Stern. Many of the same principles pioneered in Seaside were adopted in Celebration, with the exception that Disney protected the town with a 4,700-acre greenbelt and commissioned a number of well-known architects for individual civic and commercial buildings, with an overall effect of greater eclecticism than uniformity of design (Franz and Collins 1999).

Such idealized environments as Celebration have been criticized, like Disney's own theme parks, for being too sanitized. Shorn of the vital elements that make urban places interesting through the clash of visual as well as cultural experiences, they appear as manufactured as the movie sets introduced at Seaside for the shooting of *The Truman Show*, a film based on the premise that nothing actually happens in the world. 'Disney invokes an urbanism without producing a city,' the architectural critic Michael Sorkin asserts. 'Disneyzone . . . is a cartoon utopia, an urbanism for the electronic age. Like television it is a machine for the continuous transformation of what exists (a panoply of images drawn from life) into what doesn't (an ever-increasing number of weird juxtapositions)' (1992: 231–2). (See Plate 29.5.)

What Disney invented, others could build on. Themed environments could appear anywhere in a modern era dominated by what Christine Boyer calls the 'age of spectacle', marked by 'odd juxtapositions', multiple images, preserved fragments of the past, and per-vasive commodification (Boyer 1994: 47). The West Edmonton Mall in Alberta, Canada, the largest facility of its kind at 5.2 million square feet when it opened in 1986, combined ele-ments of amusement park, shopping centre, office park and heritage destination (Crawford 1992). It has been joined in ambition if not quite in size by Golden Resources Mall in

Plate 29.5. Walt Disney World, The Magic Kingdom.

northwestern Beijing, which at 3.7 million square feet represents the equivalent of six foot-ball fields. Besides being the world's largest office building, Golden Resources reproduced within its confines the ambiance of some of the world's great cities and tourist destinations, including Paris, with a re-creation of the Champs-Elysees and a full-size reproduction of the Arc de Triomphe, and Venice, complete with gondola rides through a maze of canals. In Dongguan, the new South China Mall includes a 1.3-mile artificial river lined with districts modelled on seven great water cities of the world (Barboza 2005). Such extravagance in manufacturing places represents only a part of a rising tide of fantasy constructions in the Asia-Pacific rim (Hannigan 1998: 175–86). See Chapter 62 for further discussion around these palaces of contemporary consumption.

Conclusions

From Washington DC around the world, few constraints hold back the imagination in visioning places where elements of the physical environment will advance broad social goals, be they authoritarian or liberating. While many such places have been manufactured over time, singular objectives have been difficult to achieve. The world's messy reality has a way of interfering with even the grandest of plans. That said, in places as far removed from one another as Abuja and Pullman, Chandigarh and Disneyland, real monuments have been constructed to express these visions. Fragmented as the results may seem to later generations, the message remains how important it has been for people to manufacture places that reflect but also constitute ideals in their own right.

Further reading

Creese, W.L. (1966) *The Search for Environment: The Garden City: Before and After.* New Haven: Yale University Press.

Hall, P. (1996) *Cities of Tomorrow: An Intellectual History of Urban Planning and Design in the Twentieth Century.* Oxford: Blackwell.

Hall, P. and Ward, C. (1998) *Sociable Cities: The Legacy of Ebenezer Howard.* New York: Wiley.

Parsons, K.C. and Schuyler, D. (eds) (2002) *From Garden City to Green City: The Legacy of Ebenezer Howard.* Baltimore: Johns Hopkins University Press.

Talin, E. (2005) *New Urbanism and American Planning: The Conflict of Cultures.* London: Routledge.

Williams, R.J. (2005) Modernist civic space and the case of Brasilia. *Journal of Urban History* 32 (1), 120–37.

References

Arnold, J. (1971) *The New Deal in the Suburbs, 1935–1954.* Columbus: Ohio State University Press.

Barboza, D. (2005) China, new land of shoppers, builds malls on gigantic scale. *The New York Times,* 25 May.

Barth, G. (1988) *Instant Cities: Urbanization and the Rise of San Francisco and Denver,* revised edition. Albuquerque: University of New Mexico Press.

Bender, T. (1975) *Towards an Urban Vision: Ideas and Institutions in 19th Century America.* Baltimore: Johns Hopkins University Press.

Bloom, N.D. (2001) *Suburban Alchemy: 1960s New Towns and the Transformation of the American Dream.* Columbus: Ohio State University Press.

Boxer, S. (1998) A remedy for the rootlessness of modern suburban life? *The New York Times*, 1 August.

Boyer, M.C. (1994) *City of Collective Memory: Its Historical Imagery and Architectural Entertainments*. Cambridge, MA: MIT Press.

Buder, S. (1990) *Visionaries and Planners: The Garden City Movement and the Modern Community*. New York: Oxford University Press.

Calthorpe, P. and Fulton, W. (2001) *The Regional City: Planning for the End of Sprawl*. Washington DC: Island Press.

Christensen, C. (1986) *The American Garden City and the New Towns Movement*. Ann Arbor: UMI Press.

Crawford, M. (1992) The world in a shopping mall. In M. Sorkin (ed.) *Variations on a Theme Park*, pp. 3–30. New York: Hill and Wang.

——(1995) *Building the Workingman's Paradise: The Design of American Company Towns*. London: Verso.

Dougherty, J.P. (1974) Baroque and picturesque motifs in L'Enfant's design for the federal capital. *American Quarterly* 26 (March), 23–36.

Evenson, N. (1973) *Two Brazilian Capitals: Architecture and Urbanism in Rio de Janeiro and Brasilia*. New Haven: Yale University Press.

Findlay, J.M. (1992) *Magic Lands: Western Cityscapes and American Culture After 1940*. Berkeley: University of California Press.

Fishman, R. (1977) *Urban Utopias in the Twentieth Century: Ebenezer Howard, Frank Lloyd Wright, Le Corbusier*. New York: Basic Books.

Franz, D and Collins, C. (1999) *Celebration, U.S.A.: Living in Disney's Brave New Town*. New York: Henry Holt.

Freestone, R. (2000) From city improvement to the city beautiful. In S. Hamnett and R. Freestone (eds) *The Australian Metropolis*, pp. 27–45. New York: Routledge.

Frolic, B.M. (1975) Moscow: the Socialist alternative. In H.W. Eldredge (ed.) *World Capitals: Toward Guided Urbanization*, pp. 295–339. Garden City, NY: Anchor Press.

Gans, H. (1967) *The Levittowners: Ways of Life and Politics in a New Suburban Community*. New York: Random House.

Gillette, H. Jr (1995) *Between Justice and Beauty: Race, Planning, and the Failure of Urban Policy in Washington, D.C.* Baltimore: Johns Hopkins University Press.

——(1999) Assessing James Rouse's role in American city planning. *APA Journal* 65, 150–67.

Gindroz, R. (2002) New urbanism and smart growth: city life and new urbanism. *Fordham Urban Law Journal* 29, 1419–37.

Griffin, J.G. (1911) The city beautiful: Australia's supreme opportunity. *Sydney Morning Herald*, 30 December (Available at http://www.library.cornell.edu/Reps/Docs/grif_jg.htm).

Griffin, W.B. (1955) *Commonwealth of Australia, Report from the Senate Select Committee Appointed to Inquire and Report upon the Development of Canberra*. September, Appendix B, 93–10 (Available at http://www.library.cornell.edu/Reeps/Docs/griffin.htm).

Hall, P. (1996) *Cities of Tomorrow*. Oxford: Blackwell.

Hannigan, J. (1998) *Fantasy City: Pleasure and Profit in the Postmodern Metropolis*. London: Routledge.

Holston, J. (1989) *The Modernist City: An Anthropological Critique of Brasilia*. Chicago: University of Chicago Press.

Irving, R.G. (1981) *Indian Summer: Lutyens, Baker and Imperial Delhi*. New Haven: Yale University Press.

Mumford, L. (1961) *The City in History: Its Origins, Its Transformations, and Its Prospects*. New York: Harcourt, Brace and World.

Ross, A. (1999) *The Celebration Chronicles: Life, Liberty, and the Pursuit of Property Value in Disney's New Town*. New York: Ballantine.

Scott, P (1991) 'This vast empire': the iconography of the mall, 1791–1848. In R. Longstreth (ed.) *The Mall in Washington, 1791–1991*, pp. 36–58. Washington DC: National Gallery of Art.

Smith, C. (1995) *Urban Disorder and the Shape of Belief: The Great Chicago Fire, the Haymarket Bomb, and the Model Town of Pullman*. Chicago: University of Chicago Press.

Sorkin, M. (1992) See you in Disneyland. In M. Sorkin (ed.) *Variations on a Theme Park*, pp. 205–32. New York: Hill and Wang.

465

Starr, F.S. (1976) The revival and schism of urban planning in twentieth-century Russia. In M.F. Hamm (ed.) *The City in Russian History*, pp. 222–42. Lexington, KY: University Press of Kentucky.

Stein, C. (1957) *Towards New Towns for America*. Cambridge, MA: MIT Press.

Town Planning Review (1913) http://www.library.cornell.edu/Reps/DOCS/newdel_1.htm (originally published in *Town Planning Review* 4 (October) 185–7).

Vale, L. (1992) *Architecture, Power, and National Identity*. New Haven: Yale University Press.

Wines, M. (1994) Step up, folks! Check it out! Nationhood! *New York Times*, 29 May, 1.

30

Regenerating places

The contemporary British city – sweet centre, sour surround

Brian Robson

Cities are dynamic. Their built fabric may give an impression of permanence, but it is regularly remade. Building cycles redirect capital as money is made from construction and renovation. Fashion also dictates changing land uses: a warehouse in the 1950s, derelict by the late 1970s, converted into offices or loft living in the 1990s. The waterfront as unwanted backyard morphs into a series of desirable vistas for the new millennium. People create different and constantly changing social spaces in the new quartered cities. The actors directing change themselves change over time as contexts alter. New agencies and new ways of governing the city shape different futures. New people move into the city, new kinds of livelihood are made, new household structures, new services, new kinds of employment. New, new, new: an endless wheel of change.

Cities in the developed world are in constant flux, and the regeneration process is now accepted as an orthodoxy of the urban condition across Western Europe and North America. In popular culture the word stands as a label for a whole industry. In the UK the *Guardian* advertises regeneration jobs in its Wednesday supplements. Regeneration has been the new thing, ever since the Thatcherite neo-liberal experiment developed into more interventionist management of our cities.

This chapter addresses the changes that regeneration brings to places, by focusing upon evidence from British cities. It charts the processes that have led to this urban renaissance and explains why the change has taken place, indicating how the movers and shakers have been able to alter the city. The new kinds of people living in regenerated areas are then considered, and juxtaposed with the very real problems being experienced in adjacent inner-city areas that continue to be some of the most deprived in the UK. The successes and failures of the urban policy framework are described, and the chapter concludes with some of the challenges our cities face in the future.

A sort of urban renaissance

We used to think of the big cities of Britain as places with problems – collapsing industries, high unemployment, high crime rates, poor housing, dirty streets, poor people, low educational performance, poor health. Many of these problems remain, but during the last decade we have begun to see big cities in a very different light – as places with potential as well as problems. Over the period of the last 20 years, it has become ever clearer that our big industrial cities were not in the process of complete collapse but rather, slowly, often painfully, they were reinventing themselves to meet the very different circumstances of a post-industrial world. Like the curate's egg, they are now very good in parts. Their central areas in particular have become wealthier, cleaner and more successful; and this is helping the cities to attract new investment and new residents.

There is ample evidence of this turn-around in the fortunes of big cities in Britain. The economic renaissance of cities can be seen in the patterns of Gross Value Added (GVA; which measures the generation of wealth and is the most widely used measure of economic prosperity). Table 30.1 shows that, for the three northern regions where a large number of the ex-industrial cities lie, there is a contrast between the core cities and their surrounding regions, both in the level of GVA and its rate of growth. In all cases, it is now the core cities that have the faster growth rates and often the higher levels of per capita GVA. For the North West, the fastest growth has been in Manchester and Liverpool; for Yorkshire and Humber, in York, Leeds and Sheffield; and for the North East, in Newcastle (i.e. Tyneside) and Sunderland. Of course, across Britain as a whole there remains a huge gap between the per capita levels of GVA in London and the South East, and in the rest of the country. However, the fact that per capita levels and, more especially, the growth in those levels have been higher in the main cities than elsewhere in the respective region suggests that the cities must now be recognized as the drivers of their sub-regional economies (Office of the Deputy Prime Minister 2004c; 2006b). Strong cities may not be a *sufficient* condition for regional prosperity, but they are *necessary* condition. This significant change is a reflection of the growth of the new knowledge economy and the advantage that big cities have in capitalizing on their new economic potential in the post-industrial world where services and business rely increasingly on good information and on informal contacts.

There is also evidence of a renaissance in terms of population change. While, overall, most of the big cities are still net exporters of people, they have now begun to attract significant numbers of residents to live in their central areas (Champion and Fisher 2004). Liverpool, for example, lost 75,000 people overall between 1981 and 2001, but since 1991 its central area has grown from 10,000 to 15,000 residents. This pattern is true to varying degrees of most of the big cities. The population census data show that in 1991 there were hardly any people living within a half-mile radius of the centres of such places as Birmingham, Leeds or Manchester. By 2001 this had changed significantly. For example, Central Ward in Manchester had 11,689 people, Central Ward in Liverpool had 8,648, Ouseburn Ward in Newcastle had 7,791.

There is also much evidence of new construction and new investment in city centres. The 'crane index' provides a testament to the new investment in these places. Look at the skylines and count the cranes (Plate 30.1). New housing, new offices, new leisure and entertainment facilities have multiplied in the centres of most of the big cities. And many of the old warehouse and office premises have been converted into new residential spaces with lofts, flats and apartments alongside new purpose-built housing. This growth of residential accommodation is perhaps the most dramatic aspect of the transformation of city centres. Sites alongside water have proved an irresistible lure for developers, so that now there are new residential complexes fronting the lines of old canals and waterways which earlier had been used for industry. Good examples include the dock complex on the Mersey in Liverpool, where the Albert Dock has been converted into a mix of shopping, museums and housing;

or the canal complex of the Brindley Basin in Birmingham, which has shops, bars and housing within the shadow of a major convention centre; or Canon's Wharf and Narrow Quay in Bristol alongside the Floating Dock, where there is a mix of art galleries like the Arnolfini, of offices and hotels and of apartments. Where water frontages have not existed they have often been newly created or existing ones have been extended to provide an environmental incentive for new residential development: for example, Liverpool is proposing to extend the Leeds and Liverpool canal to parallel the line of the Mersey and provide a new locational incentive for investment.

Such developments are well illustrated in Manchester (Peck and Ward 2002; Taylor 1996). The process started in the later 1980s in Castlefield (an area of canals at the heart of the site

Table 30.1. Areas[a] ranked by percentage change in per capita GVA, 1995–2001

	GVA: £ per capita 2001	% change 1995–2001
NORTH WEST		
Greater Manchester South	**17,015**	**50.6**
Liverpool	**13,317**	**44.4**
Wirral	8,611	34.4
Halton and Warrington	16,022	34.0
East Merseyside	9,165	28.9
Sefton	9,315	28.8
Lancashire	12,534	28.0
Blackpool	10,626	27.5
Cheshire	15,694	26.1
Greater Manchester North	10,361	18.5
Blackburn and Darwen	12,103	17.1
West Cumbria	10,776	13.8
East Cumbria	11,385	9.0
YORKSHIRE and HUMBER		
York	**16,833**	**38.9**
Leeds	**16,904**	**38.5**
Sheffield	**12,634**	**33.0**
Calderdale, Kirklees and Wakefield	11,815	28.4
Barnsley, Doncaster and Rotherham	9,270	28.4
Kingston upon Hull	13,143	27.9
Bradford	11,895	27.8
North Yorkshire	11,822	25.3
North and North East Lincolnshire	13,413	18.0
East Riding of Yorkshire	9,549	6.1
NORTH EAST		
Tyneside	**12,539**	**32.5**
Sunderland	**11,215**	**27.5**
South Teesside	10,114	17.9
Hartlepool and Stockton-on-Tees	12,295	17.0
Darlington	12,831	16.8
Durham County	9,285	15.3
Northumberland	8,722	6.6

Notes:

[a] The areas are the smallest ones used for European statistics (so-called NUTS3 regions) which are not always identical to local authority districts.

Source: Office of National Statistics.

of the city's old Roman settlement), stimulated by public resources through regeneration finance provided by the Central Manchester Urban Development Corporation (CMDC) which was established in 1988 (Deas *et al.* 2000). Old warehouses began to be converted to flats and lofts and some new dwellings were constructed; and new restaurants and offices for small businesses in the creative and cultural industries began to appear (Plate 30.2). By the end of CMDC's life in 1996, residential development was being undertaken entirely with private investment. The market had begun to take off. Subsequently, new residential development spread further afield, into the Northern Quarter (which had hitherto been badly neglected, but now has a mass of small cultural and creative industries as well as flats and apartments) and later across the whole central area and its fringes, so that now there are of the order of 15,000 residents living in the centre (Nathan and Urwin 2006). Between 1991 and 2004 over 7,000 flats and over 1,000 student bed-spaces were built in the city centre and there are a further 7,000 proposed residential units in the planning pipeline. Most of the developers involved at the outset were small local businesses. They had the advantage of being more knowledgeable about the area, more innovative in their designs and less risk-averse than the national volume house builders.

One such early local pioneer, Urban Splash, started with warehouse conversions in Manchester and has since become a nationally known company and has expanded its activities across the country. It is now involved in residential developments in Liverpool, in converting the gigantic Lister Mills in Bradford into flats, and redeveloping the local authority Park Hill flats in Sheffield. In Manchester it is currently involved in innovatively reconfiguring old terraced streets in Salford to convert them into larger dwellings more suited to modern family life, and in the development of the Millennium Village of New Islington which is being constructed around a new waterway that links the two existing canals to Oldham and to Rochdale. New Islington is an especially interesting development which reflects the growing maturity and confidence associated with inner-city residential development in some of the big cities. Originally a small area of post-war local-authority housing which had become unpopular, had lost many of its residents and suffered severe problems of crime and anti-social

Plate 30.1. Cranes rebuilding Manchester. Photograph by Nick Scarle.

Plate 30.2. Cultural industries in the new city: Rain Bar, Manchester. Photograph by Nick Scarle.

behaviour, it is being converted into what is marketed as a 'vibrant waterside community' with aggressively modern designs grouped around five fingers of waterways. The existing residents were offered new housing on the site – and a role in its design – and other developments are aimed at attracting a mix of new residents. The hope is that, unlike most centre-city housing, it may attract families; and a new health centre is being incorporated into the development as part of this aim. Across the city as a whole, now that city living has been well established, volume national housebuilders are an important element of the new developments being built. The sheer volume of development has had the interesting effect of changing the nature of the marketing of city-centre property. In the early stages this was very much a question of persuading potential residents of the benefits of city-centre living. Now it is more a question of enticing buyers on the basis of the quality or the innovativeness of the design of individual properties. Competition has encouraged the use of high-profile architects and designers, whilst developers and estate agents make much of attracting well-known purchasers like football players or television stars, or incorporating 'unique' features such as an emphasis on the 'green' credentials of a building (Tallon 2003).

The change makers

What have been the main processes that have helped to bring about this dramatic transition in city centres? There have been a number of obvious prompts. First is the sectoral change in the economy. The cities' traditional manufacturing industrial base has contracted whilst the service economy and 'smart' research-driven business has risen. This has transformed the role

471

of the ex-industrial cities (Amin *et al.* 2000). Previously their rationale was based on housing a large workforce and capitalizing on good transport links to assemble raw materials and to export finished products. Now their rationale is to provide information-rich environments that can offer businesses access to the range of knowledge that is vital to maintain their competitiveness. The size, density and heterogeneity of big cities have come into their own as locational advantages in the new knowledge economy. Their size and density mean that they can offer numerous informal social networks that provide a lubricant for the exchange of ideas, of information and business links that are vital for boosting the competitiveness of firms and ensuring that their products are sensitive to the requirements of the market. Much of the growth in the base of cities has been linked to the expansion of producer services, like legal and financial services, and of high value-added manufacturing in fields such as bio-technology. For all such businesses knowledge, information and dense informal contacts are vital ingredients. The concentration of universities and researchers in all the big cities is clearly important in this respect. And the same principle of size and diversity applies to the retail and leisure sectors. Cities offer opportunity-rich environments that present people with a wide choice of shopping and entertainment: a range of shops, niche bars, restaurants, theatres, clubs, concert halls and the like (O'Connor and Wynne 1996; Jayne 2005). Each of these concomitants of size and diversity can be thought of as 'agglomeration economies' which can give big cities a competitive edge in a consumption-oriented society. The consequence has been that cities now offer much more attractive locations for the new economic activities on which post-industrial economies depend. They play new key economic roles. And with that has come a new emphasis on highly paid professional jobs.

Second, the physical environment of cities has improved. The collapse of manufacturing industry has helped to make cities more attractive as places in which to live. Their environment is no longer polluted to the same degree by smoke and smog or the noise associated with heavy industry. Just as there is a 'crane index' of construction, so there is also an environmental 'shirt-collar index'. Fifty years ago the high level of particulates in the air of big cities generated the 'smogs' of London and other big cities and meant that shirts were dirty before the end of a day. Now there is little difference between town and country. The dirty urban environments of industrial cities had pushed those who could afford to do so to move to cleaner suburban and semi-rural locations. Today that is less the case. And equally for firms: service businesses, research-based establishments and 'modern' industries look for pleasant environments as one important element in their locational decisions.

Third, these economic and environmental changes have been allied with some dramatic changes in demography and in life styles. Social and demographic processes have clearly helped to fuel the striking growth in central-city living in provincial cities. People now live much longer; thereby increasing the numbers of elderly households whose children have moved away from home. And because they can enjoy many more years as small elderly households, this increases the incentive for the parents to move to smaller houses. Parents have also delayed the age at which they have their first child, hence boosting the number of small pre-child households. Divorce rates have increased – there were fewer than 100,000 in Great Britain in 1950, but since 1970 this number doubled to almost 200,000 by 2003 – hence increasing the numbers of small households in those cases where the divorcees do not re-marry (Holmans 2002).

The demographic effects of such changes can be seen by looking at the trends in the composition of households. Table 30.2 shows that over the last fifty years the percentage of one-person households increased by almost three times, and two-people households grew by one-quarter. Conversely, those with three or more people all fell. Table 30.3 then gives an

Table 30.2. Household size in Great Britain

Household size	Percentages					
	1951	1961	1971	1981	1991	2001
1 person	11	12	18	22	27	29
2 people	28	30	32	32	34	35
3 people	25	23	19	17	16	16
4 people	19	19	17	18	16	14
5 and more	18	16	14	11	7	7

Source: *Social Trends.*

Table 30.3. Household composition in Great Britain

	Percentage of households			
	1971	1981	1991	2001
One-person household				
Under pensionable age	6	8	11	14
Over pensionable age	12	14	16	15
One family				
No children	27	26	28	29
Dependent children	35	31	25	23
Non-dependent children	8	8	8	6
Lone-parent family				
Dependent children	3	5	6	7
Non-dependent children	4	4	4	3
Two or more unrelated adults	4	5	3	3
Multi-family household	1	1	1	1

Source: *Social Trends.*

indication of the make-up of households over the last thirty years. The significant growth in one-person households has overwhelmingly been a result of the doubling in the proportion of small younger households (although those of pensionable age also increased substantially). At the same time, lone-parent households have more than doubled. In contrast, the most significant decrease has been in families with dependent children which fell from over one-third to less than one-quarter.

Finally, Table 30.4 looks at the age and gender of one-person households. The biggest increase has been amongst people aged 25–44 where, both for males and females, the proportions doubled. There is a much larger percentage of males in this age group living alone than of females; conversely, for the pensionable households it is females who comprise the largest proportion of one-person households.

The other major change has been the growth of students in higher education. Table 30.5 shows the scale of this transformation. There has been an inexorable growth in numbers, with more than a doubling over the last thirty years. The rate of increase has been especially marked amongst full-time students, who are the most critical group in terms of local housing market since a larger proportion of full-time students live away from home than is the case for part-time students, and they therefore represent a more significant market for housing.

All of these demographic trends mean that there is now a much larger proportion of one-person and small households for whom central-city living can potentially be an attractive

Table 30.4. People living alone in Great Britain

	Percentages			
	Male		Female	
Age	**1986/7**	**2003/4**	**1986/7**	**2003/4**
16–24	4	6	3	3
25–44	7	15	4	8
45–64	8	14	13	15
65–74	17	19	38	34
75 and over	24	29	61	60

Source: *Social Trends.*

Table 30.5. Students in higher education

	Numbers in thousands			
	1970/71	**1980/81**	**1990/91**	**2002/03**
Full time	241	277	345	534
Part time	127	176	193	261
	Percentage change			
		70/71 to 80/81	**80/81 to 90/91**	**90/91 to 02/03**
Full time		14.9	24.5	54.8
Part time		38.6	9.7	35.2

Source: *Social Trends.*

option. And this has been further reinforced by changes in life styles. The increasing affluence of those in work – and especially those in professional jobs – has fuelled the growth of a consumer society and given people the resources to indulge their preferences in shopping and in entertainment and leisure activities. City-centre living can be seen as a response to the trend for city residents to express a sense of play, of sociability and of hedonism. How you dress, what clubs you frequent, what music you listen to, what restaurants you eat at, how you decorate your apartment, what social circles you move in, all become key talismans of who you are. To this extent, life styles have partly replaced occupation as a signifier of social standing. City centres – with the easy access they offer to the profusion of clubs, bars, clothing shops and the like – enable young people to indulge their tastes, or those of their peers, and this has been an important prompt to city living.

And there is a further reinforcement to central-city living through the increase in the employment of women in the labour force. Between 1984 and 2004, the rate of employment for men stayed the same (rising from 78 per cent to only 79 per cent) whereas that for women increased significantly; from 59 per cent to 70 per cent. For two-income households, where both the male and female partner are in work, there is therefore an additional incentive to live close to the (often central-city) locations of their workplaces since, were they to live in suburban locations, the cost and time of travel to work would be doubled where there are two earners.

One further important prompt to this growth in city-centre living has been the planning policy context that has been set by government. Its aim to increase the proportion of new development on 'brownfield' rather than 'greenfield' sites – with a target that now stands at

70 per cent – and its associated target to increase the density of development have both had the effect of encouraging developers to build in urban areas and to build smaller houses and flats (Rogers and Power 2000). Between 2001 and 2005, the number of flats as a proportion of all dwellings built each year increased from 20 to 41 per cent.

The major cities – Birmingham, Bristol, Leeds, Liverpool, Manchester, Newcastle, Nottingham, Sheffield – each now have substantial and growing numbers of residents living in flats and apartments in the central areas. This has been a real sea-change of the last two decades. Previously, amongst the large cities, it was only in London that such households were found.

Who lives in the city centres?

Some recent studies of city-centre living can give an indication of the people who have fuelled these changes. The most recent study has looked at Liverpool, Manchester and Dundee and provides a helpful insight into the nature of this central-city housing market and why people choose to live centrally (Nathan and Urwin 2006).

Not surprisingly, most of the central-city residents are young and single. Almost two-thirds of Manchester's city-centre residents are aged 18–34, and three-quarters are single. Over 40 per cent are students, but one-fifth are affluent professionals such as accountants and lawyers. There are also significant but much lower numbers of small elderly households, most of whom are retired. There are few if any families with children. In Liverpool the figures are similar, but there is a higher percentage of students (almost one-half), a lower percentage of young professionals and a larger proportion of low-income households.

In most of the big cities, about half of residents own and half rent their property. Many of the new and refurbished dwellings are therefore buy-to-let, bought by investors with an eye both to rentals and to rising prices. The disproportionate numbers of renters reflect not only the fact that many of the residents are young and lack the resources to buy property outright, but also that the nature of the job market is now very different than was once the case. At one time a new graduate could expect to stay in a company throughout his or her career. Now they have to be much more flexible. There is much greater movement from one company to another or from one career to another. New employees can expect multiple changes of job and hence often numerous changes of workplace throughout their working lives. The flexibility that renting offers, therefore, becomes a more attractive option, at least at the outset of their careers.

The incentives for choosing to live in the centre are those one might expect: proximity to jobs, shopping, restaurants, clubs, bars and entertainment, and the general 'buzz' of the city centre (Allen and Blandy 2004; Crouch 2005; Seo 2002). Almost all those in employment work in the city centre and many walk to work. The involvement of students is clearly an important part of the market. City leaders have seen the provision of city-centre housing as one of the ways in which they can retain their student populations after they graduate, and many students opt to live and work in the city centres where previously they had rented student accommodation – some, indeed, starting or joining small businesses in the cultural and creative industries in big cities (O'Connor and Wynne 1996). The city centre has thus become something of a conveyor belt, acting as a locational springboard for early employment.

There is, of course, a downside to this. Most of the households are highly mobile. In Manchester, one-third move in and out each year and, even allowing for their age structure, city-centre residents are more mobile than the national figures (Nathan and Urwin 2006). Most residents say that they intend to leave when they have children; and, in practice, almost all do leave once they start families. City centres lack the kinds of facilities that families look for – space, good schools, health facilities, security. These are clearly all disincentives associated with the decision to locate centrally.

The implication is that the continued buoyancy of city-centre living depends on there being a sufficient supply of new young residents to replace those who move out. The jury is still out on whether there is an increasing over-provision of flats and apartments. Recent evidence suggests that some of the earlier flats are proving difficult to sell and that a ceiling may have been reached in terms of the growth of resident numbers. Nevertheless, city-centre living in the big provincial cities is clearly now an established part of urban life. This is less the case with smaller places. The Dundee example (Nathan and Urwin 2006) suggests how reliant smaller places are on the student market for city-centre living. In Dundee, no fewer than 62 per cent of city-centre residents are students. Parents buy houses for their offspring and the buy-to-let market has grown substantially. Further, the city's universities are extending halls of residence and going into partnership with private developers to build housing both for students and non-students. Smaller cities have little in the way of other realistic potential markets for city-centre residents. They are smaller and more compact and they offer a less rich variety of entertainments and goods and services, so the incentives for central living for the 'ordinary' household are not so compelling as in the big cities.

While these changes have transformed the centres of our big cities, many of the areas just outside the centres have continued to suffer from the familiar problems of social and economic deprivation. To this extent, social exclusion has been exacerbated by the growth of city-centre living. Unlike the case in areas of London like Islington, city-centre colonization has not been a process of 'gentrification'. That term should be restricted to changes which involve the direct displacement of poorer residents by more affluent in-comers (despite the broader arguments about flows of capital by writers such as Smith 1996). It is usually linked with the refurbishment of old but potentially attractive housing which has fallen into disrepair or is lived in by poorer households. In contrast, so far, city-centre living in the provincial cities has involved the conversion of warehouses and offices or of new building, none of which have entailed the displacement of existing residents. The only element of gentrification that could be argued is that city centres have increasingly been commandeered by those with money to spend and life styles that are student-oriented or young-professional-oriented, and to this extent can alienate or deter poorer households and lead to the replacement of 'traditional' high street shops and services with 'trendy' premises targeted at a very different clientele.

Moving beyond the centre

Gentrification may be linked with one of the interesting challenges that the provincial cities now face: whether their inner suburbs – the areas cheek-by-jowl with city centres and which are often characterized by all the problems of deprivation – can be reconfigured to make them attractive locations for more socially mixed households with families. This would offer scope to retain the new inner-city residents once they start families. It would entail providing more attractive residential environments, new larger housing, better schools, safer contexts for children, improved public services and more public open space. Current government policies have begun to address such challenges. Theirs is but another link in the chain of urban policies which have been undertaken by successive government administrations for thirty years (Robson *et al.* 2000). There have been – and still are – many fine words addressed to the perceived problems of cities; many initiatives have been tried and discarded; financial stimuli has been introduced, but usually with strings of a particularly knotty variety. By 2000 the government tried to draw together the welter of policies and policy instruments directed at cities, with a formal White Paper on the future of towns and cities in 2000 (Department of the Environment, Transport and the Regions 2000b). Currently, there are two major policy thrusts: the Sustainable Communities Plan (Office of the Deputy Prime Minister 2003a), and the National Strategy for Neighbourhood Renewal (Social Exclusion Unit 2001).

The Sustainable Communities Plan addresses the regional disparities in the 'north' and 'south' of England. The much higher level of economic prosperity in the south has created markedly different housing markets in the two parts of the country. On the one hand, in most of the northern cities there are neighbourhoods which suffer from low demand for housing as people have abandoned unpopular areas and left whole streets empty or virtually unsaleable (Nevin *et al.* 2001). On the other hand, in London and the wider South East there are huge pressures on the housing market and difficulties of affordability for many households on medium or low incomes. The government's response has been, first, to create the Housing Market Renewal Programme (HMR) in nine 'pathfinder' areas which suffer from low housing demand. These areas are partly linked to a broader strategy for a 'growth corridor' in northern England (Office of the Deputy Prime Minister 2004b). Its aim is to create more mixed tenure structures in the low-demand areas and to improve the housing stock more generally. This will entail the refurbishment and demolition of some existing houses and the addition of newly built housing. However, as the market for housing is essentially a derived demand, the programme is also concerned with strengthening local economies, improving schooling and the environment and all the range of other aspects that create a healthy local demand. The second element of the plan aims to establish four growth zones in the South East – of which the Thames Gateway is the largest – in which new housing and new jobs will be created to cater for the pressures in the region, thereby necessitating significant investment in new infrastructure such as roads, railways, water supply and the like (Office of the Deputy Prime Minister 2003b). There are some curious anomalies in this conjuncture of strategies. The HMR programme should help to turn around the prospects of poor neighbourhoods in the big northern cities (and in the process aim to create mixed neighbourhoods which may entail displacement effects), but its success will depend on there being buoyant local economies in the provincial cities in order to attract and retain professional households. Yet the public investment in the infrastructure of the southern growth zones will inevitably provide incentives for developers and businesses to invest in southern locations at the expense of the big provincial conurbations and thereby denude the economic buoyancy of the provincial cities which they need in order to attract and retain city-centre and other residents.

The National Strategy for Neighbourhood Renewal has at its heart the aspiration to ensure that within ten to twenty years no-one is seriously disadvantaged by where they live (Social Exclusion Unit 2001). This implies both absolute improvements in employment, skill levels, crime, health, housing and the environment within the disadvantaged areas, and also relative improvements so as to narrow the gap between the most deprived areas and the rest of the country. The government has created a new administrative body – the Neighbourhood Renewal Unit (situated within the Office of the Deputy Prime Minister, ODPM) – to oversee the programme. The specific funding programmes that address neighbourhood problems include:

- the Neighbourhood Renewal Fund, which is allocated as top-up resources to 88 of the most deprived local authorities and allocated through Local Strategic Partnerships, which are bodies established in each of the local authorities and drawn from public, private and voluntary organizations;
- 39 New Deal for Communities programmes, which focus on defined neighbourhoods across the country;
- the Skills and Knowledge Programme established to improve the supply of learning opportunities and provide incentives for bottom-up action in renewal areas;
- the Safer, Stronger Communities Fund, which drew together three earlier funding streams – Neighbourhood Wardens, who were created to tackle anti-social behaviour in local areas; the Neighbourhood Management Pathfinders, which provide a model for local-area management in 35 neighbourhoods; and the Single Community Fund, which aims to develop social cohesion through community activity.

Currently, ODPM is developing a 'New Deal for Cities', which focuses on some 56 towns and cities and looks to them to propose imaginative ways of building on their potential and strengths. The clear implication is that urban issues remain to the fore of the policy agenda.

So what?

What does all this frenetic activity add up to? The cynic can say that, despite 30 years of urban policy, even though there have been dramatic changes in the centres of our big cities the deprived areas remain pretty much as deprived as ever they were. The government's own index of deprivation suggests that between the earliest index in 1991 and the most recent in 2004, the same places and the same neighbourhoods lie at the very worst end of the spectrum of deprivation (DoE 1995; DETR 2000a; ODPM 2004a; Maclennan 2000). However, there is no doubt that regeneration policy has learned much from its 30-year history. Government policy has incorporated much more appropriate fundamental principles: programmes are now of much longer duration, reflecting the deep-seated nature of deprivation; they generally recognize the importance of addressing the range of interrelated policy domains and put more emphasis on the significance of co-ordinating the work of different spending departments; they give much greater weight to the involvement of local communities, accepting that local ownership of programmes and local input into determining priorities are critical in maximizing the long-term success of policy intervention; and they embody the principle of partnership working across the public and private sectors. Each of these aims is difficult to achieve, and none has yet been mastered fully: for example, much of the community involvement sometimes smacks of tokenism; and there are still questions about the horizontal links across different central and local government spending departments. Nevertheless, ever since the advent of City Challenge in the early 1990s, urban policy has undoubtedly continued to make significant strides and has had beneficial impacts on the overall fortunes of cities and of their poorer neighbourhoods.

There are, of course, major challenges still to surmount. Amongst them, two are especially relevant to the theme of this chapter.

First is the challenge of linking poor neighbourhoods to the more prosperous areas of the city more broadly. The growing polarization between poor and affluent areas, which is most starkly reflected in the buzz of the city centres and the deprivation of areas just outside the centres, has remained a continuing difficulty despite the best efforts of policy. The aim of creating genuinely mixed communities seems well intentioned but undoubtedly difficult to achieve.

Related to this is a second challenge of better linking policy at the successive spatial scales of neighbourhood, city, region and nation (see Chapters 18–24 for a more detailed consideration of scale). Here, the absence of a meaningful policy for city regions is one of the gaps in current policy. Many of the things that would improve the economic competitiveness of cities, and would potentially help to link the fortunes of poorer and more affluent areas within them, are essentially issues best tackled at a scale that is larger than local authority districts but smaller than regions. Planning for improved transport provision and accessibility is one example; developing strategies for the supply-chains of businesses is another; linking university research to local business is a third; linking housing provision to the job market is another; so too is developing strategies for major cultural events like concerts. Many of the strategic decisions affecting the lives of city residents are effectively ones that impinge on the wider footfall that cities imprint well beyond their formal administrative boundaries. As commuting has grown and the 'reach' of cities has increased, so an increasing number of us now live 'city-region' lives – working in one district, living in another, shopping in a third, going to a theatre in a fourth (Office of the Deputy Prime Minister 2006a).

Finally, if we were to succeed in creating fully prosperous big cities, we would still be left with awkward questions about the whole new settlement system that is being created across the country as a response to post-industrial changes. The most challenging questions face the fates of smaller more specialized urban communities, not least the medium-sized towns that were based on single industries and the seaside towns that were equally reliant on one principal source of prosperity that has now largely evaporated. The cotton towns of Lancashire (places like Burnley, Oldham, Blackburn) or the mining towns and villages of Nottinghamshire have clearly lost their original rationale and cannot offer the variety of locational advantages that could help them re-create themselves in the way that has been possible for the major cities. Their future roles may be more as residential tributaries to the major centres than as post-industrial employment centres – and for this they clearly face major challenges in creating attractive residential environments. For places such as this, inner-city living is not a realistic stimulus for regeneration since they are too small to offer the appropriate incentives and too unattractive as potential residential environments. The seaside towns face similar challenges – some (and again it is the larger ones such as Blackpool) may find a new rationale through mega-casinos, but others again need to develop as dormitory towns. In both cases this reinforces the arguments about the importance of planning within the context of city regions, since jobs and growth seem likely to continue to grow in the big core cities and the challenge for strategy is to develop better links across the broader housing and labour markets on which the city cores develop.

The renaissance of our big cities is one of the key changes of the last few decades; and one greatly to be welcomed. The post-industrial economic context has breathed new life into the major provincial cities. But the process is as yet patchy. Buzzing city centres sit cheek-by-jowl with deprived neighbourhoods just outside the centres; and the smaller ex-industrial towns face difficult issues about their future rationale. The real challenge now is to link the fortunes of the booming and declining areas into a new settlement system in which the benefits of growth can be more evenly spread across regions, cities and neighbourhoods. This is why we need to explore the value that a city-region geometry can offer as a way of developing such links.

Further reading

Boddy, M. and Parkinson, M. (2004) *City Matters: Competitiveness, Cohesion and Urban Governance.* Bristol: The Policy Press.

Forrest, R. and Kearns, A. (2001) Social cohesion, social capital and the neighbourhood. *Urban Studies* 38, 2125–43.

Imrie, R. and Raco, M. (eds) (2003) *Urban Renaissance? New Labour, Community and Urban Policy.* Bristol: The Policy Press.

Jayne, M. (2005) *Cities and Consumption.* London: Routledge.

Lawless, P. (2004) Locating and explaining area-based urban initiatives: new deal for communities in England. *Environment and Planning C: Government and Policy* 22, 383–99.

Nathan, M. and Urwin, C. (2006) *City People: City Centre Living in the UK.* London: Institute for Public Policy Research.

Peck, J. and Ward, K. (eds) (2002) *City of Revolution: Restructuring Manchester.* Manchester: Manchester University Press.

Roberts, P. and Sykes, H. (eds) (2000) *Urban Regeneration: A Handbook.* London: Sage.

Robson, B., Parkinson, M., Boddy, M. and Maclennan, D. (2000) *The State of English Cities.* London: DETR.

References

Allen, C and Blandy, S. (2004) *The Future Implications of City Centre Living: Implications for Urban Policy.* ODPM website, at http://www.odpm.gov.uk

Amin, A., Massey, D. and Thrift, N. (2000) *Cities for the Many Not the Few.* Bristol: The Policy Press.

Champion, T. and Fisher, T. (2004) Migration, residential preferences and the changing environment of cities. In M. Boddy and M. Parkinson (eds) *City Matters: Competitiveness, Cohesion and Urban Governance.* Bristol: The Policy Press.

Crouch, C. (2005) Housing development in the city centre. *Planning Practice and Research* 14, 69–86.

Deas, I., Robson, B. and Bradford, M. (2000) Re-thinking the Urban Development Corporation experiment: the case of central Manchester, Leeds and Bristol. *Progress in Planning* 54, 1–72.

Department of the Environment (1995) *1991 Deprivation Index: A Review of Approaches and a Matrix of Results.* London: DoE.

Department of the Environment, Transport and the Regions (2000a) *The Indices of Deprivation 2000.* London: DETR.

——(2000b) *Our Towns and Cities: The Future*, Cm 4911. London: DETR.

Holmans, A. (2002) *Britain's Housing in 2002: More Shortages and Homelessness?* York: Joseph Rowntree Foundation.

Jayne, M. (2005) *Cities and Consumption.* London: Routledge.

Maclennan, D.(2000) *Changing Places, Engaging People.* York: Joseph Rowntree Foundation.

Nathan, M. and Urwin, C. (2006) *City People: City Centre Living in the UK.* London: Institute for Public Policy Research.

Nevin, B., Lee, P., Goodson, L., Murie, A. and Phillimore, J. (2001) *Changing Housing Markets and Urban Regeneration in the M62 Corridor.* Birmingham: Centre for Urban and Regional Studies, University of Birmingham.

O'Connor, J. and Wynne, D. (eds) (1996) *From the Margins to the Centre: Cultural Production and Consumption in the Post-industrial City.* London: Arena.

Office of the Deputy Prime Minister (2003a) *Sustainable Communities: Building for the Future.* London: ODPM.

——(2003b) *Making It Happen: The Thames Gateway and the Growth Areas.* London: ODPM.

——(2004a) *Indices of Deprivation 2004.* London: ODPM.

——(2004b) *Making It Happen: The Northern Way.* London: ODPM.

——(2004c) *Our Cities are Back: Competitive Cities Make Prosperous Regions and Sustainable Communities.* London: ODPM.

——(2006a) *A National Framework for City Regions.* London: ODPM.

——(2006b) *State of the English Cities.* London: ODPM.

Peck, J. and Ward, K. (eds) (2002) *City of Revolution: Restructuring Manchester.* Manchester: Manchester University Press.

Robson, B., Parkinson, M., Boddy, M. and Maclennan, D. (2000) *The State of English Cities.* London: DETR.

Rogers, R. and Power, A. (2000) *Cities for a Small Country.* London: Faber and Faber.

Seo, J.-K. (2002) Re-urbanisation in regenerated areas of Manchester and Glasgow: new residents and the problem of sustainability. *Cities* 19, 113–21.

Smith, N. (1996) *The New Urban Frontier: Gentrification and the Revanchist City,* London: Routledge.

Social Exclusion Unit (2001) *A New Commitment to Neighbourhood Renewal.* London: SEU.

Tallon, A. (2003) Residential transformation and the promotion of inner city centre living. *Town and Country Planning* 7, 190–91.

Taylor, Ian (1996) *A Tale of Two Cities: Global Change, Local Feeling and Everyday Life in Manchester and Sheffield.* London: Routledge.

31

Reconcentration

Ian Douglas

Introduction

New opportunities encourage people to move to hitherto sparsely populated areas, some-times in search of new agricultural areas to open up with irrigation or improved fertilizers, on other occasions attracted by new opportunities for resource exploitation, particularly mining. Yet today examples of abandoned mining and agricultural settlements abound, from the Roman centuriated fields of North Africa to the former nineteenth-century 'ghost town' mining settlements of the Californian and Australian gold rushes. What happened to the people of those settlements, especially the children born there, is seldom asked, but in many cases it would be discovered that they had migrated to cities, adding to the con-centration of people in urban areas. The phenomenon of reconcentration of people in urban areas is the subject of this chapter.

Reconcentration implies the movement back to city centres after dispersal. It is primarily driven by the failure of the enterprise and social conditions of the dispersed settlement systems, through economic change, environmental change, political change or civil conflict or war. There is also the attraction of the prospects of opportunity and a particular kind of lifestyle in the city centre. This chapter explores three possibly extreme examples, that of migration from rural areas where agricultural livelihoods have collapsed in the face of modernization, mechanization and market forces, that of forced refugees in the face of war and civil conflict, and that of new apartment living in city centres, where regeneration and new social and leisure opportunities have made living close to work and entertainment highly attractive, particularly for the 16 to 35 years age group.

Reconcentration from rural economic change

The population of Latin America as a whole demonstrates three trends: (1) a decline in the annual total population growth rate from 2.5 per cent between 1970 and 1980, to 1.7 per cent between 1990 and 1997; (2) a −0.8 per cent decline in the rural growth rate; and (3) an increase in percentage of the population living in towns and cities, from 64 per cent in 1980, to 71.9 per cent in 1990, and 77.7 per cent in 1997. A marked contrast has developed between a dwindling rural population, for whom the quality of infrastructure and local services has often declined, and growing urban centres, in which resources, government and product investment are concentrated. In much of South America, specialization of production, use of capital intensive technologies, and expansion of agro-industrial centres have deepened the segmentation among producers, pushing much of the rural population to urban areas (Cerrutti and Bertoncello 2003).

This phenomenon of urban reconcentration is, in many ways, a reconcentration of poverty. Across Latin America rural poverty accounted for 61 per cent of total poverty in 1970 but only 30 per cent in 1997. For many, rural to urban migration has been a key exit strategy to escape rural poverty in Latin America (de Janvry and Sadoulet 2000). However, the actual causes and processes of migration in individual households are complex (Bilsborrow *et al.* 1987). Case studies of rural out-migration in Peru and Bolivia demonstrate how, as the commercialization of agriculture has made it impossible for peasant households to maintain their traditional patterns of activity, the families' daughters have become migratory in new ways (Lawson 1998).

The rapid expansion of urban areas as a consequence of disadvantaged economic and social conditions of rural areas of Latin America has been augmented by flows linked to civil conflict and violence, as in Colombia and Guatemala (Cerrutti and Bertoncello 2003). Natural and economic disasters can also precipitate more migration to cities. Such was the case in the economic crisis in Argentina in 2000–2.

Reconcentration in Argentina: the rural crisis and increasing poverty

In Argentina's Pampa, the technological modernization of agriculture and cattle production has not been accompanied by an increase in population living in rural areas or even by an improvement in the capacity of these areas to retain population (Cerrutti and Bertoncello 2003). Rural infrastructure, particularly the railways, has been neglected and farm and rural industry employment has declined. Many of the remaining agricultural workers now live in towns, while others have become unemployed. Such a situation is always aggravated by downturns in the economy.

By the year 2000, Argentina was undergoing a severe economic crisis, with the government defaulting on international loans. Over half of Argentines were living below the national US $2 per day poverty level, with 43 per cent of the poor being defined as indigent (Chiarotti 2005). The social situation in the country had been deteriorating for over 30 years, with poverty and inequality increasing, even when the economy was prospering (Auyero and Moran 2005). High unemployment and an associated growth of the informal sector became persistent, with consequent movement of people from rural areas to cities. The crisis saw many people who would have regarded themselves as middle class moving into poverty. Between 1992 and 2005, 1.5 million of the 38 million Argentine population crossed the US $1 per day poverty threshold (Gasparini 2005). Poverty (measured by a head count index) rose rapidly in the 2001–2 crisis, when 7.5 million people crossed the poverty line, but subsequently declined by 6.5 million by 2005, although not to the levels before 1998 (Gasparini 2005). Inequality became more marked after 1995. By 2003, the poorest 10 per cent of the urban population of Argentina earned 2.2 per cent of the total income, while the richest 10 per cent earned 30.8 per cent of the total income. In 1980 the richest 10 per cent of the population earned 15 times more than the poorest 10 per cent, while in 2003 they earned 24 times more (Roitman 2005).

This upsurge in poverty added to the pre-existing rural–urban migration. A social survey in urban areas, including rural towns, across Argentina, inquired as to whether a household member had migrated since October 2001 or whether someone in the household was considering that option; it found that a little over 4 per cent of the households had at least one member who had migrated. The main reasons for migration included 'lack of work' (58 per cent) and seeking better quality of life (15 per cent). However, more than 20 per cent of the households reported that at least one family member was considering migrating (Fiszbein et al. 2002). The key option being considered (80 per cent of the households) was migrating to another country – particularly within the highest income groups in the city of Buenos Aires.

The increase in migration produced a rapid expansion of squatter settlements on the fringes of cities. This movement was augmented by the continuing migration of people from neighbouring countries, especially Bolivia, who for many years had been settling in peri-urban areas, contributing to vegetable-growing in the green belts surrounding bigger cities, sometimes augmenting the urban informal sector through the selling of produce by female family members (Benencia and Gazzotti 1995). There were attempts in the mid-1990s, to halt migration and imports from Bolivia, for fear that they could cause a new cholera epidemic (Grimson 2002); however, the migration was as intense as ever by 2001. The net result is a complex pattern of land-use in and around the mega-cities and provincial centres of Argentina. On the one hand, areas of accessible land, including patches of unused land close to city centres and spaces around peripheral highway intersections, are occupied by squatter settlements. On the other hand, the rich segregate themselves in gated communities, particularly around Buenos Aires, but increasingly on the edges of provincial cities such as Rosario (Bragos et al. 2002) and Mendoza (Roitman 2005).

Developers have encouraged the growth of gated communities as part of an international trend linked to inward foreign investments that bring ideas about suburban development from elsewhere, particularly the USA. However, gated communities tend to polarize social divisions. While residents of gated communities in Mendoza feel more comfortable and more secure than their neighbours as they have a variety of protective and security measures, they also feel that their poorer neighbours are envious or jealous of their security and comfort and that they may be discriminated against in local shops and be charged higher prices if their elite residence is known. In addition, they feel embarrassed, knowing that they have many advantages and privileges that others cannot have. In contrast, people living in the surrounding areas consider themselves discriminated against, segregated and deprived of the security and benefits that the gated community residents have (Roitman 2005).

The two groups of residents know little about each other and have no contact. This fuels suspicion and distrust, with feelings against the other group becoming stronger. The two different worlds appear to have almost nothing in common. The gated community residents enjoy protection from the outside world, particularly from crime and urban violence, while the others suffer from constant fear of crime, violence and insecurity (Roitman 2005). This situation is part of a worsening trend for the poor in Argentine and other Latin American cities. Rapid growth has led to sharply rising land prices which increase the difficulties faced by the poor in obtaining adequate housing. The price of peri-urban serviced land in Latin America may be as high as that in cities of North America and Europe where per capita incomes are typically seven to ten times higher (Smolka 2003). Land development is directed towards the most profitable housing; sometimes enough serviced land is not available even for the middle class (Everett 1999).

Outcomes of reconcentration in Rosario, Argentina

Rosario City, in the province of Santa Fe, Argentina, has an estimated population of 908,875 (Borghi *et al.* 2003), although other sources describe the urban area as having a population of well over 1 million. It occupies over 600 sq km on the west bank of the Parana River. The downtown core, close to the river, is characterized by high-rise apartment buildings. On the edge of the downtown area lies the Parque Independencia. Radiating from the central business district are areas of low-rise housing interspersed with factories and small business premises. These spread out to the Avenida de Circunvalacion that forms a by-pass route to the west of the city (Hall *et al.* 2001). Beyond the ring road, new urban areas are interspersed with agricultural land uses.

Rosario's population is young, with 52.6 per cent males and 47.4 per cent females, a proportion characteristic of many cities which receive young male, poorly educated migrants coming from rural areas in search of work. Fifty per cent of the population is now below the poverty line, almost 20 per cent is unemployed (Spiaggi 2005). The recent migrants, coming from impoverished rural areas, remain trapped in poverty and are unable to gain access to good housing. They, and many family members, live in squatter settlements, known as *villas miseria* (slums), without legal title to the land they occupy (Hall *et al.* 2001). Characteristic of these settlements are Molino Blanco and Villa Banana. The former is mainly sited within a triangle formed by a railway, a stream and a major highway. Villa Banana is closer to the city centre but similar in character.

By a combination of remote sensing and GIS analysis, Hall and co-workers (2001) identified areas occupied by squatter settlements in Rosario City, noting that in some places they were more prevalent than expected. They also commented that overcrowding appeared to be less of a problem than the poor materials and structure of the homes. Many of the settlements were in cramped areas along major transportation routes. Some were recent additions on the edges or adjacent to longer-established squatter settlements.

Some serious social issues are closely associated with the poverty in the reconcentration process. Women in the squatter settlements had problems gaining access to healthcare and low expectations of the quality of service that they would receive in hospitals and clinics. In Argentina generally, poor women face major problems if they seek to terminate an unwanted pregnancy. They have to resort to back-alley practitioners or attempt to terminate the pregnancy themselves. They end up in public hospitals in the aftermath of botched abortions. Unsafe abortions cause 29 per cent of maternal deaths. However, an intensive training programme with squatter settlement women helped to raise both their self-esteem and their expectations of medical assistance. The workshops transformed their perceptions about health as a human right and not as a handout. Their sense of helplessness was transformed into empowerment. This type of human rights education has to incorporate tools and mechanisms that empower people to exercise their citizenship (Chiarotti 2005).

Urban agriculture has been encouraged as one way of helping poverty-stricken families to gain good food and to raise their self-esteem (Spiaggi 2005). The advantages of the urban food production have been felt in four ways: (1) in terms of neighbourhood food supply (production of more and better crops for self-consumption and commercialization); (2) socially (strengthening of community participation and organizational capabilities); (3) economically (generation of genuine income and employment); and (4) environmentally (use of agro-ecological techniques, restoration of informal dumps, provision of environmental training). The people involved have more food for self-consumption, and gain some income from the commercialization of various products. Each family now gets about 1 kg of vegetables a day, and whenever they have surplus – something that depends on seasonal patterns – the average income (including self-consumption and barter) is equivalent to about US $1 a day. Although marketing of the surpluses should be improved, this is difficult for people living in extreme poverty without access to credit.

The Rosario reconcentration situation has parallels in many other Argentine cities. The migrants initially have problems of engaging with life in the city, but once they become part of the system, however marginally, there are ways in which they can improve their conditions. Urban agriculture, often frowned upon by authorities, is a clear path to improving diet and incomes. Support from Civil Society (NGO) groups who understand the workings of the city is often needed to get such activities started and firmly established in the eyes of the authorities. This then begins to transform the squatter settlements themselves, encouraging people to manage the land and waste surrounding their dwellings and giving them a stake in the city.

Reconcentration of refugees from war, civil conflict and environmental disasters in towns and cities

War, civil conflict and environmental change have driven millions of people to abandon their rural homes and to seek refuge in elsewhere, but mainly in the poorer countries of Africa and Asia. Asia had 6,187,800 asylum seekers, refugees and others of concern to the United Nations Commissioner for Refugees (UNHCR), while Africa had 4,285,100. World-wide a total of 17,084,100 asylum seekers, refugees and others of concern to UNHCR were reported (UNEP 2005).

While many add to the reconcentration in towns and cities, even more other forced migrants live in crowded camps in rural areas. However, the reconcentration of people has led to profound changes to many small towns and has modified the character of larger cities. Many of the refugees cross borders into neighbouring countries and set up temporary shelters around the first town they find. For example, refugees from Sierra Leone clustered in camps on the edge of Guéckédou, just across the border in southern Guinea. In January 2001, the influx of refugees had led to about 200,000 people being in temporary accommodation in the area of Guéckédou, a town that normally has about 30,000 people. Thus urban refugees can place great strains on existing infrastructure and services. In this instance, international aid to the camps close to the town was the key to survival. Later, however, conflict in 2001 in that region of Guinea led to almost 400 people being taken from that area to Faranah, 200 km further north. The fighting destroyed the town of Guéckédou and neighbouring villages and the remaining refugees in the area were temporarily cut off from sources of aid.

From August 2003, Liberian refuges began to return home, and by the end of 2004 most of the refugees from Sierra Leone had left Guinea. However, in February 2005, UNHCR officials in Guinea estimated there were still 75,000–90,000 Liberians left in the region around Guéckédou, some in refugee camps, others living in local towns and villages. The situation of the individual refugees who have moved into urban areas and have tried to establish themselves as part of the city lifestyle differs considerably from those in the camps several kilometres outside the town.

The urban settlers are usually termed 'urban refugees'. Those who come from urban areas tend to flee individually or in small groups, while those from rural areas may move as whole clans or communities (Kibreab 1996). The majority of the world's urban refugees, especially those in poor countries, support themselves through casual labour or participation in the informal economy (Lindstrom 2003). They are often illegally living in the towns and cities and may be evicted by the authorities. In many cases they add to the numbers in informal settlements. They often have difficulty in gaining access to health and education services.

Some 15,000 refugees, escapees from wars in Sudan, Rwanda, Burundi, the Democratic Republic of Congo, Eritrea, Ethiopia and Somalia, are living in the Ugandan capital, Kampala, without UNHCR assistance. Instead of seeking shelter in rural camps, they have come to the city to use their knowledge and skills to attain self-sufficiency and dignity. Many of these urban refugees are either single men or single mothers with children. Most of them have come to Kampala directly from their country of origin without having stayed in a refugee camp. Some, however, may have spent a considerable time in refugee camps. The factors attracting these two groups to Kampala are:

- opportunities to trade and use their skills to offer services to better-off city residents;
- access to hospitals and private medical services;
- accommodation, schooling and vocational training;
- Internet access to maintain contacts with relatives, transfer money and explore business opportunities;
- recreational and intellectual activities;
- opportunities to hide from the Ugandan authorities and from intelligence agents from their home countries who actively monitor those who officially register their presence.

Most of these urban refugees are educated city people. Seventy per cent of those sampled in one survey had been attending or had finished secondary education before fleeing from their home, and 30 per cent had a tertiary educational qualification. Many are academics, researchers, engineers, teachers and musicians. A large number of them are secondary school students keen to complete their education. These Kampala refugees do not see themselves as a burden on the host country. One-third of those interviewed were working in the informal sector as artisans, tailors, hairdressers, traders in precious metal and diamonds and vendors of food and second-hand clothes. A quarter of refugees depended on money sent by relatives outside Uganda. Another sixth appeared to be establishing viable livelihoods in Kampala.

Several thousand refugees, mainly Congolese, Burundians and Rwandans, live among the 3 million people of Dar es Salaam, Tanzania. They receive almost no assistance from the UNHCR and thus there are no accurate records of their numbers. Unfortunately, Tanzania's 1998 Refugee Act confines refugees to designated camp areas and criminalizes any violation of the law. Refugees who travel beyond a 4 km radius of the camps in search of work or trade opportunities, or simply to gather firewood, are subject to arrest and even imprisonment. The government rarely allows refugees to leave the camps for temporary or longer-term purposes. Many urban refugees are much worse off and survive only by begging or on charity. They are at risk of abrupt removal by the authorities.

The retention of refugees for long periods in camps or resettlements has adverse effects on both the migrants and their hosts. The presence of foreign aid workers who establish parallel services undermines the local economy by attracting the best staff, who enjoy the higher salaries paid by humanitarian organizations. The local population may be poorer than the refugees and the targeting of relief to the refugees creates resentment, and even hostility, in local communities. Camp life affects mental well-being, inhabitants often feeling despair and helplessness and becoming less and less inclined to accept their social responsibilities. These large clusters of refuges strain local resources and the environment far more that if the people were dispersed. They are also centres of health risks in which disease can spread rapidly.

Mortality rates are higher in the bigger camps. Conditions in camps make it easy for campaigners to politicize people and foster terrorism and violence (Harrell-Bond 1998).

If the locations and sites of camps are unsuitable and the shelter inappropriate, the consequences become apparent in the health of the people living there. In Ethiopian refugee camps in eastern Sudan, for example, malaria was highly prevalent because there were numerous riverbed pools and forests surrounding the site. Ten per cent of the population was infected with malaria as a result. The camp's stick and grass shelters further exacerbated the situation because they were inappropriate for the use of insecticides.

Environmentally safe disposal of human, medical and solid wastes is a major problem in most refugee camps. The hard volcanic rock underlying the Kibumba camp, in the Goma region of the Democratic Republic of the Congo, made excavation of pit latrines difficult. There would have been no easy way to manage pit latrines once they were filled. An area of 6,000 sq m was set aside for defecation, but it encroached on the buffer zones of the Virunga National Park and consequently solid, human and medical waste was continually dumped in the Virunga National Park.

The Khan Eshieh camp, in Syria, lacks a sewerage system and only has pit latrines whose proximity to water wells creates major health hazards for camp residents. Many refugees there now buy water from mobile tankers operating in the area, but the water is not safe for human consumption (UNEP 2005).

However, it may be mistaken to assume that the refugees themselves are the causes of environmental degradation. Kibreab (1997) argues that environmental change and concomitant population displacement are the consequences of war and insecurity.

It is also often alleged that HIV might be spread by increased rates of partner exchange during times of war and civil conflict (Girdler-Brown 1998), In the Magoro refugee camp in Uganda, the USAID-funded AIM programme claims that young men have given up hope and spend most of the day drinking, and that the poverty and drinking are directly related to the burgeoning rate of AIDS in Ugandan camps (see http://www.jsi.com/aim/Stories/PreventingAIDS.htm). However, elsewhere, again, the evidence from the few detailed studies suggests that the supposed effect is not always present. Of the male respondents interviewed in two large refugee camps in western Tanzania, 37 per cent denied having any sexual intercourse in the previous three months. The problem may be different in urban areas where the mixing of forced migrants with migrant workers and local people is greater.

In other health matters, refugees face many risks in camps. The absence of appropriate water and sanitation systems almost inevitably leads to outbreaks of disease. In Zaire, for example, cholera and dysentery spread through a contaminated water source, killing nearly 50,000 Rwandan refugees in 1994. Most camps managed by international agencies and humanitarian organizations have a strong emphasis on establishing water supplies and sanitation. Sometimes, however, they are overwhelmed. Exposure to non-sterile equipment such as razor blades is common. Up to 25 per cent of refugee women may be pregnant at any given time, and they have difficulties finding traditional birth assistants in the camps. Most refugees only make contact with health services once or twice a year. In some cases, horrific sexual violence, mostly perpetrated by the military, has occurred (Girdler-Brown 1998).

For governments, it may be easiest to keep refugees concentrated in camps until they can be repatriated. For humanitarian aid agencies, the camps may provide good conditions for the delivery of relief, health care, water and sanitation and the management of housing. For the refugees, the camps may offer security and protection, provided they do not get caught up in local conflicts. However, the opportunities for enterprise and advancement in camps are restricted to providing services to other refugees. In the towns and cities there are many opportunities for enterprise and initiative. For example, in the 1990s, refugees owned 25 per cent of the trucks in the Sudan and played a key role in the national transport system (Kibreab 1996). The insecurity and often illegal status of many urban refugees make their lives hard, but the opportunities give hope. The reconcentration of refugees illustrates the diversity of situations, the transformations of places and the varying attitudes and influences of governments. It is another facet of the dynamics of our diverse world, but sadly illustrates some of the worst consequences of the exploitation of political power, land and resources.

Reconcentration by city centre living in Western cities

Much of the twentieth century saw the flight to suburbia in the cities of North America, Europe and Australasia. Central cities became, with a few notable exceptions, almost dead at night, and the suburbs seemed to stretch endlessly and monotonously for tens of kilometres, creating what Pierce Lewis calls the 'galactic metropolis' (Lewis 1983). Some suburbs have exotic, exciting connotations, while others have come to symbolize monotony and dreariness. In Sydney, Australia, this is embodied by the contrast between the North Shore and Western Sydney suburbs (Dowling and Mee 2000). Western Sydney was always perceived as being disadvantaged, dreary and lacking diversity, even though there are pockets of wealth and areas of considerable ethnic diversity. All these types of suburb gradually became transformed, particularly in the USA, by 'planned sprawl', with the development of regional shopping centres along major urban highways. In the USA, between the mid-1950s and the late 1990s, about 43,000 suburban shopping centres, anchored by large chain stores, were built (Hayden 2003).

By the 1980s this suburban lifestyle, still sought by the majority, began to lose its appeal to many first-time homebuyers, especially the younger professional classes. From the late 1960s to the late 1980s a process of counterurbanization seemed dominant in Western societies. People appeared to be moving from large cities to smaller towns and rural areas: at least, the large cities were growing less rapidly. More particularly the inner cities lost people. However, by the early 1990s cities such as London and Paris had begun to regain their populations, some of the gain being caused by international migrants but some of it, perhaps only a small part, to the process known then as 'gentrification' which followed such renewal schemes as the London Docklands and its North American counterparts (Herbert 1996). To the new apartments close to London's commercial developments at Canary Wharf came the young professionals and investment analysts. These were the forerunners of a wave of young professionals who started to buy the waterfront developments in old warehouses in the redevelopment areas of many old industrial cities.

Reconcentration in the UK's regional centres

Several UK city centres have witnessed new residential developments in both former industrial and commercial buildings and newly built apartment blocks in city centres, notably Glasgow, Liverpool and Manchester (Crouch 1999; Jones and Watkins 1996; RICS 1998; Heath 2001). Local newspaper advertising campaigns promote city centre living in such cities, while property development companies, such as Manchester's Urban Splash, are held up as visionary pioneers, engaging in projects likely to be avoided by more mainstream developers and investors (Guy and Hennebury 1999).

In major British cities, city centre populations have been rising since 1991 (Table 31.1), largely through the provision of new apartments, initially in refurbished old warehouses and

Table 31.1. City centre apartment and house building in some UK regional cities

	Completed 1991–2001[a]	Total completed by end 2005	Under construction	With planning permission	City centre population 1991	Estimated city centre population 2005
Birmingham	2,360		760	640		
Bristol	842		627	699		
Dundee			189	436	1,500	3000
Leeds	860	3,493	2,950	4,400		4,200
Liverpool	1,630		3,047	1,548	10,000	15,000
Manchester	3,120	9,094	2,836	2,754	3,500	16,000
Newcastle	790		500	450		
Sheffield	450		–	450		

Note: [a] Data as at April 2001 (except Newcastle, June 2001, and Sheffield, October 2000).

Source: Based on Lambert and Boddy (2002), Nathan and Urwin (2006) and Unsworth (2005) with additional data from the appropriate city councils.

subsequently in new multi-storey buildings, especially at sites with water frontages to canals or rivers (see Chapter 30). People have moved into these apartments both from the local area and from others part of the UK. Of people interviewed in Leeds city centre residences, 225 had moved from within the Leeds metropolitan district but others came from elsewhere in the UK, with about 12 per cent from outside the UK (Unsworth 2005). Many have come to work in the city centres, sometimes as transfers within their existing employment. In smaller cities like Dundee, students make up over 50 per cent of the inner-city residents, but in larger places, such as Manchester, they are probably less than 25 per cent. However, Unsworth (2005) concluded that although many residents appreciate the Leeds city centre lifestyle and being within walking distance of work, there are frustrations over the size of accommodation and the local surroundings, which may limit the amount of time households will actually reside in the city centre. She was concerned that a serious over-supply of small apartments could develop while there would be a lack of choice of housing for older, larger households, which would be faced with little option but to move on from the city centre as family needs mature.

Since 1993, Liverpool City Council has promoted city centre living, incorporating it into the 1996 Draft Unitary Development Plan, and making it one of the strategic priorities of Liverpool Vision in 1999. The central area of the city of Manchester was thought to be the fastest growing city centre in Britain, over 7,000 people having chosen to live there since 1991. More than half of the homes in Manchester city centre are of single occupancy, with male occupants outnumbering females by a ratio of two to one. Some 42 per cent of city centre residents earn over £20,000 a year, 60 per cent own a car and 59 per cent work in the city centre itself. The main attractions cited by residents are the lifestyle, leisure facilities and the nightlife offered by a city centre. In both Liverpool and Manchester there are 2,000–3,000 resident students in the city centre, with many thousands more living close enough to enjoy the city centre facilities.

City centre housing in Bristol shows some elements of reconcentration of the regional population. Compared with London there is little of the way of recent international in-migration of poorer families. Typical purchasers are already owner-occupiers with some equity to invest; some of the cheaper units are sold to younger, mid-thirties age groups, but more typically buyers of the most expensive properties are older 'empty nesters', moving

491

into the city from the suburbs and surrounding rural areas. Some of these may be buying city centre properties as a second home. Occupations are overwhelmingly professional and managerial, public and private sector. This is mainly a local demand from with the region, with few purchasers re-locating from London and south-east England (Lambert and Boddy 2002).

Some of the purchasing is to endeavour to benefit from rising property prices, many buyers being investor purchasers, either intending to sell after a short period for speculative gains or buying to rent. Bristol property developers claimed that around 30 per cent of sales were to investors, in most cases the smaller, lower-cost properties. (One developer actually admitted that the smallest one-bed city centre flats were actually 'too small' to be permanent residences) (Lambert and Boddy 2002).

Clearly, there are mixed objectives among those who buy city centre properties and among those who live in them. However, the apartment boom is not only changing the visual skyline of the cities, but is also changing the whole atmosphere of the cities involved. Indeed, Manchester city centre sometimes seems more crowded, noisy and vibrant at midnight than at midday on Fridays and Saturdays. Clearly this aspect of reconcentration is altering the nature of the places involved.

Gentrification in Stockholm – a case study

Stockholm, the Swedish capital, with 760,000 inhabitants, is a relatively small city on the global scale. Nevertheless, Stockholm exhibits the same employment characteristics, i.e. an increasing service sector, as many post-industrial global centres with (Borgegård and Murdie 1994). The surrounding region forms the largest metropolitan area in Sweden with 1.8 million inhabitants, or 20 per cent of the total population. It is also the fastest growing region in the country. Over the last five years, the region has gained 5 per cent through a net immigration. The region is a magnet for migrants from other parts of the country, especially young people, and is also regarded as a hub for the economic growth in the rest of the country (Magnusson 2004). Stockholm's inner city is an attractive location for households with large wealth and a high income, especially young adults. But the gain of inhabitants has extensive effects on the social and economic sustainability of a growing city. This is not least evident in the housing market. Prices of owner-occupied dwellings are increasing and few vacancies exist in the rented sector. This is also affecting the formation of new households, the functioning of the labour market and the long-term conditions for a growth in the economy.

This Swedish example reinforces the observations in the UK. While beneficial for municipal budgets and leisure providers, the upsurge in city-centre living reduces choices for others. Gradually cheaper housing, particularly in older shared-occupancy dwellings, is being replaced by new developments of 'luxury apartments'. Inner-city demography is being altered, particularly in cities such as Dundee, Leeds, Liverpool and Manchester that have large university student populations (55,000 in Manchester) living on the fringe of the city centres. Possible many segments of the urban population feel alienated by the late-night youth culture of these cities. However, the reinvigoration of once dreary city centres has had a positive benefit for the majority.

Conclusions

The two distinct examples of reconcentration described here reveal some of the diversity of factors that lead people to move into city centres. One aspect of the changes to the urban landscape that ensue from this migration is the way in which both have occupied derelict or unused spaces. While the Rosario squatters have moved on to former industrial sites or abandoned market areas, the first city centre apartments in Liverpool and Manchester were in unused, derelict warehouse buildings. Later, both forms used vacant land near transportation routes: the Rosario squatter built shelters under and around the overpasses of the Avenida de Circunvalacion, while in Liverpool and Manchester new apartments were built on former canal-side industrial land and abandoned railways sidings.

However, the social contrasts could not be greater: while in Rosario urban poverty has been increased and pressure on social and health services has grown, in cities like Manchester new money has come to the city, bringing increased rateable values and new commercial activities and stimulating the realization of the 24-hour city concept. Both, however, show examples of amazing initiative, albeit at different scales. In Rosario, the women's group promoting urban agriculture for squatters and experimenting with cultivating traditional medicinal herbs has helped to raise the incomes and material and spiritual well-being of the poorest migrants. In Manchester, the entrepreneur developer Urban Splash (see Chapter 30) has led a new wave of conversion of industrial premises and adjacent new construction of city centre dwellings.

Just as many of the new apartment dwellers in Manchester were attracted by opportunities, so were the urban refugees fleeing to Khartoum, Dar es Salaam and Kampala. Although the circumstances and lifestyles are extremely different, the search for something better, to make the best of the opportunities available and the desire to make progress are common to all these movements to cities. Reconcentration in whatever form can provide opportunities. Individuals with ideas, skills and dedication are needed to turn those opportunities into real successes.

Further reading

Kibreab, G. (1987) *Refugees and Development in Africa: The Case of Eritrea*. Trenton: The Red Sea Press.

Nathan, M. and Urwin, C. (2006) *City People: City Centre Living in the UK*. London: Centre for Cities, Institute for Public Policy Research.

Smolka, M. (2003) Informality, urban poverty and land market prices. *Land Lines Newsletter* 15 (1), 4–7.

Spiaggi, E.P. (2005) Urban agriculture and local sustainable development in Rosario, Argentina: integration of economic, social, technical and environmental variables. In L.J.A. Mougeot (ed.) *AGROPOLIS: The Social, Political, and Environmental Dimensions of Urban Agriculture*. London: Earthscan; Ottawa: IDRC.

While, A., Jonas, A.E.G. and Gibbs, D. (2004) The environment and the entrepreneurial city: searching for the urban 'sustainability fix' in Manchester and Leeds. *International Journal of Urban and Regional Research* 28, 549–69.

References

Auyero, J. and Moran, T.P. (2005) *The Dynamics of Collective Violence: Dissecting Food Riots in Contemporary Argentina*. New York: Department of Sociology, State University of New York, Stony Brook.

Benencia, R. and Gazzotti, A. (1995) Frontier migration and employment: facts and questions. *Estudios Migratorios Latinoamericanos* 10, 573–611 (in Spanish).

Bilsborrow, R.E., McDevitt, T.N.M., Kossoudji, S. and Fuller, R. (1987) The impact of origin community characteristics on rural–urban out-migration in a developing country. *Demography* 24, 191–210.

Borgegård, L.-E. and Murdie, R. (1994) Social polarization and the crisis of the welfare state: the case of Stockholm. *Built Environment* 20, 254–68.

Borghi, J., Bastus, S., Belizan, M., Carroli, G., Hutton, G. and Fox-Rushby, J. (2003) Costs of publicly provided maternity services in Rosario, Argentina. *Salud Publica Mex* 45, 27–34.

Bragos, O., Mateos, A. and Pontoni, S. (2002) Nuevos desarrollos residenciales y procesos de segregacion socioespacial en la expansion oeste de Rosario. In L.F. Cabrales Barajas (ed.) *Latinoamerica: paises abiertos, ciudades cerradas*, pp. 441–80. Guadalajara, Mexico: Universidad de Guadalajara and UNESCO.

Cerrutti, M. and Bertoncello, R. (2003) Urbanization and internal migration patterns in Latin America. Paper prepared for Conference on African Migration in Comparative Perspective, Johannesburg, South Africa, 4–7. Available at pum.princeton.edu/pumconference/papers/1-Cerrutti.pdf (accessed 6 February 2006).

Chiarotti, S. (2005) Learning and transforming reality: women from Rosario's neighbourhoods demand access to public health services free of discrimination. *Intercultural Education* 16, 129–135.

Crouch, C. (1999) Housing development in the city centre. *Planning Practice and Research* 14, 69–86.

de Janvry, A. and Sadoulet, E. (2000) Rural poverty in Latin America: determinants and exit paths. *Food Policy* 25, 389–409.

Dowling, R. and Mee, K. (2000) Tales of the city: Western Sydney at the end of the millennium. In J. Connell (ed.) *Sydney: The Emergence of a World City*. South Melbourne: Oxford University Press.

Everett, M. (1999) *Evictions and Human Rights: An Ethnographic Study of Development and Land Disputes in Bogotá, Colombia*. Available from the Lincoln Institute of Land Policy website at http://www.lincolninst.edu/pubs/dl/747_everett_99.pdf (accessed 30 November 2004).

Fiszbein, A., Giovagnoli, P.I. and Aduriz, I. (2002) *Argentina's Crisis and its Impact on Household Welfare* (Argentina Poverty Update 2003, Background Paper No. 1). Washington: World Bank Office for Argentina, Chile, Paraguay and Uruguay.

Gasparini, L. (2005) *Monitoring the Socio-economic Conditions in Argentina* (updated version of a Working Paper with the same title published by the World Bank and CEDLAS). La Plata, Argentina: CEDLAS, Universidad Nacional de La Plata.

Girdler-Brown, B. (1998) Eastern and Southern Africa. *International Migration* 36, 513–51.

Grimson, A. (2002) Hygiene wars on the Mercosur border: local and national agency in Uruguaiana (Brazil) and Paso de Los Libres (Argentina). *Identities: Global Studies in Culture and Power* 9, 151–72.

Guy, C. and Hennebury, J. (1999) Realism and real estate: towards a relational understanding of urban development processes. Paper presented at the RICS Cutting Edge Conference.

Hall, G.B., Malcolm, N.W. and Piwowar, J.M. (2001) Integration of remote sensing and GIS to detect pockets of urban poverty: the case of Rosario, Argentina. *Transactions in GIS* 5, 235–53.

Harrell-Bond, B. (1998) Camps: literature review. *Forced Migration Review* 2, 21–2.

Hayden, D. (2003) *Building Suburbia*. New York: Pantheon.

Heath, T. (2001) Adaptive re-use of offices for residential use. *Cities* 18 (3), 173–84.

Herbert, D.T. (1996) Western cities and their problems. In I. Douglas, R. Huggett and M. Robinson (eds) *Companion Encyclopedia of Geography*, pp. 730–51. London: Routledge.

Jones, C. and Watkins, C. (1996) Urban regeneration and sustainable markets. *Urban Studies* 33 (7), 1129–40.

Kibreab, G. (1996) Eritrean and Ethiopian urban refugees in Khartoum: what the eye refuses to see. *African Studies Review* 49 (13), 131–78.

——(1997) Environmental causes and impact of refugee movements: a critique of the current debate. *Disasters* 21, 20–38.

Lambert, C. and Boddy, M. (2002) *Transforming the City: Post-Recession Gentrification and Re-Urbanization* (CNR Paper 6: August). Bristol: ESRC Centre for Neighbourhood Research.

Lawson, V.A. (1998) Hierarchical households and gendered migration in Latin America: feminist extensions to migration research. *Progress in Human Geography* 22, 39–53.

Lewis, P. (1983) The galactic metropolis. In R.H. Platt and G. Macinko (eds) *Beyond the Urban Fringe*, pp. 34–49. Minneapolis: University of Minnesota Press.

Lindstrom, C. (2003) Urban refugees in Mauritania. *Forced Migration Review* 17, 46–7. Available at http://www.fmreview.org/FMRpdfs/FMR17/fmr17.20.pdf (accessed 10 February 2006).

Magnusson, L. (2004) Gentrification – the prospect of European cities? Paper presented at the ENHR Conference 2–6 July 2004, Cambridge, UK.

Nathan, M. and Urwin, C. (2006) *City People: City Centre Living in the UK*. London: Centre for Cities, Institute for Public Policy Research.

RICS (1998) *Back to the Centre*. London: RICS.

Roitman, S. (2005) Who segregates whom? The analysis of a gated community in Mendoza, Argentina. *Housing Studies* 20, 303–21.

Spiaggi, E.P. (2005) Urban agriculture and local sustainable development in Rosario, Argentina: integration of economic, social, technical and environmental variables. In L.J.A. Mougeot (ed.) *AGROPOLIS: The Social, Political, and Environmental Dimensions of Urban Agriculture*. London: Earthscan; Ottawa: IDRC.

UNEP (2005) The impact of refugees and internally displaced persons on local environmental resources. *Environmental Emergencies News* 5, 1–4.

Unsworth, R. (2005) *City Living in Leeds – 2005*. Leeds: K.W. Linfoot and University of Leeds.

32

Counterurbanization

Peter Gordon

In 20 years Japanese office workers may still commute, packed shoulder to shoulder, to downtown towers. But no one else in the developed world will. Office work, rather than office workers, will do the travelling. Tomorrow's big city is no longer going to be the office centre.

The exodus is already under way . . .

The modern big city is the creation of the nineteenth century's ability to move people. Everyone in Dickens' London walked to work, except the owners who lived over their shops or their counting houses. But then, beginning in mid-century, people began to acquire wheels – the railroad first, then the omnibus and the streetcar (horse-drawn, of course, for many decades), the subway and the elevated train, the automobile, the bicycle. Suddenly large masses of people could move over great distances to where work was. And the elevator added vertical mobility. It was this ability to move people that, more than anything else, made possible large organizations, business, hospitals, government agencies and universities.

By 1914, every single one of the means to move people into an office-centred large city – and to enable the office workers to live outside it – had been developed. But they did not have their full impact until after World War II. Until then only two cities had skyscrapers – New York and Chicago. Now every mid-sized city world-wide boasts a 'skyline' and even in mid-sized cities people commute.

This trend has clearly reached its end, has indeed widely overshot the mark. Tokyo's office workers have to live more than two hours away just to get a seat on the train.

Peter F. Drucker, 'Information and the future of the city'.
The Wall Street Journal (4 April 1989)

Introduction

Cities exist because there are strong economic and non-economic reasons for people and the activities they engage in to cluster and, thereby, overcome the friction of distance. This is, of course, most applicable to non-agricultural activities. Urbanization and modernization have gone hand-in-hand for years. The countries that the United Nations puts into the 'developed' category went from 52 per cent urbanized in 1950 to 74 per cent urbanized in 2000. In fifty years, the urban population of these countries grew by 456 million, an increase of 131 per cent (see Table 32.1).[1]

As activities cluster to economize on transactions costs while engaging in economic and social exchange and interaction, the benefits of agglomeration are traded off against the associated costs of congestion. The population size at which marginal agglomeration benefits equal marginal congestion costs (on a dollar-value vs population plot) denotes the theoretic optimal city size. But what happens to all this over time and space? Transportation and communications costs fall and the spatial ambit of agglomeration economies expands. Thus, even this simple trade-off model predicts ever larger urbanized areas with flatter density gradients. Also, with increasing international competition, some firms may re-evaluate their ability to absorb rising costs; as relative costs change, high land costs prompt more and more firms to consider substituting away from central locations.

Seen in this light, rural vs urban settlement and rural-to-urban migration are no longer adequate descriptors for most developed countries. Even the well-documented move from

Table 32.1. Developed nations population settlement trends (000s)

	1950	1960	1970	1980	1990	2000
Europe						
Urban	280,324	342,842	412,654	475,081	516,223	529,058
Total	547,403	604,401	655,855	692,431	721,582	727,986
Per cent urban	51.2%	56.7%	62.9%	68.6%	71.5%	72.7%
North America						
Urban	109,649	142,714	171,172	189,312	213,889	249,995
Total	171,616	204,152	231,937	256,068	283,549	315,915
Per cent urban	63.9%	69.9%	73.8%	73.9%	75.4%	79.1%
Oceania						
Urban	7,765	10,469	13,725	16,237	18,720	22,564
Total	12,812	15,888	19,443	22,828	26,687	31,043
Per cent urban	60.6%	65.9%	70.6%	71.1%	70.1%	72.7%
Japan						
Urban	50,116	na	na	na	na	91,826
Total	83,200	na	na	na	na	126,926
Per cent urban	60.2%	na	na	na	na	72.3%
Developed						
Urban	426.674	536,185	652,298	749,061	825,246	882,465
Total	812,771	915,298	1,007,479	1,082,989	1,148,917	1,193,872
Per cent urban	52.5%	58.6%	64.7%	69.2%	71.8%	73.9%

Source: UN World Urbanization Prospects: The 2003 Revision Population Database. Available at http://esa.un.org/unup/p2k0data.asp

central cities to suburbs no longer tells the complete story. The spreading out of populations has reached the point where some say that it is no longer a difference of degree but, rather, a difference in kind – that we have entered a period of counter-urbanization. In an examination of substantial 1970s and early 1980s evidence for counterurbanization trends in the developed nations (Champion 1989), some suggested that long-standing urbanization trends had come to a halt and had actually reversed course. Others disagreed, noting that the evolution of settlement patterns was simply continuing the long-term tendency towards suburbanization, and questioning whether differences in extent had really given way to differences in kind (Gordon 1979). Part of the discussion inevitably involved difficult definitions of spatial units. If metropolitan-area boundaries overbound actual urbanization at one time but underbound it at another time, 'turnarounds' might be nothing more than statistical artefacts.

Successful spatial (and other) organization accompanies economic success. Rising incomes in the developed world have been characterized as 'mass affluence'. Suburbanization, exurbanization and the settlement of outlying areas have been described as nothing less than the form of spatial organization that accommodates and accompanies mass affluence.

These general introductory observations were made outside of any political or social or cultural context. How much does context matter? If not a lot, is it simply the case that rising incomes (and accompanying tastes) and changing technologies matter the most? As approximately the middle of the twentieth century, upwards of 95 per cent of population growth in the developed world's largest metropolitan areas (in the US, Canada, Western Europe, Japan, Australia and New Zealand; areas with 1 million population and above) has been in their suburbs (see Table 32.2). With geographical classifications always having to be redefined (and with inevitable spatial unit definitions differences across countries), one can quibble about where urban, suburban, exurban and rural designations should begin and end. Nevertheless, the dominance of centrifugal forces is clear. For the US case, Brooks (2004) has noted an ongoing Great Dispersal.

Nevertheless, powerful trends usually elicit strong responses and even backlashes. Whereas urbanization has always had its critics, large-scale urban dispersal has been condemned widely and its management (and even its reversal) has been made the object of a large number of policy (often referred to as 'smart growth') initiatives. Interestingly, data on the most recent settlement trends suggest that these have made very little difference. Dispersion continues and even accelerates in many places.

Table 32.2. High-income world metropolitan areas settlement trends: core city and suburban populations

	Share of change in population				
	Since	Areas	Core	Suburbs	Classification
United States	1950	39	7.3%	92.7%	Urbanized areas over 1,000,000
Canada	1951	4	5.3%	94.7%	Metropolitan areas over 1,000,000
Western Europe	1965	42	−14.2%	114.2%	Metropolitan areas over 1,000,000
Japan	1965	8	7.6%	92.4%	Metropolitan areas over 1,000,000
Australia and New Zealand	1965	6	7.2%	92.8%	Metropolitan areas over 1,000,000
Hong Kong	1965	1	55.5%	44.5%	Metropolitan areas over 1,000,000
Israel	1965	1	−1.6%	101.6%	Metropolitan areas over 1,000,000

Source: http://www.demographia.com/db-highmetro.htm

Views of concentrations and dispersion

The opening passage from Peter Drucker neatly summarizes the main forces behind urbanization and suburbanization. This discussion has been elaborated by many scholars. Mieszkowski and Mills (1993) refer to it as the 'natural evolution theory' and compare it with the 'flight-from-blight' theory. They suggest that there is evidence for both, and that this conclusion applies to the US as well as internationally. The forces included in both explanations are also of long-standing duration.

Modern forces that complement and augment these effects are cited by Easterlin (2000: 505, written 1994) who calls attention to the 'third computer-based industrial revolution'. Firms are ever more footloose and choose to follow the labour force into the suburbs. This process has 'broken the link that throughout history chained consumer residence to the economic dictates of place of work. For the first time, population distribution is being shaped noticeable by the independent effect of consumers' preferences rather than dictated by the locational decisions of firms'. He cites Frey (1993) as arguing that these effects will only become stronger over time.

As for the more focused discussion of counterurbanization, Champion (1989: 27) suggests:

> to be a true 'counterurbanite', a person or household not only has to take up residence in a remote rural area but also has to assume a life-style, which, if not identical with the traditional rural way of life, should essentially be the modern equivalent of it.

Brooks' more recent description of the modern American exurbanite is wide of this mark. Consider his rendering of 'Patio Man' (2002):

> I don't know if you've ever noticed the expression of a man who is about to buy a first-class barbecue grill. He walks into a Home Depot or Lowe's or one of the other mega hardware complexes and his eyes are glistening with a faraway visionary zeal, like one of those old prophets gazing into the promised land. His lips are parted and twitching slightly. Inside the megastore, the grills are just past the racks of affordable-house plan books, in the yard-machinery section. They are arrayed magnificently next to the vehicles that used to be known as rider mowers but are now known as lawn tractors, because to call them rider mowers doesn't really convey the steroid-enhanced M-1 tank power of the things.

> The man approaches the barbecue grills and his face bears a trance-like expression, suggesting that he has cast aside all the pains and imperfections of this world and is approaching the gateway to a higher dimension. In front of him are a number of massive steel-coated reactors with names like Broilmaster P3, The Thermidor, and the Weber Genesis, because in America it seems perfectly normal to name a backyard barbecue grill after a book of the Bible.

> The items in this cooking arsenal flaunt enough metal to suggest they have been hardened to survive a direct nuclear assault, and Patio Man goes from machine to machine comparing their features – the cast iron/porcelain coated cooking surfaces, the 328,000-Btu heat-generating capacities, the 1,600-degree-tolerance linings, the multiple warming racks, the lava rock containment dishes, the built-in electrical meat

thermometers, and so on. Certain profound questions flow through his mind. Is a 542-square-inch grilling surface really enough, considering that he might someday get the urge to roast an uncut buffalo steak? Though the matte steel overcoat resists scratching, doesn't he want a polished steel surface on his grill so he can glance down and admire his reflection as he is performing the suburban manliness rituals, such as brushing tangy sauce on meat slabs with his right hand while clutching a beer can in an NFL foam insulator ring in his left?

... As Patio Man walks past the empty handicapped and expectant-mother parking spots toward his own vehicle, wonderful grill fantasies dance in his imagination. There he is atop the uppermost tier of his multi-level backyard patio/outdoor recreation area posed like an admiral on the deck of his destroyer. In his mind's eye he can see himself coolly flipping the garlic and pepper T-bones on the front acreage of his new grill while carefully testing the citrus-tarragon trout filets that sizzle fragrantly in the rear. On the lawn below he can see his kids, Haley and Cody, frolicking on the weedless community lawn that is mowed twice weekly by the people who run Monument Crowne Preserve, his townhome community.

Brooks refers to himself as a 'comic sociologist'. Nevertheless, as the cited passage reveals, he is very insightful. There are emerging lifestyles all along a spectrum from the counterurbanite briefly sketched by Champion to Brooks' Patio Man. Yet there are probably many more of the latter than the former, suggesting that current exurbanization trends are a continuation, indeed an acceleration, of past trends rather than a break with them.

Urban economists in the US have noted 'neighbourhood environmentalism', the keen interest that residential property owners have in neighbourhood quality and, therefore, for clear rules of neighbourhood change and transition (Nelson 2005). Homeowners seem to shop for and find attractive rules of property in small suburban cities and/or in planned communities with a homeowners' association. Fifteen per cent of US housing units are now in such communities. The movement to cities at the edges of metro areas has been discussed in previous paragraphs. One author has elaborated the 'homevoter hypothesis' which emphasizes that the small-city governments found at the metropolitan peripheries are unique in that their focus is on the enforcement of property rules for neighbourhood change, again in response to homeowners' interests (Fischel 2001). Large and established cities are less likely to be able to respond as well to these interests, suggesting that here is another powerful force behind suburbanization/exurbanization.

The policy debate

It is widely presumed that outward urban expansion, often simply referred to by the catch-all 'urban sprawl', is a problem and that policy makers are expected to provide solutions, usually ones that favour more compact development. The list of suggested sprawl-spawned ills is long. Settlement dispersion is thought to be largely 'unplanned' and 'chaotic', wasteful of land, energy and other resources, a source of road congestion and air quality problems and inner-city unemployment and poverty. Public health researchers have also suggested that various measures of physical and emotional health are also threatened. Social pathologies stemming from mental health threats have been mentioned. Central cities' fiscal (and economic) viability is seen as at-risk, as is social cohesion and the general prospects for poor and minority groups. Yet the available research is clear that central city and the suburban growth are much more likely to be complements than substitutes (Voith 1992).

This is not the chapter to examine the policy debate. Cause and effect are always difficult to establish, and the empirical research that examines the links between spatial settlement and a variety of social and economic problems has been argued and criticized but most of the questions raised remain controversial. It is less controversial to posit that the number of policies focused on urban containment have expanded in almost all developed countries in recent years, but, as an examination of the available data in the next section shows, there is as yet no sign that they have had any significant effect.

In the next sections, there is an elaboration of the US case but also some reference to relevant evidence from the other developed countries.

Trends: the US case

The most extensive data to document trends that describe the nature of urbanization and the possible extent of counter-urbanization are probably for the US. While most of the settlement literature is about population trends, the US data are for employment (by major sector) as well as for population.

The Bureau of Economic Analysis maintains a Regional Economic Information System file which provides population and employment (one-digit SIC) data for all of the 3,140 US counties for each year since 1969 (to 2000 for Standard Industrial Codes [SIC] sectors; for North American Industry Codes [NAICs] sectors for the more recent years). The 30-plus years of data span periods that prompted some researchers to declare a reversal of long-standing urbanization trends (Berry 1976) and, later, a reversal of the reversal, the 'urban revival' (Frey 1989, 1993) Yet, the following discussion suggests that the urban revival may have been no more than temporary.

The full set of US counties can be arranged in many ways; two complementary approaches were adopted here. First, the US Census Bureau's new metropolitan and micropolitan definitions were used. These apply to the 1,764 'core-based' counties. The balance are the more 'rural' non-core based counties. The former are either 'metropolitan' or 'micropolitan', with each group further subdivided, according to their populations in 2000. The non-core based counties, in turn, were grouped according to the US Department of Agriculture's 'urban influence' index which is inspired by the 'Beale'-code classifications.

Combining these two classification systems, the full set of US counties were divided into thirteen classes (Tables 32.3a,b). Most 30-year population growth has been in the core-based counties, with the smallest metro areas (fewer than 1 million residents) growing the fastest. Yet the larger metro areas as well as the micropolitan counties adjacent to the larger metro areas (more than 1 million residents; their exurbs) also grew faster than the US rate of 1.24 per cent per year.

Looking at the concurrent growth rates for all (private sector) jobs, only two types of areas grew faster than the US rate, the 1–3 million population metro areas and the smaller than 1 million metro areas.

Growth in the number of proprietors is singled out because these include (but are not limited to) the smaller start-up firms. Proprietorships grew fastest in the largest metros, suggesting that many are likely to be reliant on the agglomeration economies and 'incubator' opportunities available to them in the largest markets.

502

Table 32.3a. US population and employment settlement trends by detailed geographic areas, 1970–2000 and 1970–80

Year	Area group			N	Population	Private	Proprietors	Con	FIRE	Services	Retail	Wholesale	TCU	Manufacture
1970–2000	Core-based	Large: in a metro area with at least 1 million residents or more	3 million residents and above	163	1.26%	2.86%	5.43%	3.33%	3.28%	6.67%	2.58%	2.12%	2.06%	−0.63%
			Fewer than 3 million and at least 1 million residents	250	1.35%	3.69%	5.43%	4.12%	4.50%	8.20%	3.70%	2.82%	2.59%	−0.19%
		Small: in a metro area with fewer than 1 million residents		676	1.44%	3.53%	4.24%	3.92%	4.04%	7.26%	3.96%	3.11%	2.46%	0.13%
		Metropolitan adjacent to a large metro area		92	1.30%	2.86%	2.92%	4.25%	3.45%	5.67%	3.55%	3.96%	2.04%	0.34%
		Metropolitan adjacent to a small metro area		301	0.93%	2.44%	2.13%	3.48%	2.93%	5.13%	3.11%	3.20%	1.27%	0.29%
		Metropolitan not adjacent to a metro area		282	0.82%	3.10%	2.20%	3.53%	3.10%	5.52%	3.28%	2.70%	1.66%	0.93%
	Non-core based	Non-core adjacent to a large metro area		123	1.13%	2.81%	1.62%	3.20%	3.16%	5.39%	2.57%	4.86%	1.95%	0.92%
		Non-core adjacent to a small metro and does not contain a town of at least 2,500 residents		185	0.78%	2.82%	1.38%	3.27%	2.82%	5.13%	1.92%	3.10%	2.99%	0.85%
		Non-core adjacent to a small metro with town of at least 2,500 residents		357	0.78%	2.49%	1.30%	3.42%	2.40%	4.16%	2.22%	3.17%	1.73%	0.97%
		Non-core adjacent to micro area and contains a town of 2,500– 9,999 residents		201	0.33%	2.16%	0.96%	2.40%	2.21%	3.88%	1.64%	2.96%	1.59%	1.10%
		Non-core adjacent to micro area and does not contain a town of at least 2,500 residents		198	0.06%	1.79%	0.40%	2.05%	1.68%	3.50%	0.65%	2.68%	2.31%	0.77%
		Non-core not adjacent to a metro/micro area and contains a town of 2,500 or more residents		138	0.65%	3.10%	1.65%	3.27%	3.53%	5.02%	2.55%	3.30%	1.74%	1.18%
		Non-core not adjacent to a metro/micro area and does not contain a town of at least 2,500 residents		174	0.23%	2.25%	0.70%	2.87%	2.44%	4.14%	1.12%	3.98%	1.36%	−0.10%
		Total		3,140	1.24%	3.18%	3.95%	3.68%	3.68%	6.89%	3.22%	2.61%	2.22%	−0.12%

(continued on next page)

Table 32.3a (continued)

Year	Area group		N	Population	Private	Proprietors	Con	FIRE	Services	Retail	Wholesale	TCU	Manufacture
1970–80	Core-based	Large: in a metro area with at least 1 million residents or more	3 million residents and above	163	0.69%	2.16%	3.48%	1.81%	3.09%	4.11%	2.24%	2.63%	0.86%	−0.07%
			Fewer than 3 million and at least 1 million residents	250	0.98%	2.86%	4.07%	2.56%	4.41%	4.95%	3.19%	2.95%	1.48%	0.51%
		Small: in a metro area with fewer than 1 million residents		676	1.44%	3.03%	3.38%	3.11%	4.90%	4.56%	3.48%	4.00%	2.15%	0.77%
		Metropolitan adjacent to a large metro area		92	1.33%	2.38%	2.12%	3.77%	4.50%	3.23%	2.53%	5.65%	1.69%	0.74%
		Metropolitan adjacent to a small metro area		301	1.18%	2.28%	1.49%	2.94%	4.17%	3.15%	2.54%	5.28%	1.69%	0.81%
		Metropolitan not adjacent to a metro area		282	1.20%	3.18%	1.98%	3.78%	4.26%	3.74%	3.10%	6.33%	2.41%	1.45%
	Non-core based	Non-core adjacent to a large metro area		123	1.28%	2.72%	0.73%	3.11%	3.98%	3.12%	1.63%	10.13%	3.41%	1.45%
		Non-core adjacent to a small metro and does not contain a town of at least 2,500 residents		185	1.13%	2.38%	0.42%	2.31%	2.81%	2.92%	1.19%	8.59%	2.37%	1.78%
		Non-core adjacent to a small metro with town of at least 2,500 residents		357	1.18%	2.49%	0.63%	3.90%	3.56%	2.43%	1.53%	7.56%	1.84%	1.88%
		Non-core adjacent to micro area and contains a town of 2,500–9,999 residents		201	0.81%	2.42%	0.47%	2.00%	3.15%	2.90%	1.23%	7.73%	1.61%	1.82%
		Non-core adjacent to micro area and does not contain a town of at least 2,500 residents		198	0.47%	2.16%	−0.26%	2.86%	1.99%	2.12%	0.21%	10.62%	2.39%	1.92%
		Non-core not adjacent to a metro/micro area and contains a town of 2,500 or more residents		138	1.48%	3.78%	1.12%	4.58%	4.89%	3.98%	2.53%	8.14%	3.32%	1.88%
		Non-core not adjacent to a metro/micro area and does not contain a town of at least 2,500 residents		174	0.85%	2.83%	0.10%	3.29%	2.97%	2.82%	0.92%	12.25%	2.25%	2.18%
		Total		3,140	1.05%	2.61%	2.81%	2.60%	3.90%	4.26%	2.78%	3.40%	1.48%	0.51%

Table 32.3b. US population and employment settlement trends by detailed geographic areas, 1980–90 and 1990–2000

Year	Area group	Population	N	Population	Private	Proprietors	Con	FIRE	Services	Retail	Wholesale	TCU	Manufacture
1980–90	Core-based	Large: in a metro area with at least 1 million residents or more — 3 million residents and above	163	1.17%	2.48%	4.47%	3.17%	2.79%	5.12%	2.28%	1.63%	1.73%	−0.97%
		Fewer than 3 million and at least 1 million residents	250	1.11%	2.62%	3.78%	3.08%	2.25%	5.53%	2.84%	1.88%	1.83%	−0.71%
		Small: in a metro area with fewer than 1 million residents	676	0.93%	2.38%	3.02%	2.34%	1.52%	5.09%	2.95%	1.68%	1.13%	−0.28%
		Micropolitan adjacent to a large metro area	92	0.70%	1.78%	1.90%	2.31%	0.00%	4.04%	2.76%	1.18%	0.79%	−0.24%
		Micropolitan adjacent to a small metro area	301	0.36%	1.58%	1.49%	1.71%	0.24%	3.64%	2.41%	0.98%	0.41%	0.14%
		Micropolitan not adjacent to a metro area	282	0.22%	1.58%	1.34%	0.78%	0.36%	3.74%	2.14%	0.29%	0.27%	0.39%
	Non-core based	Non-core adjacent to a large metro area	123	0.40%	1.38%	1.14%	0.48%	−0.22%	3.47%	1.94%	0.30%	0.01%	0.70%
		Non-core adjacent to a small metro and does not contain a town of at least 2,500 residents	185	0.02%	1.81%	0.75%	1.83%	0.05%	3.34%	1.33%	0.08%	1.89%	1.15%
		Non-core adjacent to a small metro with town of at least 2,500 residents	357	0.06%	1.25%	0.69%	0.87%	−0.37%	2.72%	1.76%	0.02%	1.15%	0.73%
		Non-core adjacent to micro area and contains a town of 2,500–9,999 residents	201	−0.31%	1.06%	0.41%	0.10%	−0.32%	2.48%	1.31%	−0.07%	0.67%	1.10%
		Non-core adjacent to micro area and does not contain a town of at least 2,500 residents	198	−0.61%	0.56%	0.00%	−0.88%	−0.82%	2.51%	0.27%	−1.13%	2.05%	1.84%
		Non-core not adjacent to a metro/micro area and contains a town of 2,500 or more residents	138	−0.13%	1.21%	1.15%	0.42%	0.28%	3.01%	1.49%	−0.18%	0.48%	0.73%
		Non-core not adjacent to a metro/micro area and does not contain a town of at least 2,500 residents	174	−0.43%	0.74%	0.43%	0.20%	−0.27%	2.76%	0.72%	−0.51%	0.98%	0.01%
		Total	3,140	0.90%	2.32%	3.04%	2.54%	2.03%	4.97%	2.56%	1.55%	1.43%	−0.47%

(continued on next page)

Table 32.3b (continued)

Year	Area group		N	Population	Private	Proprietors	Con	FIRE	Services	Retail	Wholesale	TCU	Manufacture
1990–2000	Core-based	Large: in a metro area with at least 1 million residents or more — 3 million residents and above	163	1.32%	1.81%	2.74%	2.33%	1.39%	3.19%	1.41%	0.82%	2.33%	−0.83%
		Large … — Fewer than 3 million and at least 1 million residents	250	1.28%	2.43%	2.81%	2.97%	2.66%	3.87%	1.92%	1.57%	2.65%	−0.30%
		Small: in a metro area with fewer than 1 million residents	676	1.20%	2.22%	2.43%	2.84%	2.32%	3.52%	1.96%	1.37%	2.43%	−0.10%
		Micropolitan adjacent to a large metro area	92	1.24%	2.27%	2.53%	2.78%	3.50%	3.71%	2.37%	1.96%	2.41%	0.47%
		Micropolitan adjacent to a small metro area	301	0.87%	1.79%	2.05%	2.92%	2.49%	3.38%	1.94%	1.25%	1.12%	−0.14%
		Micropolitan not adjacent to a metro area	282	0.74%	2.16%	1.86%	3.29%	2.59%	3.28%	1.98%	0.45%	1.48%	0.59%
	Non-core based	Non-core adjacent to a large metro area	123	1.22%	2.27%	2.15%	3.73%	3.73%	3.99%	2.32%	1.34%	1.50%	0.27%
		Non-core adjacent to a small metro and does not contain a town of at least 2,500 residents	185	0.92%	2.17%	2.38%	3.07%	3.85%	3.94%	2.11%	−0.01%	2.42%	−0.57%
		Non-core adjacent to a small metro with town of at least 2,500 residents	357	0.84%	2.02%	1.98%	2.87%	2.78%	3.54%	1.90%	0.72%	1.22%	−0.02%
		Non-core adjacent to micro area and contains a town of 2,500–9,999 residents	201	0.44%	1.65%	1.64%	3.77%	2.71%	2.84%	1.47%	0.40%	1.66%	−0.03%
		Non-core adjacent to micro area and does not contain a town of at least 2,500 residents	198	0.34%	1.65%	1.44%	3.43%	3.39%	2.96%	1.29%	−0.33%	0.99%	−1.36%
		Non-core not adjacent to a metro/micro area and contains a town of 2,500 or more residents	138	0.44%	2.01%	1.77%	2.55%	2.92%	3.06%	1.85%	0.81%	0.64%	0.44%
		Non-core not adjacent to a metro/micro area and does not contain a town of at least 2,500 residents	174	0.25%	1.80%	1.38%	3.25%	3.30%	3.06%	1.22%	0.08%	0.26%	−1.99%
		Total	3,140	1.19%	2.08%	2.49%	2.73%	2.04%	3.45%	1.77%	1.14%	2.30%	−0.33%

Notes: N is the number of counties Clifton Forge City of Virginia is excluded because population and employment data are not available 2000 census; new geographic definition and 2003 Urban Influence code are used to define area group.

Source: Calculated from *Regional Economic Information System 1969–2001*, Bureau of Economic Analysis , US Department of Commerce.

On a sector-by-sector basis (seven major sectors shown), the story is more complex. Three of them (finance–insurance–real estate, services and transportation–communications–utilities) grew fastest in the 1–3 million metro areas and construction employment grew fastest in the micropolitan areas adjacent to the largest metros. Yet wholesale jobs grew fastest in non-core counties adjacent to the largest metros (also exurbs but without a core) while manufacturing jobs grew most in non-core counties that were *not* adjacent to any metros – in this case, the ones with a town containing 2,500 or more residents. As interesting is the remaining pattern of wholesale and manufacturing job growth: wholesale jobs grew faster than the US average everywhere outside the largest metros; manufacturing jobs grew faster than the US average outside all the metros with positive growth everywhere except the non-core non-adjacent metros with towns of less than 2,500 population. Wholesale and manufacturing jobs can be said to have been on a counterurbanization path. Indeed, Carlino (1985) found empirical support for the hypothesis that modern manufacturing depends less than ever on agglomeration economies and can be carried out at remote locations. These increasingly 'footloose' firms may find it in their best interests to follow their labour force into the suburbs, exurbs and beyond. Capital is also much more mobile internationally than ever, vastly increasing the scope for this phenomenon

The same analysis can be carried out for the most recent decade, 1990–2000. In these recent years, three employment sectors showed fastest growth outside the core-based counties: construction, FIRE (finance, insurance and real estate) and services. The first two showed faster-than-national growth in all of the counties outside the largest metro areas. The fastest manufacturing growth was in micropolitan counties not adjacent to metro areas; the fastest wholesale growth was in micropolitan areas adjacent to large metro areas.

There is evidence, then, for complex patterns of dispersion of jobs and people in ways that denote suburbanization and exurbanization as well as counterurbanization. All three are important because as people and jobs settle in less centralized areas, they relieve urban congestion and crowding. While the relocators do so for self-serving reasons, they are helping to reduce externality costs.

According to decennial census population data, the top 75 US cities' share of the national population peaked in 1940. This reflects the well-known fact that the start of large-scale US suburbanization can be traced to the post-Second World War years. There are also decennial population data available for the urbanized areas (UAs) going back to 1950. Unlike spatial units defined by political boundaries, the UAs are geographic areas identified by the Census Bureau every ten years to reflect the actual boundaries of development. It is interesting to note that the share of population residing in the 33 largest urbanized areas increased from 33 per cent in 1950 to 40 per cent in 2000. After the spreading out of settlement is accounted for, there are still apparently agglomeration economies that limit centrifugal forces. These effects can be expected to limit the sort of counterurbanization that is unlinked to existing major centres.

Despite these generalizations, some authors look to the traditional big-city downtowns for signs of revitalization (sometimes referred to as 'regeneration'). Foremost among these writers has been Birch (2002), who presents evidence for population growth for 42 US central business districts (CBDs) through the decade of the 1990s. Yet as a group, these CBDs grew by slightly less than 10 per cent while their surrounding metro areas grew by almost 14 per cent. Fourteen of the CBDs did grow faster than their surrounding metro areas, but this has to be qualified by the fact that many downtowns received special attention and funding from various levels of government. Also, the share of regional growth of the successful CBDs was small, amounting to less than 5 per cent of the 42 metro areas' overall growth over the ten years. While there are some, mostly small, pockets of success, they are insufficient to affect the broad trends outlined here.

Evidence from other developed countries

Direct evidence for counterurbanization outside the US is harder to find. Yet Table 32.1 shows that there is strong evidence for widespread suburbanization. As already suggested, it is often a question of at what point the difference in degree becomes a difference in kind. A brief summary of these trends in the other developed nations follows.

Canada

The comparison of US–Canada settlement trends is interesting because cultural differences are presumably less pronounced than policy differences. Also, spatial area definitions in the two countries share enough commonalities so that fairly plausible comparisons are possible. This is not so for most international pairings.

Canadian population data assembled by spatial divisions that match the US data (Gordon and Lee 2003) may be compared with some of the US population growth data elaborated in the previous section aggregated to comparable spatial units for both countries (Table 32.4). The periods were chosen to match Canadian census years (shaded cells indicate growth faster than national growth; bold numbers indicate fastest growth in each column). For both countries, the fastest growing areas are the suburbs of the metro areas larger than 1 million. This is consistently the pattern for all of the periods for which comparisons could be made. US population growth outside the metro areas, however, was slightly greater than in Canada.

Japan

Such exurbanization-counterurbanization trends as exist in developed countries are constrained by; (1) population decline and (2) government policies that support and subsidize agriculture. Both these phenomena are now important in Japan.

Japan's highly urbanized population is concentrated in three major agglomerations, Tokyo–Yokohama, Osaka–Kobe–Kyoto and Nagoya. Examining data up to 1985, Tsuya and Kuroda (1989) reported slowing natural population increase in Japan's metropolitan sector and slowing net non-metro-to-metro net migration. The 1955–85 gross migration trends reveal declining non-metro–metro migration along with increasing metro-to-non-metro migration, although the former still exceeded the latter in 1985. They concluded that:

> urbanization reached a virtual plateau after 1975, due mainly to a dramatic decline in net migration into the major metropolitan regions. This, however, was not enough to produce population deconcentration, nor can a phenomenon of counterurbanization be clearly identified
>
> (Tsuya and Kuroda 1989: 218)

And

> [d]uring the 1970s ... urban concentration slowed considerably. This was due mainly to substantial decreases (and sometimes net loss) in the net population inflow into metropolitan regions, which was in turn caused by the enlarging 'doughnut' in the regions adjacent to metropolitan regions as well as by a rural population turnaround. Nevertheless, these changes were not large enough to reverse the urbanization process.
>
> (Tsuya and Kuroda 1989: 227)

Table 32.4. Comparative population settlement trends in the US and Canada: 1981–2000

	Percentage change (%)					Annual growth rate (%)[a]				
	81–86	86–91	91–96	96–00/ 96–01	81–00/ 81–01[b]	81–86	86–91	91–96	96–00/ 96–01	81–00/ 81–01[b]
US total	4.65	5.35	6.49	4.73	22.95	0.91	1.05	1.27	1.16	1.09
Metro areas with 1 million + Core	5.65	5.20	5.52	4.52	22.59	1.11	1.02	1.08	1.11	1.08
Non-core	**6.50**	**7.79**	**7.65**	**6.60**	**31.74**	**1.27**	**1.51**	**1.49**	**1.61**	**1.46**
Metro areas with fewer than 1 million	4.33	5.47	6.48	3.79	21.61	0.85	1.07	1.26	0.93	1.04
Adjacent to metros	1.94	2.93	6.51	3.92	16.14	0.38	0.58	1.27	0.97	0.79
Non-metro areas Not adjacent to metros	0.34	0.24	4.92	1.88	7.51	0.07	0.05	0.97	0.47	0.38
Canada[c] total	3.90	7.88	5.68	3.89	23.07	0.77	1.53	1.11	0.77	1.04
Metro areas with 1 million + Core	3.79	6.74	6.09	4.96	23.37	0.75	1.31	1.19	0.97	1.06
Non-core	**12.14**	**20.82**	**11.36**	**10.02**	**66.00**	**2.32**	**3.86**	**2.18**	**1.93**	**2.57**
Metro areas with fewer than 1 million	3.87	7.94	4.95	3.94	22.29	0.76	1.54	0.97	0.78	1.01
Adjacent to metros	1.30	5.11	5.10	1.12	13.16	0.26	1.00	1.00	0.22	0.62
Non-metro areas Not adjacent to metros	−0.36	0.45	1.70	−2.84	−1.10	−0.07	0.09	0.34	−0.57	−0.06

Notes:
[a] Annual growth rate is calculated with beginning value (B) and ending value (E) of each period: $R = (E/B)^{\wedge}(1/n)-1$.
[b] 1981–2000 for the US; 1981–2001 for Canada.
[c] Canada's 288 census divisions are classified into five county groups using Baldwin *et al.* (2001)'s modified Beale code provided by Ray Bollman from Statistics Canada; each year's census geography is adjusted to 1996 census division boundary in Canada.

Source: The US data are calculated from *Regional Economic Information System 1969–1999*, Bureau of Economic Analysis, US Department of Commerce, May 2001. Canada data are calculated from Statistics Canada, Census 1981, 1986, 1991, 1996 and 2001 20 per cent sample data.

Japan's economic downturn began after the period described. Central Tokyo's land values were the most severely affected and may never return to their pre-1990 highs. Among other things, markets are now placing a lesser value on centrality in Japan. More recent demographic data, however, show that the country's largest metropolitan areas are decentralizing rapidly (Tables 32.5a,b).

Table 32.5a. Japan population settlement trends: metropolitan areas and core cities: 1965–2000 (000s)

Population Metropolitan area	1965 Metropolitan area	Core city	Suburbs	Recent Metropolitan area	Core city	Suburbs	Year
Tokyo–Yokohama	21,017	8,893	12,124	33,413	8,130	25,283	2000
Osaka–Kobe–Kyoto	13,070	3,156	9,914	17,000	2,599	14,401	2000
Nagoya	6,078	1,935	4,143	8,837	2,171	6,666	2000
Sapporo	615	524	91	1,900	1,672	228	1990
Fukuoka	790	647	143	1,750	1,086	513	1990
Hiroshima	560	431	129	1,575	1,026	489	1990
Kitakyushu	1,425	1,065	360	1,525	918	499	1990
Sendai	515	425	90	1,175	18,839	257	1990
TOTAL	44,070	17,076	26,994	67,175	18,839	48,336	
Change				23,105	1,763	21,342	
Share of growth					7.6%	92.4%	
Top three areas	40,165	13,984	26,181	59,250	12,900	46,350	
Change				19,085	(1,084)	20,169	
Share of growth					−5.7%	105.7%	
Smaller areas	3,905	3,092	813	7,925	5,939	1,986	
Change				4,020	2,847	1,173	
Share of growth					70.8%	29.2%	

Source: http://www.demographia.com

Table 32.5b. Japan population settlement trends: metropolitan areas and core cities, 1965–2000 changes (000s)

Metropolitan area	Metropolitan area	Core city	Suburbs	Metropolitan area	Core city	Suburbs
Tokyo–Yokohama	12,396	(763)	13,159	59.0%	-8.6%	108.5%
Osaka–Kobe–Kyoto	3,930	(557)	4,487	30.1%	-17.7%	45.3%
Nagoya	2,759	236	2,523	45.4%	12.2%	60.9%
Sapporo	1,285	1,148	137	208.9%	219.1%	150.5%
Fukuoka	960	590	370	121.5%	91.2%	258.7%
Hiroshima	1,015	655	360	181.3%	152.0%	279.1%
Kitakyushu	100	(39)	139	7.0%	-3.7%	38.6%
Sendai	515	425				
Total	23,105	1,763	21,342	52.4%	10.3%	79.1%

Source: http://www.demographia.com

Western Europe

Since 1965, the 42 largest cities of Western Europe, as a group, experienced an overall decline in central city population accompanied by a 113 per cent increase in suburban growth (Table 32.6). If Berlin and its constrained suburbanization for most of these years were excluded, the difference would be even greater.

Suburbanization is mostly motor-car oriented development and the demand for personal travel is well known to be a function of income. As cars are more widely owned, origins and destinations disperse. Greater dispersal, in turn, augments the demand for more car owner-ship and use. This cycle is not simply a North American phenomenon. Gerondeau (1997) provides evidence for the convergence of western European and US car ownership rates; his data go to 1990 and he extrapolated to 2000 (Gerondeau 1997: 316, Figure 2). Car owner-ship figures for the 15 EU countries for 1999 are available, however, and average 460 vehi-cles per 1,000 inhabitants. For the US in the same year, the number of passenger cars per thousand residents was 474. The number may be higher when trucks for personal use are added. Nevertheless, the EU's population can be said to be almost as car-oriented as that of the US.

A recent collection of papers, *Urban Sprawl in Western Europe and the United States*, edited by Richardson and Bae (2004) includes a number of papers that echo this point. The editors' summary of the collected findings is worth noting:

> This book suggests that sprawl is not solely an American phenomenon; it is alive and well in Western Europe too. Also, United States planners have misunderstood what is happening in Europe, basing their judgments more on the compactness of the older European cities and their excellent intercity public ground transit service rather than on the statistical trends or on what is happening away from the large metropolises and the tourist towns. Furthermore, we need to be cautious about the influence of public policies. Despite strong anti-sprawl and pro-urban-centralization policies in many European countries, automobile use continues to rise much faster than in the United States and many households continue to choose suburban or quasi-rural homes. However, despite the major differences (e.g., the geographical size of countries, his-torical forces, current automobile ownership rates, travel mode shares, housing styles), there is more convergence than divergence between the United States and Western Europe.
>
> (Richardson and Bae 2004: 7)

The attention that European planners and policy makers now direct at 'sustainable' transport planning provides further evidence that current trends are following car-oriented patterns of development. In a recent position paper, *European Transport Policy: Strangling or Liberating Europe's Potential?* the writers noted that 'European land transport, freight and passenger alike, is ... based almost entirely on roads (95%), with railways accounting for only 4% ... Road traffic should be relieved by developing other means of transport' (p. 5).

Australia

The available information for fast-growing Australia suggests that trends there follow the general patterns discussed throughout this paper. The country's five major metro areas had almost 93 per cent of their population growth in the suburbs over the last 35 years of the twentieth century. Of the five, Brisbane and Melbourne had positive core city growth while the cores of Adelaide, Perth and Sydney lost population (Tables 32.7a,b)

O'Connor *et al.* (2001) reported on activities in four major zones of Australia's metropolitan areas: 'core', 'inner', 'middle' and 'outer.' These show that, '[b]y 1998, almost half of Australia's total population lived in the middle (20.7%) and outer suburbs (28.5%), with these

Table 32.6. Western Europe: metropolitan areas (1 million or more by latest estimates) and core cities populations (000s)

Metropolitan area	1965			Recent		
	Metro	Core city	Suburbs	Metro	Core city	Suburbs
Amsterdam	1,730	866	864	1,875	713	1,162
Antwerp	1,015	248	767	1,225	157	1,068
Athens	1,950	650	1,300	3,188	745	2,443
Barcelona	2,175	1,650	525	3,766	1,504	2,262
Berlin	4,025	3,241	784	4,101	3,388	713
Birmingham	2,640	1,115	1,525	2,705	966	1,739
Brussels	1,975	165	1,810	2,500	137	2,363
Copenhagen	1,380	705	675	1,524	501	1,023
Dublin	690	537	153	1,004	495	509
Dusseldorf	1,050	704	346	1,316	571	745
Frankfurt	1,450	695	755	1,897	641	1,256
Glasgow	1,885	1,030	855	1,870	663	1,207
Hamburg	2,300	1,855	445	2,593	1,726	867
Helsinki	635	476	159	1,070	559	511
Koln	1,550	855	695	1,893	968	925
Leeds	1,360	514	846	1,530	424	1,106
Lille	856	193	672	1,143	185	958
Lisbon	1,300	802	498	2,250	564	1,686
Liverpool	1,685	738	947	1,515	482	1,033
London	12,930	3,175	9,755	13,945	2,776	11,179
Lyon	1,000	545	455	1,649	422	1,227
Madrid	2,575	2,450	125	5,087	2,939	2,148
Manchester	2,850	652	2,198	2,760	403	2,357
Mannheim	1,170	323	847	1,569	308	1,261
Marseille	870	778	92	1,516	798	718
Milan	2,775	1,665	1,110	3,790	1,306	2,484
Munich	1,500	1,175	325	1,894	1,228	666
Naples	1,765	1,225	540	3,150	1,047	2,103
Newcastle	1,155	262	893	1,350	189	1,161
Nuremburg	675	466	209	1,018	491	527
Paris	8,000	2,800	5,200	11,175	2,125	9,050
Porto	750	303	447	1,035	263	772
Rhine–Ruhr	5,200	739	4,471	5,823	592	5,231
Rome	2,500	2,340	160	3,235	2,650	585
Rotterdam	1,010	732	278	1,325	599	726
Seville	750	443	307	1,180	685	495
Stockholm	1,180	800	380	1,684	758	926
Stuttgart	1,415	642	773	2,593	587	2,006
Turin	1,350	1,110	240	1,550	921	629
Valencia	660	505	155	1,398	738	660
Vienna	2,025	1,660	365	1,825	1,550	275
Zurich	715	440	275	1,220	340	880

Source: http://www.demographia.com

Table 32.7a. Australia settlement trends: metropolitan areas and core cities, 1965–2000 (000s)

Population Metropolitan area	1965 Metropolitan area	Core city	Suburbs	2001 Metropolitan area	Core city	Suburbs
Adelaide	660	21	639	1,073	18	1,055
Brisbane	650	619	31	1,628	888	740
Melbourne	2,055	75	1,980	3,367	91	3,276
Perth	485	95	390	1,340	13	1,327
Sydney	2,340	168	2,172	3,997	140	3,857
Total	6,690	1,126	5,564	12,695	1,556	11,139
				6,005	430	5,575
					7.2%	92.8%

Source: http://www.demographia.com

Table 32.7b. Australia and New Zealand settlement trends: metropolitan areas and core cities, 1965–2000 changes

Change Metropolitan area	1965–2000 population change (000s) Metropolitan area	Core city	Suburbs	1965–2000 population per cent change Metropolitan area	Core city	Suburbs
Adelaide	413	(3)	416	62.6%	−14.3%	65.1%
Brisbane	978	269	709	150.5%	43.5%	2287.1%
Melbourne	1,312	16	1,296	63.8%	21.3%	65.5%
Perth	855	(82)	937	176.3%	−86.3%	240.3%
Sydney	1,657	(28)	1,685	70.8%	−16.7	77.6%
Total	6,005	430	5,575	89.8%	38.2%	100.2%

Source: http://www.demographia.com

two broad suburban zones accounting for around half of all the population increase recorded in the nation since 1986' (p. 142). As elsewhere, these developments have spawned the typical concerns about 'sprawl' and have launched investigations into possible 'smart growth' alternatives.

Discussion

Over 40 years ago, Mel Webber predicted:

> Increasingly in the future, when high-level specialists are able to locate establishments in outlying settlements or even in the mountains … what is hinterland and what is center becomes, at best, but a difference in magnitudes of information flow and volumes of activity.
>
> (Webber 1964: 143).

It now appears that the standard geographic descriptors of urban settlements may have been rendered obsolete by events. The widespread settlement of outer suburbs and exurbs in

513

recent years can be seen as a continuation of old trends or may even qualify as 'counter-urbanization'. Either way, the trends documented in this chapter appear to be widespread and durable.

Our brief survey has found lots of suburbanization in developed country metro areas and it is unclear how much of this merits the label 'counterurbanization'. We are, after all, looking for differences of degree that can qualify as a difference in kind. It is safer to say that no reversals are anywhere in sight and at some point continuing suburbanization/exurbanization trends will be seen as something different from traditional urbanization.

It is also not clear how the study of urbanization–suburbanization exurbanization–counterurbanization impacts discussions of changing urban hierarchies. Peter Hall (1990), for example, concludes that, '[t]he new technologies are likely to promote concentration at the top of the urban hierarchy rather than the reverse' (p. 19). While the continued dispersion of people and jobs is likely to continue – even to the point that it is seen as a counterurbanizing trend – whether the relative importance and large vs mid-sized vs small centres changes remains an interesting area for further investigation.

Another remaining question is the one that has been described as 'urban decline' (see R.D. Ebel (1985) for a cross-country summary). Settlement change never stops and there are always winners and losers. At the same time, there are push and pull forces at work. Declining areas, just like declining industries, can be expected to seek help via the political processes. Some of the cited policy debates are spawned by these sorts of politics. Again, their scope and wisdom is an area for discussion that goes beyond this chapter.

The histories of cities focus on the importance of transportation hubs and cross-roads. Seaports were notable examples for many years and the giant hub airports (Chicago, Dallas, Denver, St Louis, Minneapolis) are the sites of important hubs in the US today (Hall 1990). The future is likely to include further declining travel costs and the reduce importance of scale economies. Just as cars and ubiquitous access replaced transit hubs, widely available personal air travel will one day not very far into the future diminish the role of the giant airport hubs. When that day comes, counterurbanization forces will have received another boost.

Note

1 This chapter focuses on the 'developed' or 'Western' nations. There is, however, an emerging literature that documents broad urban development similarities throughout parts of the world that also include many developing nations. See, for example, Ingram (1997: 5):

> Over time, a universal finding is that metropolitan populations have become more decentralized (population gradients become flatter) – due to the effects of increases in income (promoting housing consumption) and improvements in transport performance (higher speeds and lower costs relative to incomes).

More on urbanization in the parts of the world not covered here can be found in Rogers and Williamson (1982).

Further reading

Baldwin, J.R., Brown, M., and Vinodri, T. (2001) Dynamics of the Canadian manufacturing sector in metropolitan and rural regions. Micro-Economic Analysis Division, Statistics Canada, Research Paper Series No. 169.

Bruegmann, Robert (2005) Sprawl: A Compact History. Chicago: University of Chicago Press.

Champion, A.G. (1989) *Counterurbanization*. New York: Routledge.

Clark, W.V.A. (2000) Monocentric and policentric: new urban forms and old paradigms. In Gary Bridge and Sophie Watson (eds) *A Companion to the City*, Ch. 13, pp. 141–54. Oxford, UK: Blackwell.

Easterlin, Richard A. (2000) Twentieth-century American population growth. In S. Engerman and R.E. Gallman (eds) *The Cambridge Economic History of the United States. Vol. III: The Twentieth Century.* Cambridge, UK: Cambridge University Press.

Ebel, R.D. (1985) Urban decline in the world's developed economies: an examination of the trends. In J.P. Ross (ed.) *Research in Urban Economics (vol. 5): Causes and Consequences of Urban Change in the World's Developed Countries.* Greenwich, CT: JAI Press.

Gerondeau, Christian (1997) *Transport in Europe*. Norwood, MA: Artech House.

Gordon, P. and Lee, B. (2003) *Settlement Patterns in the U.S. and Canada: Similarities and Differences – Policies or Preferences?* (Lusk Center for Real Estate Working Paper). Los Angeles: University of Southern California.

Ingram, G.K. (1997) *Patterns of Metropolitan Development: What Have We Learned?* (Policy Research Working Paper 1841). Washington DC: The World Bank.

National Academy of Sciences (2005) *Proceedings of the National Academy of Sciences of the U.S.A.: Spatial Demography Special Feature.* Washington DC: National Academy of Sciences.

Richardson, Harry W. and Bae, Chang-Hee Christine (2004) *Urban Sprawl in Western Europe and in the United States.* Aldershot, UK: Ashgate.

Rogers, A. and Williamson, J.G. (eds) (1982) Urbanization and development in the Third World. *Economic Development and Cultural Change*, 30 (3), 463–82.

References

Berry, B. (1976) The counterurbanization process: urban America in 1970. In B. Berry (ed.) *Urbanization and Counterurbanization*, pp. 17–30. Beverly Hills: Sage.

Birch, E.L. (2002) Having a longer view of downtown. *Journal of the American Planning Association* 68 (1), 5–21.

Brooks, D. (2002) Patio Man and the sprawl people. *The Weekly Standard* 12–19 August.

——(2004) Our sprawling, supersized utopia. *The New York Times Magazine* 4 April.

Carlino, G.A. (1985) Declining city productivity and the growth of rural regions: a test of alternative explanations. *Journal of Urban Economics* 18, 11–27.

Champion, A.G. (1989) *Counterurbanization*. New York: Routledge.

Easterlin, R.A. (2000) Twentieth century American population growth. In S. Engerman and R.A. Gallman (eds) *The Cambridge Economic History of the United States, Vol, III, The Twentieth Century.* Cambridge, UK: Cambridge University Press.

Ebel, R.D. (1985) Urban decline in the world's developed economies: an examination of the trends. In J.P. Ross (ed.) *Research in Urban Economics (vol. 5): Causes and Consequences of Urban Change in the World's Developed Countries.* Greenwich, CT: JAI Press.

Fischel, W.A. (2001) *The Homeovoter Hypothesis: How Home Values Influence Local Government Taxation, School Finance and Land-Use Policies.* Cambridge, MA: Harvard University Press.

Frey, W.H. (1989) United States: counterurbanization and metropolis depopulation. In A.G Champion (ed.) *Counterurbanization*. New York: Routledge.

——(1993) The new urban revival in the US. *Urban Studies* 30, 741–74.

Gerondeau, C. (1997) *Transport in Europe*. Norwood, MA: Artech House.

Gordon, P. (1979) Deconcentration without a 'clean break'. *Environment and Planning A*, 11, 281–90.

Hall, P. (1990) *International Urban Systems* (Working Paper 514). Berkeley, CA: Institute of Urban and Regional Development, University of California at Berkeley.

Mieszkowski, P. and Mills, E.S. (1993) The causes of metropolitan suburbanization. *Journal of Economic Perspectives* 7 (3), 135–47.

Nelson, R.H. (2005) *Private Neighborhoods and the Transformation of Local Government*. Washington DC: Urban Institute Press.

O'Connor, K., Stimson, R. and Daly, M. (2001) *Australia's Changing Economic Geography: A Society Dividing*. Oxford: Oxford University Press.

Richardson, H.W. and Bae, C. (2004) *Urban Sprawl in Western Europe and in the United States*. Aldershot, UK: Ashgate.

Tsuya, N.O. and Kuroda, T. (1989) Japan: the slowing of urbanization and metropolitan concentration. In A.G. Champion (ed.) *Counterurbanization*. New York: Routledge.

Voith, R. (1992) City and suburban growth: substitutes of complements? *Federal Reserve of Philadelphia Business Review* September/October.

Webber, M.M. (1964) The urban place and the nonplace urban realm. In M.M. Webber (ed.) *Explorations into Urban Structure*. Baltimore: Johns Hopkins University Press.

33

Virtual places[1]

Martin Dodge and Rob Kitchin

Introduction

> Cyberspace. A consensual hallucination experienced daily by billions of legitimate
> operators, in every nation, by children being taught mathematical concepts ... A gra-
> phical representation of data abstracted from the banks of every computer in the
> human system. Unthinkable complexity. Lines of light ranged in the nonspace of the
> mind, clusters and constellations of data. Like city lights, receding.
>
> (William Gibson, *Neuromancer*, 1984)

Many everyday activities and social interactions take place in virtual places – places that are
dependent on networked computing infrastructure for their existence. For the most part
virtual places are created online in cyberspace, usually within Internet technologies, and we
concentrate most of our discussion on the geographies of such places. However, important
virtual spaces are also increasingly produced in the material world through the embedding of
information and communications technologies (ICTs) into the fabric of cities. Examples
include traffic management systems, electronic payment through credit/debit cards, point of
sales terminals and ATM machines, access control through swipe cards and pin numbers, and
surveillance through networks of digital cameras. Here, the virtual and material blend together,
one dependent on the other. And as we discuss later, the virtual is always accessed from the
material; they are not so easily separated. In other words, there are distinct kinds of virtual
places. We start, though, by examining the nature of cyberspace and the online virtual places
it supports through its various media.

Cyberspaces consist of information flows and social interactions that are continually
beckoned into being *within* the infrastructural ensemble of digital computing hardware,
software code and high-speed telecommunications networks. Cyberspace has emerged in the
last 150 years from the convergence of two sets of technologies: those for the transmission of
information and those for the automation of computation. Since the Second World War the
technologies of computing and communication have grown dramatically in capacity and
fallen in per unit cost (see Chapter 16). Of particular importance has been the development
of the Internet – literally a network of computer networks. The Internet traces its roots to a

US military-funded network called ARPANET launched in 1969 (Salus 1995). This network quickly grew to link together a number of computers across the US, and by the early 1970s via satellite and underwater cable to other Western countries (Kitchin 1998). The first social application was the development of email in 1970, followed quickly by mailing lists. The first bulletin board came online in 1978. Throughout the 1970s a number of non-military networks were established and the PC revolution of the 1980s ensured a steady growth in numbers of users. The launch of the World Wide Web in 1992, and the growth in visual interfaces, led to an exponential increase in Internet users and the development of numerous other Internet technologies and applications (e.g. webcams, multiplayer games), along with rapid commercial exploitation leading to the dot.com boom in the late 1990s (Zook 2005). In 2004 it was estimated that worldwide there were 840 million Internet users contributing to numerous multi-billion dollar industries (including online shopping, gambling, games, distance education, and so on). As Internet usage has grown so has cyberspace itself. Everyday, tens of thousands of new web pages are added so that by the end of 2005 Google indexed over 8 billion pages. It is not unsurprising, then, that Internet technologies and the cyberspaces they support have diffused throughout society and have had a significant transformative agency in the nature of everyday living, including radically altering space–time relations in complex ways through convergence, compression and distanciation (Janelle 1969; Harvey 1989; Giddens 1990).

Cyberspaces are not the technology or infrastructure themselves (although they cannot exist independently of these), but the *experience* of virtual places that these engender. The word 'cyberspace' literally means 'navigable space' and is derived from the Greek world *kyber* (to navigate). As a description of online virtual places it was conceived by William Gibson in his novel *Neuromancer* (1984) as a three-dimensional 'data-scape' inside the global matrix of computer networks where disembodied users interact with 'clusters and constellations of data'. As an everyday human experiential phenomena, online virtual places are much more mundane than William Gibson's science-fiction imaginary, but are nonetheless powerful in mediating social relationships and shaping the material world. For example, they are:

> the 'place' where a telephone conversation appears to occur. Not inside your actual phone, the plastic device on your desk. Not inside the other person's phone, in some other city. The place between the phones. The indefinite place out there, where the two of you, two human beings, actually meet and communicate.
>
> (Sterling 1992: 1)

Cyberspace is also the 'place' where your money is (to paraphrase John Perry Barlow, cited in Jordan and Taylor 1998) and is fast becoming the primary archive of memories (emails and text messages, homepages, blogs, digital photographs, and so on).

Online virtual places are not 'real' in terms of common-sense definitions of material 'stuff' that can be touched; they are, in Gibson's phrase, a 'consensual hallucination' created by software code and visual interfaces, and made tangible by access devices (touch screens, keyboards, stereo speakers, joysticks, and so on). However, they are perceived as real places and they can have very real, material consequences (e.g. money being electronically stolen from one's bank account). This is because virtual places are produced as hybrid space that is folded into everyday lived experience and physical environment, rather than being some exotic, dissociated para-space (as frequently depicted cinematically in the 1990s; see Kitchin and Kneale 2001). Uses of ICTs are themselves intrinsically embodied practices and the experiences of virtual places form a complex continuum from purely material ones to wholly cyber ones, with many social activities now liminally combining the 'virtually real and the actually real' (Madge and O'Connor 2005: 83). For example, when taking part in a multi-player game on the Internet, while the interactions are occurring online as characters take part in shared social activities (fighting, flying, driving and conversing), the virtual characters are made real by the typing fingers of players staring at a computer screen, who might also be drinking Coke and chatting to friends co-present in geographic space. The player is in both the virtual world and the geographic world simultaneously. Later in the chapter, we discuss more fully the idea of material spaces becoming virtualized in particular contexts at specific times.

This experiential continuum of cyberspace and hybrid nature of virtual places is differentiated in two ways: first, the material context and social characteristics of the people using the technologies (see, for example, various empirical analyses presented in Wellman and Haythornthwaite 2002); second, the technologies themselves and how they work to shape the way in which interaction occurs. Focusing on the latter, we can construct a typology of online virtual places.

Typology of online virtual places

Online virtual places composed of infinitely malleable software code can exist in numerous forms including web pages and their hyperlinks, social interactions through text in chat rooms and email mailing lists, three-dimensional virtual reality (VR) environments, large multiplayer games, and huge distributed file corpuses on peer-2-peer networks – all with 'their own sense of place and space, their own geography' (Batty 1997a: 339). These forms of virtual places are always contingent on the time and place of their production. They are also heterogeneous in structure and operation, and are typically fast changing.

To make sense of these virtual places we can categorize them into a simple typology, demarcated by the temporality of social exchange and the configuration and numbers of users (Table 33.1). The time dimension divides online virtual places into two groups: asynchronous (participants can communicate at different times) and synchronous (participants must be present at the same time). In communications in general, letter-writing is the archetypal asynchronous mode of social interaction and face-to-face spoken conversation is the archetypal synchronous mode. The number of users dimension divides online virtual place in relation to how many people are participating through a particular social medium and how they are configured (in terms of senders or receivers of information). Clearly this dimension is a continuum ranging from a minimum of two people, small conversations with a group of friends or family, up to large parties, seminars and concerts, and perhaps even the many millions who participate in large events like the World Cup final or the Olympics via mass media broadcasting. We impose a logical, simplifying break in this continuum, dividing social media into three groups – one-to-one being social media for interactions between two people, one-to-many being media for simultaneous one-way communication with more than one other person, and many-to-many being media that supports several simultaneous conversations and information distribution. Table 33.1 takes these two dimensions to create a typology of six categories which characterize the principal online virtual places used for social interaction.

Email is the archetypal example of an asynchronous and one-to-one form of communication. Messages are sent from one individual to another, with the message being stored in a mailbox for reading at leisure. The users of email never need to be online at the same time to successfully communicate. It is the ideal form of interaction for people in divergent time zones where arranging a convenient time for a 'live' conversation can be difficult. Email

Table 33.1. Typology of online virtual places

	Asynchronous	*Synchronous*
One-to-one	Email	Talk/instant messaging (ICQ) Private chat rooms 'Whispering' in MUDs/virtual worlds Internet telephony Video conferences
One-to-many	Web homepages Ftp archives Blogs Moderated email Newsletters	'Live' websites Webcams Podcasts
Many-to-many	Mailing lists/listservs Usenet Bulletin-boards Peer-2-peer file sharing	Chat rooms/IRC MUDs Graphical virtual worlds Networked games

remains the most popular reason to use the Internet; for example Oxford Internet Institute's 2005 survey found that 92 per cent of British Internet users check email regularly. One-to-many, asynchronous media include personal homepages and blogs on the web and are the nearest in form to conventional mass media communication of newspapers. Here, information is published by one source and communicated to a group of people, but in an asynchronous form that allows them to access the material at any time. Asynchronous many-to-many media include mailing lists, bulletin boards, Usenet groups and peer-2-peer file sharing, wherein there are multiple authors of information sharing the same place, accessed by many different people.

One-to-one synchronous communications are similar in form to private conversations between two people in the same location, except that they take place online between geographically distant participants. Typically a conversation takes place by typing short sentences which are displayed in real-time on the screen of the other 'speaker'. Examples include instant messaging, the most prevalent commercial examples being ICQ, Yahoo Messenger and AIM (AOL instant messaging) and private conversations in 'public' media using a private chat channel or room or the whisper mode in virtual worlds. Many-to-many synchronous communications typically take the form of broadcasts and include 'live' websites that are updated in real-time, such as sports results web pages and broadcasting radio shows or concerts. Finally, synchronous one-to-many media are spaces in which many people can converse and interact in real-time and include chat rooms, multi-user domains (MUDs), virtual worlds and networked games. One must also be aware that digital information and communications are mutable in nature and the virtual spaces set out above can be modified in operation to be used in different ways (e.g. the publishing of information on Web homepages can be made into a one-to-one media by password protection). Information can also be presented in different virtual spaces at the same time (e.g. blog entries being distributed to subscribers over RSS – really simple syndication).

The differing nature of each of these media leads to different forms of social interaction. The degree to which these media have a differentiated sense of spatiality, how they are complementing, reshaping or replacing social interactions in geographic space, and what that means for understanding socio-spatial relations are important questions. Indeed, to what extent can different forms of communication be said to generate new virtual places that have a sense of community similar to existing place-bound communities?

Online virtual places: remaking community, replacing geography?

Very few commentators now doubt that virtual communities exist. However, to date, virtual communities have been conceived and examined in largely aspatial terms, and tellingly the lack of geography is considered by many social scientists one of the key features in the development and sustenance of online social and economic relations. Indeed, many commentators have argued that cyberspace is essentially spaceless and free of the constraints of place (e.g. Rheingold 1993; Negroponte 1995). It is thus argued that online communities are sustained and grounded by communicative practice, not geographic propinquity. In other words, a sense of community is based upon new ways of communicating and shared interests and affinity, not on sharing the same geographic environment; what is important is what people think, say, believe and are interested in, rather than on where they live. As we have argued previously (Dodge and Kitchin 2001), we believe that this could not be further from the truth. To the contrary, virtual communities are ripe for geographic enquiry because they display remarkably complex socio-spatial relations and because they have been hailed as alternatives to geographic communities.

Online communities as placeless communities

The idea that cyberspace has no spatiality and thus no sense of place has been challenged by a number of commentators. They argue that online interactions are often structured through a complex set of geographic metaphors that are employed precisely because they work to create a 'sense of place' and a tangible spatiality. As we, and others such as Adams (1997) and Graham (1998), have noted, cyberspace is replete with the vocabulary of place – nouns, such as rooms, lobbies, highway, frontier, cafes; and verbs, such as surf, inhabit, build, enter. Cyberspace is 'made real' through the language of place; geographic metaphors supply a familiar spatiality that fosters social interaction. In other words, such interactions are socio-spatial in nature. As Taylor (1997: 190) states, 'to be within a virtual world is to have an intrinsically geographic experience, as virtual worlds are experienced fundamentally as places'. The case example below of AlphaWorld, a three-dimensional, collaborative virtual environment (CVE), illustrates this quite clearly (discussed later).

Online communities as an alternative to geographic communities

For some commentators such as Rheingold (1993) and Mitchell (1995), virtual communities are providing more sustainable alternative communities to those in geographic space which they perceive to be fragmenting and becoming increasingly placeless. The demise of geographic communities has been commented on for a number of years. Analysts have suggested that cultural and economic globalization (the coalescing of cultural signs and symbols, increased geographic mobility, a de-significance of the local, and changing social relations; cf. Castells 1996; Dicken 2003; Klein 2000) is leading to social alienation and a condition of placelessness – that is, 'a weakening of the identity of places to the point where they not only look alike, but feel alike and offer the same bland possibilities for experience' – is occurring (Relph 1976: 90). Online communities thus are perceived to provide an antidote to such conditions, providing an alternative form of community to one underpinned by a sense of place. This view can be contrasted to that of Robins (1995). He severely criticizes the idea that one can simply turn away from the problems of geographic communities and further questions the salience of online relationships, which he sees as fleeting and self-selecting, a view also expressed by Gray:

We are who we are because of the places in which we grow up, the accents and friends we acquire by chance, the burdens we have not chosen but somehow learn to cope with. *Real* communities are always local – places in which people have to put down some roots and are willing to put up with the burdens of living together. The *fantasy* of virtual communities is that we can enjoy the benefits of community without its burdens, without the daily effort to keep delicate human connections intact. Real communities can bear those burdens because they are embedded in particular places and evoke enduring loyalties. In cyberspace, however, there is nowhere that a sense of place can grow, and no way in which the solidarities that sustain human beings through difficult times can be forged.

(Gray 1995, our emphases)

Wellman and Gulia (1999) argue that it is a mistake to characterize online and geographic communities as being opposed to one another. In many respects they are remarkably similar, consisting of social networks that vary in range and often overlap in many ways (e.g. keeping in contact with friends through email). Indeed, many people's communities, the people that make up their social networks, do not live within the same geographical location. These networks are sustained through various forms of communication beyond face-to-face conversations. What is perhaps different about online communities is that members might never meet. That said, online social networks are not pale imitations of 'real' networks, or substitutions for them; they are just merely another form, a subset of an individual's total network.

Further, one of the common uses of cyberspace is as a forum in which to mobilize and debate a plethora of 'real world' issues such as community development. Many communities are using the Internet to develop cross-community and cross-issue alliances to help fight particular concerns from local (e.g. anti-road protests) to global issues (e.g. opposition to the Iraq war) (cf. Jordan 2002; Pickerill 2003). In addition, e-government initiatives are increasingly allowing residents to communicate directly with state agencies and local political representatives, helping to manage changes in a globalizing world. In other words, rather than replacing geographic communities, the online virtual places in these examples are augmenting them.

AlphaWorld case study

Many of these arguments around community and spacelessness online can be illustrated with respect to collaborative virtual environments (CVEs), often suggested to be the nearest thing to geographic communities available online due to their synchronous, many-to-many nature, their shared three-dimensional graphical environment, and the use of avatars[2] to represent participants. The graphical environment offers more than just an interface, it provides an immersive, spatial context for social activities (e.g. Figure 33.1). This is achieved by differentiating ground and sky, granting the freedom to move in different directions, and providing an awareness of things that are nearby and locations that are distant. It is productive, therefore, to think of CVEs as hybrid virtual places – lacking the materiality of geographic and architectural space, yet having a powerful mimetic quality, containing enough geographical referents and spatial structure to make them experientially tangible (Schroeder 2002). Avatars provide participants with an embodied form, a tangible sense of self within the environment (Figure 33.2). Often the virtual world is seen in first-person perspective through the eyes of the avatar, which can be made to move, manipulate objects, talk to others (via text presented in speech bubbles) and make simple gestures (wave, dance, shake a fist in anger). They also set the scale of the world in context, particularly in terms of the size and layout of buildings. The fact that avatars can modify the virtual world to varying degrees helps engender a sense of community: lifeless online media are rendered into *places* that have meaning to regular users, who in turn develop a sense of belonging.

Figure 33.1. A screenshot of the three-dimensional graphic environment of AlphaWorld.
Source: Martin Dodge.

Figure 33.2. Avatars interacting in AlphaWorld at 'Ground Zero'.
Source: Martin Dodge.

523

The CVE we examine here, AlphaWorld, is one of a number of commercially developed systems that are publicly available. It is the flagship virtual world produced by ActiveWorlds. The system can be tried for free but requires downloading a special 3D browser (more details are available at http://www.activeworlds.com). AlphaWorld measures 429,000 square kilometres (about the size of California). Since 1995 over 158 million objects have been placed on to this landscape by over a million different users, as of June 2004 (Roelofs and van der Meulen 2004). Like other social CVEs – such as Second Life (http://secondlife.com/) – AlphaWorld is expressly designed as a space in which people can meet, interact and build new forms of community. These CVEs differ in relation to the interface and the rules explicitly built into the system. Other CVEs have been designed for pedagogic use as virtual learning environments or as training simulators for the military (Taylor 1997).

From the perspective of social geography, the analysis of CVEs is worthwhile because it can shed light on how social interaction and the spatial environment combine to create a virtual place. This can considered in four different ways: (1) the built environment and the social meaning inscribed into homes; (2) the changing notion of distance and accessibility in an environment with virtualized location and instantaneous travel; (3) the emergent morphology of virtual urban development; and (4) persistence of place and the manifestation of community memory. The virtual nature of AlphaWorld actively shapes the socio-spatial practices that occur there by shaping how people interact (through typing at a keyboard at a remote location), masking identity (using avatars), regulating how people make things (using a virtual toolkit) and get around the world (using teleporting), and so on. That said, social and spatial behaviour is infused with the social norms, rules and meanings of the 'real' world that people take online with them.

Built environment and making homes

AlphaWorld enables inhabitants to claim their own plot of land and design and build homes, thereby constructing their own places for social interaction. This 'homesteading' facility was a conscious part of the design and has been enthusiastically grasped by many thousands of people since AlphaWorld opened. Building in AlphaWorld is much like using a Lego construction set with predefined objects (such as road sections, wall panels, doors, windows, flowers and furniture) and the citizens have built a huge, sprawling city in the centre of the world (Figure 33.3), along with many smaller settlements and isolated homesteads.

Building in AlphaWorld is time-consuming and represents a real investment in the virtual world. It also provides a powerful new mode of personal self-expression with many thousands of people becoming virtual architects. Virtual homesteads, like web homepages, are tangible expressions of presence and a fixed point of reference. 'Building a home provides an opportunity to showcase one's craftsmanship, and create a feeling of ownership as the home is a territorial marker for a virtual habitat' (Jeffrey and Mark 1998: 26). The ability to own land and to build is also one of the major sources of social conflict in AlphaWorld. For example, virtual vandalism is possible by deliberately placing annoying/offensive objects (like flames, bogus teleports and even large billboards with pornographic pictures on them) as close as possible to other people's homesteads. Further, the homestead, whilst owned by one individual, does not really operate as private space as other users can go anywhere, including entering buildings without the owner's permission.

From informal observation of the homes and other structures which users have built it is clear that they are firmly rooted in users' quotidian experience of real-world places. Many designs use vernacular architectural forms (e.g. the mock Tudor mansion shown in Figure 33.1)

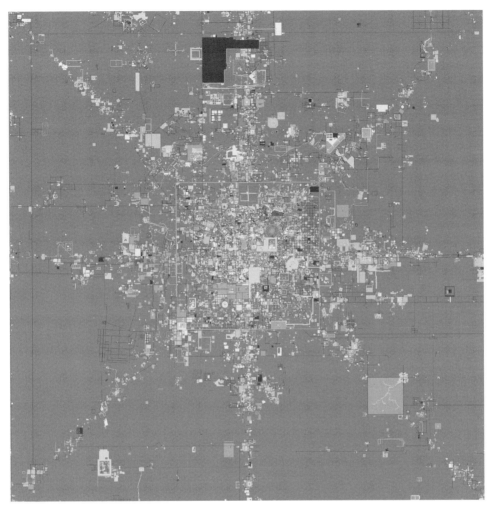

Figure 33.3. A satellite image of the building at the centre of AlphaWorld in December 1996.
Source: Roland Vilett, http://www.activeworlds.com/community/maps.asp

and grid street layouts despite the ability to stretch and warp conventional architectural notions of the material world. Indeed, it is perfectly possible to build abstract structures floating in mid-air and other architectural designs that would be impossible with real-world building materials and gravity. And yet the ideal of a spacious Californian-style home with sun decks and a pool is common in AlphaWorld, because of, in part, the North American background of many users and the aspirations of many others based on Americanized media representations of 'dream' homes. Importantly, there is also a strong tendency to scale the buildings to the height of the 'human' avatar, just like the environment of the real world.

Location and movement

AlphaWorld's 'geography' consists of a rectangular plain with a pre-defined Cartesian co-ordinate system delineating location around an origin point in the centre of the world

525

(designated 0,0). This centre point is known as Ground Zero (GZ) to regular users and is the focal point for the world because it is the default entry point for avatars arriving in Alpha-World. (Figure 33.3 shows the town that has grown up around GZ.) Consequently, the area around Ground Zero tends to be the most densely populated. When people give addresses in AlphaWorld they use co-ordinates such as 67N, 42W which translates to 670 metres north and 420 metres west of GZ. Regular users know the co-ordinates of their homesteads in these terms and use them as the primary address location scheme.

Social stratification is played out in spatial terms, with 'newbies' tending to cluster at GZ while regular users are more wide-ranging, exploring more of the territory and holding meetings and events at specific locations (Schroeder 1997). This is the result of their greater familiarity with the system and what is available in the world – they know the good places to go. Also, regulars have often built homesteads that they can invite people to visit, a facility denied to casual users (known as 'tourists').

The movement of avatars in AlphaWorld is enhanced compared to embodied human movement. Avatars can dispense with the real-world convention of doors and simply walk through walls by holding down the shift key. Second, avatars can as easily fly in the air as stick to *terra firma*. So while AlphaWorld encourages the construction of a built environment with solid walls using the metaphors of the material world, it also provides superhuman powers to shatter the illusion and allow avatars to effortlessly glide through and above structures.

The nature of time–space is also warped in virtual worlds such as AlphaWorld by the power to teleport avatars to a specified location. Teleportation side-steps geographical accessibility based on the friction of distance because any location in the expanse of Alpha-World can be reached instantaneously from any other point, at no cost in time or money. Consequently, every point in AlphaWorld is equally accessible – this is truly the 'death of distance' (Cairncross 1997). The ability to teleport is a powerful feature; however, it was not available at the beginning of AlphaWorld's history. It has been progressively introduced for fear of its effects on the world. Teleportation does cause problems. In terms of navigation, when users become dependent on it they tend to lose their understanding of the geographic context of features and the spatial relations between them. When combined with the lim-itations on avatar vision (by default only 40 metres), it is hard to build up a mental map of local AlphaWorld neighbourhoods, which in turn means it is difficult to find buildings and features of interest unless their x and y co-ordinates are known. Teleportation also has a negative impact on the social life of the virtual place as it reduces the opportunities for chance encounters and discoveries. AlphaWorld citizens can teleport directly to their homesteads without encountering other people. In a similar manner to car travel in cities, teleportation has the tendency to diminish spontaneous social interaction.

While the 'tyranny of distance' may be rendered obsolete by teleportation, location remains important. When people are choosing a location to visit or, more importantly, a place to build their homestead, they want a *good* location. In the context of AlphaWorld a good location is determined by two main factors: first, being as close as possible to Ground Zero, the centre of the world; and second, having a location with memorable co-ordinates – for example, the Pink Village is located at 2222S and 2222E. These parameters have interesting impacts on the evolving urban morphology.

Urban morphology

AlphaWorld has undergone concerted urban development since it came online in 1995. The initial *terra nullius* state has been transformed by the placing of millions of objects into the

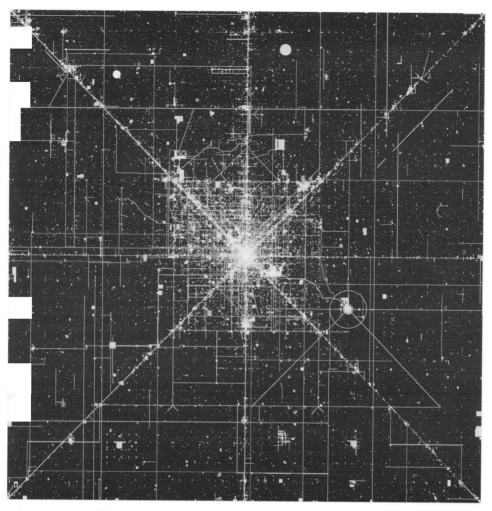

Figure 33.4. A density map of the whole of Alpha World, with light intensity relating the amount of building. Map computed in June 2004.

Source: Roelofs and van der Meulen (2004).

landscape. Yet it is evident that a large amount of AlphaWorld's expansive plain, beyond the central core at GZ, remains undeveloped with only a small percentage of the land containing any buildings (Figure 33.4).

It is clear that the most developed part of AlphaWorld is the densely built city around GZ, which sprawls out in all directions for about 35 kilometres. Ribbons of urban growth project out from this city along the principal compass axes to form a distinctive star shape. Towns and other small settlements lie along these axes, looking like bright beads strung along a necklace. The spatial structure of urban development is largely the result of the power of the co-ordinate system as a form of addressing in AlphaWorld. Once a pioneer has started building, other citizens will build alongside either by invitation or just to be close to other potentially interesting people.

At the local scale, the urban morphology of the city around GZ (shown in Figure 33.3, from 1996) is chaotic and disorganized because it has accreted over time from the efforts of lots of individuals with little or no co-ordination. In AlphaWorld there are no building controls or planning zones. One could argue that AlphaWorld's towns are similar to the informal squatter settlements described in Chapter 31, that characterize many rapidly urbanizing cities in the third world. These settlements are unplanned and built by the residents themselves from whatever materials they have to hand.

Manifest community memory

Specific events and social acts are performed in particular places and at set times in Alpha-World. CVEs such as AlphaWorld have socio-spatial persistence, unlike other online spaces, which is manifest as a communal memory. AlphaWorld exhibits the best and worst of human culture in this regard. Social activities mirror 'real' materially based culture and include virtual weddings, religious ceremonies (Schroeder 1997), political meetings and poetry readings, educational classes in building, contests for the best homestead, guided tours and games (such as hide-and-seek). The first AlphaWorld wedding took place in May 1996:

> Citizens floated their avatars down the aisle, crowded the altar to witness the words 'I do' from both the bride and groom, and then floated in around the couple to wish them well … When the bride tried to toss her bouquet, she discovered that it was permanently glued to her avatar. Immediately after the wedding, the groom drove 3,100 miles from San Antonio, Texas to Tacoma Washington to kiss his bride.
>
> (Damer 1997: 134)

The activities are accompanied by social memory in the form of communally recorded histories. For example, there is an AlphaWorld Historical Society, with an actual museum, in the world (see http://www.awcommunity.org/awhs/ for details). There have also been several attempts to form specific communities in AlphaWorld by formally planning and building an actual township. The most well-documented of these has been the Sherwood Forest community project run by the Contact Consortium (Damer 1997).

Social institutions have also been forged to deal with problems in AlphaWorld. For example, the AlphaWorld volunteer police, called Peacekeepers, have taken on a proactive role to intervene in cases of verbal abuse and to investigate avatar stalking and incidents of vandalism, and they have the powers of ejection and banning users from the world (see http://www.peacekeeper.net/ for details). They are organized with a duty roster to provide continuous police cover. Some users have expressed serious concerns over how the peacekeeper role is executed, with accusations of heavy-handed policing and summary expulsions, and an inadequate appeals systems. The evidence of formalized social activities and regulation nonetheless illustrates the vitality of socio-spatial relations.

The material world as virtual place

So far the discussion has focused on characterizing online virtual places. In this final section we want to turn things on their head and consider the extent to which the material world is becoming virtualized: that is, to consider how everyday geographic spaces are becoming virtual places due to the embedding of distributed, networked computing infrastructure into

Figure 33.5. Plane ticket.
Source: Martin Dodge.

their physical fabric and diffusing of software mediation throughout their social reproduction. In some cases, we argue, this embedding and mediation has become so pervasive that if the networked computing infrastructure fails then the geographic space cannot function as intended. An archetypal example in this case is the airport. It is no exaggeration to say that nearly all essential operations within an airport are dependent on software, with several consisting of dedicated intranets that sift and profile passengers – ticket purchasing, checking in, baggage handling, security checks, immigration and passport control, and air traffic control (Dodge and Kitchin 2004). The development and implementation of these systems are driven by issues of security and safety, fears over fraud and illegal immigration, and the desire to increase productivity and efficiency. A prime example of the former is the US system known as Secure Flight which uses routine transaction information (e.g. how a ticket was paid for) to identify 'suspicious' passengers. Even planes are dependent on software for their operation, with a Boeing 747–400 reliant on some 400,000 lines of code to power its numerous cockpit avionics systems, while a Boeing 777 aircraft has some 79 different computer systems, requiring in excess of 4 million lines of code (Pehrson 1996). A mundane view into the software-mediated extent of air travel is given when one examines a typical flight ticket (Figure 33.5), which contains a myriad of code numbers that tie the passenger into databases (Dodge and Kitchin 2005b). Of course, the ticket itself as a material object carried by passengers is itself virtualizing through the move to e-tickets. The airport, we would argue, is a virtualized place – it depends on cyberspace in order to function as an airport. Many other spaces are similar, although with varying degrees of virtualization dependent on software: for example, city spaces, workspaces and 'money-spaces' (Dodge and Kitchin 2005a).

City spaces

The built environment is increasingly overlain and augmented by virtual systems and software in complex ways, resulting in what Graham (2004) defines as cybercities (see also Batty 1997b; Mitchell 1995). New buildings come supplied with 'intelligent' management systems that monitor environmental conditions, sense occupation level and then control lighting, heating and other utilities appropriately to produce spaces that have a more sustainable 'footprint'. Buildings are also made safer through software, for example controlling a sensor network of smoke detectors and sophisticated alarm systems, emergency lighting and automatic door closures. Even seemingly mundane mechanical items such as elevators and public toilets are now literally brought to life through software. Bodies are moved up and down by the same physics but the control algorithms are now held virtually, such that 'smart' lifts 'learned to skip floors when they are already full, to avoid bunching up, and to recognise human behaviour patterns. They can anticipate the hordes who gather on certain floors and start pounding the DOWN button at 4.55 p.m. each Friday' (Gleick 1999, quoted in Thrift and French 2002: 314). In many toilets the mechanics of flushing, turning on taps, dispensing soap and activating dryers is going 'hand-free' to maximize hygiene. Here, sensors and software become crucial to mediate bodily encounters with the environment.

Another facet of diffusion of software systems throughout buildings operations is to make access control more sophisticated, for example through automatic doors and turnstile barriers, while keys for entry to secure sections are authenticated by swipe cards or transponders. Importantly, the move to software-mediated access enables the potential logging of individual movement patterns. Similarly, many road networks are continuously monitored and managed in real time via dedicated intranets that link up cameras around the city with a management programme which calculates the optimal phasing of traffic lights. Other systems monitor access to certain parts of the network, such as bus lanes, toll roads and congestion charge zones, automatically logging which vehicles are using them and administering payments or fines as required. Much of this information is collated together and presented on multiple displays for human operators to interpret and manage in dedicated traffic control centres (Figure 33.6). Other transport systems such as rail are also becoming virtualized, with safety systems that automatically monitor all train movements and work to second-guess decisions made by operators, intervening to override drivers if necessary. In addition, smart ticketing systems are being introduced, along with enhanced safety features.

As these complex process of virtualizing material spaces proceed, the result, according to Amin and Thrift (2002: 125) is that '[t]he modern city exists as a haze of software instructions. Nearly every urban practice is becoming mediated by code'. However, much of the haze is unseen and subject to little external scrutiny. Software itself is largely invisible and the assemblage of networked computing infrastructure is small in scale and has few noxious externalities in operation (particularly in relation to earlier communications technologies).

Workplaces

We would argue that there are few workplaces in the Western world that are not infused with software, a great many of which are distributed in nature. Indeed, distributed communication and information systems are now the structural glue that binds distanciated corporate activities together. They enable companies to maintain complex systems of customer orders, production and logistics. Moreover, they have enabled companies to change how and where they operate by transforming how work is undertaken (Graham and Marvin 1996). To take one example, that of grocery retail: supermarkets are very much virtualized places with many seemingly 'low-skill' working practices being mediated thoroughly by software. Stores now monitor their stock levels using PDAs, automatically ordering new supplies; the checkout system monitors employee performance; computer systems monitor work hours, calculate pay, process payments and organize logistics. Other similar service industries rely on such systems to organize and run their businesses. Workplaces, then, are increasingly virtual places.

Figure 33.6. Los Angeles Department of Transportation's automated traffic surveillance and control centre.

Source: Center for Land Use *Interpretation* (2004).

Money-spaces

A final example is the increasing virtualization of money, most of which now only exists in virtual form as credit (see also Chapter 54). In Britain there were 8.1 billion payment transactions made with debit and credit cards in 2004, amounting to some £443 billion spent (APACS 2005). A person withdrawing money from an ATM maybe stood in material space withdrawing material cash, but the withdrawal can only take place because of the ATM's virtual connection to the bank's intranet that verifies account details and authorizes payment. At the checkout, a networked payment system allows the use of virtual money via credit/debit cards to pay for goods, and another system administers the loyalty card scheme, automatically updating records held on a central database. The widespread use of online virtual places (Internet banks) instead of material banking spaces for many transactions is a tangible manifestation of software in everyday practices. Yet it is not without risks: for example, it gives rise to some novel forms of virtual criminality, including so-called phishing (the attempt to lure people by email to divulge valuable information such as passwords to access bank accounts by constructing fake web pages). The virtualization of money also has significant wider social risks, for example in terms of individual privacy over purchases. The swiping of a payment card by necessity undermines the anonymity of the transaction and leaves a data trail that is of interest to both commercial firms and state bodies to profile individual behaviour – the maxim being that you are what you buy. Given that the geographic locations of ATMs and points-of-sales terminals reveal the place of the person making the transaction, these profiles also map important aspects of time–space paths.

Conclusions

In this chapter we have argued for a broad conception of the notion of a virtual place – as a place that is dependent on networked infrastructure for its existence. Such places can exist online through the various media of cyberspace, or in the material world as it becomes increasingly virtualized. In both cases, virtual places are a hybrid mix of virtual and material – online spaces are accessed from the material world and embodied with its customs and conventions; material spaces are virtualized through the embedding of virtual architecture into its fabric. In both cases, the nature of place is altered in interesting ways through the modes of interaction (e.g. temporality, degree of anonymity, ease of use), but as our examples and discussion have highlighted they retain many of the characteristics of non-virtual places. For example, AlphaWorld is a complex society that has built and inhabits a complex space. Its diverse socio-spatial relations work to turn the virtual environment into a place, engendering its inhabitants with a rich sense of place and community. In this sense, AlphaWorld is just as tangible and real as the neighbourhoods of the pre-virtual era. Similarly, the airport still looks and operates in much the same way as it did 50 years ago, but now with many of operations are virtualized. And while some would call an airport a non-place (Augé 1995), the large community who work there every day and its defined role clearly make it a place – and also a virtual place. Much more work needs to be done to think through the complex nature and implications of these interactions between the virtual and the real.

Notes

1 This chapter draws on our previous work, particularly Dodge and Kitchin (2001, 2005a), Kitchin and Dodge (2002) and Dodge (2002).
2 The word 'avatar' comes from Sanskrit and is commonly translated as 'God's appearance on Earth'; it was first used in the context of CVEs in the pioneering Habitat system developed in the late 1980s (Morningstar and Farmer 1991).

Further reading

Dodge, M. and Kitchin, R. (2001) *Mapping Cyberspace*. London: Routledge.
——(2005a) Code and the transduction of space. *Annals of the Association of American Geographers* 95 (1), 162–80.
Gibson, W. (1984) *Neuromancer*. London: HarperCollins.
Graham, S. (2004) *The Cybercities Reader*. London: Routledge.
Zook, M.A. (2005) *The Geography of the Internet Industry: Venture Capital, Dot-coms and Local Knowledge*. Oxford: Blackwell.

References

Adams, P.C. (1997) Cyberspace and virtual places. *Geographical Review* 87 (2), 155–71.
Amin, A. and Thrift, N. (2002) *Cities: Reimagining Urban Theory*. Cambridge: Polity Press.

APACS (2005) Plastic cards in the UK and how we used them in 2004. *Association for Payment Clearing Services*. Available at http://www.apacs.org.uk/resources_publications/card_facts_and_figures.html

Augé, M. (1995) *Non-places: Introduction to an Anthropology of Supermodernity*, trans. John Howe. London: Verso.

Batty, M. (1997a) Virtual geography. *Futures* 29, 337–52.

——(1997b) The computable city. *International Planning Studies* 2, 155–73.

Cairncross, F. (1997) *The Death of Distance: How the Communications Revolution Will Change Our Lives*. Boston: Harvard Business School Press.

Castells, M. (1996) *The Rise of the Network Society*. Oxford: Blackwell.

Center for Land Use Reclamation (2004) http://www.clui.org/clui_4_1/ondisplay/loop/index.html

Damer, B. (1997) *Avatars! Exploring and Building Virtual Worlds on the Internet*. Berkeley: Peachpit Press.

Dicken, P. (2003) *Global Shift: Reshaping the Global Economic Map in the 21st Century*, fourth edition. London: Sage.

Dodge, M. (2002) Explorations in AlphaWorld: the geography of 3D virtual worlds on the Internet. In P. Fisher and D. Unwin (eds) *Virtual Reality in Geography*, pp. 305–31. London: Taylor & Francis.

Dodge, M. and Kitchin, R. (2001) *Mapping Cyberspace*. London: Routledge.

——(2004) Flying through code/space: the real virtuality of air travel. *Environment and Planning A* 36 (2), 195–211.

——(2005a) Code and the transduction of space. *Annals of the Association of American Geographers* 95 (1), 162–80.

——(2005b) Codes of life: identification codes and the machine-readable world. *Environment and Planning D: Society and Space* 23 (6), 851–81.

Gibson, W. (1984) *Neuromancer*. London: HarperCollins.

Giddens, A. (1990) *The Consequences of Modernity*. Cambridge: Polity Press.

Graham, S. (1998) The end of geography or the explosion of place? Conceptualizing space, place and information technology. *Progress in Human Geography* 22 (2), 165–85.

——(2004) *The Cybercities Reader*. London: Routledge.

Graham, S. and Marvin, S. (1996) *Telecommunications and the City: Electronic Spaces, Urban Places*. London: Routledge.

Gray, J. (1995) The sad side of cyberspace. *Guardian* 10 April.

Harvey, D. (1989) *The Condition of Postmodernity*. Oxford: Blackwell.

Janelle, D. (1969) Spatial reorganization: a model and concept. *Annals of the Association of American Geographers* 59, 348–64.

Jeffrey, P. and Mark, G. (1998) Constructing social spaces in virtual environments: a study of navigation and interaction. In K. Höök, A. Munro and D. Benyon (eds) *Workshop on Personalised and Social Navigation in Information Space* pp. 24–38. Stockholm: Swedish Institute of Computer Science.

Jordan, T. (2002) *Activism! Direct Action, Hacktivism and the Future of Society*. London: Reaktion.

Jordan, T. and Taylor, P. (1998) A sociology of hackers. *Sociological Review* 46 (4), 757–80.

Kitchin, R. (1998) *Cyberspace: The World in the Wires*. Chichester, England: John Wiley and Sons.

Kitchin, R. and Dodge, M. (2002) Exploring the emerging geographies of cyberspace. In R. Johnston, P. Taylor and M. Watts (eds) *Geographies of Global Change*, pp. 340–54. Oxford: Blackwell.

Kitchin, R. and Kneale, J. (2001) Science fiction or future fact? Exploring imaginative geographies of the new millennium. *Progress in Human Geography* 25, 17–33.

Klein, N. (2000) *No Logo*. London: Flamingo.

Madge, C. and O'Connor, H. (2005) Mothers in the making? Exploring liminality in cyber/space. *Transactions of the Institute of British Geographers* 30, 83–97.

Mitchell, W.J. (1995) *City of Bits: Space, Place and the Infobahn*. Cambridge, Mass.: MIT Press.

Morningstar, C. and Farmer, R. (1991) The lessons of Lucasfilm's Habitat. In M. Benedikt (ed.) *Cyberspace: First Steps*, pp. 273–301. Cambridge, Mass.: MIT Press.

Negroponte, N. (1995) *Being Digital*. New York: Vintage Books.

OII (2005) *The Oxford Internet Survey (OxIS) Report 2005: The Internet in Britain*. Oxford: Oxford Internet Institute, University of Oxford. Available at http://www.oii.ox.ac.uk/research

Pehrson, R.J. (1996) Software development for the Boeing 777. *CrossTalk, the Journal of Defense Software Engineering*, January. Available at http://www.stsc.hill.af.mil/crosstalk/1996/01/Boein777.asp

Pickerill, J. (2003) *Cyberprotest: Environmental Activism Online*. Manchester: Manchester University Press.

Relph, E. (1976) *Place and Placelessness*. London: Pion.

Rheingold, H. (1993) *The Virtual Community: Homesteading on the Electronic Frontier*. New York: Addison-Wesley.

Robins, K. (1995) Cyberspace and the world we live in. In M. Featherstone and R. Burrows (eds) *Cyberspace, Cyberbodies and Cyberpunk: Cultures of Technological Embodiment*, pp. 135–56. London: Sage.

Roelofs, G. and van der Meulen, P. (2004) *AlphaWorld Mapping Project*. Available at http://mapper.-activeworlds.com/

Salus, P.H. (1995) *Casting the Net: From ARPANET to Internet and Beyond*. Reading, Mass.: Addison-Wesley.

Schroeder, R. (1997) Networked worlds: social aspects of multi-user virtual reality technology. *Sociological Research Online*, 2 (4). Available at http://www.socresonline.org.uk/2/4/5.html

——(2002) *The Social Life of Avatars: Presence and Interaction in Shared Virtual Environments*. London: Springer.

Sterling, B. (1992) *The Hacker Crackdown: Law and Disorder on the Electronic Frontier*. New York: Bantam Books.

Taylor, J. (1997) The emerging geographies of virtual worlds. *The Geographical Review* 87, 172–92.

Thrift, N. and French, S. (2002) The automatic production of space. *Transactions of the Institute of British Geographers* 27, 309–35.

Wellman, B. and Gulia, M. (1999) Virtual communities as communities: net surfers don't ride along. In M.A. Smith and P. Kollock (eds) *Communities in Cyberspace*, pp. 167–94. London: Routledge.

Wellman, B. and Haythornthwaite, C. (2002) *The Internet in Everyday Life*. Oxford: Blackwell.

Zook, M.A. (2005) *The Geography of the Internet Industry: Venture Capital, Dot-coms and Local Knowledge*. Oxford: Blackwell.

Index

I